D1380888

28.97
29.8.2

MRCS
System Modules:
Essential Revision Notes

7 DAY

DOS

NOV 2007

PASTEST
Dedicated to your success

MRCS
System Modules:
Essential Revision Notes

Edited by

Catherine Parchment Smith
Catherine Hernon

Chapter authors

Sudipta Banerjee MBChB MRCS
Jeremy J Elkabir MBBS FRCS (Eng) FRCS (Urol) FEBU
Catherine Hernon BSc MBChB AFRCS (Edin)
Clive Morris MBChB MRCS
Catherine Parchment Smith BSc (Hons) MBChB (Hons) MRCS

PASTEST
Dedicated to your success

©PASTEST LTD
Egerton Court
Parkgate Estate
Knutsford
Cheshire WA16 8DX

Telephone: 01565 752000

First edition 2000
Reprinted 2001

ISBN: 1 901198 41 3

A catalogue record for this book is available from the British Library.

PasTest Revision Books and Intensive Courses

PasTest has been established in the field of postgraduate medical education since 1972, providing revision books and intensive study courses for doctors preparing for their professional examinations.

Books and courses are available for the following specialties: **MRCP Part 1 and Part 2, MRCPCH Part 1 and Part 2, MRCOG, DRCOG, MRCGP, DCH, FRCA, MRCS, PLAB.**

For further details contact:

PasTest Ltd, Freepost, Knutsford, Cheshire WA16 7BR
Tel: 01565 752000 Fax: 01565 650264
E-mail: enquiries@PasTest.co.uk

Design and typesetting by **EDITEXT**, Charlesworth, Derbyshire (01457 857622).
Printed and bound by Hobbs the Printers, Totton, Hampshire.

Contents

Contributors

Sudipta Banerjee MBChB MRCS
Senior House Officer, Department of Otorhinolaryngology, Hope Hospital, Salford, Manchester
Head, Neck, Endocrine and Paediatrics

Jeremy J Elkabir MBBS FRCS (Eng) FRCS (Urol) FEBU
Senior Registrar in Urology, St George's Hospital, London
Urinary System and Renal Transplantation

Catherine Hernon BSc MBChB AFRCS (Edin)
Senior House Officer, Plastic Surgery Department, St James' Hospital, Leeds
Locomotor

Clive Morris MBChB MRCS
Research Fellow, Department of Surgery, Hope Hospital, Salford, Manchester
Vascular

Catherine Parchment Smith BSc (Hons) MBChB (Hons) MRCS
Specialist Registrar in General Surgery, The Yorkshire Deanery, Harrogate District Hospital
Abdomen

Preface

'The times they are a'changing ...'

Times change and so do teaching styles. Many of us who trained not so long ago would barely recognize parts of the new style medical curricula, let alone the examination formats which accompany them. EMQs and OSCEs now complement MCQs; what we need is a glossary to help us come to terms with the changes themselves!

Such changes in medical education have not been applied solely to undergraduate training — postgraduate training has undergone a similar upheaval and from this has arisen the MRCS examination that allows 'entry' to higher surgical training programmes in the candidate's chosen specialty.

The syllabus for this exam is broad, but the emphasis is always on the application of basic principles to the care of the individual patient. This book concentrates on various specific systems and presents facts on both the normal and pathological states. As in the Core Modules book, essential facts are presented in bullet form. One of the strengths of this book is that it is written for trainees and thus there is a greater focus on areas where concepts are know to be difficult to grasp, controversy exists or recent developments have taken place.

This book is indeed what it says it is — a book of essential revision notes — and its success relies on prior exposure to clinical material and more specialist texts. It allows examination candidates to confirm the facts they know and to identify holes in their knowledge base that may be filled before their meeting with the examiner.

All in all, this book should allow revision for the MRCS to become a less physiologically upsetting process, leading to greater success in the stressful environment of the examination hall.

Deborah M Eastwood FRCS
Consultant Orthopaedic Surgeon
Honory Senior Lecturer
Royal Free Hospital/Royal National Orthopaedic Hospital

Introduction

This book is aimed specifically at doctors sitting the AFRCS/MRCS Systems MCQ and the viva voce exams. It provides short notes on all aspects of the System Modules syllabus as set out by the Royal Colleges and is designed to be used in conjunction with the Royal College Step Course. A companion volume covering the Core Modules is available, along with four titles for the MCQ and EMQ papers. Books covering the clinical component and the viva exam are planned for publication in 2001.

At the time of writing, the Membership of the Royal College of Surgeons examination is still slightly different, depending on which British or Irish college has set the exam, but the basic principle is common to all. A pass in all sections of the MRCS and completion of Basic Surgical Training means that a doctor is eligible to apply for a National Higher Surgical Training position in his or her chosen specialty.

A pass in the final 'exit' Intercollegiate specialty examination awards candidates with the 'full' Fellowship of the Royal College of Surgeons (FRCS). Providing training has been adequately completed, trainees may then apply for a certificate of completion of Surgical Training (CCST) and be placed on the GMC register and so be eligible to apply for a consultant post.

Membership of the Royal College of Surgeons of England (MRCS) examination consists of the following sections:

- **Paper 1 Core Modules multiple choice paper**
  Tests knowledge of peri-operative management, trauma, intensive care, neoplasia, techniques and outcomes of surgery.
- **Paper 2 System Modules multiple choice paper**
  Involves specific systems: locomotor, vascular, abdominal, head, neck, endocrine and paediatric, urology and renal transplantation.
- **Clinical Examination**.
- **Viva Voce**.

These subjects are tested using a combination of multiple choice questions and extended matching questions. Candidates may sit each of the MCQ papers as often as they wish. There is full reciprocity of recognition of a 'pass' in the whole MCQ section between all three UK Royal Surgical Colleges and the Royal College of Surgeons of Ireland.

The clinical examination tests candidates' clinical knowledge, examination and communication skills with real patients.

The viva voce testing comprises knowledge of applied surgical anatomy, operative surgery, applied physiology and critical care, clinical pathology and principles of surgery — usually six vivas conducted by surgeons and academic non-clinicians.

The writers of this book have either experienced the MRCS examination for themselves or have knowledge through teaching on MRCS revision courses. We found that one of the most frustrating aspects of working towards the exam was not having one single tailor-made text which covered all the topics needed. The STEP course provided by the Royal College was indispensable, and working through the modules using the long list of detailed, weighty and authoritative reference texts was essential. However, when it came to revision we had to rely on our own notes. We wanted to share these revision notes with future candidates, incorporating reminders of the anatomy, physiology, pathology, operative surgery and principles of surgery covered in the Systems syllabus.

We hope that by having one small book instead of ten large ones in your on-call room or hospital library you will feel more inclined to get on with some useful revision in your spare hours. These notes helped us get through the exam successfully and we hope they do the same for you.

GOOD LUCK!

Catherine Parchment Smith   **Catherine Hernon**

Acknowledgements

To Jon, Mum and Isabel

Lady surgeons are still far too thin on the ground for me not to feel extremely lucky. I am able to do a job I enjoy and come home (most nights!) to a wonderful family. If my husband wasn't so understanding (and also so medical!), my mother so supportive and my daughter so good at sleeping through the night, this book would never have been finished. Certain people I have been taught by or worked with have, probably unknowingly, encouraged, helped and inspired me. They include Neil Hulton, Nigel Womack, Trudi Roberts, Finlay Curran and Andy Parry. Thanks also to Sue Harrison and all at PasTest.

Catherine Parchment Smith

Many thanks to all at PasTest, especially Sue Harrison. I would also like to thank my parents and my sister for their unfailing support.

Catherine Hernon

Permissions

The following figures in this book have been reproduced from *Clinical Anatomy for Medical Students*, R Snell, 6th ed., 2000 by kind permission of the publisher Lippincott, Williams and Wilkins.

Anatomy of the ear, p. 183	Fig 11-52A
Tympanic membrane, p. 184	Fig 11-52C
Middle ear, p. 185	Fig 11-55A
Internal ear, p. 186	Fig 11-55B
Anatomy of the nose, p. 192	Fig 11-62A
Anatomy of the paranasal sinuses, p. 194	Fig 11-63C
Anatomy of the pharynx, p. 204	Fig 11-59A
Interior of the pharynx, p. 205	Fig 11-59B
Anatomy of the tongue, p. 212	Fig 11-57A
The inferior surface of the tongue, p. 213	Fig 11-57B
The eye, p. 227	Fig 11-51A
Muscles of facial expression, p. 233	Fig 11-20
Sensory supply of the face, p. 234	Fig 11-18A
Fascial layers of the neck, p. 236	Fig 11-3
Posterior triangle of the neck, p. 237	Fig 11-6
Anterior triangle of the neck, p. 238	Fig 11-8
Anatomy of the inguinal region, p. 301	Fig 4-13
Saggital section of abdominal wall, p. 327	Fig 4-8B
Transverse section of abdomen showing arrangement of peritoneum, p. 334	Fig 5-4
Structures entering and leaving porta hepatis, p. 559	Fig 5-34

The following figures in this book have been reproduced from Langman's *Medical Embryology*, Sadler T, 6th ed.,1990 by kind permission of the publisher Lippincott, Williams and Wilkins.

Formation of the neural tube (transverse section), p. 266	Fig 20-2
Formation of the neural tube (dorsal view), p. 267	Fig 20-3
Transverse section of the diaphragm at the fourth month of gestation, p. 268	Fig 11-5C
Sagittal section through embryo showing the formation of the primitive endoderm-lined duct, p. 269	Fig 14-1
Formation of GI Tract at fourth week of gestation showing fore-, mid- and hind gut, p. 270	Fig 14-7
The foregut during the fourth week of gestation, p. 270	Fig 14-2 B,C
The cloacal region at successive stages in development, p. 272	Fig 14-23

The following figures in this book have been reproduced from *The New Aird's Companion in Surgical Studies*, Burnand K et al., 3rd ed., 1992 by kind permission of the publisher Churchill Livingstone.

Variable sites of the appendix, p. 377	Fig 36.33
Excision of Meckel's diverticulum, p. 385	Fig 36.37
Operative treatment of duodenal ulcer, p. 412	Fig 37.5
Palliative treatment for gastric cancer, p. 425	Fig 37.16
Goodsall's rule, p. 528	Fig 39.4

The following figures in this book have been reproduced from *ABC of Colorectal Diseases*, Jones D, 2nd ed., 1999 by kind permission of the publisher BMJ Books.

Gross anatomy of the large bowel, p. 467	Fig 1.1
Venous drainage of the large bowel, p. 471	Fig 1.3
Activity of the large bowel, p. 472	Fig 1.5
Movement of electrolytes and metabolites across the bowel wall, p. 473	Fig 1.4
Findings on rectal examination, p. 475	Fig 2.1
Three types of rectal prolapse, p. 534	Fig 11.3
Overlapping sphincter repair, p. 541	Fig 12.6
Post-anal repair, p. 542	Fig 12.7

The following figures in this book have been reproduced from Calder SJ. Fractures of the hip. *Surgery* 1998; 16: 253–8, by kind permission of the publisher The Medicine Publishing Group.

Blood supply of the femoral head, p. 24
Intra-capsular fractures, p. 25
Extra-capsular fractures, p. 26

The following figures in this book have been reproduced from Chester TJS. Forearm fractures. *Surgery* 1998; 16: 241–8, by kind permission of the publisher The Medicine Publishing Group.

Smith's fracture; Volar Barton's fracture, p. 19
Salter-Harris classification, p. 20

The following figures in this book have been reproduced from *Clinical Orthopaedic Examination*, McRae R, 3rd ed., 1996

Anatomy of the foot, p. 52
Schematic diagram of vertebra and spinal cord, p. 93

The following table in this book has been reproduced from *Effective Head and Neck Cancer Management*, 2nd consensus document, 2000, by kind permission of the British Association of Otorhinolaryngologists, Head and Neck Surgeons

Classifications TNM, p. 199

The following figures in this book have been reproduced from An Introduction to the *Symptoms and Signs of Surgical Disease*, Browse N, 3rd ed., 1977 by kind permission of the publisher Arnold:

Reduction *en masse* of a hernia, p. 321
Richter's hernia, Maydl's hernia, p. 322

Chapter 1
Locomotor

CONTENTS

Locomotor

1. COMMON FRACTURES AND JOINT INJURIES

1.1 Bones and fractures

Types of fracture

- Traumatic
- Incomplete (e.g. greenstick)
- Complete
- Comminuted: when bone splinters into multiple fragments
- Open: when fracture site communicates with skin surface
- Closed: when the overlying skin is intact

- Stress: slowly developing fracture in a bone subjected to repetitive loads (e.g. sports training, military marches)
- Pathological: in a bone altered by a disease process

Radiographs
For fracture diagnosis:

- Always two views of whole bone with its two joints
- If one bone of a pair is broken look very carefully at the other one
- If there is no fracture look for dislocation
- Look for soft tissue injuries on radiographs

Stages of bone healing

Bone is unique in its ability to repair itself as it reactivates processes that normally occur during embryogenesis.

- **Haematoma** (immediately after fracture): rupture of the blood vessels within the medullary cavity forms a haematoma that fills the fracture gap and spills out into the surrounding tissue; this haematoma provides a fibrin mesh that seals off the fracture site and provides a framework for the influx of inflammatory cells, fibroblasts and capillary vessels

- **Inflammation** (initially): inflammatory cells release PDGF, TGF-ß, FGF, ILS, which activate osteoprogenitor cells which, in turn, stimulate production of osteoclastic and osteoblastic activity
- **Callus formation**: by the end of the first week the organized haematoma is known as the **callus**; it provides some anchorage but no structural rigidity. Osteoblasts from activated osteoprogenitor cells deposit a subperiosteal layer of woven bone perpendicular to the cortical axis within the medullary cavity. The activated mesenchymal cells in the surrounding soft tissues may also differentiate into chondroblasts to make fibrocartilage and hyaline cartilage which envelope the fracture site. As the intramedullary and subperiosteal woven bone approaches the newly formed cartilage, the cartilage undergoes ossification such as that which normally occurs at the growth plate. Thus the fracture ends are bridged by a bony callus that gains strength as it mineralizes in order to support weight-bearing.
- **Remodelling** (over months): in the early stages of callus formation, excess amounts of callus are formed; if the bone is not aligned the volume of callus is greatest in the concave portion of the fracture site in order to counteract this site of potential weakness. As the callus matures and transmits weight, the portions that are not stressed are resorbed thus decreasing its size and shape until the bony ridge has been restored. The medullary cavity is also restored.

Complications which impede fracture healing

- Infection
- Diabetes mellitus
- Vascular insufficiency
- Displaced and comminuted fractures: frequently result in deformity; the devitalized fragments of splintered bone require resorption which delays healing, enlarges the callus and requires longer periods of remodelling
- Calcium/phosphate/vitamin D deficiency
- Inadequate immobilization: if there is constant movement of fracture site, the normal constituents of callus do not form; callus may comprise mainly fibrous tissue and cartilage perpetuating instability and resulting in delayed union and non-union

Fracture management

- Reduce (if necessary)
- Hold
- Rehabilitate

Non-operative methods

- Analgesia
- Bed rest
- Traction
- Slings
- Splints
- Plaster casts

Non-operative fracture management

- **Advantages**
  No surgery or complications
  associated with surgery
  No complications associated with
  fixation methods
  Relatively safe and simple

- **Disadvantages**
  Difficult to maintain precise
  reduction
  Cumbersome for patient
  Prolonged hospitalization
  Joint stiffness
  Immobility — prone to pressure
  sores and chest infections

Operative methods

- **Internal fixation** (e.g. plates, screws, intramedullary nails): used when precise reduction required, for example, near joints in an attempt to avoid post-traumatic osteoarthritis. Used in situations where angulation or rotation will compromise function; allows early mobilization. It is used when closed reduction techniques have failed; also in pathological fractures and in those with a neurovascular deficit.
- **External fixation**

Internal fixation

- **Advantages**
  Early mobilization
  Precise reduction
  Less pain
  Decreased complications such as fat
  embolus, ARDS

- **Disadvantages**
  Requires an operation
  Expensive
  Plating: requires soft tissue
  stripping and exposure of bone
  which may compromise blood supply
  Infection: which may necessitate
  removal of metalwork fixation

External fixation

- **Advantages**
  Versatile
  Simple
  Safe
  Fast
  Can re-use fixators
  Often indicated if infection is a risk
    (e.g. open fractures)

- **Disadvantages**
  Cumbersome
  Pin–track infection

1.2 Humerus

Anatomy of the humerus

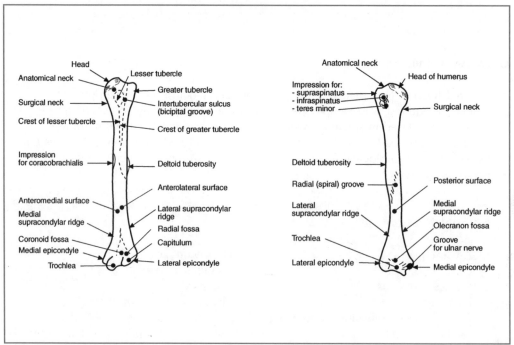

Humerus (front and back)

The humerus is a long bone

* The upper half is cylindrical, consisting of a head facing medially. The head is separated from the greater and lesser tubercles by the anatomical neck. The tubercles are separated by the bicipital groove and the shaft is separated from the upper half by the surgical neck.
* The lower half of the humerus is flattened. Its lower end bears the capitulum laterally which articulates with the radial head and the trochlea medially which articulates with the trochlea notch of the ulna. The medial and lateral epicondyles are extracapsular. The medial is larger and extends more distally.

Important nerve relationships

* **Surgical neck**: the axillary nerve and circumflex humeral vessels
* **Spiral groove** (running along the posterior aspect of the shaft): the radial nerve and profunda brachii vessels
* **Posterior aspect of the medial epicondyle**: the ulnar nerve

Sites of humeral fracture

* Proximal humerus
* Shaft
* Supracondylar
* Condylar
* Epicondylar

Fracture of the proximal humerus

These fractures may involve the anatomical neck, surgical neck, greater tuberosity or lesser tuberosity and are described in terms of how many fragments are involved, e.g. two-part, four-part.

Mechanisms

* A fall onto side or direct blow to side of arm
* Fall onto outstretched hand

The upper limb acts as a strut between the hand and torso through which force is transmitted. These fractures are common in the elderly and range in severity from minimal displacement fractures with minor angulation to multiple part fractures associated with dislocation at the shoulder joint.

Neer's classification of the proximal humeral fracture

- **Group I**
  All fractures with: displacement
  < 1 cm; angulation ≤45°

- **Group II**
  Anatomical neck fractures displaced
  > 1 cm
  Can be complicated by avascular
  necrosis of humeral head

- **Group III**
  Surgical neck fracture with significant
  displacement or angulation
  Can be complicated by axillary nerve
  injury

- **Group IV**
  Greater tuberosity fracture:
  displaced by pull of suprasinatus
  Can be complicated by painful arc
  syndrome due to impingement of
  greater tuberosity on the acromion
  process and coracoacromial ligament

- **Group V**
  Lesser tuberosity fractures

- **Group VI**
  Fracture dislocations: can involve
  two- to four-part fractures

Management
Ranges from conservative treatment with collar and cuff or broad arm sling for Group I to formal open reduction and internal fixation or hemi-arthroplasty for more complicated injuries.

Shaft fractures

Mechanisms

- Fall onto outstretched hand, indirect and twisting force resulting in spiral fracture
- Direct force to arm resulting in short oblique or comminuted fracture

Classification
These fractures are seen in adults of any age, but seldom in children. They are described in relation to the position of fracture along the shaft:

- **Upper third**: proximal fragment is adducted by pull of the now unopposed pectoralis major muscle
- **Middle third**: proximal fragment tends to be abducted by action of deltoid muscle
- **Lower third** or supracondylar fractures

Associated radial nerve injury may occur in the middle third fracture due to the course of the radial nerve in the spiral groove on the posterior aspect of the humeral shaft.

Management

Ranges from conservative treatment for simple fracture, e.g. plaster slab immobilization, to formal open reduction and internal fixation or intramedullary nailing.

Supracondylar fractures

Mechanism

- Fall onto outstretched hand

Fracture characteristics

- Most common in childhood — peak age 8 years
- The distal fragment is usually displaced and tilted backwards
- Reduction is required if: displacement of distal fragment is 15° backwards or more; lateral displacement is 10° or more; medial displacement is 10° or more

Management

- An uncomplicated, minimally displaced fracture should be immobilized with the elbow flexed — but in a position with no vascular compromise
- Manipulation under anaesthesia (MUA) plus open reduction plus internal fixation (ORIF), e.g. percutaneous pins in children. In displaced fracture, lower fragment brought into position by longitudinal traction and pressure applied behind olecranon with elbow flexed
- Vigilant observation for signs of brachial artery and median nerve damage due to proximal fragment impingement

Signs of brachial artery damage

- Excessive bruising and swelling around the elbow
- Pain and paraesthesia
- Loss of distal pulses
- Pallor and coldness of hand and forearm
- Progressive weakness
- Gangrene of digits due to emboli

Volkmann's ischaemic contracture may result if these signs are missed

Condylar fractures

These are uncommon and occur mainly in children. They can cause permanent disability if not reduced adequately. They mostly involve the lateral condyle.

The major problem in children is growth arrest at the fracture site which causes a deformity that increases with age.

Lateral condylar fracture (fracture of capitulum)
May be undisplaced or displaced by forearm extensors.

Management:

- Simple immobilization to MUA plus, occasionally, ORIF, e.g. percutaneous pins in children
- Vital to detect early slippage — weekly check X-rays
- Observe for ulnar nerve neuritis — may require transposition of nerve from posterior groove to soft tissues in front of the elbow

Epicondylar fracture

These fractures are usually medial and occur more often in children.

- Usually caused by direct violence or avulsion injury (e.g. avulsed by outstretched flexors during a fall)
- Medial epicondyle may be avulsed by ulnar collateral ligament when elbow abducted
- Occasionally medial epicondyle trapped in elbow joint requires MUA or ORIF
- Injury to ulnar nerve is a known complication

1.3 Radius and ulna

Anatomy of the radius and ulna

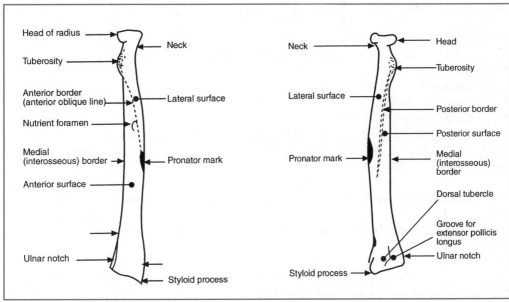

Radius   front   back

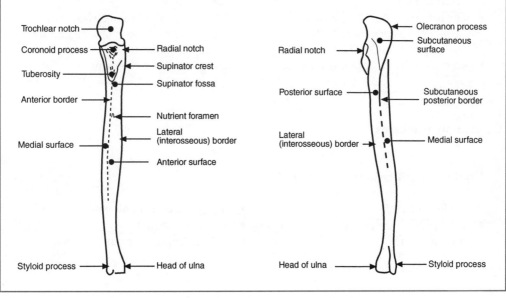

Ulna   front   back

Hints for orientating the radius and ulna in the viva

- **Radius**
  Distal end large $\Big\}$ Reverse arrangement to ulna
  Proximal end small
  Anteroposteriorly: distal end — prominent dorsal tubercle posteriorly
  Mediolaterally: ulnar notch faces medially to articulate with ulna distally

- **Ulna**
  Proximal end large
  Distal end small
  Anteroposteriorly: proximal end — trochlear notch projecting anteriorly
  Mediolaterally: radial notch faces laterally to articulate with radius proximally

The two bone shafts are joined by an interosseous membrane. In pronation and supination, the head of the radius rotates against the radial notch of the ulna. The radial shaft swings around the relatively fixed ulna shaft. The distal end of the radius rotates against the head of the ulna.

Fractures of the radius and the ulna

- Olecranon
- Head of radius
- Fracture of upper third ulna with associated dislocation of the radial head: MONTEGGIA
- Fracture of shafts of radius and ulna

- Coronoid
- Radial neck
- Fracture of shaft radius with dislocation of the inferior radio-ulna joint: GALEAZZI
- Lower end of radius/ulna

Olecranon fractures

Colton classification

- I Undisplaced
- II Displaced (by pull of triceps tendon)
- IIa Avulsion

- IIb Oblique + transverse
- IIc Comminuted
- IId Fracture dislocation

Mechanism

- Fall onto elbow point — usually adults

Management

- **Undisplaced**: immobilization with elbow flexed to 90° without distracting fracture further
- **Displaced**: screw fixation, tension band wiring
- **Comminuted**: excise fragments of olecranon and secure triceps insertion to ulna

Coronoid fractures

Most commonly associated with posterior dislocation of elbow.

Classification

- Simple avulsion
- Half or less of coronoid
- More than half of coronoid

Management
Conservative unless more than half of coronoid involved. May be fixed internally to prevent recurrent dislocations.

Head of radius fractures

Mason classification of radial head fractures

- Type I undisplaced
- Type II fracture part radial head with displacement
- Type III comminuted fracture of head
- Type IV fracture dislocation

Mechanism
Fall onto outstretched hand (the force is transmitted along radial shaft to the head — striking the head on the capitulum). These fractures are common in young adults.

Management
Dependent on severity of damage to the radial head.

- Simple immobilization for undisplaced fracture to excision of severely comminuted radial head fracture with silastic replacement
- Always check for associated subluxation of distal ulna in cases where interosseous membrane is torn and there is upward drift of radial shaft

Fractures of the radial neck

These fractures commonly occur in children after a fall onto outstretched hand. In adults a similar mechanism of injury may produce a radial head fracture.

Management

- If angulation <30%: simple immobilization
- If >30%: MUA
- If residual angle >45° or dislocated: ORIF in adults. Open reduction only in children
- Radial head should not be excised in a child

Complications of fractures around the elbow joint

- Loss of range of movement: prolonged immobility
- Posterior interosseous nerve damage: in surgery near radial head
- Myositis ossificans
- Ulnar nerve damage

Monteggia and Galeazzi fractures

If one forearm bone is fractured and angled with its humeral and wrist attachments intact, the other forearm bone must be dislocated.

- Fracture of the upper end of the ulna with dislocation of the radial head is called a **Monteggia fracture**; it is relatively uncommon
- It is due to a fall with forced pronation of forearm or direct blow on back of upper forearm — during, for example, warding off an assault
- The radius is forced against the ulna, fracturing it and is itself forced away from the capitulum

A **Galeazzi fracture** is a fracture of the shaft of the radius, usually at the junction of middle and lower third, with dislocation of distal ulna. It is often due to a fall on the hand. A single forearm fracture should never be accepted as a definitive diagnosis until Monteggia or Galeazzi are ruled out.

Management of Monteggia and Galeazzi fractures

Perfect reduction is seldom attainable by closed manipulation. ORIF is often required to restore full function.

Forearm bone shaft fractures

It is possible to sustain a fracture of either forearm bone in isolation (e.g. warding off a direct blow or falling on a sharp edge). More commonly, a fall onto the outstretched hand subjects the forearm bones to indirect force which causes both to fracture.

The ulna may angulate or be displaced, whereas the radius may be subject to axial rotation due to insertion of pronator teres midway along the radial shaft.

If the radius is fractured proximal to this insertion, the proximal fragment will supinate due to unopposed biceps insertion action and the distal fragment will be pronated. The forearm should be immobilized, supinated to match the supinated proximal end. If the fracture is distal to the insertion of pronator teres, the actions of biceps plus pronator muscles are equalised. The forearm is immobilized in the neutral position.

Management

- From MUA in children — to formal ORIF in adults
- In children, angulation of up to 20° is acceptable in those under the age of 10
- Over 10 years: angulation of no greater than 10° accepted

Complications of forearm shaft fractures

- Compartment syndrome
- Non-union
- Synostosis
- Malunion
- Refracture (first six months)
- Neurological damage

Fractures of lower end of radius

Mechanism

- Fall onto outstretched hand

Fractures of lower end of radius

- **Adult fractures**
  (peak age 60–80)

  Colles'
  Barton's
  Smith's

- **Children's fractures**
  (peak age 6–14)

Colles' fracture

- Fracture of the radius within 2.5 cm of the wrist joint
- Extra-articular fracture with dorsal and radial displacement of distal fragment
- The classic 'dinner fork' deformity

Commonly associated with fracture through ulnar styloid. Radial displacement of distal fragment causes avulsion of ulna styloid through its attachment via the triangular fibrocartilage.

Management of Colles' fracture depends on the degree of displacement and age. MUA or ORIF may be necessary.

- In younger patients, it is essential to restore the congruity of the radial articular surface and of the distal radio ulnar joint as there is a risk of loss of forearm rotation and a predisposition to developing arthritic change
- Elderly patients can gain reasonable function even with considerable deformity at the expense of weakened grip strength

Reduction of Colles' fracture

The main aim is to dis-impact the radial fragment

- **Exaggerate deformity**: traction; dorsal displacement
- **Restore anatomical position**: volar displacement
- **Plaster in ulnar deviation and slight flexion**

May be performed under local (haematoma block), regional (Bier's block) or general anaesthetic

Smith's fracture
This is an extra-articular distal radial fracture with volar displacement. It usually occurs as a result of a fall onto the dorsum of the hand (see diagram).

Barton's fracture (intra-articular)
This is a fracture of the dorsal or volar lip of the distal radius with subluxation of carpus.

Management is MUA and ORIF.

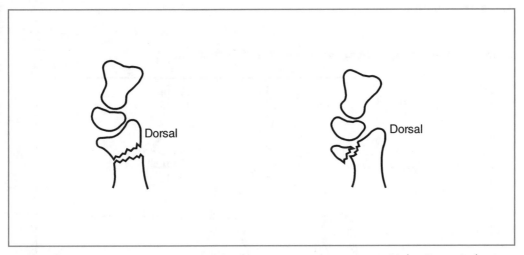

Smith's fracture   Volar Barton's fracture

Complications of lower end of radius fractures

- Malunion
- Rupture of tendon of extensor pollicis longus (after fracture of lower end of radius)
- Compression of median nerve
- Stiffness
- Reflex sympathetic dystrophy (RSD)

- Subluxation inferior radio-ulnar joint: painful subluxation of the inferior radio-ulnar joint can be managed by excising the head of the ulna with approximately 3 cm of distal shaft — Darrach's procedure

Fractures of forearm bones in children

Mechanism

- Fall onto outstretched hand (e.g. in roller-blading accidents, climbing trees)

Common forearm bone fractures in children

- Epiphyseal injuries
- Greenstick fracture
- Torus or buckle fracture
- Complete fracture both distal forearm bones

Epiphyseal injuries

Salter–Harris classification — most are Type I and II

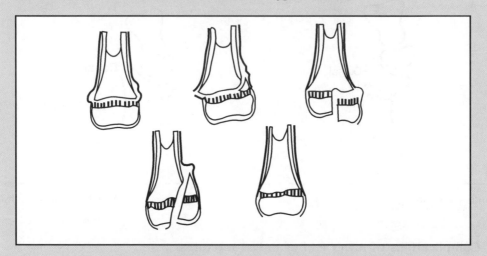

- **Type I**
  A tear through the growth plate
  Seldom growth disturbance

- **Type II**
  A fracture through the physis with
  a metaphyseal fragment
  Seldom growth disturbance

- **Type III**
  A portion of epiphysis associated with
  its adjacent growth plate fractures from
  the epiphysis — this is intra-articular,
  therefore needs early reduction and
  fixation

- **Type IV**
  This involves a separation of a portion
  of metaphysis, physis and epiphysis —
  intra-articular

- **Type V**
  Crush injury to the physis
  Disrupts growth
  Difficult to diagnose

The distal radial and ulnar physes provide approximately 75–80% of total growth of forearm. There is therefore excellent remodelling potential of distal, radial and ulnar fractures in the plane of the joint only.

Complete and greenstick fractures
Both complete and incomplete fractures may occur in children but incomplete fractures are common due to the increased plasticity of children's bones.

A **greenstick fracture** is an incomplete fracture where one cortex breaks and the other does not. It is due to forced angulation. The bone buckles on the side opposite to the causal force. There may be minimal periosteal tearing.

A **Torus fracture** is due to compression. The side of the cortex buckles when it is subjected to compression.

Management

- **Torus fracture**: POP for pain relief
- **Complete and greenstick fractures**: require MUA or, occasionally, ORIF; above-elbow POP to prevent supination/pronation of the forearm

1.4 Carpus

Common injuries of the carpus

- Fracture of scaphoid bone
- Dislocation of carpal bones
- Fractures of other carpal bones

Scaphoid fracture

The most commonly fractured wrist bone is the scaphoid which is involved in both the radiocarpal joint and the joint between the distal and proximal carpal rows. The blood supply is variable. It commonly enters the distal part of the ligamentous ridge between the two main articular surfaces. Thus there is a risk of avascular necrosis of the proximal part of the bone if a fracture of the waist is sustained. Due to the role of the scaphoid in two major joints, movement of fracture fragments is difficult to control. The prognosis is good in stable fractures, but poor in unstable fractures.

Mechanism

- Fall onto outstretched hand
- 'Kick-back' when using jump start handles or pulleys

Sites of fracture

- Waist (most common)
- Proximal half
- Distal half (least common)

Management

- Treatment is by plaster immobilization
- Using scaphoid plaster: wrist pronated; radially deviated; moderately dorsiflexed; extending from MCP joints, including thumb in mid abduction, extending along forearm but not involving the elbow joint

Complications

- Delayed union
- Non-union
- Avascular necrosis (of the proximal third)
- Osteoarthritis

Fractures of other carpal bones

These fractures are uncommon. Treatment principles are the same as those applying to un-complicated fractures of the scaphoid, i.e. short period of plaster immobilization.

Kienboch's disease of lunate bone
A minor fracture or contusion to the lunate can cause significant degeneration of the bone as a result of disruption of blood supply. This destroys the articular surfaces and causes severe osteoarthritis. In some cases of Kienboch's disease no history of injury can be obtained, but usually an injury is sustained with the hand dorsiflexed.

Dislocation of lunate

- The lunate is a wedge-shaped bone with its base anteriorly
- If subjected to excessive force with hand extended it can be squeezed out of position
- Characteristic displacement: the lunate lies anterior to wrist; it is rotated through 90° or more on a horizontal axis so that its concave lower articular surface faces anteriorly

Management

- MUA
- ORIF

Complications

- Median nerve injury
- Osteoarthritis

Perilunar dislocation of carpus

The whole carpus is dislocated posteriorly except for the lunate which remains congruous with the radius.

1.5 Proximal femur

The types of proximal femur fractures are different in different age groups:

- **Adolescents**: slipped upper femoral epiphysis
- **Adults**: hip dislocation as opposed to fracture
- **Elderly**: fracture neck of femur; approximately 75–80 years; male:female ratio 1:4

Blood supply of the femur

- Through diaphysis
- Retinacular branches from medial and lateral femoral circumflex arteries which pass proximally within joint capsule to anastamose at junction of neck and articular surface
- Ligamentum teres

The retinacular vessels are therefore easily disrupted in intracapsular fractures.

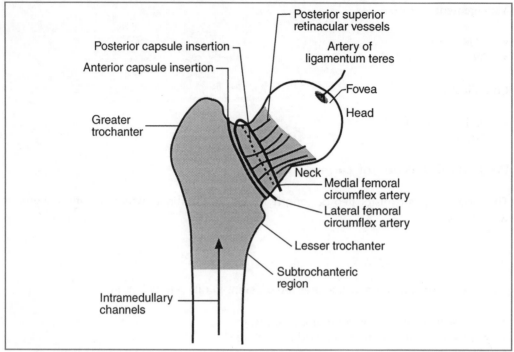

Blood supply of the femoral head

Types of femur fracture:

- The neck fracture: subcapital; cervical; basal (all intracapsular)
- Trochanteric fracture (extracapsular)

Neck fractures of the femur disrupt the blood supply from the diaphysis. The nearer the neck fracture is to the head, the greater the chance of disruption of retinacular blood supply also. Hence increased risk of avascular necrosis.

Intracapsular fracture

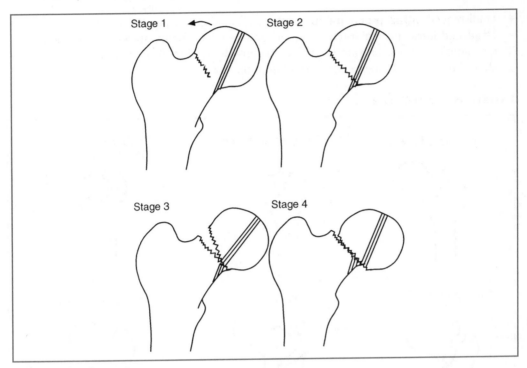

Stage 1   Stage 2

Stage 3   Stage 4

Intracapsular fractures

Garden's classification

Based on integrity of trabecular lines in an AP projection

- **Stage I**
  Impacted fracture: medial cortical;
  trabeculae intact but angulated
  — undisplaced similar prognosis

- **Stage II**
  Complete but undisplaced fracture
  Medial cortical trabeculae are
  interrupted but not angulated

- **Stage III**
  Complete, partially displaced
  fracture with loss of trabecular
  alignment

- **Stage IV**
  Completely displaced fracture

Management

- **Undisplaced intracapsular fracture**: internal fixation: 2–3 parallel screws
- **Displaced intracapsular fracture**: in UK preference for hemiarthroplasty in elderly, e.g. simple unipolar prosthesis such as Austin–Moor, Thompson; fit patients <65 years should be treated by reduction and internal fixation

Extracapsular fracture

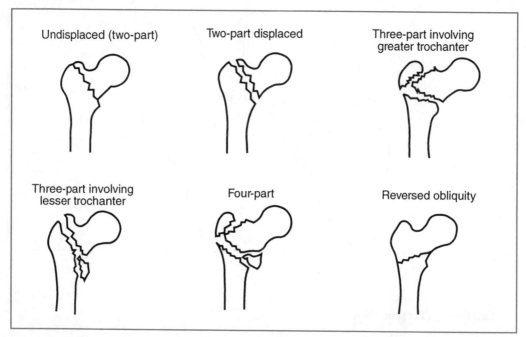

Extracapsular fractures

These fractures occur from the basal part of the femoral neck to approximately 5 cm below lesser trochanter. They include:

- Intertrochanteric
- Basal
- Subtrochanteric

Essentially distal to the insertion of the joint capsule through an area of well-vascularized metaphyseal bone. Classification is based on the number of fragments produced by the fracture:

- Undisplaced (two-part)
- Displaced (two-part)

- Three-part involving the greater trochanter
- Three-part involving the lesser trochanter
- Four-part
- Reversed obliquity

Management

- **Intertrochanteric and basal fractures**: dynamic hip screw; closed reduction using traction on fracture table; the main lag screw should be parallel to the femoral neck in all planes: extending up to the subchondral bone within 5 mm
- **Subtrochanteric fracture**: ORIF

Complications
Due to co-morbid factors, the mortality rate for unselected hip fracture patients is 14–36% at 1 year. Highest mortality risk occurs within the first 4–6 months. After 1 year the mortality rate approaches that for age- and sex-matched control subjects. Other complications include:

- Infection
- Dislocation
- Femoral stem loosening
- Acetabular erosion

1.6 Knee

The inherent stability of the knee joint is dependent on the associated soft tissues.

Main structures at risk in knee injury

- **Ligaments**
  Extra-articular
  Intra-articular

- **Menisci**
- **Extensor apparatus**

Extra-articular ligaments

Medial collateral ligament
The most common mechanism of injury is a blow to the lateral aspect of the knee — abducting the tibia on the femur and stressing the medial collateral ligament. Severity of injury varies from simple strain to complete rupture, involving medial meniscus due to its attachment to the medial collateral ligament. The posterior capsule can be torn and ultimately the anterior cruciate can be involved.

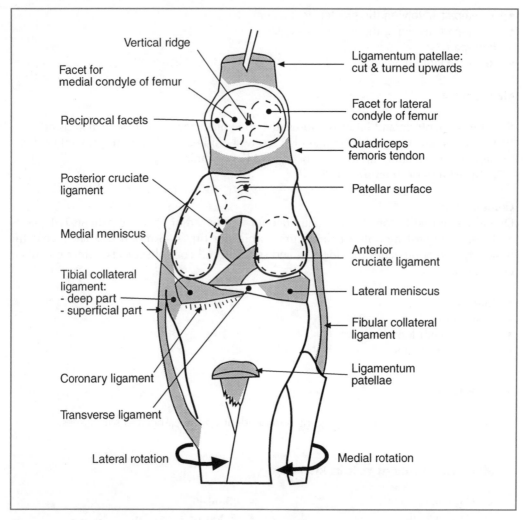

Anatomy of the knee

Lateral collateral ligament

This is a less common injury as knees are mostly injured from a lateral blow. The lateral collateral ligament is part of a complex that includes biceps femoris tendon and fascia lata — forming attachments to tibia, fibula and patella. All three structures may be damaged including the cruciates in severe varus stress. The common peroneal nerve may be damaged resulting in weakness of dorsiflexion of foot and toes, numbness in dorsum of foot and lateral aspect of lower leg.

Intra-articular ligaments

Posterior cruciate ligament injuries (rare)
Common when tibia is struck with knee flexed and forced backwards (e.g. lower leg against dashboard in front seat passenger road traffic accident; during fall). Loss of profile of knee when flexed as tibia sags backwards. Use posterior draw test.

Anterior cruciate ligament (common)
After forced hyperextension or forced flexion.

How to differentiate a serious ligamentous knee injury from a strain

- **Serious ligamentous injury**
  Rapid swelling within 1-2 hours
  of injury
  Significant haemarthrosis (complete
  rupture of collateral ligament
  may allow haemarthrosis to
  escape into soft tissues)
  Large effusion (allowing minimal
  movement)
  Sometimes surprisingly painless
  Localized tenderness
  (however, no localized tenderness
  may be elicited in cruciate injuries)
  X-ray: bony avulsion of ligamentous
  attachments sometimes seen

- **Strain**
  Swelling develops over 12–24 hours

  Moderate effusion

  Painful
  Localized tenderness

  No bony injury

If in doubt, examine under anaesthesia and arthroscope knee

Meniscal injuries (semi-lunar cartilages)

Mechanism is rotation of tibia on femur in flexed weight-bearing knee. Internal rotation of femur results in medial meniscal tears. External rotation of femur results in lateral meniscal tears. Medial meniscal injuries are more common — 20 times that of lateral meniscal tears. Majority of tears are vertical splits in body of meniscus — longitudinal tear. The free edge may be displaced centrally — bucket-handle tear.

The meniscus may rarely be congenitally discoid in shape. These are more prone to tears and even if untorn may give rise to loud clunks in the knee. A meniscal cyst may arise from a direct blow to the knee.

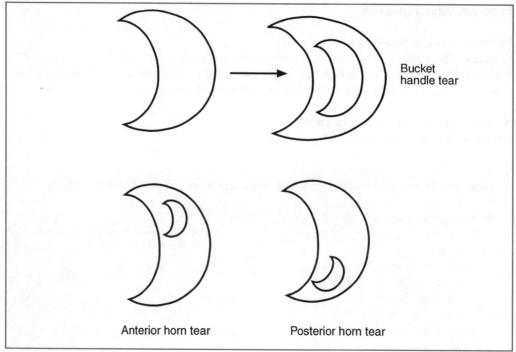

Anterior and posterior horn tears

Clinical feature of meniscal tears

- **Haemarthrosis**: absence of haemarthrosis may be deceptive as these occur with peripheral tears but not with more centrally based tears. Injuries at the meniscus are relatively avascular. Once torn, they do not heal.
- Joint line tenderness
- **Extension block to knee**: secondary to displaced tears
- **Locking of joint**: prevention of full flexion or full extension
- Clicking, clunking
- Medial or lateral pain

Investigations

- Need to X-ray to exclude other pathology
- MRI
- Arthroscopy

Extensor apparatus

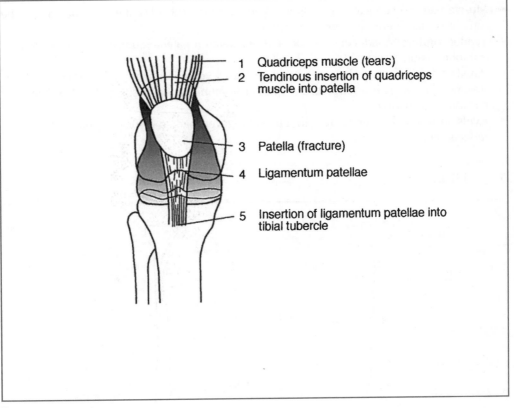

1	Quadriceps muscle (tears)
2	Tendinous insertion of quadriceps muscle into patella
3	Patella (fracture)
4	Ligamentum patellae
5	Insertion of ligamentum patellae into tibial tubercle

Extensor apparatus

Mechanisms of injury

- Direct violence (e.g. falls against hard surface)
- Indirect violence (e.g. sudden muscular contraction)

Clinical features

- Mostly unable to extend knee
- Swelling
- Bruising
- Palpable gap above patella (tear of tendinous insertion of quadriceps muscle into patella)
- Obvious displacement of patella — gap in patella

Require X-ray (AP and lateral). Tangential projections are difficult due to pain. Do not mistake congenital bipartite or tripartite patella for a fracture.

Management

- **Muscle tear**: no surgical intervention. When swelling subsides, the proximal end of the muscle is prominent on thigh contraction.
- **Tendon rupture**: quadriceps tendon and ligamentum patella. Surgical repair or plaster immobilization.
- **Patella fractures**: vertical do not show on lateral view, frequently missed, conservative treatment; horizontal undisplaced — plaster immobilization, displaced — ORIF mostly tension band wiring
- **Avulsion of tibial tubercle**: rare in adults, however marked displacement must be reduced and fixed.

1.7 Tibia

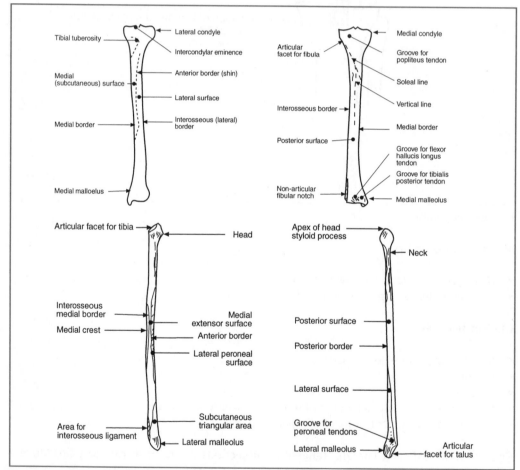

Anatomy of the tibia/fibula

Tibial fracture sites

- **Proximal**
  Intra-articular
  Extra-articular

- **Shaft**
  (± fibula fracture)
- **Distal tibia** (ankle fractures)
  — see Section 1.8

Articular fractures

Lateral tibial plateau

- Most common of intra-articular fractures
- Secondary to impaction of lateral femoral condyle on plateau during severe valgus force abducting tibia

With increasing force:

- Tibial fragment depressed
- Associated fibula neck fracture
- Rupture of medial collateral ligament
- Rupture of cruciates
- Subluxation of tibia
- Crushing lateral meniscus
- Conversion to bicondylar fracture

Medial tibial plateau fracture

- Less common
- May be associated with lateral ligament ruptures and common peroneal nerve palsy

Clinical features of intra-articular fractures

- Haemarthrosis
- Lateral/medial bruising
- Valgus/varus deformity of knee

Investigation
X-ray, CT scan

Management
For undisplaced, no ligament damage or tibial subluxation, use skin traction. Otherwise, ORIF ± ligament repair.

Extra-articular fractures

• Fracture tibial tuberosity

Tibial shaft ± fibula fracture

These are caused by direct or indirect violence.

Direct

• Road traffic accident (RTA): direct blow from car bumper
• Fall from motorbike combining impaction and bending forces
• Kicks during football

The resultant fractures are oblique or transverse and occur at the same level in both bones. They can be associated with a butterfly segment or more extensive comminution. They are often open due to external trauma to subcutaneous tibia or from a bony spike from within. Skin closure is difficult due to the tibia being partly subcutaneous. Plastic surgical intervention is often required to provide soft tissue cover in the form of local or free flaps as vascular soft tissue cover is essential to prevent infection and ensure healing of fracture site. When the fibula remains intact the displacement of the tibial fracture is often slight and plaster immobilisation is all that is required. Delayed union, however, is a complication, possibly due to the fibula acting as a strut preventing the fracture ends from uniting, as in malunion.

Indirect
Caused by:

• Torsions of the body on a fixed foot base (e.g. a fall during skiing)
• Bending of a fixed tibia and foot during a sideways fall of body (e.g. in a football game)

Indirect tibial fractures tend to be spiral or oblique. Muscle tone of soleus, gastrocnemius and tibialis anterior tend to produce shortening and displacement.

Complications

• The popliteal artery is susceptible to damage in upper-third fractures
• Interruption of the nutrient artery may lead to ischaemia of the distal fragment
• Angulation must be corrected to avoid abnormal loading of the knee and ankle joint surfaces and subsequent secondary osteoarthritis

Management of tibial shaft fracture ± fibula fracture
Minimally displaced and slightly displaced **stable fractures** (e.g. transverse) are readily amenable to conservative treatment with an above-knee plaster of Paris (PoP). **Oblique and**

spiral fractures are potentially unstable, although conservative management is an option if there is minimal displacement.

Displaced unstable fractures require reduction and internal fixation with intramedullary nailing or plates. The latter carries the risk of further devitalizing the fractured bone and skin coverage may be difficult.

External fixators are used in **open fractures**. Fractures of the tibia are more commonly open than in any other bone, and skin closure is particularly difficult because the bone is subcutaneous. The nature of the injury also often involves skin and tissue loss.

- **Double fractures** (both fibula and tibia involved): mostly require closed intramedullary nailing as they are too unstable for plaster immobilization and there is a risk of nonunion
- **Gross comminution**: alignment is restored by manipulation and fixed by Steinmann pins and PoP immobilization. Comminuted fractures are particularly slow to heal. On average, tibial fractures take 16 weeks to heal, but a grossly comminuted fracture may take up to 24 weeks.
- **Fracture of distal shaft**: can mostly be treated by MUA and PoP immobilization.
- **Isolated fracture of the fibula**: these are treated symptomatically only, such as a below-knee walking PoP for six weeks to aid pain relief and provide support.

Gustuilo and Anderson 1976 classification of open fractures

- **Type I**
  A wound <1 cm long with little soft tissue damage
  Fracture pattern is simple with little comminution

- **Type II**
  A wound >1 cm long without extensive soft tissue damage
  Contamination and fracture comminution are moderate

- **Type III**
  Extensive soft tissue damage contamination and fracture comminution
  (A) Soft tissue coverage is adequate. Comminuted and segmental high-energy fractures are included regardless of wound size
  (B) Extensive soft tissue injury with massive contamination and severe fracture comminution requiring a local or free flap for coverage
  (C) Arterial injury requiring repair

Complications associated with tibial fracture

- **Compartment syndrome**: see Section 1.10, p. 40
- **Skin damage**: tibial fractures are often associated with skin damage and tissue loss. It is vital to aid fracture healing and avoid infection by having viable skin cover. Stabilization is provided by external fixation and later skin cover, provided by local or free flaps ± split skin grafting as a second-stage procedure.
- **Vascular injury**: displaced fracture of proximal shaft may damage the trifurcation of the popliteal artery
- **Delayed union and non-union**: in up to 20% of cases. If union not present at 16–20 weeks, may need to progress to internal fixation and bone grafting. Often occurs secondary to significant initial displacement, comminution and distraction, secondary to intact fibula.
- **Malunion**: shortening, malrotation, varus and valgus deformity, >10° may lead to secondary OA.
- **Ankle and subtalar joint stiffness**: due to prolonged immobilization.

1.8 Ankle

Anatomy of the ankle

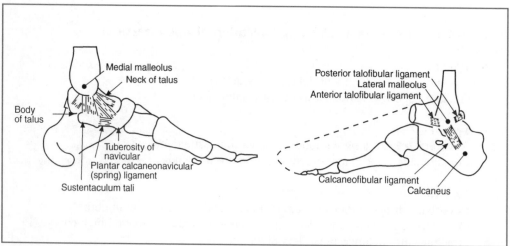

Anatomy of the ankle

The ankle is essentially a hinge joint. It is formed by the malleoli and lower end of the tibia and the body of the talus. As in every hinge joint, it is weak anteriorly and posteriorly but reinforced laterally and medially by ligaments. The ankle may be dorsiflexed and plantar flexed. The body of the talus is wider anteriorly and in full dorsiflexion becomes firmly wedged between the malleoli with the fibula slightly displaced laterally. In plantar flexion, there is a greater degree of movement possible between the talus and malleoli and the ankle is hence more susceptible to injury in this position. This is because the talus is narrower posteriorly.

The principle ligaments that provide stability are:

- **Inferior tibio-fibular ligaments**: anterior and posterior; these attach the fibula to the tibia, along with a weak interosseous membrane
- **Lateral ligament**: this originates from the fibula and consists of three parts; distally, the anterior and posterior slips attach to the talus and the central slip attaches to the calcaneus
- **Medial ligament** (deltoid ligament): is triangular in shape and extremely strong. It originates from the medial malleolus. Distally its deep fibres attach to the medial surface of the talus and the superficial fibres attach to the navicular, spring ligament and calcaneus.

Mechanisms of injury

Inversion injury
Damages lateral ligament — grades of severity dependent on how much of the ligament is involved. Range from sprain (some fibres) to complete tear or detachment from fibula. In complete tears the talus is free to tilt leading to chronic instability of the joint if untreated.

Eversion injuries
These stress the medial ligament which, due to its strength, tends to avulse the medial malleolus rather than tear.

Forced dorsiflexion
When the foot is dorsiflexed, the distal end of the fibula moves laterally. This movement is restricted by the inferior tibio-fibular ligaments and interosseous membrane. Damage to these structures may lead to lateral displacement of the fibula and lateral drift of the talus (diastasis).

Fracture of the ankle

There are numerous classifications of ankle fracture which are extremely complex. The two most widely used systems are the Weber–AO system, which depends on the level of the fibula fracture, and the Lange–Hansen system, in which the first term refers to the position of the foot and the second term refers to the direction of the deforming force.

In the Weber–AO system:

* **Type A** fractures are below the tibial plafond and are typically transverse fractures
* **Type B** fractures begin at the level of the tibial plafond and typically extend proximally in a spinal or short oblique fashion
* **Type C** fractures of the fibula are initiated above the tibial plafond and are associated with syndesmotic injuries

There are five main mechanisms that result in recognized patterns of injury:

* **Inversion/lateral rotation**: the rotating talus carries the fibula with it disrupting the anterior tibiofibular ligament. As rotation continues the fibula fractures in a spiral fashion. The fibula fragment can in turn displace a fragment of the posterior malleolus to which it is attached. The fourth structure to be damaged is the medial ligament or its attachment.
* **Eversion/abduction injuries**: the foot everts and the talus is abducted thus the structures initially damaged are the medial structures. The medial ligament rarely tears due to its strength, more commonly there is an avulsion fracture of the medial malleolus. The fracture line is transverse. As eversion continues the next structures to be damaged are the tibiofibular ligaments. Then the fibula fractures.
* **Eversion/lateral rotation**: the rotating talus produces an oblique fracture of the medial malleolus or rarely ruptures the medial (deltoid) ligament. As rotation continues, the anterior tibiofibular ligament is put under tension often avulsing the tibial attachment of the ligament. The fibula is then fractured in a spiral or oblique manner. The fibula may fracture proximally at the neck (the Maisonneuve fracture). If the talus continues to be pushed laterally, the posterior tibiofibular ligament ruptures and in turn ruptures the interosseous membrane resulting in marked talar shift (diastasis).
* **Inversion/adduction**: the first structure to be damaged as the talus externally rotates is the lateral ligament — either partial disruption or complete disruption of all three slips. Occasionally, avulsion fracture of lateral malleolus-transverse lie. The adducting talus then strikes the medial malleolus causing a verticular high oblique fracture.
* **Eversion/dorsiflexion**: as the talus dorsiflexes, its wide anterior part is forced between the malleoli shearing off the medial malleolus. As this continues, the anterior tibial margin is fractured followed by the lateral malleolus.

Treatment of ankle injuries

Aims of treatment

* To restore and maintain normal alignment of the talus with the tibia
* To ensure no future problems with instability
* To ensure re-alignment of articulating surfaces to reduce the chance of developing secondary osteoarthritis

Excellent results can be obtained by conservative management in the stable, one-malleolar fracture. However, ORIF is method of choice for unstable fractures, i.e. those with talar shift or potential talar shift. If a fibular fracture is above the inferior tibiofibular joint, the fracture is unstable requiring ORIF.

1.9 Clavicle

Most clavicle fractures are secondary to a direct blow on the shoulder (e.g. a fall on the side). Less commonly, they result from transmitted force from a fall onto outstretched hand. A fracture is most common at the junction of the middle and outer thirds and through the middle third. This is due to the strong ligament attachments via the costoclavicular ligament and the coracoclavicular ligament.

Subluxations and dislocations may involve the acromioclavicular joint and the sternoclavicular joint. Greenstick fractures are common — healing of this type of fracture is rapid and reduction is not required.

In the adult, undisplaced fractures are common — conservative treatment only is required. With greater violence there is separation of the bone ends. The proximal end under the pull of sternocleidomastoid muscle often becomes elevated. With greater displacement of the distal fragment there is overlapping and shortening. However, union is rapid and remodelling is so effective even in adults that conservative treatment suffices.

1.10 Complications of fractures

Early general

Hypovolaemic shock
Approximate blood loss in closed fracture:

- Pelvis   1–5 L
- Femur   1–2.5L
- Tibia   0.5–1.5L
- Humerus 0.5–1.5L

Disseminated intravascular coagulation
In severe blood loss.

Systemic inflammatory response syndrome (SIRS)
In the multiply injured, shocked patient.

Fat embolism

Occurs as a result of:

- Release of lipid globules from damaged bone marrow fat cells
- Increased peripheral mobilization of fatty acids
- Increased synthesis of triglycerides by liver

Results in thrombo-embolism of the microvasculature with lipid globules. As any part of the microvasculature can be affected the clinical manifestations are varied:

- **Pulmonary**: ventilation/perfusion mismatch
- **Cerebral**: ischaemia, infarction, oedema
- **Cardiac**: arrhythmias and impaired mechanical performance
- **Renal**: ischaemic glomerular/tubular dysfunction
- **Skin**: capillary damage, petechial haemorrhage

Diagnosis is made by detections of fat globules in body fluids in association with pulmonary and at least one other organ system failure/dysfunction.

Early local

Arterial/nerve injury

Compartment syndrome

This may occur after any injury to a limb, even without an associated fracture. In the forearm and lower leg there are compartments made up of bone, interosseous membranes and investing layers of deep fascia in which are muscles, nerves and vessels.

If swelling occurs in a compartment either secondary to oedema, inflammation or haematoma, this will impede venous outflow, increasing the compartment pressure further, preventing forward flow of oxygenated blood. This leads to muscle ischaemia and ultimately necrosis.

Causes of compartment syndrome

- Crush injuries
- Prolonged compression of limb (e.g. tight PoP, prolonged surgery)
- Open/closed fractures
- Reperfusion injury

Clinical features of compartment syndrome

- Pain out of proportion to the injury sustained
- Pain on passive stretching of the affected muscle

- Muscle tenderness
- Sensory loss
- Weakness

Pale cool limb and loss of pulses are very late signs. Initially, distal circulation and pulses are normal with warm, pink skin

If compartment syndrome is suspected clinically then plaster immobilization and any bandaging must be removed immediately. Compartment pressures should be measured if there is doubt about the diagnosis, and, if elevated, urgent fasciotomy must be performed.

Infection

Wounds at risk of faecal contamination (e.g. those allowing clostridial spores in soil to enter tissues) can give rise to anaerobic gas, producing infections 80% due to *Clostridium perfringens*. Invasion of traumatized muscle leads to infection of the entire muscle. Subcutaneous tissues can be affected in isolation — spreading extensively foul-smelling necrotic tissues.

Diagnosis is made by:

- Crepitus on palpation
- X-ray: air in muscles or subcutaneous plane

Local skin loss

Requiring split skin grafting or local/free flaps if bone/tendon/joint exposed. Fracture blisters complicate healing and choice of fracture fixation.

Late complications

- **General**
  DVT
  PE
  UTI
  Respiratory tract infection
  Disuse atrophy
  Osteoporosis
  Psychosocial/economic factors

- **Local**
  Delayed union/non-union/malunion
  Infection
  Interposition of soft tissues
  Poor blood supply
  Distraction of fracture fragments
  Joint stiffness
  Secondary osteoarthritis
  Avascular necrosis
  Myositis ossificans
  Sudeck's atrophy

Avascular necrosis
Intracapsular fracture of proximal femur, resulting in avascular necrosis of femoral head. Proximal scaphoid from a fracture of waist of scaphoid, humeral head from proximal humeral fracture. Body of talus from neck of talus fracture.

Myositis ossificans
May occur following a fracture or soft tissue injury that involves avulsion of periosteum and local haematoma. It is thought that periosteal cells proliferate within the haematoma and ossify it, therefore markedly reducing the range of movement often resulting in permanent limitation.

Sudeck's atrophy/complex regional pain syndrome/reflex sympathetic dystrophy (RSD)
An autonomic neuropathy of uncertain aetiology. Fracture complication most frequently seen after Colles' fracture.

Clinical features:

- Localized swelling
- Warm, well perfused periphery
- Marked restriction of movements due to diffuse tenderness

Treatment:

- Usually self-limiting 4–12 months but may result in permanent decreased function
- Intensive physiotherapy

Typical X-ray changes:

- Union of the fracture
- Diffuse osteoporosis

2. ARTHRITIS

This is a degenerative joint disease.

Differentiating between rheumatoid and osteoarthritis

- **Rheumatoid arthritis (Inflammatory)**

- **Osteoarthritis (Mechanical)**

Symptoms	
Worst on waking	Worst at end of day
Relieved by exercise	Worse with exercise
Worse with rest	Relieved by rest
Early morning stiffness (>30 min)	Limited early morning stiffness (<30 min)
Stiffness after rest (>5 min)	Limited stiffness after rest (<5 min)
Relieved by NSAIDs	Relieved by simple analgesics
Systemic effects	No systemic effects
Possible family history	Previous injury
Autoimmune disease	Particular occupation

Signs	
Soft tissue swelling	Bony swelling
Joints warm ± erythema	Joints cool no erythema
Systemic signs	No systemic signs
Associated pathology	No associated pathology

Investigations	
Increased ESR, CRP	Normal ESR, CRP
Anaemia of chronic disease	Normal full blood count
Positive autoantibodies	Negative autoantibodies
Inflammatory synovial fluid	Non-inflammatory synovial fluid

X-ray changes	
Peri-articular osteoporosis	Heberden's nodes
Joint space narrowing	Bouchard's nodes
Marginal erosions	Joint space narrowing
Boutonnière deformity	Subchondral sclerosis
Subluxations and dislocations	Osteophytes
Soft tissue swelling, symmetric, fusiform	

2.1 Osteoarthritis

Osteoarthritis affects synovial joints. It used to be considered a simple degenerative process. It is now described as a dynamic condition characterized by:

- Breakdown of articular cartilage
- Loss of joint space
- Reparative bone response

Pathogenesis

Cartilage is composed of chondrocytes in an extracellular matrix with water accounting for 70–80% of weight. The matrix is composed of proteoglycans and non-collagenous proteins in a network of collagen fibres. The extra-cellular aggressin is the predominant proteoglycan synthesized and secreted by chondrocytes. Proteoglycans are hydrophilic but swelling due to hydration is restrained by collagen network. With normal ageing, decreased proteoglycans lead to lower water binding capacity. This results in a thinner, stiffer cartilage with lower resilience and higher vulnerability to injury.

In early osteoarthritis increased matrix turnover is followed by a loss of proteoglycan and collagen. This increases the space in which the remaining proteoglycan can hold water resulting in chondromalacia. The swollen, soft cartilage is less resistant to force allowing further damage to the collagen network. Breakdown products activate the immune system leading to inflammation and tissue destruction by cytokines and degradative enzymes.

Attempts at repair lead to formation of new cartilage which may undergo endochondral ossification forming marginal osteophytes. Also causes bony protrusions at the margins of distal interphalangeal joints — **Heberden's nodes**. Subchondral new bone formation leads to sclerosis.

Clinical patterns

Primary OA

- Men: middle age
- Women: old age
- 80% >70 years

Secondary OA

- Previously damaged or congenitally abnormal joint
- Any age

2.2 Rheumatoid arthritis

Rheumatoid arthritis is a symmetrical inflammatory polyarthropathy with systemic manifestations — affecting vasculature, skin, heart, lungs, nerves, eyes in approximately 20% of patients.

Pathology

Mainly severe chronic synovitis. Initially affects small proximal joints of the hands and feet but then usually progresses symmetrically to wrists, elbows, ankles and knees.

- Infiltration of synovium of predominantly macrophages and T-lymphocytes
- Inflamed synovium: **pannus**. This eventually fills the joint space and impinges on joint surfaces. Pannus formation and release of destructive enzymes and cytokines destroy underlying cartilage.
- Bony erosion at joint margin follows. Inflammation of other synovial structures, such as tendon sheath, contribute to deformity and disability by leading to tendon rupture.
- 20% have rheumatoid nodules. These are lesions of the subcutaneous collagen. Each nodule consists of a central zone of necrotic collagen surrounded by a cellular infiltrate of macrophages and fibroblasts. Mostly occur on extensor surfaces of arms and elbows.

Proposed aetiologies

Aetiology of rheumatoid arthritis is uncertain but there are two main theories.

- **Microbial trigger**: Epstein–Barr virus prime suspect, also *Mycobacterium tuberculosis* and *Proteus mirabilis*
- Linkage to HLA-DR4 points to genetic susceptibility. Once inflammatory synovitis is initiated, an autoimmune reaction ensues. CD4 cells are activated with release of many cytokines. Autoantibodies are produced. Autoantibody against the FC portion of autologous IgG is called **Rheumatoid Factor**. Rheumatoid factor is usually IgM but can be IgG, IgA or IgE. These factors form complexes within the synovium and synovial fluid and are partly responsible for the characteristic changes. Rheumatoid factor occurs in only 20% of cases.

Clinical features

- Warm joints
- Swelling, joint thickening and effusion
- Muscle wasting
- Tendon rupture
- **Boutonnière deformity**: flexion of PIP joint and extension DIP joint of finger due to detachment of central slip of extensor tendon which is attached to base of middle phalanx and dislocation of lateral slips

- **Swan neck deformity**: DIP joint is flexed and PIP joint extended. Causes: shortening of extensor digitorum communis, tight interossei, rupture flexor digitorum superficialis.
- **Z-thumb**: due to displacement of extensor tendons or rupture of flexor pollicis longus

2.3 Surgery for arthritis

Indications for surgery

- Significant pain in a joint with instability
- Significant pain in a joint where analgesia is ineffective or contraindicated

Surgical options — excise, fuse, replace

- **Primary surgery for OA**
  Arthrolavage
  Osteotomy
  Replacement arthroplasty
  Excision arthroplasty
  Arthrodesis

- **Primary surgery for RA**
  Synovectomy
  Arthrodesis
  Replacement arthroplasty
  Osteotomy

- **Revision surgery for RA and OA**
  Arthroplasty following osteotomy
    or arthrodesis
  Exchange arthroplasty
  Salvage procedures

Non-surgical options

- Splintage
- Occupational therapy
- Physiotherapy

Surgical anatomy of the knee

Anteromedially
The knee joint can be exposed by incisions through the vasti and alongside the patella tendon. This is the medial parapatellar approach. This gives unrivalled exposure of the whole joint and is used for total knee joint replacement surgery.

Medially
A much more restricted approach is used to access the medial meniscus. This is achieved by incising along the medial side of the patella with the knee flexed. Care must be taken not to

extend the incision more than 1 cm below the upper margin of the tibia as damage to the infrapatella branch of the saphenous nerve can occur. This can lead to the development of a painful neuroma. The area of anaesthesia produced is not usually troublesome.

Posteriorly
This is used rarely. This approach exposes the back of the joint capsule. It involves dissecting the tibial nerve from semimembranosus then displacing the nerve and popliteal vessels laterally and detaching the medial head of gastrocnemius from its origin. The head is also displaced laterally to protect the neurovascular bundle whilst exposing to joint capsule.

Superficial structures to avoid: small saphenous vein, posterior femoral cutaneous nerve, medial sural cutaneous nerve.

Deep structures to avoid: tibial nerve, popliteal vein, popliteal artery. Common peroneal nerve.

Aspiration
Knee joint flexed approximately 30°. This is carried out from the side at the upper lateral margin of the patella — which allows entry to the suprapatellar bursa.

Injection
Is carried out at the lower lateral margin of the patella on either side of the ligament.

Arthroscopy
The approach is on the lateral side of the patellar ligament.

Surgical anatomy of the hip

Anterior approach
Through the interval between sartorius and tensor fascia lata detaching the tensor fascia lata, rectus femoris, anterior parts of gluteus medius and iliacus from hip so that upper and anterior parts of the joint capsule can be accessed. Structures to avoid: lateral femoral cutaneous nerve, femoral nerve, ascending branch of lateral femoral circumflex artery.

Antero-laterally
Between tensor fascia lata and gluteus medius. It also involves partial or complete detachment of some or all of the abductor mechanism so that the hip can be abducted during reaming of the femoral shaft and so that the acetabulum can be more fully exposed. Beware of femoral nerve as it is the most laterally placed structure in the neurovascular bundle in the femoral triangle, mostly compression neuropraxia from misplaced retraction results. The femoral artery and vein are at risk from retractors that penetrate iliopsoas. Beware of the ascending branches of the lateral circumflex femoral vessels which are deep to the tensor and gluteus medius.

Posteriorly
This approach involves splitting of the middle of gluteus maximus in the line of its fibres. Piriformis, obturator internus and the gemelli are divided at their femoral attachments to expose the joint. The sciatic nerve is retracted medially and protected by turning the cut ends of obturator internus and gemelli backwards over the nerve.

2.4 General complications of orthopaedic surgery

Complications of orthopaedic surgery

- **General**
  Deep vein thrombosis (DVT)
  Pulmonary embolism (PE)

- **Local**
  Soft tissue swelling
  Haematoma
  Complications of implants
  Infection
  Neurovascular damage

Venous thromboembolism and pulmonary embolism

Orthopaedic surgery carries a high risk of development of DVT (40–80%), and proximal vein thrombosis (10–30%).

Risk factors

- Prolonged immobility (>4 days)
- Surgery of pelvis, hip, lower limb
- Prolonged operating time in both elective and emergency surgery
- Elderly population
- Fracture NOF
- Often associated with blood transfusion, increased risk of deep vein thrombosis
- Joint replacement

Diagnosis
Doppler USS: for iliofemoral or more proximal lesions. Venography is the method of diagnosis for peripheral sites.

Treatment
Full anticoagulation — 3 months

Complications
Pulmonary embolus can be fatal (0.1%). It is diagnosed with radioisotope perfusion lung scan and treated by full anticoagulation as for deep vein thrombosis. Sometimes surgery is

contemplated for a major embolism — specialist centres only. The best method is to prevent occurrence of deep vein thrombosis.

Prevention
Measures are employed to minimize stasis, endothelial trauma and increased coagulability — **Virchow's triad**.

- **Pre-operative measures**: low molecular weight heparin two hours before surgery and until patient is fully mobile
- **Intra- and post-operative measures**: calf pumps throughout surgery; TED stockings — graduated pressure stockings; minimize bleeding and transfusion; strict fluid balance; minimize tissue trauma good surgical technique; avoid hypothermia; early mobilization.

2.5 Local complications of orthopaedic surgery

Soft tissue swelling

This can be avoided by:

- Elevating the limb during surgery and post-operatively
- Ensuring dressings are not too tight
- Early mobilization

Haematoma

This can be avoided by:

- Meticulous haemostasis
- Use of suction drains

Complications of implants in joint replacement surgery

Fracture dislocation
Metal-work reduces the natural elasticity of the bone to which it is attached. Thus, the loads to which the bone is subjected are not absorbed evenly. The areas under most stress are at the end of the internal fixation devices or prosthetic joint components. This increases the susceptibility to fracture with less violence required.

Infection risk

- Increased if ongoing infection elsewhere (e.g. UTI)

- **Poor operative technique**: contamination, inadequate haemostasis, ischaemic tissue, inadequate antibiotic prophylaxis
- **Late infection**: up to one year post-surgery
- *Staphylococcus aureus*: thickening of capsule
- *Staphylococcus epidermidis*: polysaccharide slime, loosening the prosthesis, causing pain, necessitating removal

To minimize infection risk:

- Prophylactic antibiotics before insufflation of limb tourniquet
- Antibiotic cement
- Special precautions in the theatre

3. THE FOOT

3.1 Peripheral nerves of the lower limb

Before the anatomy of the foot can be discussed it is important to consider the peripheral nerves of the lower limb and the muscles they innervate as most exert their actions on the foot.

Common peroneal nerve

(The smaller terminal branch of the sciatic nerve.)

Motor distribution

- **Muscles of anterior compartment**: tibialis anterior; extensor hallucis longus; extensor digitorum longus; peroneus tertius; extensor digitorum brevis (all deep branch of common peroneal nerve)
- **Muscles of the peroneal (lateral) compartment**: peroneus brevis; peroneus longus (superficial branch of common peroneal nerve)

Common peroneal nerve also supplies extensor digitorum brevis in the foot.

Sensory distribution

- First web space (deep peroneal branch)
- Dorsum of foot, anterior and lateral side of lower limb (superficial peroneal branch)

Mechanisms of injury

- Fracture of fibula neck (e.g. direct blow to leg)
- Lateral ligament injuries of knee
- Pressure from plaster casts

Classical peroneal nerve injury

- Loss of anterior (deep) and lateral (superficial) leg muscles
- Loss of ankle and foot dorsiflexion and toe extension (foot drop)
- High-stepping gait to ensure plantar fixed foot clears the ground
- The foot is of normal appearance

Test: dorsiflexion against resistance, deep branch
             evert foot against resistance, superficial branch

Tibial nerve

(The larger terminal branch of the sciatic nerve.)

Motor distribution

- Soleus
- Tibialis posterior
- Flexor hallucis longus
- Flexor digitorum longus
- Plantaris
- Popliteus
- Gastrocnemius

All the muscles of the sole of the foot via its division into medial and lateral plantar nerves.

Sensory distribution

- Sole of foot
- Nail beds
- Distal phalanges
- Lower lateral calf skin
- Lateral foot and little toe skin

NB. Lateral side of foot and lower lateral calf skin supplied by the sural nerve (single cutaneous branch from tibial nerve).

Mechanism of injury

- Tibial shaft fracture
- Compartment syndrome of posterior calf
- Tight plasters

- Injuries posterior to medial malleolus
- Injuries involving tarsal tunnel

Classical tibial nerve injury

- Loss of ankle and toe flexors
- Clawing of toes
- Trophic ulceration
- Shuffling gait as the take-off phase of walking is impaired

- Muscle wasting in sole of foot
- Loss of sensation in sole of foot and distal phalanges
- Foot will be flat as the lateral longitudinal arch will have lost most of its principal supports and the medial longitudinal arch is compromised by the loss of tibialis posterior (see later)

Test: toe flexion, sensation on sole

3.2 Anatomy of the foot

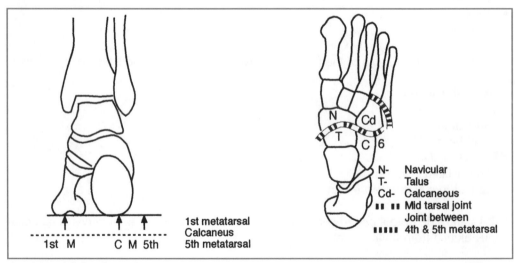

N- Navicular
T- Talus
Cd- Calcaneous
▮▮ ▮▮ Mid tarsal joint
▮▮▮▮▮ Joint between 4th & 5th metatarsal

1st metatarsal
Calcaneus
5th metatarsal

1st M   C M 5th

Anatomy of the foot

On standing, the prominence of the heel is aligned with the tibia. The calcaneus and the first and fifth metatarsal heads form a tripod. The forefoot is connected to the hind foot by the calcaneo-cuboid joint and the talo-navicular joint. As the heel goes into varus (inverts) it is projected downwards and medially. This movement is accompanied by plantar flexion and adduction of the forefoot. These movements cannot be separated due to the calcaneo-cuboid joint. Beyond the calcaneus is the mid-tarsal joint which is formed by the talus and navicular on one side and the calcaneus and cuboid on the lateral side. Valgus tilting or everting of the heel is accompanied by dorsiflexion and abduction of the forefoot.

The arches

Medial longitudinal arch (most important)
Bony components — calcaneus, talus, navicular, cuneiforms plus medial three metatarsals. Flattening of the arch is common (pes planus).

Principal supports of the medial longitudinal arch

- **Spring ligament** (plantar calcaneo-navicular ligament), supports head of talus
- **Plantar fascia** (acts as a tie by means of its attachments to the heel and metatarsal heads)
- **Abductor hallucis** and **flexor digitorum brevis** (spring ties)
- **Tibialis anterior**: elevates arch and with peroneus longus forms a stirrup-like support for it
- **Tibialis posterior**: adducts mid tarsal joint and reinforces the action of the spring ligament
- **Flexor hallucis longus**

The lateral longitudinal arch
Bony components — calcaneus, cuboid, fourth and fifth metatarsals. Shallow, flattens on weight-bearing.

Principal supports of the lateral longitudinal arch

- Long and short plantar ligaments
- Plantar fascia
- Flexor digitorum brevis
- Flexor digiti minimi
- Abductor digiti minimi
- Peroneus tertius
- Peroneus brevis

Anterior arch

Lies in the coronal plane. Bony compartments — metatarsal heads. This arch is only present in the non-weight-bearing foot. Under a load the metatarsal heads flatten out and the arch disappears. The metatarsal heads are prevented from spreading out by the intermetatarsal ligaments and the intrinsic foot muscles. The interosseous and lumbrical muscles, through their attachment to the extensor expansions, extend the toes at the PIP and DIP joints. If they become weak or frail, the unopposed flexor digitorum longus results in clawing of the toes.

3.3 Common disorders of the foot

Claw toes

Clawing of toes results from weakness of the interosseous and lumbrical muscles which normally extend the PIP and DIP joints of the toes by their attachment to the extensor expansions. The unopposed action of flexor digitorum longus results in clawing via flexion of DIP and PIP joint. When standing, the toe pads do not contact the ground so the weight bearing forces are transmitted through the metatarsal heads which are in a state of hyperextension. The result of this downward pressure is pain and callosity of the skin of the sole. Callosities form on the dorsal aspect of the toes due to their prominence in their flexed state.

Causes of claw toes

- Idiopathic
- Pes cavus
- Hallux valgus
- Poor footwear (e.g. high heels)
- Rheumatoid arthritis
- Underlying neurological abnormality

Treatment

- Treat cause
- Exercises for the intrinsic muscles of the foot
- Insoles to relieve weight from the metatarsal heads
- Padding to callosity
- Surgical intervention: flexor to extensor tendon transfer; excision of metatarsal heads (effective in rheumatoid arthritis); forefoot arthroplasty

Hammer toes

This affects the second, third and fourth toes and is characterized by hyperextension of the MTP and DIP joints and flexion of PIP joint. It is associated with hallux valgus and overcrowding of toes (e.g. in pointed or small shoes). Callosities form over the bony prominence on the dorsum of the PIP joint and eventually adventitious bursae develop.

Secondary contractions of tendons and ligaments can occur. There is pain beneath the metatarsal head due to pressure transmitted from PIP joint.

Treatment

- Remove the cause
- Corrective splinting
- Arthrodesis PIP joint with extensor tenotomy and dorsal capsulotomy of MTP joint

Pes cavus (claw foot)

Characterized by abnormally high longitudinal arches produced by an imbalance in the muscles controlling the maintenance and formation of the arches. The muscle imbalance is mostly between the peroneals and the extensor compartment and weakness of the intrinsic muscles of the toes producing clawing.

The abnormal distribution of weight in the foot leads to extensive callosities forming under the metatarsal heads and the heel. The deformity becomes worse during the growth period. A neurological cause should always be sought.

Neurological causes of pes cavus

- Poliomyelitis
- Spino-cerebellar degenerative diseases (e.g. Friedreich's ataxia, peroneal muscular atrophy)
- Spastic diplegia

Treatment

- Symptomatic (e.g. insoles)
- Surgery (only if sufficient disability exists)
- Lengthening Achilles tendon
- Calcaneal osteotomy
- Flexor to extensor tendon transfers

Hallux valgus

Lateral deviation of the great toe may be initiated by wearing footwear too narrow for forefoot. Abnormally broad forefoot predisposes to this condition. Hereditary short and varus first metatarsal may also contribute. Once the valgus position of the great toe has developed, it tends to progress due to the pull of the extensor and flexor hallucis longus which increase the deformity by a bowstring mechanism.

Complications of hallux valgus

- An exostosis on the medial aspect of the first metatarsal head — secondary to pressure on the periosteum
- A bunion (inflamed adventitious bursa) produced over the prominent head of the first metatarsal by pressure and friction
- Osteoarthritis of first MTP joint secondary to malalignment of proximal phalanx
- Further lateral drift of the great toe results in crowding of the other toes. The great toe may pass over the second toe or, more commonly, the second toe may override it
- A displaced second toe may develop a painful callosity, later dislocating at the MTP joint
- Dislocation of the second toe is an indication for surgery even in the younger patient

The aim of surgery is to correct the deformity and maintain the function of the great toe. Treatment varies depending on the age of the patient.

SUGGESTED TREATMENT OF HALLUX VALGUS

Age of patient	Treatment
15 years	Soft tissue correction: at level of MTP joint by tightening the stretched medial collateral ligament after division of the contracted adductor in the first web space.
	Metatarsal osteotomy: laterally based wedge osteotomy to narrow the angle between the first and second metatarsal shafts; used when there is no OA at the MTP joint. This is supplemented by the soft tissue procedures which involve tightening the medial capsule of the MTP joint to re-align the toe in the correct position. Mitchell's procedure (1958) most useful as simple and gives good results. Osteotomy is made at junction of metatarsal head and neck. Other methods involve basally placed osteotomies or oblique neck osteotomies.
45 years	Metatarsal osteotomy

Continues …

... Continued

75 years	Keller's: excision arthroplasty of proximal half of proximal phalanx and excision of prominent part of metatarsal head. Optional stabilization of the great toe with intra-medullary wire and elongation of extensor hallucis longus. Silastic MTP joint replacement, arthrodesis of MTP joint, MTP joint fusion
95 years	Soft shoes

Hallux rigidus

Osteoarthritis of the MTP joint of the great toe can be primary but is mostly secondary. It is more common in men.

There are two types:

- **Adolescent**: synovitis of MTP joint following injury (e.g. kicking football with toe); may develop osteochondritis dessicans of first metatarsal head
- **Adult**: osteoarthritis occasionally precipitated by injury; painful, decreased movement secondary to destruction of articular surfaces and interlocking of osteophytes

Treatment

- Fusion MTP joint
- Keller's arthroplasty

Diabetic foot

The multiple problems of the diabetic foot are related to three main pathological processes:

- **Arteriopathy**: leading to ischaemic and atrophic changes
- **Neuropathy**: leading to pressure necrosis
- **Predisposition to infection**: leading to development of soft tissue infection and osteomyelitis

Principles of treatment

- Wide surgical debridement cutting back to viable tissue
- Antibiotics
- Close control of diabetes
- Amputation should be as conservative as possible

4. AMPUTATION

4.1 Indications for amputation

The main indications for amputation are:

- Dying (e.g. vascular disease, gangrene)
- Dangerous (e.g. tumour, severe infection)
- 'Damned nuisance' (e.g. useless painful limb following trauma, neurological damage)

In the UK the most common reason for amputation is peripheral vascular disease, but world-wide, trauma is the main indication.

Indications for amputation in the UK

- Vascular disease and diabetes (80%)
- Trauma (10%)
- Tumour and other reasons (10%)

The incidence of limb amputation varies:

- In the UK it is 1 per 1000 of the population
- In Angola it is 1 per 380 of the population

4.2 Levels of amputation

The level for amputation needs to be selected carefully. It needs to be proximal enough for good healing, but more distal amputations have better long term outcome and rehabilitation. A correctly functioning knee joint should be preserved whenever possible. In below-knee amputation, ideally, 15 cm of bone below the knee should be conserved. However, a shorter stump is preferable to an above-knee amputation.

Upper limb amputations are much rarer than lower limb amputations and the principles are slightly different. The aims of maintaining length and function by carrying out minimal debridement are paramount. Loss of function is more disabling and less amenable to prosthetics than lower limb loss.

Levels of lower limb amputation (proximal to distal)

- **Hip disarticulation**: mainly for soft tissue/bony malignancy in the upper thigh; very rare for vascular disease
- **Above knee**: bone section 25–30 cm below greater trochanter, leaving 12 cm above the knee joint for the knee mechanism; equal anterior and posterior semicircular skin flaps
- **Supra-condylar (Gritti Stokes)**: supracondylar femoral division, patella fixed to end of femur with wire/sutures; useful if more length required than obtained from above-knee amputation, such as in bilateral amputees, to aid changing position in bed, etc. Unpopular as tendency for non-union of patella to femur, and difficult to fit prosthesis.
- **Through-knee**: quick to perform, relatively atraumatic, but poor healing in ischaemic disease and difficult to fit a prosthesis due to the bulbous stump.
- **Below-knee**: most popular level in severe ischaemia (can be done in 80%). Oximetry, thermography and arteriography can be used to help gauge the likelihood of success, but are not standard practice. The best guide to success is clinical judgement and flap bleeding at the time of surgery. The two most widely used methods are the long posterior flap (Burgess), using the posterior calf muscles to cover the bone ends 15 cm below the tibial tuberosity, and the skew flap (Kingsley Robinson). Little difference in healing rates.
- **Syme's**: rarely in vascular disease, heel disarticulated and malleoli excised then covered with long posterior skin flap; 30% require revision at a higher level
- **Transmetatarsal**: useful in diabetic gangrene of the forefoot; require no prosthesis; individual rays can be amputated, being left to heal by secondary intention
- **Toes**: trauma or diabetic infective gangrene in the presence of a good blood supply only

4.3 Principles of surgery for amputation

Amputations for peripheral vascular disease and neoplasia tend to be more radical than those for trauma or diabetes in the absence of peripheral vascular disease. In peripheral vascular disease the healing of the distal stumps tends to be compromised by poor blood supply. In neoplastic disease good clearance is a priority.

As a general rule, the total length of flaps will need to be at least one and a half times the diameter of the leg at the level of the bone section.

During surgery, a tourniquet may be applied to provide a bloodless field in trauma or neoplasia, but not in cases where there is peripheral vascular disease.

4.4 Post-operative management

Post-operative management of amputation

- Analgesia
- Care of the unaffected limb
- Physiotherapy
  Prevention of flexion contractures
  To build-up muscle power and co-ordination
- Mobilization

4.5 Complications of amputation

Complications of amputation

- **Early**
  Haemorrhage and haematoma formation
  Infection (high stumps may have faecal
    contamination and develop
    gas gangrene)
  Wound dehiscence
  Ischaemia and gangrene of flaps
  Deep vein thrombosis and
    pulmonary embolus

- **Late**
  Pain: phantom limb pain;
    amputation neuroma; causalgia
    (intractable burning pain due to
    sympathetic nerve growth down
    somatic nerves); painful scar due
    to adherence to bone
  Chronic infection: osteitis;
    sinus formation
  Ulceration of stump

Following amputation in children, the growing humerus or tibia can stretch the stump tissues and skin, causing painful weight-bearing, skin breakdown and ulceration.

4.6 Prostheses

Prostheses

- Sleeve
- Straps
- Suction
- Silicone: suspension

- Foot and ankle: depending on the level of activity — 'solid ankle, cushioned heel' foot — minimal maintenance, multi-axial ankles optimize gait; more active users may benefit from an energy-storing foot
- Knee mechanisms: free, locking, controlled, intelligent

4.7 Amputations for trauma

The Mangled Extremity Severity Score (MESS) (Helfet et al., 1990) gives a quantitative assessment of the severity of injury to a limb and therefore a guide in making the difficult decision of a primary amputation.

Four components of the MESS scoring system

- Skeletal/soft tissue injury
- Shock — hypovolaemic
- Limb ischaemia
- Age

Advantages of early amputation in trauma setting

Prevention of firmly established pain pathways that will not be alleviated by late amputation.

- Reconstruction can take months or years
- Often even the most sophisticated techniques can result in failure. This can lead to depression and suicidal ideation in patients.

4.8 Amputations for tumour

Indications for amputation for tumour

- Extensive soft tissue or percutaneous involvement of tumour
- Tumour invasion of neurovascular bundle
- Pathological fracture

Special consideration must be employed when taking biopsies as this may limit the choice of amputation method at a later stage.

Amputation for vascular disease is covered in Chapter 2, *Vascular*, Section 2.8.

5. INFECTIONS OF BONES AND JOINTS

5.1 Osteomyelitis

Acute and chronic bone infections used to be common and often fatal in children. Antibiotics have made these eminently treatable.

Bacteria are blood-borne — often no obvious primary focus of infection. In 80% of cases the organism is *Staphylococcus aureus*. Other organisms causing infection are streptococcus, pneumococcus, *Haemophilus influenzae* (common in under-twos), *Staphylococcus albus*, salmonellas.

Pathology

Bone infections almost always begin at the metaphysis. They progress through the cortex via haversian canals, causing thrombosis of blood vessels, eventually reaching the subperiosteal region. In the first 24–48 hours inflammatory exudate forms deep to the periosteum elevating the membrane. Periosteum is innervated and inelastic so this stretching causes pain.

After 24 hours frank pus develops subperiosteally. This rarely affects the growth plate as it contains no blood vessels and periosteum is firmly attached to plate at this level. The inflammatory process progresses along the medulla causing venous and arterial thrombosis.

The pus tracks subperiosteally, stripping the periosteum and interrupting its blood supply; thus progressively larger areas of cortex become involved and infarcted. The bony infarct is known as a sequestrum. Surrounding the sequestrum, the elevated periosteum lays down new bone that encloses the dead bone within. The ensheathing mass of new bone is known as the involucrum. In the absence of treatment the pus bursts through periosteum, tracking through muscle to reach skin, eventually forming a sinus connecting bone to broken down skin surface. Where pus has broken through the periosteum sinuses develop within the involucrum which are known as **cloacae** (Latin, 'a drain'). Advanced pathology such as this is rare due to modern treatment.

The intraosseous abscess cavity is prevented from resolving by its bony walls which are impenetrable to both the body's normal defence mechanisms and antibiotic treatment.

Clinical features

- Pain, increasing in severity
- Localized bony tenderness
- Systemic toxicity and pyrexia
- Joint effusion: adjacent joints may contain an effusion, however the joint itself will not be tender and some movement is possible as opposed to an infective arthritis in which no movement is permitted

Investigations

- **X-ray**: no abnormal radiological signs in first few days. Periosteal elevation plus new bone deposition may be seen after 10 days, but diagnosis is mostly clinical.
- **Isotope bone scanning**: useful in areas of difficult localization: where bone infection is to be distinguished from adjacent soft tissue infection; and when joint infection must be distinguished from transient synovitis
- **Blood cultures**: should be taken before antibiotics are commenced
- FBC, ESR, CRP

Treatment

Intravenous antibiotics and surgical evacuation of abscess is required.

Differential diagnosis of osteomyelitis

- Acute suppurative arthritis → distinguish joint pain from bone pain
- Acute rheumatic arthritis — polyarticular
- Haemarthrosis (e.g. haemophilia)
- Scurvy — subperiosteal haematoma mimics pain
- Bone infarct secondary to sickle crisis
- Ewing's tumour

Post-operative osteomyelitis

Intra-operative precautions to minimize post-operative infection:

- Meticulous technique
- Minimizing haematoma formation
- No wound tension
- Peri-operative prophylactic antibiotics especially in patients with predisposing illness (e.g. diabetes mellitus, rheumatoid arthritis, corticosteroid therapy)
- Do not perform surgery with ongoing chest/urinary tract infection

The most common infecting organism is *Staphylococcus aureus*. Often the picture is mixed — *Staphylococcus aureus*, proteus, pseudomonas. Skin commensals that are not normally pathogenic, such as *Staphylococcus epidermidis*, may also be involved.

The first-choice prophylactic antibiotic is usually a cephalosporin — peri-operatively and two further post-operative doses. Commence 10 minutes before incision or application of tourniquet.

5.2 Acute joint infections

Septic arthritis is a potentially life-threatening condition. It can progress to systemic sepsis and destroy the affected joints. Treat as a surgical emergency.

Causes of acute joint infections

* Direct inoculation (e.g. penetrating trauma)
* Local extension from nearby osteomyelitis
* Blood-borne from distal site or systemic infection

Most common causative organisms include streptococcus, staphylococcus and pneumococcus. Less commonly, gonococcus. *Haemophilus influenzae* may be found in those aged under four years.

Clinical features

* Increased pain and inability to move joint
* General malaise
* Spiking pyrexia, rapid onset
* Joint is hot, red and swollen
* More common in neonates, in the immunocompromised and in children with sickle cell disease

Treatment

Joint immobilized
In position of optimum function until pain allows mobilization:

* **Shoulder**: 40–50° abduction with elbow joint anterior to coronal plane and hand in front of mouth
* **Elbow**: flexed at 90° semi-pronated
* **Wrist**: dorsiflexed to maintain strong grip
* **Hip**: neutral abduction and rotation
* **Knee**: 5–10° flexion to allow foot to clear ground when walking
* **Ankle**: at 90°

Aspiration
This is both diagnostic and therapeutic. If frank pus is aspirated this is an indication for formal washout under general anaesthetic. Send pus for urgent Gram stain plus microbiological identification.

Intravenous antibiotics
Aims of early diagnosis and treatment are to avoid the destruction of articular cartilage, necrosis of the epiphysis in children and pathological dislocation.

Later complications
Secondary osteoarthritis, joint stiffness, fibrous/bony ankylosis. In septic arthritis of the hip, destruction of the head of the femur leads to dislocation of the hip and growth plate arrest. This requires reconstructive surgery.

5.3 Tuberculosis of the skeleton

Bone/joint TB is haematogenous in origin from bacilli lying previously dormant in regional lymph nodes from an initial gut or lung infection. The disease starts in synovial membrane or intra-articular bone. This means that any synovial joint may be affected and also structures ensheathed in synovium (e.g. finger flexor tendons or bursae). The spine is commonly involved.

Pathology

Tubercles develop in the synovial membrane which becomes bulky and inflamed. There is a collection of infected effusion within the synovial cavity. If this progresses it causes destruction of articular cartilage and adjacent bone resulting in loss of function and fibrous ankylosis. Spinal TB escapes diagnosis until two adjacent vertebral bodies are involved so that the end result is replacement of intervertebral disc and adjacent bone by fibrous tissue. Should treatment be delayed abscess formation occurs leading to vertebral body collapse and kyphosis (forward angulation).

The pus often tracks along tissue planes to present superficially (e.g. T12, involvement can lead to pus tracking along psoas muscle to present as a 'cold' abscess in the groin). TB abscesses are described as cold abscesses because the skin is not red and only slightly warm. The combination of pus and spinal angulation may damage the spinal cord. The blood supply via the anterior spinal arteries may also be compromised resulting in paraplegia.

Clinical features

- Aching: localized; worse on exertion or at night
- Increased stiffness
- Increased pain on joint movement: due to adhesion formation, muscle spasm and bone destruction
- Kyphosis and abscess collection (late signs)
- Synovial thickening and effusion in superficial joints
- X-ray changes (not obvious in early disease): soft tissue swelling; narrowing joint or disc space; osteolytic lesions in adjacent bone

Early diagnosis and treatment is essential to preserve function. Early biopsy of involved tissue for histological and bacteriological examination should be performed and shows acid-fast bacilli and typical tubercles.

Management

Medical treatment comprises 6–12 months' antituberculous chemotherapy or until X-ray shows resolution in bone changes. Compliance is often problematic. Patients may need hospitalization for immobilization and splintage in the acute phase.

Surgical intervention is not indicated at the synovial stage as antibiotics will arrest the progression of disease. Abscesses need incision and drainage under antibiotic cover and continued chemotherapy after the procedure.

Where the abscess has occupied a joint space, the articulating surfaces will have been destroyed and so arthrodesis of the joint must be performed. The gap left may be filled with bone grafts that act as struts. Other surgical indications are in marked bone destruction and threatened severe kyphosis or paraplegia.

6. THE NECK

6.1 Examination of the neck

When examining the neck, it is important to assess possible involvement of spinal nerves rather than peripheral nerves. Myotomes and dermatomes are muscle masses and areas of skin supplied by single spinal nerves. Weakness or sensory loss in these areas will locate spinal nerve involvement.

Myotomes

Normally two roots produce movement of a joint in a particular direction and two in another:

- Elbow flexion (biceps) C5, 6
- Elbow extension (triceps) C7, 8
- Shoulder abduction (deltoid) C5
- Shoulder adduction (pectoralis major) C6, 7
- Wrist dorsiflexion C6, 7
- Wrist palmar flexion C6, 7
- Pronation forearm C6
- Supination forearm C6
- Abduction fingers T1
- Adduction fingers T1

Dermatomes

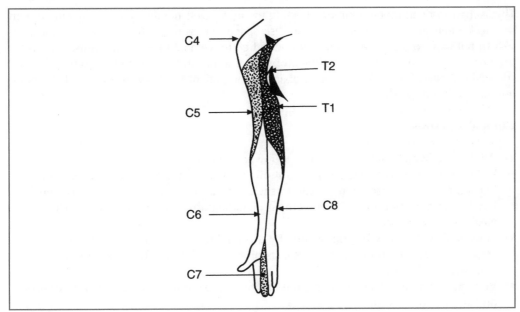

Dermatomes

The middle finger is supplied by C7 and there is an easily remembered sequence of sensory distribution around the pre-axial line of the upper limb.

Neck examination

- **Inspection**
  Asymmetry
  Torticollis

- **Palpation**
  Mid-line C-spine
  Lateral aspects of vertebrae —
    tenderness localized to one
    intervertebral space is common
  Supraclavicular fossae
  Anterior structures
  Paravertebral muscles most common
    site of tenderness

- **Movements**
  Active
  Flexion (chin to chest)
  Extension: normal range between
    flexion and extension is 130°
  Lateral flexion (ear to shoulder)
  Rotation: normal range 80° each side

Assessment of segmental nerve distribution in upper limb is essential to complete a neck examination.

6.2 Cervical spondylosis (osteoarthritis of c-spine)

This is the most common condition affecting the neck. Degenerative changes occur early in the neck often in the third decade. The disc space between C5, 6 is most commonly involved but may go unnoticed clinically due to free movement of adjacent joints. The disc is the first structure to be involved followed by facet joints and uncovertebral joints. Cervical spondylosis often does not cause complaint to the patient but may be triggered by minor trauma (e.g. a whiplash injury).

Clinical features

- Pain centrally radiating to occiput or to lower scapulae
- With nerve root involvement due to arthritic changes in the facet or uncovertebral joints there may be radiation of pain to shoulders, arms, hands with a sensory deficit
- Rarely, there is neurological involvement including absent arm reflexes, muscle weakness and sensory loss
- The cervical cord may be compressed by a central disc protrusion or, for example, osteophytes arising from posterior aspects of vertebral bodies. This gives rise to long tract signs and gait abnormalities.
- Vertebral artery involvement from osteophyte outgrowth may present as drop attacks on extremes of movement of the neck.

Treatment

- Analgesia plus neck support
- If root symptoms are prominent, can consider cervical traction
- Manipulation of c-spine is advocated in younger age groups with no neurological involvement

6.3 Rheumatoid arthritis

Ligamentous stretching accompanies rheumatoid arthritis so a picture of progressive subluxation of the cervical spine (especially at atlanto-axial and mid cervical levels) is common. Pain and stiffness are complicated by root and cord symptoms. Gait ataxia and progressive paralysis may occur.

Treatment involves local cervical fusion if patient's condition will allow.

7. THE SHOULDER

There is a complex arrangement of joints in the shoulder. It is best to consider the shoulder as separate components.

7.1 Movements of the shoulder

Glenohumeral movement

- Abduction
- Comes to an end when greater tuberosity of humerus impinges on glenoid rim
- Range of movement 90° — this can be increased if arm is externally rotated thus delaying impingement

Scapular movement

The scapula articulates with the clavicle and carries the glenohumeral joint. It can move independently over the underlying thoracic cage and serratus anterior. It may be elevated, depressed, rotated medially or laterally around the chest wall. It may also be tilted, changing the angle of the glenoid.

During the first 90° of abduction, the glenohumeral joint is the primary effector. Beyond 90° the scapula continues the movement. During the last 30° there may be a spinal contribution, i.e. lateral flexion of thoracic spine. An intact supraspinatus is necessary for initiation of abduction which is then complemented by deltoid which raises the head of the humerus relative to the glenoid.

7.2 The rotator cuff

This is an almost complete ring of muscle attached to the humerus around the anatomical neck. The joint capsule is fused with the insertion of:

- **Subscapularis** in front
- **Supraspinatus** above
- **Teres minor** plus **infraspinatus** behind

The most important structure in this arrangement is the supraspinatus which runs through a tunnel formed by the acromion and the coracoacromial ligament.

7.3 Examination of the shoulder

Inspection

Anteriorly, posteriorly and from above.

Anteriorly

- Prominent sternoclavicular joint: subluxation
- Deformity of clavicle: previous fracture
- Prominent AC joint: osteoarthritis, subluxation
- Deltoid wasting: axillary nerve palsy with loss of sensation in 'regimental badge' region, disuse atrophy
- Joint effusion/erythema

Posteriorly

Scapula: normal shape, small, high. Winged due to paralysis of serratus anterior (long thoracic nerve damage).

Palpation

- Anterior aspect glenohumeral joint: tenderness — infection, calcifying supraspinatus tendonitis
- Head of humerus in axilla
- AC joint
- Press below acromion and abduct arm to assess tenderness during arc of abduction: rotator cuff tear; subdeltoid bursitis
- Palpate clavicle

Movements

- **Abduction**: difficulty in initiating abduction suggests:
    a supraspinatus tendon tear: pain 60–120°
    rotator cuff tear; pain 120–170°
    osteoarthritis AC joint
  Repeat with arm in external rotation — if eased, suggestive of impingement on acromion from inflamed rotator cuff tear
  Abduct by fixing scapula — if no movement without scapula, suggests fixed glenohumeral joint
- **Adduction**: 0–50°
- **Forward flexion**: 0–165°
- **Backward extension**: 0–60°

Place hand behind opposite shoulder blade — internal rotation in extension. Place hand behind head — external rotation in abduction.

7.4 Disorders of the shoulder

Rotator cuff tears

Result from sudden traction to the arm. Supraspinatus is most commonly involved. This manifests as difficulty in abducting the arm. In other cases a torn rotator cuff impinges on the acromion during abduction giving rise to a painful arc of movement — 60–120°. Pain during abduction between 120° and 170° is suggestive of osteoarthritis of the acromioclavicular joint. Painful abduction in impingement from a torn rotator cuff is eased when the arm is abducted in full external rotation. Revascularization plus healing of tears and of degeneration lead to calcium deposition and sub-deltoid bursitis thus aggravating the condition.

Treatment is via local steroid injection plus NSAIDs. Surgical intervention involves decompression of the rotator cuff by excising the coraco-acromial ligament and part of the acromion. Tendon repairs are also opted for in complete tears.

Osteoarthritis of acromioclavicular joint

- Usually localized tenderness with obvious prominence of joint from osteophyte formation
- Physiotherapy is first-line treatment
- Acromionectomy may be considered in severe cases
- Referred pain from cervical spondylosis
- Pain from irritation of nerve roots is referred from neck to shoulder

Adhesive capsulitis — frozen shoulder

Numerous aetiologies but occurs most commonly in the middle-aged with degenerative changes at the rotator cuff.

Clinical features

- Decreased range of movement of shoulder joint, often severe with no movement at glenohumeral joint
- Internal rotation is the first movement to be restricted
- Frequently there is a history of minor trauma which exacerbates existing degenerative changes and develops into a prolonged inflammatory response. Occasionally develops after a period of immobilization. X-rays are mostly normal.

Anterior dislocation of the shoulder

This is much more common than posterior dislocation. The humeral head lies anterior to the glenoid. This is caused by a fall, often resulting in forced external rotation of shoulder.

Features of anterior dislocation of the shoulder

- Anterior structures are damaged — capsule is torn from its attachment to the glenoid — Bankart lesion
- Axillary nerve and brachial plexus injury are risks

- Displacement of glenoid labrum
- Damage to rotator cuff
- Greater tuberosity may fracture

Clinical features

- Painful
- Patient resists movement
- Altered contour due to displacement of humeral head
- Axillary nerve palsy results in reduction — loss of sensation in 'regimental badge' region

X-ray

Most show clearly on AP views. An axial lateral view is helpful in confirming diagnosis but often the shoulder is too painful to allow this view. An associated fracture of the greater tuberosity is common. This does not affect decision to reduce shoulder initially but may need attention afterwards.

Reduction

Kocher's method
After administration of sedative and analgesia:

- Flex elbow and pull down on upper arm slowly, externally rotating shoulder
- It should be possible to reach 90° of external rotation

The shoulder reduces with a clear clunking sensation — if this does not happen, adduct the elbow below the chest. Once reduction is complete internally rotate the shoulder with hand on opposite shoulder and protect in sling. Repeat X-ray. If unsuccessful may need general anaesthetic.

Hippocratic method
Traction is applied to arm by putting heel against chest and levering humeral head back into position.

Gravitational traction
Strong analgesia required. Patient is prone with sandbag under clavicle of dislocated shoulder. Arm is hanging over table acting as gravitational traction. Leave up to one hour before attempting other methods.

Post-reduction
Patients require broad-arm sling immobilization for one month. There is an approximately 50% risk of recurrence within two years. If shoulder dislocates four times or more, reconstructive surgery should be considered. Older patients are mobilized within two weeks to prevent stiffness and loss of function. Most greater tuberosity fractures reduce with shoulder reduction. If it remains displaced it may require open reduction and screw fixation.

Posterior dislocation of the shoulder

In posterior dislocation the humeral head lies posterior to the glenoid. It usually results from fall onto outstretched internally rotated hand or direct blow to front of shoulder (electric shock or a fit). Often the AP view looks normal. Lateral view required to show dislocation.

Reduction
Apply traction to arm with elbow flexed and arm abducted to 90° and slowly externally rotate. The shoulder is then immobilized in sling as for anterior dislocations.

Pain will eventually subside after many months (up to two years) but patients will be left with a permanently restricted range of movement — due to adhesions forming between capsule and humeral head. The mainstay of treatment is graduated shoulder physiotherapy.

Occasionally steroid injections are used or manipulations under anaesthesia with follow-up physiotherapy.

8. THE ELBOW

8.1 Anatomy of the elbow

This is a very stable joint due to the close fit between the ulna and trochlea aided by strong collateral ligaments.

- At full flexion the coronoid process lies in coronoid fossa
- At full extension, the olecranon process lies in the olecranon fossa
- Due to the proximity of these components only a small disruption in their position or a small loose foreign body in one of the fossae can cause a significant restriction of movement

The axis of pronation and supination passes through the radial head and the attachment of the triangular fibro-cartilage.

- **Pronation**: pronator teres, pronator quadratus
- **Supination**: biceps + supinator

Important neurovascular relations

The median nerve and brachial artery lie medial to the biceps tendon and superficial to brachialis muscle. Medially, in the subcutaneous plane lies the medial cutaneous nerve of forearm, basilic and median cubital veins. The radial nerve and its posterior interosseous branch lie lateral to biceps tendon. Laterally, in the subcutaneous plane lies the lateral cutaneous nerve of forearm, cephalic and median cubital veins. The ulnar nerve at the elbow lies behind the medial epicondyle. The main extensor origin is from the lateral epicondyle. The main flexor origin is from the medial epicondyle.

8.2 Examination of the elbow

Inspection

- Earliest sign of effusion is filling out of the hollow as seen in the flexed elbow above the olecranon
- Rheumatoid nodules
- Muscle wasting
- **Carrying angle**: male approximately 11°; female approximately 13°
- **Cubitus valgus**: increase in carrying angle
- **Cubitus varus**: decrease in carrying angle

Movements

- **Extension**: full 0°; loss of full extension is common in osteoarthritis, old fractures
- **Hyper-extension**: up to 15° is normal, especially in women but consider Ehlers–Danlos and other connective tissue disorders
- **Flexion**: 145°; restriction is common in osteoarthritis, rheumatoid arthritis and old fractures
- **Pronation**: range from neutral position, 75°
- **Supination**: range from neutral position, 80°
- **Pronation/supination**: reduced in old forearm, wrist fracture rheumatoid arthritis, osteoarthritis
- **Pure supination**: loss in children with pulled elbow (occurs in under-fives after sudden traction on arm) or congenital synostosis/dislocation

Palpation

- **Epicondyles**: lateral tenderness, tennis elbow; medial tenderness, golfer's elbow
- **Olecranon**
- **Radial head**: palpate while pronating, supinating forearm
- **Ulnar nerve**

8.3 Common disorders of the elbow

Tennis elbow

Strain or small tears in the common extensor origin followed by inflammatory reaction. Usually presents in the 35–50 age group. Main complaint is pain on the lateral side of the elbow exacerbated by movement and holding heavy objects at arm's length with the forearm pronated. There may be a history of excessive activity (e.g. dusting, sweeping, playing tennis!).

Treatment

- Local steroid injections and local anaesthetics
- Avoidance of pain provoking movement
- If conservative measures are unsuccessful, surgical exploration of extensor carpi radialis brevis may be advocated

Golfer's elbow

Similar complaint to tennis elbow but much less common. Pain is localized to the medial epicondyle at the common flexor origin.

Cubitus varus and cubitus valgus

Decrease (varus) or increase (valgus) in the carrying angle of the elbow follows a supracondylar or other elbow fracture in childhood. If, however, after some years of observation, there is interference with function, corrective osteotomy may be performed. In later life, a cubitus valgus deformity may be associated with a tardy ulnar nerve palsy.

Tardy ulnar nerve palsy

This is an ulnar nerve palsy characterized by slow onset. Typically presents at 30–50 years following injury to elbow, often sustained in childhood. Mostly seen with a cubitus valgus deformity. Ischaemic and fibrotic changes are seen in the nerve. Treatment is transposition of nerve from behind medial epicondyle to in front of joint.

Ulnar neuritis and ulnar tunnel syndrome

Ulnar nerve is susceptible to trauma at the elbow. Where the nerve is abnormally mobile it can be exposed to frictional damage as it slips repeatedly in front of and behind the medial epicondyle. It is susceptible to pressure as it passes through the two heads of flexor carpi ulnaris and as it lies in the ulnar tunnel in the hand. Nerve conduction studies are very helpful in determining the level of insult.

Pulled elbow

Occurs in under-fives after sudden traction on arm. Radial head slides out from under cover of orbicular ligament. Presents as pain and loss of supination. Treatment: spontaneous reduction (broad-arm sling). Reduction by forced supination while pushing radius proximally.

9. THE HAND

9.1 Examination of the hand

Inspection

- In proportion?
- Any finger hypertrophy (e.g. Paget's, neurofibromatosis, AV fistula)?
- Fusiform swelling of interphalangeal joint (e.g. collateral ligament tears, rheumatoid arthritis)
- Mallet finger/thumb deformity
- Swan neck deformity
- Boutonnière deformity
- Z-thumb
- Dupuytren's
- Ulnar deviation of fingers at MCP joint due to joint subluxation and later dislocation in rheumatoid arthritis
- Unilateral wasting: root, plexus or peripheral nerve lesion
- Widespread wasting: generalized peripheral neuropathy, MS, muscular dystrophies
- **Heberden's nodes**: dorsal aspect DIP joints, seen in osteoarthritis
- **Bouchard's nodes**: dorsal aspect PIP joints, seen in osteoarthritis
- Rheumatoid nodules/synovial swellings
- Appearance of nails and skin

Palpation

- Palpate individual finger and thumb joints
- High temperature
- Thickening, tenderness, oedema

Movements

- Should measure active and passive range with goniometer
- MCP joint 0–90°
- PIP joint 0–100°

- DIP joint 0–80°
- Thumb IP joint — flexion 80°, extension 20°
- Thumb MCP joint — 55°

Fingers

- **Flexion**: DIP — flexor digitorum profundus; PIP joint — flexor digitorum superficialis
- **Extension**: extensor digitorum communis — all fingers; extensor digiti indicis — index finger; extensor digiti minimi — little finger
- **Abduction**: dorsal interossei — abduct from axis of middle finger and flex MCP joints whilst extending IP joints
- **Adduction**: palmar interossei — adduct to axis of middle finger and flex MCP joints whilst extending IP joints

Thumb

- **Flexion**: flexor pollicis longus plus thenar eminence muscle; flexor pollicis brevis
- **Extension**: extensor pollicis longus; extensor pollicis brevis
- **Abduction**: abductor pollicis longus; abductor pollicis brevis
- **Adduction**: adductor pollicis
- **Opposition**: opponens pollicis

Assess pinch grip, grip strength. Objective measurements may be obtained with dynamometer. A reading of 200 mmHg should be achievable with the normal hand.

Assessing hand injuries requires a thorough knowledge of hand anatomy to determine any structural damage accurately. Hand trauma examination can be facilitated by the use of local anaesthetic blocks (e.g. ring block at base of digit; wrist block involving ulnar, median and radial nerves; brachial plexus block). Remember to assess any sensory deficit before giving local anaesthetic. Some structural damage may only be partial and therefore can be misleading in the clinical setting (e.g. patient may be able to flex a distal interphalangeal joint but have a partial severance of the corresponding flexor digitorum profundus tendon). In partial tears the movement, although present, will be painful and often cannot be performed against resistance. Hand trauma assessment requires radiological assessment. Tetanus status should be assessed.

Ask the patient about:

- Hand dominance
- Occupation
- Specialized hobbies
- Concurrent illness

9.2 Tendon injuries

Extensor tendon divisions from wounds on the back of the hand carry an excellent prognosis and are treated by primary suture and splintage in extension for approximately six weeks in association with hand physiotherapy.

The index and little fingers have a double extensor mechanism. In addition to extensor digitorum tendon the index has an extensor indicis and the little finger has extensor digiti minimi.

Flexor tendon injuries

Prognosis depends on level of injury, whether one or both flexor tendons are involved and whether injury occurs at a point at which the tendons are within the flexor sheath.

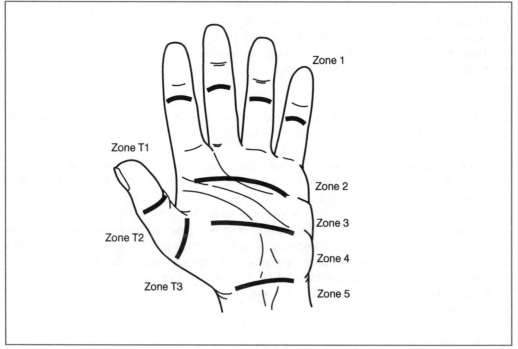

Zones of the palmar surface of the hand and wrist

The level of injury can be described in zones of palmar surface of hand and wrist. Verden (1972) described five flexor tendon zones in the hand based on anatomic factors influencing prognosis of repair.

- **Zone 1**: between the DIP and PIP joint creases distal to the insertion of FDS. This contains the FDP tendon within the distal flexor sheath.
- **Zone 2**: between distal palmar crease and mid-point of middle phalanx. This corresponds to the proximal part of the flexor tendon sheath, A1 pulley, and extends to the FDS insertion containing FDS and FDP tendons.
- **Zone 3**: between distal margin of carpal tunnel and distal palmar crease; contains both FDS and FDP tendons but are unsheathed
- **Zone 4**: area of carpal tunnel; contains both FDS and FDP tendons
- **Zone 5**: area of wrist and forearm up to carpal tunnel
- In the thumb, Zone 1 is distal to the IP joint, Zone 2 is over the proximal phalanx from the AI pulley to the IP joint. Zone 3 is the thenar eminence and zones 4 and 5 are the same as for fingers.

Mostly primary repair can be carried out. Occasionally, free tendon grafting is necessary due to tissue loss or chronicity of condition. If repair is delayed significantly it is very difficult to re-oppose severed ends as the proximal end tends to retract proximally and loses elasticity.

These injuries often involve divisions of digital nerves. These are repaired primarily. Suturing is of the epineurium only. One digital artery is sufficient blood supply to a finger/thumb, however, repair of digital arteries should be attempted using magnification.

Mallet finger
The DIP joint is flexed and cannot be extended. Traumatic — forcible flexion of an extended finger. The distal extensor tendon slip is torn at its attachment to bone or it avulses a bony fragment. Occasionally there is involvement of more than 20% of the articular surface of the distal phalanx, sometimes with anterior subluxation. This requires formal repair. Less extensive injuries can be treated with six weeks of splintage with DIP in hyperextension plus two weeks of further night splintage.

Mallet thumb
Delayed rupture of EPL may follow Colles' fracture or in rheumatoid arthritis. This can be repaired via tendon transfer of extensor indicis. If tendon damaged by incised wound primary repair is indicated

Boutonnière deformity
Characterized by flexion of PIP joint and hyper-extension of DIP joint. Due to detachment of central slip of extensor tendon which is attached to base of middle phalanx. Often seen in wounds of dorsum of finger, rheumatoid arthritis.

Swan neck deformity

Characterized by flexion of DIP joint and hyperextension of PIP joint. There are several causative factors:

* Shortening of extensor digitorum communis
* Tight interossei
* Rupture of FDS

Z-thumb deformity

Flexed MCP joint and hyper-extended IP joint due to displacement of extensor tendons or rupture FPL. Seen in rheumatoid arthritis

9.3 Hand infections

Paronychia

Infection between the tip of the nail and the cuticle.

Apical infections

Occur between the top of the nail and underlying nail bed.

Pulp infections

These occur in the fibro fatty tissue of the fingertips. These are exquisitely tender and can lead to destruction of the distal phalanx.

Tendon sheath infections

Produce rapid swelling leading to a painful swollen flexed finger. Extension exacerbates pain which is localized to the sheath — often the base. There is always a risk of tendon sloughing and adhesion formation. Require urgent incision, drainage and washout, elevation, splintage and IV antibiotics.

Web space infections

Marked swelling extending to back of hand. Painful, associated with systemic upset. Can spread to adjacent web spaces or anterior aspect of palm. Require elevation, i.v. antibiotics and occasionally incision and drainage.

Mid-palmar and thenar space infections

These two compartments lie between the flexor tendons and the metacarpals. Gross swelling involving both dorsal and palmar aspect of the hand. Unless rapid response to antibiotics, elevation and splintage — early incision and drainage is essential to preserve function.

'Safe' or 'intrinsic plus' position of the hand (Stern, 1993)

- Wrist slightly extended (20°)
- MCP joints flexed to 70°
- Interphalangeal joints fully extended.

The described joint positions are those in which the collateral ligaments and volar plates are fully extended. Thus, once movement is recommenced there should be no shortening of these ligaments or plates and, therefore, no functional problems that cannot be overcome with physiotherapy.

9.4 The rheumatoid hand

Rheumatoid disease frequently affects the hands and will involve joints, tendons, muscles, nerves and arteries.

- **Early changes**: hand warm and moist
- **Later changes**: joint swelling and tenderness; synovial tendon sheath and joint thickening with effusion, muscle wasting and ultimately deformity

Tendon involvement

- Local infiltration from synovitis of surrounding synovial tendon sheath
- Repeated trauma from rubbing over rough bony prominences

Tendon rupture and joint subluxation are the main factors leading to severe deformity.

Conservative management

To alleviate pain, preserve movement and minimize deformity:

- Analgesia
- Rest
- Splintage
- Physiotherapy

Surgical management

- **Synovectomy:** synovial thickening before joint destruction is amenable to synovectomy. This relieves pain and quells the progression of the disease.
- **Joint replacement:** in joint destruction with functional impairment, joint replacement is very helpful.
- **Tendon repair:** for spontaneous rupture of tendons in rheumatoid arthritis, surgical exploration is warranted. It is often difficult to perform direct end-to-end repair due to poor quality of tendon from long-term trauma. Often need to use tendon transfer either in the guise of a free tendon interposition graft or employ end-to-side technique hitching the ruptured tendon onto an intact extensor mechanism. This results in mass action effect.
- **Arthrodesis:** where stability is more important than flexibility (e.g. wrist, cervical spine)

Physiotherapy is an essential part of management — as in all hand surgery.

9.5 Dupuytren's contracture

This is thickening and contracture of the palmar fascia. The palm is affected first, then the disease involves the slip projections of the palmar fascia to the fingers resulting in flexion contractures.

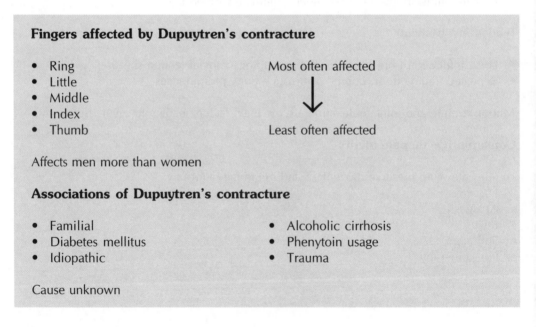

Fingers affected by Dupuytren's contracture

- Ring   Most often affected
- Little
- Middle
- Index
- Thumb   Least often affected

Affects men more than women

Associations of Dupuytren's contracture

- Familial   • Alcoholic cirrhosis
- Diabetes mellitus   • Phenytoin usage
- Idiopathic   • Trauma

Cause unknown

Fibromatosis of plantar fascia (in the foot) and Peyronie's disease (of the penis) are associated with Dupuytren's contracture.

Treatment

If contracture causes a functional problem, surgical intervention is indicated:

- **Fasciotomy**: division of thickened fascial bands
- **Fasciectomy**: excision of thickened palmar fascia (aponeurosis)

Often difficult dissection as digital nerve sheaths may blend with fascia. Involvement of skin may necessitate Z–plasty or skin excision and full-thickness skin grafting.

Post-operative management

Splintage, physiotherapy

9.6 Hand lumps and bumps

Ganglions

Arise from tendons or from the wrist joint itself. Can recur after surgical excision so avoid surgery if no functional problem as they can resolve spontaneously.

Implantation dermoid cysts

Occur after minor trauma. Commonly on volar aspect of fingers and palms.

Mucous cysts

- Arise from joints
- Mostly arthritic joints
- Mostly occur below the nail or overlying DIP joints
- Excision must extend down to joint otherwise will recur

9.7 Peripheral nerves in the hand

Radial nerve

Nerve roots
Posterior cord brachial plexus — C5, C6, C7

Radial nerve supplies

- **Above elbow**
  Muscles
    Triceps
    Lateral part brachialis
    Brachioradialis
    Extensor carpi radialis longus
  Joints
    Elbow
  Skin
    Posterior cutaneous branch
    to back of arm and forearm

- **Below elbow**
  Divided into:
    posterior interosseus nerve
    (between the two heads of
    supinator passing into posterior
    compartment) *supplies* supinator,
    all forearm extensors
    superficial radial nerve
    (under brachioradialis and lateral
    to radial artery) *supplies* skin of
    dorsum of radial side of hand
    and lateral three and-a-half digits

Vulnerable sites

- **In axilla**: Saturday night palsy from putting arm around back of chair
- **Mid-humerus**: fractures of humerus; tourniquet palsies
- **Below elbow**: dislocations; Monteggia fracture; surgical trauma

Radial nerve palsy
Motor effects

- Triceps wasting
- Forearm extensor wasting
- Wrist drop (inability to extend wrist)
- Loss of supination in proximal lesions
- Brachioradialis and triceps weakness suggest very high nerve lesions

Sensory effects

- Loss confined to anatomical snuffbox in distal lesions
- Loss of sensation along back of forearm suggests higher lesions

Examination

- Extension of wrist
- Extension of fingers
- Sensation over anatomical snuffbox

Ulnar nerve

Nerve roots
Medial cord C8, T1.

Ulnar nerve supplies

- **In forearm**
  Flexor carpi ulnaris
  Ulnar half of flexor digitorum
    profundus

- **Joint** — elbow

- **Sensation**
  Dorsal cutaneous branch
    medial skin of dorsum of hand
    and medial one-and-a-half digits
  Palmar cutaneous branch
    medial skin of the palm

- **In the hand**
  Muscles
    hypothenar muscles
    interossei
    two medial lumbricals
    adductor pollicis — variable supply

Causes of damage

- **Ulnar tunnel syndrome**: where nerve passes between pisiform and hook of hamate (e.g. due to ganglion, fracture of hook of hamate). The most distal lesions affect the deep palmar branches and are entirely motor.
- **At the wrist**: from lacerations, ganglion
- **Distal to the elbow**: by compression as it passes between the two heads of flexor carpi ulnaris
- **At the level of the medial epicondyle**: local friction; cubitus valgus; OA; trauma
- **At brachial plexus level**: trauma; traction; Pancoast's tumour

Examination
Inspection

- Hypothenar muscle wasting
- **Claw hand**: claw deformity most marked in the little and ring fingers due to loss of action of interossei and lumbricals. The MCP joints are thus extended and the IP joints flexed. If the ulnar nerve lesion is distal to the FDP muscle belly then the function of FDP to the ring and little fingers will be intact, giving a more marked flexor deformity
- **Interosseus wasting**: seen in the dorsal first web space
- **Medial forearm wasting**: FCU; FDP (medial half)
- Look for scars

Palpation
Along course of nerve

Test power

- Interossei
- Abductor digiti minimi
- **Froment's test**: for adductor pollicis weakness. Put a sheet of paper between the thumb and index finger. If no adductor pollicis power then the patient will flex thumb at the interphalangeal joint to maintain hold on paper.

Test sensation

- Ulnar side of palm and dorsum of hand; loss of dorsum indicates lesion proximal to wrist
- Ulnar one-and-a-half digits

Median nerve

Nerve roots
Lateral and ulnar cord C(5), 6, 7, 8, T1.

Median nerve supplies

- **Near the elbow**
  Flexor digitorum superficialis
  Flexor carpi radialis
  Palmaris longus
  Pronator teres

- **Hand**
  Thenar (LOAF) muscles:
    Lateral two lumbricals
    Opponens pollicis
    Abductor pollicis brevis
    Flexor pollicis brevis

- **Forearm**
  (via anterior interosseus branch)
  Flexor pollicis longus
  Radial half of flexor digitorum profundus
  Pronator quadratus

- **Sensation**
  Lateral palm and thumb $\Big\}$ Palmar
  Lateral two-and-a-half fingers
  Lateral two-and-a-half fingers $\Big\}$ Dorsally
  Tip of thumb

Causes of damage

- **Carpal tunnel syndrome**: arthritis, wrist fractures
- **At the wrist**: especially from lacerations
- **In the forearm** (anterior interosseus nerve): from forearm bone fractures
- **Distal to elbow**: pronator teres nerve entrapment syndrome
- **At elbow**: (e.g. after dislocations in children, supracondylar fractures)

Examination
Inspection

- Thenar wasting
- Simian thumb
- Cigarette burns (skin trauma)
- High lesions: wasting of lateral aspect of forearm; index finger extended

Sensation
See above

Palpation
Along course of nerve

Test motor function of abductor pollicis brevis
This muscle is invariably and exclusively supplied by the median nerve. Can patient with hand flat on table, palm down, lift his thumb off the table against resistance?

Carpal tunnel syndrome

This is compression and ischaemia of the median nerve in the carpal tunnel deep to the wrist flexor retinaculum. It commonly affects women (F:M 8:1) aged 30–60 years.

Causes of carpal tunnel syndrome	
• **Can occur in healthy people** Idiopathic Pregnancy Obesity Occupation Trauma	• **Can occur as a sign of underlying disease** Myxoedema Rheumatoid arthritis Acromegaly Diabetes

Clinical features

- Pain and paraesthesia in the distribution of the median nerve in the hand (thumb and lateral two fingers)
- Wasting of the thenar muscles
- Pain worse at night, especially in the early hours
- Relieved by hanging arm out of bed and shaking it
- During the day little pain is felt unless wrists are held still (e.g. knitting, holding a paper)

Diagnostic tests

- **Phalen's test**: ask patients to hold both wrists flexed for 1–2 minutes to see if this worsens or reproduces symptoms
- **Tourniquet test**: apply sphygmomanometer just above systolic pressure for 1–2 minutes and see if this reproduces symptoms
- **Nerve conduction test**: differentiate from cervical spondylosis involving C6 and C7

Treatment

- **Conservative**: wrist splints at night to prevent flexion
- **Surgical**: division of flexor retinaculum and decompression of nerve

10. COMMON ORTHOPAEDIC PROBLEMS OF CHILDHOOD

10.1 Congenital dislocation of the hip (CDH)

CDH is characterized by enlargement and inversion of the labrum, enlarged ligamentum teres and laxity of the capsule in its severe form. Females predominate over males. There is thought to be a multifactorial inheritance. It is more common in first-born children, possibly because maternal abdominal muscles are tighter and therefore restrict foetal movement. The same reasoning accounts for higher incidence in oligohydramnios and breech births. Malposition also increases the risk of other conditions, such as congenital muscular torticollis and metatarsus adductus. The presence of these conditions necessitates careful hip examination. The important signs to elicit are if the hip is dislocated, if so, is it reducible? Congenital dislocation of the hip may be associated with neuromuscular abnormalities, such as spina bifida.

This term is often used to cover a spectrum of hip instability, ranging from an irreducibly dislocated hip to a correctly placed hip sited in a shallow acetabulum. Hence, incidence is controversial and is dependent on definition of the condition. The age of the baby at examination as well as the expertise of the screener has influenced the frequency of reported incidences. All babies are now screened for this condition as development of a normal hip is possible if the condition is recognized and correctly managed after birth.

Diagnosis

Ortolani's test
Flex knees, place hands so that thumbs overlie medial aspect of thigh and fingers overlie the trochanters. Flex hips to right angle. Slowly and gently abduct hips. If a hip is dislocated the femoral head will be felt slipping into the acetabulum as full abduction is approached. If abduction is restricted, this may represent an irreducible dislocation.

Barlow's provocative test
If the Ortolani test is negative, the hip may still be unstable. Fix pelvis between the symphysis and sacrum with one hand. With the thumb of the other hand, attempt to dislocate the hip by gentle but firm backward pressure. If the head is subluxed backwards, its reduction should be achieved by forward finger pressure or wider abduction. Hence these tests, when used in combination, can elicit a dislocated hip, assess its reducibility and diagnose an unstable hip which is dislocatable.

These tests are verified by ultrasound examination and are best performed at the two week stage when a large percentage of lax capsules will have tightened up. This will lessen the likelihood of unnecessary splintage which does have a complication of aseptic necrosis of the femoral head.

An X-ray at birth is not diagnostic but is helpful at 3–4 months when the femoral capital epiphysis begins to ossify.

Diagnosis in the older child

- Presentation after walking age
- The affected leg may appear shorter and lie in external rotation
- Asymmetry of skin folds of the thigh
- In bilateral cases there is widening of the perineum and there is a compensatory increase in lumbar lordosis
- There is always limited abduction in flexion of hip

Gait

Trendelenburg's test will be positive due to impairment of the abductor mechanism secondary to the dislocation. Child will dip to the affected side. In bilateral cases, the child will have a waddling gait.

Management

Depends largely on the age of the patient. When diagnosed early, conservative treatment with a harness or splint is likely to be successful. After walking age, surgery is usually required.

Neonate

- Hip is reduced and held in abduction and flexion
- Pavlik harness is widely used and will be successful in approximately 85% of cases, this allows controlled movement
- Rigid splinting can cause avascular necrosis of the femoral head due to excessive pressure

Six months to two years
In those older than 6½ months of age or in those who do not respond to splintage, a short period of traction can be helpful. Then an EUA with an image intensifier is advocated to elicit which structures block reduction. If closed reduction is possible, then the patient will need six months in plaster immobilization. Otherwise, open reduction and realignment is required. In those older than two years, management is much more difficult as secondary changes will have occurred as a result of dislocation. Regular follow-up until skeletal maturity is required. In those that require open reduction there is an increased risk of avascular necrosis and then osteoarthritis. Eventually total joint replacement may be necessary.

10.2 Congenital talipes equinovarus (club foot)

Most common of congenital foot abnormalities. Incidence 1:1000 live births.

Aetiology

- Mostly idiopathic
- Increased incidence if first-degree relative has condition
- Found in association with neuromuscular conditions: important to perform full neurological examination of child presenting with club foot
- More common in males, 2:1
- The diagnosis is usually obvious from birth but fixed (pathological) club foot must be distinguished from a postural deformity
- The new-born child often holds the foot in plantar flexion and inversion; therefore observe as child kicks
- If foot is maintained in that position lightly scratch the lateral side of the foot. If normal the child will respond by dorsiflexing the foot and fanning the toes
- In a normal foot it should be effortless to dorsiflex the foot into contact with the tibia
- In club foot, both the hind foot and forefoot are abnormal:
  Hind foot: fixed in equinus and varus, the heel is not in line with the lower leg
  Forefoot: fixed in varus, with subluxation of talo-navicular joint, posteromedial soft tissues are tight and under-developed
- True club foot has a range of severity.

Severe cases: characterized by rigidity of foot, constriction rings, deep sole clefs. Calf muscle wasting is a common and permanent feature.

Management

Remains controversial, regarding timing and nature of surgery. Each case should be considered and treated according to the severity of the deformity. Stretching and strapping or plaster casts should be commenced early. The response to conservative treatment dictates the need for surgery. Unsuccessful cases require lengthening of tight structures, open reduction and fixation of subluxed joint. After-care involves a period of immobilization and then physiotherapy to rehabilitate. Sometimes secondary surgery is required.

10.3 The limping child

There are a number of conditions affecting the hip in childhood which cannot reliably be distinguished from each other in the initial presentation, although age at presentation helps.

Features

- Limp
- Decreased range of movement
- Pain

Differential diagnosis of the limping child

- Irritable hip
- Slipped upper femoral epiphysis
- Perthes' disease
- Septic arthritis

Irritable hip

- Transient synovitis
- Age 3–6, M:F 2:1
- Essentially a diagnosis of exclusion
- There may be a history of preceding minor trauma or viral illness
- Decreased extension and internal rotation and abduction
- No systemic upset
- May have a normal ESR
- X-rays may show signs of synovitis
- Hip aspirate: no bacterial growth
- Full recovery with bed rest, 24 hours may be adequate

Perthes' disease

Growth disturbance associated with temporary ischaemia of the upper end of the femur leading to a cycle of avascular necrosis followed by deformation and subsequent revascularization. The cycle is approximately 3–4 years. Cause unknown.

- Age 3–12 (commonly 5–7) Male: Female 4:1
- Condition is self-limiting. There is usually some residual deformity, growth arrest and flattening of the femoral head that can predispose to degenerative changes in later life.
- More common in children who are small for age or who have delayed bone maturation
- <1% transient synovitis cases get Perthes' disease
- Episodic vague pain in region of hips, thighs or knees. Decreased internal rotation and abduction. The radiological changes are usually well-established by the time the child presents.

The condition can be classified on the radiological appearance into groups of varying severity. In general, prognosis is dependent on the extent of the area of the femoral head that is involved.

Management

Rest and restriction of activities is needed to relieve pain. Physiotherapy is required to maintain movement. Avoid formation of flattened irregular head by 'containment' of femoral head within acetabulum. A more spherical head and therefore a more congruous joint will decrease the risk of degenerative arthritis in the future. Containment can be achieved by maintaining movement or by surgical osteotomy. Long-term series are difficult to evaluate because different types of treatment are not matched for age, sex, stage and extent of epiphyseal involvement.

Slipped upper femoral epiphysis

- Uncommon
- Affects approximately 3/100,000 children. Males more often than females. Usually related to puberty: boys 14–16, girls 11–13.
- Seen in overweight children who are slow to mature
- Postulated susceptible hip in which the strength of the growth plate and its resistance to shear forces is decreased as a result of mechanical, hormonal and possibly genetic factors
- Under such circumstances normal forces, perhaps exacerbated by obesity, are sufficient to cause slippage
- Difficult to diagnose — thought to be a strain. Pain localized to thigh or knee. Acute on chronic presentation often.
- Leg externally rotated with mild shortening, decreased abduction, increased adduction
- Epiphysis almost always slips backwards

- If severe, can be seen on AP view. Otherwise, essential to obtain lateral view.
- Slips are graded radiologically on the extent of the displacement of the epiphysis on the neck.

Management
Slight degrees of slip are treated by internal fixation of epiphysis without reduction (reduction carries a risk of developing avascular necrosis). If there is a large amount of acute displacement reduction is attempted before fixation. If this slip is longstanding, osteotomy of femoral neck may be needed. The incidence of bilateral slip is variable but at least 20%, therefore should monitor other hip during treatment and follow-up.

Septic arthritis

See Section 5.2.

11. LOW BACK PAIN

11.1 Anatomical features of the spine

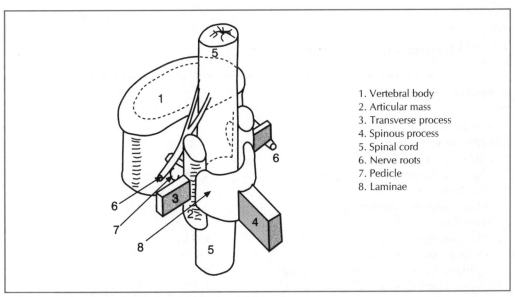

1. Vertebral body
2. Articular mass
3. Transverse process
4. Spinous process
5. Spinal cord
6. Nerve roots
7. Pedicle
8. Laminae

Schematic diagram of the vertebra and spinal cord

- Vertebral body
- Horseshoe-shaped neural arch which is divided into pedicles (anteriorly) and laminae (posteriorly) by two articular processes. The articular processes take part in the inter-articular or facet joints.
- Transverse processes
- Spinous processes

This arrangement forms a protective covering for the cord and nerve roots.

Each vertebra articulates with one above and one below by means of facet joints and intervertebral discs. Each disc is composed of a nucleus pulposus surrounded by concentric sheets of fibrous tissue (annulus fibrosis). At all levels of the spine flexion, extension and lateral flexion to both sides are possible.

In the thoracic spine the plane of the facet joint lies in the arc of a circle which has its centre in the nucleus pulposus — hence axial rotation is possible in this part of the spine only. In contrast, the orientation of the facet joints in the lumbar region is such that rotation is blocked.

As a result of the elasticity of the annulus, the nucleus pulposus is under constant pressure and may herniate into a vertebral body anteriorly or centrally. More commonly, the annular fibres tear (secondary to trauma or degenerative changes) so that the nucleus bulges posteriorly or laterally.

11.2 Dermatomes and myotomes

MYOTOMES

Hip flexion (iliopsoas)	L2, 3
Hip extension (gluteus maximus + hamstrings)	L4, 5
Knee extension (knee jerk) (quadriceps)	L3, 4
Knee flexion (hamstrings)	L5, S1
Ankle dorsiflexion (tibialis anterior) (long toe extensors)	L4, 5
Ankle plantar flexion calf muscles	S1, 2

Dermatomes

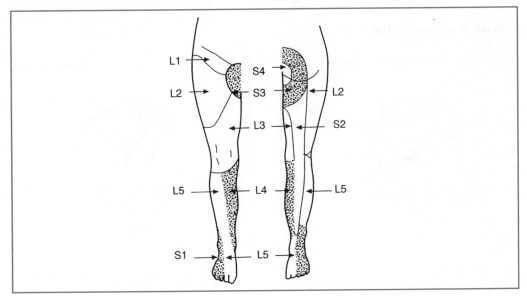

Dermatomes

11.3 Back pain

Causes of back pain

- Mechanical back pain
- Spinal cord compression

- Nerve root pain

Mechanical back pain

Irritation of facet joints, ligaments and muscles may produce dull, aching pain in the buttocks and thighs which is aggravated by activity. There may be a history of minor injury. Mechanical back pain often radiates to the buttock and sometimes the knees. There is a good range of movement of the spine and no positive neurological signs.

Nerve root pain

This is caused most commonly by lateral disc protrusion but can also be caused by other space occupying lesions such as tumour or osteophytes. Nerve root irritation or compression may be manifested as sciatic pain, paraesthesia, muscle weakness, sensory disturbance, reflex loss. The neurological disturbance is segmental and dependant on the level of prolapse. Sciatic pain extends past the knee and on to the foot/ankle.

Lateral disc protrusion

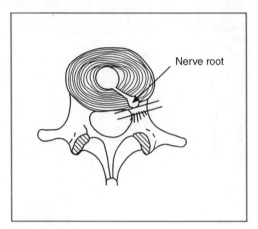 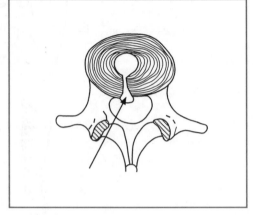

Lateral disc protrusion   Central disc protrusion

May affect one or two nerve roots only. Signs are mostly unilateral and localized to the particular nerve root that is involved. It is rare in the thoracic region and common in the lumbar region. Can be diagnosed clinically but confirmed by MRI/CT scan. The disc between L5/S1 is most commonly implicated, followed by L4/5 and L3/4.

It is commonly caused by an annular tear which allows nucleus pulposus to herniate through. The back pain component is produced by the tear itself and the resulting protective lumbar muscle spasm at the affected level. The muscle spasm results in loss of lumbar lordosis, decreased range of movement and a protective scoliosis.

Patients usually recover completely with rest and physiotherapy but the process is usually long with variable responses to treatment modalities.

Spinal cord compression

This is commonly caused by central disc protrusion but can also be caused by tumours, infection, ankylosing spondylitis and Paget's which narrow the spinal canal.

Central disc protrusion

(See diagram above.)

May affect the cord directly or the cauda equina in the lower lumbar spine. If there is bladder disturbance and bilateral lower limb signs this warrants immediate emergency surgical exploration.

Management of disc prolapse

Once significant neurological signs are excluded, all cases of acute disc prolapse are first treated by conservative methods:

*   Rest
*   Analgesia
*   Physiotherapy

If, however, there is an unsatisfactory response or where residual symptoms are severe, further investigation by MRI scanning (preferably) or CT scanning is undertaken with a view to exploratory surgery. Prior to discectomy:

*   Routine bloods
*   Lumbosacral spine X-rays
*   MRI/CT scan

Discectomy considerations

Traditionally, full laminectomy, thorough decompression of nerve root and clearing of debris from intervertebral disc space. This makes the operated segment unstable. Now, less invasive techniques are employed (e.g. percutaneous disc removal via unilateral approach with minimal stripping of paraspinous muscles). Sometimes fenestrations of lamina may be necessary to provide adequate visualization.

12. DISORDERS OF BONE

12.1 Bone physiology

Bone is a type of connective tissue. It is unique in that it normally mineralizes. It consists of an organic and inorganic matrix.

*   **Organic matrix (35%)**: composed of bone-forming cells — osteoprogenitor cells, osteoblasts and osteocytes. The generation and stimulation of these cells is regulated by cytokines and growth factors. Osteoclasts are responsible for bone resorption.
*   **Inorganic matrix (65%)**: composed of mainly calcium hydroxyapatite which contains 99% of body calcium store and 85% of body phosphorus. The inorganic matrix also houses 65% of sodium and magnesium stores.

Bone cells

Osteoprogenitor cells
These are located in the vicinity of all bony surfaces. They are pluripotential mesenchymal stem cells. When stimulated they produce osteoblasts which, in turn, differentiate into osteocytes. Osteoblasts and osteoclasts act in co-ordination and are considered the functional unit of bone. The processes of bone formation and resorption are tightly coupled.

Osteoblasts
Located on surface of bone:

- Synthesize, transport and arrange the many proteins of the matrix
- Initiate mineralization
- Exhibit cell surface receptors which bind to parathyroid hormone, vitamin D, oestrogen, cytokines, growth factors and extracellular matrix proteins
- Control osteoclast activity; once osteoblasts are surrounded by matrix they are known as osteocytes

Osteocytes
Osteocytes are osteoblasts that have been surrounded by matrix. They are the most numerous of bone cells. Although encased in bone, they communicate with each other and with surface cells via a network of tunnels through the matrix called canaliculi. This network may control the fluctuations in serum calcium and phosphate by altering the concentration of these minerals in the local extracellular fluid. They translate mechanical forces into biological activity.

Osteoclasts
These are responsible for bone resorption. The osteoclast is derived from haematopoietic progenitor cells. Cytokines are crucial for osteoclast differentiation and maturation. Osteoclast activity is initiated by binding to matrix adhesion proteins. The pits they produce are known as **Howship lacunae**. The osteoclast cell membrane becomes modified by villous extensions on the matrix interface which increases the surface area. The plasmalemma bordering this region forms a seal with the underlying bone preventing leakage of digestion products and creating a self-contained extracellular space. The osteoclast acidifies this space with a hydrogen pump system that solubilizes the mineral. It then releases a multitude of enzymes which break down the matrix proteins into amino acids and liberate and activate growth factors and enzymes. Thus, as bone is broken down to its elemental units, substances are released that initiate its renewal.

Bone proteins

The proteins of bone include type I collagen and non-collagenous proteins that are derived from osteoblasts.

Type I collagen
Ninety per cent of organic component. Osteoblasts deposit collagen either in a random weave — **woven bone** or orderly layered manner — **lamellar bone**.

- **Woven bone**: seen in foetal skeleton, growth plates. It is indicative of pathological state in adult (e.g. in circumstances requiring rapid repair such as fractures). It forms around infection, comprises the matrix of bone forming tumours.
- **Lamellar bone**: gradually replaces woven bone, is deposited much more slowly and is stronger than woven bone. There are four types of lamellar bone of which three occur in the cortex — **circumferential**: subperiosteal endosteal; **concentric**: about vascular cores creating haversian systems; **interstitial**: fills the spaces between haversian system. The fourth type, **trabecular**, composes bone trabeculae. These extend from the endosteal surface.

Non-collagenous proteins
Bound to the matrix. These are adhesion proteins, calcium binding proteins, mineralization proteins, enzymes, cytokines and growth factors.

12.2 Rickets and osteomalacia

Rickets (in children) and osteomalacia (adults) arise from deranged vitamin D absorption or metabolism or, less commonly, from disorders that disturb calcium or phosphate homeostasis. The major role of vitamin D is the maintenance of normal plasma levels of calcium and phosphorus. There are two major sources of vitamin D:

- Endogenous synthesis in the skin: the precursor, 7-dihydrocholesterol in the skin is converted to vitamin D_3 by UV light
- Diet

The active form of vitamin D (produced by the kidney):

- Stimulates absorption of calcium and phosphorus in the gut
- Collaborates with parathyroid hormone (PTH) in the mobilization of calcium from bone
- Stimulates the PTH-dependent re-absorption of calcium in the distal renal tubules

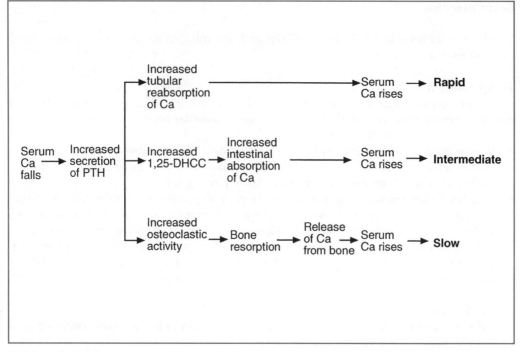

Calcium haemostasis

Although vitamin D collaborates with PTH in the resorption of calcium and phosphorus from bone to support blood levels, it is required for normal mineralization of epiphyseal cartilage and osteoid matrix. It is not clear how the resorptive mechanism is mediated. The mechanism of mineralization is also not known.

Predisposing conditions for rickets or osteomalacia

- **Inadequate synthesis or dietary deficiency of vitamin D**
  Inadequate exposure to sunlight
  Dietary deficit
  Poor maternal nutrition
  Dark skin pigmentation

- **Decreased absorption of fat-soluble vitamin D**
  Cholestatic liver disease
  Pancreatic insufficiency
  Biliary tract obstruction
  Small bowel disease

Continues …

... Continued

- **Derangements in vitamin D metabolism**
  Drugs can increase degradation of vitamin D (e.g. phenytoin, phenobarbital, rifampicin)
  Liver disease
  Renal disease

- **Phosphate depletion**
  Poor absorption — due to chronic use of antacids (phosphate binds to aluminium hydroxide)
  Excess renal tubule excretion of phosphate
  X-linked inherited hypophosphataemia secondary to enzyme deficiency

In both rickets and osteomalacia, there is an excess of unmineralized matrix.

In children, there is the complication of inadequate calcification of epiphyseal cartilage deranging endochondral bone growth. This leads to:

- Overgrowth of epiphyseal cartilage due to inadequate calcification and failure of cartilage cells to mature and disintegrate
- Persistence of distorted irregular masses of cartilage
- Deposition of osteoid matrix on inadequately mineralised cartilaginous remnants — enlargement and lateral expansion of osteochondral junction
- Deformation of the skeleton due to loss of rigidity of developing bones, in response to stresses to which individual bones are subjected

During the non-ambulatory stage of infancy the head and chest sustain the greatest stresses leading to:

- Flattening of occipital bones
- Inward buckling of parietal bones
- Frontal bossing $\left.\vphantom{\begin{array}{c}a\\b\end{array}}\right\}$ due to excess osteoid
- Squared appearance to the head
- Pigeon chest (due to pull of respiratory muscles on weak ribs)

In the ambulatory child the stresses are on the pelvis, spine and long bones. This causes:

- Increased lumbar lordosis
- Bowing of legs

Main radiological features in rickets

- Flaring/cupping of metaphysis
- Bowing of diaphysis

- Thickening, wide growth plate

Investigations

- Low calcium
- Low phosphate
- Increased alkaline phosphatase (this is increased in young children normally)

In adults the newly formed osteoid matrix laid down by osteoblasts is inadequately mineralized, thus producing excess of osteoid. Although the contours are not affected, the bone is weak and subject to gross fracturing. It is most likely to affect vertebral bodies and femoral necks.

Less dramatic manifestations include proximal muscle weakness and bone pain, most often localized to the pelvis, scapula and ribs, possibly related to microfractures or pseudo fractures, commonly called Looser's zones. These are radiolucent lines several millimetres thick and sharply demarcated from the adjacent bone. They are attributed to resorption of the thin bone by overlying pulsating arteries.

The best way to make the diagnosis of osteomalacia in most instances is a therapeutic trial of vitamin D and calcium. The serum Ca^{2+} + 25-OD-D levels are not usually helpful as they may be normal or low.

Persistent failure of mineralization leads to loss of skeletal mass, thus making the distinction between osteoporosis difficult.

12.3 Osteoporosis

This is the increased porosity of bone secondary to decrease in bone mass. Peak bone mass, achieved in early adulthood, is determined by the type of vitamin D receptor inherited, the state of nutrition, levels of physical activity, age and hormonal status. Approximately 5–10% of the skeleton is remodelled yearly and the amount of bone resorbed is equal to the amount of bone formed. At the start of the fourth decade, the amount of bone resorbed exceeds that which has been formed so there is a steady decrease in skeletal mass. Osteoblasts from elderly individuals have impaired reproductive and biosynthetic potential. Also the non-collagenase proteins bound to the extracellular matrix, such as growth factors, lose their full impact on osteoblastic stimulation over time.

Causes of osteoporosis

- **Primary osteoporosis**
  Post-menopausal
  Senile
  Idiopathic

- **Neoplasia**
  Multiple myeloma
  Carcinomatosis

- **Drugs**
  Anticoagulants
  Chemotherapy
  Corticosteroids
  Anticonvulsants
  Alcohol

- **Secondary osteoporosis**
  Endocrine disorders
  Hyperparathyroidism
  Thyroid disorders
  Hypogonadism
  Pituitary tumours
  Addison's DM — type I

- **Gastrointestinal**
  Malnutrition
  Malabsorption
  Vitamin C, D deficiency

Reduced physical activity
Mechanical forces are important stimuli for normal bone remodelling. There is evidence to support physical activity as a prevention of bone loss (e.g. observation of bone loss in paralysed, immobile limbs compared to higher bone density in athletes). Muscle contraction is the dominant source of skeletal loading.

Genetic factors
The type of vitamin D receptor molecule that is inherited accounts for approximately 75% of peak bone mass achieved.

Nutritional state
Calcium deficiency occurs during a period of rapid bone growth stunting the peak bone mass achieved if not replaced via dietary intake.

Hormonal influences
Decreased oestrogen levels result in increased stimulation of IL-1, IL-6 and TNFα by blood monocytes and bone marrow cells. These are potent stimulators of osteoclast activity. Compensatory osteoblastic activity occurs but it does not keep up the pace.

Clinical features

- Depends on which bone is involved
- Commonly, vertebral fracture in thoracic and lumbar spine occur — pain, loss of height, kyphosis
- Fracture neck of femur, pelvis, Colles' fracture

Investigations

Osteoporosis cannot be reliably detected in plain X-ray until 30–40% bone mass is lost. Measurement of serum calcium, phosphorus and alkaline phosphatase are not diagnostic. Difficult to diagnose accurately since it is asymptomatic until advanced skeletal fragility manifests itself in the form of complications.

- Bone biopsy
- Radiographic imaging (e.g. quantitative CT, single energy proton absorptiometry, bone density scan)

Treatment

- Exclude secondary cause
- Calcium supplements
- Oestrogen replacement — HRT

12.4 Paget's disease (osteitis deformans)

Characterized by:

- Initial osteolytic stage mediated by osteoclasts
- Rapid bone formation mediated by an osteoclastic/osteoblastic stage which ends with a predominance of osteoblastic activity. This results in a gain of bone mass. The newly formed bone is disordered and structurally unsound.
- Finally, burnt out quiescent osteosclerotic stage

Aetiology

Evidence suggests a slow virus infection by a paramyxovirus, targeting the osteoblast and osteoclast. It is thought to increase their activity and overcome the normal regulatory mechanism. Usually begins in mid-adulthood. Common in white people in Europe and Australia.

Clinical features

- Occurs in one or more bones
- It is monostotic in about 15% of cases
- The axial skeleton or proximal femur is involved in up to 80% of cases
- Any bone can be affected

Diagnosis

- Radiological appearance: enlarged with thick, coarse cortices and cancellous bone. Increased alkaline phosphatase. Increased urinary excretion of hydroxyproline.
- Variable clinical picture: can be asymptomatic, however can cause skeletal, neuromuscular and cardiovascular complications.

Skeletal and neuromuscular effects

- Painful affected bone
- Bone overgrowth can compress spinal and cranial nerve roots
- Overgrowth in craniofacial skeleton: leading to leontiasis ossea (lion-like facies) and a cranium so heavy that it becomes difficult for patient to hold head erect
- Invagination of base of skull secondary to increased weight with compression of posterior fossa structures
- Anterior bowing of femur and tibia
- Distortion of femoral head leading to severe osteoarthritis
- Long bones of lower limbs are affected leading to chalk stick fractures
- Compression fracture in spine may result in spinal cord injury and kyphosis

Cardiovascular effects

Hypervascularity of pagetic bone leads to increased blood flow which acts as an AV shunt leading to high output cardiac failure or exacerbation of underlying cardiac disease.

A variety of tumour and tumour-like conditions develop in pagetic bone

- **Benign**
  Giant cell reparative granuloma

- **Malignant**
  Sarcoma: in 5–10% with severe polyostotic disease
  Osteosarcoma
  Malignant fibrous histiocytoma
  Chondrosarcoma
  Giant cell tumour

Paget's can be treated with calcitonin and diphosphonates.

13. BONE TUMOURS

13.1 Metastatic disease

Metastatic tumours are the most common form of skeletal malignancy via:

* Direct spread
* Lymphatic/vascular dissemination
* Intraspinal seeding

Any cancer can spread to bone but in adults more than 75% originate from:

* Prostate
* Breast
* Kidney
* Lung
* Thyroid

Usually skeletal metastases are multifocal but kidney and thyroid carcinomas tend to produce solitary lesions. The following bones are commonly affected:

* Vertebral column
* Pelvis
* Ribs
* Skull
* Sternum
* Proximal femur
* Humerus

The red marrow in these areas facilitates implantation and growth of tumour cells because it has:

* Rich capillary network
* Slow blood flow
* Nutrient environment

X-ray changes of bony metastatic disease

* Lytic
* Blastic
* Combination of lytic and blastic

In **lytic** lesions the tumour cells secrete factors that stimulate osteoclastic bone resorption — the tumour cells do not directly resorb bone. Examples: cancer of kidney, lung, gastrointestinal tract and malignant melanoma.

Malignancies that elicit a sclerotic response, e.g. adenocarcinoma of prostate do so by stimulating osteoblastic formation. Most metastases produce a mixed lytic/blastic reaction.

Clinical findings

- Pain
- Hypercalcaemia
- Pathological fracture
- Neurological complications
- Marrow suppression

It is generally accepted that a fracture is inevitable when 50% of a single cortex of a long bone has been destroyed by metastatic disease. Prophylactic fixation should be performed in such cases if radiotherapy is to be given.

Aims of surgery:

- Immediate stability in a fracture that is assumed will not unite
- Fixation to last for the lifetime of the patient

13.2 Pathological fractures

Common causes of pathological fractures

- **Children**
  Bone cysts
  Rickets
  Osteogenesis imperfecta

- **Young people**
  Chrondroma
  Sarcoma
  Osteomalacia

- **Elderly**
  Osteoporosis
  Metastatic tumour
  Paget's disease

The commonest causes of pathological fractures overall are:

- Osteoporosis
- Metastatic tumours

Pathological fractures are usually low-energy fractures resulting from minor trauma or twisting movements in bones already significantly weakened by the pathological process.

13.3 Primary bone tumours

- Rare
- Represent <1% of all diagnosed tumours

PRIMARY BONE TUMOURS

	Benign	Malignant
Bone forming	Osteoid osteoma Osteoblastoma	Osteosarcoma
Cartilage forming	Osteochondroma Chondroma Chondroblastoma	Chondrosarcoma
Fibrous/fibro-osseus	Non-ossifying fibroma Fibrous dysplasia	Fibrosarcoma
Vessel forming	Angioma	Angiosarcoma
Marrow		Plasma cell myeloma Reticulum cell sarcoma Ewing's tumour
Miscellaneous	Giant cell tumour Brown tumour of hyperparathyroidism	

Osteoid osteoma

- Occurs in the 10–30-year age group
- Commonly in shaft of long bones
- Presents with pain:
    worse at night
    relieved by aspirin as pain is caused by excess prostaglandin E_2 production
- Mostly <2 cm in diameter

- Radiographic appearance: small radiolucent nidus, composed of osteoblastic tissue laying down woven bone, surrounded by reactive bone formation
- Treatment with curettage

Osteoblastoma

Essentially the same as ostoid osteoma, but lesions involve vertebrae and are larger. There is less surrounding reactive bone formation.

Osteosarcoma

This is the most common primary bone tumour accounting for 20% of cases. It has a bimodal distribution, 75% of cases affecting the 10–25-year age group, and a second smaller peak in incidence in the elderly, most of whom have Paget's disease.

Aetiology

- 90% idiopathic: found in young before epiphyseal closure
- 10% secondary to underlying bone disorder (e.g. Paget's)
- Genetic: surviving retinoblastoma patients have a 500x risk of developing osteosarcoma

Most arise in medullary cavity in metaphyseal ends of long bones.

Lower femur > upper tibia > upper humerus > upper femur > pelvis

Radiographic appearance

- May be lytic or sclerotic
- Extend through cortex and periosteum forming bulky mass
- A triangular shadow seen between the cortex and raised periosteum, known as Codman's triangle
- Seldom penetrates the epiphyseal plate or invades into the joint

Presentation

- Typically with a painful, enlarging mass
- These are aggressive tumours mostly with extensive blood-borne metastases on diagnosis
- 20% have pulmonary metastases on presentation

Advances in combination chemotherapy and limb-sparing surgery have significantly improved survival.

Five-year survival rate is 75%.

Prognosis is better in young adults, in those with more distally located tumours and in jaw tumours.

Multi-focal osteosarcomas and those arising against a background of Paget's disease have a poor prognosis.

Osteochondroma

- Most common benign tumour of bone
- Bony outgrowths from the surface of bone that are capped with a layer of cartilage
- Single or multiple
- Found in long bones, pelvis, scapula and ribs from a developmental anomaly of the epiphyseal growth plate
- Growth of lesions usually ceases with skeletal maturity
- Range in size 1–2 cm
- Slow growing
- Most are incidental findings
- Malignant change is rare in solitary lesions, but malignant transformation to chondrosarcoma occurs in 10% of patients with multiple lesions

Chondromas

Benign tumours of hyaline cartilage that arise within the medullary cavity or from the surface of bone.

Usually <3 cm in diameter.

Composed of lobules of cartilage which are well-circumscribed with benign chondrocytes lying in lacunae.

Most are asymptomatic and are incidental findings.

Solitary chondromas do not show malignant transformation, however, 25–30% of patients with multiple enchondromas (within the medullary cavity) develop chondrosarcoma.

Chondrosarcoma

- Second most common primary maligant bone tumour
- Occur within the medulla of bone (central) or on bone surface (juxta cortical)
- Affect middle-aged and elderly
- Occur *de novo* or as a result of malignant transformation of a previously benign cartilage tumour

- Grading is determined by examining cellularity, degree of cytological atypia and mitotic activity
- Sites most commonly affected: pelvis, ribs, proximal humerus/femur
- Radiographic appearance: prominent endosteal scalloping, cortical thickening and destruction, bone expansion

Most chondrosarcomas are slow-growing and are of low to intermediate grade = 85%.

Five-year survival rates:

- Grade 1 — 90%
- Grade 2 — 81%
- Grade 3 — 43%

Seldom metastasize, but pulmonary metastases are the most common.

Non-ossifying fibroma

- Common developmental abnormality
- Metaphyseal fibrous cortical defects
- Usually in the 5–20-year age group
- May self-heal or disappear spontaneously
- May enlarge to involve medullary cavity then can cause pathological tumours
- Radiographic appearance: eccentric, well-defined lucencies in metaphyseal cortex of long bones
- Treatment by curettage

Fibrous dysplasia

- Fibro-osseus abnormality of unknown aetiology
- May affect any bone
- Monostotic
- Polyostotic
- Malignant change is rare
- Radiographic appearance: lytic lesions with well-defined margins and a 'ground glass' appearance

Fibrosarcoma

- Affect a wide age range, 20–60 years
- Present with pain, swelling, pathological fractures
- Most arise *de novo*
- Prognosis depends on size and grade
- Ewing's sarcoma + primitive neuroectodermal tumour (PNET)

- These are closely related tumours
- 85% have characteristic chromosomal translocation between chromosomes 11 and 22

Ewing's sarcoma usually arises in diaphysis of long tubular bones, especially the femur and flat bones of the pelvis.

- 80% younger than 20 years
- Radiographic appearance: lytic lesions with permeative margins giving a 'moth-eaten' appearance

The characteristic periosteal reaction produces layers of reactive bone deposited in an 'onion skin' pattern.

Presents with pain, enlarging mass and sometimes associated systemic upset.

The development of effective combination chemotherapy has significantly improved five-year survival rate to ≃ 75%.

Giant cell tumour

- Neoplasm of the mature skeleton
- 20–40-year age group
- 50% arise around the knee
- Radiographic appearance: lytic, eccentric lesions; commonly reactive bone formation
- Benign but locally agressive tumour and difficult to manage
- Conservative surgery is associated with 15–60% recurrence rate, depending on surgical experience

14. PERIPHERAL NERVE INJURIES

14.1 Types of nerve injury

There are three grades of severity of peripheral nerve injury.

Neuropraxia

This is a block to conduction of electrical impulses down a nerve without disruption of the axonal transport system. Wallerian degeneration does not occur.

Mechanism of injury
Typically blunt trauma:

- Bony fragment compression
- Tourniquet or plaster cast compression

Recovery is complete if the cause is removed. Time of recovery — hours to days.

Axonotmesis

This is a disruption of the axon but not of the surrounding nerve sheath. The axon swells and the Nissl granules which represent endoplasmic reticulum disappear — chromatolysis. The lipid rich myelin sheath of the axon splits. The surrounding Schwann cells proliferate. New neurofibrils sprout from the proximal end of the severed axon and invaginate the Schwann cells at a rate of 1 mm/day. As the endoneurial channels are intact the regenerating axons mostly reach the correct end organs, and therefore give a good functional result. Traction is usually the mechanism of injury and the time of recovery is usually weeks to months.

Neurotmesis

This is a disruption of both the axon and supporting cells. There is chromatolysis proximally and Wallerian degeneration distally. The regenerating axons have to cross a gap filled with organising repair tissue and have no guiding endoneurial channels. The prognosis of recovery even if surgical repair is performed is very little. The end result may be a tangle of undirected new nerve fibres growing into a mass of fibrous tissue — traumatic neuroma. The mechanism of injury is usually laceration (e.g. stab wounds). It often leads to permanent disability. The treatment varies depending on the site of injury and functional deficit.

14.2 Sequelae of nerve injury

Motor deficit

Muscle paralysis, decreased joint function, joint stiffness, muscle contractures. Need daily physiotherapy, splintage in a position of function.

Sensory deficit

Sensory end organs rapidly deteriorate following Wallerian degeneration of a nerve. This cannot be prevented. Skin must be protected against friction, burns and other trauma. This is called sensory retraining. This is time-consuming and difficult to maintain in the long-term.

Autonomic deficit

The return of autonomic function is dependent on nerve recovery. Lack of sweat — dry, shiny skin prone to trauma. Delayed healing. Loss of pulp bulk in digits.

When an expected recovery does not occur, nerve conduction studies may be of use but surgical exploration is mandatory.

14.3 Surgical repair

Principles of surgical repair of nerves

- Accurate opposition of nerve ends
- Healthy surrounding tissue
- No tension
- Minimal dissection

May need to consider nerve grafting where deficit too large to allow direct closure without tension (e.g. sural nerve graft). If primary nerve repair is not appropriate (e.g. contaminated wounds, devitalized tissue) then suture the nerve end to local soft tissue to minimize retraction and to aid identification at second-look surgery.

There is no advantage to performing interfascicular repair as opposed to epineural repair so the latter is always performed. The aim is to provide epineural cover to nerve bundles without tension. Post-operative plaster immobilization is applied to minimize tension on suture line.

14.4 General prognostic factors

Age

Children recover from nerve injuries to a far greater degree than adults. However, growth abnormalities can occur in children secondary to failed nerve repair. In patients of over 50 years, there is a very poor prognosis for proximal nerve injuries.

Level of injury

Proximal worse than distal lesions

Severity of injury

Traction injuries can produce multi-level neurotmesis and axonotmesis thus associated with poor prognosis.

Type of nerve

Motor nerves to large muscle groups that do not require fine control have a better prognosis than those supplying the small muscles of the hand. Pure sensory nerve division often associated with chronic pain phenomena.

Delayed repair

Injuries which are not repaired within 10 days have a poorer prognosis.

Surgical technique

Several surgical factors adversely affect the outcome. These include:

- Damage to associated structures
- Degree of retraction and deficit
- Nerve grafting introduces an extra suture line for axonal regeneration to cross. The longer the nerve graft, the worse the prognosis.

15. PARALYTIC DISORDERS

In paralytic disorders deformity results from an imbalance of muscle groups. The deformity is initially correctable passively but can become fixed due to the development of contractures over time. This will inevitably lead to joint disorganisation. Surgery has a valuable role but only in the context of continuing physiotherapy, occupational therapy, orthotic splintage and good family support.

Strength of muscle contraction (and hence the strength of each joint movement) is recorded via the MRC scale.

THE MRC SCALE, 1976

M0	No active contraction detected
M1	Flicker of muscle contraction seen or felt but activity is insufficient to cause any joint movement
M2	Contraction very weak but can just produce movement with careful positioning of limb to minimize weight
M3	Contraction weak but can produce movement against gravitational resistance
M4	Strength not full but can produce movement against gravity with added resistance
M5	Normal power

15.1 Poliomyelitis

1–2% of patients infected with polio virus develop neurological disease. The virus affects the anterior horn cells particularly in cervical and lumbar enlargements.

Muscle weakness is proportional to the number of motor units destroyed. Paralysis is twice as common in the lower limb than in the upper limb.

Acute phase

Treatment
Physiotherapy: to prevent unaffected muscles from becoming hypertrophied, to prevent paretic muscles from being over-exercised, to prevent contracture formation in paretic muscles.

Chronic phase

Treatment
Surgery may be indicated. Common deformities are flexion contractures of knee, hip and calcaneus. If all muscles acting on a joint become paralysed, the joint will be weak and unstable. If paraspinal muscles are involved scoliosis results.

Surgical techniques

* Tendon transfer to augment weak muscle function
* Soft tissue release of contractures
* Stabilization of joints by arthrodesis
* Spinal fusion for scoliosis

15.2 Spina bifida

Spina bifida is a developmental neural tube defect marked by a defect in closure of the vertebra around the spinal cord. Disability depends on level of lesion. Spina bifida patients classically have lower motor neurone lesions resulting in motor and sensory loss. Most are complicated by upper motor neurone involvement resulting in coexisting spasticity. The lack of protective sensation means that minor cuts are a major infection risk as they will go unnoticed.

Surgical techniques

* **Foot**: tenotomy can be performed to produce a flat ankle and foot that can be controlled in an orthosis (splint)
* **Hip**: psoas tendon transfer to augment weak abductors
* **Kyphosis**: may require spinal fusion

If there is a progressive worsening of clinical signs the following surgically correctable causes should be considered:

- Tethering of nerve roots during growth
- A syrinx

15.3 Cerebral palsy

Non-progressive injury to developing brain usually occurring in neonatal period (e.g. anoxia, intracerebral haemorrhage, infection), all associated with prematurity.

- **Manifestations**: wide variation
- **Spasticity**: affecting flexor muscle groups more than extensors

Distribution

- Monoplegia
- Hemiplegia
- Diplegia
- Quadriplegia

Treatment

This is aimed at correcting and preventing deformity:

- Physiotherapy
- Splintage
- Surgery

Hemiplegics
Deformity mainly confined to foot. Commonly equinus contracture. Consider percutaneous lengthening if no improvement with ankle and foot orthosis or if contracture is fixed.

Diplegics
Equinus at ankles. Consider percutaneous lengthening, fixed flexion of knees, medial hamstring release at knee, adduction, internal rotation and flexion of hips. Consider adductor transfer at hip.

Quadriplegics
There is commonly a scoliosis. There is hip instability due to acetabular dysplasia, valgus, anteverted femoral necks, adductor tightness. Treatment is based on surveillance to prevent dislocation. If indicated, soft tissue release, varus femoral osteotomy and acetabular augmentation.

Chapter 2
Vascular

CONTENTS

Vascular

1. ARTERIAL DISEASE

1.1 Atherosclerosis

Atherosclerosis can be defined as a focal intimal accumulation composed of lipids and fibrous tissue, associated with smooth muscle proliferation. It is found mainly in the large and medium-sized arteries and develops as a plaque beneath the endothelium. It is responsible for 90% of arterial disease in the West, but is less common in the far east/Africa where the vasculitides are a more common cause.

The initial lesion is a fatty streak composed of a collection of lipids. This has been recognized even in young children. The lipids collect within macrophages derived from blood monocytes beneath the overlying endothelium. They may break down at the plaque base leading to the formation of a lipid-rich pool. This may disrupt the endothelium, which encourages platelet adhesion, leading to the release of thromboxane and platelet derived growth factor (PDGF). This promotes smooth muscle migration and proliferation and further platelet aggregation. The roughened surface is highly thrombogenic. The cause of atheroma is still unknown, although a number of theories exist. It is suggested that intimal damage may lead to platelet adherence, with the release of mitogen leading to smooth muscle cell proliferation. These cells are thought to encourage the deposition of lipid. Hypertension, low shear stress (reduces the transport of atheroma promoting substances away from the wall), turbulent flow and chemical damage due to nicotine and hyperlipidaemia have all been implicated in causing the intimal damage.

Risk factors for atherosclerosis

- Male sex
- Smoking
- High fat diet
- Hypertriglyceridaemia
- Hypercoagulability
- Myxoedema

- Diabetes
- Hypertension
- Hypercholesterolaemia
- Obesity
- Family history
- Older age

Atheroma can lead to vascular events by occluding vessels itself, the formation of thrombus on the plaque, haemorrhage into the plaque or embolization of plaque/thrombus.

1.2 Physiology of the arterial system

Arterial system functions include blood distribution and conversion of pulsatile to steady flow, as this requires less work. This is accomplished by the elasticity in the vessel walls. This elasticity is known as **compliance**.

Mean arterial pressure $P_a = P_d + 1/3(P_s - P_d)$

where P_a is mean arterial pressure; P_d is diastolic pressure and P_s is systolic pressure.

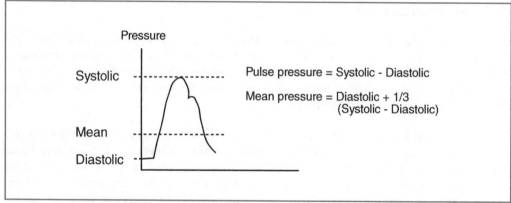

Arterial pressure wave

It is also related to cardiac output by:

$$P_a - P_{RA} = CO.SVR$$

where SVR = systemic vascular resistance; CO = cardiac output and P_{RA} is right atrial pressure.

NB. Arterial pressure is determined by the rate blood enters the system (cardiac output), and at the rate at which blood leaves the system (systemic vascular resistance). Factors such as heart rate and stroke volume affect arterial pressure by altering the cardiac output. The less compliant the system (stiff arteries) the more work the heart must do to pump a given stroke volume. Compliance decreases with age.

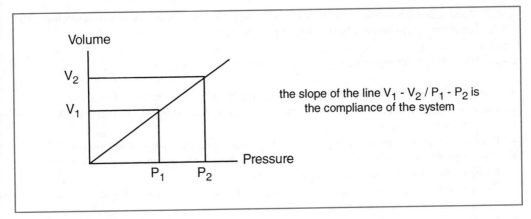

the slope of the line $V_1 - V_2 / P_1 - P_2$ is the compliance of the system

Vascular compliance

Haemodynamics

Flow $(Q) = \Delta P/\text{Resistance}$

where ΔP is pressure change across vessel, therefore in the systemic circulation:

$P_a - P_{RA} = \text{CO.SVR}$

(The same equation format can be applied to the pulmonary circulation.)

Flow in smooth vessels should be laminar, i.e. along the longitudinal axis. Poiseuille's law then governs it:

Flow $= \Delta P \pi r^4 / 8 \eta L$

where η is blood viscosity, L is the length of the vessel segment and r is it's radius.

NB. Strong dependence of flow on vessel radius. If the radius doubles, the flow will increase 16-fold.

In dehydration or polycythaemia the viscosity of blood increases (effect is exaggerated as haematocrit increases) leading to an increase in pressure to maintain the flow. There is a decrease in the apparent viscosity of blood when it flows in smaller vessels; therefore in small vessels there is a lower resistance to flow. Lower blood pressure reduces shear rate and therefore increases blood viscosity. This has implications for flow distal to stenoses. Small arteries and arterioles provide the greatest resistance to flow in the systemic circulation by altering smooth muscle tone in their walls and are therefore the main determinants of systemic vascular resistance.

The greatest cross-sectional area is in the capillary bed and the velocity is therefore least here. This allows maximum opportunity for exchange.

Capillary beds are arranged in parallel, allowing:

- The flow to each bed to be adjusted independently, according to its metabolic needs. If there is a large increase in flow to a particular area, then the flow to other beds will be decreased to compensate.
- Flow that can preferentially be directed to certain vital areas if cardiac output falls
- The overall SVR can be adjusted by increasing the resistance in many capillary beds
- Oxygenated blood to reach all capillary beds
- Certain individual beds to maintain their blood flow locally, despite variation in cardiac output — auto regulation
- Feeding artery occlusions to only affect the particular bed

To calculate systemic vascular resistance:

$1/SVR = 1/R_1 + 1/R_2 + 1/R_3$, etc. as each resistance $R_1/R_2/R_3$, etc. all lie in parallel.

Haemodynamics and stenosis

As there is a pressure drop across a segment of increased resistance, leading to a lower pressure distal to the resistance, the pressure distal to an area of vascular stenosis will be decreased.

NB. Assuming the flow rate remains relatively constant, the reduction of lumen diameter will result in an increased velocity through the stenosis. As velocity increases, the smooth laminar flow is lost and a turbulent pattern emerges. The likelihood of turbulent flow can be estimated by calculating Reynolds' number (N_R).

$[N_R < 2000$-laminar flow, $N_R > 3000$-turbulent$]$

This turbulence dissipates some energy, and may be heard as a murmur/bruit.

Critical stenosis

Clearly, as the stenosis increases, a point is reached where flow can no longer be maintained, and the stenosis is now termed critical. This tends to occur at approximately 70% stenosis. As the resistance in the vessel is proportional to r^4 the flow rate through the vessels will now sharply decline, and the pressure drop becomes significant.

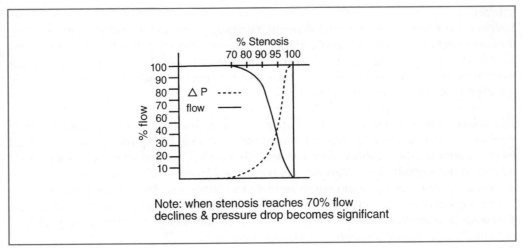

Relationship of flow to degree of stenosis

Cutaneous circulation

This circulation serves a number of important functions. The prime regulator of flow to the cutaneous capillary bed is not local tissue nutrition and excretion, as the skin has a relatively low nutrition requirement. The prime regulator of flow is the need for regulation of body temperature. Other factors include sympathetic nervous supply, nutrition of surrounding tissues, reflexes such as the baroreceptor reflex, trauma and local hormones such as bradykinin.

Skeletal muscle circulation

Low blood flow at rest (15 ml/min/100 g in red muscle, 4 ml/min/100 g in fast twitch muscles). This can increase by 20 times during exercise, at the expense of blood supply to the viscera. Vasoactive metabolites are the most important dilatory mechanism, but there are also a large number of β-receptors responding to circulating adrenaline. As skeletal muscle represents a large proportion of body weight, even at rest its low flow of blood per kg means it can receive 30% of the cardiac output. This means that the resistance offered by skeletal muscle capillary beds must be a significant fraction of the total SVR.

Peripheral vascular control

Intrinsic
Local mechanisms serve to match the flow through a capillary bed to its metabolic activity. Examples include the vasodilatation produced in response to products of metabolism, including CO_2, endothelial-derived relaxing factor (nitric oxide), lactic acid and H^+ ions. These lead to an increased blood flow.

Extrinsic

Systemic mechanisms involve the autonomic nervous system and hormones, and generally they are integrated with the whole cardiovascular system. Not only does this provide control over flow to specific beds but it will also control the total vascular resistance. The sympathetic nervous system releases noradrenaline as a transmitter, which acts at smooth muscle α-receptors to cause vasoconstriction.

The balance between the two systems varies between tissues. Skin has a strong extrinsic component, whereas the brain has a chiefly intrinsic auto-regulation. The control is achieved by the arterioles, which contain abundant smooth muscle. This smooth muscle is intimately related to the endothelium allowing agents released by the endothelium in response to blood-borne stimuli (e.g. hormones) to regulate its contraction. The baroreceptor reflex involves increased afferent nerve signals from the baroreceptors in response to hypertension. This leads to a decreased output from the medullary cardiovascular centres, lowering blood pressure. It is an important short-term control measure.

1.3 Measurement of blood flow

USS

This method utilizes duplex scanning to calculate flow by measuring the velocity of red cell movement, and the cross-sectional area of the vessel. The system produces ultrasound waves and measures the phase shift of reflected signals, using the Doppler principle to calculate blood velocity.

Indicator dilution

Widely used to estimate cardiac output. A known quantity of indicator (dye/isotope) is injected rapidly into central vein. Arterial blood is continuously passed through a detector, and the indicator concentration measured. The greater the blood flow (cardiac output) the greater the dilution of the indicator. Currently, the most common indicator is a bolus of cold saline injected via a PA catheter. This is also known as the **thermodilution** technique.

Plethysmography

A sphygmomanometer cuff is placed around a dependent part of the body and inflated to pressure greater than that of venous pressure, but less than arterial pressure. This prevents blood from leaving the region while allowing the arterial supply to continue. The rate of increase in the dimensions of the limb will depend on the arterial flow. Several methods exist to measure the dimensions, including strain gauges and water displacement.

2. PERIPHERAL VASCULAR DISEASE

Atherosclerosis with thrombosis is the most common cause of PVD, with connective tissue diseases and thromboembolic disease occurring less frequently. Disease is more extensive in diabetic patients. In the 50–75-year age group, 30% of the UK population has detectable occlusive disease, with about 15% of these being symptomatic.

Flow in a vessel is governed by **Poiseuille's law**

$$\text{Flow} \sim \frac{r^4}{\eta L}$$

Initial decreases in diameter have little effect due to effective compensation. When $d < 75\%$ of normal, flow cannot be increased by distal dilatation, leading to tissue ischaemia at times of exercise — angina/claudication.

The mechanism of the pain is unknown but possibly related to anoxia, acidosis, metabolite accumulation and substance P accumulation.

NB. Musculoskeletal causes of pain (most common cause of lower limb pain) and spinal claudication in the differential diagnosis.

2.1 Anatomy of the lower limb arterial supply

Femoral artery

The femoral artery enters the thigh at the mid-inguinal point (i.e. halfway between the symphysis pubis and the anterior superior iliac spine). It descends almost vertically through the femoral canal to enter the adductor canal continuing towards the adductor tubercle. It enters the popliteal fossa via the adductor hiatus in adductor magnus to become the popliteal artery. Its branches are the superficial circumflex iliac, superficial epigastric, superficial and deep external pudendals and the profunda femoris. The profunda is the largest branch, which arises laterally before descending medially to enter the adductor compartment. It gives off the medial and lateral circumflex femoral branches then three perforators before ending as the fourth perforator.

Popliteal artery

The popliteal artery is deeply placed as it enters the popliteal fossa. Posteriorly lies the popliteal vein and tibial nerve, while anteriorly it is in contact with the joint capsule. It ends at the lower border of the popliteus muscle by dividing into anterior and posterior tibial branches.

Anterior tibial artery

The anterior tibial artery is the smaller of the terminal branches. It enters the anterior compartment of the leg via an opening in the interosseous membrane. It descends with the deep peroneal nerve. As it enters the foot under the extensor retinaculum it becomes the dorsalis pedis artery. On its medial side is the extensor hallucis longus tendon while the extensor digitorum longus tendons lie laterally.

Posterior tibial artery

The posterior tibial artery passes deep to soleus and gastrocnemius. The tibial nerve is initially medial but crosses posteriorly to lie on the lateral side. The artery passes behind the medial malleolus and divides into the medial and lateral plantar arteries. It supplies the posterior compartment muscles and gives off the peroneal artery.

Peroneal artery

The peroneal artery arises near the origin of the posterior tibial artery and descends behind the fibula. It gives numerous perforating branches to supply the lateral compartment of the leg before ending in the anastomosis around the ankle.

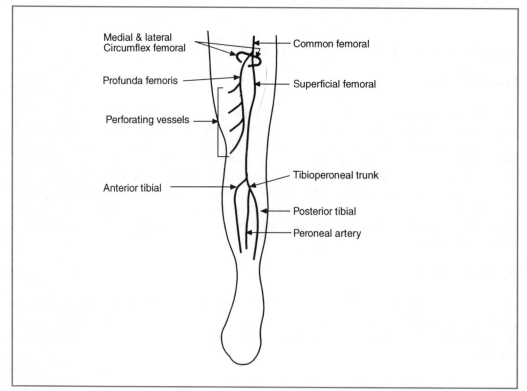

Arterial supply of the lower limb

2.2 Investigation of vascular disease

Investigations

General

- FBC (polycythaemia, anaemia, leukaemia)
- Fasting lipids
- ESR (vasculitis)
- Exclude diabetes
- CXR (chest disease, concurrent Ca)
- ECG (arrhythmia) (exercise ECG, positron emission tomography (PET), Thallium scans in special cases)

Specific

- Doppler pressures — resting/post exercise confirms diagnosis and provides a baseline for treatment
- The ankle/brachial pressure index should be ~1. An index of 0.5–1 indicates a moderate occlusion, <0.5 severe

At present contrast angiography is the investigation of choice, though magnetic resonance angiography is developing.

Complementary

- Duplex scanning
- Intravenous Digital Subtraction Angiography (i.v. DSA)
- Intra-arterial Digital Subtraction Angiography (i.a. DSA) (see overleaf)

Complementary investigations

- **Advantages**
  Duplex
  Relatively cheap
  Non-invasive
  Accurate measurement of stenosis
  Continually developing

  i.a. DSA
  Small contrast volume
  Can dilate at same time
  Good images

  i.v. DSA
  No arterial puncture

- **Disadvantages**

  View obscured by bowel gas
  Operator-dependent
  Poor in calcified vessels

  Invasive
  Arterial damage

  Poor images below knee
  Large contrast volume
  Poor in heart failure

2.3 Intermittent claudication

Cramping pain ± rigidity/spasm. Felt in the calf, thigh, buttock (if aorta/iliac vessels involved), upper limb occasionally.

Only occurs on exercise and always relieved by rest. The most common site of stenosis in the lower limb is the superficial femoral artery in the adductor canal. The more distal the occlusion the greater the likelihood of symptoms due to the decreased prospect of collateral vessels.

Rest pain is a sign of critical ischaemia. It is usually felt in the skin of the foot, precedes gangrene and is relieved by having the limb dependent.

Leriche's syndrome comprises lower limb claudication, erectile dysfunction and muscle wasting and is due to distal aortic stenosis.

If severe stenosis precedes an acute occlusion, collateral channels may reduce the changes of acute ischaemia/gangrene, but usually symptoms deteriorate, then improve as new channels open. The system of collateral circulations develops not through the growth of new vessels, but by the enlargement of existing vessels. The stimulus to enlargement appears to be increased blood flow through the channels. The efficiency of collateral flow depends on the location (lower limb — good, upper limb — poor). Collateral vessel dilatation takes several weeks; therefore slowly developing occlusions are best tolerated. There are, however, a number of problems with collateral circulations:

- Increased resistance offered by the new system
- Maximally dilated distal vessels due to reduced flow, therefore poor exercise tolerance
- Poor compensation in multiple occlusions

Fate of claudicants
Mortality increased by about three times, 75% dying of vascular causes, especially myocardial infarction. Most cases do not progress to critical ischaemia and can be managed conservatively.

Management

Aim to decrease symptoms **and** reduce risk of vascular mortality.

- Investigation as outlined above
- Stop smoking
- Increase exercise — this improves cardiovascular fitness and collateral circulation
- Improve diet — low fat/moderate alcohol
- Lose weight
- Aspirin 75–300 mg/day, optimal dose unknown (dipyridamole if allergic). Shown to decrease vascular complications in claudicants including reducing MI/CVA rates by about 25%. Little evidence to support formal anticoagulation.
- Blood pressure management — avoid β-blockers as these may reduce walking distance. Care with ACE inhibitors due to raised prevalence of renal artery stenosis.
- Blood lipid management — reduce cholesterol if > 5.5 mmol/l
- Surgery/interventional radiology — indicated in lifestyle-limiting disease despite medical treatment

2.4 Critical ischaemia

Chronic critical ischaemia

Critical ischaemia implies that without intervention, limb loss may be imminent. It is often due to progressive disease at multiple levels. It can be defined as rest pain, ulceration or gangrene in the presence of an ankle pressure < 30 mmHg (40 mmHg in diabetics due to stiffened vessels giving falsely high readings). It may be precipitated by a reduction in perfusion of the limb (e.g. heart failure/AF or respiratory disease reducing oxygenation).

Management of chronic critical ischaemia

- Treat causes of decreased cardiac output
- Reduce peripheral oedema (this helps improve perfusion)
- Dependent limb position
- Treat infection
- Angiography (± angioplasty, thrombolysis or surgery where appropriate)

Acute critical ischaemia

A surgical emergency. 5000 patients/year in the UK. Usually due to embolic impaction, or acute thrombosis. Rarer causes include aortic dissection, thrombosed popliteal aneurysm, intra arterial injection and trauma. Atheromatous plaque may rupture leading to thrombosis within the wall occluding the lumen. Symptoms depend on speed of occlusion and collateral circulation. Symptoms are bursting pain, paraesthesia (stocking distribution), pallor, cold, leading to wet gangrene.

Arterial embolism

Most emboli originate in the left heart (atrial fibrillation, myocardial infarction, cardiomyopathy, infective endocarditis) but may arise from thrombosis within an aneurysm or the surface of an atheromatous plaque. Rarer causes include tumours, endocarditis vegetations and paradoxical emboli. They commonly lodge at arterial bifurcations (e.g. aorta, femoral, popliteal, carotid).

Investigations

- **Arteriography**: usually shows a sharp cut off at the upper aspect of occlusion with poor collateral vessels
- **Echocardiography**: may detect a source of thrombus

Management of acute critical ischaemia (see flow chart below)

- Anticoagulate with heparin initially
- Angiography if thrombosis suspected or the cause of occlusion unclear
- Surgical embolectomy/thrombectomy — occlusions above the knee
- Local, regional or general anaesthesia; mortality reaches 20%
- Thrombolysis — for occlusions below the superficial femoral. Also the treatment of choice in acute on chronic ischaemia. The most effective agent is r-tpa, however, streptokinase is still popular as it is less expensive. The major complications include retroperitoneal, cerebral and local haemorrhage. Contraindications include old age, recent stroke, recent surgery/CPR, bleeding tendency, and peptic ulceration.

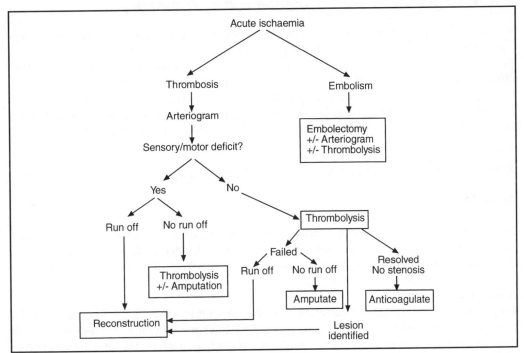

Management of acute lower limb ischaemia

NB. Skin can withstand 48 hours of ischaemia but nerve and muscle are more sensitive leading to tissue death, and contractures/neuritic pain. In advanced cases revascularization/embolectomy/thrombolysis is hazardous due to release of toxic metabolites, myoglobin and potassium. These can lead to a reperfusion injury with myocardial dysfunction, pulmonary oedema/ARDS and renal failure. These account for the high mortality associated with reperfusion and therefore in advanced cases of ischaemia amputation is carried out.

Femoral embolectomy

- Local, general or regional anaesthesia
- Prepare leg and both groins; foot placed in clear bag to aid inspection
- Longitudinal skin incision over femoral artery
- Slings placed around common, superficial and profunda femoral vessels, for control
- Longitudinal arteriotomy
- 5 F catheter inserted proximally and withdrawn with balloon inflated
- 3 F then 4 F catheters inserted distally to clear distal thrombus
- Heparinized saline injected proximally and distally then arteriotomy closed with continuous non-absorbable suture

---

2.5 Buerger's disease (thromboangiitis obliterans)

A progressive obliteration of distal arteries in young men who smoke heavily. The vessels show transmural inflammation, intimal proliferation and commonly lamina thrombosis. Patients usually present with evidence of poor peripheral circulation, chronic paronychias, ulcers or digital gangrene. Popliteal pulses usually preserved with loss of pedal pulses. Management includes stopping smoking and sympathectomy. Antibiotics, foot care, analgesia and prostaglandins may be tried to overcome acute ischaemia and allow collaterals to open. Bypass is usually fruitless and many end up with one or more amputations.

2.6 Principles of reconstructive arterial surgery

Aortoiliac disease

Direct aortoiliac reconstruction by aortobifemoral grafting using a prosthetic graft is the most definitive means of revascularization. In those patients deemed high risk for direct repair, endo-vascular techniques or extra-anatomic bypass procedures should be considered.

Aortobifemoral grafting

This is the preferred method for treating symptomatic aortoiliac disease. Initial graft patency approaches 100% with 80% five-year patency. Operative mortality is in the region of 5% in specialist centres. The good long term results in this method of treatment are due to a number of factors, including the elimination of graft failure due to iliac disease progression and improvements in graft technology. The proximal anastomosis is usually constructed in an end-to-end fashion as this results in less turbulence, better flow characteristics and eliminates competitive flow within the native iliac vessels compared to an end-to-side anastomosis. The graft can also be covered more easily to reduce the incidence of aorto-enteric fistulae. However, some surgeons prefer the end-to-side anastomosis especially in the presence of bilateral external iliac occlusion; aortic transection in this instance may devascularize the pelvis due to lack of retrograde flow from the femoral anastomoses. The limbs of the graft are then tunnelled to the groins retro-peritoneally, avoiding the ureters and autonomic plexus. The distal anastomoses are then formed in an end-to-side manner.

Extra-anatomical bypass
These procedures are carried out if the patient is deemed unfit for major vascular reconstruction. If the iliac occlusive disease is limited to one side then **femoral crossover grafting** can be undertaken. Here the contralateral femoral system is grafted to the affected side via a prosthetic graft. Concerns that the bypass may produce a 'steal' phenomenon by reducing flow to the donor limb appear to be unfounded as long as there is no significant disease in the donor leg inflow. Operative mortality is small and five-year patency rates of 75–80% have been reported. If the disease process involves the aortic segment or bilateral iliac systems then **axillo-bifemoral grafting** would be required. This involves anastomosis of a graft tunnelled subcutaneously to the axillary artery, the ipsilateral femoral artery then the contralateral femoral vessel. The procedure requires general anaesthesia though the initial groin and axillary exploration can be done under local anaesthesia. Although inferior to the results in aortobifemoral or femoral crossover grafting, it can provide a compromise for the high-risk case.

Peripheral disease

The choice of operation for patients with peripheral occlusive disease depends on the site and extent of the occlusion, experience of the operator and availability of graft materials. The most common procedure is a bypass from the common femoral artery to a distal vessel, usually the popliteal artery, although it may involve the tibio-peroneal trunk or any of the three crural vessels. Generally, anastomosis should be to the most proximal suitable vessel (i.e. popliteal better than tibio-peroneal better than crural). The technique, first described by Kunlin in 1948, involves formation of a separate path around the occlusion to allow blood to flow in parallel to the original vessels without damaging any collateral circulation.

The two main types of graft used for reconstruction are **autogenous saphenous vein** and **synthetic PTFE**.

Autogenous saphenous vein
This is the best material for peripheral vascular bypass procedures and is usually explored and assessed at the time of surgery. Contraindications to its use include:

- Small calibre
- Useable length too short
- Thrombosed
- Markedly varicose
- Previously removed

The short saphenous, cephalic or basilic veins may be used as alternatives in some circumstances. Occlusion rates when used for femoro-popliteal bypass are around 20% in the first year and 10% in each subsequent year. Occlusion rates increase as the anastomosis becomes more distal (e.g. femoro-distal).

Reversed autogenous saphenous vein grafting
In femoro-popliteal bypass grafting the popliteal artery is exposed via a medial incision, and the femoral vessel is exposed in the groin. The vein is explored and an adequate length excised following ligation of all tributaries. The vein is then tested for leaks with saline, these being repaired with fine non-absorbable sutures.

A tunnel is formed by blunt dissection to connect the two anastomosis sites and the reversed vein is passed via the tunnel.

NB. As the vein contains valves it needs to be reversed before anastomosis, to allow blood flow from proximal to distal.

The patient is heparinized and end-to-side anastomoses are carried out with continuous non-absorbable sutures.

In situ saphenous vein grafting
The use of the *in situ* long saphenous vein is an alternative procedure that is gaining in popularity. Here, the vein is not excised but left *in situ* and anastomosed in the same way as for reversed vein grafts. Tributaries must be recognized and ligated to prevent the formation of A-V fistulae. Generally, the proximal anastomosis is made first and blood allowed to fill the vein down to the first valve. The valves are then disrupted with a valvulotome and the distal anastomosis completed. Advantages over the reversed vein technique are that the blood supply to the vein is not disturbed and the larger end of saphenous vein is anastomosed to the larger artery. Disadvantages are the risk of A-V fistulae and the technical experience required to construct the smaller distal anastomosis.

Synthetic grafts
If no suitable vein is available a synthetic graft is required. The most popular is expanded poly-tetrafluoroethylene (PTFE). This is an inert material, relatively resistant to thrombosis and available in many calibres (6 mm is usually used for femoro-popliteal bypass). Early patency rates are similar to those for vein grafts, but the long-term patency is lower with 15–20% occlusion per year. This is thought to be due to neo-intimal hyperplasia particularly at the distal anastomosis. Other materials such as Dacron are available though are less popular due to higher occlusion rates.

Complications of arterial reconstruction

- **Early**

  Graft thrombosis: usually due to
  inadequate outflow or inflow
  or poor surgical technique

  Haemorrhage: may be due to poor
  anastomosis formation which may be
  resolved by inserting further sutures,
  or bleeding from vein side branches

  Lymph leaks: usually from the groin
  and thigh wounds. They generally stop
  spontaneously and until this time graft
  infection should be prevented by
  administration of antibiotics.

  Wound infection: relatively uncommon
  and usually affects the groin. Antibiotic
  treatment usually prevents graft infection,
  though when this does occur the graft
  will generally need to be removed

  Leg oedema: commonly seen due to
  increased interstitial fluid following
  reperfusion of an ischaemic limb and
  immobility, though may be due to DVT

- **Late**

  Thrombosis: the main cause of
  late graft failure. It is usually due
  to progression of the occlusive
  disease or neo-intimal hyperplasia

  False aneurysm: due to anastomotic
  leak near the time of surgery

  Anastomotic aneurysm: a true
  aneurysm due to failing strength
  of the vessel wall near the
  anastomosis

2.7 Gangrene

May be wet or dry, with a spectrum in-between.

Dry gangrene

Occurs due to gradual interruption of arterial supply to tissues free from oedema and remaining uninfected. The black discoloration of the skin is due to staining by haemoglobin liberated from the vascular compartment. Commonly occurs at the tips of toes and pressure points. Sensation is lost, affected part becomes cold, dry and shrivelled. Progresses until a level of adequate perfusion reached. Eventually the gangrenous part demarcates and may separate (auto-amputation).

Wet gangrene

Usually follows an acute arterial occlusion. Ischaemic necrosis is associated with infection by putrefactive organisms. Must differentiate from primary infective gangrene. The bacterial contamination is often resistant to systemic anti-bacterial agents due to lack of perfusion, however they may prevent spread of infection. It has a dusky appearance, with a poorly defined edge. There may be blistering and an offensive odour.

2.8 Principles of amputations in vascular disease

The subject of amputations in general, along with details of the procedures and complications are covered in Chapter 1, *Locomotor*, Section 4.

In the UK, 60% of amputations are carried out for vascular disease but, world-wide, trauma is the main indication. In general the amputation should be at the most distal level that is compatible with sound wound healing as more distal amputations have been shown to have better long term outcome and rehabilitation. If the patient has the mental and physical capacity to regain mobility then a correctly functioning knee joint should be preserved whenever possible, ideally along with 15 cm of bone below the joint. However, a shorter stump is preferable to an above knee amputation. Below-knee amputation can be carried out in approximately 75% of cases. The desire for improved rehabilitation, however, has to be weighed against the increased risk of complications due to a compromised blood supply when amputations are carried out for vascular disease. Too distal an amputation level leads to failure of new vessel formation in granulation tissue, impairment of the metabolic processes of tissue repair and decreased ability to fight infection. Approximately 50% of amputees die within three years and early mortality ranges from 10% to 20%. Thirty per cent of initial survivors become bilateral amputees within two years. The main consideration in performing the amputation should always therefore be rapid wound healing.

The skin that is to form the flaps must obviously be viable from the outset. Evidence of demarcation, ulceration, excoriation or anaesthesia of the skin are obvious contraindications to its preservation within the flap. The tissues deep to the skin must also be healthy, and muscle tenderness or loss of function may signal deep necrosis or sepsis that is likely to compromise healing. The absence of the next most proximal pulse to the amputation site has been said to be a contraindication, but is probably an unreliable marker for choosing the site. The most commonly employed methods of assessment are clinical examination and flap bleeding at the time of surgery, though the latter can be greatly affected by anaesthetic agents and transient hypotension.

A variety of other techniques such as thermography, transcutaneous oxygen measurement, cutaneous perfusion measurement and Doppler ultrasound have been described for assessing the blood supply to amputation flaps. All improve the proportion of amputations carried out at the correct level in the hands of enthusiasts, but require a degree of expertise and are not readily available in most hospitals. No single technique has been shown to be sufficiently superior to the others to attain widespread acceptance but transcutaneous oxygen measurement is probably the most valuable.

The difficulties with wound healing are often aggravated by the co-existence of poor cardio-respiratory function or diabetes, and attempts should always be made to control these prior to surgery.

2.9 Vascular supply of the upper limb

Axillary artery

The axillary artery is the continuation of the subclavian artery at the outer border of the first rib; it becomes the brachial artery at the lower border of teres major. It is closely related to the brachial plexus and both are enclosed in the fascial axillary sheath. The pectoralis minor muscle divides the artery into three parts. The main branches of each part are:

- **1st part**: highest thoracic
- **2nd part**: thoracoacromial, lateral thoracic
- **3rd part**: subscapular, anterior and posterior circumflex humeral

Axillary vein

The axillary vein is formed by the union of the brachial and basilic veins, and continues at the first rib as the subclavian vein. Its tributaries correspond to the artery but it also receives the cephalic vein.

Brachial artery

The brachial artery provides the main blood supply to the upper limb. It descends in the anterior compartment of the arm dividing into the radial and ulnar arteries at the neck of the radius. Its branches supply the arm, with its profunda branch supplying the posterior compartment. The median nerve initially lies laterally but then crosses anteriorly to lie medial to the artery in the ante-cubital fossa.

Ulnar artery

The ulnar artery passes medially and inferiorly in the anterior compartment of the forearm, running deep to flexor carpi ulnaris, lateral to the ulnar nerve. It ends by forming the superficial palmar arch with the superficial branch of the radial artery. Its upper part gives off the common interosseous artery, which divides into anterior and posterior branches.

Radial artery

The radial artery passes downwards and laterally under brachioradialis, emerging on its medial side near the wrist. Distally it lies on the radius, only covered by skin and fascia. It is here that its pulsation is felt. It then winds laterally before entering the palm between the two heads of the first dorsal interosseous muscle. It supplies its neighbouring muscles and ends as the deep palmar arch.

2.10 Raynaud's syndrome (Raynaud's disease if idiopathic)

Characterized by extreme sensitivity of digital vessels to cold. Three distinct clinical phases are recognized:

- **Digital blanching**: due to arterial spasm (hands go white)
- **Cyanosis/pain**: due to stagnant anoxia (hands go blue)
- **Reactive hyperaemia**: due to accumulation of vasoactive metabolites (hands go red)

Causes of Raynaud's syndrome

- **Connective tissue disorders**
  Scleroderma
  SLE
  PAN
  Rheumatoid arthritis
  Sjögren's syndrome

- **Blood disorders**
  Cold agglutinins
  Cryoglobulinaemia
  Polycythaemia

- **Arterial disease**
  Atherosclerosis
  Buerger's
  Cervical rib

- **Trauma**
  Vibration-induced
  Post-frostbite

- **Drugs**
  Ergot
  β-blockers
  Contraceptive pill

Attacks are episodic, in response to cold or emotion. Seventy-five per cent of sufferers are female, the majority young. Unilateral disease suggests a local organic cause. Management includes keeping hands warm, stopping smoking, and medical treatment, such as methyl-dopa or nifedipine. Prostacyclin and PGE_1 have been used with effect especially in acute attacks and gangrene. Some, however, require regular prostacyclin, plasmapheresis or sympathectomy.

3. ANEURYSMS

As age increases, arteries become stiffer, calcified, wider and longer. The increased length leads to tortuosity. Dilatation by more than 50% is named **arteriomegaly**. Dilatation by 100% is named an **aneurysm**. Aneurysms can be classified as:

- **False**: due to a traumatic breach in the wall, with the sac made up from the compressed surrounding tissue
- **True**: dilatation involving all layers of the wall

True aneurysms can further be divided into:

- **Fusiform**: spindle-shaped involving whole circumference
- **Saccular**: small segment of wall ballooning due to localized weakness

Most aneurysms are caused by degenerative disease affecting the vessel (aka atherosclerotic). There is damage to, and loss of intima, and a reduction in the elastin and collagen content of the media. The risk factors are the same as for atherosclerosis, with 25% being associated with occlusive vascular disease. Why some develop stenotic disease and others dilatation is not known.

Rarer causes of aneurysm formation

- **Congenital**
  (e.g. Berry aneurysms)

- **Mycotic**
  Usually due to infective emboli
  (e.g. in endocarditis) and tend to
  occur at bifurcations

- **Syphilis**
  Rare today
  Characteristically saccular aneurysms

- **Connective tissue disorders**
  (e.g. Marfan's or Ehlers–Danlos
  syndromes)

As tension in the wall **T α radius^4** (Laplace's law), for every increase in radius there is a large increase in tension, leading to further enlargement of the aneurysm.

- Over 90% of atherosclerotic aneurysms occur in the abdominal aorta, with 30% also having associated iliac disease
- 95% are infra-renal; they also occur in the popliteal and occasionally femoral arteries, though any artery (and the heart) can be involved
- Incidence increases with age, with 5% of the over-50 population affected, and 15% of the over-80s
- M:F ratio ~6:1, with an increased risk of 12-fold in first-degree relatives compared to the general population

3.1 Anatomy of the abdominal aorta

The aorta enters the abdomen between the diaphragmatic crura anterior to the T12 vertebra. It descends on the vertebral bodies until its bifurcation on the body of L4 forming the common iliac arteries with the small median sacral artery between. It is crossed anteriorly by splenic vein, body and uncinate process of pancreas and the third part of the duodenum. On its right lie the cisterna chyli, IVC and azygos vein, whereas the left sympathetic trunk lies to the left.

Its surface markings are from just above the transpyloric plane in the mid-line to a point to the left of the midline on the supracristal plane. Its branches are shown below.

Branches of the abdominal aorta

- **Paired visceral branches**
  Suprarenal
  Renal
  Gonadal

- **Paired abdominal wall branches**
  Subcostal
  Inferior phrenic
  Lumbar

- **Unpaired visceral branches**
  Coeliac axis
  Superior mesenteric
  Inferior mesenteric

3.2 Clinical features of abdominal aortic aneurysms

Seventy-five per cent are asymptomatic, and found incidentally during clinical examination or radiographic investigations. The most common symptom is pain, commonly referred to the back. It may be chronic due to stretching the vessel wall or compression/erosion of surrounding structures, or acute, usually due to a complication. The main complications being:

- **Rupture**: severe central abdominal pain radiating to the back and flanks. If intra-peritoneal there will be exsanguination and shock. Many however are retroperitoneal, with the patient initially surviving due to tamponade by surrounding tissues. This temporary stability may last hours before a second fatal haemorrhage. The risk of rupture has been shown to correlate to the aneurysm size (remember Tension α radius[4]). In a study from the Mayo Clinic (1989) the median growth rate was 0.21 cm/

year, though 25% grew at 0.4 cm/year. The five-year rupture rate was 0% for aneurysms <5 cm and 25% for those >5 cm. The diastolic blood pressure and the degree of obstructive airways disease have also been reported to predict the risk of rupture.

- **Fistulation**: rarely, aneurysms may rupture into the gut, IVC or left renal vein
- **Thrombosis**: leads to acute lower limb ischaemia. Rare, more often seen in popliteal aneurysms.
- **Distal embolism**: emboli of thrombus/atheroma from the aneurysm give rise to a clinical spectrum from acute limb ischaemia to small areas of distal infarction (trash foot).
- **Distal obliteration**: they may also present with symptoms of distal occlusive disease such as claudication, rest pain or gangrene.

3.3 Investigations for abdominal aortic aneurysms

- **CXR**: to evaluate thoracic extension and pulmonary disease
- **ECG**: to detect cardiac arrhythmia/ischaemia; consider exercise test, etc. to evaluate function
- **ESR**: if elevated may suggest an inflammatory aneurysm
- **U&Es**: to detect renal impairment
- **Abdominal USS**: for measurement and to image extent; accurate to within 10%; poor at defining juxtarenal anatomy
- **CT scanning**: improved imaging of juxtarenal anatomy and retroperitoneal structures; important if an inflammatory aneurysm suggested
- **Arteriography**: not an accurate investigation of size, as it only outlines the lumen, not the sac containing thrombus; useful in multiple/uncommon aneurysms

3.4 Management of abdominal aortic aneurysms

Most surgeons would offer elective repair for aneurysms >6 cm diameter which carries a post-operative mortality of about 5%. Overall mortality in ruptured aneurysms is about 75%, with a 50% mortality in those who reach hospital and undergo surgery. The question arises regarding the management of smaller aneurysms. This is currently under investigation in the UK small aneurysm trial where patients aged 60–76 with aneurysms of 4–5.5 cm diameter are randomized to receive early surgery or USS every six months. It is hoped this will provide details on the natural history of aneurysms in addition to results of surgery. Most centres accept 85 years as an upper age cut-off for surgery.

Surgical management of abdominal aortic aneurysms

- **Surgery — Elective**
  Six-unit cross-match
  Systemic heparinization
  Aneurysm neck defined and
    controlled
  Control of normal vessels distal
    to aneurysm
  Aneurysm sac opened and thrombus
    removed
  Back bleeding from lumbar arteries
    controlled with sutures
  Choice of inlay synthetic graft —
    straight tube if iliacs not involved,
    otherwise trouser graft;
    3-0 Prolene suture
  Closure of aneurysm sac over graft

- **Surgery — ruptured aneurysm**
  No investigation in unstable patient;
    consider USS/CT if stable and
    diagnosis uncertain
  Ten-unit cross-match
  Urinary catheter and two large-bore
    i.v. lines
  Resuscitate to systolic BP ~100 mmHg
    higher pressures may increase
    bleeding
  'Crash' anaesthetic induction with
    patient draped for surgery
  No anticoagulation
  Rapid entrance to abdomen and
    control of aneurysm neck; if difficult
    can clamp supra-renal aorta for
    short period
  Proceed as elective surgery

- **Complications of aortic surgery**
  Haemorrhage
  CVA
  Colonic ischaemia
  Spinal ischaemia
  Aorto-enteric fistulae
  Graft thrombosis

  Myocardial ischaemia
  Renal failure/ARDS/DIC (especially
    after emergency surgery)
  False aneurysms at anastomosis
  Distal embolism

3.5 Inflammatory aneurysms

Aneurysm is characterized by a marked degree of fibrosis extending from the wall into the adjacent tissues on the lateral and anterior aspects only. It is associated with a profuse inflammatory cell infiltrate of T- and B-lymphocytes and plasma cells. Tissues resemble those in idiopathic retroperitoneal fibrosis, some believing it to be part of the same disease. The fibrosis may compress other structures such as the ureters leading to renal failure. Rupture is less common than in atherosclerotic aneurysms and usually posterior. Patients present with abdominal pain, weight loss and a raised ESR. Surgery is more difficult due to the inflammation and fibrosis and management is often therefore conservative.

3.6 Femoral aneurysms

Can occur in isolation but usually part of a generalized arterial dilatation. Often symptomless and rarely rupture. Occasionally a source of distal emboli and may thrombose. Repair is by insertion of a prosthetic graft or reversed saphenous vein.

3.7 Popliteal aneurysms

Second most common site of atherosclerotic aneurysms. Occasionally present with an expansile swelling, but more commonly with aneurysm thrombosis or distal emboli leading to peripheral ischaemia. Confirm diagnosis by USS/CT or arteriography (which will also assess distal vasculature). Repair by resection/ligation and vein bypass graft.

3.8 Splenic aneurysms

The only aneurysms where the usual male predominance is reversed with a female: male ratio of 4:1. Mainly occur during childbearing years. Symptomless unless rupture (25%) which is most common in pregnancy (3rd trimester), treatment is by resection with anastomosis/graft if size > 3 cm or patient is pregnant.

4. CAROTID DISEASE

This is a common and treatable cause of cerebral infarction, TIA and retinal infarction. It is thought that 25–30% of strokes are caused by extra-cranial carotid disease. Atherosclerosis is common at the carotid bifurcation. It is initially asymptomatic but may cause the complications mentioned above due to thrombotic occlusion or embolism. Once one of these events has occurred it is termed a **symptomatic carotid stenosis**. A patient with a 50% asymptomatic stenosis has a CVA risk of 1–2% per year. This increases with further stenosis, with the greatest risk between 75% and 90% stenosis. The risk of CVA is also higher in symptomatic stenoses, with a 10% rate of subsequent CVA in the first year after the defining event and 5% per year thereafter.

The diagnosis is usually made during the investigation of focal neurological deficits, but may be found incidentally during clinical examination for other purposes or during a thorough vascular work-up for surgery. Carotid bruits are caused by the turbulent blood flow in a stenosed artery. They are however an unreliable guide to the degree of stenosis, with a high false positive rate due to patients with transmitted cardiac murmurs, etc. and a significant number of people with moderate to severe stenoses who have no bruit.

4.1 Carotid anatomy

The common carotid artery ascends the neck within the carotid sheath, along with the internal jugular vein, vagus nerve and ansa cervicalis (nerve supply to strap muscles). The common artery can be exposed surgically by retracting the lower part of sternocleidomastoid posteriorly and incising the carotid sheath. At the upper level of the thyroid cartilage the common carotid artery divides into internal and external branches. The external branch travels anterior to the internal branch to reach the parotid gland and divides into terminal branches.

Branches of the external carotid artery

- Superior thyroid
- Lingual
- Occipital
- Superficial temporal

- Ascending pharyngeal
- Facial
- Posterior auricular
- Maxillary

The internal branch continues within the carotid sheath to enter the skull via the carotid canal. It gives no branches in the neck. At its commencement there is a slight bulge — the **carotid sinus**. This contains baroreceptors and is supplied by the glossopharyngeal nerve. Lying behind the carotid bifurcation is the **carotid body**, containing chemoreceptors for O_2, CO_2 and pH.

4.2 Physiology of cerebral circulation

The brain has a large blood supply per unit weight of tissue — 55ml/min/100 g (100 ml/min/100 g for grey matter) and is very intolerant of ischaemia. It has a number of methods by which it is able to regulate a constant blood supply despite an inconsistent supply to other body parts (auto-regulation). This auto-regulation is extremely effective between mean blood pressures of 60–160 mmHg. The sympathetic nerve supply to cerebral vessels is weak allowing local factors to predominate.

Cerebral vessels are very sensitive to $PaCO_2$ elevations, which lead to marked vasodilatation locally. The converse is also true. This effect is thought to be mediated by changes in perivascular pH. Any ischaemia affecting the medulla leads to an increase in systemic blood pressure to improve supply, by alteration in outflow from the medullary centres. The carotid baro and chemoreceptors ensure that blood supply to the brain is one of the main determinants of systemic blood pressure.

Measurement of cerebral flow

The Fick principle

This principle can be used to calculate the blood flow to an organ by application of the law of conservation of mass. If the blood flowing into an organ contains a marker of known concentration and some of this marker diffuses into the organ, then its concentration in the blood leaving the organ will be lower. Remember:

quantity = concentration x volume

therefore the quantity of marker entering the organ per unit time depends on the concentration of marker and volume per unit time, i.e. *Flow*. The quantity of marker leaving the organ per unit time depends on the blood concentration and the same blood flow.

The Fick principle

• As flow in = quantity$_{in}$/concentration$_{in}$

and

• Flow out = quantity$_{out}$/concentration$_{out}$

then

• Flow = (quantity$_{in}$ – quantity$_{out}$)/(concentration$_{in}$ – concentration$_{out}$)

NB. Concentration$_{in}$ – concentration$_{out}$ is the quantity of marker taken up by the brain per unit time. Nitrous oxide (N_2O) can be used as a marker to calculate cerebral bloodflow.

Positron emission tomography (PET)

PET is a nuclear medicine technique. Radio-chemicals produced in a cyclotron are injected intravenously. These substances emit positrons that interact with the body to produce photons. The patient passes through a ring of detectors that receive the photons and create an image. These images reflect physiology rather than anatomic detail and can be used to assess metabolism in tumours, etc.

4.3 Carotid stenosis assessment

- **Duplex USS**: Doppler measurement of flow in the vessels associated with real time ultrasound imaging for anatomy. It is non-invasive and requires no contrast, but is highly operator-dependent. Colour flow Doppler is a newer refinement where different velocities are assigned colours to aid interpretation.
- **Arteriography**: invasive procedure, requiring contrast. Detailed anatomical information including intra-cerebral vessels obtained. Complications include CVA (1%) and TIA (4%) in symptomatic stenoses, contrast allergy and local complications related to arterial puncture.
- **Magnetic resonance angiography**: newer non-invasive technique currently being evaluated. May overestimate stenosis and cannot assess plaque morphology. Some studies have suggested evaluation with MRI and Duplex scanning correlates well with angiography.

4.4 Medical management of carotid disease

Important to gain diabetic and hypertension control, and to stop smoking.

Anti-platelet agents

Aspirin
Proven to reduce vascular events in atherosclerotic disease (approx. 40 events per 1000 patients treated for three years). Higher dose (150–300 mg) on confirmation of ischaemic event, reducing to 75 mg after one month (to reduce GI side-effects). Asymptomatic patients should take a prophylactic low dose (75 mg).

Dipyridamole
No conclusive evidence of increased effectiveness when compared to aspirin alone or in combination with aspirin. Restrict to use in patients with a symptomatic stenosis who are aspirin intolerant.

Lipid-lowering drugs

Proven benefit in reducing the risk of CVA ($\sim 30\%$) when used in secondary prevention of all atherosclerosis complications. No evidence to support their use in primary prevention in asymptomatic disease. They will also help reduce the rate of other cardiovascular events.

4.5 Surgery in carotid stenosis

Carotid endarterectomy

This involves the removal of atheromatous plaque from the diseased vessel. In the recent *Asymptomatic Carotid Disease Study* of patients with a 60% or greater stenosis, it has been shown to reduce the risk of CVA when compared to medical therapy alone (despite a 2.3% peri-operative mortality). However, smaller trials have failed to show similar results. The results in symptomatic disease are more convincing. Two large trials — the *MRC European Carotid Surgery Trial* (ECST) and the *North American Symptomatic Carotid Endarterectomy Trial* (NASCET) compared surgery in combination with medical therapy to medical treatment alone in patients who had a vascular event in the preceding six months and severe (70–90%) symptomatic stenoses. Both trials showed a significant reduction in the risk of CVA compared to surgery alone. The ECST trial also showed that patients with mild/ moderate stenoses (10–70%) derived no benefit from surgery. Therefore the only patients who should currently be offered surgery are those with a severe stenosis (70–99%) who have recently become symptomatic. The procedure should ideally be performed in specialist centres, or the decreased mortality/CVA rate may be negated by increased operative complications.

Complications of carotid endarterectomy

- About 5% 30-day CVA/mortality in symptomatic disease
- 3.5% in asymptomatic stenoses
- Risk increased if female, age > 75, peripheral vascular disease or
  have contralateral carotid disease
- Other complications include: myocardial infarction (3%); nerve injury
  in neck (20% but usually transient); local wound complications

---

Carotid angioplasty ± stenting is a newer procedure that is less invasive and has been shown to dilate severe stenoses with a good success rate. There is, however, a re-stenosis rate and the procedure is yet to be fully evaluated.

4.6 Carotid body tumours

These present as masses in the neck adjacent to the hyoid bone anterior to sternocleido-mastoid. They are relatively smooth, compressible and pulsatile, (though not classically expansile) due to their vascular component. They may be mobile horizontally but not vertically, and often have a bruit. Approximately 5% are malignant, this percentage increasing with size. They are occasionally bilateral and easily diagnosed on CT scanning. Angiography classically demonstrates splaying of the carotid bifurcation by a vascular mass. The preferred method of excision is dissection of the tumour off the vessel in the sub-adventitial plane. In elderly patients or in recurrent malignant tumours radiotherapy may be beneficial.

5. VASCULAR TRAUMA

5.1 Arterial injury

Most commonly seen during times of war, but increasingly common in civilian life due to penetrating/blunt injuries. There are also an increasing number of iatrogenic injuries. Mechanisms include:

- Penetrating injury (e.g. stab/gunshot wounds)
- Blunt injuries (e.g. RTA or associated with fractures/dislocations)
- Iatrogenic (e.g. ligation, arterial puncture damage or compression by plasters/splints)
- Intra-arterial drug injection (e.g. barbiturates, benzodiazepines, quinine)
- Cold injury

Remember to examine for associated bony, nerve, visceral and soft tissue injury.

Classification of arterial injury

- **Puncture/incomplete transection** can lead to haematoma, delayed haemorrhage, false aneurysm, thrombosis embolism or A-V fistula

- In a **closed injury** the vascular injury may be more severe than suggested by external appearance. Examples include blunt trauma or compression by fractures, which lead to spasm, thrombosis, intimal haematoma/ occlusion or intimal dissection

- **Complete transection** leading to vessel contraction, haematoma and distal ischaemia

- **Laceration** often associated with soft tissue loss, similar complications to puncture/incomplete transection group but can be more severe

---

All injuries lead to arterial spasm and platelet deposition to reduce haemorrhage. There may be prolonged bleeding if the defect is large/held open.

Management

- **Prompt resuscitation**: with large-bore venous access
- **Direct pressure**: on wound or artery more proximal
- **Avoid tourniquets** and application of haemostats to bleeding vessels
- No place for initial investigation if arterial bleeding is massive, but blood should be cross-matched
- **Intra-operative angiography**: can be considered once control has been achieved. In less urgent cases Doppler/Duplex scanning and arteriography are useful in defining the site, nature and extent of injuries.
- Once control has been achieved by vascular tapes, clamps or balloon occlusion, the distal vasculature should be protected by injection of heparin
- Repair is preferable to ligation, though single vessels in the forearm or calf can be ligated if required. The type of repair depends on the extent of the injury but commonly employed methods are shown below.

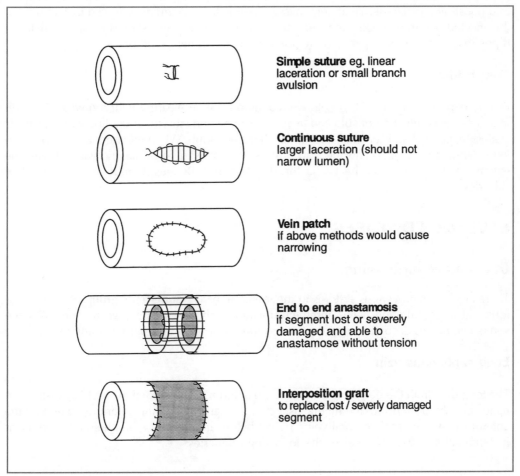

Simple suture eg. linear laceration or small branch avulsion

Continuous suture larger laceration (should not narrow lumen)

Vein patch if above methods would cause narrowing

End to end anastamosis if segment lost or severely damaged and able to anastamose without tension

Interposition graft to replace lost / severely damaged segment

Methods of arterial repair

5.2 Venous injury

Damage to small or medium-sized veins due to trauma can usually be simply treated with local pressure and elevation, though a haematoma may develop. Similar injuries during surgery can be controlled by diathermy or ligation. Larger veins should always be repaired to prevent haemorrhage or acute/chronic venous occlusion. Simple lacerations can be sutured, but larger injuries require repair with a vein patch or interposition graft.

5.3 Cold injury

Frostbite

First signs are reddening due to oxygen surplus and pain. These may occur at + 10 °C. Tissue destruction occurs at –4 to –10 °C. This is caused by protein denaturation, pH changes, cell membrane rupture and enzymatic destruction. Blood flow is decreased eventually leading to thrombosis and gangrene. Treatment involves whole-body warming followed by warming of the affected part in warmed water. Amputations of necrotic digits should ideally be delayed if possible, and fasciotomy may be required for compartment syndromes.

Trench foot

Due to exposure of the feet to cold/wet conditions while wearing tight footwear. The wet increases the conduction of cold and heat losses preventing the super-cooling which protects against frostbite. Pain is unusual but the feet become numb. When released, the feet become hyperaemic and swollen and the skin blisters. Patients should be gently warmed with the extremities protected from heat, and the skin kept dry. Bed-rest is required until swelling subsides.

6. VENOUS DISEASES

6.1 Lower limb veins

There are two main venous systems in the lower limb. The **superficial group** comprises the long and short saphenous veins and their tributaries, whereas the **deep group** consists of the venae comitantes accompanying the anterior/posterior tibial and peroneal arteries.

Long saphenous vein

The longest vein in the body. It runs from 1 cm anterior to the medial malleolus, passing one hands breadth posterior to the medial aspect of the patella, winding anteriorly to end on the anteromedial side of the femoral vein, 3.5 cm below and lateral to the pubic tubercle. Near its termination it usually receives the following tributaries:

- Superficial and deep external pudendals
- Superficial circumflex iliac
- Superficial inferior epigastric

The main sites of deep-superficial venous communication are:

- Sapheno-femoral junction
- Mid-thigh perforators (Hunter's canal)
- Medial calf communicator (just below, just above and 10 cm above the medial malleolus and just below the knee)

The lower perforators are often joined to form the posterior arch vein, which usually joins the long saphenous just below the knee. Some of the perforators join the posterior tibial venae comitantes, others joining the plexus below soleus.

Short saphenous vein

Begins as the continuation of the lateral side of the dorsal venous arch behind the lateral malleolus. It passes cranially in the subcutaneous tissues to pierce the deep fascia prior to entering the popliteal vein. It communicates by several channels with the long saphenous system.

6.2 Venous return

Return flow from the lower limbs is primarily due to the pumping action of the heart maintaining a pressure gradient across the veins, but this is greatly influenced by the effect of gravity, action of the calf pump and venomotor tone.

Gravity

Impedes the return of blood from dependent limbs leading to pooling peripherally (gravity also acts to increase arterial inflow in dependent areas). The pooling may reduce cardiac output by 2 l/min and can lead to fainting. Other measures are therefore needed to increase the venous return from dependant parts.

Venomotor tone

Maintained by smooth muscle within the vein wall which is under the control of the sympathetic nervous system. On assuming an upright position, the decreased cardiac output due to dependant pooling leads to an increased sympathetic discharge, which increases venous tone to reduce the capacitance of the system and increase venous return.

Muscular activity and the calf pump

Normally as the calf muscles contract, blood is forced cranially and prevented from retrograde flow by valves within the veins. This results in lower pressure in the deep veins during muscular activity. This allows flow of blood from the superficial to deep veins via the communicating vessels. These also have valves to ensure uni-directional flow. The flow is shown in the diagram below.

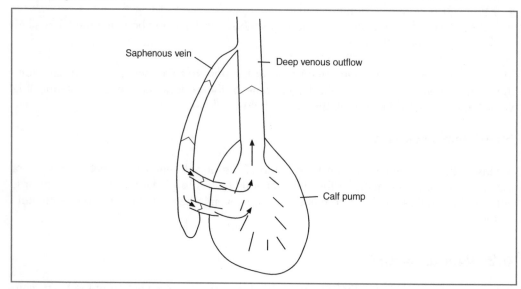

Calf pump

If the deep system outflow is obstructed or the communicating veins are incompetent then blood is forced from the deep system into the superficial veins leading to an increased pressure. On persistent standing at rest blood continues to enter the veins, despite inadequate emptying due to muscular inactivity. Endoluminal valves normally support the blood, but as the pressure in a segment of vein between valves exceeds the pressure in the segment above, the valve opens. Eventually all the valves are open and there is a continuous column of blood below the heart leading to greatly increased venous pressures in the legs.

6.3 Varicose veins

Defined by the World Health Organization as **saccular dilatations of veins, often being tortuous**. The veins involved are usually the long and short saphenous and their tributaries plus other superficial veins. Histologically, the veins show fibrous scar tissue dividing the smooth muscle within the media into separate bundles and extending through all layers.

Primary varicosities occur in 2% of the population; with about one million affected people in the UK. Their frequency increases with:

- Age; peak in sixth decade
- Female sex; F:M = 4:1 ? hormonal effect
- Obesity
- Occupations with long periods of standing
- Family history; 50–80% of first-degree relatives affected

Secondary causes include:

- Venous/valve damage secondary to thrombosis
- Pelvic malignancy
- Congenital absence of valves, or other abnormalities

Klippel–Trenaunay syndrome

- Congenital varicose veins
- Port wine stains

- Bone and soft tissue hypertrophy in affected limb
- Deep venous abnormalities (often)

Symptoms of varicose veins include:

- Cosmetic disfigurement
- Discomfort on prolonged standing
- Night cramps and ankle swelling

Clinical examination

Examine with the patient standing up. Look for pigmentation, eczema, lipodermatosclerosis or ulceration. Then note the extent and distribution of varicosities. Palpate for dilated short saphenous vein suggestive of incompetence in the popliteal fossa. Feel for saphena varix near the SFJ (1 cm medial to the femoral artery in the groin skin crease). There may be a transmitted cough impulse in long saphenous varicosities if SFJ incompetence is present. Test for incompetence by emptying the veins (elevation) and applying a mid-thigh tourniquet. If veins remain empty but refill on removal of the tourniquet, the incompetence must lie above the level of the tourniquet (Brodie–Trendelenburg test). Perthes' walking test involves placing a tourniquet around the thigh, and walking/heel raising. If the surface veins empty, this signifies saphenous incompetence with an intact deep system. Incompetence can easily be identified by hand-held Doppler examination. The venous signal is found in the groin. Squeezing the calf augments the signal, with a biphasic signal if the junction is incompetent due to retrograde flow. Retrograde flow can also be heard on coughing.

NB. Duplex scanning is mandatory in all patients with a history of DVT or trauma prior to varicose vein treatment to ensure a patent deep venous system.

Complications of varicose veins

- Eczema
- Thrombophlebitis
- Ulceration

- Bleeding
- Lipodermatosclerosis (inflammation, pigmentation and induration of calf skin)

Management

Minor varicosities can be treated with support stockings or injection sclerotherapy with sodium tetradecyl sulphate (Fibro-vein). Those with evidence of long/short saphenous incompetence should undergo sapheno-femoral/sapheno-popliteal ligation, respectively. Branch varicosities can then be treated by avulsion/ligation via multiple stab incisions. If incompetent perforating veins have been isolated preoperatively by Duplex scanning these can be ligated individually.

Sapheno-femoral junction ligation (Trendelenburg procedure)

- 15° head-down tilt, patient flat with legs abducted
- A short oblique incision is placed in the skin crease, centred 1 cm medial to the artery
- The long saphenous vein is identified and traced through the cribriform fascia to the sapheno-femoral junction (SFJ)
- All tributaries (see Section 6.1) should be ligated
- The SFJ is then doubly ligated
- The saphenous vein can be tied off or removed to the knee with an endoluminal stripper

6.4 Venous ulcers

These are common ulcers, affecting approximately 150,000 people in the UK. The cost of NHS treatment of ulcers is £400 million annually. They occur due to venous insufficiency with 40% due to superficial vein insufficiency (varicose veins). The remainder are caused by dysfunction of the calf pump action, such as outflow obstruction or neuromuscular disorders leading to an increased pressure in the venous system which is transmitted via the perforating veins to the superficial system. Exactly how this leads to ulceration is not known, but theories include:

- Formation of a fibrin cuff around vessels leading to decreased nutrient diffusion
- WBC entrapment and capillary occlusion leading to decreased nutrition and inflammation

A flowchart for the management of ulcers is shown opposite.

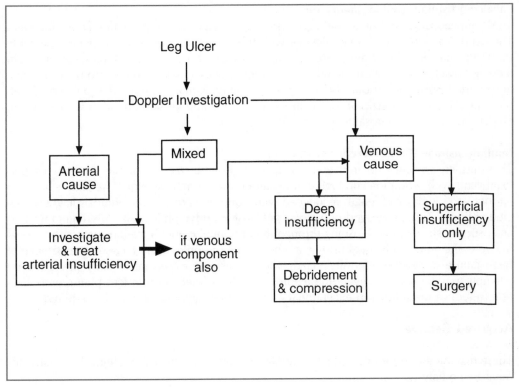

Management of leg ulceration

NB. Compression bandaging should be used with care in patients with concomitant arterial disease. An ankle brachial pressure index (ABPI) <0.5 being an absolute contraindication, and an ABPI between 0.5 and 0.8 requiring less compression. Ulcers which have failed to heal after 12 weeks' bandaging, or larger than 10 cm² often require skin grafting in the form of split-skin or pinch grafts.

6.5 Arterio-venous fistulae

These can be defined as an abnormal connection between the arterial and venous systems. They may be congenital or acquired, and may be between large (macrofistulae) or small (microfistulae) vessels.

Congenital fistulae

These are rare, being seen in approximately one per million live births and are most commonly seen in the head/neck or extremities. Although present from birth they often enlarge during puberty or pregnancy. They may be **localized** or **multiple**.

Localized fistulae (cirsoid aneurysm)

These appear as soft pulsatile swellings, which are unsightly and may cause an aching pain. The overlying skin/mucosa may ulcerate with brisk haemorrhage. There is often a palpable thrill and machinery murmur present, which may be abolished by compressing the main feeding vessel. Investigation includes CT scanning and selective arteriography. Those that arise during pregnancy should be treated expectantly as many regress after delivery. Treatment may be by embolization or occlusion of the feeding vessel combined with excision. Direct injections of sclerosants have not been effective.

Multiple fistulae (Parkes–Weber syndrome)

These usually present with an overall enlargement in limb size. There may be dilated superficial veins with ulceration and high output cardiac failure may develop. The limb is hot with an increased width and length associated with bone overgrowth. Differential diagnoses include Klippel–Trenaunay syndrome, local gigantism and lymphoedema. Arteriography characteristically shows rapid blushing through the abnormal communications with early arrival of dye in the veins. Individual fistulae are not visualised unless very large. In the absence of heart failure or severe deformity management is usually expectant in early life. Later on attempts may be made to ligate the feeding vessels or injection of microspheres/embolization to reduce the inflow. In exceptional circumstances amputation may be required.

Acquired fistulae

These may be the result of accidental trauma (traumatic A-V fistula) or surgically created for renal hemodialysis.

Traumatic arteriovenous fistulae

These usually follow simultaneous adjacent arterial and venous injury with a common haematoma. They take days to form and there is usually a thrill and bruit. Adjoining veins may become dilated and arterialized eventually leading to venous hypertension and possibly ulceration. Limb hypertrophy and lengthening may occur. If blood flow through the distal artery is sufficiently decreased distal ischaemia may occur. A fistula between larger vessels may be sufficient to create a left to right shunt, which may lead to heart failure if severe. Methods for closure include the application of Duplex directed pressure, insertion of a covered stent or surgical closure.

Arteriovenous fistulae for haemodialysis

These are usually created for long-term dialysis access and once formed can remain patent indefinitely. The connection of the artery to a vein results in a dilated vein, which is suitable for repeated cannulation and can deliver a high flow of blood for dialysis. The ideal site, originally described by Brescia is the radio-cephalic fistula in the forearm, but other sites may be used. The general rule in fistula formation is that the most distal site on the non-dominant arm is used. The procedure can be carried out under local anaesthesia by side-to-side anastomosis of the radial artery and cephalic vein, though some surgeons ligate the distal vein or perform an end-to-side anastomosis to prevent the possibility of distal venous hypertension. Post-operatively maintaining a warm limb and adequate hydration are necessary for successful fistula formation. Recently GTN patches have been used on the distal limb to encourage vasodilatation. Expected patency rates are 60–90% at one year and 60–75% at five years. Generally, fistulae are not closed following a renal transplant as they may subsequently be required again, though many thrombose spontaneously following transplantation. Indications for fistula closure are cosmetic, large flows leading to heart failure and occasionally sepsis or distal embolization.

7. THROMBO-EMBOLIC DISEASE

Virchow first described the factors responsible for the formation of thrombosis:

- **Stasis** (intra/post-operative)
- **Vessel wall damage** (leading to decreased nitric oxide/vasodilatory prostaglandin secretion locally)
- **Abnormalities in blood constituents**

These are known as **Virchow's triad**. Abnormalities in the endothelium structure/function may allow platelet–vessel wall interaction and initiation of platelet aggregation and thrombosis. If combined with stasis or hypercoagulability the thrombus may propagate. The hypercoagulability may be due to:

- **Alteration in the coagulation homeostasis**: either too much pro-coagulation factors (fibrinogen, factor VII) or a deficiency/dysfunction of natural anti-coagulation factors (antithrombin III or protein C-S-thrombomodulin system)
- **Increased blood viscosity**: (raised immunoglobulins, polycythaemia or dehydration)
- **Increased platelet count**: or alteration of their function (increased adhesion)
- **Malignancy**: (especially mucin secreting adenocarcinomas, e.g. pancreas) can lead to clotting factor activation or thromboplastin release

Fibrin and red cells are deposited in layers with platelets giving a laminated appearance to the clot. Loosely attached thrombus may dislodge and form emboli, whereas a firmly adherent clot contracts causing luminal occlusion.

7.1 Deep vein thrombosis (DVT)

Ninety-eight per cent of all venous thrombi arise in the deep veins of the legs and pelvis. If no prophylaxis were used the approximate incidences would be:

- **General population**: 0.5%
- **Major surgery, age > 40**: 30%
- **Serious medical illness** (e.g. MI): 30%
- **Major hip surgery**: > 60%

Known risk factors for DVT

- Immobility
- Obesity
- Varicose veins
- Pelvic disease
- Oral contraceptives

- Age
- Previous DVT
- Malignancy
- Major surgery
- Blood disorders (e.g. polycythaemia or coagulation defects)

Clinical features are unilateral limb swelling, pain, tenderness and low-grade pyrexia, though many may be asymptomatic. The most common presenting symptoms are swelling (50–80%) and calf muscle tenderness (50–60%). Massive proximal thrombosis may cause **phlegmasia cerulea dolens** (blue leg) which may progress to gangrene, or occasionally **phlegmasia alba dolens** (white oedematous limb). The more proximal the thrombus, the greater the signs. Homan's dorsiflexion test is inaccurate, may dislodge thrombus and should be avoided.

Differential diagnoses of DVT

- Cellulitis
- Torn gastrocnemius
- Acute ischaemia
- Thrombophlebitis

- Ruptured Baker's cyst
- Ruptured popliteal aneurysm
- Pathological fracture
- Knee acute arthritis/haemarthrosis

The 'gold standard' investigation is bipedal ascending phlebography, which outlines both the extent and type of thrombus. B-mode ultrasound scanning is useful in the diagnosis of above-knee thrombosis, but poor in the calf vessels. The radioactive I^{125} fibrinogen uptake test needs to be done early in the course of thrombus formation, and is too expensive for routine use, though it has been useful in the comparison of prophylaxis methods.

Complications of deep venous thrombosis include chronic leg oedema, varicose veins, venous ulceration, post-phlebitic leg syndrome and pulmonary emboli.

7.2 Thromboprophylaxis

Despite advancement in the management of PE, its mortality is increasing with >21,000 deaths per year in the UK, and >60% occurring within 30 minutes of the embolic event. It is logical therefore not to wait for the events before treatment, but to institute prophylaxis. All surgical patients should therefore undergo risk assessment and appropriate prophylaxis should be given. There are three main types of prophylaxis.

Physical methods

This group aims to reduce blood stasis:

- **Pneumatic calf compression and TED stockings** decrease DVT by ~60% but is not proven to reduce mortality due to PE
- **Dextran-70** expands the plasma volume leading to decreased stasis, and also alters the structure of thrombi leading to a less organized thrombus, which is less likely to produce large emboli. It has been shown to reduce PE by 70% in orthopaedic patients, though is less effective in DVT prevention than heparin. However, it has to be given for >3 days post-operatively, may cause fluid overload and has a risk of anaphylaxis.

Oral anticoagulation

Warfarin antagonises the action of vitamin K in the liver, reducing production of prothrombin and factors VII, IX and X. Risk of DVT is reduced by 60% and PE by 80%, but at the expense of increased haemorrhage (itself with a 0.1% mortality).

Low-dose heparin (5,000 iu t.d.s)

This has been shown to result in a 60% reduction in DVT and 50% reduction in PE. Minor increase in bleeding (but no increase in fatalities). However, must be commenced pre-operatively, continuing until at least discharge, and multiple injections are involved.

Low molecular weight heparins (LMWH) have molecular weights between 2000 and 8000 Daltons (conventional heparin 5000–30,000). They act by inhibiting factor X and binding with antithrombin III. They reduce the risk of DVT by 70%, being at least as good as any other prophylaxis, and it is suggested that they confer a similar benefit on PE prevention as conventional heparin. It is given once daily, but is considerably more expensive than conventional heparin.

A Royal College working party has established the THRIFT guidelines for DVT prophylaxis in general surgery (see table overleaf).

THRIFT GUIDELINES FOR DVT PROPHYLAXIS

Risk	Prophylaxis
Low	
Minor surgery (<30 min) and no risk factors	Early mobilization only
Moderate	
Major surgery (age >40)	Subcutaneous heparin
Minor surgery with past history DVT/PE	Low muscular weight heparin (LMWH)
High	
Major pelvic/abdominal surgery for cancer	Subcutaneous heparin/LMWH
Major surgery, previous DVT/PE	and graduated compression stockings
Acute abdominal surgery (age >40)	

7.3 Pulmonary embolism

An embolus is an abnormal tissue mass transported in the bloodstream from one part of the circulation to another, finally impacting in vessels smaller than the embolus. They may consist of thrombus (99%), atherosclerotic plaques, tumour cells, air or fat. When the origin of thrombus is venous the impaction will usually be in the pulmonary vasculature.

The clinical presentation of pulmonary embolism (PE) depends on:

- Size of embolism
- Duration
- Pre-existing cardio-respiratory disease and the degree of pulmonary congestion

Eighty per cent have no signs/symptoms of peripheral thrombosis.

Acute minor PE

Involves <50% of the pulmonary vasculature. They may present with pleuritic chest pain, shortness of breath and haemoptysis (blood streaking not frank), but many are asymptomatic creating difficulty in establishing an incidence. There may be a pleural rub/fine crepitations on examination and mild pyrexia. There is no haemodynamic disturbance. CXR may show a wedge shaped area of consolidation. VQ scanning may help with the diagnosis but often cannot distinguish a small PE from pneumonia. They usually resolve spontaneously, but may herald a larger event therefore anticoagulation should be undertaken.

Acute massive PE

By definition involves >50% of the pulmonary circulation. The embolus is formed from thrombus/clot formed in a long venous segment, namely the ilio-femoral veins. There may be minor herald emboli in 50% of patients. The symptoms often appear while the patient is straining (e.g. at stool). As there is a sudden reduction in blood return to the left heart, there is a consequent drop in cardiac output which may lead to 'shock' (90%), syncope (70%) or even cardiac arrest. The right heart dilatation can lead to central chest pain leading to a clinical situation similar to an acute MI. There will be a marked tachycardia and a low-volume pulse. The increased pressure in the right heart leads to dilatation and failure. The JVP is raised and there may be a gallop rhythm. Due to the large V/Q mismatch there will be shortness of breath (85%) and arterial desaturation.

Chronic thromboembolic pulmonary hypertension

The least common presentation with the poorest prognosis. Presentation is with a long history of progressive dyspnoea, decreasing exercise tolerance and syncope. There may be evidence of pulmonary hypertension (RV hypertrophy/loud pulmonary valve sound) but it is often difficult to diagnose requiring cardiac/pulmonary angiography studies.

Radiological investigations

A CXR done initially will help to exclude other causes of chest symptoms such as pneumonia or a pleural effusion. In pulmonary emboli there may be an area of lucency seen peripherally and occasionally a small pleural effusion.

The most commonly performed investigation is a **ventilation-perfusion (VQ) scan**. Perfusion is measured using Technetium[99]-labelled microspheres. Areas of VQ mismatch suggest emboli. Matched defects indicate other pathology e.g. emphysema. The gold standard investigation is **pulmonary angiography** (usually via the femoral vein) and is useful if the VQ scan is equivocal.

Prevention of pulmonary embolism

This falls into two categories:

- Reduction of thrombosis (see Section 7.1, p. 159)
- Preventing embolism from established thrombus

The latter entails either:

- **Prevention of further growth of the thrombus**: all patients should be anticoagulated, although this only prevents the formation of new thrombus. Anticoagulation prevents embolism in adherent thrombus but non adherent thrombus may still produce emboli.
- **Confinement of the thrombus to the limb by venous blockade**: ligation of the superficial femoral vein can prevent emboli if the thrombus is confined below the ligation and doesn't appear to cause any additional complications above those of the pre-existing thrombus. Multiple emboli, despite anticoagulation, can be prevented by the insertion of a vena caval filter such as the Greenfield filter or Mobin Uddin umbrella (shown below). They can also be used if anticoagulation is contraindicated.
- **Therapeutic removal of the thrombus**: thrombus may be removed surgically by balloon catheter or thrombolysis may dissolve clot if fresh. These may need to be combined with a 'locking in' procedure to isolate the thrombus from the systemic vasculature.

Thirty per cent of patients surviving a PE are known to have a second with 20% of these being fatal. Ascending phlebography can help to define the extent and nature of the thrombus.

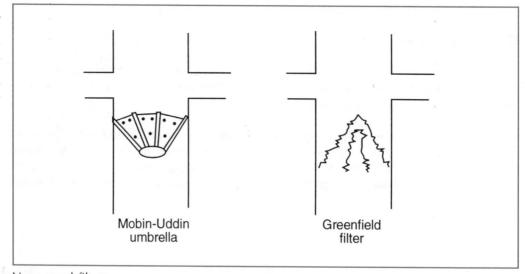

Mobin-Uddin umbrella

Greenfield filter

Vena caval filters

Fat embolism

Probably occurs in 90% of patients who sustain significant trauma but can occur in other situations:

- Long bone fractures
- Severe burns
- Hyperlipidaemia
- Ischaemic marrow necrosis in sickle cell disease
- Pancreatitis
- Cardiac bypass

Probably due to a mixture of mechanical factors (marrow-derived fat globule release due to fractures, etc.) and biochemical factors (suggested that free fatty acids directly affect the air space lining in the lungs leading to gas exchange abnormalities). Clinical consequences are rare but may be severe. May present with respiratory distress 24–72 hours post-injury, or central agitation/coma due to cerebral involvement.

8. LYMPHORETICULAR SYSTEM

This comprises the spleen, lymph nodes and mucosa-associated lymphoid tissue (MALT).

8.1 The spleen

This, the largest lymphoid organ was previously considered dispensable, with splenectomy being the only procedure for management of its disorders until the 1970s. As awareness of its functions and side-effects of removal have become known, the management of splenic disease/trauma has become more conservative.

Splenic functions

- **Immune**
  Antigen processing, IgM and
  opsonin production

- **Filtering**
  Macrophages important in
  removing cellular and
  non-cellular material, including
  bacteria such as pneumococci
  and defective/old red cells and
  platelets

- **Haemopoiesis**
  In foetus and later if demand
  exceeds marrow capacity

- **Iron re-utilization**

- **Platelet pooling**

Anatomy

The numbers 1, 3, 5, 7, 9, and 11 summarize the anatomy of the spleen. It measures 1 x 3 x 5 inches, weighs 7 oz and lies between ribs 9 and 11 in the left hypochondrium. Its long axis lies along the 10th rib. On its medial aspect the kidney leaves an impression posterior to the hilum with the posterior leaf of the greater omentum (the lieno-renal ligament) passing from the hilum to the kidney. The tail of the pancreas lies within the lienorenal ligament. The anterior leaf (gastrosplenic ligament) joins the hilum to the greater curve of the stomach, the area between the leaves forming part of the boundary of the lesser sac. There is a notch in the anterior surface of the spleen, left over from its embryonic development. As a spleen enlarges it grows towards the umbilicus, and needs to double in size before it extends beyond the costal margin and becomes palpable. The blood supply is from the splenic artery (from coeliac axis) which enters the hilum via the lieno-renal ligament and divides into smaller segmental branches (up to four). Venous drainage is via the splenic vein to the portal system. 'Accessory spleens' (splenunculi) occur in 1:10 individuals and result from the failure of fusion of embryonic segments. They are usually found along the splenic vessels or peritoneal attachments and may be multiple.

Traumatic rupture of the spleen

Usually due to blunt trauma to the abdomen/lower ribs. Injury may occur due to more minor trauma in children (due to the proportionally larger spleen and less robust rib cage) or in adults with splenomegaly. The main signs are those of haemorrhage and may follow three presentations.

Injury involving the capsule with continuing bleeding
Usually present with evidence of haemorrhage continuing to be unstable despite resuscitation.

Extra-capsular rupture
If small may initially be closed by adherent omentum/clot. Patients initially have evidence of haemorrhage and often left shoulder tip referred pain (Kehr's sign). A period of recovery follows lasting hours to days. There may then be a second more profound bleed, with collapse, shock and generalized abdominal pain.

Intra-capsular rupture leading to haematoma formation
This is initially contained due to the shock, but as blood pressure is elevated further bleeding occurs leading to intra-peritoneal rupture.

Intra-capsular rupture
With haematoma formation only, presents with pain and minimal evidence of blood loss.

Investigations

If the patient is haemodynamically stable the possibility of splenic injury can be assessed with USS or CT scanning (both have diagnostic accuracy >90%). If the patient is unstable with obvious abdominal injuries, laparotomy is indicated after initial attempts at resuscitation. Diagnostic peritoneal lavage is indicated only if there is doubt as to the cause of hypovolaemia (e.g. in unconscious multiply injured patients). Some argue that it has **no role**, as less invasive investigations can be carried out if the patient is stable with laparotomy being indicated if the patient is unstable.

Management

Non-operative management can be cautiously undertaken if there is absence of progressive haemorrhage (<4-unit transfusion in 48 hours) and no other intra-abdominal injuries. Non-operative treatment is easier in children, and where it is possible, bleeding will usually stop within 12 hours. Patients should be closely observed for at least 7–10 days due to the risk of secondary rupture.

Where laparotomy is required every effort should be made to conserve the spleen, with experience showing it is possible to conserve enough to be of value in 30–50%. Small tears may be managed by pressure and haemostatic agents, fractures can be sutured with large liver needles. Arterial branch ligation may be of benefit and may aid partial splenectomy. Multiple fractures may be treated by omental wrapping or enclosing the spleen within a mesh bag. Occasionally total splenectomy is required, sometimes being combined with implantation of splenic fragments within the omentum. There is evidence that these fragments function, though their efficacy is unknown.

Medical indications for splenectomy

- **Regularly**
  Autoimmune thrombocytopenia
  Autoimmune haemolysis
  Hereditary spherocytosis/elliptocytosis
  Splenic vein thrombosis
  Gaucher's disease

- **Occasionally**
  Myelofibrosis
  Hodgkin's disease
  Hairy cell leukaemia
  Sickle cell disease
  Thalassaemia major

Splenomegaly

The normal spleen weighs 200 g but this can be massively increased by various pathological processes. Gradual splenomegaly may develop with minimal symptoms, these being more common in sudden enlargement, which usually causes upper abdominal discomfort. Massive enlargement may compress the stomach leading to early satiety/weight loss.

Causes of splenomegaly

- **Congestion**
  Portal hypertension due to liver cirrhosis*
  Portal/splenic vein thrombosis
  CCF

- **Viral infections**
  HIV
  CMV
  Infectious mononucleosis
  Measles

- **Protozoal infections**
  Malaria
  Leishmaniasis

- **Storage diseases**
  Gaucher's disease

- **Haematological/lymphoreticular disorders**
  Haemolytic anaemias
  Leukaemias*
  Other myeloproliferative disorders*
  Lymphoma and thrombocytopenic purpura

- **Bacterial infections**
  TB
  Typhoid
  Syphilis

- **Autoimmune**
  Rheumatoid arthritis
  SLE

- **Miscellaneous**
  Amyloidosis
  Cysts

*Most common causes

Hypersplenism is defined as splenomegaly with anaemia, leukopenia or thrombocytopenia. There is compensatory bone marrow hyperplasia.

Elective splenectomy

Splenectomy is only indicated in splenomegaly to treat hypersplenism, cysts, tumours or abscesses, or to improve symptoms due to a massive spleen. Following access via an upper midline incision (dependent on spleen size), the short gastric vessels are ligated to free the spleen from the stomach. The spleen is then mobilized by lifting it to the right using a hand between it and the diaphragm. This allows access to the vessels located within the lieno-renal ligament. The vessels may be ligated individually or *en masse* and the spleen removed. A careful search should be made for splenunculi as these can lead to a recurrence of hypersplenism. Normal changes seen in the blood after splenectomy include:

- A transient neutrophilia
- Increased size and number of platelets
- The presence of nucleated red cells and target cells

Complications of splenectomy

- Intra-operative haemorrhage
- Gastric/colonic perforation
- Pancreatic trauma leading to wound dehiscence/pancreatic fistula

- Post-operative haematoma which can become infected leading to abscess formation
- Increased risk of sepsis, including overwhelming post-splenectomy infection

Overwhelming post-splenectomy infection
Caused by infection by one of the encapsulated organisms normally destroyed by the spleen. These are *S. pneumoniae*, *N. meningitidis* and *H. influenzae*. Infection with these pathogens can lead to overwhelming sepsis with a mortality of 50–90%. Incidence is about 2% in children and 0.5% in adults, the highest incidence being in those undergoing splenectomy for lymphoreticular malignancy. All patients should have prophylaxis following splenectomy.

Current guidelines for post-splenectomy prophylaxis

- Explanation of risk to patient, with card to carry
- Vaccination with pneumovax, HiB and meningococcal vaccines; remember boosters at 5–10 years
- Antibiotic prophylaxis with amoxil (erythromycin if allergic) until age 15 only; NOT lifelong; Patients should commence amoxil at first sign of febrile illness
- Malaria prophylaxis if required

8.2 Lymph nodes

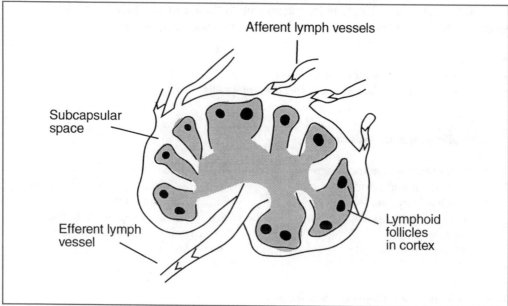

Afferent lymph vessels

Subcapsular space

Efferent lymph vessel

Lymphoid follicles in cortex

Internal structure of a lymph node

Afferent lymphatics drain into the sub-capsular sinus. Lymph then penetrates into the node via a series of sinuses, which eventually regroup to form the efferent lymphatic. Phagocytic cells and macrophages that filter the lymph line the sinuses. The lymphoid follicles contain B-cells, which become active and enlarge when exposed to antigen. T-cells and their antigen presenting cells (dendritic cells) lie between the follicles. Lymph nodes can enlarge as a reaction to infection in the territory drained by the node or by generalized disease (e.g. sarcoid, HIV or tumour), TB.

Lymphoma

This is the primary neoplastic disorder of lymphoid tissue and accounts for 5% of all new malignancies in the UK. It may be divided into Hodgkin's and non-Hodgkin's types. Hodgkin's disease is diagnosed on specific criteria namely the presence of Reed–Sternberg cells in an appropriate cellular background, whereas others are diagnosed on absence of these criteria.

Hodgkin's disease

The Reed–Sternberg cell is thought to be the neoplastic cell in Hodgkin's disease. There is a bimodal age distribution with a peak in young adults and an increase in the elderly. It usually presents with painless lymphadenopathy, mainly in the axial groups (cervical, tracheal, para-aortic). It usually spreads from group to group sequentially and extra-nodal involvement is rare. The composition of the cellular background forms the basis of the **Rye classification**.

RYE CLASSIFICATION OF HODGKIN'S DISEASE

Type	Incidence (%)	Prognosis
Lymphocyte predominant	< 10	Very good
Nodular sclerosing	50–70	Good
Mixed cellularity	17	Moderate
Lymphocyte depleted	3–5	Poor

Staging

This is accomplished using the Ann Arbor classification

Ann Arbor staging of Hodgkin's disease

- **Stage I**
  Confined to a single lymph node region or localized extra-lymphatic involvement

- **Stage II**
  Involvement of two or more node regions or localized extra-lymphatic sites on the same side of the diaphragm

- **Stage III**
  Involvement of node regions on both sides of the diaphragm ± spleen

- **Stage IV**
  Diffuse/disseminated involvement of one or more extra-lymphatic organs/tissues

The presence of the systemic symptoms of weight loss, fever or sweating adds a B to the stage (e.g. III B).

The role of staging laparotomy and splenectomy has been greatly reduced due to the sensitivity of CT scanning, which now forms the basis of staging. Treatment involves radiotherapy in combination with chemotherapy, with cure rates in excess of 60% for those with disseminated disease attained.

Non-Hodgkin's lymphoma

Usually arise in the lymph nodes, lymphoid organs and organs with a significant lymphoid content (e.g. bowel). They usually present in the fifth and sixth decades and initially form discrete tumours but later disseminate widely, often in a non-sequential manner with groups being skipped. There are many classification schemes such as the Kiel system (widely used in UK/Europe) where tumours are initially split into B and T cell types before final classification, and the REAL (Revised European American Lymphoma) classification where clinical features are also included. They are divided into a low-grade group, which run an indolent course with frequent relapses and a median survival of 5–10 years and a high-grade group with more aggressive disease and a survival of 12–24 months if untreated. Treatment has not produced great improvements in cure-rate in the low-grade group, but up to 30% of the high grade group may be cured.

8.3 Leukaemias

These are malignant neoplasms of the haematopoietic stem cells within the bone marrow that flood the blood and other organs. They may be defined as the uncontrolled proliferation of haematopoietic cells lacking the capacity to differentiate normally into mature cells. Acute leukaemias are characterized by the presence of immature cells (blasts), whereas chronic forms are associated with mature cell types and a more indolent course.

In **acute leukaemia** the blasts suppress normal haematopoietic stem cells leading to a pancytopenia. Patients may present with anaemia, infection or bleeding due to marrow suppression, generalized lymphadenopathy, splenomegaly or bone pain. There may also be infiltration of other tissues (e.g. skin or meninges). There are two types.

Acute lymphoblastic (ALL)
Mainly a disease of children and young adults with a peak incidence at the age of 4. Eighty per cent are B-cell types and 60% have chromosomal abnormalities. With chemotherapy 90% achieve complete remission, with 60% of patients being alive at 5 years.

Acute myeloblastic (AML)
Usually presents between the ages of 15 and 40, are derived from myeloid stem cells and seven types have been recognized. Ninety per cent have chromosomal abnormalities. Prognosis is worse than in ALL with an 80% initial remission rate, who usually relapse within 12–18 months. Long term survival occurs in 15% and bone marrow transplantation may help some.

Chronic myeloid leukaemia (CML)
Mainly affects adults, 25–60 years old with a peak in the fourth and fifth decades. Presentation is non-specific with fatigue, weight loss and anorexia. There is a markedly raised leukocyte count and often a raised platelet count initially. Some may enter an accelerated phase with increasing anaemia, thrombocytopenia and transformation into acute leukaemia (blast crisis). Remission may be attained with chemotherapy though survival remains at three to four years.

Chronic lymphocytic leukaemia (CLL)
Occurs mainly after the age of 50 and accounts for 25% of all leukaemias. May present with non-specific symptoms and lymphadenopathy but often asymptomatic and found on routine

blood investigation. There is a marked lymphocytosis with mainly small mature-looking cells. Median survival is four to six years and blast crisis is rare.

8.4 Plasma cell dyscrasias

These are uncontrolled, monoclonal proliferation of immunoglobulin-secreting cells. Along with the immunoglobulin (M protein) there may be an excess of light chains (Bence–Jones proteins) or heavy chains and these may sometimes be secreted alone. The most common type is multiple myeloma. Rarer types include Waldenström's macroglobulinaemia and heavy-chain disease.

Multiple myeloma

A neoplasm characterized by a monoclonal proliferation of mature and immature plasma cells. The plasma cell tumours form osteolytic lesions in bones containing red marrow. These cause bone pain and may lead to pathological fractures. Bone resorption leads to hypercalcaemia. Extension of tumours from bone may lead to cranial nerve or spinal cord compression. There is an increased susceptibility to infection with recurrent episodes of sepsis due to encapsulated organisms particularly. This is due to a lack of normal Ig and defects in lymphocyte numbers and function. Occasionally the **POEMS syndrome** may develop (**P**olyneuropathy, **O**rganomegaly, **E**ndocrinopathy, **M**onoclonal protein, and **S**kin lesions).

Laboratory findings include a monotypic Ig peak on serum electrophoresis and the presence of abnormal plasma cells in the bone marrow. There may be anaemia and a raised ESR. Renal failure is common due to the large filtered load of Ig, which forms eosinophilic inclusions in the renal tubular cells, and hyaline casts that injure the epithelium. Amyloidosis (AL type) occurs in 10% and may lead to arthropathy, skin lesions, cardiomyopathy and tongue enlargement. Median survival is two to four years with most deaths due to renal failure and infection.

8.5 Myeloproliferative disorders

Polycythaemia rubra vera

An increase in red cells leading to an increased red cell volume. There is also an increase in the number of white cells and platelets suggesting an abnormal drive to proliferation of multipotent stem cells. The cause is unknown and there is an insidious onset. Blood viscosity is increased by 5–10 times and there is a greatly increased risk of arterial and venous thrombosis. 30% die from thrombotic complications, with a total median survival of 10 years with repeated venesection. Secondary polycythaemia affects only red cells and is usually due to an increase in erythropoietin (EPO). This may be appropriate (high altitude, congenital heart disease, COAD and heavy smoking) or inappropriate (renal cell carcinoma, hepatic carcinoma).

Myelofibrosis

A clonal neoplasia of haematopoietic stem cells associated with marrow fibrosis. Usually presents in the elderly with anaemia, massive splenomegaly, and hyperuricaemia. Bone marrow aspiration may be difficult due to the fibrosis.

Essential thrombocythaemia

A clonal proliferation of megakaryocytes leading to a raised platelet count. It presents as an increased bruising/bleeding tendency and an increased thrombo-embolic risk.

8.6 Lymphoedema

Lymphoedema is an accumulation of tissue fluid secondary to a faulty lymphatic system. Affects the lower limbs in 80% of cases. It initially presents as pitting oedema though as the condition becomes chronic, fibrosis ensues and the classical non-pitting oedema becomes evident.

Differential diagnoses of lymphoedema

- Cardiac failure
- Liver cirrhosis/hypoproteinaemia
- Post-thrombotic states/
  venous occlusion

- Renal failure
- Allergic disorders
- Arterio-venous malformations
- Disuse oedema

The most common cause of unilateral ankle oedema is long-standing venous disease. Venous occlusion alone does not cause lymphoedema unless there is an underlying lymphatic dysfunction. True lymphoedema may be primary or secondary to lymphatic damage, most commonly due to surgery/radiotherapy in the UK but commonly due to infection worldwide. The most common infections are TB and filariasis, which produce an inflammatory reaction within the lymphatic system, particularly the lymph nodes. Infiltrating malignant disease in the pelvis may obstruct the lymphatic channels leading to unilateral or bilateral swelling. Surgery alone can cause lymphatic dysfunction though this is greatly increased when combined with radiotherapy as the fibrosing reaction prevents lymphatic regeneration. The cause of the majority of cases of primary lymphoedema is unknown. Milroy's disease (hereditary aplasia of the lymph trunks) is extremely rare. Most patients appear to have a congenital inadequacy of the lymphatic system, which copes until it is stressed by fluid overload, trauma or infection. The abnormality can be classified on lymphography as distal, distal and pelvic or pelvic obliteration, or hyperplasia of the lymph nodes and lymphatics. Ninety per cent of patients have obliterated distal lymphatics.

Investigations may include a radionucleotide lymphatic clearance to ascertain clearance from the limb and uptake into the inguinal nodes. A low ilioinguinal uptake may indicate primary lymphoedema while a raised uptake occurs in venous oedema due to the increased flow. Contrast lymphography is indicated to aid identification of the site of dysfunction if treatment is to be attempted.

Management is conservative in >90% of patients with compression stockings (>40 mmHg pressure), intermittent mechanical compression and vigorous systemic treatment of infection or cellulitis. Diuretics should be avoided due to the minimal improvement but lifelong need and risk of fluid depletion.

Surgery for this condition has two main aims:

- Improving lymphatic drainage by lymphatic-venous anastomosis or bypass operations such as anastomosis of sectioned lymph nodes to isolated small bowel pedicles to aid lymph drainage via mesenteric lymphatics (small number of patients with pelvic obliteration).
- Debulking surgery such as the Homén's or Charles procedures to remove excess tissue.

These surgical options are limited, and appropriate in less than 10% of patients.

9. ANAEMIA

This is defined by low haemoglobin and haematocrit values (see below). There is usually an increased erythropoietin level and red cell formation leading to marrow hyperplasia. Normal values for red cells are shown below

NORMAL VALUES FOR RED CELLS

Haemoglobin (g/dl)	Males 14–18; Females 12–16
Red-cell count (x10^{12}/l)	Males 4.4–6.0; Females 4.8–5.5
Haematocrit (PCV)	Males 0.4–0.54; Females 0.37–0.47
Mean corpuscular volume (MCV) (fl)	82–101
Mean corpuscular haemoglobin (pg/cell)	27–34
Mean corpuscular haemoglobin concentration (g/dl RBCs)	31.5–36

Normal red cells are referred to as **normocytic** (normal size) and **normochromic** (normal Hb concentration). Marked size variation is called **anisocytosis**, and marked shape variation is called **poikilocytosis**. Cells with a low Hb concentration are termed **hypochromic** and have a pale centre on a blood film. They may contain a small central Hb aggregation and are then called **target cells**.

Anaemias are classified depending on their mechanism of production (below)

9.1 Increased requirements

Blood loss

This may be acute such as in trauma or a large GI bleed. After a few days increased marrow activity is evident by a raised reticulocyte count. Chronic causes (e.g. from the GI or gynaecological systems leads to iron depletion and a hypochromic, microcytic anaemia.

Pregnancy

The increased metabolic demands of pregnancy increase the requirements of iron to an extra 8 mg daily at term. In addition, there is a physiological dilutional anaemia of pregnancy due to the 30% increase in plasma volume although the total mass of haemoglobin is increased by 15%. A haemoglobin level of 11 is regarded as the lower limit of normal during pregnancy. Relative iron and folate deficiency in the diet may contribute to anaemia.

9.2 Increased destruction (haemolytic anaemia)

This is characterized by haemolysis with accumulation of degradation products such as bilirubin and a marked increase in erythropoiesis. It may be due to intrinsic red cell abnormalities — spherocytosis, elliptocytosis, enzyme deficiencies (G6PD), abnormal haemoglobin (thalassaemia, sickle cell) and membrane defects (paroxysmal nocturnal haemoglobinuria), or extrinsic abnormalities such as antibody mediated, mechanical trauma (DIC), infections (malaria), chemical injury (lead poisoning) and sequestration (hypersplenism).

9.3 Impaired production

This may be due to a stem cell disturbance, such as aplastic anaemia or anaemia of renal failure, or an erythroblast proliferation/maturation defect — defective DNA synthesis (vitamin B12/folate deficiency) and defective haemoglobin synthesis (iron deficiency).

Sickle cell disease

A hereditary haemoglobinopathy resulting from a point mutation at the sixth position of the β globin chain. This transforms HbA to HbS. Heterozygotes (sickle-cell trait) have ~40% HbS with a low tendency to sickle compared to homozygotes. On deoxygenation the cells sickle. These can then occlude small vessels leading to infarction, or are broken down in the spleen, resulting in anaemia. They may present with haemolytic anaemia, hyperbilirubinaemia (leading to gallstones), painful crises due to infarction (bones, lung, liver, spleen) or infections due to encapsulated organisms or salmonella (splenic damage, complement impairment). Diagnosis is on blood films or SickleDex testing.

Megaloblastic anaemia

Megaloblastic anaemia is most commonly caused by a vitamin B12 or folate deficiency, these being important co-enzymes in the DNA synthetic pathways. Vitamin B12 is normally found in dietary animal products and absorbed in the terminal ileum in conjunction with intrinsic factor (IF) from the gastric parietal cells. B12 deficiency may be caused by:

- Gastrectomy, leading to loss of IF
- Autoimmune damage leading to atrophic gastritis and parietal cell damage — pernicious anaemia; in 75% there is also demyelination in the spinal cord leading to neurological symptoms
- Ileal resection or disease (Crohn's)

Folic acid deficiency causes a megaloblastic anaemia clinically and haematologically indistinguishable from that in B12 deficiency, but without the gastric atrophy and neurological features. Deficiency may be dietary (alcoholics, elderly), malabsorption syndromes (coeliac disease), increased demand (pregnancy, malignancy) or in the presence of folate antagonists (methotrexate).

Abnormally large erythrocyte precursors (megaloblasts) with poor nuclear maturation are present. Abnormally large red cells are produced with an MCV > 100.

Iron deficiency anaemia

The Western diet contains 10–20 mg of iron/day, mostly in the form of animal haem (20% absorbable compared to 2% of non-haem iron in vegetables). It is absorbed in the duodenum and either bound to ferritin or transported in the blood in conjunction with transferrin. The iron storage pool (haemosiderin and ferritin bound iron) represents 15–20% of body iron, and ferritin is a good indicator of storage levels. Negative iron balance may be caused by:

- Chronic blood loss, especially GI and female genital tracts
- Low dietary intake alone (rare in West)
- Malabsorption (coeliac disease, gastrectomy)
- Increased demand not met by intake (pregnancy, infants)

Diagnosis relies on clinical and haematological features along with a low serum iron and ferritin, increased total iron binding capacity and reduced plasma transferrin saturation.

Chapter 3
Head, Neck, Endocrine and Paediatric

CONTENTS

Head, Neck, Endocrine and Paediatric

1. THE EAR

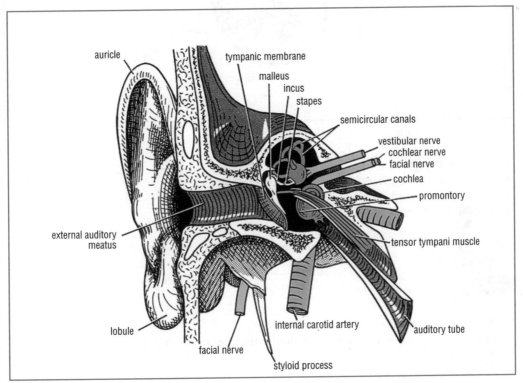

Anatom

1.1 Anatomy of the ear

External ear

- **Auricle**: elastic cartilage covered by skin
- **External acoustic meatus**
- **Lateral one-third**: cartilaginous, contains ceruminous wax-producing glands (modified sweat glands)
- **Medial two-thirds**: bony

Tympanic membrane

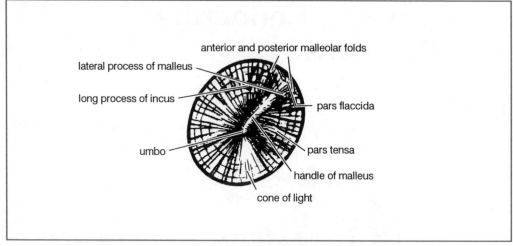

Tympanic membrane

- 1 cm in diameter
- Forms partition between external and middle ears
- Externally covered by single layer of epithelium
- Internally covered by mucous membrane

The tympanic membrane moves in response to air vibrations and causes movement of the auditory auricles.

Nerve supply

- **External surface**
  Auriculotemporal nerve (from mandibular division of the trigeminal nerve)
  Vagus nerve
  Facial nerve
  Glossopharyngeal nerve

- **Internal surface**
  Tympanic branch of glossopharyngeal nerve

Middle ear

This is an air space within the petrous part of the temporal bone, also known as the tympanic cavity. The cavity connects within the mastoid air cells via the **mastoid antrum** superiorly. The **promontory**, on the medial wall of the tympanic cavity, is due to the underlying first turn of the cochlea.

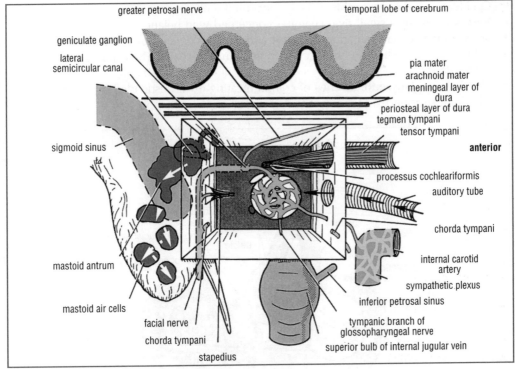

Middle ear

Auditory ossicles

- **Malleus**: connects to the tympanic membrane
- **Incus**
- **Stapes** (the foot process): articulates with the oval window

Nerve supply

- Glossopharyngeal nerve
- Facial nerve

The middle and external sections of the ear are supplied by the Vth, VIIth, Xth and XIth cranial nerves. Therefore, pain may be referred to the larynx, pharynx, teeth and posterior part of the tongue.

Internal ear

Within the petrous part of the temporal bone. This is divided into the bony and membranous labyrinth. The bony labyrinth consists of cochlea, vestibule and semi-circular canals.

- **Cochlea**: contains the cochlear duct, concerned with hearing
- **Vestibule**: this is a small oval chamber concerned with balance
- **Semi-circular canals**: anterior, posterior and lateral; contain ducts; they are placed at right angles to each other and occupy three planes in space. The canals are concerned with balance.
- **Membranous labyrinth**: a series of communicating ducts suspended within the bony labyrinth; surrounded by perilymph and containing endolymph

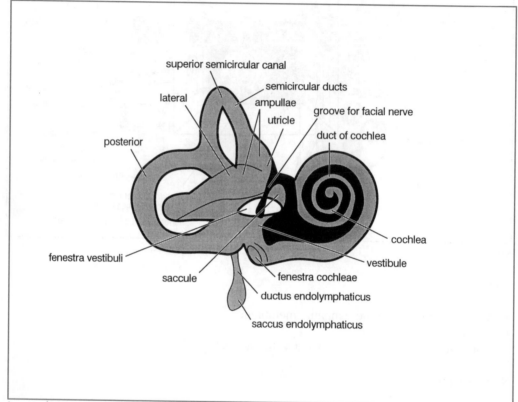

Internal ear

Facial nerve within the ear
Passes through the petrous part of the temporal bone, enters through the internal acoustic meatus and emerges at the stylo-mastoid foramen. It then runs laterally, posteriorly and downwards and enters the parotid gland.

Auditory tube

This connects the middle ear to the nasopharynx. The lateral one-third is bony, whereas the medial two-thirds are cartilaginous. The ostium drains posterior to the inferior meatus.

1.2 Inflammatory conditions of the ear

Otitis externa

Definition: *Acute diffuse infection of the skin of the external auditory canal.*

Organisms

- Haemolytic streptococcus
- *S. aureus*
- *P. pyocyaneus*
- *P. aeruginosa*

Risk factors

- Local trauma (e.g. cotton bud)
- Eczema
- Swimming

Clinical features

- Pain
- Otorrhoea
- Itching
- Blocked ear
- Debris in ear canal
- Mucopurulent discharge
- Swelling and obliteration of lumen

Management

- Analgesia
- Removal of debris — cleaning of canal
- Topical antibiotics
- Ribbon-gauze wick, which is changed daily if the lumen is narrowed

Furunculosis (acute circumscribed otitis externa)

Definition: *A staphylococcal abscess arising within a hair follicle of the external canal.*

Organisms
Mainly *S. aureus*

Clinical features

- Severe local pain
- Tenderness
- Swelling over tragus or mastoid
- Unusual to have hearing loss
- On examination swelling is seen in outer one-third of auditory canal

Management

- Analgesia
- Wick (ribbon gauze) in canal
- Antibiotics
- Puncture if furuncle is pointing

Mastoiditis

Infection of the bone of the mastoid antrum and air cell system. Caused by direct spread of acute otitis media.

Clinical features

- Low-grade pyrexia
- Pain
- Tenderness maximal over mastoid
- Marked hearing loss
- Eardrum is red and bulging
- X-ray can show destruction and cloudiness of the mastoid air cells

Management

- Antibiotics (IV): if no evidence of pus under pressure
- Myringotomy: if no improvement after 24 hours
- Mastoidectomy: if subperiosteal abscess present or no improvement with the above

1.3 Intra-cranial complications of suppurative otitis media (SOM)

Acute SOM, cholesteatoma and chronic SOM can all lead to complications that have an associated high morbidity and may be life-threatening. These include the following.

Intra-cranial complications of suppurative otitis media

- Extra-dural abscess
- Perisinus abscess
- Subdural abscess
- Brain abscess: temporal lobe abscess, cerebellar abscess
- Meningitis
- Lateral sinus thrombosis
- Otitic hydrocephalus
- Cortical thrombophlebitis

Infection can spread via the following routes:

- **Extension through bone**: demineralized by acute infection, reabsorbed by cholesteatoma/osteitis
- **Propagation**: of infected clot
- **Through normal anatomical pathways** (e.g. oval window, round window, internal acoustic meatus, cochlear and vestibular aqueducts)
- **Along periarteriolar spaces**: leads to temporal or cerebellar lobe abscess
- **Through non-anatomical bony defects** (e.g. traumatic fracture)

Clinical features
Symptoms are those of infection and compression of brain tissue:

- Headache
- Malaise
- Fever
- Drowsiness
- Otalgia
- Vomiting
- Visual disturbance
- Altered level of consciousness

Signs

- Focal neurology
- Seizure
- Raised BP
- Lowered pulse
- Papilloedema

Investigations

- High-definition CT scan
- MRI with gadolinium enhancement (is the investigation of choice for intracerebral venous thrombosis)

Principles of treatment

* Systemic antibiotics
* Neurosurgical opinion
* Treatment of underlying ear disease

Extra-dural and peri-sinus abscess

A collection of pus between the dura and bone. Usually a result of bone erosion. If the pus lies against the dura of the posterior fossa, medial to the sigmoid sinus, the abscess is termed **extra-dural**. If pus encloses the lateral sinus, it is called a **peri-sinus** abscess.

Sub-dural abscess

A collection of pus between the dura and arachnoid mater, a less common complication than extra-dural abscess. It can occur by propagation of infection through veins or direct bony and dural erosion. Symptoms include focal neurology and seizures. Treatment consists of drainage of the abscess and cortical mastoidectomy.

Brain abscess

Otogenic abscesses occur most commonly in the temporal lobe or cerebellum. They can occur due to bony erosion or thrombophlebitis. Patients may present with cerebellar signs, nominal aphasia or hemiparesis according to the side of the lesion.

Treatment consists of high-dose antibiotics, surgical drainage and treatment of the ear disease at a later stage. Organisms include *Strep. pneumoniae, H. influenzae*, pseudomonas, proteus and bacteroides.

Meningitis

This is the most common intracranial complication from suppurative otitis media. It presents with headache, neck stiffness, vomiting and pyrexia. Children may experience convulsions. Management includes CT scan, lumbar puncture and systemic antibiotics. Treatment of the underlying condition occurs when the patient's condition improves.

Lateral sinus thrombosis

This usually develops due to erosion of the lateral sinus plate. A peri-sinus abscess is formed, followed by a mural thrombus in the walls of the sinus, which becomes infected and spreads distally and proximally. The lumen of the sinus becomes occluded by a clot which then disseminates and fragments into the circulation.

Organisms are proteus, staphylococcus, bacteroides and *E. coli*. In addition to headache and malaise, patients may experience persistent spiking fever. They may also exhibit Griesinger's sign, oedema and tenderness over the mastoid process due to thrombophlebitis of the mastoid emissary vein. Diagnosis is confirmed by FBC, blood cultures and MRI angiography.

Treatment consists of antibiotics, cortical mastoidectomy, evacuation of clot from the lateral sinus. Some surgeons ligate the internal jugular vein high in the neck to reduce infective embolization.

Otitic hydrocephalus

A syndrome of increased intra-cranial pressure (ICP) during or following middle ear infection without a brain abscess. Aetiology is unknown. Condition is seen most commonly in children and adolescents. Patients present with headache, VIth cranial nerve palsy and papilloedema. The aim of treatment is to reduce ICP, i.e. diuretics, steroid, lumbo-peritoneal or ventriculoperitoneal shunt. Prognosis is good.

2. THE NOSE AND PARANASAL SINUSES

2.1 Anatomy of the nose

The nose consists of the external nose, nasal septum and nasal cavity:

- The external nose is largely cartilaginous
- The lateral and alar cartilages are made up of hyaline cartilage
- It is lined by respiratory epithelium

Nasal cavity

This extends from the nostrils to the posterior nasal aperture at the posterior end of the nasal septum and is lined by respiratory epithelium. The olfactory area is located in the roof and lateral walls above the superior conchae.

Nasal conchae

Three scroll-shaped elevations on the lateral walls of the nose. The cavity below each conchae is known as the **meatus**; above the superior conchae is the spheno-ethmoidal recess. The inferior meatus receives the nasolacrimal duct; the superior meatus drains the posterior ethmoidal air cells. The middle meatus drains the maxillary sinus, middle ethmoidal sinus, frontal and anterior ethmoidal sinuses. The spheno-ethmoidal recess drains the sphenoidal air sinuses.

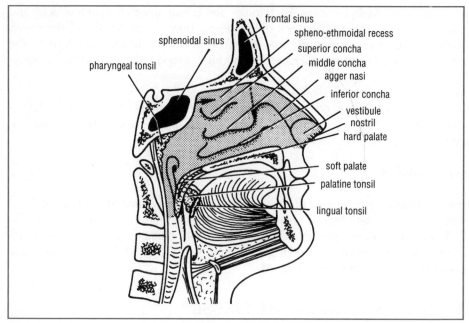

Anatomy of the nose

Blood supply of the nose

- **Anterior and posterior ethmoid vessels**: supply roof, anterior and lateral walls
- **Sphenopalatine artery**: supplies conchae, meati and septum
- **Little's area**: at anterior part of nasal septum

The sphenopalatine, superior labial and greater palatine arteries form an anastomosis known as **Kiesselbach's plexus**.

Venous drainage
Pterygoid venous plexus

Lymph drainage
Drain to the submandibular, deep cervical and retropharyngeal nodes

Nerve supply

- **Nasopalatine nerve**: (branch of maxillary nerve)
- **Anterior ethmoidal nerve**: (from the ophthalmic division of the trigeminal nerve)
- Nasal branches of the **maxillary nerve**
- **Greater palatine nerve**

2.2 Epistaxis

Two types: anterior and posterior nasal bleeds

- **Anterior**: usually Little's area
- **Posterior**: bleeding point not usually visible

Causes of epistaxis

- **Local**
  Idiopathic
  Traumatic
  Inflammatory
  Neoplastic

- **Systemic**
  Hypertension
  Blood disorders (e.g. leukaemia,
    haemophilia)

Blood vessels involved in epistaxis

- Greater palatine
- Sphenopalatine
- Anterior and posterior ethmoidal
- Superior labial

Treatment

- Manual pressure and ice
- Cauterization — anterior nasal bleed
- Nasal packing
- Foley catheter — tamponade post-nasal space
- Ligation of blood vessels (e.g. inferior maxillary artery, anterior ethmoidal artery)
- Correction of clotting disorder

2.3 Anatomy of the paranasal sinuses

These are air-filled extensions of the respiratory part of the nasal cavity and are named according to the bones they extend into. They are lined by respiratory epithelium and drain into the nasal cavity via ostia. They are mucus-producing, but their function is unknown.

THE PARANASAL SINUSES

Sinus	Nerve supply	Location of ostia
Maxillary	Anterior, middle and posterior superior alveolar nerves (from maxillary nerve)	Middle meatus
Frontal	Supra-orbital nerve (from ophthalmic nerve)	Infundibulum (hiatus semilunaris of the middle meatus)
Ethmoidal		
Anterior	Anterior ethmoidal branch of the nasociliary nerve	Infundibulum
Posterior	Posterior ethmoidal branch of the nasociliary nerve	Superior meatus
Sphenoidal	Posterior ethmoidal nerve	Spheno-ethmoidal recess (above and behind the superior meatus)

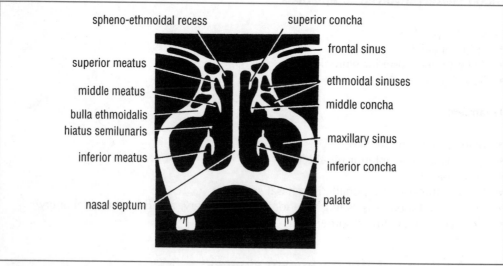

Anatomy of the paranasal sinuses

2.4 Acute sinusitis

Organisms

- *Strep. pneumoniae*
- *S. aureus*
- *H. influenzae*

Aetiology

- Acute infective rhinitis
- Dental extraction or infection
- Fractures involving sinuses
- Swimming or diving (spread of infection through ostia)
- Nasal obstruction
- Neighbouring infection (e.g. tonsillitis)

Clinical features

- Pain over sinus and tenderness
- Nasal obstruction
- Nasal discharge
- Systemic symptoms (e.g. malaise, pyrexia)
- Post-nasal drip
- Facial tenderness

Differential diagnosis

- Toothache
- Migraine
- Neoplasia of sinuses
- Trigeminal neuralgia

Treatment

- **Non-operative**: analgesia, antibiotics, decongestant nasal drops
- **Operative**: when non-operative treatment is not effective, drainage and irrigation

Complications of acute sinusitis

- **Intracranial**
  Meningitis
  Extra-dural/subdural abscess
  Cavernous sinus thrombosis
  Cerebral abscess

- **Osteomyelitis**
  Most commonly caused by
    frontal sinusitis; this is rare

- **Orbital**
  All the sinuses contact the
    boundaries of the orbit and the walls
    are thin and easily eroded
  Orbital cellulitis
  Subperiosteal abscess (points through
    the eyelids)
  Destruction of the eyeball

3. THE LARYNX AND THE TRACHEA

3.1 Anatomy of the larynx

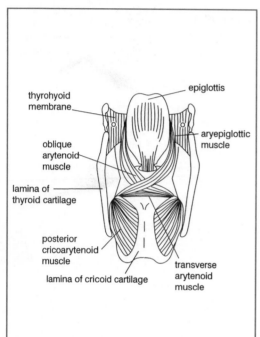

Cartilage

- Thyroid
- Cricoid
- Epiglottis
- Arytenoid
- Corniculate } paired
- Cuneiform

Ligaments and membranes

- Thyrohyoid membrane
- Cricothyroid ligament
- Cricotracheal ligament
- Quadrangular membrane

Anatomy of the larynx

Vestibular folds (the **false vocal cords**) are the lower border of the quadrangular membrane.

Cricovocal ligaments (the **true vocal cords**) extend from the vocal process of the arytenoids to the thyroid laminae.

Phonation is produced by the vocal cords being held together and blown apart by discrete jets of air.

Nerve supply of the larynx

Motor
The recurrent laryngeal nerve supplies all muscles except the cricothyroid which is supplied by the external laryngeal.

Sensory
Above the vocal cords, the mucosa is supplied by the internal branch of the superior laryngeal nerve; below the vocal cords, the mucosa is supplied by the recurrent laryngeal nerve.

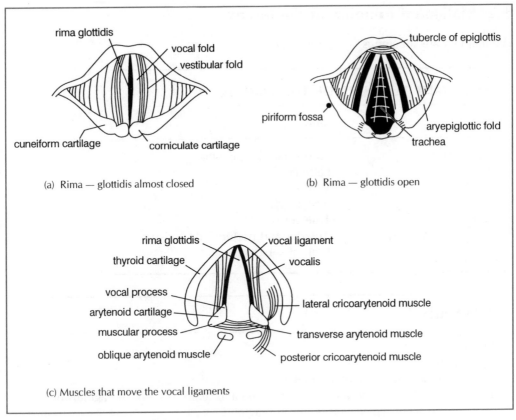

(a) Rima — glottidis almost closed

(b) Rima — glottidis open

(c) Muscles that move the vocal ligaments

Muscles of the larynx

BLOOD SUPPLY AND LYMPHATIC DRAINAGE OF THE LARYNX

	Blood supply	Lymphatic drainage
Above vocal folds	Superior laryngeal branch of the superior thyroid artery	Upper group of deep cervical nodes
Below vocal folds	Inferior laryngeal branch of the inferior thyroid artery	Lower group of deep cervical nodes

Lymphatic drainage also occurs to the pretracheal and tracheobronchial nodes.

3.2 Malignant tumours of the larynx

The majority are squamous cell carcinoma.

MALIGNANT TUMOURS OF THE LARYNX

Regions	Sites
Supraglottic	Lower part of epiglottis
	False cords
	Ventricles
	Arytenoids
Glottic	True cords
(most common)	Anterior and posterior commissures
Subglottic	Wall of subglottis

SUIMMARY

Larynx

Supraglottis

T1	One subsite, normal mobility
T2	Involving mucosa of more than one adjacent subsite of supraglottis or adjacent region outside the supraglottis
T3	Limited to larynx with vocal cord fixation or invades postericoid area, pre-epliglottic tissues, base of tongue

Glottis

T1	Limited to vocal cord(s), normal mobility
T2	Supraglottis, or subglottis, or impaired cord mobility
T3	Cord fixation
T4	Extends beyond larynx

Subglottis

T1	Limited to the subglottis
T2	Extends to vocal cord(s) with normal/impaired mobility
T3	Cord fixation
T4	Extends beyond the larynx

All sites

N1	Ipsilateral single < 3 cm	
N2	(a)	ipsilateral single > 3 cm to 6 cm
	(b)	ipsilateral multiple < 6 cm
	(c)	bilateral, contralateral < 6 cm
N3	> 6 cm	

TNM Classification

T — primary tumour — salivary

TX	Primary tumour cannot be assessed
T0	No evidence of primary tumour
Tis	Carcinoma *in situ*
T1	Tumour 2 cm or less in greatest dimension without extraparenchynmal extension*
T2	Tumour more than 2 cm but no more than 4 cm in greatest dimension without extraparenchymal extension*
T3	Tumour having extraparenchymal extension without seventh nerve involvement and/or >4–6 cm in greatest dimension*
T4	Tumour invades base of skull, seventh nerve, and/or exceeds 6 cm in greatest diameter

N – regional lymph notes

NX	Regional lymph nodes cannot be assessed	
N0	No regional lymph nodes	
N1	Ipsilateral single <3 cm	
N2	a)	Ipsilateral single >3–6 cm
	b)	Ipsilateral multiple <6 cm
	c)	Bilateral, contralateral <6 cm
N3	>6 cm	

*Extraparenchymal extension is clinical or macroscopic evidence of invasion of skin, soft tissues, bones or nerve. Microscopic evidence alone does not constitute extraparenchymal extension for classification purposes.

Risk factors

- Males
- Smoking
- Over 40
- Excess alcohol

Clinical features

- Hoarseness
- Cough
- Palpable lymph node
- Referred pain in ear
- Stridor

Management

- Staging using CT or MRI of neck
- T_1/T_2: radiotherapy or endoscopic resection
- T_3: depends on tumour volume, options include radiotherapy, total laryngectomy
- T_4: primary surgery with neck dissection with post-operative radiotherapy

If nodal involvement, neck dissection is performed. For supraglottic tumours, radiotherapy is performed; can be combined with surgery but this depends on the medical suitabilty of the patient.

3.3 Anatomy of the trachea

The total length of the trachea is 10 cm, extending from the level of C6 in continuity with the larynx. It is made up of C-shaped hyaline cartilage rings, trachealis muscle posteriorly and a fibro-elastic membrane.

Relations

Anteriorly
- Inferior thyroid vein
- Anterior jugular venous arch
- Thyroidea ima artery
- Isthmus of the thyroid gland (2nd, 3rd and 4th rings)

Posteriorly
- Oesophagus
- Recurrent laryngeal nerve

Laterally
- Carotid sheath
- Thyroid lobes (down to the level of the 6th ring)

Blood supply

Inferior thyroid artery.

Lymphatic drainage

Postero-inferior group of deep cervical nodes (supply smooth muscle and blood vessels).

Nerve supply

- **Parasympathetic**: vagi and recurrent laryngeal nerves (supply pain)
- **Sympathetic**: upper ganglia of the sympathetic trunk

3.4 Stridor

'Bovine-like' inspiratory noise associated with laryngeal obstruction more common in children.

Causes of stridor

- **Adults**
  Extra-luminal
  Neurological — MND
  Iatrogenic — thyroidectomy
  Trauma

  Mural
  Angioneurotic oedema
  Granuloma
  Malignancy
  Laryngomalacia

  Luminal
  TB
  Foreign body

- **Children**
  Extra-luminal
  Trauma
  Mediastinal tumours
  Anomalous blood vessels
  Vagal or recurrent laryngeal
    nerve paralysis

  Mural
  Angioneurotic oedema
  Laryngeal web
  Subglottic stenosis
  Laryngotracheobronchitis (croup)
  Laryngeal papilloma or
    haemangioma
  Acute laryngitis/acute epiglottitis

  Luminal
  Foreign body

Management

- Remove false teeth and secretions
- **In emergency situation**: ET tube, laryngotomy (cricothyroidotomy), jet insufflation
- **If time**: laryngoscopy for removal of foreign body, ET tube if intubation required for few days, tracheostomy for longer period of intubation

Maintenance of airway and ventilation in trauma is covered in Chapter 3, *Trauma*, Section 1.2 of the *MRCS Core Modules: Essential Revision Notes*.

3.5 Tracheostomy

Indications for tracheostomy

Relief of airway obstruction

- Congenital (e.g. laryngeal cysts, subglottic stenosis, tracheoesophageal anomalies)
- Trauma to larynx and trachea

- Infection (e.g. acute epiglottitis, laryngotracheobronchitis)
- Tumour (e.g. tongue, larynx, pharynx, thyroid)
- Trauma (Le Fort II and III fractures, haemorrhage)
- Bilateral vocal cord paralysis
- Foreign body
- Sleep apnoea syndrome

Protection of the tracheobronchial tree
For temporary or permanent protection:

- Neurological diseases (e.g. myasthenia gravis, MS)
- Trauma — burns to the face and neck
- Coma (e.g. drug overdose, head injury)
- Head and neck surgery — supraglottic laryngectomy, oropharyngeal resection

Treatment of respiratory insufficiency

- Tracheostomy reduces upper airway dead space by 70%
- Chest injury (flail chest)
- Pulmonary disease

Performing a tracheostomy

Anaesthetic
GA and intubation; LA (in emergency).

Position
Head moderately extended.

Skin incision
Transverse 2 cm below cricoid cartilage (elective); mid-line from thyroid cartilage to manubrium (emergency).

Procedure

- Separate strap muscles
- Retract thyroid isthmus or divide
- Cut circular disc from 2nd/3rd tracheal rings (injury of the first ring leads to subglottic stenosis)
- Vertical incision in children (do not remove cartilage, can lead to tracheal collapse)
- Aspirate trachea
- Insert tube

Closure
Skin edges closed, tapes tied to secure tube.

Post-operative management

- Nurse upright
- Regular suction
- Humidified O_2 with 5–7% CO_2 to prevent apnoea

Complications of tracheostomy

- **Early**
  Asphyxia
  Aspiration
  Haemorrhage or haematoma
  Obstruction
  Subcutaneous emphysema
  Pneumothorax, pneumomediastinum
  Mal-positioned tube
  Injury to cricoid cartilage

- **Late**
  Cellulitis
  Subglottic stenosis
  Vocal cord palsy
  Tracheo-cutaneous or tracheo-oesophageal fistula
  Delayed haemorrhage
  Displacement of tube
  Atelectasis and pulmonary infection
  Tracheomalacia
  Dysphagia
  Difficult decannulation
  Tracheal stenosis

4. THE PHARYNX AND TONGUE

4.1 Anatomy of the pharynx

The pharynx conducts food from the mouth to the oesophagus. It extends from the base of the skull to C6 vertebra and is 12 cm long.

The pharynx has four layers:

- Mucous membrane
- Submucous (fibrous) layer
- Muscular layer
- Buccopharyngeal membrane

The muscular layer consists of:

- External circular layer (the constrictors)
- Inner longitudinal layer (palatopharyngeus, stylopharyngeus, salpingopharyngeus)

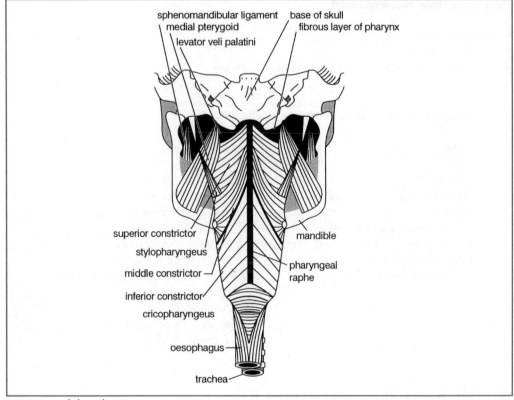

Anatomy of the pharynx

Killian's dehiscence

This is a potential weak area between thyropharyngeus and cricopharyngeus. A diverticulum of mucosa protrudes to produce a pharyngeal pouch.

Nerve supply

Motor

- **Pharyngeal plexus**: pharyngeal branches of vagus, glossopharyngeal and cervical sympathetic — motor supply to all muscles except stylopharyngeus
- **Glossopharyngeal nerve**: supplies stylopharyngeus
- **Recurrent or external laryngeal nerves**: may supply cricopharyngeus

Sensory

- **Nasopharynx**: supplied by the maxillary nerve
- **Oropharynx**: supplied by the glossopharyngeal nerve — the vallecula is supplied by the internal laryngeal nerve

Interior of the pharynx

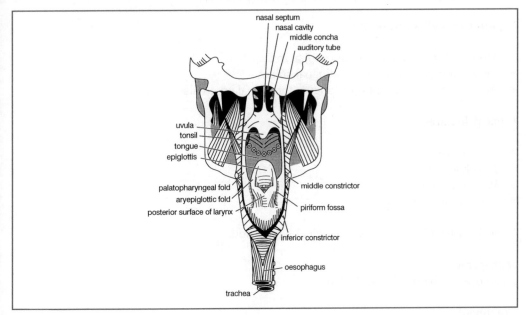

nasal septum
nasal cavity
middle concha
auditory tube

uvula
tonsil
tongue
epiglottis

palatopharyngeal fold
aryepiglottic fold
posterior surface of larynx

middle constrictor

piriform fossa

inferior constrictor

oesophagus

trachea

Interior of the pharynx

The interior of the pharynx is divided into:

- **Nasopharynx**: from the base of the skull to the lower border of the soft palate
- **Oropharynx**: from the lower border of the soft palate to the upper border of the epiglottis
- **Laryngopharynx/hypopharynx**: from the upper border of the epiglottis to the level of the cricoid cartilage (C6)

Nasopharynx
This contains the opening of the auditory tube. The pharyngeal tonsils (adenoids) are located high on the posterior wall.

Oropharynx
This contains the palatine tonsils, which:

- Lie in the tonsillar fossa between the palatopharyngeus and palatoglossus
- Are covered by the pharyngeal submucosa
- Are supplied by the tonsillar branch of the facial artery
- Drain to the jugulodigastric lymph node below the angle of the mandible
- Are supplied by the tonsillar branch of the glossopharyngeal nerve

Laryngopharynx
This contains the laryngeal inlet and piriform recesses which lie at each side of the larynx.

4.2 Malignant tumours of the oropharynx

Squamous cell carcinoma

- Most common tumour of the oropharynx
- Most common site is tonsillo-lingual sulcus
- Also from: posterior third of tongue, tonsil, palate, uvula

Clinical features

- Sore throat
- Dysphagia
- Pain in the ear
- Lump in the neck

Spread via lymphatics to upper cervical lymph nodes.

Management
Diagnosis via biopsy (exclude TB).

Treatment

- Radiotherapy
- Commando operation (*en bloc* dissection of mandible, tongue, cheek, tonsil and palate)

Prognosis
Depends on stage:

- Stage I (<2 cm) has 93% five-year survival rate
- Stage IV (deep invasion of nodes or metastasis) has 17% five-year survival rate

Adenocarcinoma

Occurs in palatal and faucial region. Most are 'mixed' salivary gland tumours.

Sarcoma

Can occur in tonsils in children and young adults. Presents as unilateral enlargement of the tonsil. Treated with radiotherapy.

4.3 Malignant tumours of the nasopharynx

Squamous cell carcinoma

This is the most common tumour of the nasopharynx.

Clinical features

- Palpable neck nodes
- Conductive deafness (due to infiltration of the Eustachian tube)
- Elevation of ipsilateral soft palate (direct infiltration)
- Pain in side of head (Vth CN involvement at the foramen lacerum)
- There is also nasal obstruction and epistaxis

Management

- Visualize with post-nasal mirror, nasopharyngoscope, CT
- Biopsy

Treatment
Radiotherapy.

Other malignant tumours

Lymphosarcoma and reticulosarcoma: younger patients, highly sensitive to radiotherapy.

4.4 Tonsillitis

Aetiology

Inflammation due to:

- **Bacterial**
  Streptococci (ß-haemolytic)
  Staphylococci
  Pneumococci
  H. influenzae
  E. coli

- **Viral**
  Rhinovirus
  Adenovirus
  Enterovirus
  Epstein–Barr

Continues

... Continued

- **Other infective**
  Bacteroides fragilis
    (chronic or recurrent)
  Corynebacterium diphtheriae
  Treponema pallidum
  Mycobacterium tuberculosis
  Vincent's spirillum without
    fusobacterium
  Candida (without HIV)

- **Non-infective**
  Leukaemia
  Lymphoma

Pathological types

Acute parenchymatous

- Whole tonsil is infected
- Generalized swelling
- Reddened and oedematous

Acute follicular

- Crypts filled with infected fibrin
- Spotted or membranous appearance

Clinical features

- Sore throat
- Cervical lymphadenopathy
- Chills
- Malaise
- Headache
- Pyrexia
- Otalgia (nerve supply from glossopharyngeal)
- Abdominal pain (mesenteric adenitis in children)

On examination: swollen, reddened tonsils, uvula oedematous, exudate of pus (in established cases), patchy membrane.

Differential diagnosis: glandular fever, AIDS (especially candidiasis).

Complications

- Peritonsillar abscess or quinsy (leading to laryngeal oedema in children)
- Retropharyngeal abscess
- Rheumatic fever ⎫ post-streptococcal
- Glomerulo-nephritis ⎭ (rare)

Non-surgical treatment

- Soft diet
- Antibiotics in severe infection (penicillin or erythromycin for 10 days)
- Antiseptic gargles

Tonsillectomy

Indications

- Repeated attacks (more than six episodes per year for two consecutive years) interfering with health or life
- Peritonsillar abscess — not absolute
- Sleep apnoea syndrome

Patient must be free of acute tonsillitis for at least two weeks prior to operation.

Haemorrhage post-tonsillectomy

- **Reactionary/primary**
  Within two days of operation
  due to incomplete haemostasis
  at time of operation

- **Secondary**
  Usually days 5–10 post-operatively
  due to build-up and then
  removal of slough

Treatment

- Inspect
- Control bleeding
- Infection of tonsillar bed — antibiotics

4.5 Acute epiglottitis

A bacterial infection of the throat characterized by progressive acute laryngitis which affects all the supraglottis, but predominantly the loose connective tissue of the epiglottis.

Aetiology

- Usually *H. influenzae*, Type B is the causative organism
- Staphylococci, β-haemolytic streptococci and pneumococci have been found, particularly in adults

Clinical features

- Usually occurs in children aged 2–7 years
- Initially, the child complains of a sore throat which rapidly progresses to inspiratory stridor
- Pyrexia (temperature of 38–40 °C)
- The child tends to lean forwards and drools

> **Do not attempt to examine the child as this may precipitate laryngospasm**

Management

- The child's airway must be secured
- An experienced paediatric anaesthetist and otolaryngologist must be in attendance
- Child and parent are moved to an induction area with operating facilities adjacent
- Anaesthesia is induced by inhalation
- An endotracheal tube is passed; at this time, a cherry red epiglottis will be seen
- Rigid bronchoscopy can be used to intubate if initial attempts at intubation fail
- Tracheostomy is rarely required
- Intravenous access, blood cultures and throat swabs are performed after the airway has been secured
- Patients respond quickly to intravenous antibiotics (e.g. chloramphenicol) and usually can be extubated after 24–48 hours
- Steroids may be of value before decannulation to reduce oedema

The incidence of acute epiglottitis in children has been declining, which may be due to Hib vaccine administration.

4.6 Dysphagia

Definition: *Difficulty in swallowing and eating (**not** pain)*

Causes of dysphagia

- **Mouth**
  Dental (e.g. ill-fitting
    dentures, caries)
  Aphthous ulcers
    (e.g. UC)
  Carcinoma
  Anaemia (e.g. B12,
    folate deficiency)
  SLE
  Sjögren's syndrome

- **Oropharynx**
  Tonsillitis
  Carcinoma
  Pharyngitis

- **Oesophageal**
  See Chapter 4, *Abdomen*,
    Section 4.2, p. 349

- **Hypopharynx**
  Pharyngeal pouch
  Achalasia
  Carcinoma
  Neurological disease
    (e.g. MS, MND)

Assessment of dysphagia

History then examination

- Mouth: direct vision
- Oropharynx: viewing mirror
- Endoscopy
- Barium swallow (e.g. pharyngeal pouch)

Management

- Symptomatic relief from gargles, sweets, mouth washes
- Treat specific cause of dysphagia

4.7 Anatomy of the tongue

- **Functions**: speech, swallowing, mastication, taste
- **Parts**: dorsum, tip, inferior surface, root, lingual frenulum

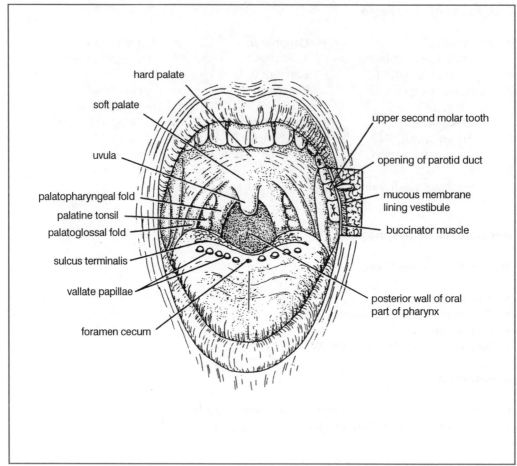

Anatomy of the tongue

The **dorsum** is divided into the anterior two-thirds and posterior one-third by the sulcus terminalis. The **foramen caecum** is the remnant of the opening of the thyroglossal duct. The anterior two-thirds of the tongue has numerous papillae projecting from it (as shown):

- **Filiform**: scattered throughout, they do not contain taste receptors
- **Fungiform**: located peripherally, they contain taste receptors
- **Vallate**: lie in front of the sulcus, they have numerous taste receptors

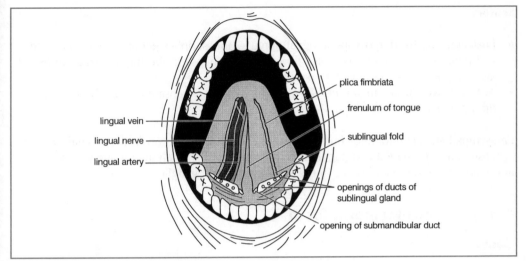

The inferior surface of the tongue

Muscles of the tongue

- **Intrinsic**
  Superior and inferior longitudinal
  Transverse
  Vertical

- **Extrinsic**
  Genioglossus: protrudes the tongue
  Hyoglossus
  Styloglossus: retracts the tongue
  Palatoglossus

Blood supply

Lingual artery and vein.

Lymphatic drainage

- **Posterior one-third**: this drains to the deep cervical nodes
- **Anterior two-thirds**: this drains via the submandibular nodes to the deep cervical nodes
- **Tip**: this drains via the submental nodes

Nerve supply of the tongue

Motor
All muscles are supplied by the hypoglossal nerve, except palatoglossus which is supplied by the pharyngeal plexus and the cranial root of the accessory nerve.

Sensory

- **Posterior one-third**: glossopharyngeal nerve — this supplies general sensation, taste and parasympathetic secretomotor fibres which synapse in the lingual ganglion (NB. It also supplies taste to the vallate papillae)
- **Anterior two-thirds**: lingual nerve — supplies ordinary sensation (branch of the mandibular nerve); chorda tympani — supplies taste

Parasympathetic secretomotor fibres from the chorda tympani run in the lingual nerve and synapse in the submandibular ganglion. Sympathetic fibres reach the tongue with the lingual artery and have their cell bodies in the superior cervical ganglion.

4.8 The infra-temporal fossa

Contents

- Insertion of temporalis
- Maxillary artery and branches
- Pterygoid venous plexus
- Mandibular nerve and branches
- Medial and lateral pterygoid
- Otic ganglion
- Chorda tympani
- Posterior superior alveolar nerve

Boundaries of the infra-temporal fossa

- **Medial**
  Lateral pterygoid plate
  Pterygomaxillary fissure
  Superior constrictor of the pharynx
  Tensor palati
  Levator palati

- **Roof**
  Greater wing of the sphenoid
  Squamous part of the temporal bone

- **Lateral**
  Ramus of the mandible

- **Anterior**
  Posterior surface of the maxilla
  Inferior orbital fissure

- **Posterior**
  Carotid sheath

Lateral pterygoid muscle

Origin
Infra-temporal surface of the skull (upper head), lateral surface of the lateral pterygoid plate (lower head).

Insertion
Pterygoid fossa on mandibular head.

Nerve supply
Branch from anterior division of the mandibular nerve.

Action
Draws the condyle forward, i.e. opens the mouth.

Medial pterygoid muscle

Origin

- Medial surface of the lateral pterygoid plate (deep head)
- Tuberosity of the maxilla   } superficial
- Pyramidal process of the palatine bone } head

Insertion
Inner surface of the angle of the mandible.

Nerve supply
Branch from the main trunk of the mandibular nerve.

Action
Closes the mouth; moves the mandible to the opposite side in chewing.

Maxillary artery

Passes between the two heads of lateral pterygoid to enter the pterygopalatine fossa. It has 15 branches, including the inferior alveolar artery, middle meningeal artery, sphenopalatine artery and infra-orbital artery.

Mandibular nerve

This emerges from the skull through the foramen ovale. It has nine branches, including the nerves to medial and lateral pterygoid, lingual nerve, inferior alveolar and auriculotemporal nerves.

Mylohyoid

This muscle forms the floor of the mouth.

Origin
Mylohyoid line.

Insertion
Body of the hyoid (posterior quarter); mid-line raphe (from chin to hyoid).

Nerve supply
Nerve to mylohyoid from the mandibular division of the trigeminal nerve.

Action
Supports the tongue and elevates the hyoid and tongue during swallowing.

5. FOREIGN BODIES IN THE EAR, NOSE AND THROAT

Foreign body in the ear

- May cause otorrhoea
- Inspect both ears
- Inspect ear after removal of foreign body

Foreign body in the nose

- May cause malodour
- Remove with curved Eustachian catheter
- Risk of inhalation in children, therefore should be removed urgently

Foreign body in the throat

Sites of impaction

- **Mouth**: tonsils
- **Pharynx**: base of tongue, oropharynx
- **Oesophagus**: oesophageal inlet, at the level of the arch of aorta cardio-oesophageal junction

Diagnosis of site of impaction

- **Mouth**: local anaesthesia to throat
- **Pharynx**: indirect laryngoscopy and remove with forceps

Oesophagus
With sharp objects urgent oesophagoscopy due to risk of perforation.

6. THE SALIVARY GLANDS

6.1 Anatomy of the salivary glands

The parotid gland

A salivary gland, situated in the space between the mastoid process, styloid process and ramus of the mandible. It has a surrounding layer of investing fascia, the parotid sheath. Mainly a serous gland, with a few mucous acini. There are upper and lower poles, and lateral, anterior and deep surfaces.

Relations

*   **Anterior**: masseter, medial pterygoid, stylomandibular ligament, superficial temporal and maxillary artery, facial nerve
*   **Deep surface**: sternocleidomastoid, posterior belly of digastric muscle, external carotid artery, mastoid process, styloid process with attached muscles and ligaments
*   **Within the gland**: facial nerve (superficial), retromandibular vein, external carotid artery, auriculotemporal nerve (deep)

The parotid duct runs across masseter and pierces the buccinator and drains opposite the second upper molar tooth.

Blood supply
Branches from the external carotid artery; venous drainage via the retromandibular vein.

Lymphatic drainage
To the deep cervical nodes.

Nerve supply

*   **Parasympathetic**: secretomotor
*   **Sympathetic**: vasoconstrictors from the superior cervical ganglion, the fibres travel from the external carotid artery plexus
*   **Sensory**: auriculotemporal nerve

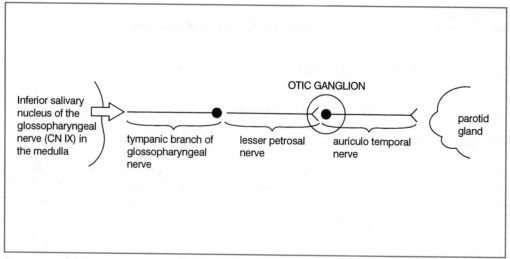

Parasympathetic secretomotor fibres reach the parotid gland via the otic ganglion by 'hitch-hiking' along with three nerves

Submandibular gland

The submandibular gland is divided into deep and superficial parts by the posterior border of mylohyoid. It is a mixed salivary gland, secreting mucous and serous saliva. The submandibular duct emerges from the superficial part of the gland. It enters the floor of the mouth next to the frenulum. In its course it runs between the mylohyoid and hyoglossus.

Relations of superficial part of submandibular gland

- **Lateral**
  Submandibular fossa of mandible
  Medial pterygoid
  Facial artery

- **Inferior**
  Skin
  Platysma
  Facial vein
  Cervical branch of facial nerve

- **Medial**
  Mylohyoid muscle
  Hyoglossus muscle
  Lingual nerve (superior to deep
    part of gland)
  Submandibular ganglion
  Hypoglossal nerve (inferior to deep
    part of gland)
  Deep lingual vein
  Submandibular duct (inferior to deep
    part of gland)

Blood supply
Facial artery and vein.

Lymph drainage
Submandibular lymph nodes.

Nerve supply

- **Parasympathetic**: secretomotor fibres
- **Sympathetic**: vasoconstrictor from the plexus around the facial artery

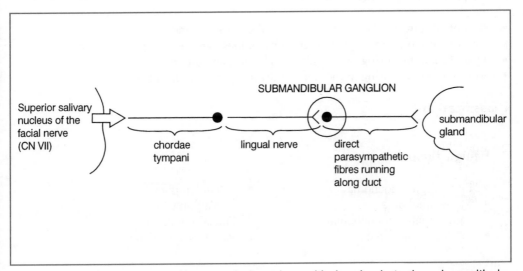

Parasympathetic secretomotor fibres reach the submandibular gland via the submandibular ganglion by 'hitchhiking' along with two nerves

Sublingual gland

A mucus-secreting gland which lies in front of the anterior border of the hyoglossus and medial to genioglossus.

Relations

- **Lateral**: sublingual fossa of the mandible
- **Medial**: genioglossus
- **Posterior**: stylomandibular ligament, submandibular gland
- **Anterior**: opposite glands meet anteriorly
- **Inferior**: mylohyoid
- **Superior**: causes the sublingual fold of mucosa in floor of mouth

Blood supply
Lingual artery.

Nerve supply
Submandibular ganglion.

6.2 Salivary gland neoplasms

These can be divided into benign and malignant tumours. Furthermore, malignant tumours can be primary or secondary tumours.

- 80% of all salivary gland tumours are in the parotid gland
- 80% of parotid tumours are benign; 80% of these are pleomorphic adenomas
- 33% of tumours arising in the submandibular gland are malignant
- 50% of tumours arising in the minor salivary glands are malignant

Classification

Benign tumours

- Pleomorphic adenoma
- Myoepithelioma
  (myoepithelial adenoma)
- Oncocytic adenoma

- Adenolymphoma
  (Warthin's tumour)
- Ductal papilloma
- Papillary cystadenoma

Pleomorphic adenomas account for 80% of benign parotid gland tumours. They occur (most frequently in the fifth decade), equally in males and females. They have a pseudocapsule and arise from myoepithelial cells and intercalated duet cells. They present as a painless enlarging smooth mass.

Adenolymphomas are seen mainly in males (male:female ratio is 7:1) aged 60–70 years. They are thought to arise from lymph nodes within the parotid gland. One in 10 patients have bilateral tumours, but these rarely occur synchronously.

Malignant tumours

- Adenoid cystic carcinoma
- Adenocarcinoma
- Carcinoma in pleomorphic adenoma

- Squamous cell carcinoma
- Undifferentiated carcinoma

Adenoid cystic carcinoma is a slow-growing tumour which often spreads along nerve sheaths. The most common malignant tumour of the salivary glands, it occurs more frequently in minor rather than major salivary glands. Patients may present with facial pain and facial nerve palsy. Tumours do not metastasize early and lymph node metastasis is uncommon. It occurs equally in men and women.

Adenocarcinomas make up 3% of parotid tumours and 10% of submandibular and minor salivary gland tumours.

Tumours of variable malignancy

- Mucoepidermoid carcinoma
- Acinic cell carcinoma

Mucoepidermoid tumours arise mainly in the parotid gland. They can behave in a benign or malignant fashion depending on degree of differentiation. Undifferentiated tumours metastasize early and carry a poor prognosis. They are the most common salivary neoplasms in children.

Non-epithelial tumours

- Lymphangioma
- Lymphoma
- Neurofibroma
- Haemangioma

Staging of malignant parotid tumours

The AJC system (American Joint Committee)

- T_0 No clinical evidence of tumour
- T_1 <2 cm diameter, without extraparenchymal extension
- T_2 2–4 cm diameter, without extraparenchymal extension
- T_3 4–6 cm diameter, and/or extraparenchymal extension
- T_4 Base of skull, VIIth nerve involvement and/or >6 cm

A parotid lump with involvement of the facial nerve (i.e. facial nerve palsy) is highly suggestive of malignancy

---

Investigations

- **CT scan**: helps to assess relation of tumours to anatomical structures (e.g. facial)
- **FNA**: a controversial issue, current guidelines recommend FNA at the first presentation and examination of the aspirate by an experienced cytopathologist

Management of salivary gland tumours

The aim is to resect the tumour with a margin of macroscopically normal tissue with preservation of the facial nerve. This is known as a **formal conservative parotidectomy**. If the patient has a pre-operative facial nerve palsy, then total parotidectomy is undertaken.

Primary grafting of the facial nerve is considered, but frozen section of the facial nerve must be undertaken to ensure clear resection margins of the nerve.

Post-operative radiotherapy is indicated in certain cases:

- Incomplete removal of pleomorphic adenoma or rupture at the time of removal
- If there is any doubt regarding resection margins
- If there is evidence of extracapsular spread
- High grade tumours with high risk of locul recurrence
- Recurrent disease

T_1 and T_2 tumours and pleomorphic adenomas removed with clear resection margins do not require post-operative radiotherapy.

Complications of superficial parotidectomy

- Post-operative haemorrhage
- Sensory loss
- Salivary fistula

- Facial nerve palsy
- Frey's syndrome — gustatory sweating

6.3 Non-neoplastic salivary gland disease

Infectious

Acute sialoadenitis
Viral
- Mumps: this infection by paramyxovirus usually affects children aged 4–10 years; it is characterized by bilateral parotid swelling, malaise and trismus; it can also lead to orchitis, pancreatitis, nephritis, encephalitis, cochleitis and meningitis; usually self-limiting

- Coxsackie
- HIV
- Echovirus

Bacterial
Usually staphylococcal infection leading to pain, tenderness and discharge from the duct. It is most commonly seen in the dehydrated and immunocompromised. Treatment consists of systemic antibiotics and rehydration.

Chronic recurrent sialoadenitis
Recurrent slightly painful enlargement of the gland. It is due to decreased salivary flow homeostasis. Treatment consists of sialogogues, massage and hydration or sialoadenectomy in refractory cases.

Granulomatous sialoadenitis

- Sarcoidosis
- TB
- Syphilis
- HIV

Non-infectious

Sialolithiasis

- Stones in the salivary glands lead to pain and swelling, worse at mealtimes
- Most commonly seen in middle-aged men
- 80% of stones affect the submandibular gland; 65% of submandibular gland stones are radio-opaque, whereas 65% of parotid stones are radiolucent
- Stones can be removed trans-orally
- Sometimes submandibular gland resection must be undertaken

Inflammatory conditions
Sjögren's syndrome is an autoimmune disease defined by periductal lymphocytes in multiple organs. Classified into:

- **Primary Sjögren's syndrome** (sicca complex): identified by xerostomia, xerophthalmia and no connective tissue abnormality
- **Secondary Sjögren's syndrome**: comprises xerostomia, xerophthalmia and a connective tissue disorder, most commonly rheumatoid arthritis.

40% of patients have salivary gland involvement and 1 in 6 patients will develop lymphoma.

Benign lymphoepithelial lesion: a mass of lymphoid tissue within a salivary gland containing scattered foci of epithelial cells of ductal origin. It is associated with HIV infection. The incidence of lymphoma from this condition is 10%.

Pseudoparotomegaly

The following may be confused with sialo-megaly:

- Winged mandible
- Mandibular tumours
- Dental cysts
- Branchial cyst
- Hypertrophic masseter
- Neuroma of the facial nerve
- Preauricular lymph node
- Lipoma
- Sebaceous cyst

Drug-induced sialo-megaly

- OCP
- Thiouracil
- Co-proxamol
- Isoprenaline
- Phenylbutazone

Metabolic causes for sialo-megaly

- Diabetes
- Myxoedema
- Cushing's disease
- Cirrhosis
- Gout
- Alcoholism
- Bulimia

Sialectasis

A disease of unknown origin recognized by progressive destruction of the alveoli and parenchyma of the gland, with duct stenosis and cyst formation. Calculi may be found in the main ducts and patients often give a history of swelling exacerbated by eating.

Clinical features: all the major salivary glands must be examined bimanually. Facial nerve palsy can be an indication of malignancy. Examination of the pharynx may show a lesion in the deep lobe of the parotid pushing the tonsil medially. In addition, a full ENT and general examination must be performed.

Investigations

- ESR
- FBC
- Rheumatoid factor
- Antinuclear factor   } Sjögren's syndrome
- Electrophoresis
- SSRO and SLA antibodies
- TFTs
- Blood glucose
- RLFTs
- Urate
- Plain film — submandibular calculus (NB. Most parotid calculi are radiolucent)
- Sialogram — duct stenosis, calculi, sialectasis
- CT/MRI — if neoplastic disease is suspected

Biopsy

- Incisional or Trucut biopsy should not be performed due to the risk of seeding of tumours
- FNA may be useful
- Sublabial biopsy is the investigation of choice in patients with suspected Sjögren's syndrome

7. THE EYE

7.1 Anatomy of the orbit

This is a pyramidal cavity, which has its apex posteriorly and base anteriorly.

It has bony walls which consist of:

- **Roof**: frontal air sinuses and the frontal bone
- **Lateral**: zygoma and the greater wing of sphenoid bone
- **Floor**: maxilla and the greater wing of sphenoid
- **Medial**: maxilla, lacrimal, ethmoid, sphenoid bones

The orbit has the following relations:

- **Superiorly**: anterior cranial fossa
- **Medial**: ethmoidal air cells, nasal cavity
- **Lateral**: temporal fossa, lateral surface of the face
- **Inferior**: maxillary air sinus

Contents of the orbit

- Eyeball
- Cranial nerves II, III, IV, V, VI
- Lymphatics
- Extra-ocular muscles
- Blood vessels
- Fat

Extra-ocular muscles

- **Muscle**
  Lateral rectus
  Superior oblique
  Medial rectus
  Inferior rectus
  Superior rectus
  Inferior oblique

- **Nerve supply**
  Abducens nerve (VI)
  Trochlear nerve (IV)

  Oculomotor nerve (III)

(The oculomotor nerve also supplies levator palpebrae superioris)

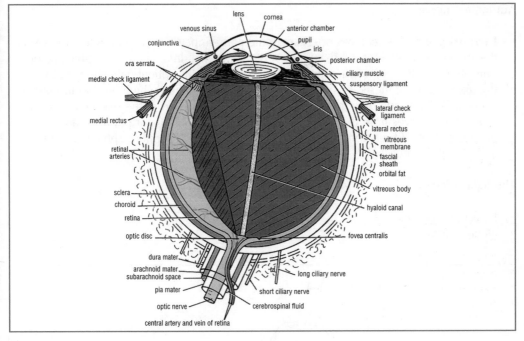

The eye

The eyeball has an incomplete fascial covering, the **fascia bulbi**, which facilitates movements of the eyeball. Within each eyelid, the **orbital septum** is thickened to form a **tarsal plate**, which is perforated by the **palpebral fissure**. The **lacrimal gland** is located at the superolateral angle of the orbit, its duct draining into the **conjunctival sac**. The **nasolacrimal canal** drains the **lacrimal punctum**, at the medial end of the lower lid, into the inferior meatus of the nose.

Nerve supply

Optic nerve
This enters the orbit through the optic canal with CSF, meninges and ophthalmic artery. It conveys visual sensation.

Nerves passing through the superior orbital fissure

* Trochlear nerve
* Abducens nerve
* Lacrimal ⎫ branches of the ophthalmic
* Frontal ⎬ division of the trigeminal
* Nasociliary ⎭ nerve (Va)
* Oculomotor nerve — superior division/inferior division

Autonomic nerves

- **Lacrimal gland**: this receives post-ganglionic parasympathetic secretomotor fibres from the zygomatic branch of the maxillary nerve via the lacrimal nerve. The preganglionic fibres travel in the nervus intermedius and synapse in the sphenopalatine ganglion.
- **Pupillary muscles**: these are supplied by the ciliary ganglion which lies behind the eyeball, lateral to the optic nerve. Receives sensory fibres from the nasociliary nerve, sympathetic nerves from the carotid plexus (which supply dilator pupillae) and parasympathetic fibres from the oculomotor nerve (which supplies sphincter pupillae and the ciliary muscles).

The light reflexes

- Direct and consensual
- Neural pathway

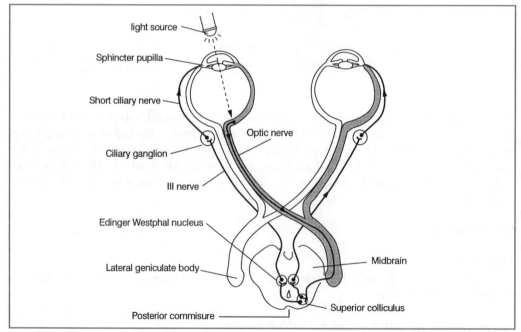

Light reflexes

Some fibres from the optic tract reach the pretectal nucleus in the mid-brain. These synapse with cell bodies in the Edinger–Westphal nuclei on both sides. These cell bodies then synapse in the ciliary ganglion and post-ganglionic fibres pass in the short ciliary nerves to the sphincter pupillae.

Sympathetic pupillary dilatation

Sympathetic innervation of the eye descends from the hypothalamus through the spinal cord via anterior roots of C8 and T1 to the superior cervical ganglion. Post-ganglionic fibres ascend on the wall of the internal carotid artery to the ciliary ganglion and thence to the eye and cranial nerves III, IV, V and VI.

Interruption of the sympathetic supply (e.g. by a supraclavicular extension of a bronchial carcinoma in Horner's syndrome) affects:

- Pupillary dilatation (dilated pupil)
- Levator palpebrae muscle (ptosis)
- Vasoconstrictor fibres to orbit, eye and face

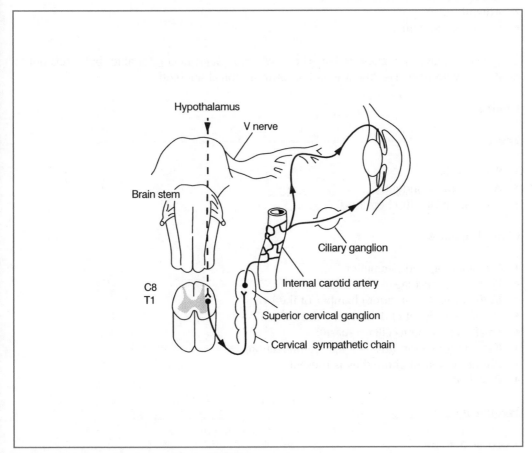

Pathway of sympathetic pupillary dilatation

7.2 Corneal infections

These can be subdivided into:

- **Viral**: the most common is *Herpes simplex* keratitis which is treated with topical aciclovir; it can result in corneal opacity
- **Fungal**: *Candida albicans*, this is treated topically with antifungals
- **Bacterial**: the most common are staphylococcal and pneumococcal; these are treated with topical antibiotics

Conjunctivitis

- **Bacterial**: streptococci and pneumococci are the most common affecting organisms
- **Viral**: most commonly adenovirus
- Allergic
- Secondary to toxins

Conjunctivitis gives a watery, inflamed eye which is often uncomfortable, but tends not to produce severe pain. Treatment is in the form of topical antibiotics.

Uveitis

Causes

- Sarcoidosis
- Ankylosing spondylitis
- Toxoplasmosis (in choroiditis)

Clinical features

- Circumcorneal inflammation
- Posterior synechiae
- Cells within the anterior chamber of the eye
- White cells (keratic) deposits on the cornea
- Small pupil (due to ciliary spasm)
- Cataract formation (this is a late complication)
- Blurred vision (if choroiditis is present)
- PAINFUL

Treatment

- Local steroids
- Mydriatic drops
- β-blockers if intra-ocular pressure is raised
- In choroiditis: antibiotics — systemic steroids

7.3 Acute glaucoma

Clinical features

- Painful red eye
- Visual loss
- Severe pain
- Corneal oedema

Symptoms occur with sudden onset.

Treatment

- Pilocarpine drops (to produce miosis)
- Acetazolamide (to reduce intra-ocular oedema)
- Iridectomy

7.4 Foreign bodies in the eye

These can be divided into those on the surface and those which are intra-ocular:

- **Foreign bodies** on the surface of the eye can be removed with local anaesthetics
- **Intra-ocular foreign bodies** can be diagnosed on X-ray, ultrasound or CT

If foreign bodies are iron or copper, they may pose a potential hazard to vision. They can be removed by microsurgical methods. Some foreign bodies can be left *in situ*.

8. THE FACIAL NERVE

8.1 Anatomy

- **Origin**: junction of the pons and medulla
- **Components**: motor root, special sensory — taste, parasympathetic, somatic sensory

During its course, the facial nerve traverses the following:

- Posterior cranial fossa
- Internal acoustic meatus
- Facial canal in the temporal bone
- Stylomastoid foramen
- Parotid gland

ANATOMY OF THE FACIAL NERVE

Branches	Type of nerve	Structure supplied
Posterior auricular Temporal Zygomatic Buccal Mandibular Cervical } Motor		Muscles of facial expression Occipitalis Auricular muscles Posterior belly of digastric Stylohyoid Stapedius
Greater petrosal nerve	Parasympathetic secretomotor	Lacrimal gland (the nerve synapses in the pterygopalatine ganglion)
Chorda tympani	Parasympathetic secretomotor	Submandibular and sublingual glands (synapses in the submandibular ganglion)
	Taste (chorda tympani joins the lingual nerve to supply the tongue)	Anterior two-thirds of tongue
Fibres from the geniculate ganglion*	Somatic sensory	Area of skin around the external acoustic meatus

*The sensory ganglion of the facial nerve is known as the geniculate ganglion and is located at the medial wall of the middle ear.

8.2 Corneal reflex

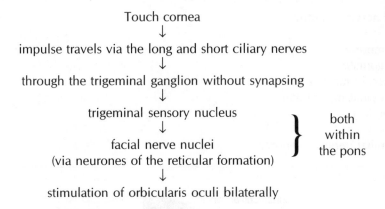

Touch cornea
↓
impulse travels via the long and short ciliary nerves
↓
through the trigeminal ganglion without synapsing
↓
trigeminal sensory nucleus ⎫ both
↓ ⎬ within
facial nerve nuclei ⎭ the pons
(via neurones of the reticular formation)
↓
stimulation of orbicularis oculi bilaterally

8.3 Muscles of facial expression

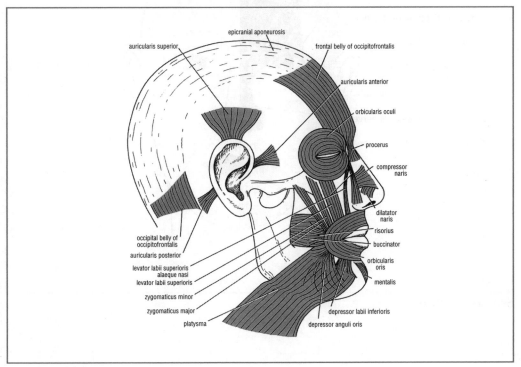

Muscles of facia

The muscles are derived from the mesoderm of the second pharyngeal arch and are members of the panniculus carnosus.

Nerve supply

Facial nerve — motor

- Temporal
- Zygomatic
- Buccal branches
- Marginal mandibular
- Cervical

Trigeminal nerve — sensory

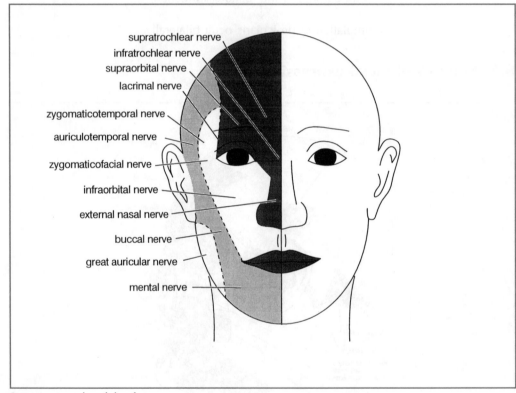

Sensory supply of the face

Divisions of the trigeminal nerve

- **Ophthalmic**
  Lacrimal
  Supra-orbital
  Supratrochlear
  Infratrochlear
  External nasal

- **Maxillary**
  Zygomaticotemporal
  Zygomaticofacial
  Infra-orbital

- **Mandibular**
  Auriculotemporal
  Buccal
  Mental

8.4 Facial nerve palsy

Upper motor neurone lesions: forehead tends to be spared

Causes of facial nerve palsy

- **Intracranial**
  Brainstem lesions
  Tumours
  CVA
  MS
  Acoustic neuroma
  Cholesteatoma
  Meningitis

- **Bell's palsy**
  (Approximately 40%)
  A spontaneous idiopathic facial
    nerve palsy, often following a viral
    illness and usually self-limiting

- **Intratemporal**
  Otitis media
  Ramsay Hunt syndrome
    (*Herpes zoster* oticus)
  Trauma (temporal bone fracture)
  Iatrogenic

- **Infratemporal**
  Parotid tumours
  Trauma
  Surgery

Management

- Eye: protection of eye (lubricating drops, tarsorrhaphy if prolonged)
- Surgery
- Bell's palsy: steroids
- Ramsay Hunt: aciclovir

9. THE NECK

9.1 Anatomy

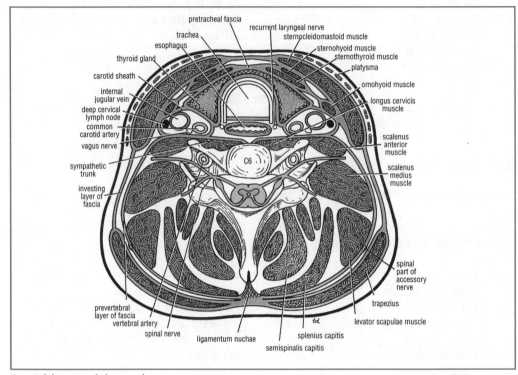

Fascial layers of the neck

Fascial layers

Investing
This extends from the base of the skull and lower border of the mandible to the spine of the scapula, lateral part of the clavicle and sternum. It splits into two layers to form the parotid fascia and also forms the stylomandibular ligament.

Prevertebral
This lies in front of the prevertebral muscles and covers the muscles forming the floor of the posterior triangle. The accessory nerve lies superficial to this fascia.

Pretracheal
This splits to enclose the thyroid gland and provides a slippery surface for the trachea to move during swallowing. It blends with the carotid sheath laterally.

Carotid sheath
Surrounds the internal jugular vein, common carotid artery and the vagus nerve. Loose areolar tissue which allows expansion of the internal jugular vein.

The posterior triangle of the neck

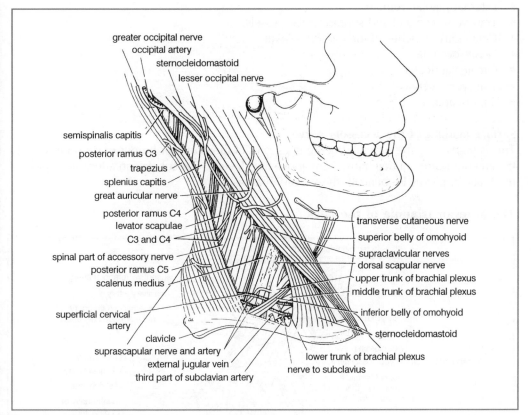

Posterior triangle of the neck

Boundaries

- **Anterior**: sternocleidomastoid
- **Posterior**: trapezius
- **Base**: middle third of clavicle
- **Roof**: investing fascia
- **Floor**: prevertebral fascia overlying prevertebral muscles (splenius capitis, levator scapulae, scalenus anterior, middle and posterior)

Contents

- Accessory nerve
- Lymph nodes (see figure on p. 242)
- Occipital artery
- Inferior belly of omohyoid
- External jugular vein
- Transverse cervical and suprascapular vessels
- Cutaneous branches of the cervical plexus
- Lesser occipital
- Greater auricular
- Transverse cervical
- Suprascapular

Surface marking of the accessory nerve
This is marked by the line joining the mid-point of the posterior border of sternomastoid to the anterior border of trapezius, 5 cm above the clavicle. The subclavian artery and trunks of the brachial plexus lie beneath the prevertebral fascia.

The anterior triangle of the neck

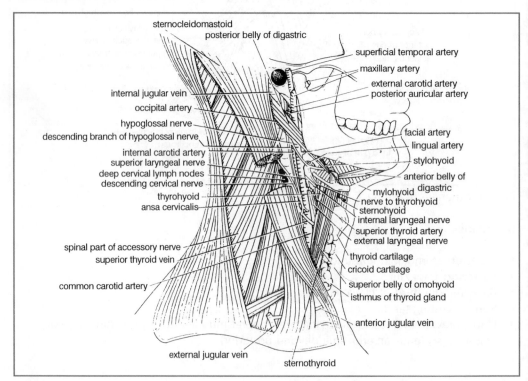

Anterior triangle of the neck

Boundaries

- **Medial**: the mid-line
- **Lateral**: anterior border of sternocleidomastoid
- **Superior**: lower border of the mandible
- **Roof**: investing fascia
- **Floor**: prevertebral fascia

Suprahyoid muscles

- Digastric
- Stylohyoid
- Geniohyoid
- Mylohyoid

Infrahyoid (strap) muscles

- Sternohyoid
- Omohyoid
- Thyrohyoid
- Sternothyroid

Contents of the anterior triangle of the neck

- **Submental triangle**
  Submental lymph nodes
  Anterior jugular vein

- **Carotid triangle**
  (NB. All are contents of the carotid sheath)
  Common carotid artery
  Internal carotid artery
  External carotid artery and its branches
  Internal jugular vein and its tributaries
  Hypoglossal nerve and its descending branch
  Internal and external laryngeal nerves
  Deep cervical lymph nodes
  Accessory nerve
  Vagus nerve

- **Digastric (submandibular triangle)**
  Submandibular salivary gland
  Facial artery
  Facial vein
  Submandibular lymph nodes
  Hypoglossal nerve
  Hypoglossus muscle
  Nerve and vessels to mylohyoid
  Carotid sheath (see Carotid triangle)
  Stylopharyngeus
  Glossopharyngeal nerve
  Parotid gland

- **Muscular triangle**
  Sternohyoid muscle
  Sternothyroid muscle
  Structures underlying these muscles:
  thyroid gland, larynx, trachea, oesophagus

9.2 Embryology

The pharyngeal arches

These occur in the fourth and fifth weeks of gestation, they contribute to the development of the neck and face. The pharyngeal arches consist of mesoderm, endoderm and ectoderm and each has its own arterial and nerve supply.

First pharyngeal arch

- **Nerve supply**: mandibular branch of the trigeminal nerve
- **Derivatives**: incus, malleus, maxilla, zygoma, part of the temporal bone, mandible
- **Muscles**: temporalis, masseter, pterygoideus, anterior belly of digastric, tensor palati and tympani, mylohyoid

Second pharyngeal arch

- **Nerve supply**: facial nerve
- **Derivatives**: stapes, styloid process, lesser horn and upper half of the body of the hyoid, stylohyoid ligament
- **Muscles**: muscles of facial expression, posterior belly of digastric, stapedius, stylohyoid

Third pharyngeal arch

- **Nerve supply**: glossopharyngeal nerve
- **Derivatives**: greater horn and lower part of the body of the hyoid, stylopharyngeus

Fourth and sixth pharyngeal arches

- **Nerve supply**: fourth — superior laryngeal branch of vagus; sixth — recurrent laryngeal nerve to vagus
- **Derivatives**: cartilage of the larynx, cricothyroid, constrictors of the pharynx, levator palatini, intrinsic muscles of the larynx

The pharyngeal pouches

These are outpouchings along the lateral pharyngeal wall; there are five pairs. The endoderm lining these pouches give rise to the following:

Pharyngeal pouches

- **First pharyngeal pouch**
  Middle ear cavity
  Pharyngotympanic (Eustachian) tube

- **Second pharyngeal pouch**
  Palatine tonsils

- **Third pharyngeal pouch**
  Inferior parathyroid gland
  Thymus

- **Fourth pharyngeal pouch**
  Superior parathyroid gland

- **Fifth pharyngeal pouch**
  Parafollicular (C) cells

9.3 Lumps in the neck

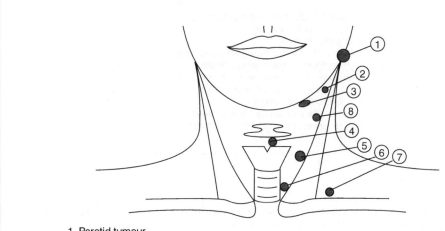

1. Parotid tumour

2. Tonsillar node

3. Swollen submandibular gland

4. Thyroglossal cyst

5. Branchial cyst

6. Thyroid nodule

7. Virchow's node

8. Carotid body tumour

Differential diagnosis of a lump in the neck

Cervical lymph nodes

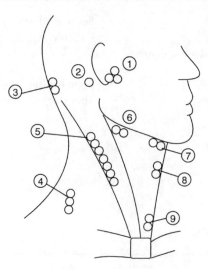

1. Parotid (scalp, face, parotid gland)
2. Mastoid (scalp, auricle)
3. Occipital (scalp)
4. Superficial cervical (along external Jugular vein)
   (breast, lung, viscera, face, parotid)
5. Deep cervical (along internal Jugular vein)
   (all neck nodes ultimately drain to here)
6. Submandibular (tongue)
7. Submental (antrum and floor of mouth, lips)
8. Anterior cervical (oesophagus, front of neck)
9. Tracheal (thyroid)

Lymph nodes of the head and neck

Deep cervical nodes

These are found around the internal jugular vein and include the jugulodigastric node and the jugulo-omohyoid node. They drain the superficial cervical nodes.

Superficial cervical nodes

(See diagram above.)

10. THE THYROID

10.1 Anatomy

The thyroid gland is surrounded by its own capsule and pretracheal fascia. Each lobe has three surfaces: lateral, medial and posterior.

Relations

Lateral surface

* Sternothyroid
* Sternocleidomastoid
* Sternohyoid

Medial surface

* External laryngeal nerve
* Recurrent laryngeal nerve
* Larynx
* Pharynx
* Oesophagus
* Trachea

Posterior surface

* Parathyroid glands
* Carotid sheath and content
* Inferior thyroid artery
* Thoracic duct (on the left)

Relations of isthmus

* Anastomosis between superior thyroid arteries
* Tributaries of the inferior thyroid veins
* Pyramidal lobe (remnant of the thyroglossal duct)

Relations of recurrent laryngeal nerves
These are both given off by the vagi, but the left nerve hooks around the arch of the aorta whilst the right passes beneath the subclavian artery. They ascend between the trachea and oesophagus and pass behind the pretracheal fascia to lie next to medial surface of the lobes. They then pass under inferior constrictor.

Blood supply

- **Superior thyroid artery** (branch of the external carotid artery)
- **Inferior thyroid artery** (branch of thyrocervical trunk of the subclavian artery)
- **Thyroidea ima artery** (present in 3%, branch from brachiocephalic artery, right common carotid or arch of the aorta)

Venous drainage

Superior thyroid vein (drains into the internal jugular or facial vein). **Middle thyroid vein** (drains into the internal jugular vein). **Inferior thyroid vein** (form a plexus inside the thyroid capsule which drains into the brachiocephalic veins).

Lymphatic drainage

- **Upper pole**: anterior–superior group of the deep cervical nodes
- **Lower pole**: posterior–inferior group of the deep cervical nodes

Nerve supply

- **Sympathetic**: vasoconstrictor from the middle cervical ganglion
- **Parasympathetic**: via vagus, of unknown function

Development of the thyroid gland

The thyroid gland first appears at the site of the foramen caecum in the floor of the pharynx and descends to reach its final position by the seventh week of gestation. It remains connected to the tongue by the thyroglossal duct and so thyroglossal cysts can be found along this path of descent. They are cystic remnants of the thyroglossal duct. Accessory thyroid tissue can be found in the tongue, near the hyoid bone, deep to sternocleidomastoid and in the superior mediastinum.

10.2 Physiology

The thyroid gland is an endocrine gland which produces:

- Thyroxine
- Tri-iodothyronine (T3)
- Calcitonin

T3 and thyroxine are synthesized in the colloid of the thyroid gland by the iodination of tyrosine molecules bound to thyroglobulin. Iodide (I^-) is absorbed from plasma and converted to iodine (I_2) by thyroid peroxidase in the follicular cells.

Most thyroxine and T3 circulate in plasma bound to proteins, including thyroxine binding globulin (TBG), thyroxine binding pre-albumin (TBPA) and albumin. T3 is more potent than thyroxine and so thyroxine is converted to tri-iodothyronine by de-iodination.

The thyroid hormones act by entering the cell and attaching to nuclear receptors. These bind to DNA which leads to increased production of mRNA and increased expression of certain genes.

Control of thyroid function

Via a negative feedback mechanism, with increased levels of thyroxine and T3 detected by the hypothalamus and anterior pituitary. The hypothalamus releases thyroid releasing hormone (TRH) which travels through the portal system of blood vessels to reach the anterior pituitary. Thyroid stimulating hormone (TSH), a glycoprotein, travels in the bloodstream to act on the thyroid gland.

TSH acts by binding to receptors on the cell membrane which causes increased c-AMP production within the cell.

Actions of thyroid hormones

Thyroid hormones stimulate oxygen consumption in most of the body's cells and increase the sensitivity of β-receptors to catecholamines. Their actions include:

- Increased protein catabolism
- Increased fat mobilization and degradation
- Increased gluconeogenesis, glycogenolysis and glucose absorption from the gut
- Normal development of the central nervous system
- Regulation of gut motility and hair and skin development

From the above, the features of cretinism, myxoedema and hyperthyroidism can be explained.

10.3 Hyperthyroidism (thyrotoxicosis)

Causes of hyperthyroidism

- Graves' disease
- Solitary toxic nodule
- Toxic multinodular goitre
- Overdose of thyroxine
- Thyroid carcinoma
- Iodine therapy
- Hyperfunctioning ovarian teratoma

Clinical features of hyperthyroidism

- Heat intolerance
- Low blood cholesterol
- Anxiety and irritability
- Diarrhoea

- Muscle wasting and weight loss
- Tremor
- Tachycardia and arrhythmias
- Menstrual irregularities

Treatment of hyperthyroidism

- Medical (e.g. carbimazole)
- Radioactive iodine
- Surgery

10.4 Hypothyroidism

Causes of hypothyroidism

- Autoimmune thyroiditis (Hashimoto's, atrophic thyroiditis)
- Iodine deficiency
- Post-irradiation
- Tumour infiltration
- Anti-thyroid drugs
- Hypopituitarism

Clinical features of myxoedema

- Cold intolerance
- Increased blood cholesterol
- Sluggish mental ability
- Menstrual irregularities

- Weight increase
- Tiredness
- Bradycardia
- Cretinism, if occurring perinatally: mental retardation, slow growth velocity, arrest of puberty, short stature

Treatment of hypothyroidism

- Thyroxine

10.5 The thyroid swelling

Causes of a thyroid swelling

- **Solitary nodule**
  Multinodular goitre
  Adenoma
  Carcinoma
  Haemorrhage into a cyst

- **Diffuse swelling**
  Multinodular goitre
  Hashimoto's thyroiditis
  Graves' disease
  Carcinoma

Investigation of thyroid swellings

- Thyroid function tests (T3, T4 and TSH)
- TRH test
- Ultrasound
- FNA
- Thyroid auto-antibodies (e.g. in Hashimoto's disease)

10.6 Thyroid tumours

Benign tumours

Adenomas
Common and often multiple. Can be solid or filled with colloid and can produce hyperthyroidism.

Malignant tumours

(0.5% of cancer deaths.)

Papillary adenocarcinoma (70% of thyroid tumours)
The most common malignant thyroid cancer, seen in younger patients with a history of irradiation to the neck. Multifocal disease can be seen and frequently spreads to cervical lymph nodes. Histological appearance includes the presence of 'Orphan Annie' nuclei, pale empty-looking nuclei. Most tumours are TSH-dependent. The treatment of papillary carcinoma is controversial. Treatment can consist of total thyroidectomy with thyroxine (to prevent TSH excretion) or unilateral lobectomy with thyroxine. Ten-year survival is 90%.

Follicular carcinoma (20% of thyroid tumours)
A unifocal tumour of the thyroid, composed of malignant glandular tissue. Can spread via the bloodstream in addition to lymph nodes. Treated by total thyroidectomy, 85% ten-year survival.

Anaplastic carcinoma (<5% of thyroid tumours)
Seen in older patients and have the worst prognosis. They metastasize to lymph nodes rapidly and also spread directly to adjacent tissues. Treatment consists of debulking surgery and external beam radiotherapy. Five-year survival is very poor.

Medullary carcinoma (5% of thyroid tumours)
A tumour of C cells (calcitonin-secreting cells). A familial tendency therefore screen for multiple endocrine neoplasia (MEN) syndromes. These tumours can be multifocal and spread via blood and to lymph nodes. The treatment consists of total thyroidectomy.

10.7 Thyroidectomy

Indications for thyroid surgery

- Overactivity, where other treatments have failed
- Cosmesis
- Compression symptoms
- Carcinoma

Pre-operative preparation

Pre-operative preparation of hyperthyroid patients is imperative because operating on toxic patients precipitate a thyroid crisis. Includes administration of carbimazole and β-blockers. Patients must also have vocal cord examination pre-operatively.

Procedure

Patient is placed supine, with neck extended using a head ring. The skin, subcutaneous fat and platysma are incised horizontally, whilst investing fascia and connective tissue between the strap muscles is incised vertically. Strap muscles may be divided if necessary. Thyroid lobe is mobilized. The superior thyroid artery is tied off close to the gland to avoid the external laryngeal nerve. The inferior artery is tied off laterally far from the gland to avoid the recurrent laryngeal nerve which crosses it. Some tie the inferior thyroid artery in continuity to avoid transecting the laryngeal nerve.

In a subtotal thyroidectomy it is acceptable to leave a sliver of gland laterally in front of the parathyroids and recurrent laryngeal nerve.

In a total thyroidectomy or lobectomy the thyroid must be dissected free from these structures. The isthmus is dissected with care avoiding damage to the trachea and oversewn in a lobectomy. Closure is in layers with a drain and clips to skin.

Possible complications of thyroidectomy

- Post-operative bleeding
- Superior laryngeal nerve damage
- Recurrent laryngeal nerve damage
- Temporary and permanent hypocalcaemia

11. THE PARATHYROIDS

11.1 Anatomy

Usually four in number and can be located inside or outside of the pretracheal fascia. The superior glands lie at the level of the first tracheal ring whilst the inferior glands lie closely applied to the inferior pole of the thyroid below the inferior thyroid artery. However, the position of the lower parathyroids can be much lower, for example in the superior mediastinum. They are supplied by the inferior thyroid artery and are approached operatively as for the thyroid gland.

11.2 Physiology

Calcium homeostasis

The normal serum calcium level is 2.2–2.6 mmol/l. Only 1% of the total body calcium is not contained in bone. The serum calcium level assay can be altered by a patient's albumin level, due to 40% of calcium in the blood being transported bound to albumin.

The functions of calcium include:

- Blood clotting
- Muscle contraction
- Nervous impulse conduction
- Cofactor in many enzyme reactions
- Constituent of bone and teeth
- Maintaining normal permeability of cell membrane
- Maintaining excitability of nerve and muscle

The hormones involved in the balance of calcium within the body are:

- Parathyroid hormone (PTH)
- Vitamin D
- Calcitonin

Actions of parathyroid hormone

• Increases resorption of calcium from bone
• Decreases excretion of calcium in the urine by the kidney
• Increases phosphate excretion in the urine

Actions of calcitonin

• Reduces calcium resorption from bone
• Reduces calcium resorption from the gut

Vitamin D and its derivatives

Vitamin D3 (cholecalciferol) is derived from the diet and UV light falling on skin. In the liver it is converted to 25-hydroxy-cholecalciferol. On arrival in the kidney it is converted to 1,25-dihydroxycholecalciferol. The actions of this are:

• Increased calcium absorption from the gut
• Decreased excretion by the kidney
• Inhibits parathyroid hormone gene transcription

11.3 Hyperparathyroidism

The incidence of asymptomatic mild hypercalcaemia is 1:1000 and is usually due to primary hyperparathyroidism. It is often found on routine blood testing.

Classification of hyperparathyroidism

• **Primary**: usually due to single or multiple parathyroid adenomas or rarely carcinoma or primary parathyroid hyperplasia
• **Secondary**: this is in response to a low serum calcium (e.g. renal failure) therefore, serum PTH levels are raised whilst serum calcium is low or normal
• **Tertiary**: occurs after long-standing secondary hyperparathyroidism; the parathyroids become hyperplastic after long-term stimulation; it is most often seen in chronic renal failure; both PTH and serum calcium levels are raised

Other causes of hypercalcaemia

It must be remembered that 80% of patients with hypercalcaemia have hyperparathyroidism or malignancy. It can also be caused by the following:

- Excess vitamin D action
  (e.g. sarcoidosis)
- Addison's disease
- Long-term immobility
- Paget's disease
- Tuberculosis

- Milk-alkali syndrome
- Multiple myeloma
- Thiazide diuretics
- Familial hypocalciuric
  hypercalcaemia

Clinical features

'Stones, bones and psychic moans'

- Renal stones
- Bone pain, osteoclastomas, pepper pot skull and phalangeal subperiosteal erosions
- Depression and general malaise
- Abdominal pain, peptic ulcer disease, acute pancreatitis and constipation
- Hypertension
- Hypercalcaemic crisis

Treatment

Symptomatic patients and those with renal or bone involvement warrant parathyroidectomy.

11.4 Hypoparathyroidism

In surgical practice hypoparathyroidism and hypocalcaemia are most often seen post-operatively (e.g. after thyroidectomy, parathyroidectomy or radical neck surgery). However, other causes include:

- Acute pancreatitis
- Chronic renal failure
- Massive transfusion
- Vitamin D deficiency

Clinical features

- Paraesthesia
- Cramps

- Tetany
- Circumoral numbness
- Chvosteck's sign: twitching of facial muscles when tapping the facial nerve
- Trousseau's sign: spasm of fingers and wrist when sphygmomanometer cuff is tightened around the arm for three minutes
- Dystonia
- Psychosis
- Convulsions

Treatment of hypocalcaemia

- 10 ml IV calcium gluconate over 5 minutes
- 40 ml IV calcium gluconate over 24 hours
- Vitamin D derivatives
- Oral calcium preparations
- Monitor serum calcium levels closely

11.5 Parathyroidectomy

Among patients with primary hyperparathyroidism, 80% have a single adenoma, 10–15% have hyperplasia and 2% have two adenomas. Therefore, it is reasonable to explore both sides of the neck and visualize all four parathyroids. However, parathyroid glands may be located at the level of the hyoid bone, in the mediastinum, inside the thyroid gland, in the carotid sheath, in the retro-oesophageal space or re-tracheal space. Pre-operative investigations to localize the glands can include ultrasound or thallium technetium or iodine isotope scans.

The principles of the parathyroidectomy operation are:

- All possible sites are explored
- Any possible parathyroid adenoma is completely removed and sent for frozen section
- At least one normal parathyroid is biopsied
- Multiple adenomas are looked for carefully
- Accurate chart of findings and biopsy sites
- If hyperplasia is found, three and a half glands are removed and the remnant marked with a suture or implanted into brachioradialis muscle

Operative procedure

- GA, neck extended, head draped
- Transverse incision 2 cm above sternal notch
- Lift flaps of skin and platysma
- Divide pretracheal fascia and retract strap muscles
- Expose thyroid lobe and identify recurrent laryngeal nerve and inferior thyroid artery
- Identify parathyroids and proceed as outlined above
- Haemostasis, drain and close skin with clips

Operative hazards

- Inability to find all glands
- Bleeding
- Damage to recurrent laryngeal nerve

Post-operative complications

- Hypocalcaemia
- Hypercalcaemia (in unsuccessful operation)
- Bleeding which may necessitate urgent removal of clips or re-operation to avoid airway obstruction

12. THE ADRENALS

12.1 Anatomy

Each gland lies on top of the kidney. They are enclosed within the renal fascia but separate from the kidney. The left adrenal gland lies more medially than the right.

Adrenal glands — relations

- **Left**
  Anteriorly
    Splenic artery
    Body of the pancreas
    Peritoneum of the lesser sac
  Posteriorly
    Left crus of diaphragm
    Left inferior phrenic artery
  Medially
    Coeliac ganglion
    Left gastric vessels
  Laterally
    Left kidney

- **Right**
  Anteriorly
    Right lobe of the liver
    IVC
  Posteriorly
    Right crus of the diaphragm
  Medially
    Right inferior phrenic vessels
  Superiorly
    Bare area of liver
  Inferiorly
    Right kidney

Blood supply

Arterial supply

- Inferior phrenic vessels
- Branches from the aorta
- Branches from the renal artery

Venous return

- Right adrenal vein drains into the IVC
- Left adrenal vein drains into the left renal vein

Structure

Cortex

- Zona glomerulosa secretes aldosterone
- Zona fasciculata secretes cortisol
- Zona reticularis secretes sex hormones

Medulla
This secretes catecholamines and dopamine.

12.2 Physiology

PHYSIOLOGY OF THE ADRENAL GLANDS

	Produces	Example
Adrenal cortex		
Zona glomerulosa (outer zone)	Mineralocorticoids	Aldosterone
Zona fasciculata (middle zone)	Glucocorticoids	Cortisol
	Androgens	Testosterone
Zona reticularis (inner zone)	Oestrogens	Oestradiol
		Progesterone
Adrenal medulla	Adrenaline (80%)	
	Noradrenaline (20%)	

The products of the adrenal cortex are derived from cholesterol. Synthesis is limited by the conversion of cholesterol to pregnenolone which occurs in the mitochondria (see figure opposite).

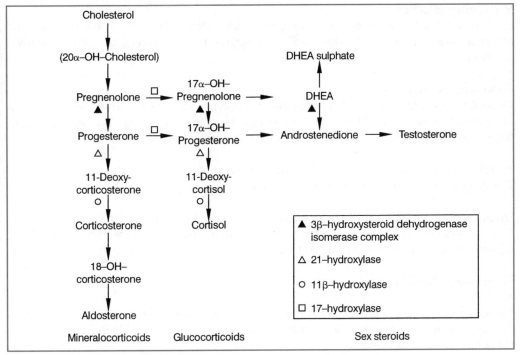

Synthesis of cortisol, testosterone and aldosterone from cholesterol

Glucocorticoids (cortisol, cortisone)

Actions of glucocorticoids

- Glycogenolysis
- Gluconeogenesis
- Protein catabolism
- Lipolysis
- Anti-inflammatory
- Mineralocorticoid actions: ↓ lymphocytes, ↑ neutrophils, ↓ bone marrow, ↑ calcium excretion, ↑ acid/pepsin secretions in stomach

Transport of glucocorticoids
75% of cortisol in plasma is bound to cortisol-binding globulin, 15% to albumin and 10% unbound and active.

Mechanism of action

Cortisol acts via hormone receptor complex in the cytosol. The steroid binds to specific receptor inside target cells. The complex migrates to the nucleus to increase mRNA synthesis.

Control of secretion

Cortisol is controlled via ACTH, a 39 amino acid polypeptide secreted from the basophils of the anterior pituitary. ACTH in turn is controlled by cortisol-releasing hormone CRH from the hypothalamus which is under negative feedback from cortisol.

ACTH acts via cyclic AMP to: - cortisol formation and secretion, and ↑ adrenal blood flow. There is a circadian rhythm to cortisol secretion.

Stimuli for release of cortisol include: stress (e.g. shock), ↓ sugar, exercise, fever. Excess cortisol production is known as Cushing's syndrome (see Section 12.3 page 258). Deficiency of cortisol secretion is known as Addison's disease (see Section 12.4 page 260).

Mineralocorticoids

Aldosterone is a mineralocorticoid from the zona glomerulosa which promotes the absorption of sodium chloride and water and the excretion of potassium and hydrogen ions in the collecting ducts of the kidneys.

Control of secretion

- Changes in the extracellular volume via the renin angiotensin system
- ACTH has a negligible role
- Increased plasma K^+
- Decreased plasma Na^+

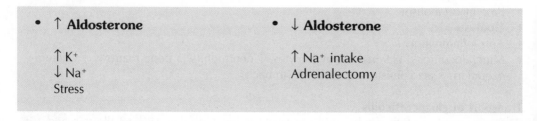

- ↑ **Aldosterone**

  ↑ K^+
  ↓ Na^+
  Stress

- ↓ **Aldosterone**

  ↑ Na^+ intake
  Adrenalectomy

The renin angiotensin system

Aldosterone helps control blood volume via the renin angiotensin system (see figure opposite).

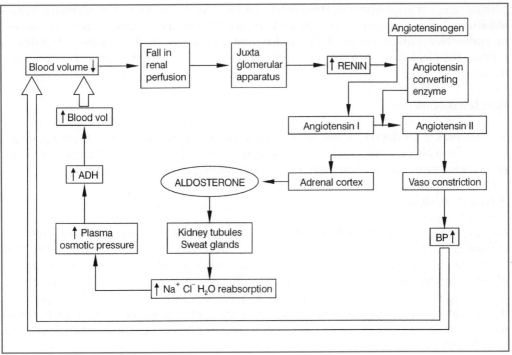

The renin angiotensin system

Actions of angiotensin II

- Arterial and venous vasoconstriction
- ↑ Aldosterone
- ↑ Antidiuretic hormone (ADH)
- ↑ Thirst

Control of renin secretion

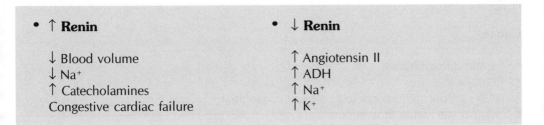

• ↑ **Renin**	• ↓ **Renin**
↓ Blood volume	↑ Angiotensin II
↓ Na⁺	↑ ADH
↑ Catecholamines	↑ Na⁺
Congestive cardiac failure	↑ K⁺

Aldosterone excess (hyperaldosteronism) can be primary or secondary. **Primary hyperaldosteronism** is covered in Section 12.6, p.261. **Secondary hyperaldosteronism** is due to congestive cardiac failure (CCF) and cirrhosis of the liver. It has similar features to primary hyperaldosteronism except renin and angiotensin are increased and oedema is a feature.

Sex hormones

Testosterone is produced by the zona fasciculata of the adrenal cortex. Oestrogens and progesterone are produced in the zona reticularis of the adrenal cortex. The adrenal glands are a minor supply of sex hormones compared with the gonads (ovaries or testicles).

Adrenal medulla

The adrenal medulla is derived from the neural crest cells which form chromaffin cells. The adrenaline and noradrenaline is produced by chromaffin cells. The adrenal medulla is innervated by the greater splanchnic nerves and can be considered part of the sympathetic nervous system. The plasma half-life of adrenaline and noradrenaline is about three minutes. They are taken up by the sympathetic nerve endings and are destroyed by monoamine oxidase (MAO). They are released due to fear, stress and hypoglycaemia by impulses from the hypothalamus via the greater splanchnic nerves. The effects of adrenaline and noradrenaline include:

- ↑ Glycogenolysis (from liver and muscle)
- ↑ Gluconeogenesis
- Lipolysis
- CVS effects

12.3 Cushing's syndrome

This is the clinical syndrome produced by excess circulating glucocorticoids. This can occur due to excess ACTH levels (referred to as Cushing's disease) or an excess of glucocorticoid alone.

Causes

- Steroid administration
- Pituitary lesions
- ACTH producing tumours (e.g. oat cell carcinoma)
- Adrenal carcinoma or adenoma

Clinical features of Cushing's syndrome

- Truncal obesity
- Hair growth and acne
- Weakness
- Hypertension
- Oedema
- Striae

- Easy bruising
- Polyuria/polydipsia
- Depression
- Osteoporosis
- Kyphosis
- Glycosuria

Diagnosis

- 24-hour urinary free cortisol — elevated in Cushing's syndrome
- Overnight dexamethasone suppression test: in non-affected patients, 2 mg dexamethasone given at midnight will reduce the morning plasma cortisol level, but is not reduced in Cushing's patients
- Morning and evening plasma cortisol measurement: a loss of the circadian variation is seen

Investigations of the cause of Cushing's syndrome include:

- Plasma ACTH level
- Adrenal CT scan
- Pituitary CT scan
- CXR for ACTH producing bronchial carcinoma

Treatment

Treat the cause

Pituitary

- Trans-sphenoidal excision of pituitary adenoma
- External irradiation (can take years to work)
- Yttrium irradiation (can also be slow to be effective)

Adrenal

Resection of adenomas and carcinomas. Bilateral adrenalectomy is indicated when other measures have failed, ACTH producing tumour is not found, severe Cushing's syndrome requiring rapid treatment, or in the presence of bilateral adrenal nodular hyperplasia.

12.4 Adrenocortical insufficiency (Addison's disease)

Causes of adrenocortical insufficiency

- Bilateral adrenalectomy
- Infection (e.g. TB, histoplasmosis)
- Metastatic deposits within the adrenal glands
- Amyloidosis
- Sudden cessation of steroid therapy
- Sarcoidosis
- Meningococcal septicaemia
- Autoimmune disease

Signs and symptoms

Postural hypotension and pigmentation of the buccal mucosa and skin are classical. Other symptoms include weakness, loss of body hair, drowsiness, confusion and coma.

Diagnosis is made by the short Synacthen test, which does not raise the plasma cortisol level in affected patients.

Management

Those presenting with acute hypotension must be given fluids and 100 mg hydrocortisone six-hourly. Long-term replacement therapy consists of hydrocortisone 20 mg in the morning and 10 mg in the evening.

Surgical patients who usually take steroids long-term must be given hydrocortisone 100mg with their pre-medication and thereafter six-hourly until they are able to resume their normal dose of hydrocortisone. If this is prolonged, an intermittent dose of 50 mg eight-hourly should be given.

12.5 Phaeochromocytoma

A tumour of the adrenal medulla arising from chromaffin cells. Secretes excess catecholamines. It is known as the 10% tumour because 10% are malignant, bilateral, familial and extra-adrenal.

Extra-adrenal sites include thorax, neck, bladder, kidney and scrotum.

It can occur alone or as part of other genetic conditions, namely von Hippel–Lindau syndrome, neurofibromatosis and multiple endocrine neoplasia (MEN) Types I and II.

Clinical features

These are explained by the excess plasma levels of catecholamines and include sustained or intermittent hypertension, anxiety, palpitations, tachycardia, stroke, angina and excessive sweating.

Pathological features: they are often soft, vascular tumours which can have areas of haemorrhage and necrosis within.

Diagnosis

- 24-hour urinary VMA (vanillylmandelic acid) measurement shows an elevated result
- CT and MRI are used to localize the tumour once the diagnosis of phaeochromocytoma is made

Management

Treatment of choice is adrenalectomy, except in those with metastatic disease or who are unfit for surgery. However, patients must be thoroughly prepared prior to surgery due to potentially fatal changes in the CVS which can occur under anaesthesia and whilst handling the tumour.

12.6 Aldosteronism

Aldosterone is secreted by the zona glomerulosa, and acts on the loop of Henle and the proximal convoluted tubule to increase water retention by the kidney.

Causes of aldosteronism include:

- Conn's syndrome (aldosterone-secreting adrenocortical adenoma)
- Aldosterone producing adenocarcinoma
- Bilateral adrenocortical hyperplasia

Clinical signs include hypertension, muscle weakness, headaches, polydipsia, polyuria and nocturia. The diagnosis is made by measuring plasma aldosterone and suppressed plasma renin levels. CT or MR scanning can be used to localize aldosterone secreting adenomas.

Management of patients with adenomas consists of removal of the affected adrenal gland, following adequate pre-operative preparation with spironolactone and potassium supplementation.

12.7 Congenital adrenal hyperplasia

This occurs as a result of 2,1-hydroxylase deficiency, although a lack of other enzymes can lead to this syndrome. This deficiency leads to reduced cortisol and aldosterone levels whilst androgens are increased. The resulting clinical picture in females is one of virilization. In males the syndrome leads to short stature and penile enlargement in childhood. Reduced aldosterone can lead to wasting, vomiting and failure to thrive in infants. Diagnosis is confirmed by radioimmunoassay of 17-hydroxyprogesterone,which shows elevated levels. Treatment is with hydrocortisone and mineralocorticoid therapy if required.

12.8 Adrenalectomy

Peri-operative care of the patient is co-ordinated between the anaesthetic and surgical staff and starts prior to operation.

Pre-operative preparation

Alpha- and beta-adrenergic blockade should be started, consisting of phenoxybenzamine and propranolol. Alpha blockade should be started at least one week prior to surgery, whereas propranolol is started four days pre-operatively. IVU demonstrates the function of the kidneys in case of unavoidable nephrectomy.

Per-operatively

- Tempered handling of the tumour is required to minimize changes in blood pressure
- Nitroprusside is used intravenously to control blood pressure intra-operatively
- Removal of the tumour often precipitates hypotension and is managed with fluids, blood and dopamine

Post-operative care

Appropriate fluid replacement is essential to avoid hypotension and fluid overload. This is achieved by monitoring central venous pressure, arterial pressure, pulse rate and urinary output. Hypoglycaemia can occur so blood glucose must be monitored. Hydrocortisone may be required intra- and post-operatively.

Surgical approaches to the adrenal gland include bilateral subcostal, transverse epigastric or lumbar incisions.

Nelson's syndrome

This occurs following bilateral adrenalectomy and is characterized by continued enlargement of the pituitary gland and hyperpigmentation.

12.9 Secondary hypertension

Causes

- **Renal disease**: glomerulonephritis, renal artery stenosis
- Coarctation of the aorta
- **Endocrine**: phaeochromocytoma, Cushing's syndrome, Conn's syndrome, hyperparathyroidism, acromegaly
- **Drugs** (e.g oral contraceptive pill)

13. PAEDIATRIC PHYSIOLOGY

13.1 Paediatric statistics

To calculate a child's approximate weight:

Weight = (age + 4) x 2 kg

PAEDIATRIC STATISTICS

Statistic	Age (years)			
	Neonate	**0.5**	**1–2**	**3–6**
Pulse rate (beats/min)	120–160	120–140	100–120	80–100
Repiratory rate (breaths/min)	30–60	30–45	25–35	20–30
Hb (g/dl)	14.5–21.5	8.5–13.5	10.5–13.5	11.5–14.0
WCC (x10⁹/l)	5–26	6–15	6–15	6–15
Daily maintenance requirements:				
Water (ml/kg)	150	150	100	80
Na⁺ (mmol/kg)	2.5	2.5	2.5	2.0
K⁺ (mmol/kg)	2.5	2.5	2.5	2.0
Calories (per kg)	100	100	75	50

Classification of children

Premature infants are those born before 38 weeks' gestation. A child is a **neonate** between birth and 44 weeks' gestation. Children between the ages of four weeks and 52 weeks are **infants**. One to four-year-old children are **pre-school**.

13.2 Physiological differences between children and adults

Nervous system

The blood-brain barrier is underdeveloped and myelination is not complete at birth. This means that opiates and fat-soluble drugs have more efficacy on the brain and can lead to respiratory depression.

Temperature control

Neonates are more susceptible to hypothermia. They have a larger surface area to weight ratio, less subcutaneous fat and less vasomotor control over skin vessels. Neonates cannot shiver and have no voluntary control over temperature regulation. In addition, premature infants have smaller stores of brown fats.

Respiration

Respiratory rate in neonates is usually between 30 and 60 breaths per minute, but can vary from minute to minute. When increased respiratory effort is required the respiratory rate increases but not tidal volume. At birth, 50% of alveoli are not developed and tidal volume is approximately 20 ml (7 ml/kg). Hypocalcaemia leading to convulsions can result from respiratory distress. At birth oxygen consumption is 6–8 ml/kg/min.

Cardiovascular system

At birth, right atrial pressure decreases, left atrial pressure rises and so the foramen ovale closes. The ductus arteriosus is completely closed at the eighth week. A neonate only has to lose 30 ml of its 300 ml blood volume to suffer circulatory collapse.

Gut and liver function

Vitamin K can be given to premature infants due to the immature liver not producing clotting factors. Drug doses must be reduced due to reduced clearance of drugs. Glycogen stores are small resulting in hypoglycaemia after short periods of starvation. The absorptive capacity of the neonate gut is reduced due to a smooth surface. Fatty acids and glycerol are used for energy after birth, whereas *in utero* glucose is the main source of energy.

Kidney function

Neonates are less able to concentrate urine and so dehydrate more easily. They have a lower GFR and lose more sodium in their urine.

13.3 Fluid replacement therapy

Fluid deficiency in children manifests (in order of severity) as thirst, oliguria, dry mucous membranes, sunken fontanelle, tachycardia, reduced skin turgor and capillary return and finally drowsiness and hypotension.

Mild dehydration can be treated with oral rehydration or IV crystalloids, whereas more severe fluid depletion requires 10–20 ml/kg colloid (albumin) as a bolus and maintenance crystalloids.

Intravenous access

The following methods can be used for vascular access:

- **Central venous catheterization** (under expert supervision only): internal jugular, femoral vein
- **Peripheral long line**: cubital fossa, long saphenous vein
- **Peripheral line**: cubital fossa, dorsum of hand, scalp, femoral vein, long saphenous vein, foot
- **Intraosseous trephine needle into tibia** (1–3 cm below tubercle); in children less than six years old. Complications: through and through bone penetration, sepsis, osteomyelitis, haematoma, abscess, growth plate injury
- **Arterial access**: radial artery

14. CONGENITAL PAEDIATRIC DISORDERS

14.1 Embryology of the neural tube

Development of the neural tube

By the third gestational week the embryo is trilaminar. It consists of:

- Notochord
- Intra-embryonic mesoderm
- Intra-embryonic coelom
- Neural plate (the ectoderm overlying the notochord)

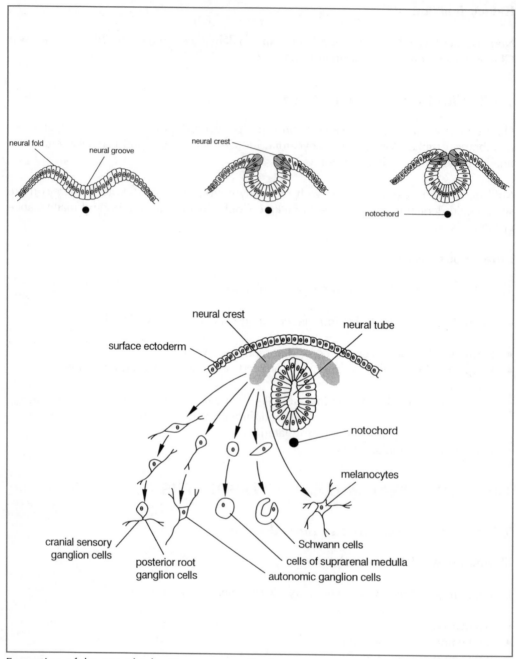

Formation of the neural tube (transverse section)

Two ridges run the length of the neural plate . The mesoderm underneath folds on either side to approximate with each other to form the neural tube.

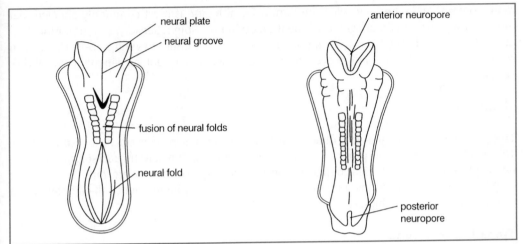

Formation of the neural tube (dorsal view)

Closure of the tube begins centrally and extends caudally on day 26 and rostrally on day 24. Failure to close rostrally results in **anencephaly**, whereas dorsal failure results in **spina bifida**.

Not all neural ectoderm is incorporated into the neural tube. These cells are known as **neural crest cells**. They form the following tissues:

- Dorsal root ganglia
- Chromaffin tissue in the adrenal medulla
- Melanocytes
- Sheath cells of the peripheral nervous system
- Ganglia of the autonomic nervous system

The vertebrae develop from the mesodermal somites. Cartilaginous rings form in the mesoderm surrounding the neural tube. The vertebrae ossify in hyaline cartilage and this process occurs by the eighth gestational week.

14.2 Neural tube defects

The incidence of neural tube defects has fallen in the last 30 years from 3:1000 live births to 1:1000. This is due to pre-natal screening and possibly better maternal nutrition. Folic acid deficiency has been implicated as a causative factor for neural tube defects, hence folic acid supplementation is recommended for women trying to conceive.

Myelomeningocele

This condition is characterized by complete unfolding of the spinal cord which lies on the surface of the patient's back. Unfortunately this condition has a much worse prognosis and is more common than meningocele. The lumbo-sacral region is most commonly affected, but the extensive lesions can affect the whole thoraco-lumbar spine. Sensory and motor function are reduced or absent from the nipple distally in those children with severe defects, in association with bladder and bowel dysfunction. Eighty per cent of patients have hydrocephalus.

Meningocele

This indicates a meningeal sac filled with CSF and normal placement of the spinal cord. These defects have a good prognosis but are less common. They are treated surgically in the neonatal period. Neurological deficit in the legs and hydrocephalus are rare. The bladder may be affected. Urinary incontinence can be treated with intermittent self-catheterization or use of an artificial sphincter.

Spina bifida occulta

This condition is said to affect up to 20% of the population but most are asymptomatic. It may be associated with a hairy patch or birth-mark. Occasionally it can cause a spastic gait or bladder dysfunction.

14.3 Embryology of the diaphragm

The diaphragm develops from the following embryonic structures:

- Transverse septum (the origin of the central tendon)
- Oesophageal (dorsal) mesentery
- Pleuroperitoneal membranes
- Third, fourth and fifth cervical somites

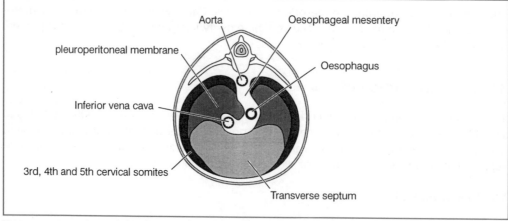

Transverse section of diaphragm at the fourth month of gestation

14.4 Congenital diaphragmatic herniation

Incidence of 1:2200 due to a defect of the hemidiaphragm, usually left-sided. It can be diagnosed pre-natally on ultrasound or post-natally on CXR. Respiratory distress develops soon after birth and bowel sounds can be heard within the chest. Treatment consists of insertion of a nasogastric tube to empty the stomach and urgent surgery. Pre-operative intubation may be required. The condition may present along with other congenital malformations (e.g. neural tube defects, trisomy 18 and other syndromes (Pierre Robin and Beckwith–Weidemann syndromes)).

14.5 Embryology of the gastro-intestinal tract

As stated before, by the third gestational week the embryo is trilaminar and consists of the notochord, intra-embryonic mesoderm, intra-embryonic coelom and neural plate. The intra-embryonic coelom is formed by the re-absorption of intra-embryonic mesoderm.

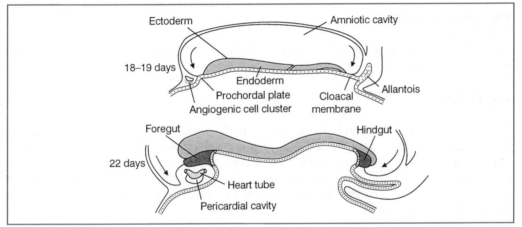

Sagittal section through embryo showing the formation of the primitive endoderm-lined gut

In the fourth gestational week the previously flat embryonic disc folds in the cephalo-caudal direction and transversely. This leads to the endoderm-lined cavity which forms the primitive gut. It extends from the buccopharyngeal membrane to the cloacal membrane. It is divided into the pharyngeal gut, foregut, midgut and hindgut. The endodermal lining of the primitive gut gives rise to the epithelial lining of the gut whilst mesoderm provides the muscular parts.

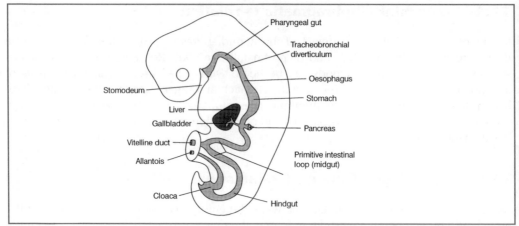

Formation of gastro-intestinal tract at fourth week of gestation showing, fore-, mid- and hindgut

The pharyngeal gut

Extends from the buccopharyngeal membrane to the tracheobronchial diverticulum and has been discussed in Section 9.2, p.240.

The foregut

This gives rise to the trachea and oesophagus, stomach, duodenum, liver, pancreas and spleen. The **trachea** develops from the tracheobronchial diverticulum, which becomes separated from the foregut by the **oesophagotracheal** septum. The lung buds develop from the blind end of the trachea. These lung buds give rise to the segmental bronchi and expand into the pericardioperitoneal cavity. Abnormal closure of the oesophagotracheal septum can lead to tracheo-oesophageal fistula.

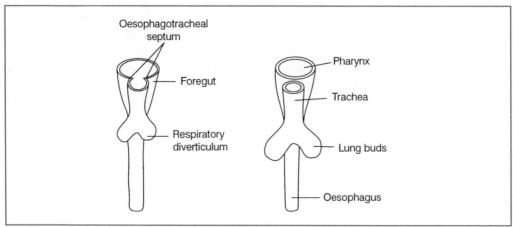

The foregut during the fourth week of gestation

Formation of the **stomach** occurs when the dorsal mesentery lengthens, the gut tube rotates clockwise and the liver bud migrates to the right side of the dorsal body wall. This also gives the **duodenum** its 'C' shape.

The **liver** develops from the hepatic diverticulum which is an endodermal outgrowth from the distal end of the foregut. The bile duct is formed from the connection between the liver and foregut.

The uncinate process of the **pancreas** is formed from the ventral pancreatic bud which is closely associated with the hepatic diverticulum. The body of the pancreas is formed from the dorsal pancreatic bud. The ventral pancreatic duct rotates clockwise to join the dorsal pancreatic duct.

The **spleen** is a foregut derivative of the left face of the dorsal mesentery.

The midgut

This extends from the entrance of the bile duct to the junction of the proximal two-thirds and distal one-third of the transverse colon.

The dorsal mesentery of the midgut extends rapidly producing physiological herniation in the sixth week.

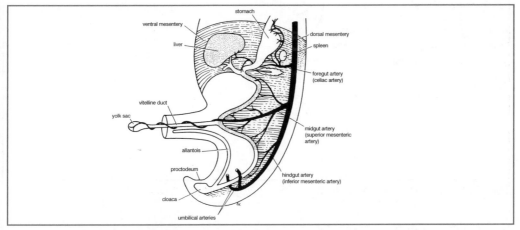

The midgut of a fifth week embryo

The cephalic limb of the midgut grows rapidly to hang down on the right side of the dorsal mesentery. The gut rotates around the axis formed by the superior mesenteric artery 270° in an anticlockwise direction. The gut returns to the abdominal cavity in the tenth week.

The hindgut

This gives rise to the distal one-third of the transverse colon, descending colon, sigmoid colon, rectum and upper half of the anal canal.

In addition, the endoderm of the hindgut gives rise to the lining of the bladder and urethra. The **urorectal**, a transverse ridge arising between the allantois and the hindgut, grows to reach the cloacal membrane, to divide it into the urogenital membrane anteriorly and the anal membrane posteriorly. The **anal pit** forms in the ectoderm over the anal membrane and this ruptures in the ninth week to form connection between the rectum and outside.

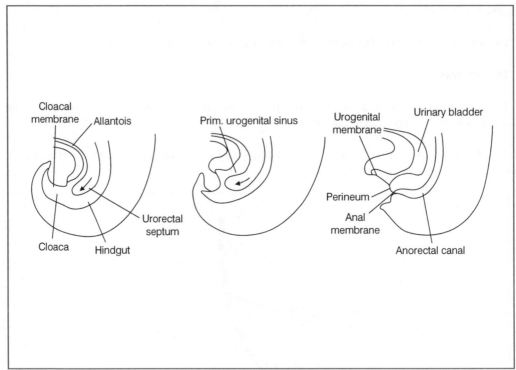

The cloacal region at successive stages in development

14.6 Congenital disorders of the gastro-intestinal tract

Gastroschisis

This is a protrusion of gut through a defect in the abdominal wall usually to the right of a normal umbilicus. Incidence of 1:3000 live births.

- There is no covering of the gut
- Associated malformations are significantly less common than with exomphalos
- The defect is between 2 and 4 cm and through intact rectus muscles
- The ovary and fallopian tube may be involved in females

Treatment consists of normal vaginal delivery, NG tube, IV fluids and antibiotics. The loops of bowel are placed in a sterile surgical bag, maintaining the bowel in a warm temperature. Early surgical closure. In 30% of patients this has to be staged.

Exomphalos

Also has an incidence of 1:3000 and occurs due to the failure of the primitive gut loop to return to the abdominal cavity in the tenth gestational week. The umbilical ring is enlarged up to 10 cm. Diagnosis is usually made antenatally.

- The bowel has a membranous covering
- Half of affected patients have other severe malformations

Treatment consists of covering of the bowel with cling-film, insertion of a nasogastric tube, intravenous fluids and antibiotics and prompt surgical closure.

Malrotation and volvulus neonatorum

Pathology

- Failure of rotation leaves the duodenojejunal junction to the right of the mid-line and the caecum in the upper abdomen
- Ladd's bands are peritoneal bands which cross from the caecum across the second part of the duodenum to the posterior abdominal wall
- These bands can cause intermittent obstruction
- A volvulus of the mid-gut is more likely as the mid-gut mesenteric base is narrow; it is rare in the absence of malrotation
- Volvulus of mid-gut causes high intestinal obstruction and can lead to ischaemia and perforation

Clinical features

Typically presents at three months with intermittent pain and bile-stained vomiting. Abdominal distension is not a prominent feature due to high obstruction. Rectal bleeding and abdominal tenderness suggest intestinal ischaemia progressing to gangrene.

Investigations

- **Plain abdominal X-rays**: usually inconclusive, may demonstrate dilated first part of the duodenum

- **Barium enema**: shows malrotation
- **Ultrasound scan**: identifies orientation of superior mesenteric vessels

Management

- Urgent laparotomy is indicated if obstruction or volvulus is present
- Entire mid-gut delivered into wound and mesenteric volvulus is identified
- Volvulus corrected by rotating anticlockwise
- Ladd's bands and adhesions must be divided
- Small bowel is returned to the right of the abdomen and caecum and colon to the left (not to the normal position); this widens the base of the mesentery stabilizing it
- Appendicectomy is performed as it is now, confusingly, on the left
- If >50 cm viable small bowel exists, excise the ischaemic bowel
- If <50 cm viable small bowel exists, untwist and return it all to the abdomen and have a second-look laparotomy

Oesophageal atresia

Incidence is 1:4500 and has equal sex distribution. Clinical features include maternal poly-hydramnios, excessive saliva, and choking on feeds. 50% have other problems (e.g. cardio-vascular, anorectal, genito-urinary and gastro-intestinal). Diagnosis can be made pre-natally. A radio-opaque tube is passed into the oesophagus and CXR taken. The tube will be seen in the upper thorax. An associated tracheo-oesophageal fistula may be indicated by air in the stomach. Definitive treatment is surgical. This is not performed as an emergency unless respiratory distress has occurred. Oesophageal dysmotility may persist into adult life.

Duodenal atresia and stenosis

- **Duodenal atresia:** results from the failure of the duodenum to recanalize in the tenth week of foetal life
- **Duodenal stenosis:** can be caused by malrotation, volvulus, diaphragmatic herniation, annular pancreas and peritoneal bands

Incidence is 1:6000, and is associated with Down's syndrome and congenital heart disease. Diagnosis can be made antenatally. Clinical signs include bile-stained vomiting and 'double gas bubble' on abdominal X-ray.

Treatment is laparotomy and duodenostomy performed urgently to avoid aspiration.

Small bowel atresia

Incidence is 1:20,000 and in 10% are multiple. There are three types:

- Mucosal membrane
- Atretic segment
- Mesenteric defect

Diagnosis can be made antenatally. Clinical features include bilious vomiting, abdominal distension, lack of stools following meconium, and distended loops of bowel with fluid levels on plain abdominal X-ray. Laparotomy and primary anastomosis is performed.

Meconium ileus

This is an abnormality found in 15% of infants born with cystic fibrosis where the meconium has a concentration of 70% (normal is 9%). Prenatally, the meconium will obstruct the terminal ileum. Volvulus of this distended ileum can lead to ischaemic perforation and meconium peritonitis. The infant is born with a distended abdomen and bilious vomiting. Masses of meconium may be palpable but the rectum is empty and meconium is not passed.

Prenatal diagnosis by ultrasound scanning may detect dilated loops of small bowel and bulky meconium. Abdominal X-rays after birth confirm the presence of dilated loops of bowel. Flecks of calcium suggest prenatal perforation with meconium peritonitis. A barium enema will demonstrate the collapsed empty colon. Gastrografin enema may be therapeutic in an uncomplicated case because the detergent effect will loosen the meconium if it refluxes into the ileum. The patient must be prepared for laparotomy.

Laparotomy may be indicated, as 50% will have an associated atresia, perforation or volvulus. The ileum is usually blocked by a rubbery mass of meconium. Dilated ileum is opened; meconium is washed out; grossly dilated ileum is resected. Temporary ileostomy may be needed, which if double-barrelled allows introduction of acetyl cysteine to loosen remaining meconium.

10% mortality in infancy can be expected in cystic fibrosis (confirmed by serum immunoreactive trypsin level and a sweat test).

Hirschsprung's disease

Hirschsprung's disease is characterized by an absence of the ganglia in Auerbach's plexus and an increase in unmedullated innervation to the bowel wall muscle. It has an incidence of 1:5000.

There is usually a well-demarcated segment of abnormal bowel in the rectum, varying in length. The aganglionic segment may affect the entire colon and even the small bowel, but typically the sigmoid colon is involved.

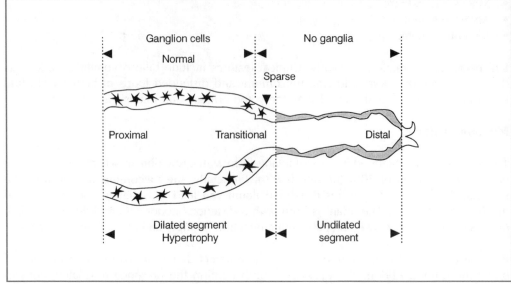

Histopathology of Hirschsprung's disease

Clinical presentation

- Congenital condition
- M:F is 4:1
- Associated with other abnormalities (e.g. Down's syndrome)
- The neonate fails to pass meconium, may have abdominal distension, feeding difficulties and vomiting
- The removal of a mucous plug on rectal examination leads to dramatic decompression, but symptoms recur
- 66% of children are diagnosed after the age of six months
- Older children present with failure to thrive, chronic constipation and distended abdomen
- Children with short affected segments may not be diagnosed until the teenage years

Investigations

- Hirschsprung's disease must be differentiated from other conditions such as: meconium ileus due to cystic fibrosis; infective gastro-enteritis; chronic constipation without aganglionosis
- Barium enema with plain X-ray showing retained barium after 24 hours is highly suggestive
- Biopsy specimens per rectum or at laparotomy exclude the disease if ganglia are present, or confirm it in large specimens if no ganglia are present

- Acetylcholinesterase activity may also be measured in small specimens
- Anorectal manometry may be helpful in making the diagnosis in children with a short, low segment affected

Treatment
Ideally the surgery is carried out between the ages of three and nine months. However, this is increasingly being performed on neonates. The principles of treatment of Hirschsprung's disease are:

- Deflate the bowel either by colostomy, rectal washouts or early laparotomy (colostomy preferred)
- Delay operation if possible while child gains weight, becomes well-nourished and dilated colon returns to normal
- Excise aganglionic segment at laparotomy using one of a variety of procedures (e.g. a 'pull through' operation) to anastomose normal bowel to anus
- The bowel is excised 3 cm proximal to the margin of the diseased segment (which is confirmed by frozen section)
- Close colostomy at a later date when anastomosis has healed satisfactorily

Complications
The most common cause of death in children with Hirschsprung's disease is enterocolitis (often clostridial in origin). After treatment, 90% of children have normal bowel habit but some have continued soiling or constipation.

Congenital anorectal anomalies

Anal anomalies occur in 1:5000 births. There are many types of abnormality but the basic distinction is whether the bowel ends above the levator ani muscle (high anomaly) or below it (low anomaly) (see the figure overleaf). More than half the children with anorectal anomalies have at least one other abnormality, usually of the urinary tract, heart, skeleton or other part of the gastro-intestinal system. The perineum is routinely inspected in newborns to exclude these conditions.

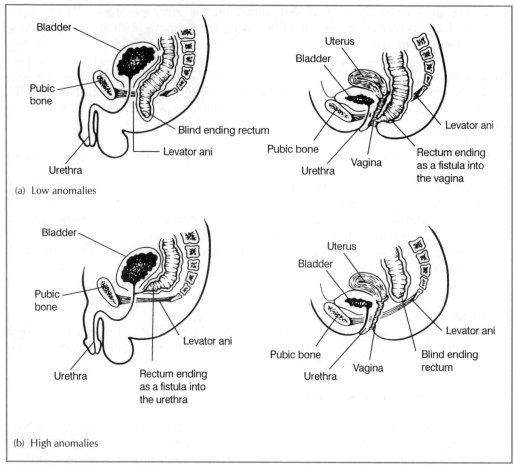

Congenital anorectal anomalies

Low anomalies

In females, most anomalies are of the low variety. The bowel usually passes through a normal levator ani muscle. It may end blindly a few centimetres from the anus (imperforate anus), enter the perineum in an abnormal position or form a fistula to the vagina or penile shaft. The fistulous opening is carefully sought, and the fistula is surgically cut back to a normal anus. If the sphincter muscle is normal, continence may be achieved.

High anomalies

In males, high anomalies are more common. In these children, the bowel ends above the levator ani which is often poorly developed. It is important to distinguish between a low imperforate anus and the more serious high anomaly.

A lateral inverted radiograph 24 hours after birth shows intestinal gas ending above the pubococcygeal line.

Treatment entails a colostomy with subsequent 'pull through' of the colon through the pelvic muscles. The earlier such reconstructive surgery is carried out, the more likely the child is to develop normal continence. Various surgical approaches (abdominal, sacral or perineal) have been attempted. Due to the poor quality of the levator ani, even with strenuous post-operative physiotherapy, continence levels are not as good as in patients with low anomalies.

14.7   Congenital genito-urinary malformations

The embryology of the genito-urinary system is covered in detail in Chapter 5, *Urinary System and Renal Transplantation*, Section 1.1.

Urinary tract malformations

Malformations causing impaired renal drainage via obstruction of the ureter can lead to hydronephrosis.

- Horseshoe kidney
- Ureteric duplication
- Ureterocele (more common in girls)
- **Pelviureteral junction obstruction**: the most common cause of hydronephrosis caused by intrinsic, extrinsic or mural compression, treatment is by pyeloplasty
- **Vesicoureteric junction obstruction**: treated by re-implantation of the ureters
- **Posterior urethral valves**: the most common cause of obstruction in boys and is treated endoscopically

Other congenital urinary tract anomalies include renal agenesis (Potter syndrome), renal hypoplasia and polycystic kidneys.

Hypospadias

In this condition the external urethral meatus lies on the ventral surface of the penis. Severity varies from a slightly displaced meatus to a perineal meatus. The incidence is 1:125 boys. Associated features include undescended testis, inguinal hernia, bifid scrotum, chordee and renal and ureteric abnormalities.

Classification
These describe the position of the meatus after correction of the chordee:

- Glandular
- Coronal
- Anterior penile
- Middle penile

- Posterior penile
- Penoscrotal
- Scrotal
- Perineal

Management
Surgery is performed between the ages of nine and 18 months and varies according to the classification of the deformity.

- **Meatal advancement and granuloplasty (MAGPI)**: this procedure is carried out for glandular abnormalities and consists of creation of a new meatal pit, advancement of the new pit and closure of a sleeve of glandular tissue
- **Mathieu flap**: in coronal hypospadias, a flap is created based on the ectopic meatus; this is folded over and the lateral flaps are closed over the new urethra; complications of this operation include fistulae and strictures
- **More proximal deformities**: require reconstructive surgery in the form of pedicle grafts, tubes or patches; complications include fistulae, urethral stenosis and meatal regression

Epispadias and bladder exstrophy

This results from failure of mid-line fusion of mid-line structures below the umbilicus. The bladder mucosa is present as a small plaque on the anterior abdominal wall and the penis is upturned with the meatus opening on to the dorsum. Other features can include split symphysis, low umbilicus, bifid clitoris, apparently externally rotated lower limbs, undescended testes and poorly developed scrotum. It is more common in boys.

Treatment is surgical reconstruction of the bladder. However, complications include damage to the upper tracts due to obstruction and reflux and adenocarcinoma of the original bladder mucosa. In adult life, incontinence, renal damage and vaginal stenosis can occur.

Maldescent of the testes

The testes develop within the abdomen during fetal life and enter the inguinal canal in the seventh month *in utero*. Testes which are not found in the scrotum can be retractile, ectopic or incompletely descended. The incidence of maldescended testes is 2–3%.

Retractile testes
The testes can be elevated to the upper scrotum by the cremasteric muscles. However, retractile testes are of normal size, can be manipulated to the fundus of the scrotum and remain there some time after examination.

Incompletely descended testes

These account for 20% of maldescended testes and lie along the path of descent but have failed to reach the scrotum. The main anatomical sites are:

- Intra-abdominal
- Inguinal
- Intra-canalicular
- Emergent (external inguinal ring)
- High scrotal

Emergent and high scrotal testes are palpable on examination. Undescended testes may descend in to the scrotum in the first few weeks of life, but descent after one year is rare.

Ectopic testes

Testes which leave the normal course of descent account for 80% of maldescended testes. They can be found at one of the following sites:

- Superficial inguinal pouch (most common site)
- Base of the penis
- Perineum
- The femoral region

Maldescended testes become hypoplastic due to them not being maintained at a cooler temperature. Also, the risk of malignancy in a maldescended testis is 1:70 in comparison to 1:5000 in the general population. Therefore, orchidopexy through an inguinal skin crease incision by the age of two years is recommended.

Intersex

Congenital adrenal hyperplasia

This is an autosomal recessive disorder characterized by the absence of certain enzymes in the pathway of cortisol and aldosterone synthesis from cholesterol. This results in excess androgen levels and so virilization in affected females. Affected males may present with adrenal crisis early in life. The most common form is 21-hydroxylase deficiency.

Management consists of intravenous fluids, glucose and hydrocortisone. Long-term management includes hydrocortisone and surgical correction of virilized external genitalia in females in the first year.

Klinefelter's syndrome

In this condition males have an extra X chromosome — 47, XXY. The incidence is 1:1000 males. Clinical features include increased height, mild mental retardation, gynaecomastia and infertility. Testes may be small and incompletely descended.

Testicular feminization

Affected individuals are chromosomally XY but present as females due to complete andro-gen insensitivity of the genitalia. Patients may present with an inguinal hernia containing a testis or later in life with amenorrhoea.

14.8 Embryology of the face and palate

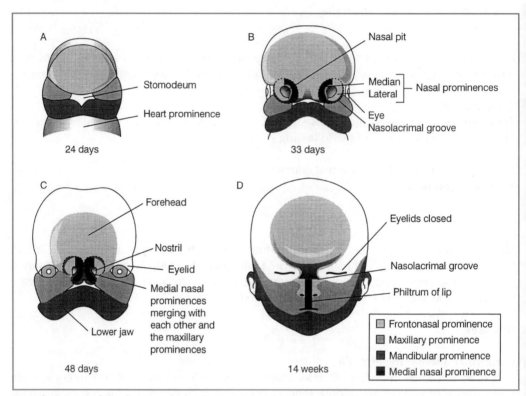

Development of the human face

The facial primordia appear in the fourth week around the stomodeum. The five facial primordia are:

- Frontonasal prominence
- Maxillary prominences (paired)
- Mandibular prominences (paired)

They are active centres of growth and the face develops mainly between the fourth and eighth weeks.

Nasal placodes (the primitive nose and nasal cavities) develop in the frontonasal prominence by the end of the fourth week. The mesenchyme around the placodes proliferate to form elevations, the medial and lateral nasal prominences.

The **maxillary prominences** proliferate and grow medially towards each other. This pushes the medial nasal placodes into the mid-line, and a groove is formed between the lateral nasal prominence and the maxillary prominence merge by the end of the sixth week.

As the medial nasal prominences merge they give rise to the **intermaxillary segment**. This develops into the philtrum of the upper lip, septum of the premaxilla and the primary palate and nasal septum.

The maxillary prominences form the upper cheek and most of the upper lip, whereas the mandibular prominences give rise to the chin, lower lip and lower cheek region.

Development of the palate

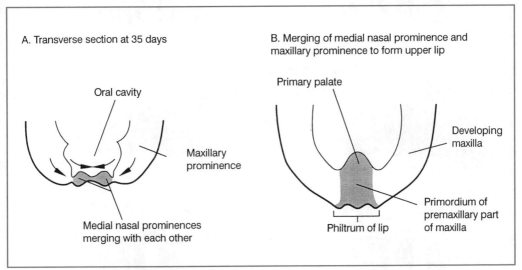

Transverse section of palate during development

The palate develops from the fifth week to the twelfth week. It develops from the primary palate and secondary palate.

The primary palate develops from the deep part of the intermaxillary segment of the maxilla, during the merging of the medial nasal prominences. It forms only a small part of the adult palate.

The secondary palate forms the hard and soft palates. It forms from the lateral palatine processes which extend from the internal aspects of the maxillary prominences. They approach each other and fuse in the mid-line, along with the nasal septum and posterior part of the primary palate.

14.9 Cleft lip and palate

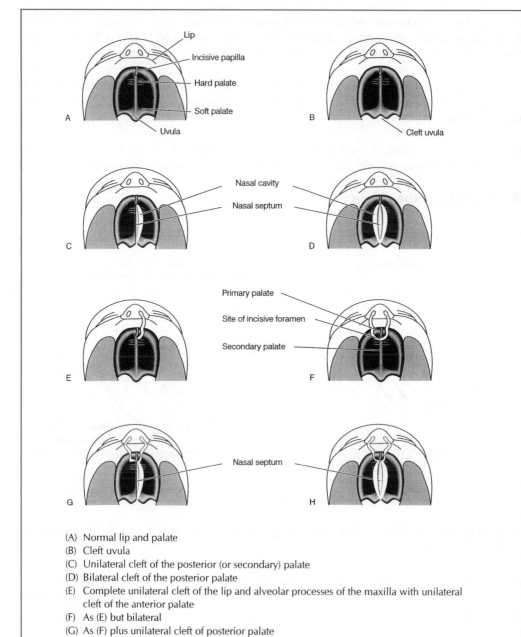

(A) Normal lip and palate
(B) Cleft uvula
(C) Unilateral cleft of the posterior (or secondary) palate
(D) Bilateral cleft of the posterior palate
(E) Complete unilateral cleft of the lip and alveolar processes of the maxilla with unilateral cleft of the anterior palate
(F) As (E) but bilateral
(G) As (F) plus unilateral cleft of posterior palate
(H) As (F) plus bilateral cleft of posterior palate

Types of cleft lip and palate

There are two major groups of cleft lip and palate:

- Clefts involving the upper lip and anterior part of the maxilla, with or without involvement of parts of the remaining hard and soft regions of the palate
- Clefts involving hard and soft regions of the palate

The various types of cleft lip and palate are shown in the diagram. Cleft lip and palate is thought to have some genetic basis. Teratogenic factors are largely unknown, but vitamin B complex deficiency in pregnancy may have an aetiological role. The risk of having a second affected child is 4% in comparison to 0.1% in the general population.

15. ACQUIRED PAEDIATRIC DISORDERS

15.1 Urinary tract disease in children

Presentation

- Infection
- Haematuria
- Lethargy
- Failure to thrive
- Vomiting
- Pain
- Mass
- Abdominal distension

Renal function tests

Urinalysis
Infection may be indicated by haematuria, leucocytes and nitrites. Proteinuria can indicate nephrotic syndrome. Normal urinary pH is between 5 and 7. Abnormalities can be caused by renal tubular acidosis.

Microscopy
Red blood cells, white blood cells, casts and bacteria can be seen on microscopy. Red blood cell casts are suggestive of glomerulonephritis.

Blood tests
FBC, urea, creatinine, calcium, albumin, phosphate and bicarbonate are all useful.

Radiological investigations
Ultrasound is used to illustrate the renal tract. Isotope renography demonstrates renal function and drainage of the kidney.

Endoscopy

Cystoscopy and urethroscopy are used to visualize the lower urinary tract directly.

Children with more than two episodes of UTIs should be considered for investigations for vesico-ureteric reflux (see Chapter 5, *Urinary System and Renal Transplantation,* Section 11).

15.2 The acute scrotum

This is characterized by pain, a rapidly growing mass, erythema and oedema of the scrotum and testes.

Common causes

- Torsion of the testis
- Epididymo-orchitis
- Torsion of the appendage of the testis or epididymis
- Idiopathic scrotal oedema

Other causes include hernia, hydrocele, haematoma, cysts, leukaemia, varicocele and tumours, including orchioblastoma and rhabdomyosarcoma.

Torsion of the testis

This can occur at any age but has its peak incidence during puberty and the neonatal period.

Clinical features

- Acute onset of severe testicular pain
- Enlarged, exquisitely tender testis which may be lying horizontally
- Nausea and vomiting
- Occasionally abdominal rather than testicular pain is present

Management

If there is any doubt as to the cause of an acutely swollen testis IT MUST BE EXPLORED.

- Doppler ultrasound has been used to detect the flow of blood through the testicular artery but even though this reduces the number of negative explorations there is potential for error.
- A transverse incision is made over the affected testis and the torsion released
- After 10 minutes, assessment is made of the viability of the testis: black, non-viable testes should undergo orchidectomy with fixation of the remaining testis; if viable, both testes should be fixed by invaginating the tunica vaginalis and suturing the testes to the mid-line septum with non-absorbable sutures.

It is said that most testes are salvageable within six hours of torsion whilst most are necrotic after 24 hours.

Torsion of the appendages of the testes

90% of torsions of the appendages of the testis are due to torsion of the hydatid of Morgagni, the remnant of the Mullerian duct. The appendage of the epididymis, the organ of Giraldés and remnant of the Wolffian duct can also undergo torsion.

A more insidious onset of pain is seen, but the eventual severity of pain can vary from mild to extreme. Swelling of the testis and hydrocele may be seen.

Treatment consists of excision of the appendage if pain is severe and analgesics if mild.

Epididymo-orchitis

In children this is commonly due to Gram-negative bacilli and may be associated with a structural abnormality of the urethral tract. However, in young adult men venereal infection is a more likely cause, with 70% being due to Chlamydia. Epididymitis may also follow instrumentation of the urinary tract.

Clinical features
This disease has a more insidious onset of symptoms than testicular torsion. In addition patients may experience the following:

- Fever and feeling generally unwell
- Dysuria, frequency and pyuria
- Throbbing, constant pain
- Tender, swollen epididymis

Management

- Exploration may be required if there is doubt regarding diagnosis
- Urine culture is performed
- Broad spectrum antibiotics are given
- Ultrasound of the urinary tract should be carried out to exclude anatomical abnormalities

Idiopathic scrotal oedema

This is a rare condition, occurring in children. Erythema and oedema of the scrotal skin is seen which resolves spontaneously. Even though clinically the testes are non-tender it may be difficult to exclude a diagnosis of testicular torsion or the other causes of acute scrotum.

15.3 Circumcision

Indications in children and adults

- Phimosis
- Paraphimosis
- Recurrent balanitis
- Balanitis xerotica obliterans
- Carcinoma of the penis
- Recurrent urinary tract infections
- Religious

Complications

- Haemorrhage
- Infection
- Post-renal failure due to tight dressing

15.4 Groin hernias

Inguinal hernias

Occur in 4% of live male births in the UK due to a patent processus vaginalis and are more common on the right side possibly due to the later descent of the right testis. They can also occur after birth most frequently presenting in the first three months of life and are uncommon after three years of age.

Indirect inguinal hernias are much less common in female neonates but do occur. Testicular feminization syndrome should be excluded using chromosomal studies in female babies with an inguinal hernia.

Management
60% of inguinal hernias in children present with incarceration due to infants having a narrow external inguinal ring. The majority do not become obstructed or ischaemic. However, the testis is at risk of infarction due to pressure on the testicular vessels. Also, in girls the ovary may undergo incarceration and torsion.

Incarceration is treated by sedation and taxis, supported by IV antibiotic and observation due to risk of sepsis. Herniotomy is performed 48 hours later. Prompt elective surgery is indicated in non-incarcerated inguinal hernias in both male and female neonates and infants. Preterm babies can be observed.

Femoral hernias in children are rare and should be operated on promptly at all ages, except premature infants who can be observed. (For more details on hernias and the operations for them see Chapter 4, *Abdomen*, Section 1, p. 299.)

Hydroceles in children

A hydrocele occurs when excess fluid accumulates within some portion of the processus vaginalis. The most common form is a vaginal hydrocele but hydroceles of the spermatic cord are seen also. Hydroceles transilluminate on examination unlike hernias, but groin hernias can cause hydroceles, making diagnosis difficult. Hydroceles should be treated operatively at the age of two years, but observed before this time.

15.5 Acute appendicitis

3:1000 per year have their appendix removed. Can occur at any age but is more common > 5 years. Children may present with abdominal pain, vomiting and peritonism (McBurney's triad). Peritonism can be demonstrated in children by the jump test.

Infants may show more non-specific features such as anorexia, vomiting, irritability and fever.

Treatment consists of appendicectomy following appropriate intravenous fluid replacement and antibiotics. (*See* Chapter 4, *Abdomen*, Section 6.1, p. 375.)

15.6 Mesenteric adenitis

Vague central abdominal pain accompanies an URTI, due to inflammation of the mesenteric lymph nodes and subsequent mild peritoneal reaction. Features which distinguish it from appendicitis include cervical lymphadenopathy, headache, mild abdominal pain, shifting tenderness and pyrexia above 38 °C. It occurs most commonly between the ages of 5 and 10 years. (For more details *see* Chapter 4, *Abdomen*.)

15.7 Meckel's diverticulum

May mimic the presentation of appendicitis or present with bleeding, perforation, intussusception, volvulus or intestinal obstruction. Haemorrhage or perforation may be due to gastric mucosa being present within it. (*See* Chapter 4, *Abdomen*, Section 6.3, p. 384.)

15.8 Pyloric stenosis

Hypertrophy of the circular pyloric muscles of unknown aetiology. 2–4:1000 live births. It has a lower incidence amongst Negroes, Indians and Chinese. M:F is 4:1. It has a preponderance amongst first-born males. One in seven patients has a positive family history.

Clinical features of pyloric stenosis

- Projectile vomiting 10–20 minutes after feeding
- Hunger following vomiting
- Dehydration and weight loss
- An olive-shaped mass can be palpated in the right upper quadrant, particularly following feeding
- Visible peristalsis may be seen
- Biochemical investigations reveal metabolic alkalosis, hypokalaemia, hypochloraemia and hyponatraemia (serum potassium and sodium levels may be normal)

Diagnosis is made by a test feed and ultrasound scanning. A positive diagnosis is made if the pylorus is more than 4 mm thick or 19 mm long.

Treatment

- Rehydration
- Ramstedt's pyloromyotomy: this can be performed through an upper right transverse incision or circum-umbilical incision; the tumour is incised longitudinally until the mucosa pours through to the level of the serosa

15.9 Intussusception

An intussusception occurs when a segment of bowel (the intussusceptum) invaginates into an adjoining segment (the intussuscipiens). It is reported in 2–4:1000 children. It is more common in children than in adults. The majority present between six and nine months of age.

Most are ileo–colic but ileo–ileo–colic, ileo–ileal and colo–colic are also described. Fewer than 10% have an identified lead point such as a Meckel's diverticulum or a polyp. Nine of ten intussusceptions are associated with lymphoid hyperplasia in Peyer's patches of the ileum and may occur after an URTI. It is therefore seen most commonly in winter.

An increased incidence is seen with Henoch–Schönlein purpura.

Prolonged intussusception leads to strangulation, necrosis of the gut and perforation.

Clinical features of intussusception

- Spasms of pain associated with pallor and the child drawing up its legs; patient may appear well between attacks
- A sausage-shaped mass may be palpable in the abdomen (commonly the upper abdomen)

- Increasing irritability
- Passage of a 'redcurrant jelly' stool after 24 hours
- Abdominal distension and dehydration
- Blood on rectal examination
- The apex of the intussusception may be palpable per rectum

Diagnosis

By barium enema or ultrasound scan. Barium enema does not generally pass beyond the apex of the intussusception but may show a 'coiled spring' appearance. Ultrasound scan shows a diagnostic 'doughnut' appearance.

Treatment

- Rehydration (with intravenous fluids) and analgesia
- Pneumatic or hydrostatic reduction by an expert in a paediatric centre is indicated if there are no signs of peritonitis or perforation and symptoms have been present for less than 24 hours
- Laparotomy is indicated if there is evidence of perforation, evidence of peritonitis or failure of radiological reduction
- Reduction at laparotomy is achieved by squeezing the distal portion and pushing the intussuscepted portion proximally
- Resection of the bowel is indicated if the intussusception is irreducible, non-viable bowel is present or a specific cause (e.g. Meckel's diverticulum) is found
- Laparotomy should be performed in the 3% of patients presenting with a recurrence of intussusception so that a precipitating cause can be sought

15.10 Constipation

Causes of constipation in childhood include:

- Hypothyroidism
- Hypercalcaemia
- Neuromuscular disorders
- Hirschsprung's disease
- Febrile illness in older children

Chronic constipation may lead to abdominal pain, anorexia, vomiting, failure to thrive, urinary tract infections and faecal soiling. Soiling occurs due to the accumulation of faeces within the rectum and thus an acquired megacolon. This leads to distension of the external sphincter and eventual failure of the external sphincter. Anal irritation and tears can occur due to pain on defaecation leading to a cycle of faecal retention.

Management

- Treat the precipitating cause if applicable
- A short course of oral laxatives is most often successful
- A course of enemas can be considered in more refractory cases
- This should be supplemented with high fluid and roughage intake

15.11 Jaundice in the neonate

Physiological
Bilirubin is less than 200 μmol/l. This can be due to hepatic immaturity or breast-feeding amongst other causes.

Medical

- Rhesus haemolytic disease
- ABO incompatibility
- Congenital spherocytosis
- G6PD deficiency
- Hypothyroidism
- Congenital and acquired infections

Surgical

- Biliary atresia
- Choledochal cysts
- Spontaneous perforation of the bile duct
- Inspissated bowel syndrome (within the common bile duct)
- Tumours of the extrahepatic bile ducts

Gallstones and acute gall bladder distension must not be forgotten when managing children with an unknown cause of jaundice.

Biliary atresia

Unknown aetiology. Extra-hepatic bile ducts are destroyed by inflammation. It occurs in 1:14,000 live births and is equally common in males and females. Clinical features include jaundice, hepatosplenomegaly, pale stools and dark urine. The inflammation can be confined to the common bile duct or extend to the right and left hepatic ducts.

Treatment includes biliary-enteric anastomosis, porto-enterostomy or liver transplant if these fail. Long-term sequelae include portal hypertension and cirrhosis.

Choledochal cysts

These occur due to a congenital weakness in the wall of the biliary tree and a functional obstruction at the distal end. Investigated by ultrasound scanning and ERCP and treatment consists of excision of the cyst.

15.12 Inflammatory bowel disease in children

There are about 1000 children with inflammatory bowel disease in the UK. The number of children with Crohn's disease is increasing. The presentation, diagnosis and treatment is similar to those in adults (see Chapter 4, *Abdomen*, Section 6.6, p. 391).

Children tend to present with extra-gastro-intestinal symptoms. Surgery for children who are malnourished because of the severity of their inflammatory bowel disease should be performed early to avoid growth stunting.

Chapter 4
Abdomen

CONTENTS

Abdomen

1. HERNIAS

1.1 Types of abdominal hernia

A hernia is the protrusion of all or part of a viscus through the wall of the cavity in which it is normally contained.

Types of abdominal hernias

- Inguinal
- Femoral } groin hernias
- Umbilical
- Paraumbilical
- Incisional

- Epigastric
- Spigelian
- Lumbar
- Gluteal
- Sciatic

1.2 Groin hernias

Inguinal and femoral hernias are two of the most common types of hernia and repairs make up a large proportion of elective surgery.

Incidence of groin hernias

- **Male children**
  4% of male infants have an indirect inguinal hernia
  60% of childhood inguinal hernias present with incarceration
  Indirect inguinal > direct inguinal > femoral (very rare)

- **Female children**
  All groin hernias are rare in female children and the presence of a
  hernia should alert the clinician to the possibility of testicular
  feminization syndrome
  Indirect inguinal > direct inguinal > femoral (very rare)

Continues ...

... Continued

- **Male adults**
  Direct inguinal > indirect inguinal > femoral

- **Female adults**
  Indirect inguinal = femoral > direct (rare)

All hernias are more common on the right than on the left, this may be due to the later descent of the right testis or a previous appendicectomy.

Anatomy of inguinal region

The inguinal canal
This is an oblique intermuscular slit 6 cm long above the medial half of the inguinal ligament between the deep and superficial ring. It transmits the spermatic cord in the male and the round ligament of the uterus in the female.

The deep inguinal ring
This is an oval opening in the transversalis fascia, 1.3 cm above inguinal ligament, midway between the anterior superior iliac spine and the pubic tubercle. This is the midpoint of the inguinal ligament — just lateral to the midinguinal point. The deep ring is bounded laterally by the angle between the transversus abdominis and the inguinal ligament. It is bounded medially by the transversalis fascia and the inferior epigastric vessels behind this.

The superficial inguinal ring
A triangular opening in the external oblique aponeurosis. The lateral crus attaches to the pubic tubercle. The medial crus attaches to the pubic crest near the symphysis. The base of the superficial ring is the pubic crest.

Floor of the inguinal canal
The inguinal ligament forms most of the floor of the inguinal canal. The lacunar ligament forms the medial part of the floor filling in the angle between the inguinal ligament and the pectineal line.

Ceiling of the inguinal canal
Lateral to medial, this is formed by the transversus abdominis, internal oblique and the conjoint tendon.

The **transversus abdominis** arises lateral to the deep ring from the lateral half of the inguinal ligament. It arches over the roof of the inguinal canal to become the conjoint tendon.

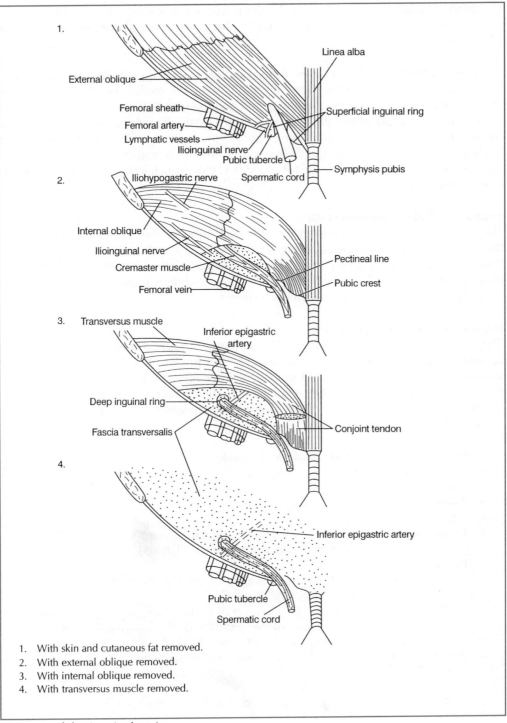

1. With skin and cutaneous fat removed.
2. With external oblique removed.
3. With internal oblique removed.
4. With transversus muscle removed.

Anatomy of the inguinal region

The **internal oblique** arises in front of the deep ring from the lateral two-thirds of the inguinal ligament and, lying superficial to the transversus abdominis, behaves in the same ways.

The **conjoint tendon** is formed by the fusion of the aponeurosis of the internal oblique and transversus abdominis. It arches over the canal forming the medial roof and strengthening the posterior wall. It inserts into the pubic crest and the pectineal line at right angles to the lacunar ligament which forms the floor here. Transversus abdominis, internal oblique and conjoint tendon can contract and lower the roof of the inguinal canal thereby strengthening it. They are supplied by L1 from the iliohypogastric and the ilioinguinal nerves. These nerves are at risk in muscle-splitting incision for appendicectomy which leads to an increased risk of direct hernia.

Anterior wall of the inguinal canal
The anterior wall of the canal is formed mostly by external oblique strengthened laterally by the internal oblique. The superficial ring is a defect in the anterior wall. The anterior wall is strongest opposite the weakest point of the posterior wall — the laterally placed deep ring. Here the anterior wall is strengthened by the internal oblique fibres that originate anterior from the lateral two-thirds of the inguinal ligament.

Posterior wall of the inguinal canal
The posterior wall of the canal is formed by transversalis fascia strengthened medially by conjoint tendon. The deep ring is a defect in the posterior wall. The posterior wall is strongest opposite the weakest point of the anterior wall — the medially placed superficial ring. Here it is strengthened by the conjoint tendon fibres, formed from the internal oblique and transversus abdominis as they curve over to insert posterior into the pubic crest and the pectineal line.

Contents of the inguinal canal in the male

- **Vas**
- **Arteries**: testicular, artery to vas, cremasteric
- **Veins**: the pampiform plexus
- **Lymphatic vessels**: the testis drains to the paraaortic lymph nodes; the coverings of the testis drain to the external iliac nodes
- **Nerves**:
  Genital branch of genitofemoral (supplies cremaster muscle)
  Sympathetic nerves accompanying arteries
  Ilioinguinal nerve (enters via anterior wall of the canal, not via the internal ring and runs in front of the spermatic cord) supplying the skin of inguinal region, upper part of thigh and anterior one-third of scrotum or labia
- **Processus vaginalis**: the obliterated remains of the peritoneal connection to the tunica vaginalis

All of the above are in the spermatic cord except the ilioinguinal nerve

Coverings of the spermatic cord

- Internal spermatic fascia (from transversalis fascia)
- Cremasteric fascia (from internal oblique and transversus abdominus)
- External spermatic fascia (from external oblique)

The inguinal canal is a natural point of weakness in the abdominal wall. There are several features which reduce this weakness:

- The rings lie some distance apart (except in infants)
- The anterior wall is reinforced by internal oblique in front of the deep ring
- The posterior wall is reinforced by the conjoint tendon opposite the superficial ring
- When abdominal pressure increases, the internal oblique and transversus abdominus contract, lowering the roof
- When abdominal pressure increases, we automatically squat so the anterior thigh presses against the inguinal canal and reinforces it

Indirect inguinal hernias

- 60% of adult male inguinal hernias are indirect
- 4% of male infants have an indirect inguinal hernia

This is the most common type of groin hernia in children. It is thought to be caused by a congenital failure of processus vaginalis to close (saccular theory of Russell).

Predisposing factors for indirect inguinal hernias

- **Males**: bigger processus vaginalis than in women
- **Premature twins or low birth weight**: processus vaginalis not closed
- **Africans**: the lower arch in the more oblique African pelvis means the internal oblique origin does not protect the deep ring
- **On the right**: right testis descends later than the left
- **Testicular feminization syndrome**: genotypic male but androgen insensitive so phenotypic female
- **Young men**: direct hernias become more common with age
- **Patients with increased intraperitoneal fluid** from whatever cause (e.g. cardiac, cirrhotic, carcinomatosis or dialysis); this tends to open up the processus vaginalis

The indirect inguinal hernia sac is the remains of the processus vaginalis. The sac extends through the deep ring, canal and superficial ring. The inferior epigastric artery lies medial to the neck. In a **complete sac** the testis is found in the fundus. In an **incomplete sac**, the sac is limited to the canal or is inguinoscrotal or inguinolabial. The indirect hernia commonly descends into the scrotum.

Direct inguinal hernias

- 35% of adult male inguinal hernias are direct
- 5% of adult male inguinal hernias are a combination of direct and indirect

This is an acquired weakness in the abdominal wall so tends to develop in adulthood as compared with indirect hernias which are common in children.

Predisposing factors for direct inguinal hernias

- Males
- Old age
- Increased intra-abdominal pressure
  (e.g. chronic cough, obesity, constipation, prostatism)
- Smoking
- Aortic aneurysm (associated with a collagen defect)
- Anatomical variant (10% of adult white males have no lateral extension
  of the conjoint tendon, which makes them more liable to
  direct hernias)

The direct inguinal hernia sac lies behind the cord. The inferior epigastric artery lies lateral to the neck. The hernia passes directly forward through the defect in the posterior wall (fascia transversalis) of the inguinal canal. This hernia does not typically run down alongside the cord to the scrotum but may do so.

Anatomy of femoral region

Femoral sheath

The femoral sheath is a downward protrusion into the thigh of the fascial envelope lining the abdominal walls. It surrounds the femoral vessels and lymphatics for about 1″ below the inguinal ligament. The sheath ends by fusing with the tunica adventitia of the femoral vessels. This occurs close to the saphenous opening in the deep fascia of the thigh.

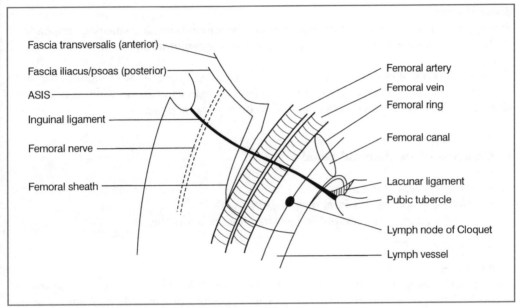

The femoral region

The anterior wall is continuous above with fascia transversalis, the posterior wall is continuous above with fascia iliacus/psoas fascia. It does not protrude below the inguinal ligament in the foetal position.

The femoral sheath exists to provide freedom for vessel movement beneath inguinal ligament during movement of the hip.

Contents of the femoral sheath

- Femoral artery in lateral compartment
- Femoral veins in intermediate compartment
- Lymphatics in medial compartment or femoral canal
- The femoral branch (L1) of the genitofemoral nerve pierces the anterior wall of the femoral sheath running on the anterior surface of the external iliac artery

NB. The femoral nerve lies in the iliac fossa between psoas and iliacus behind the fascia. Therefore it enters the thigh outside the femoral sheath.

Femoral canal

The femoral canal is the medial compartment of the femoral sheath containing lymphatics. It is about 1.3 cm long with an upper opening called the **femoral ring**.

The femoral canal allows lymph vessels to be transmitted from the lower limbs to the abdomen and is also a dead space into which the femoral vein can expand when venous return increases. The femoral canal is the path taken by femoral herniae.

Contents of the femoral canal

- Fatty connective tissue
- Efferent lymph vessels from deep inguinal nodes
- The deep inguinal node of Cloquet draining the penis/clitoris

Femoral ring

The top of the femoral canal is called the femoral ring. It is covered by the femoral septum, a condensation of extraperitoneal tissue. This is pushed downwards into the canal in a hernia.

Relations of the femoral ring

- Anteriorly the inguinal ligament
- Posteriorly the superior ramus of the pubis and the pectineal ligament
- Medially the lacunar ligament or ileopubic tract
- Laterally the femoral vein

These are also the margins of the neck of a femoral hernia. Note that three of the four are rigid making the femoral hernia prone to strangulation.

The lacunar ligament may have to be incised to release a strangulated hernia risking an accessory (abnormal) obturator artery.

Femoral hernia

Epidemiology

In females, femoral hernias are as common as indirect inguinal hernias. They are found 2.5 times more commonly in females because:

- Inguinal ligament makes a wider angle with the pubis in the female
- Enlargement of the fat in the femoral canal in fat middle-aged ladies stretches the femoral canal; this fat then disappears in old age leaving a bigger canal
- Pregnancy increases intra-abdominal pressure and stretches fascia transversalis

Mechanics of femoral hernia

Femoral hernia enters femoral canal through the femoral ring. The hernia arrives in the thigh next to the saphenous opening of the femoral sheath. The cribriform fascia over the saphenous opening becomes stretched over the hernia. Hernia enlarges upwards and medially into the superficial fascia of the inguinal ligament. Typically it lies between the superficial external pudendal and superficial epigastric veins compressing the saphenous vein as it emerges through the saphenous opening.

Characteristics of a typical femoral hernia

- Small (hard to find in an obese patient)
- Not reducible
- No cough impulse
- Often contains only omentum
- May contain a knuckle of bowel (most common site for a Richter's hernia)
- More common on the right
- 35–50% of all strangulated groin hernias in adults are femoral hernias

Differential diagnosis of femoral hernia

- Inguinal hernia
    Femoral hernia emerges below and lateral to the pubic tubercle
    Inguinal hernia emerges above and medial to the pubic tubercle
- Saphena varix
- Enlarged lymph node
- Lipoma
- Femoral artery aneurysm
- Sarcoma
- Ectopic testis
- Obturator hernia
- Psoas bursa
- Psoas abscess

Management of groin hernias

INDICATIONS FOR GROIN HERNIA REPAIR

Non-mandatory	Small
	  easily reducible
	  direct
		Follow-up in one year
		  (same for recurrent
		  hernias)

Elective
  (to be prioritized
  by job)
	Indirect
	Symptomatic
	  direct
		Because rate of
		  strangulation of inguinal
		  hernia is 0.3–2.9% per year
		  ↑ risk if irreducible or
		  indirect

Prompt	Irreducible
	  inguinal hernia
	History of <4
	  weeks
		More risk of strangulation
		  in first three months after
		  appearing

Urgent	All femoral
	  hernias
		Within a month 50%
		  strangulate

Emergency	Painful irreducible hernias	

Royal College of Surgeons' Guidelines of Management of Groin Hernias

- Appropriately trained surgeon performs/supervises operation
- Special hernia centres and special interest consultants recommended
- Suggest aiming to do 30% of elective hernias as a day case (8% at present)
- Criteria for surgery should be assessed:
    type of hernia (inguinal, femoral, reducible, partially reducible, primary, recurrent, complex)
    type of patient (social circumstances for discharge, ASA grade)
    and matched to surgeon, operative technique, day case or inpatient, GA or LA
- Recommends aiming for a recurrence rate of 0.5% at 5 years

Repair of inguinal hernia

The Royal College of Surgeons' guidelines on hernia management suggest the Shouldice technique or mesh repair for primary uncomplicated inguinal hernias.

- **Surgical approach**
  Patient is positioned supine
  Anaesthetic is general or local
  Incision is 2.5 cm above the medial two-thirds of the inguinal ligament along a skin crease
  Superficial veins are ligated and divided
  External oblique is slit along its fibres using scissors as far as the superficial inguinal ring
  Ilioinguinal nerve is identified and preserved if possible
  Spermatic cord is identified and the external spermatic fascia is incised
  Cremasteric muscles may be divided
  Cord is protected with a tape or hernia ring
  Spermatic cord is inspected for the presence of an indirect hernial sac; if found, the sac is held with clips and separated from the spermatic cord structures as far as the deep inguinal ring
  Sac is opened and its contents are released into the abdominal cavity
  Sac is then transfixed close to the deep ring using Vicryl and divided just distal to the ligature
  Shouldice or mesh repair is carried out

- **Mesh repair**
  Prophylactic antibiotics should be given
  Posterior wall of the inguinal canal is reinforced by use of a prolene mesh
  Mesh is applied on the transversalis fascia and internal oblique muscle
  Lateral end is slit in order to accommodate the spermatic cord
  Inferior margin of the mesh is sutured to the inner surface of the inguinal ligament using continuous prolene or nylon suture
  Medial and superior margins are fixed to the internal oblique muscle using interrupted sutures
  Medial end should reach the pubic tubercle
  Lateral tail ends are sutured to one another around the cord

---

Advantages and disadvantages of the prosthetic mesh repair

- **Advantages**
  Easier to learn and perform by trainees
  Lower recurrence rate (1:1000)
  Tension-free repair
  Reduced analgesic requirement

- **Disadvantages**
  Main disadvantage is the risk of infection; incidence may be reduced by avoiding haematomas and use of prophylactic antibiotics

- **Shouldice repair**

  In the Shouldice repair the cremaster muscle should always be divided to give good access to the deep ring

  Margins of the deep ring are dissected from the cord

  Fascia transversalis is opened from the deep ring medially down to the pubic tubercle

  Fascia transversalis is cleaned of extraperitoneal fat to expose:

  (1) the deep surface of the conjoint tendon above and medially
  (2) the fascia transversalis as it plunges into the thigh below and laterally to become the anterior layer of the femoral sheath

  Lower lateral fascia transversalis flap is sutured to the under-surface of the conjoint tendon

  Upper flap is overlapped and sutured to the anterior surface of the lower lateral flap of the fascia transversalis

  This reconstructs the posterior wall of the inguinal canal

  Suturing is taken laterally to make a new deep ring flush with the emergent cord

  Repair is reinforced medially by suturing the conjoint tendon to the aponeurosis of the external oblique

---

Advantages and disadvantages of the Shouldice repair

- **Advantages**
  Low risk of infection
  Indicated in the presence of
    strangulated bowel where mesh
    is not recommended
  Low recurrence rate in the right hands*

- **Disadvantages**
  More technically difficult than
    the mesh repair
  High standard of training needed
  Longer operative time than mesh repair
  Difficult to perform tension-free repair
  Higher post-op analgesic requirement
    than mesh repair

*This technique was popularized by the Shouldice Clinic. Recurrence rate is < 1% there, but approaches 3.5% elsewhere. At the Shouldice Clinic, the trainee surgeon is required to assist in 50 hernia repairs then perform 100 hernia repairs under supervision before being allowed to repair inguinal hernias independently.

- **Closure**

  This is similar for both the shouldice and mesh repair:

  Before closure, one should inspect for potential femoral hernia

  The external oblique aponeurosis is closed with a continuous absorbable suture
    (e.g. P.D.S.) over the cord

  Scarpa's fascia is closed with interrupted Vicryl

  Skin is closed with undyed subcuticular Monocryl

  The ipsilateral testicle is drawn down to the bottom of the scrotum

Other types of inguinal hernia repair
Laparoscopic repair is indicated in bilateral inguinal hernias and in recurrent hernias. The mesh is stapled between the peritoneum and the fascia transversalis.

In the **McVay–Cooper ligament operation** the fascia transversalis is opened and the upper medial flap is sutured to the iliopectineal ligament (Cooper's ligament).

The **Bassini (darn) repair** is no longer recommended due to high recurrence rates.

Repair of femoral hernia
The main aims are to:

* remove peritoneal sac
* repair defect

There are three main approaches: the low crural, the high inguinal and the high extra-peritoneal.

* **The crural or low approach (Lockwood approach):** this is the simplest and can be done under general or local anaesthetic. It is used for elective repair but is controversial for strangulated hernia. It is difficult to resect the compromised bowel through this incision and if compromised bowel slips through the canal back into the abdomen, a laparotomy is needed to retrieve it.
  Oblique incision 1 cm below and parallel to the medial inguinal ligament is performed
  Femoral sac in the subcutaneous tissue is exposed and opened
  Contents are examined and reduced into the abdomen. In an elective repair
    usually only omentum present. Compromised bowel should never be returned to the abdomen.
  Once the contents are reduced into the abdomen the sac neck is transfixed using Vicryl
    and excised 1 cm distal to the ligation
  Repair is performed by suturing the inguinal and pectineal ligaments for 1 cm laterally
    using interrupted nylon sutures on a J-shaped needle
  Care is taken to protect the laterally located femoral vein and avoid constricting it
  Subcutaneous tissue is closed using Vicryl
  Skin is closed with subcuticular Monocryl

* **The high inguinal approach (Lotheissen approach):** approaches the femoral canal through the inguinal canal. The dissection proceeds as for inguinal hernia repair except that the transversalis fascia is opened to expose the femoral vessels and the canal beneath it. This approach has the disadvantage of disrupting the normal inguinal canal but can, therefore, be used to repair a co-existing inguinal hernia. Although it provides better access to the contents of the peritoneal sac than the low approach, it is still not ideal for access to strangulated contents which may need a bowel resection. These strangulated hernias are best approached through the high extra-peritoneal approach (see later).

Approach is identical to that for Shouldice repair of an inguinal hernia (see earlier)

Once in the inguinal canal, the posterior fascia transversalis is divided to gain access to the femoral canal

Hernia sac is opened, the contents are examined and reduced if safe to do so

Neck of the sac is transfixed, ligated and divided 1 cm distal to the ligature

Femoral canal defect is then repaired by suturing the pectineal ligament to the medial inguinal ligament

Transversalis fascia must be reconstituted, otherwise there is a high recurrence rate

Inguinal hernia orifices are examined and the inguinal canal is closed as described in the mesh repair of the inguinal hernia

- **High extra-peritoneal approach (McEvedy approach):** the most useful approach for strangulated hernia because it facilitates bowel resection if necessary. It can also be used for bilateral hernias through a Pfannenstiel incision.

Incision is transverse 6 cm above and parallel to the inguinal ligament over the lateral border of the rectus sheath

Rectus sheath is divided vertically at the lateral border to expose the peritoneum

Peritoneum and bladder are swept away from the back of the anterior abdominal wall exposing the femoral canal and the neck of the sac

Sac is reduced into the wound (the lacunar ligament may be divided to facilitate this)

Sac is opened and the contents examined

If the bowel looks doubtful, wrap it in a warm pack for 10 minutes and re-inspect

If the bowel is non-viable, resect it and do an end-to-end anastomosis

Reduce the contents of the sac, transfix the neck of the sac with a Vicryl suture and excise it 1 cm distal to the ligature

Close the defect by medial apposition of the inguinal and pectineal ligaments, protecting and avoiding compression of the femoral vein laterally

Use strong, non-absorbable suture and a J-shaped needle

After repair, the femoral canal should just admit the tip of the little finger

Repair the rectus with continuous, non-absorbable sutures

Close the subcutaneous tissue with Vicryl and use a subcuticular undyed Monocryl to skin

---

Royal College of Surgeons' Guidelines on Repair of Femoral Hernias

- The Royal College of Surgeons recommends the high inguinal approach, except in thin females when a low crural approach is acceptable
- In complex, recurrent or obstructed hernias the high extraperitoneal approach is advised

Post-operative care of groin hernia repair

- Analgesia
    local anaesthetic
    oral analgesia
- Early mobilization
- Stockings and heparin
- Return to sedentary job in two weeks
- Laxatives if necessary
- Audit results
    aim for 0.5% five-year recurrence

Post-operative complications of groin hernia repair

- **Wound**
  Bleeding
  Haematoma
  Sepsis
  Sinus

- **Scrotal**
  Ischaemic orchitis
  Testicular atrophy
  Hydrocoele
  Genital oedema
  Damage to vas and vessels

- **Special complications**
  Nerve injuries
  Persistent post-op pain
  Compression of femoral vessels
  Urinary retention
  Impotence

- **General complications**
  Chest infection
  DVT
  PE
  Cardiovascular problems
  Visceral injury

- **Operation failure**
  Recurrence
  Missed hernia
  Dehiscence

- **Mortality**

Groin hernia repair under local anaesthetic

* **Advantages**
  Early mobilization
  Decreased urinary retention, DVT/PE
  Safer in high-risk patients
  Decreased cost, increased patient turnover
  No reduction in outcome or increase in recurrence if not fit for general anaesthetic

Not suitable in obese/anxious/unco-operative patients or in complex hernias.

* **Precautions**
  Safe dose/kg recorded in notes (patient weighed)
  Monitoring:
    pulse oximeter
    IV access
    BP before and after local anaesthetic
    observations
  Nurse
  Anaesthetist in the building
  Nearby resuscitation equipment
  Two hours' pre-op fasting
  IV access before local anaesthetic given
* **Method**
  Subcutaneous wheal in line of incision
  Deep injection at ilioinguinal + iliohypogastric nerves (one finger breadth medial to anterior superior iliac spine)
  Further injection deep to proposed incision
  Deep infiltration as needed
  Bupivacaine block before closure in both general anaesthetic and local anaesthetic
* **Agents**
  Lignocaine
  Bupivacaine
  Hypnoval (not encouraged due to varying response)
* **Complications of repair under local anaesthetic**
  Systemic excitation (increased anxiety or rarely convulsions)
  Hypotension
  Dysrhythmias
  Respiratory depression
  May have to go to general anaesthetic due to inadequate analgesia or technical problems

1.3 Other hernias

Paraumbilical hernias

More common within increasing age, M = F.

Causes
Increased intra-abdominal pressure, e.g. ascites, multiple pregnancy, malignancy, chronic obstructive airway disease or obesity.

Anatomy
The sac protrudes through a defect in the linea alba near the umbilical cicatrix but, unlike the true umbilical hernia, not through the cicatrix itself. Progressively increases in size. Usually contains omentum and transverse colon, sometimes small intestine. The neck of the sac is often very narrow compared with the sac contents and very fibrous. Contents adhere to each other, the coverings and the omentum.

Coverings
Skin, superficial fascia, rectus sheath, transversalis fascia and sac. These stretch and fuse into a thin membrane, through which peristalsis may be seen.

Complications
Redness, excoriation, ulceration, gangrene, pendulousness, infection, faecal fistula, strangulation, incarceration and obstruction.

Clinical features
Usually irreducible. May present with pain due to incarceration and subacute obstruction. Strangulation is common due to narrow neck.

Surgical repair
This may have significant mortality in old patients with large hernias. Problems include:

- Patients tend to be old with co-morbidity
- High risk of strangulation
- Difficult anatomy and reduction
- May have increased intra-abdominal pressure after reduction, which exacerbates respiratory problems. Pre-operative weight loss and chest physiotherapy may help.

Surgical repair of paraumbilical hernia

Mayo's Operation ('vest over pants')

1. Stretched skin is excised as a horizontal ellipse
2. Incision is deepened to rectus sheath to expose neck of sac
3. Incision enlarged laterally to give a long transverse exposure
4. Sac opened near neck where adhesions are least likely
5. Protruding bowel examined and returned
6. Protruding omentum excised to lessen volume of contents
7. Sac and overlying skin removed
8. Lower edge of rectus is brought up and fixed by non-absorbable mattress sutures to behind the upper flap ('pants')
9. Upper flap is pulled down to overlap lower flap ('vest')
10. Superficial fascia and skin are closed

Mesh repair
Steps 1–7 as above, then mesh is sutured over defect
Antibiotic prophylaxis should be given

Umbilical hernia in infants

Remember the rule of 3s

- 3% live births have umbilical hernia
- Only 3:1000 need an operation
- Operate on after the age of 3
- Recur in third trimester of pregnancy

Incidence

- 3% neonates have umbilical herniae, most resolve spontaneously
- 3:1000 live births need further surgery
- More common in Negro children

Anatomy
Peritoneal sac penetrates through linea alba at umbilical cicatrix to lie in subcutaneous tissues beneath skin cicatrix. There is a narrow rigid neck at the aponeurosis.

Prognosis

- All decrease in size as child grows
- Few persist after puberty
- Some cause disfigurement or incarcerate
- Only a minority need an operation
- Must preserve the umbilicus to avoid stigmatizing child
- Similar Mayo 'vest over pants' repair to adult repair (see above)
- Absorbable polymer used

Incisional hernia

Diffuse extension of peritoneum and abdominal contents though a weak scar.

Incidence

- 6% of abdominal wounds at 5 years
- 12% at 10 years
- M = F

Clinical features
Can present as a lump increasing in size, subacute intestinal obstruction, incarceration, pain, strangulation, skin excoriation and rarely spontaneous rupture (more common in Caesarean section and gynaecological wounds). Smaller incisional hernias can cause persistent discomfort in abdominal wound caused by impalpable extraperitoneal protrusion.

Causes of incisional hernia

- **Technical failure by the surgeon**
  Post-operative haematoma,
    necrosis, sepsis
  Inept closure
  Drains or stomas
  Inappropriate incision

- **Tissue factors**
  Age
  Immunosuppression (diabetes,
    jaundice, renal failure)
  Obesity
  Malignant disease

- **High-risk incisions**
  Lower mid-line
  Upper mid-line
  Lateral muscle splitting
  Subcostal
  Parastomal
  Transverse

- **Pre-operative conditions**
  Cardiopulmonary disease
  Obesity
  Local skin/tissue sepsis

Surgical repair

- **Layer-to-layer anatomical repair**: if there is no tissue loss
- **Mesh repair**: mesh inserted across defect; essential if there is tissue or aponeurosis loss
- **Keel repair**: the sac is invaginated by successive lines of non-absorbable sutures
- **Recurrence rates**: vary from 1% to 46%; recurrence rates with mesh are lower (10%)

Epigastric hernia

This is a protrusion of extra-peritoneal fat or peritoneum through one of the lozenge-shaped fissures commonly found between the latticed fibres of the linea alba. Epigastric hernias can occur in children or adults and may cause disproportionate epigastric pain and upper gastro-intestinal symptoms. They are cured by excision of sac and repair of linea alba. 30% have co-existing intra-abdominal disease causing symptoms and so should be fully investigated.

Spigelian hernia

These are also known as **semilunar line hernias** and account for 1% of abdominal hernias. The hernia protrudes through bands of internal oblique muscle as it enters the semilunar line. Most occur below the umbilicus adjacent to line of Douglas. It is usually deflected laterally by the external oblique and can be found near the iliac crest. The sac may enter rectus sheath and be confused with rectus muscle haematoma. They are more common in women than men. They present as an aching lump, and are diagnosed by ultrasound scan. They may strangulate. Repair is by excision of peritoneal sac and closure of the aponeurotic defect.

Lumbar hernia

These tend to occur after renal operations, lumbar abscesses or paralysis of lateral lumbar muscles by poliomyelitis or spina bifida. Spontaneous lumbar hernias occur through the lumbar triangle of Petit (formed by the iliac crest, posterior external oblique and anterior latissimus dorsi) or the quadrilateral lumbar space (formed by the 12th rib, lower border of serratus posterior inferior, anterior border of erector spinae and internal oblique).

Other types of hernias

Other, rarer hernias include gluteal (through greater sciatic notch) and sciatic (through lesser sciatic notch).

1.4 Complications of hernias

Incarceration

The contents are fixed in the sac because of their size or adhesions. The hernia is irreducible but the contents are not necessarily strangulated or obstructed.

Obstruction

The lumen of the bowel is obstructed by the neck of the hernia itself or the fibrosis or swelling of the peritoneum or bowel. The afferent loop will be distended, the efferent will be empty.

Strangulation

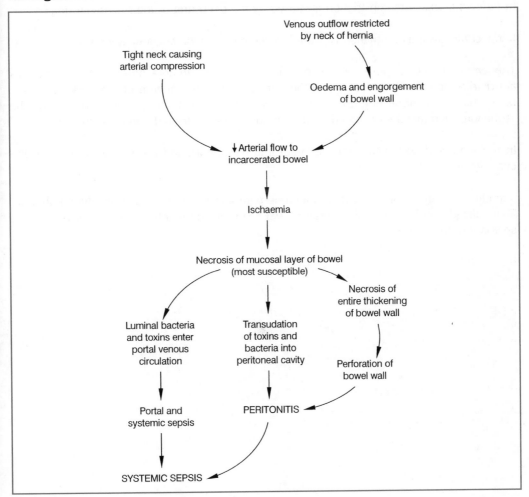

Pathophysiology of bowel strangulation

In strangulation the blood supply of the contents of the hernia is cut off leading to ischaemia. When a loop of gut is strangulated, there will also be intestinal obstruction. The swelling and oedema increases the strangulation, which normally starts with venous obstruction leading to oedema, arterial obstruction and finally ischaemia.

> The longer the strangulated length of bowel, the more the consequent systemic morbidity. The more distal the bowel strangulated, the more the toxicity and morbidity.

The constricting agent is usually the neck of the peritoneal sac, which is often fibrosed and rigid where it crosses the parietal defect.

In *indirect hernias* the constriction is caused by the deep ring or the superficial ring.

In *direct hernias* the constriction is caused by the defect in the fascia transversalis.

The *femoral hernia* is more constricting due to the inflexible neck (three of its four margins are rigid). The constriction is due to the fibrosis of the peritoneum of the neck of the sac rather than the femoral ring itself, which is why the femoral vein is rarely obstructed. The saphenous vein may be occluded by the fundus as it exits from the femoral sheath.

In the *umbilical hernia* the rigid aponeurotic margins around the peritoneal sac are the constricting agents.

The clinical features of strangulation include pain and tenderness in an irreducible hernia. Strangulated hernias containing small bowel are more frequently on the right due to the anatomy of the mesentery.

Reduction *en masse*

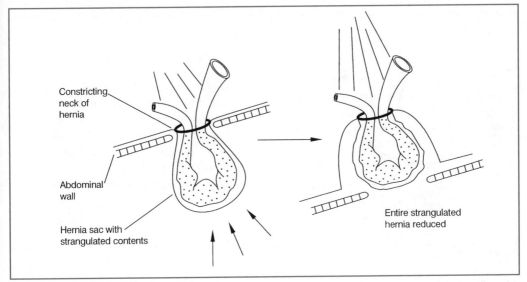

Reduction *en masse* of a hernia

Pushing a hernia back into the abdomen without surgery may relieve the obstruction or strangulation, but you risk the following complications:

- Rupture of the bowel at the neck of the sac
- Return of devitalized bowel to abdomen
- Reduction *en masse* of entire hernia sac complete with strangulating neck out of sight through the abdominal wall. In reduction *en masse* of an inguinal hernia the cord is foreshortened and the testicle is drawn up. Traction on the testicle gives pain and a tender mass is felt in the abdomen (Smiddy's sign).
- Even after successful reduction, the returned bowel can develop stricture at either of the two sites of constriction of the efferent and afferent loops (internal stenosis of Garré).

Richter's hernia

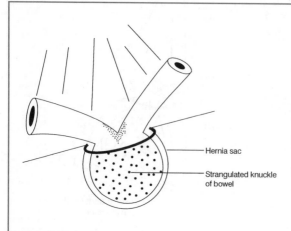

Hernia sac

Strangulated knuckle
of bowel

This is a partial enterocoele when only the antimesenteric margin of the gut is strangulated in the sac. The obstruction may be incomplete but there will be a tender, irreducible hernia with a varying amount of toxaemia and gangrene.

Richter's hernia

Maydl's hernia

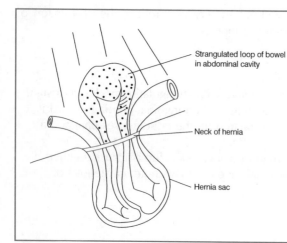

Strangulated loop of bowel
in abdominal cavity

Neck of hernia

Hernia sac

This occurs when a W-shaped loop of small gut lies in the hernia sac and the intervening loop is strangulated within the main abdominal cavity. This is seen in very large hernial sacs, especially in developing countries.

Maydl's hernia

Afferent loop strangulation

Another rare problem seen in large hernias when the gut of the afferent loop becomes entwined about the afferent and efferent loops.

Littre's hernia

This is a hernia sac containing strangulated Meckel's diverticulum. It can progress to gangrene, suppuration and formation of a local fistula.

Spontaneous rupture of hernia sac

This can occur in incisional hernia. It is surprisingly benign and peritonitis is rare. It needs an urgent laparotomy. The adhesions and oedema at the neck of the sac probably prevent the main peritoneal cavity from immediate contamination.

Traumatic rupture of hernia

This is usually due to blunt trauma to the abdomen or a hernia when it is 'down'. It may occur during over-enthusiastic attempts at reduction. Rupture usually occurs at the neck of the sac. Urgent laparotomy is needed.

Involvement in peritoneal disease process

- **Mesothelial hyperplasia**: repeated incarcerations of gut in the hernial sac in infancy can lead to local peritoneal hyperplasia. This is an exuberant reactive phenomenon, not a malignant condition such as adult peritoneal mesothelioma from which it must be distinguished.
- **Metastatic disease**: this occurs by transcoloemic seeding or direct invasion. If ascites or thickening in hernia sac is detected at operation, the fluid should be sent for cytology and the sac for histology. Only occurs in one in three million hernia repairs. It is advised to then complete the hernia operation and return the patient to the ward to prepare and consent for laparotomy.
- **Intra-abdominal mesothelioma**: this can spread to the hernia sac
- **Endometriosis**: is found most often in incisional hernias after gynaecological operations or Caesarean sections
- **Peritonitis**: this can lead to a pus-filled hernia sac
- **Appendicitis**: this can be found in inguinal, femoral or umbilical hernias.

Sliding hernia (hernia *en glissade*)

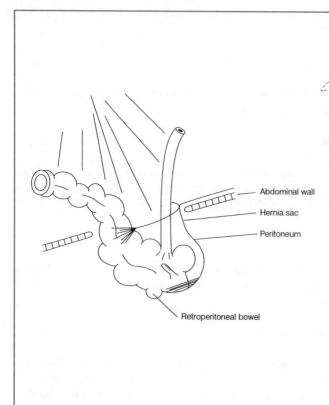

This occurs when the sac wall is composed in part by retroperitoneal viscus, like caecum or colon. The bowel forms part of the hernia but anatomically lies outside the cavity of the sac. In children, sliding hernias of the bladder (in boys) or ovary and tubes (in girls) can occur. Large hernias in old people may contain huge loops of sigmoid or caecum with only a small sac in the upper part. Surgical treatment should be carried out with care as there is a danger of opening the bowel instead of the sac. The patulous redundant sac is removed, hernia contents are mobilized and reduced.

Sliding hernia

Herniation of female genitalia

The ovary and tubes are commonly found in inguinal hernias in small girls. They must be carefully preserved and returned to the abdomen. In older women, sliding hernias of the ovary and tubes can occur in femoral, inguinal and obturator hernias. The uterus is a rare finding in a hernia sac, but pregnancy in incarcerated hernias is documented!

2. ABDOMINAL WALL

2.1 The anterior abdominal wall

Layers of abdominal wall

When you make an incision in the anterior abdominal wall you will go through the following layers.

Layers of abdominal wall

- Skin
- Superficial fascia
- Deep fascia (vestigial)
- Muscles (depending on incision)

- Transversalis fascia
- Extra-peritoneal fat
- Peritoneum

Skin
The skin has horizontal Langer's lines over the abdomen.

Superficial fascia

- Superficial fatty layer (Camper's fascia)
- Deep membranous layer (Scarpa's fascia). This is absent above and laterally and fuses with the deep fascia of the leg inferior to the inguinal ligament. It is continuous with Colles' fascia over the perineum which forms a tubular sheath for the penis/clitoris and a sac-like covering for the scrotum/labia.

Deep fascia
This is a vestigial thin layer of areolar tissue over the muscles.

Muscles
The muscles you pass through depend upon the site of your incision:

- **External oblique**: a large sheet of muscle fibres run downwards from lateral to medial, like a 'hand in your pocket'. Medially it becomes a fibrous aponeurosis which lies over the rectus abdominus muscle (see below) forming part of the anterior rectus sheath.
- **Internal oblique**: another large sheet of muscle fibres lying deep to external oblique and at right angles to it. Medially it forms a fibrous aponeurosis which splits to enclose the middle portion of the rectus abdominus as part of the anterior and posterior rectus sheath.

- **Transversus abdominus**: the third large sheet of muscle lying deep to internal oblique and running transversely. Medially it forms a fibrous aponeurosis which contributes to the posterior rectus sheath lying behind the rectus abdominus.
- **Rectus abdominus**: this muscle and its pair are joined at the linea alba in the midline and form a wide strap running longitudinally down the anterior abdominal wall. It lies within the rectus sheath formed by the aponeuroses of the three muscles described above. It is attached to the anterior rectus sheath, but not the posterior rectus sheath, by three tendinous insertions. These insertions are at the level of the xiphisternum, umbilicus and halfway between (giving the 'six pack' appearance in well-developed individuals!).
- **Pyramidalis**: a small unimportant muscle arising from the pubic crest and inserting in the linea alba. 4 cm long and lies behind the anterior rectus sheath in front of the rectus abdominus.
- **Rectus sheath**: any incision over the rectus abdominus will go through the anterior rectus sheath. The arrangement of the rectus sheath is best considered in three sections:

Above the level of the costal margin, the anterior rectus sheath is formed by the external oblique aponeurosis only. There is no internal oblique or transversus abdominus aponeurosis at this level. Therefore, there is no posterior rectus sheath and the rectus abdominus lies directly upon costal cartilages 5–7.

From the costal margin to just below the umbilicus, the anterior rectus sheath is formed by the external oblique aponeurosis and the anterior leaf of the split internal oblique aponeurosis. It is attached to the rectus abdominus by tendinous intersections. The posterior rectus sheath is formed by the posterior leaf of the internal oblique aponeurosis and the transversus abdominus aponeurosis.

Below the line of Douglas: about 2.5 cm below the umbilicus is a line called the 'arcuate line of Douglas' (see figure opposite). At this level, the posterior rectus sheath (that is, the posterior leaf of the internal oblique aponeurosis along with the transversus abdominus aponeuroses) passes anterior to the rectus abdominus. Therefore, below the arcuate line of Douglas there is no posterior rectus sheath. The rectus abdominus lies directly on transversalis fascia which is thickened here and called the iliopubic tract. The anterior rectus sheath is now formed by all the combined aponeuroses of the external oblique, the internal oblique and the transversus abdominus.

Apart from the rectus abdominus muscle, the other contents of the rectus sheath are the pyramidalis muscle, the segmental nerves and vessels from T7 to T12 and the superior and inferior epigastric vessels (see figure opposite).

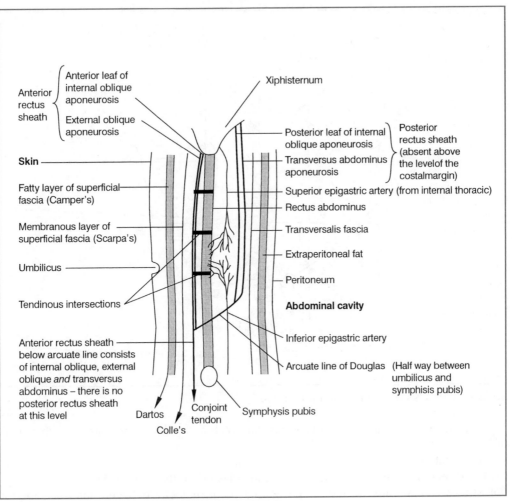

Saggital section of abdominal wall

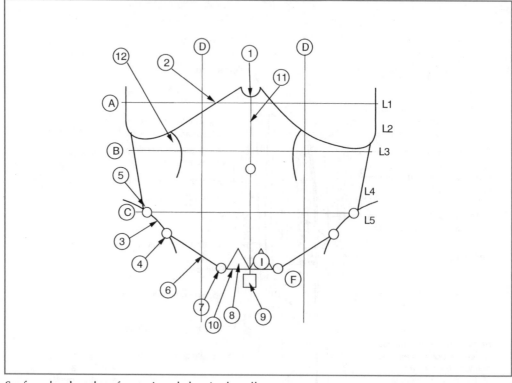

Surface landmarks of anterior abdominal wall:

(A) **Transpyloric line**: halfway between jugular notch and pubic symphysis at L1 (pancreas lies here)

(B) **Subcostal line**: under lowest rib (rib 10 at L3)

(C) **Intertubercular line**: between the two tubercles of the iliac crest (L5)

(D) **Mid-clavicular line**: through mid-inguinal point, halfway between anterior superior iliac spine and symphysis pubis

(1) **Xiphoid process**: Xiphisternal junction is at T9

(2) **Costal margins**: ribs 7–10 in front and 11 and 12 behind. Tenth costal cartilage is the lowest at L3

(3) **Iliac crest**: anterior superior iliac spine (ASIS) to posterior superior iliac spine (PSIS). Highest point L4

(4) **ASIS**

(5) **Tubercle of iliac crest**: 5 cm behind ASIS at L5

(6) **Inguinal ligament**: running from ASIS to pubic tubercle

(7) **Pubic tubercle**: tubercle on superior surface of pubis. Inguinal ligament attaches to it, as the lateral end of the superficial inguinal ring

(8) **Superficial inguinal ring**: inguinal hernia comes out above and medial to the pubic tubercle at point marked (I). Femoral hernia below and lateral to the pubic tubercle at point marked (F)

(9) **Symphysis pubis**:mid-line cartilaginous joint between pubic bones
(10) **Pubic crest**: ridge on superior surface of pubic bone medial to pubic tubercle
(11) **Linea alba**: symphysis pubis to xiphoid process mid-line
(12) **Linea semilunaris**: lateral edge of rectus. Crosses costal margin at ninth costal cartilage (tip of gall bladder palpable here)

Surface markings of abdominal organs and vessels

- **Gall bladder**: tip of right ninth costal cartilage where linea semilunaris intersects the costal margin
- **Spleen**: under ribs 9, 10 and 11 on the left; long axis lies along rib 10; palpable in infants
- **Pancreas**: lies along transpyloric plane (L1)
- **Kidney**: from the level ot T12 to L3 the hilum lies on the transpyloric plane (L1). Right kidney is lower. Kidneys move 2–5 cm in respiration
- **Appendix**: McBurney's point is the surface marking of the base of the appendix one-third of the way up the line joining the anterior superior iliac spine to the umbilicus.
- **Aortic bifurcation**: at the level of L4 vertebra to the left of the mid-line
- **External iliac artery**: palpable at the mid-inguinal point halfway between anterior superior iliac spine and symphysis pubis

Diseases of the umbilicus

- **Congenital**
  Hernias of the cord
  Gastroschisis
  Exomphalos

- **Tumours**
  Primary
    benign (papillomas, lipoma)
    malignant (SCC, melanoma)
  Secondary
    breast
    ovarian
    colon (via lymphatic, transcoloemic and direct spread along falciform ligament)

- **Endometriosis**

- **Hernia**
  Childhood (umbilical)
  Adult (paraumbilical)

- **Fistula**
  Urinary tract (via urachal remnant)
  Gastro-intestinal tract (via vitello-intestinal duct)

- **Suppurations**
  Primary
    obesity
    pilonidal
    fungal infections
  Secondary
    from intra-abdominal abscess

Abdominal incisions

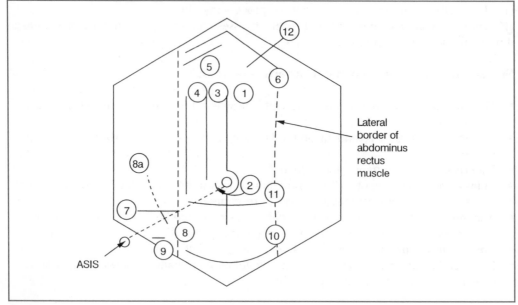

Abdominal incisions:

(1) **Mid-line incision through the linea alba**: this provides good access, can be extended easily and is quick to make and close. It is relatively avascular. Is more painful than transverse incisions. Incision crosses Langer's lines. Poor cosmetic appearance. Narrow linea alba below umbilicus. Some vessels cross the mid-line. May cause bladder damage.

(2) **Subumbilical incision**: used for repair of paraumbilical hernias and laparoscopic port

(3) **Paramedian incision**: 1.5 cm from mid-line through rectus abdominus rectus. Was the only effective vertical incision in the days when the only available suture material was catgut. Takes longer to make than mid-line incision Does not lend itself to closure by 'Jenkins rule' (use four time the length of the suture as the length of the wound). Poor cosmetic result. Can lead to infection in the rectus sheath. Other hazards include: the tendinous intersections must be dissected off; need to divide falciform ligament above umbilicus on the right; if rectus is split more than 1 cm from medial border, the intercostal nerves are disrupted leading to denervation of the medial rectus (the rectus can be retracted without splitting to avoid this).

(4) **Pararectal**: now abandoned due to damage of nerves entering rectus sheath

(5) **Kocher's incision**: 3 cm below and parallel to the costal margin from the mid-line to the rectus border. Good incision for cholecystectomy on the right and splenectomy on the left, **but** beware superior epigastric vessels. If wound is extended laterally, too many intercostal nerves are severed. Cannot be extended caudally.

(6) **Double Kocher's (rooftop) incision**: good access to liver and spleen. Useful for intrahepatic surgery. Used for radical pancreatic and gastric surgery and bilateral adrenal-ectomy

(7) **Transverse muscle-cutting incision**: can be across all muscles. Beware intercostal nerves.

(8) **McBurney's/Gridiron**: classic approach to appendix 'through the junction of the outer and middle third of a line from the ASIS to the umbilicus at right angles to that line'. It may be modified into a skin crease horizontal cut. The external oblique aponeurosis is cut in the line of the fibres and the internal oblique and transversus abdominus are split transversely in the line of the fibres. **Beware** — scarring if not horizontal — the iliohypogastric and ilioinguinal nerve — the deep circumflex artery.

(8a) **Rutherford Morrison incision**: the gridiron can be extended cephalad and laterally, obliquely splitting the external oblique to afford good access to the caecum, appendix and right colon.

(9) **Lanz**: this is a lower incision than the McBurney's and closer to the ASIS. It has a better cosmetic result (covered by bikini in ladies) but tends to divide the iliohypogastric and ilioinguinal nerves, leading to denervation of the inguinal canal mechanism which can result in increased risk of inguinal hernia.

(10) **Pfannenstiel incision**: most frequently used transverse incision in adults. Excellent access to female genitalia for Caesarian section and for bladder and prostate operations. Also used for bilateral hernia repair. The skin is incised in a downwardly convex arc into the suprapubic skin crease 2 cm above the pubis. The upper flap is raised and the rectus sheath incised 1 cm cephalic to the skin incision (not extending lateral to the rectus). The rectus is then divided longitudinally in the mid-line.

(11) **Transverse incision**: particularly useful in neonates and children who do not have the subdiaphragmatic and pelvic recesses of the adult. It heals securely and cosmetically with less pain and fewer respiratory problems than the longitudinal mid-line incision, **but** division of red muscle involves more blood loss and less secure closure than a longitudinal incision. It cannot be extended easily. It takes longer to make and to close. Limited access in adults to pelvic or subdiaphragmatic structure.

(12) **Thoracoabdominal incision**: access to lower thorax and upper abdomen. Used for liver and biliary surgery on the right. Used for oesophageal, gastric and aortic surgery on the left.

NB. **The ideal abdominal incision**: should allow easy and rapid access to the relevant structures; should allow easy extension, if necessary; should favour secure healing for the short-term (dehiscence) and long-term (herniation); should be relatively pain free post-operatively; should have a satisfactory cosmetic appearance.

2.2 The peritoneum

Anatomy of the peritoneum

The peritoneum is a thin serous membrane. It consists of a single layer of flattened cells (mesothelium).

Parietal peritoneum
Lines the walls of abdominal and pelvic cavities

Visceral peritoneum
Covers the organs

Peritoneal fluid
Lubricates surfaces and facilitates free movement

Extraperitoneal tissue
Lies between fascia of abdominal/pelvic wall and the parietal peritoneum. It varies in different regions. It forms loose areolar tissue over lower abdominal wall, is a thick fascial layer over iliacus, psoas and in the pelvis and is fatty over the kidney.

Peritoneal cavity
This is closed in the male but has tiny communications with exterior through the uterine tubes in the female.

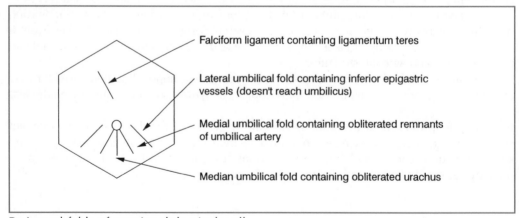

Falciform ligament containing ligamentum teres

Lateral umbilical fold containing inferior epigastric vessels (doesn't reach umbilicus)

Medial umbilical fold containing obliterated remnants of umbilical artery

Median umbilical fold containing obliterated urachus

Peritoneal folds of anterior abdominal wall

The **greater sac** is the main component of the peritoneal cavity (see figure opposite). The **lesser sac** is a small diverticulum from the greater sac with which it communicates via the epiploic foramen of Winslow. It lies behind the stomach and is also known as the omental bursa.

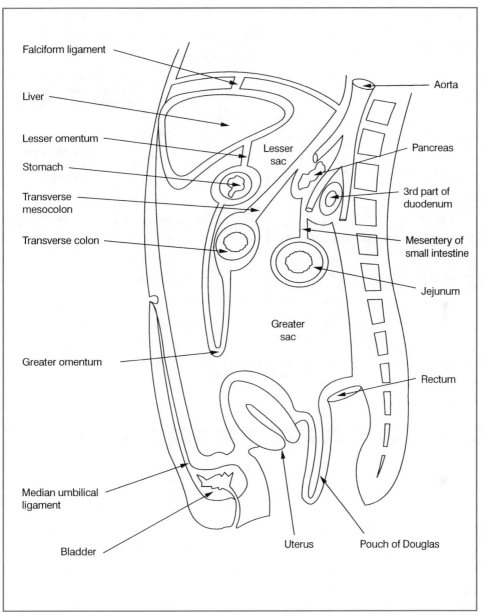

Falciform ligament

Liver

Lesser omentum

Stomach

Transverse mesocolon

Transverse colon

Greater omentum

Median umbilical ligament

Bladder

Lesser sac

Greater sac

Aorta

Pancreas

3rd part of duodenum

Mesentery of small intestine

Jejunum

Rectum

Uterus

Pouch of Douglas

Saggital section of abdomen showing arrangement of peritoneum

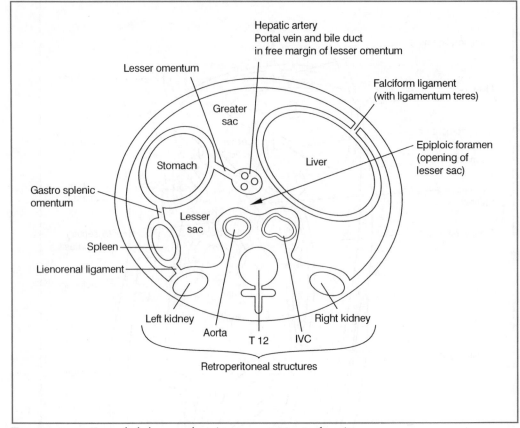

Transverse section of abdomen showing arrangement of peritoneum

Borders of the lesser sac

- **Anterior wall**: lesser omentum and stomach
- **Right side**: epiploic foramen and right free border of greater omentum
- **Left side**: hilum of spleen, lienorenal and gastrosplenic ligaments
- **Roof**: peritoneum over caudate lobe of liver
- **Posterior wall**: diaphragm, pancreas, left kidney and adrenal gland and transverse mesocolon

Functions of peritoneum

- Movement of viscera
- Absorption of contaminants (contains leucocytes in fluid)
- Seals off infected/ulcerated surfaces
- Suspends viscera in cavity
- Conveys blood vessels, lymphatics and nerves to viscera
- Stores fat (especially greater omentum)

Terms relating to peritoneum

Mesentery
Two-layered folds of peritoneum attaching intestines to posterior abdominal wall, e.g. mesentery of:

- small intestine
- transverse mesocolon
- sigmoid mesocolon

The viscus is suspended by and enclosed in the peritoneum, and the mesentery contains fat, blood vessels and lymphatics, sandwiched between the two layers of the peritoneum.

Omentum
Two-layered fold of peritoneum attaching stomach to another viscus. The **greater omentum** from greater curve of stomach, hangs down like an apron in front of the small intestine. It folds back on itself and attaches to the inferior border of the transverse colon. The **lesser omentum** runs from the stomach to the liver. The **gastrosplenic omentum/ligament** runs from the stomach to the spleen.

Peritoneal ligament
For example, falciform ligament — double layer of peritoneum attaching liver to anterior abdominal wall and diaphragm.

Peritoneum — boundaries and spaces

Boundaries of epiploic foramen

- **Anterior**
  Free border of lesser omentum with bile duct, hepatic artery and portal vein

- **Posterior**
  Inferior vena cava

- **Superior**
  Caudate process of caudate lobe of liver

- **Inferior**
  First part of duodenum

The epiploic foramen is the entrance to the lesser sac.

Subphrenic spaces

- Right and left anterior subphrenic spaces lie between diaphragm and liver, one each side of falciform ligament
- Right posterior subphrenic space lies between the right lobe of liver, right kidney and right colic flexure
- Right extraperitoneal space lies between the two layers of coronary ligament between the liver and diaphragm

For more details see section on subphrenic abscesses in Section 5.8, p.371.

Paracolic gutters

These lie on the lateral and medial side of ascending and descending colon (see figure opposite).

- Right lateral paracolic gutter is in communication with right posterior subphrenic space
- Left lateral paracolic gutter is separated from the area around the spleen by phrenocolic ligament but is in communication with the pelvic cavity

Roots of the mesenteries

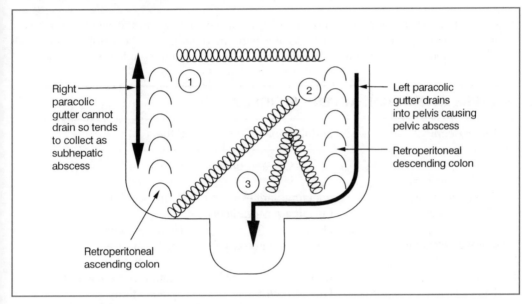

Right paracolic gutter cannot drain so tends to collect as subhepatic abscess

Left paracolic gutter drains into pelvis causing pelvic abscess

Retroperitoneal descending colon

Retroperitoneal ascending colon

Roots of the mesenteries

1. **Transverse mesocolon** attaches along the posterior abdominal wall and pancreas. The transverse colon is suspended from it.
2. The origin of the **mesentery of the small intestines** begins on the left posterior abdominal wall near the root of the transverse mesocolon and runs to the right iliac fossa. It is attached to the jejunum and ilium.
3. The root of the **sigmoid mesocolon** is an inverted 'V' in the left corner of the infracolic compartment. It overlies the bifurcation of the left common iliac vessels and left ureter.

2.3 Minimal access surgery (MAS)

This is conducted by remote manipulation. It is carried out within the closed confines of body cavities or lumens of hollow organs. It is performed under visual control via telescopes which incorporate the Hopkins rod lens system linked to charge couple device cameras.

TYPES OF MINIMAL ACCESS SURGERY

Laparoscopic	Endoluminal	Others

Biliary tract
Cholecystectomy
Cholecystotomy
Common duct
  examination
Cholecystojejunostomy
Deroofing hepatic cysts
	*Upper GIT and biliary
	  tract*
	Injecting varices
	Injecting gastric ulcers
	ERCP
	  ± sphincterotomy
		*Intra-articular joint
		  surgery*
		(arthroscopic)
		
		Thoracoscopic
		Thoraco dorsal
		  sympathectomy

Upper GIT
Cardiomyotomy
Cardiopexy
Fundoplication
Suturing perforated
  duodenal ulcers
Vagotomy
	Urology
	Diathermy/biopsy
	  bladder tumours
	Dilating urethral
	  strictures
	TURP
		Ligature of bullae and
		  pleurectomy
		Pulmonary resections
		Pericardiectomy
		Oesophageal vagotomy
		Oesophagectomy

Urology
Varicocele
Rectopexy
Nephrectomy
	Lower GIT
	Snaring of polyps
	Biopsy of tumours/
	  mucosa
		Perivisceral endoscopic
		
		Combined
		Endoscopic/open
		  (e.g. hemicolectomy)

Lower GIT Appendicectomy Hernia repair		

Advantages of minimal access surgery

* ↓ **Trauma to tissues**
* ↓ **Post-operative pain** leading to:
  * ↑ mobility (↓ DVT)
  * ↑ respiration (↓ chest infections)

↓ post-operative analgesia (↑ respiration, ↑ bowel function)
↓ post-operative lethargy/mental debility
- ↓ **Cooling and drying** of the bowel which may decrease intestinal function and threaten anastomosis; more marked in elderly and children
- ↓ **Retraction and handling** which causes iatrogenic injury and tissue compression leading to decreased perfusion and bowel function
- ↓ **Adhesions**
- ↓ **Wound complication** (e.g. infection, dehiscence, hernia formation)
- ↓ **Risk of Hep B and AIDS transmission**
- **Better view** on monitors for teaching purposes

Disadvantages of minimal access surgery

- Lack of tactile feedback
- Problems controlling bleeding
- Needs more technical expertise
- Longer operation times
- Significant ↑ in iatrogenic injuries to other organs (may not be seen)
- Difficulty removing bulky organs
- Expensive to buy and maintain cameras, monitors, laparoscopic instruments and disposables

How to establish a pneumoperitoneum

- Supine patient; usually general anaesthetic and muscle relaxation
- Prep anterior abdominal wall for open surgery
- Sub-umbilical stab incision with scalpel through the skin
- Introduce Veress needle (spring-loaded needle with blunt probe) through tented abdominal wall
- Confirm position with normal saline in needle (as abdominal wall is lifted, this creates decreased intra-abdominal pressure which moves the saline in the needle)
- Insufflation with 2–3 litres of CO_2 to a pressure of 15 mmHg pressure

Contraindications to laparoscopic surgery

- Previous laparotomies
- Peritonitis
- Bowel distension
- Ascites

NB. These depend on the case and the surgeon and are not absolute.

3.   ABDOMINAL STOMAS

3.1 Stomas

Incidence

There are 100,000 colostomies and 10,000 ileostomies in the UK at present. Incidence declining due to improved medical treatment of IBD and new stapling techniques enabling low resections.

Indications

- **Feeding** e.g. gastrostomy following GI surgery, in CNS disease, in coma
- **Decompression** e.g. gastrostomy (usually temporary), caecostomy (on table only)
- **Lavage** e.g. caecostomy on table before resecting distal colonic disease with primary anastomosis
- **Diversion** e.g. ileostomy to protect at risk distal anastomosis, colostomy to achieve bowel rest for Crohn's. Loop colostomies and double-barrelled colostomies facilitate closure later but are more difficult to manage
- **Exteriorization** e.g. double-barrelled colostomy (not used for malignancy), resection with end colostomy and rectal stump (Hartmann's) when primary anastomosis is impossible (e.g. perforation, ischaemia, obstruction). Resection with end colostomy and mucous fistula (like Hartmann's but easier to rejoin). Permanent colostomy (e.g. after abdomino-perineal resections in low rectal tumours). Permanent ileostomy (e.g. after panproctocolectomy for ulcerative colitis or familial polyposis coli).

Selecting a stoma site

Assess	Avoid	Problem patients
Before operation	Wound site	Wheelchair-bound
With clothes	Bony prominences	Amputees
Lying and standing	Existing scars	Obese
Good visibility	Umbilicus	Allergies
	Groin crease/	Psychological problems
	skin fold	

Pre-operative preparations

For elective colonic procedures, the following should be considered:

- Laxatives
- Enemas
- Antibiotic prophylaxis
- DVT prophylaxis
- Mark stoma site
- Counselling

3.2 Types of stoma

Gastrostomy

- **Main indications**: feeding
- **Pre-operatively**: empty stomach then fill with air
- **Methods**: commonly endoscopic (percutaneous endoscopic gastrotomy PEG) under sedation or general anaesthetic. May be done as an open procedure or under radiological control.

Jejunostomy

- **Main indications**: feeding
- **Methods**: T-tube jejunostomy sewed with purse string. A Witzel jejunostomy is a fine catheter into the jejunum and with the proximal 5-6 cm buried with interrupted sutures.

Ileostomy

Indications
Temporary:

- To protect ileorectal anastomosis
- Persistent low intestinal fistula
- Right colonic trauma
- Preliminary to construction of ileo-anal reservoir

Permanent:

- Panproctocolectomy for: ulcerative colitis; severe Crohn's; familial polyposis coli; multiple colonic cancer

Forming an ileostomy

Usually in the right iliac fossa. A circular skin defect 2–3 cm in diameter is excised. A cruciate incision is made in the underlying rectus. The peritoneum is incised. The clamped ileum is passed through the incision in the peritoneum. A peritoneal tunnel lessens the risk of herniation and prolapse. The main abdominal wound is closed and dressed. Intestinal clamp is then removed. A 4–5 cm spout is formed by everting the stump and suturing the mucosa to the skin with interrupted Vicryl sutures. A bite of the serosa is taken a few cm proximal to the stump with each stitch to evert the stoma.

(NB. 500 ml/day of high enzyme content fluid is lost from a low output ileostomy. One litre per day in a high output ileostomy.)

Caecostomy

- **Indications**: a formal caecostomy is seldom performed nowadays but tube caecostomies are still used for on table lavage, to protect awkward lower anastomoses and as a decompressing 'blowhole' for distal colonic obstruction
- **Methods**: usually performed with a large bore catheter through a stab incision in the caecum, protected by a purse string

Colostomy

Indications
Temporary:

- To protect distal anastomosis
- To achieve bowel rest (e.g. for Crohn's)
- If primary anastomosis is not possible after resection (e.g. in the presence of perforation, sepsis, ischaemia or obstruction)

Permanent:

- After abdomino-perineal resection of low rectal tumours

Types of colostomy

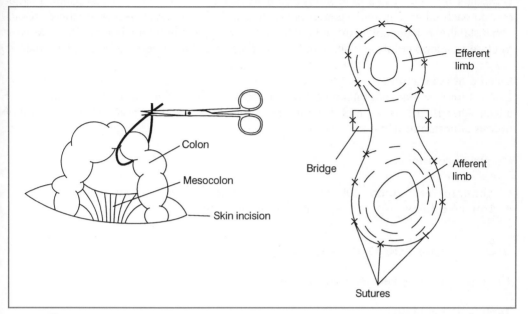

Loop colostomy

Loop colostomy

- Used for diversion not resection
- Usually in right transverse colon, proximal to middle colic artery
- Colostomy bridge passed around loop of colon through small avascular window in mesocolon
- Loop is brought out through abdominal wall incision
- Bridge is secured, laparotomy wound (if present) closed then stoma opened and formed

End colostomy and rectal stump (Hartmann's procedure)

- If a primary anastomosis is contraindicated
- After resection, colostomy is brought out using proximal end of colon
- Distal (usually rectal stump) is oversewn and left in the abdomen
- Difficult to rejoin later as the rectal stump is hard to find

End colostomy and mucous fistula

Used in similar circumstances to a Hartmann's but instead of dropping the rectal stump back into the abdomen, it is brought out as a separate stoma which, being an efferent limb, only produces mucus. This makes the distal limb more accessible when the bowel is rejoined later.

Double-barrelled colostomy
Used after resection when both limbs of the stoma can be brought to the skin surface adjacent to each other (e.g. mid-sigmoid perforation or volvulus). After resection, the proximal and distal limbs of the colon are sutured together along antimesenteric border. This is as easy to close as a loop colostomy and can be closed using a side-to-side stapler at a later date.

Closure of colostomies
Best left for 6 weeks until inflammation and oedema have settled, so minimizing the risk of a leak. After 10–12 weeks, mobilization of the bowel may become more difficult because of fibrous adhesion formation.

Output of colostomies

- **Mid-transverse colon**: 200–300 ml/day, significant enzyme content
- **Low colostomy**: 100 ml/day, virtually no enzyme

3.3 Complications of stomas

These are technical, general and practical.

Technical problems

Ischaemia/gangrene

- Abdominal wall defect too tight
- Injury to mesenteric vessels
- Re-siting is necessary

Prolapse or intussusception

- When bowel is not anchored to abdominal wall internally
- Reduction is easy but re-siting is needed if prolapse is recurrent

Parastomal hernias

- May cause difficulties with appliances
- May contain bowel at risk of obstruction/strangulation
- Re-siting may be needed

Stenosis

- Poor initial siting ✓
- Ischaemia ✓
- Underlying disease process (carcinoma, inflammatory bowel disease) ✓
- Re-siting may be necessary if there is obstruction

Bowel contents spill over into efferent loop

- Especially in loop colostomy
- Distal bowel is not adequately defunctioned if this occurs ✓
- Split or double-barrelled stomas solve this
- The efferent loop should always be sited cephalic to (above) the afferent loop

Reservoir ileostomies have specific problems: ✓

- Valve failure
- Incontinence
- Obstruction
- Impaired blood supply

General problems

Stoma diarrhoea

- Due to underlying disease
- Due to inappropriate diet
- Can lead to water and electrolyte imbalance especially after ileostomy

Nutritional disorders

- Vitamin B deficiency (megaloblastic anaemia)
- Chronic microcytic normochromic anaemia (?)

Kidney stones and gallstones

- Caused by loss of terminal ileum
- Failure of bile salt absorption
- Excessive water loss

Short gut syndrome

- Profuse fluid and electrolyte loss

Underlying disease

- May cause recurrent symptoms
- Crohn's may cause peristomal fistulae or proximal obstruction

Psychological and sexual problems

Practical problems

Odour
Advice can be given on hygiene, diet and deodorant sprays.

Flatus
This can be improved by diet and special filters.

Skin problems
This is usually due to an ill-fitting device. The problem is worsened as the stoma shrinks post-operatively. The problem can be counteracted by a barrier cream or two-piece appliance. Ileostomies with their irritant, copious output, can be particularly troublesome. The patient may need a supporting belt if spout is not big enough.

Leakage
Transverse loop colostomies are especially prone to leakage. A poor site may be responsible. Methyl cellulose bland paste around the appliance can help.

Parastomal hernia
A flexible pouch, supporting belt and filler paste can all help with this problem. Resiting may be necessary.

Stoma prolapse
Needs surgical correction.

3.4 Stomas — post-operative practicalities

Stoma appliances must be secure, comfortable, skin friendly, adhesive and odour proof.

Two types of appliance:

- **One-piece**: adhesive, surrounding pouch adheres to skin; whole appliance is changed
- **Two-piece**: base plate with flange; pouch only changed regularly

Two types of pouch:

- **Drainable**: used in immediate post-operative period when output is large and fluid
- **Closed**: has charcoal filter to release flatus without odour

Post-operative advice

- Patient warned of problems: oedematous stoma; copious offensive early output; transparent pouch to monitor stoma
- Self-care programme: patients observe, help then manage their own stomas
- Counselling and support: from stoma care nurse

Alternative methods of colostomy management

- **Irrigation**: flushing fluid into colon via stoma (no appliance needed); patient needs suitable bathroom facilities; not satisfactory for Crohn's
- **Colostomy plug**: foam plug which clips to a flange; plug fills lumen and blocks bowel for 8–12 hours

4. THE OESOPHAGUS

4.1 Anatomy of the oesophagus

Muscular tube extending from cricoid cartilage (C6) to the cardiac orifice of the stomach (T10 and left seventh costal cartilage) 25 cm long. Divided into upper, middle and lower third.

SUMMARY OF ANATOMY OF OESOPHAGUS

	Upper (cervical)	Middle (thoracic)	Lower (thoracic and abdomen)
Relations	C6, C7 Trachea Thyroid Recurrent laryngeal nerve Thoracic duct	T_1 body Descending aorta Thoracic duct Trachea and left main bronchus Right pulmonary artery Pericardium Arch of the aorta Azygous vein	Pierces diaphragm 2.5 cm left of mid-line at T_{10} 1–2 cm in abdomen Through left crus fibres of diaphragm Right crus fibres form sling Left lobe of liver Left gastric artery Left inferior phrenic artery

Continues ...

... Continued

	Upper (cervical)	**Middle (thoracic)**	**Lower (thoracic and abdomen)**
Blood supply	Inferior thyroid artery	Oesophageal branches from aorta and bronchial arteries	Branches from left gastric and left inferior phrenic arteries
Venous drainage	Inferior thyroid vein Vertebral vein Brachiocephalic vein	Azygous and hemiazygous veins	Left gastric vein draining to the portal system (portosystemic anastomosis at T_8)
Lymph	To deep cervical nodes	Posterior mediastinal and tracheo-bronchial nodes	Left gastric and coeliac nodes
Muscles	Skeletal	Mixed	Smooth
Nerves	Recurrent laryngeal Sympathetic from middle cervical ganglion	Vagus (left vagus eventually runs anteriorly on abdominal oesophagus) Sympathetic trunk Greater splanchnic nerve	Vagus forms anterior and posterior vagal plexuses
Surgical approach	Between trachea and carotid sheath	From the right In front of the vertebral canal transecting azygous arch Beware posterior vessels and thoracic duct	From the left Above the diaphragm Beware heart

Histology

- All the way down there is an inner circular and outer longitudinal muscle and a submucosal layer with sparse mucus glands (fewer in the middle)
- Thick muscularized mucosa
- Mucosa has lymphoid follicles and longitudinal folds. Stratified squamous epithelium (distal few centimetres are gastric mucosa).

4.2 Physiology of the oesophagus

Swallowing

Swallowing can be initiated voluntarily, thereafter is entirely reflex. Touch receptors in the pharynx are set off. These impulses are sent to the medulla and lower pons (swallowing centre). The impulses from the swallowing centre are transmitted to the pharynx and oesophagus via cranial nerves, and to the oesophagus via the vagus.

Three phases of swallowing

- **Oral**: tongue sends bolus of food to pharynx and initiates reflexes by touch receptors
- **Pharyngeal**: takes less than one second during which time respiration is reflexly inhibited. The soft palate is pulled up, the vocal cords are pulled together, the upper oesophageal sphincters relax and the superior constrictor muscle contracts. A peristaltic wave is initiated.
- **Oesophageal**: the upper oesophageal sphincter reflexly constricts. The peristaltic wave (primary peristalsis) continues at 5 cm per second. If food is still present, distension initiates secondary peristalsis beginning above site of distension and moving down.

Dysphagia

Difficulty (not pain) on swallowing. It may be associated with an uncomfortable sensation of bolus arrested during progression.

Site

- Pharynx
- Oesophagus
- Gastro-oesophageal region

Causes

- Constriction of pharyngeal/oesophageal lumen (extrinsic or intrinsic)
- Inflammation

- Infection of pharynx or oesophagus
- Dysmotility

Progressive dysphagia over several weeks, starting with solids leading to liquids is typical of oesophageal cancer.

Areas of narrowing of the oesophagus

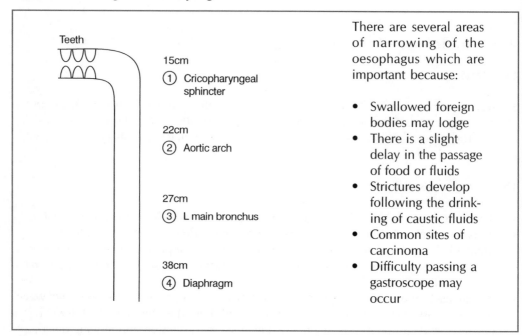

Teeth

15cm
① Cricopharyngeal sphincter

22cm
② Aortic arch

27cm
③ L main bronchus

38cm
④ Diaphragm

There are several areas of narrowing of the oesophagus which are important because:

- Swallowed foreign bodies may lodge
- There is a slight delay in the passage of food or fluids
- Strictures develop following the drinking of caustic fluids
- Common sites of carcinoma
- Difficulty passing a gastroscope may occur

Areas of narrowing of the oesophagus

Odynophagia

This is the correct term for pain on swallowing. It is usually felt within 10–15 seconds of swallowing.

Causes

- Reflux oesophagitis
- Peptic ulceration of oesophagus
- Candidiasis
- Herpes simplex
- Diffuse oesophageal spasm

4.3 Motor disorders of the oesophagus

Achalasia

Epidemiology
The absence of relaxation of the lower oesophageal sphincter affects 1:100,000 people, usually aged 30–60 years.

Pathogenesis
Unknown. There is a theory that a neurotropic virus affecting the vagal nucleus may be responsible.

- **Early phase**: vigorous achalasia and chest pain; simultaneous peristaltic contractions
- **Later phase**: dilatation of oesophagus with retention of solids and liquids; dysphagia and regurgitation are typical; liquids and solids are equally difficult to swallow, unlike mechanical obstruction

Diagnosis

- **Barium swallow**: shows a 'bird's beak' abnormality of the lower oesophageal sphincter. Dilated oesophagus. No gastric air bubble.
- **Manometry**: shows the absence of peristaltic waves in the oesophagus with high resting intra-oesophageal pressure and impaired relaxation. The normal pressure is 0–30 mm Hg.
- **Pseudoachalasia**: typically occurs in the over 50s and is caused by carcinoma of lower oesophageal sphincter, cardia or extrinsic tumour (e.g. pancreas, lymphoma). There is increased resistance on passing the endoscope unlike true achalasia.

Complications of achalasia include nocturnal aspiration, bronchiectasis and lung abscess. Carcinoma develops in 3%, usually a squamous cell carcinoma in the mid-oesophagus which is bulky with a poor prognosis.

Treatment

- **Balloon dilatation**: to a pressure of 300 mm Hg for 3 minutes; this works in 67% of patients but there is a 3% perforation rate
- **Heller's cardiomyotomy**: a 7 cm single myotomy no more than 1 cm into stomach at the oesophageal–gastric junction (recognized by small transverse extra mucosal veins). The procedure leads to reflux in 3% of patients.

Diffuse oesophageal spasm (DOS)

30% of patients admitted with 'anginal' chest pain have normal angiograms. 50% of these have DOS. Retrosternal pain radiating to jaw and inter scapular region is described and the patient is clammy and pale. The symptoms are intermittent and hard to diagnose but manometry may reveal a 'Nutcracker oesophagus' with high amplitude peristalsis of long duration. Nifedipine, reassurance and balloon dilatation are mainstays of treatment.

Chagas' disease

Chronic infection with *Trypanosoma cruzi* found in Brazil. Is very similar to achalasia. Caused by destruction of intermuscular ganglion cells. Also associated with cardiomyopathy, mega-colon, megaduodenum and megaureter.

Scleroderma

80% of scleroderma patients have oesophageal involvement. Oesophagitis is also seen in CREST (**C**alcinosis, **R**aynaud's, o**E**sophagitis, **S**cleroderma and **T**elangiectasia) syndrome. An adynamic oesophagus and gastro-oesophageal reflux leads to the formation of a stricture. The lower oesophageal sphincter is found to be hypotensive on manometry, unlike in acha-lasia. Nissen fundoplication is surgical treatment.

Pharyngeal pouch

This is a pulsion diverticulum of the pharynx through the gap between the lower most hori-zontal and oblique fibres of the inferior constrictor muscle (Killian's dehiscence) posteriorly.

Cause
Unco-ordinated swallowing.

Symptoms
The typical patient is middle-aged or elderly; M>F; the spectrum of clinical features in-cludes halitosis, recurrent sore throat, regurgitation of undigested food, aspiration pneumo-nia, lung abscesses, dysphagia, swelling in neck and gurgling sounds. This eventually leads to a malnourished patient with weight loss.

Diagnosis
Barium swallow, careful endoscopy.

Treatment
Excision of pharyngeal pouch. Starve for 24 hours preoperatively. Beware inhalation during induction of general anaesthesia (Mendelson's syndrome). Nasogastric tube if possible. Pouch packed with proflavine gauze for easy identification. Incision inferior to superior constrictor muscle. Dissect pouch, remove gauze via mouth and then excise pouch. Should incise cricopharyngeus (myotomy). Send excised pouch to pathology to exclude cancer. An alter-native is Dohlman's endoscopic resection in high risk patients. This method may miss a carcinoma.

4.4 Gastro-oesophageal reflux (GOR)

Epidemiology

7% of healthy people have heartburn. 5% will eventually need an operation. Reflux is usually (but not always) associated with hiatus hernia. 50% of over 50s have a hiatus hernia, one-third of these suffer reflux.

Aetiology

- Lower oesophageal sphincter (LOS) incompetence; the LOS should have a pressure >5 mm Hg over a distance of >1 cm
- Duodenogastric reflux (e.g. after gastric resection) worsens symptoms
- Defective oesophageal action (e.g. scleroderma); this may be part of a vicious circle because defective oesophageal action can be caused by reflux and, in turn, predisposes to more reflux
- Gastric outlet obstruction (this increases acid reflux)

Clinical features of GOR

- Epigastric/retrosternal pain ('heartburn' is pathognomonic)
- Angina-type pain (reflux may be exercise-related)
- Painful dysphagia (especially when swallowing hot drinks)
- Reflux of food (this is not vomiting, it is effortless especially on bending)
- Globus (lump in throat); the cricopharyngeal 'bar' may be seen on barium swallow
- Pulmonary aspiration (nocturnal coughing, hoarse voice)

Diagnosis

- History (effect of posture and antacids)
- Barium swallow (diagnosis in 60% also shows other pathology)
- Endoscopy (diagnosis in 70%, shows changes proximal to squamo-columnar junction
- Biopsy (diagnosis in 80%; 5 cm above gastro-oesophageal junction shows increased eosinophils and hypoplasia)
- Bernstein acid perfusion tests: this reproduces symptoms in 70%; 0.1mmol/L hydrochloric acid is introduced at 6 ml/min 5 cm above the gastro-oesophageal junction
- Spencer pH monitoring: this is the gold standard and is 90% sensitive. A glass or antinomy pH probe is placed above the gastro-oesophageal junction for 24 hours. The diagnosis is made if pH is <4 for more than 1% of the time when supine or more than 6% of the time when erect.
- Oesophageal manometry: this also plays a minor role; it is used to assess motility disturbance

Stages of endoscopic gastro-oesophageal reflux

I	Discrete linear ulceration
II	Areas of more confluent oesophagitis
III	Circumferential oesophagitis
IV	Stricture formation

Complications of gastro-oesophageal reflux

Oesophageal stricture

Occurs in 10% of patients with gastro-oesophageal reflux. Endoscopy, biopsy and brush cytology diagnose 95% of cases. Other causes include drugs (slow K, tetracycline, non-steroidal anti-inflammatory drugs) and disease (tuberculosis, Crohn's). It is treated by dilatation, using balloon dilators, Mercury or Celestin bougies. These are usually 44–45 French (divide by 3 to get mm in diameter). Surgery is indicated by certain criteria, for example young people, recurrent stricture, undilatable (rare) or shortened oesophagus.

Haemorrhage

This is rare. One should suspect Barrett's oesophagus or cancer. Reflux does not explain anaemia so another cause should be sought.

Barrett's oesophagus

In 1950 Barrett described a gastric lined oesophagus; it is a latent irreversible metaplastic response to reflux. If the squamocolumnar junction is more than 3 cm above the gastro-oesophageal junction, this is Barrett's oesophagus.

- **Epidemiology**: 10% of patients who have endoscopy for reflux would demonstrate signs of Barrett's oesophagus. There is a 30-fold increased risk of adenocarcinoma of the oesophagus in these patients. It may be multi-focal.
- **Follow-up**: if dysplastic the patient should have an annual endoscopy/biopsy. If invasive malignancy is demonstrated then oesophagectomy is indicated. Prophylactic oesophagectomy is not indicated as it has a 10% mortality.
- **Treatment**: usually does not regress with medical treatment. Treatment is normally symptomatic, for example dilatation for strictures, anti-reflux surgery, surveillance for dysplasia and resection for carcinoma.

NB. There is a high incidence of colonic polyps in Barrett's oesophagus patients.

Treatment of GOR

Medical
This works for 90% of patients.

- Conservative treatment: weight loss, raise the bedhead, decrease the size of the evening meal, reduce alcohol intake
- Antacids (helps 36%)
- Metoclopramide: increases the lower oesophageal sphincter pressure and increases the gastric emptying. It helps about half of patients.
- H_2 blockers (e.g. cimetidine 800 mg b.d. and ranitidine 150 mg b.d.)
- Omeprazole, 90% short-term healing; a proton pump inhibitor

Surgical
Limits reflux by decreasing hiatus hernia and increasing lower oesophageal sphincter tone. The procedure may also have the effect of a flap valve.

- **Floppy Nissen fundoplication**: the fundus is wrapped around the oesophagus. You should be able to pass your finger within the wrap. It has a 90% success rate. Complications include gas bloat 5%, dysphagia 5%, recurrent reflux 5%.
- **Belsey mark IV**: this is a transthoracic fundoplication, less satisfactory than the Nissen fundoplication.
- **Hill repair**: in this repair, the fundoplicated oesophageal gastric junction is fixed to the median arcuate ligament of the diaphragm.
- **Angelchick prosthesis**: this is a silicon collar with two tapes which is anchored below the diaphragm. It can increase dysphagia. The prosthesis can also migrate or cause erosion. It is also more costly than a Nissen fundoplication.
- **Roux-en-Y procedure**: may be indicated if reflux is recurrent. This has a high morbidity and mortality.

4.5 Oesophageal carcinoma

Epidemiology

- M:F 1.5–3:1
- Rare under 40 years of age
- Has an increased incidence in China, Russia and South Africa
- Incidence in the USA and Europe is 2–8:100,000 people

Site

Thought to be most common at points of physiological narrowing of oesophagus: (see figure on p. 350). 55% of cases occur in the upper and middle oesophagus; 34% in the lower oesophagus and 8% in the cervical oesophagus.

Pathology

Mostly squamous cell carcinoma. Adenocarcinomas are responsible for 0.8–8% and are mostly from Barrett's oesophagus. Oat cell carcinoma is very rare with a poor prognosis. Other rare causes include adenoid cystic carcinoma, melanoma and carcinoid.

Aetiology

- Smoking
- Alcohol
- Strictures (lye strictures increase the incidence of carcinoma by a factor of x22, webs x9, achalasia x7, peptic ulcer disease x6)
- Diet — mouldy food, nitrosamines and vitamin deficiencies have all been implicated in increased oesophageal carcinoma rates

Prognosis

This is poor due to spread which is direct, lymphatic or blood borne to the liver or lungs.

Presentation

Oesophageal carcinoma may present with the following features:

- Dysphagia
- Retrosternal discomfort
- Atypical chest pain
- Pseudoachalasia
- Pulmonary symptoms
- Aspiration pneumonia
- Coughing during eating
- Recurrent laryngeal nerve palsy
- Anaemia (rare)
- Massive haematemesis
- Lymphadenopathy

Investigations

FBC, CXR, U&Es, LFTs, albumin, CT scan, including the liver. Barium swallow, endoscopy and biopsy are diagnostic.

Staging

For full staging, the following features need to be taken into account:

- Length of tumour
- Depth of tumour
- Nodal status
- Metastatic spread

Ultrasound scan, CT, laparoscopy and bronchoscopy can help with the staging.

Pre-operative preparation

- Correct U&Es/anaemia
- Optimize nutrition: withdraw solid food; start high-protein liquid diet; parenteral feeding via nasogastric tube may be necessary
- Optimize respiratory function: encourage the patient to give up smoking; intensive physiotherapy; treat any chest infection

Surgical approaches to oesophagus

Curative surgery, especially for radiation resistant adenocarcinoma has a 10% mortality. There are several approaches used depending on the site and extent of the tumour.

- **Thoraco abdominal excision** of lower oesophagus through 6th rib space on the left. Although this gives a good view, it can lead to respiratory problems.
- **Ivor Lewis procedure** for middle oesophagus. This is through a right thoracotomy through the 4th or 5th rib space.
- **McKeown three-stage oesophagectomy** for high lesions. This is an Ivor Lewis procedure plus a cervical incision. The patient needs to be turned halfway through the procedure.
- **Trans-hiatal dissection** for lower lesions. This is done through a laparotomy and the stomach is pulled down. The oesophagus has to be mobilized in the neck.
- **Cervical incisions** or trapdoor incisions with reflection of sternum and clavicle. Used for cervical tumours. Luckily these are rare.

Perioperative treatment of oesophageal cancer

- Minimize pain using PCA or epidural
- Minimize respiratory failure by careful patient selection, pre-operative physiotherapy, post-operative intensive care and good pain control
- Minimize post-operative nutritional deficiency (e.g. by siting a feeding jejunostomy during the operation)

357

Management of advanced oesophageal cancer

- **Radiotherapy**: better for squamous cell carcinoma. May produce strictures.
- **Chemotherapy**: good for adenocarcinomas.
- **Laser treatment**: good for short, intrinsic tumours to restore swallowing. May need repeating. Danger of perforation.
- **Intubation**: via fibre optic endoscope and/or X-ray control using a guide wire. The old rigid tube intubation is now thought to be very dangerous. Although intubation can keep the oesophagus patent, a special diet needs to be followed otherwise the stent can become blocked. Problems include migration of the stent or tumour growing over or through it.
- **Bypass or resection**: Kirschner operation: the oesophagus is divided in neck and abdomen. The stomach is brought up subcutaneously and anastomosed to the cervical oesophagus. The upper end of the oesophagus is closed and the lower end is joined to the jejunum. The mortality of this procedure approaches 50%.

NB. Tracheo-oesophageal fistula is an incurable, dangerous complication. Endo-oesophageal stenting is the usual treatment.

4.6 Oesophageal perforation

Causes of oesophageal perforation

Spontaneous rupture
Spontaneous rupture usually results in a torn left posterior aspect of oesophagus, just above the cardia. Classically, patients present with severe chest pain/upper abdominal pain after an episode of vomiting (Boerhaave's syndrome). May lead to cardiovascular collapse ± peritonitis. Clinically, there may be subcutaneous emphysema. CXR typically shows a pneumothorax, mediastinal gas and pleural effusion. A gastrografin swallow is helpful. Early diagnosis is the key to a successful outcome.

Penetrating injury
This is rare, since the oesophagus is smaller than other vital intrathoracic organs. Resection may be needed.

Instrumental perforation
There are five typical sites of perforation during endoscopy.

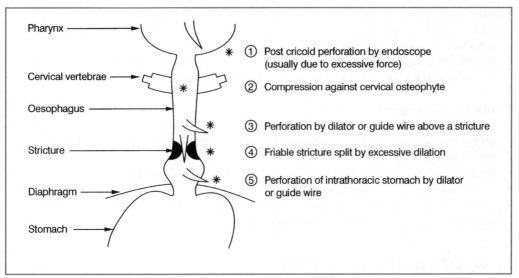

①	Post cricoid perforation by endoscope (usually due to excessive force)
②	Compression against cervical osteophyte
③	Perforation by dilator or guide wire above a stricture
④	Friable stricture split by excessive dilation
⑤	Perforation of intrathoracic stomach by dilator or guide wire

Typical sites of perforation during endoscopy

The clinical picture may be less acute and dramatic than with spontaneous rupture, however, mediastinitis usually develops.

Mediastinitis is a dangerous condition which can lead to severe systemic disturbance and cardiovascular collapse. Cardiac dysrhythmias are common (tachycardia, atrial fibrillation). Classically mediastinal 'crunch' (like footsteps on soft snow) may be heard with the heart sounds.

Treatment of oesophageal perforation

There is some controversy between non-operative and operative management depending on the type of perforation. The principles of initial management are:

- Nil by mouth
- Broad-spectrum antibiotics
- H$_2$ blockers
- Chest drain

Principles for the different types of presentation are as follows:

- Small contained perforation (intramural or mediastinal); may be managed conservatively with contrast study after five days to confirm healing
- Delayed presentation (two days or longer after injury); manage conservatively, usually too friable to suture

- Large perforation, recognized immediately with little contamination (e.g. at endoscopy in a starved patient); try conservative management for 12 hours; if patient deteriorates, surgery is indicated
- Boerhaave's syndrome (rupture induced by vomiting); early surgery is recommended as there is usually massive contamination

Principles of surgery

- Incise muscle layer of oesophagus to see mucosal defect (which is always larger than the muscle defect)
- Repair may be strengthened by intercostal flap or fundus of stomach
- Excise any abnormal strictures
- May need excision of oesophagus with delayed or immediate reconstruction; if so, a gastrostomy for feeding should be considered

5. ACUTE ABDOMINAL PAIN

5.1 Abdominal pain

The acute abdomen is one of the most frequent referrals to the general surgeon on call. This unit is concerned with the understanding, diagnosis and management of the common causes of acute abdominal pain.

Visceral pain

- This is pain arising from the abdominal, pelvic and thoracic viscera
- The visceral peritoneum, including the mesentery, is sensitive to stretch and is innervated by autonomic nerves
- Afferent fibres from these sensory receptors travel with sympathetic and para-sympathetic fibres to reach the central nervous system
- Visceral pain is generally vague and poorly localized and is generated by stretching of the viscera. Due to activation of the autonomic nervous system, visceral pain may be associated with warmth, flushing, pallor and dizziness.
- The visceral pain of the foregut (stomach and duodenum) is felt in the epigastrium, the mid-gut (jejunum to transverse colon) in the peri-umbilical region and the hindgut (transverse colon to anal canal) in the lower abdomen.

Somatic pain

This is pain arising from the surface structures. The neuroreceptors in the skin and skeletal muscles detect the type and location of the pain very accurately. Abdominal pain arising from the parietal peritoneum is of the somatic type and can be precisely located to the site of the origin.

Peritonism

This is the pain arising from peritonitis, the inflammation of the peritoneum. It can be detected by the clinical signs of tenderness, rebound and guarding. It can be localized or generalized. It is eased by lying still and exacerbated by movement.

Referred pain

This is the phenomenon wherein visceral pain is perceived not in the affected viscus but instead at a somatic site some distance from the viscus (e.g. testicular pain felt in the periumbilical area rather than the scrotum itself).

Radiation of pain

The phenomenon wherein pain is felt diffusely in and around the region of the affected viscus, in addition to being perceived remotely. An example of this is ureteric colic radiating to the ipsilateral testicle.

5.2 Causes of acute abdominal pain

Causes of acute abdominal pain

- **Inflammation and infection**
  Acute
    appendicitis
    cholecystitis
    diverticulitis
    pancreatitis
    salpingitis
  Mesenteric adenitis
  Primary peritonitis
  Crohn's disease
  Ulcerative colitis
  Pyelonephritis
  Terminal ileitis
  Yersinia infection
  Meckel's diverticulitis

- **Obstruction**
  Renal colic
  Biliary colic
  Small bowel obstruction
    congenital (bands, atresia)
    meconium ileus
    malrotation of gut
    adhesions
    hernia
    intussusception
    gallstone
    tumours
    Crohn's
  Large bowel obstruction
    tumour
    volvulus
    inflammatory stricture

- **Perforation**
  Gastric ulcer
  Duodenal ulcer
  Diverticular disease
  Colon cancer
  Ulcerative colitis
  Lymphoma
  Foreign body perforation
  Perforated cholecystitis
  Perforated appendicitis
  Perforated oesophagus
  Perforated strangulated bowel
  Abdominal trauma

- **Haemorrhage**
  Rupture of the aortic aneurysm
  Mesenteric artery aneurysm
  Aortic dissection
  Ruptured ovarian cyst
  Ruptured ectopic pregnancy
  Ovarian bleed
  Endometriosis
  Rupture of liver tumour
  Rectus sheath haematoma
  Abdominal trauma

- **Infarction**
  Torsion of a viscus
  Ischaemic bowel (arterial
    thrombosis/embolus)
  Venous thrombosis
  Aortic dissection

Non-surgical causes of acute abdominal pain

- **Intra-abdominal**
  Diseases of the liver
    tumours
    abscesses
  Primary peritonitis
    bacteria/TB
    Candida
    glove lubricants
  Infection
    viral gastroenteritis
    food poisoning
    typhoid
    mesenteric adenitis
    Yersinia
    Curtis–Fitz-Hugh syndrome
    (*Chlamydia* causing right
    upper quadrant pain)

- **Neurological causes**
  Spinal disorders
  Tabes dorsalis

- **Abdominal wall pain**
  Rectus sheath haematoma
  Neurovascular entrapment

- **Retroperitoneal causes**
  Pyelonephritis
  Acute hydronephrosis

- **Infections**
  Infectious mononucleosis (EBV)
  Herpes zoster

- **Metabolic disorders**
  Diabetes
  Addison's
  Uraemia
  Porphyria
  Haemochromatosis
  Hypercalcaemia
  Heavy metal poisoning

- **Immunological**
  Polyarteritis nodosa
  Systemic lupus

- **Haematological**
  Sickle cell
  Haemolytic anaemia
  Henoch–Schönlein purpura
  Leukaemia
  Lymphomas
  Polycythaemia
  Anticoagulant therapy

- **Intra-thoracic causes**
  Myocardial infarction
  Pericarditis
  Pneumothorax, pleurisy
  Coxsackie B virus
  Strangulation of diaphragmatic
    hernia
  Aortic dissection
  Boerhaave's syndrome

5.3 Sites of acute abdominal pain

The diagram below shows the common sites of abdominal pain and their causes.

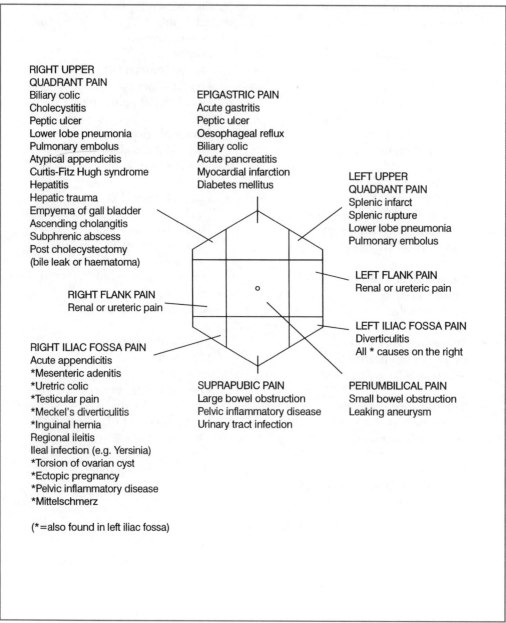

RIGHT UPPER
QUADRANT PAIN
Biliary colic
Cholecystitis
Peptic ulcer
Lower lobe pneumonia
Pulmonary embolus
Atypical appendicitis
Curtis-Fitz Hugh syndrome
Hepatitis
Hepatic trauma
Empyema of gall bladder
Ascending cholangitis
Subphrenic abscess
Post cholecystectomy
(bile leak or haematoma)

EPIGASTRIC PAIN
Acute gastritis
Peptic ulcer
Oesophageal reflux
Biliary colic
Acute pancreatitis
Myocardial infarction
Diabetes mellitus

LEFT UPPER
QUADRANT PAIN
Splenic infarct
Splenic rupture
Lower lobe pneumonia
Pulmonary embolus

LEFT FLANK PAIN
Renal or ureteric pain

RIGHT FLANK PAIN
Renal or ureteric pain

LEFT ILIAC FOSSA PAIN
Diverticulitis
All * causes on the right

RIGHT ILIAC FOSSA PAIN
Acute appendicitis
*Mesenteric adenitis
*Uretric colic
*Testicular pain
*Meckel's diverticulitis
*Inguinal hernia
Regional ileitis
Ileal infection (e.g. Yersinia)
*Torsion of ovarian cyst
*Ectopic pregnancy
*Pelvic inflammatory disease
*Mittelschmerz

(*=also found in left iliac fossa)

SUPRAPUBIC PAIN
Large bowel obstruction
Pelvic inflammatory disease
Urinary tract infection

PERIUMBILICAL PAIN
Small bowel obstruction
Leaking aneurysm

Sites of abdominal pain

5.4 History of acute abdominal pain

A full history from a patient with abdominal pain should include the following features.

* **The patient's history**
* **Details of the pain**: site, intensity, radiation, onset, duration, character, alleviating and exacerbating factors, symptoms associated with the pain, previous episodes

---

WELL-RECOGNIZED SITES OF RADIATION OF ABDOMINAL PAIN

Right shoulder tip	from	Ruptured liver
Left shoulder tip	from	Ruptured spleen
Between scapulae	from	Gall bladder
To centre of back	from	Pancreatitis
		Aortic aneurysm
To ipsilateral testicle	from	Ureteric colic
To ipsilateral flank	from	Testicular pain

---

* **Review of the relevant systems**
* **Other relevant history**: regular medications and allergies, smoking and drinking, social and family history, review of other systems, anaesthetic problems

5.5 Examination of acute abdominal pain

* General overview
* Abdominal examination: inspection, palpation, percussion, auscultation, external genitalia
* Rectal examination
* Review of general fitness

SPECIFIC SIGNS ON EXAMINATION OF THE ABDOMEN

Sign	Indicates	Definition
Psoas stretch sign	Appendicitis	Passive extension or hyper-extension of the hip increases the abdominal pain due to psoas muscle being in contact with the inflamed appendix
Rovsing's sign	Appendicitis	Palpation in the left iliac fossa may produce pain at the site of tenderness in the right iliac fossa due to movement of the inflamed parietal peritoneum
Grey–Turner's sign	Acute pancreatitis (usually severe haemorrhagic pancreatitis)	Bruising in the flanks due to extra-vasated blood
Cullen's sign	Acute pancreatitis (usually severe haemorrhagic pancreatitis)	Bruising in the area of the umbilicus
Murphy's sign	Acute cholecystitis	Patient catches breath due to pain on inspiration while the right hypochondrium is deeply palpated, but not when the left hypochondrium is deeply palpated. This is due to the downward movement of the inflamed gallbladder on to the examining hand during inspiration
Boas' sign	Acute cholecystitis	Pain radiating from an inflamed gall bladder to the tip of the right scapula renders an area of skin below the scapula hyperaesthetic

5.6 Investigation of acute abdominal pain

- **Bedside tests**: pulse, blood pressure, temperature, urinalysis

A bedside pregnancy test on the urine is mandatory in a woman of reproductive age with lower abdominal pain to exclude potentially disastrous ectopic pregnancy and to check on pregnancy status in case of later surgery.

- **Blood tests**: FBC, U&Es, amylase, group and save, clotting, LFT, ABGs
- **Radiological investigations**: plain abdominal X-ray, erect CXR, erect abdominal X-ray, lateral decubitus abdominal X-ray, ultrasound scan, CT/MRI, contrast studies
- **Endoscopy**: gastroscopy, colonoscopy, laparoscopy
- **Peritoneal lavage**: (limited role except in trauma)
- **Other investigations**

In the acute scenario, urgent laparotomy should not be delayed for time-consuming tests if the clinical indications for surgery are clear.

5.7 Peritonitis

Peritonitis is inflammation of the peritoneum which may be generalized or localized.

Causes of peritonitis

Bacterial peritonitis
Bacteria may enter the peritoneal cavity via four portals:

- **From the exterior**: penetrating wound or infection at laparotomy
- **From intra-abdominal viscera**: gangrene of a viscus (e.g. appendicitis, diverticulitis or intestinal strangulation); perforation of a viscus (e.g. perforated duodenal ulcer, perforated appendix, rupture of intestine); from trauma (post-operative anastomotic leak)
- **Via the bloodstream**: as part of a septicaemia — 'Primary peritonitis' occurs without any obvious source for the infection being demonstrated, but is usually secondary to some initial source of infection
- **Via the female genital tract**: acute salpingitis or puerperal infection may lead to peritonitis

The most common causes of peritonitis are as follows:

- Post-operative complications   30%
- Acute appendicitis   20%
- Perforated peptic ulcer   20%

CAUSATIVE ORGANISMS IN BACTERIAL PERITONITIS

Type of peritonitis	Causative organisms
From bowel	Mixed flora (*E. coli, Strep. faecalis,* Pseudomonas, Proteus, Clostridia, Bacteroides)
From genital tract	Gonococcus, Streptococcus
Blood-borne	Streptococcus, Pneumococcus Staphylococcus, Tuberculosis

Aseptic (chemical) peritonitis
Perforated duodenal or gastric ulcer. This usually progresses to bacterial peritonitis after several hours. It is one of the most common causes of peritonitis.

Biliary peritonitis
This may occur as a result of:

- **Iatrogenic damage**: leakage from the liver, gall bladder or its ducts after a biliary tract operation. Dislodging of a 'T' tube can also cause leakage. Percutaneous liver biopsy or percutaneous cholangiography can also cause damage to the gall bladder.
- **Trauma**: gunshot wounds, stabbing or blunt trauma can rupture the gall bladder
- **Acute cholecystitis**: this rarely leads to biliary peritonitis because, unlike the appendix, the inflamed gall bladder rarely becomes gangrenous or perforates. It tends to become thickened and walled off by adhesions.
  It also has good blood supply from the liver bed, so is not dependent on one end artery like the appendix, which quickly becomes ischaemic. However, perforation of the acutely inflamed gall bladder or transudation of bile through a gangrenous but non-perforated gall bladder may occur.
- **Idiopathic**: this is a rare but well-recognized condition in which bile peritonitis occurs without obvious cause, possibly because of a small perforation due to a calculus which then becomes sealed.

Laparotomy is usually required to deal with any of the above problems.

Pancreatitis
(See Section 14.12, p. 597.) Acute uncomplicated pancreatitis causes peritonitis but does not require laparotomy.

Blood in peritoneal cavity
Blunt abdominal trauma can release blood, pancreatic enzymes and urine into the peritoneal cavity. Blood in the peritoneal cavity causes pain and peritonitis. Sources of bleeding include ovarian cyst, endometriosis, trauma and leaking aortic aneurysm.

Meconium peritonitis
Occurs in neonates after intestinal rupture. The bowel perforation has usually closed before birth. Atresia, volvulus or hernia are usually responsible. Treatment entails relief of obstruction and closure of any perforations that are present.

Tuberculous peritonitis
Always secondary to TB elsewhere. It spreads from mesenteric lymph nodes, via female genital tract or from miliary TB. Rare in the UK but still seen in immigrants and immunocompromised patients. The peritoneum is studded with tubercles in the initial phase with an accompanying serous effusion. Local abscesses may develop, abdominal viscera become matted together with dense adhesions. Clinically, there are three forms: the acute form which mimics bacterial peritonitis; the ascitic type in which the serous effusion predominates and the plastic type in which adhesions, abscesses and obstruction are a feature. Treatment is anti-tuberculous chemotherapy and laparotomy for relief of adhesions if indicated.

Drugs and foreign bodies
Clinical symptoms similar to acute peritonitis have been described during treatment with **isoniazid** and a beta-blocker **practolol** (now withdrawn). Intra-peritoneal chemotherapy for malignant disease may also cause a peritoneal reaction. **Talc** and **starch** may stimulate foreign body granulomata if they are introduced into the peritoneal cavity on surgical gloves.

Pathology

The pathological effects of peritonitis are:

- Widespread absorption of toxins from the large inflamed surface
- An associated paralytic ileus leading to loss of fluids, electrolytes and proteins
- Gross abdominal distension with elevation of the diaphragm which can lead to lung collapse and pneumonia

Clinical features

Signs of underlying condition
For example, appendicitis, peptic ulcer disease.

Pain
Characteristically constant, worse on movement and severe. It may be localized but often becomes generalized. Pain may be referred to the shoulder tip because of diaphragmatic irritation. The abdomen is held **rigidly** and **rebound tenderness** is present.

Signs of ileus
The abdomen may become distended and tympanic. Bowel sounds are reduced on auscultation. Vomiting is frequent and may become faeculent.

Signs of systemic shock
For example, tachycardia, tachypnoea, ↓BP, ↓urine output.

Investigations

The diagnosis is usually a clinical one and in many cases an urgent laparotomy is indicated. Investigations are, therefore, of limited value and should not delay prompt treatment unless the diagnosis is in doubt. Four simple tests are generally necessary:

- **FBC**: will usually show a marked leucocytosis and underlying anaemia
- **U&Es**: can guide fluid resuscitation and enable correction of electrolyte imbalances
- **Serum amylase**: may help differentiate acute pancreatitis, but may also be elevated in a patient with perforated viscus or other cause of peritonitis
- **Erect CXR**: will reveal free gas in 80% of cases of a perforated viscus

Other investigations, depending on the underlying pathology.

Differential diagnosis

Other causes of severe abdominal pain, such as intestinal obstruction, ureteric or biliary colic tend to lead to restlessness in the patient. Basal pneumonia, myocardial infarction, intra-peritoneal haemorrhage or leakage of an aortic aneurysm can lead to mis-diagnosis.

Treatment

- **Analgesia**: usually with IV opiates and an appropriate anti-emetic
- **Fluid resuscitation**: with IV crystalloids or colloids depending on the degree of dehydration or shock. Hourly urine output is useful so the patient should be catheterized. Electrolyte replacement, especially potassium, is also important. CVP monitoring may be indicated in severe cases, or those complicated by co-morbidity. Blood should be cross-matched for surgery.
- **NG tube and aspiration**: reduces the risk of aspiration pneumonia and alleviates vomiting
- **Antibiotics**: initially with broad spectrum antibiotics, such as a cephalosporin and metronidazole (to cover the anaerobic bacteria)
- **Oxygen**: may be required to support the respiration and if the patient is shocked it is essential. Hypoxia can be monitored by pulse oximetery or arterial blood gas measurements.
- **Surgery**: is indicated if the source of peritonitis can be removed or closed, (e.g. perforated viscus or gangrenous appendix)

• **Conservative treatment**: this may be indicated if the infection has been localized (e.g. an appendix mass), if the cause of the peritonitis is inoperable (e.g. acute pancreatitis) or if the patient is not fit for a general anaesthetic (e.g. moribund elderly patient with severe, pre-existing co-morbidity). The mainstays of conservative treatment are IV fluid, gastric aspiration and antibiotics.

5.8 Subphrenic abscesses

The two main sequelae of peritonitis are adhesive obstruction (see Section 10.3, p. 434) and intra-peritoneal abscesses.

An intra-peritoneal abscess occurs when peritonitis remains localized or when generalized peritonitis fails to resolve completely. Rarely, infection occurs as a result of a haematogenous spread. Localized abscesses are most commonly found in the subphrenic spaces or in the pelvis.

Anatomy

There are seven anatomical spaces in relation to the abdominal surface of the diaphragm where pus can collect. Four are intra-peritoneal (right and left subphrenic and right and left subhepatic), two are perinephric and, therefore, retro-peritoneal, and one is contained above the bare area of the liver and so is also extra-peritoneal (see figure overleaf).

Clinical features

General
Usually, subphrenic infection follows generalized peritonitis after 10–21 days but it may manifest weeks or months after the original episode. Malaise, nausea, weight loss, anaemia and pyrexia. Many cases have the typical swinging pyrexia.

Local
There may be localizing features, such as upper abdominal pain, lower chest pain, abdominal or chest wall tenderness. There may be signs of fluid or collapse at the lung base. The abscess may point superficially as described in the figure overleaf. Pain may be referred to the chest wall, loin, upper abdomen, back or shoulder. Hiccoughing may be a feature.

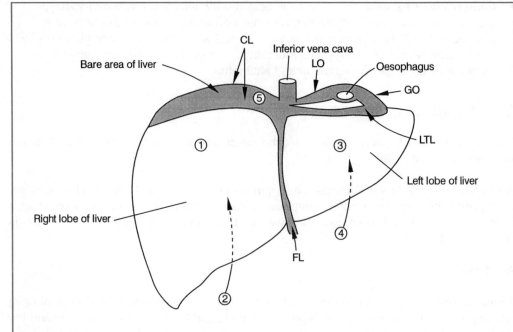

	Source of infection	**Abscess points to**
(1) Right subphrenic space	Gall bladder Stomach Duodenum	Right costal margin
(2) Right subhepatic space (Pouch of Rutherford Morrison)	Appendix Gall bladder Right colon Duodenum Right kidney	Right loin
(3) Left subphrenic space	Stomach Left colon Pancreas Spleen	Left costal margin
(4) Left subhepatic space (lesser sac)	Pancreas Stomach (especially post-op)	Below greater curve of stomach
(5) Right extra-peritoneal subphrenic space	Right kidney (rare)	Epigastrium between layers of falciform ligament

Subphrenic spaces

Diagnosis

A **WCC** usually shows a polymorph leucocytosis of 15–20,000

An **erect CXR** may show any of the following signs:

- Elevation of the diaphragm on the affected side
- Diminished or absent mobility of the diaphragm on screening, pleural effusion and/or collapse of the lung base
- Gas and a fluid level below the diaphragm

Ultrasound or **CT scan** accurately localize the collection and drainage under radio-logical control may be undertaken at the same sitting. **Radio-labelled leukocyte scans** can highlight a collection of pus in an abscess cavity and are an alternative to CT in some situations.

Treatment

Conservative treatment

In early cases where there is an absence of gas and free fluid on X-ray, broad-spectrum antibiotic therapy may be sufficient. In cases of spreading cellulitis of the subphrenic space, a rapid response to antibiotics may occur preventing progression to an abscess. Clinical or radiological evidence of a localized abscess or failure to respond to antibiotics are indications for drainage.

Percutaneous draining under radiological control

Placing a drainage tube under local anaesthetic by the radiologist has the advantage of avoiding a general anaesthetic and a laparotomy. The drain may be left in place for re-peated aspirations or the instilling of antibiotics or contrast for subsequent sinograms. Progress can be monitored clinically and radiologically. Deterioration is an indication for surgical drainage.

Surgical drainage

Depending on the location of the subphrenic abscess (indicated by CT or by a superficial swelling), there are two main approaches. The posterior extra-peritoneal approach is through the bed of, or below, the 12th rib. The anterior approach is via a subcostal incision. The cavity should be opened widely and explored to prevent loculi developing, and a large bore drain inserted as for radiological drainage.

5.9 Pelvic abscess

Anatomy

A pelvic abscess is the most common type of intra-peritoneal abscess. It may follow any generalized peritonitis but is common after acute appendicitis, gynaecological infections or other pelvic inflammatory disease, including diverticulitis. In the male, the abscess lies between the bladder and the rectum. In the female, the abscess lies behind the uterus and posterior fornix of the vagina and in front of the rectum (in the pouch of Douglas).

Clinical features

The general features are similar to a subphrenic abscess, i.e. swinging pyrexia, toxaemia, weight loss and leucocytosis some days after a pre-disposing condition or operation. The local features which may be present include diarrhoea, mucus discharge per rectum, a tender, boggy mass palpable on rectal or vaginal examination. Occasionally, urinary frequency may occur.

Diagnosis

Ultrasound and CT scans confirm the diagnosis. There is usually an ↑WCC.

Treatment

Conservative treatment: may be all that is necessary as many pelvic abscesses drain spontaneously into the rectum. An early pelvic cellulitis may respond rapidly to a short course of antibiotics but prolonged antibiotic treatment of an unresolved infection may produce a chronic inflammatory mass, studded with small abscess cavities in the pelvis.

Digital drainage: gentle finger pressure at the site of maximal swelling can encourage drainage into the rectum.

Surgical drainage: if spontaneous drainage does not occur, the abscess should be formally drained under general anaesthesia with the patient in lithotomy position. The procedure is performed via a proctoscope or sigmoidoscope. Occasionally, pelvic abscesses drain through the vagina but rectal drainage is usually preferable.

6. COMMON ACUTE ABDOMINAL EMERGENCIES

Peptic ulcer disease, biliary disorders and intestinal obstruction are covered later in this chapter. This section deals with common acute abdominal emergencies which are not covered in detail elsewhere.

6.1 Appendicitis

Incidence

Most common emergency surgical operation. 80,000 per year in the UK are admitted with this diagnosis. Declining in recent years.

Pathology

The aetiology is unknown. May be linked with a lack of fibre, familial tendency or viral infections which increase lymphoid tissue.

The original insult may be due to, or precipitated by faecaliths, lymphoid tissue hyperplasia, foreign bodies, congenital/inflammatory strictures, tumours or congenital band adhesions.

The appendix wall becomes inflamed and the lumen fills with pus. Oedema decreases blood supply, leading to infarction. Organisms from lumen enter devitalised wall. Liquefaction and perforation of appendix occurs. Either localized peritonism (if gradual with adhesions) or generalized peritonitis results.

Clinical features

- **Abdominal pain**: central colicky and vague, localizing to RIF after 24 hours and becoming constant
- **Nausea**: ± vomiting and anorexia
- **Pyrexia**: may be present ± a high WCC
- **Dry tongue**: coated, with fetor
- **RIF pain**: sharp and localized, worse on movement and is found at McBurney's point (one-third of the way from the anterior superior iliac spine to the umbilicus). Tenderness, guarding and rebound are features. Rovsing's sign is present (see table on p. 366).

Special patients

- **Babies:** appendicitis is rare under three years of age but has increased mortality. Diarrhoea and vomiting are common.
- **Children under five years:** account for only 7% of cases but 37% of deaths.
- **Pregnant women:** appendicitis is less common after seven months' gestation. 1/10 die, 3/10 have foetal loss and 6/10 perforate. Problems include nausea mistaken for symptoms of pregnancy; upwards displacement of the appendix and guarding masked by uterus.

Anatomy of appendix

The appendix is a blind-ending tube usually 6–9 cm long, opening into the posterior medial wall of the caecum, 2 cm below the ileocaecal valve at the point of convergence of the three taeniae coli. It has its own short mesentery (mesoappendix). The appendicular artery is normally a branch of a posterior caecal artery and is an end artery, thus rendering the appendix susceptible to infarction.

Investigating appendicitis

- **WCC:** 90% have leucocytosis; 75% have neutrophilia; 10% have normal WCC
- **Urinalysis:** pelvic or retrocaecal appendicitis may lead to haematuria or white cells in urine. Urinary or serum HCG mandatory in females of reproductive age
- **Cusco's speculum examination:** to exclude pelvic inflammatory disease in young women — obvious purulent discharge from os, cervical excitation
- **USS:** to exclude ovarian cyst, pyosalpinx or ectopic pregnancy in young women
- **Laparoscopy:** especially in young women. May proceed to laparoscopic appendicectomy
- **AXR:** rarely needed but if obstruction, perforation or ureteric colic are suspected, it may be useful

Differential diagnosis of appendicitis

- **Mesenteric appendicitis**
- **Gastroenteritis**
- **Disorders of female pelvis:** Mittelschmerz; pelvic inflammatory disease; ectopic pregnancy; ovarian rupture/bleed/torsion
- **Ileocaecal disorders:** Meckel's diverticulitis; Crohn's regional ileitis; Yersinia; EUCca caecum; foreign body perforation
- **Renal tract disorders:** renal colic; pyelonephritis
- **Rarer causes:** osteomyelitis of pelvis, psoas abscess, haematoma of rectus

Variable sites of the appendix

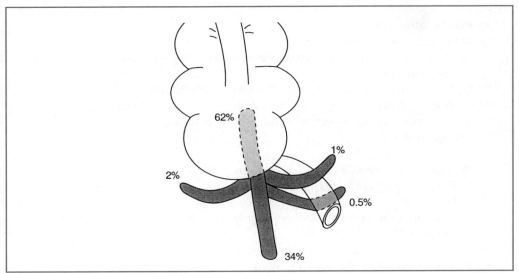

Variable sites of the appendix

- **62% are retrocaecal**: usually free in retrocaecal fossa. May be bound to the caecum leading to poorly localized signs. May lie retro-peritoneally between caecum and psoas leading to the psoas stretch sign (increased pain on the passive extension of right hip). May lie next to ureter (leading to white cells in urine).
- **34% are pelvic**: appendix hangs down into the pelvic brim. Causes more nausea and vomiting. Easily felt on examination p.r. Internal rotation of hip increases pain (obturator sign). Also may have positive psoas stretch sign.
- **1% are pre-ileal**: obvious abdominal signs.
- **0.5% are post-ileal**: poorly localized pain, harder to diagnose.

Rarely:

- Mal-descended caecum leads to right upper quadrant appendix
- Long appendix with an inflamed tip can be anywhere (appendix may be up to 25 cm long)
- Transposition of viscera leads to left iliac fossa pain

Appendicectomy

- **Pre-operative care**
  Rehydration may be needed
  Antibiotics — one dose pre-operatively (usually cefuroxime and metronidazole)
  Consent — must include removal of normal appendix and any other procedure thought necessary at operation (e.g. removal of Meckel's diverticulum, bowel resection in older patients with atypical symptoms/mass)

- **Incisions (see Figure, Section 2.1, p. 330)**
  McBurney's or gridiron incision
  Lanz incision
  Right paramedian or lower midline — only if carcinoma of caecum is suspected.

- **Procedure (using McBurney's incision)**
  Incise external oblique in line of fibres
  Split internal oblique and transversus abdominus in the line of their fibres exposing the peritoneum
  Incise peritoneum ensuring no bowel is in the peritoneal fold
  If free pus is present, send microbiology swab
  Locate caecum and deliver it into wound using fingers or Babcock's forceps
  Turn caecum to deliver appendix
  May have to extend incision or mobilise caecum if difficult
  Mesentery to appendix is clipped with artery forceps, divided and ligated
  Base of appendix is crushed, ligated and appendix is excised
  Stump may be inverted using purse string
  If appendix is normal, look for Meckel's diverticulum and feel pelvic organs
  If free pus or perforated, wash out with warm saline
  Close in layers

- **Post-operative care**
  Three days of antibiotics if perforated with peritonitis
  Fluids on day one, eat when tolerating fluids.

Complications of appendicitis and appendicectomy

- **Pre-operative**
  Perforation
  Peritonitis
  Abscess

- **Early post-operative**
  Residual abscess
  Faecal fistula
  Ileus
  Inguinal hernia
  Urinary retention
  Chest problems
  Thromboembolism
  Persistent sinus

- **Late post-operative**
  Ventral hernia
  Adhesions

Conservative treatment of appendicitis

Advocated if:

- No surgical treatment available
- Surgery contraindicated by patient's poor condition
- Appendix mass with no peritonitis
- Late presentation (3–5 days after onset of pain) — controversial
- Late presentation and abdominal mass known to be appendicitis

This non-surgical approach involves a course of antibiotics and observation.

Interval appendicectomy
This is where appendicectomy is carried out electively some time after successful conservative management. The benefits are unproven and in some studies one-third of appendices are normal and 25% have recurrence.

Other conditions of appendix

'Grumbling' appendicitis
This is a controversial entity which may be linked to helminth infestation. It may also be mimicked by a number of conditions, including Crohn's disease, adhesions, salpingitis, recurrent UTI or psychological problems.

Crohn's disease of the appendix
This is usually associated with Crohn's disease of the ileocaecal region, so local resection of the terminal ileum and caecum may be better than appendicectomy alone.

Effect of perforated appendicitis on subsequent fertility
Decreased fertility is suggested but not proven.

6.2 Diverticular disease

Definitions

- Diverticulum is an out-pouching of the wall of a luminal organ. In diverticular disease this refers to the colon, but diverticula also occur in the rest of the gut and other organs (e.g. the bladder).
- Congenital diverticula involve all layers of the colonic wall (rare)
- Acquired diverticula are areas of colonic mucosa that herniate through the muscular wall of the colon (common)
- Diverticulosis means that diverticula are present
- Diverticular disease means that diverticula are symptomatic
- Diverticulitis refers to acute inflammation of diverticula
- Complicated diverticulitis includes the sequale of diverticulitis, such as abscesses, fistulae, bowel obstruction, haemorrhage and perforation

Epidemiology

- Common in developed countries (with low fibre diet)
- Increasing in incidence
- Increases with age (10% of all 40-year-olds)
- 60% of 80-year-olds have diverticulosis

Aetiology

- Lack of dietary fibre leads to high intraluminal pressures and increased segmentation and muscular hypertrophy in the colonic wall
- Acquired diverticula occur at the site of weakness in the now non-compliant colonic wall
- The main sites of weakness are where mesenteric blood vessels penetrate the bowel wall

Distribution of diverticulosis

- 45% in sigmoid colon only
- 35% in sigmoid and descending colon
- 10% in sigmoid, descending and transverse colon
- 5% pan colonic
- 5% caecal

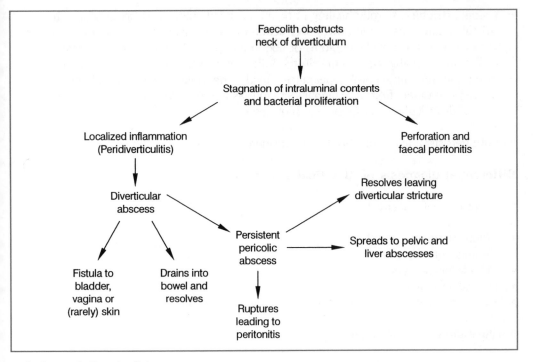

Pathology of diverticulitis

Clinical presentation

- **Diverticular disease**: in the absence of inflammation, may cause change in bowel habit, pellet-like stools, abdominal discomfort and bloating
- **Uncomplicated diverticulitis**: usually low abdominal pain (often left iliac fossa), change in bowel habit ± passage of mucus p.r. Urinary symptoms, anorexia and nausea can occur. In more severe cases, patients have pyrexia, tachycardia, peritonism ± mass, distension and diminished bowel sounds
- **PR bleed**: this usually occurs in the absence of acute diverticulitis. Is caused by erosion of mural vessels by a diverticula.
- **Pericolic abscess**: these result from a partial localization of a diverticular perforation. They can develop in the mesentery, pelvis or retro-peritoneum. They can track and 'point' as a perineal, scrotal, psoas or flank abscess. Typical presentation includes tachycardia, spiking temperature and a palpable mass.
- **Peritonitis**: is a result of a ruptured pericolic abscess (purulent) or free perforation of a diverticulum (faecal). Patient is acutely unwell with tachycardia, a rigid silent abdomen and maybe shocked and tachypnoeic.
- **Fistulae**: as a result of diverticulitis. Colonic diverticulitis may fistulate into the vagina or uterus, resulting in faeculent vaginal discharge. Colovesical fistulae produce pneumaturia, recurrent UTIs and faecaluria. Direct colocutaneous fistulae may occur but are less common.

- **Colonic stricture**: fibrotic healing of recurrent diverticulitis leads to stenosis. These strictures may cause large bowel obstruction or can present on barium or endoscopic investigations for bowel symptoms or abdominal pain. Barium enema appearance differs from a malignant stricture in the following ways: smooth-walled; no mucosal disruption; no 'apple core' appearances; tend to be longer strictures. Endoscopic appearance differs from a malignant stricture as follows: overlying mucosal integrity; area of diverticular disease; benign biopsies

If doubt persists, a resection should be considered.

Differential diagnosis of diverticular disease

If patient presents electively:

- Colon carcinoma
- Crohn's colitis
- Irritable bowel syndrome
- Ulcerative colitis
- Subacute small bowel obstruction secondary to adhesions

If patient presents as an emergency:

- Pelvic inflammatory disease
- Appendicitis
- Complications of ovarian cyst
- Exacerbation of Crohn's disease
- Ischaemic colitis
- Perforated Ca colon

Investigations

Routine tests
FBC, urine microscopy (if entero-vesical fistula is suspected), **erect CXR** (if perforation is suspected), **AXR** (if bowel obstruction or ileus secondary to abscess is suspected).

Contrast studies
Double-contrast barium enema allows diagnosis of diverticular disease, assessment of the extent of the disease, demonstration of stenoses, fistulae and pericolic abscesses. Problems — may miss small polyps or carcinoma. Barium is not ideal if urgent sugery is planned or perforation is suspected. **Single-contrast water soluble enema** is safer if mechanical obstruction or colonic perforation is suspected. **Sinography** can be used to outline the track of an entero-cutaneous fistula. **Cystography** may also be useful.

Other investigations

Colonoscopy is often used as the primary diagnostic tool in elective cases, as up to 20% of patients with sigmoid diverticular disease harbour small polyps which can be seen, biopsied or removed. This is contraindicated during an attack of diverticulitis. **CT** is the investigation of choice in complex diverticulitis. It allows diagnosis of phlegmon, abscess or free gas suggesting perforation. Using contrast, colovesical fistulas and intra-peritoneal collections can be identified. If CT is not available, **US** can confirm the presence of a diverticular mass but accuracy may be limited by surrounding bowel loops.

Non-surgical treatment of diverticular disease

Conservative
(In uncomplicated diverticular disease)

- Increased dietary fibre
- Antimuscarinics (e.g. propantheline bromide)
- Antispasmodics (e.g. mebeverine hydrochloride)

Medical
(In uncomplicated acute diverticulitis)

- Bowel rest
- Intravenous fluids
- Parenteral antibiotics (e.g. cefuroxime and metronidazole)
- Nasogastric suction if ileus is a feature
- Repeated clinical observation to detect treatment failure or development of complications

Radiological
(In diverticulitis complicated by abscess formation)

- Percutaneous drainage under radiological guidance is successful in 75% of patients with a localized collection and avoids emergency laparotomy and temporary colostomy.
- Subsequent resection with primary anastomosis may then be undertaken when nutritional markers are restored and physical signs of inflammation have resolved.

Elective surgery

Indications

- Patients who have recovered from acute diverticulitis but are considered to be at high risk of future attacks (e.g. one episode age < 50 years or two episodes in over 50-year-olds, chronically immunosuppressed patients, proven abscess or perforation treated conservatively).

- Patients with chronic complications of diverticulitis (e.g. colovaginal and colovesical fistulas, symptomatic large bowel strictures).
- Patients in whom a large bowel carcinoma cannot be excluded.

Results of elective surgery

- The risk of recurrent diverticulitis following limited colonic resection is similar to that following medically treated diverticular disease (7–15%).
- The main benefit of elective surgery is avoidance of future emergency surgery.

Emergency surgery

There is a five-fold increase in the mortality rate when emergency surgery is undertaken; in 30–50% of patients, emergency surgery results in a colostomy which is never reversed.

Indications
20% of patients with acute diverticulitis undergo a laparotomy usually for the following reasons:

- Faecal peritonitis
- Purulent peritonitis
- Pelvic or intra-abdominal abscess (if not amenable to radiological percutaneous drainage)
- Bleeding unresponsive to supportive care
- Bowel obstruction

6.3 Meckel's diverticulum

- A Meckel's ileal diverticulum is present in 2% of people, 2 ft (60 cm) from the caecum and is 2″ (5 cm) long. (This is true two-thirds of the time!)
- A true diverticulum containing all the layers of the intestinal wall
- The most common congenital anomaly of the small bowel
- Remnant of the omphalomesenteric (vitelline) duct
- Apex may be adherent to the umbilicus or attached to it by a fibrous cord
- May contain ectopic tissue, most frequently gastric or pancreatic mucosa

Abdominal pain caused by Meckel's diverticulum

- **Volvulus** or kinking of a loop of small bowel around the fibrous band from the diverticulum to the umbilicus leading to obstruction. In children, this may present as rectal bleeding and abdominal pain.
- **Haemorrhage or perforation** which may be due to gastric mucosa being present within it.

- **Intussusception** with the diverticulum as the apex of the intussusception.
- **Meckel's diverticulitis** clinically identical to appendicitis. 50% incidence of perforation.

Management
A Meckel's diverticulum may be identified by small bowel meal or radionucleide scan if gastric mucosa is present, but is commonly discovered at operation.

Simple excision
This is more difficult if broad-based. An editorial in the *Lancet* suggested that Meckel's found incidentally which are normal should not be resected in patients over 40.

Suggested methods of excision

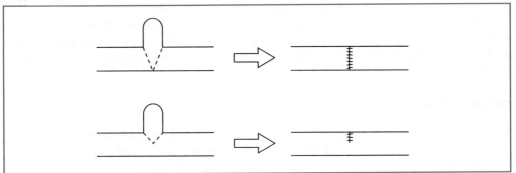

Excision of Meckel's diverticulum

There is an increased risk of complications if:

- Ectopic mucosa is present
- The diverticulum is more than 4 cm long
- The base of the diverticulum is less than 2 cm wide

6.4 Gynaecological causes of acute abdominal pain

Several gynaecological disorders present as an acute abdomen:

- Ruptured ectopic pregnancy
- Endometriosis
- Torsion or rupture of ovarian cyst
- Mittelschmerz (ruptured ovarian follicle)
- Pelvic inflammatory disease

Ectopic pregnancy

- A fertilized ovum is deposited outside the uterine cavity
- Less than 1% of pregnancies
- Increased incidence with previous salpingitis, intrauterine device or previous ectopic pregnancy
- Can occur in a sterilized woman
- Usually occurs in the Fallopian tube
- Fertilized ovum lodges in the tube causing vascular engorgement, followed by rupture
- Patient may be shocked if bleeding is rapid
- Typical history of missed period (breast tenderness ± crampy abdominal pain ± systemic disturbance
- Guarding and rebound tenderness in lower abdomen
- p.v. examination is contraindicated as it may induce haemorrhage
- Investigations should include pregnancy tests, FBC and X-matching blood
- Early referral to gynaecologist is vital, as laparoscopy is the most useful diagnostic test
- Prompt surgical intervention is vital, and usually involves salpingectomy or salpingo-oophorectomy

Endometriosis

- Functioning endometrial tissue is found as deposits outside the uterine cavity
- Commonly affects ovaries, Fallopian tubes, peritoneum, the serosal surface and ligaments of the uterus, the sigmoid colon and small intestine
- Women aged 30–50 years
- Symptoms are dysmenorrhoea and low abdominal pain starting a week before the period
- Other presentations include low back pain; painful defaecation, dysuria, haematuria and partial intestinal obstruction
- Large ovarian endometrial cysts may rupture leading to acute lower abdominal pain, tenderness, guarding and rebound
- Diagnosis is by laparoscopy or at laparotomy for the acute abdomen
- Treatment is hormonal manipulation, progesterones or synthetic androgens (e.g. Danazol) are often successful
- Complicated endometrial cysts require elective surgery

Torsion or ruptured ovarian cyst

- Ovarian cysts are either functional or proliferative
- Can cause acute abdominal pain when they rupture, twist or infarct
- Rupture or torsion produces severe, acute lower abdominal pain with guarding and rebound

- Cyst may be palpable on bi-manual examination
- Diagnosis may be confirmed by ultrasound or laparoscopy
- Treatment is surgical excision or aspiration

Mittelschmerz (ruptured ovarian follicle)

- Extensive bleeding from a Graafian follicle at the time of ovulation can produce severe lower abdominal pain with tenderness and guarding
- It typically occurs in mid-cycle and may have occurred before
- Diagnosis is confirmed by laparoscopy or at laparotomy for the suspected appendicitis

Pelvic inflammatory disease (PID)

- This is the syndrome due to ascending infection of the vagina, cervix, endometrium, Fallopian tubes and/or contiguous structures
- It is commonly caused by *Chlamydia trachomatis* or *Neisseria gonorrhoeae*
- PID may occasionally be secondary to a gastro-intestinal infection, such as appendicitis or to a systemic infection, such as tuberculosis
- Patients present with acute lower abdominal pain and a high fever associated with tenderness in the lower abdomen
- On vaginal inspection and examination, a discharge may be seen and there is cervical excitation on palpation
- Laparoscopy can be used to confirm the diagnosis
- Treatment is by antibiotics (metronidazole and erythromycin) after vaginal and cervical swabs have been taken
- IUCD should be removed if present
- Complications include tubo-ovarian abscess, infertility and recurrent infections if partner is not treated

6.5 Perforation of abdominal viscus and abdominal trauma

Perforation of an abdominal viscus causes sudden onset of acute abdominal pain and peritonitis.

Causes of perforation of the abdominal viscus

- **Oesophagus**
  Cancer
  Instrumentation
  Trauma, vomiting

- **Duodenum**
  Peptic ulcer

- **Colon**
  Diverticular disease
  Carcinoma
  Radiation damage
  Crohn's disease
  Ischaemia
  Tropical infections (typhoid,
    amoebic infections,
    tuberculosis)

- **Stomach**
  Cancer
  Peptic ulcer

- **Small bowel**
  Trauma
  Foreign bodies
  Crohn's disease
  Leukaemia
  Lymphoma
  Peptic ulcer (from ectopic gastric
    mucosa, e.g. in the Meckel's
    diverticulum)
  Meckel's diverticulitis
  Potassium chloride tablets
    (terminal ileum ulceration)

Clinical presentation

- Abdominal pain — may be localized to site of perforation initially but becomes generalized
- Rigid tender silent abdomen
- Patient may be systemically unwell, tachycardic, tachypnoeic, febrile, hypotensive
- Shoulder tip pain and loss of liver dullness on percussion may be elicited
- Symptoms and signs may be minimal in elderly sick patients

Investigations

- Erect CXR demonstrates free air in 80–90% of visceral perforation
- Gastrograffin swallow may be helpful

Management
This is described in detail in the sections covering each of the underlying conditions. As a general rule, once perforation is confirmed, immediate resuscitation is mandatory and early laparotomy is usually required.

Abdominal trauma

This subject is covered in detail in Chapter 3, *Trauma*, of the *MRCS Core Modules: Essential Revision Notes*, but it is worth mentioning a few specific points here.

Principles of management of abdominal trauma:

- Primary survey and resuscitation
- Secondary survey
- Definitive management

Indications for laparotomy in abdominal trauma

- Hypotension with evidence of abdominal injury: gunshot wounds; stab wounds; blunt trauma with positive diagnostic peritoneal lavage
- Peritonitis — early or subsequent
- Recurrent hypotension despite adequate resuscitation
- Extraluminal air on X-ray
- Injured diaphragm
- Intra-peritoneal perforation of urinary bladder on cystography
- CT evidence of injury to the pancreas, gastrointestinal tract and specific injuries to the liver, spleen and/or kidney
- Positive contrast study of upper and lower gastrointestinal tracts
- Persistently elevated amylase with abdominal findings

Blunt abdominal trauma

- This is usually caused by road traffic accidents
- Injuries to liver, spleen and kidneys are common, but small bowel injury and (less commonly) colorectal injury may occur
- Shearing and rotational forces lead to burst bowel and torn mesentery. The types of injury dictate the management of the bowel injury. Simple tears can be safely repaired without the aid of a proximal defunctioning colostomy. Mesenteric tears require control of haemorrhage and resection of any bowel of dubious viability. Primary

anastomosis is only performed in selected cases. Complex injuries usually necessitate resection and exteriorisation of the bowel ends.
- Primary anastomosis is contraindicated in the presence of: shock; extreme faecal contamination; extensive tissue damage; associated injuries; delay in treatment; gross faecal loading.

Penetrating trauma
Usually caused by stabbings and low-velocity firearms in the UK. More serious penetrating injuries are inflicted by high-velocity weapons and debris from bomb blasts. There is a move away from exploring all abdominal stab wounds. An expectant policy is now preferred in patients with no signs of major intra-abdominal haemorrhage or peritonitis. Laparotomy is performed if the patient develops signs of such injury. All patients with gunshot wounds which may have involved the abdomen should undergo a laparotomy.

Specific injuries

- **Swallowed objects**: sharp, ingested objects may lacerate the bowel or anal mucosa. Patients may present with signs of perforation or with acute anal pain. A laparotomy for the former and examination under anaesthetic for the latter may be indicated.
- **Foreign bodies in the rectum**: foreign bodies may be introduced through the anus for self-gratification or during drunken pranks or assaults. Most foreign bodies can be removed through the anus under anaesthesia, after which the rectum is examined for underlying injury.
- **Iatrogenic injury**: this may occur during sigmoidoscopy, colonoscopy, endoscopic removal of rectal tumours etc. Immediate closure of a perforation and formation of a defunctioning colostomy may be necessary. Minor injuries can be managed conservatively with active observation and antibiotics.
- **Impalement**: impalement injuries are usually caused by accidental falls onto railings or sharp spikes. They may cause severe internal injuries with little external evidence, especially if the object enters through the anus. Evidence of such internal injury is an indication for exploratory laparotomy.
- **Pelvic fractures**: the rectum may be punctured by bone fragments after major pelvic fracture. There will usually be a coincident bladder, prostate and urethral injuries. Bone fragments and dislocation of the prostate may be felt on rectal examination. A defunctioning colostomy or Hartmann type resection may be indicated.

6.6 Inflammatory bowel disease (IBD)

Ulcerative colitis and Crohn's disease may present as an acute abdomen. Crohn's disease may be mistaken for acute appendicitis or an appendix abscess. It may also present with chronic subacute or even acute small bowel obstruction. Occasionally, Crohn's disease can cause perforation and present with severe peritonitis. Ulcerative colitis may progress to toxic megacolon which can also perforate. The treatment of these conditions is discussed in Section 12.3, p. 477.

6.7 Abdominal wall pain

Pain arising in the abdominal wall rather than the abdominal cavity may occasionally be mistaken for an acute abdomen.

Neurovascular bundle entrapment presents as a recurrent abdominal pain with one or two trigger points which can be accurately localized using one finger. Injection of local anaesthetic is diagnostic and may be curative.

Rectus sheath haematoma is an uncommon condition which may arise spontaneously after minor trauma or bouts of coughing or sneezing. It may be associated with an underlying disorder of coagulation, degenerative vascular disease, infectious disease or haematological condition, such as leukaemia. The patient presents with acute onset of localised (usually lower) abdominal pain, worse when the abdominal muscles are tense. An ultrasound or CT scan may reveal the haematoma and the treatment is conservative.

NB. Acute abdominal pain in children is dealt with in Chapter 3, *Head, Neck, Endocrine and Paediatric*, Section 15, p. 285.

7. ANATOMY AND PHYSIOLOGY OF THE STOMACH AND DUODENUM

7.1 Anatomy of the stomach

The stomach is the most dilated part of the gastrointestinal tract and sits between the oesophagus and the duodenum. The capacity varies from 30 ml in the newborn to 1.45 L in adults. The major structural features are summarized in the diagram below.

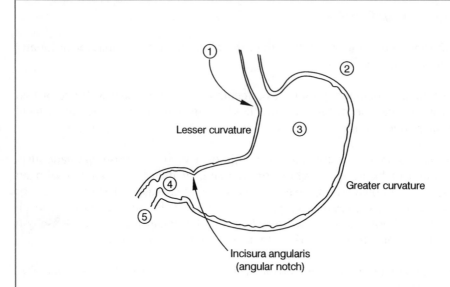

Lesser curvature

Greater curvature

Incisura angularis
(angular notch)

Structure of the stomach

Landmarks of the stomach
(1) **Cardia**: most fixed part of the stomach — left of midline at T10 — cardiac orifice (gastro-oesophageal junction) has four factors guarding it against reflux: 1 Lower oesophageal muscle fibres; 2 Fibres of right crus; 3 Mucosal flaps of muscularis mucosa; 4 Difference between intrathoracic and intra-abdominal pressure.
(2) **Fundus**: projects above cardia. Usually touches diaphragm. Full of swallowed air.
(3) **Body**: largest part of stomach, from fundus to incisura angularis which is a prominent feature that does not change with peristalsis.
(4) **Pylorus**: from incisura angularis to gastroduodenal junction: (a) pyloric antrum — proximal dilated portion; (b) pyloric canal; (c) pyloric sphincter — thickened circular muscle; (d) pylorus — narrow lumen of pyloric sphincter.
(5) **Pyloric opening**: in recumbant position with stomach empty lies right of midline at L1.

Muscle layers of the stomach

- Outer longitudinal
- Inner circular
- Incomplete innermost oblique

The innermost layer loops over the fundus. It is thickest at the notch between the oesophagus and the stomach. It is oblique when the stomach is empty. It is vertical when the stomach is full and the trunk is erect (supporting the weight of the gastric contents).

Relations of the stomach

Three double layers of peritoneum form important connections between the stomach and other organs:

- The **lesser omentum** is a double layer from liver to lesser curvature of the stomach
- The **greater omentum** is a large apron running from the greater curvature of the stomach to the transverse colon
- The **gastrosplenic omentum** runs from the stomach to the spleen

The posterior relations of the stomach are referred to as the **stomach bed** and include many clinically important structures:

- Peritoneum (anterior and posterior wall of the lesser sac)
- The left crus and dome of the diaphragm
- Upper left kidney and adrenal
- Pancreas, spleen and splenic artery
- Transverse mesocolon
- Aorta and coeliac trunk
- Coeliac ganglia and lymph nodes

Functions of the stomach

- Reservoir
- Regulates passage of food to duodenum
- Bacterial death (by hydrochloric acid)
- Oxidizes iron
- Mixes food with secretions
- Protein digestion (by pepsin)
- Intrinsic factor production (needed for vitamin B12 absorption)
- Mechanized food breakdown

Blood supply

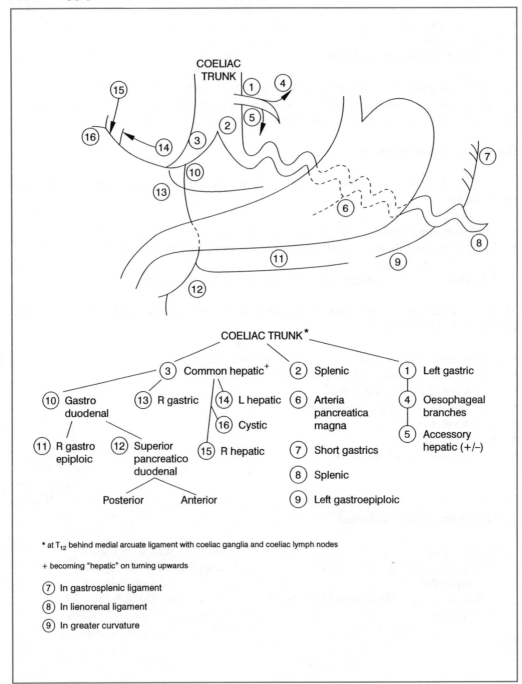

Blood supply of the stomach

The blood supply of the stomach is summarized in the diagram opposite. The lesser curvature is supplied by branches from the left and right gastric arteries (may be double) running between layers of lesser omentum. These branches meet in an end-to-end anastomosis.

The fundus and the upper left side of the greater curvature are supplied by the short gastric arteries from the splenic artery running in the gastrosplenic ligament.

The lower greater curvature is supplied by the left and right gastro epiploic arteries (rarely double) from the splenic and gastroduodenal artery running between two layers of greater omentum. They may or may not anastamose.

Venous drainage of stomach

Veins follow arteries and drain into portal veins with two exceptions:

- There is no gastroduodenal vein
- The prepyloric vein of Mayo overlies the pylorus and drains into the portal or right gastric vein

Oesophageal branches are one of the five portosystemic anastomoses.

Lymphatic drainage of stomach

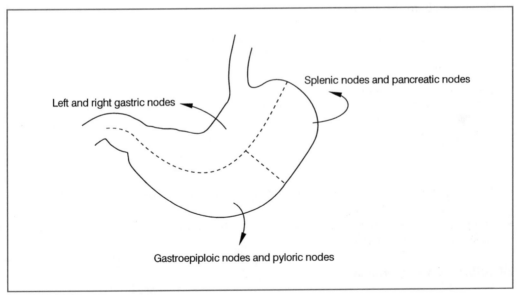

Lymphatic drainage of the stomach

Lymphatic drainage is to the coeliac nodes via a network of freely anastomosing vessels (see the diagram above). Valves direct lymph in the direction shown in the figure.

Nerve supply to the stomach

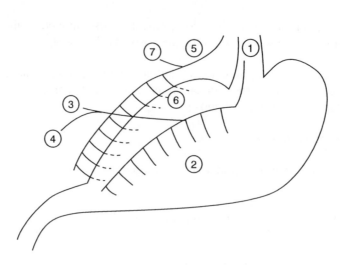

Nerve supply to the stomach

(1) **Anterior vagal trunk**: mostly left vagus. At gastro-oesophageal junction, it lies in contact with the anterior oesophagus. Runs down lesser omentum with left gastric artery. Double in 20% of people.
(2) **Gastric branches**.
(3) **Large hepatic branches**.
(4) **Branches to pyloric antrum**.
(5) **Posterior vagal trunk**: mostly right vagus. Lies in loose tissue behind and to the right of the right oesophageal margin. Runs in lesser omentum behind anterior trunk. Rarely double.
(6) **Numerous branches to posterior of stomach**.
(7) **Large coeliac branch**: coeliac ganglia.

- The sympathetic nerve supply to the stomach is from the coeliac plexus and runs with the vessels
- The parasympathetic nerve supply to the stomach is via the vagus nerves which are shown in the figure above

Histology of the stomach

At the cardio-oesophageal junction, the stratified squamous epithelium changes to single layered columnar epithelium. This epithelium has specific characteristics in different areas of the stomach:

- **Cardia**: short glands; mucus-secreting cells only
- **Body**: mucus-secreting cells; peptic cells secreting pepsin; parietal cells secreting acid and intrinsic factor; gastric pits with test-tube-like glands
- **Pylorus**: mucus-secreting cells; gastrin-producing G cells; somatostatin secreting D cells; entero-chromaffin EC cells; serotonin and endorphin-secreting cells

There is no external landmark between the acid secreting body cells and the gastrin producing (G) pyloric cells.

7.2 Anatomy of the duodenum

- The duodenum is the first part of the small intestine and runs from the pylorus of the stomach to the jejunum
- It curves over the convexity of the aorta and the inferior vena cava
- Its structure is described and relations listed in the figure below

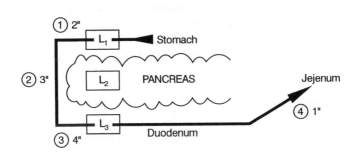

Structure and relations of the duodenum

(1) **First part**: 2" long. Runs right, upwards and backwards. The first inch is intra-peritoneal, the rest is retroperitoneal. Forms the lower border of the epiploic foramen. Lies behind the right lobe of the liver. Posterior relations include the inferior vena cava, right kidney and the liver pedicle including the bile duct, hepatic artery and portal vein.

(2) **Second part**: 3" long, running inferiorly to the right of the head of the pancreas. The bile duct and main pancreatic duct open at the major duodenal papilla (ampulla of Vater) on the posteriomedial wall, 4 cm from the pylorus. (The accessory pancreatic duct opens 2 cm proximal to this at the minor duodenal papilla). Second part of duodenum retroperitoneal and is crossed by the transverse mesocolon attachments. It lies in front of the hilum of the right kidney.

(3) **Third part**: the longest part, it is retroperitoneal, 4" long, running transversely inferior to the pancreas and behind the transverse mesocolon and curls of jejunum.

(4) **Fourth part**: the last inch of retroperitoneal small intestine before the duodenojejunal flexure (D-J flexure). The duodenum is retroperitoneal, whereas the jejunum hangs from a mesentry. The ligament of Treitz fixes the duodeno-jejunal flexure to the left psoas fascia. There are four paraduodenal recesses around the D-J flexure which can cause internal herniae.

Blood supply of duodenum

The **duodenal cap** (the most common site of bleeding duodenal ulcers) is supplied by branches of many arteries, including:

- Hepatic artery
- Common hepatic artery
- Gastroduodenal artery
- Superior pancreatico-duodenal artery
- Right gastric artery
- Right gastro-epiploic artery

The **proximal duodenum** (proximal to the bile duct) is supplied by:

- Superior pancreatico-duodenal artery — a branch of the hepatic artery from the coeliac trunk

Distal to the bile duct the duodenum is supplied by the inferior pancreatico-duodenal artery (a branch of the superior mesenteric artery)

The veins correspond with the arteries with some blood also entering the small prepyloric vein.

Lymphatic drainage

Lymph from the duodenum drains to the coeliac and superior mesenteric nodes.

Nerve supply

- Parasympathetic supply of the duodenum is from the vagus nerve
- Sympathetic supply of the duodenum is from the coeliac and mesenteric plexus
- Nerves run with the blood vessels

7.3 Physiology of the upper gastro-intestinal tract

The movement of food through the gastro-intestinal tract (GIT) and its digestion is controlled by a complex combination of neural and hormonal feedback mechanisms. Neural control of the gastro-intestinal system is mediated by the enteric and the extrinsic nervous systems. Hormonal control of the gastro-intestinal system is mediated by blood-borne, paracrine and neurocrine hormones.

Physiology of the upper GIT (summary)

- **Neural control**
  Enteric nervous system
    Meissner's plexus
    Auerbach's plexus
  Extrinsic nervous system
    Sympathetic from coeliac plexus
    Parasympathetic from vagus

- **Movement of food through the GIT**
  Inner circular, outer longitudinal layer
  Peristalsis
  Migrating myoelectric complex
  Different muscular activity in each section of GIT

- **Hormonal control**
  Blood-borne hormones (e.g.
    gastrin, secretin, CCK)
  Paracrine hormones (e.g.
    histamine, somatostatin)
  Neurocrine hormones (e.g.
    VIP, GRP)

The enteric nervous system

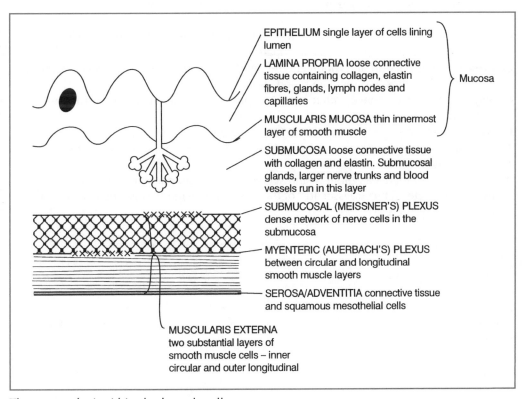

EPITHELIUM single layer of cells lining lumen

LAMINA PROPRIA loose connective tissue containing collagen, elastin fibres, glands, lymph nodes and capillaries

MUSCULARIS MUCOSA thin innermost layer of smooth muscle

} Mucosa

SUBMUCOSA loose connective tissue with collagen and elastin. Submucosal glands, larger nerve trunks and blood vessels run in this layer

SUBMUCOSAL (MEISSNER'S) PLEXUS dense network of nerve cells in the submucosa

MYENTERIC (AUERBACH'S) PLEXUS between circular and longitudinal smooth muscle layers

SEROSA/ADVENTITIA connective tissue and squamous mesothelial cells

MUSCULARIS EXTERNA two substantial layers of smooth muscle cells – inner circular and outer longitudinal

The nerve plexi within the bowel wall

- The enteric nervous system consists of two interlinking nerve plexi running in the bowel wall (see the Figure opposite), the submucosal **Meissner's plexus** and the myenteric **Auerbach's plexus**
- The nerve plexus of the GIT contain 10^8 neurones (as many as the spinal cord)
- **Auerbach's myenteric plexus** consists mostly of **motor neurons** to smooth muscle cells of muscularis externa
- These motor neurons usually produce acetylcholine as a neurotransmitter for muscarinic receptors
- The inner circular muscle is more richly innervated than the longitudinal muscle
- **Meissner's submucosal plexus** consists mostly of **secretomotor neurons** to the glandular, endocrine and epithelial cells
- These secretomotor neurons usually produce acetylcholine and VIP neurotransmittors to stimulate effector cells, but over 25 other neuromodulatory substances have been identified
- Both Auerbach's and Meissner's plexi also contain sensory neurons and interneurons which form intrinsic reflex arcs responding to intestinal pH, luminal pressure and pain
- Both plexi have connections with the sympathetic and parasympathetic nervous system which modulate their motor and secretory activity

The extrinsic nervous system

- Gastro-intestinal system is supplied with sympathetic nerves from the coeliac plexus and parasympathetic nerves from the vagus
- Extrinsic nerves act on and modulate the enteric nervous system, influence secretory and motor activities and regulate blood supply
- Sympathetic nerves convey afferent pain impulses and efferent vasomotor impulses. They run with the blood vessels
- Parasympathetic innervation is via the vagus nerve
- 90% of the parasympathetic nerves carry sensory afferent impulses which form extrinsic reflex arcs
- The vagus also increases motility and secretion of the stomach and innervates the pyloric sphincter. Thus transsection of the vagus trunks reduces gastric acid secretion and causes gastric stasis

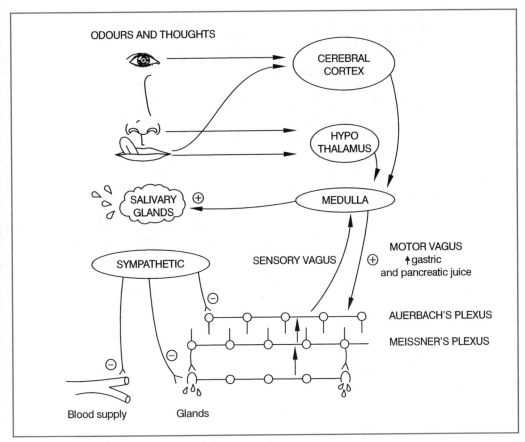

Cephalic stage of neural control of the stomach

Neural control of the stomach

Neural control of the stomach occurs in three stages:

- **Cephalic** (see the figure above): an excitory stage responsible for saliva production, some pancreatic juice production and 10% of gastric secretion
- **Gastric**: responsible for 80% of gastric secretion; mediated by a short gastric reflex and a long vagus reflex; there is also an inhibitory element to the gastric stage
- **Intestinal**: the final stage, mostly inhibitory, although responsible for 10% of gastric secretion. The acid, increased osmolarity, fatty acids and peptides in the duodenum act on the stomach via neural and hormonal feedback mechanisms to decrease gastric motility and regulate the volume of chyme being propelled through the pylorus.

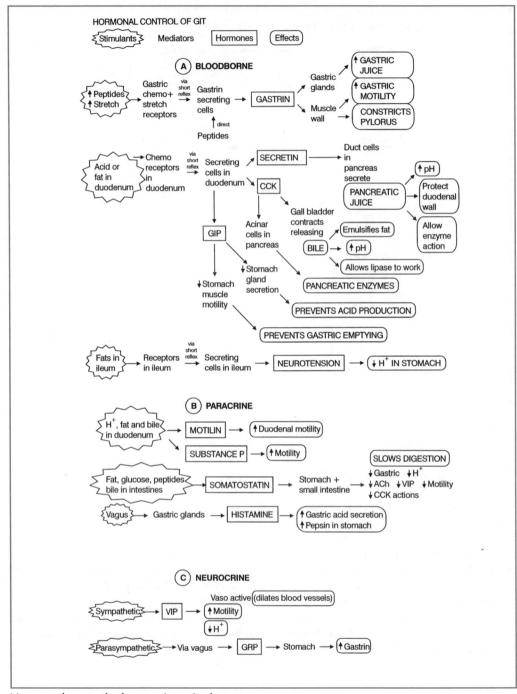

Hormonal control of gastro-intestinal tract

Blood-borne hormones acting on the gastro-intestinal tract
Some of the many blood-borne hormones acting on the GIT are shown in the Figure opposite. In general, receptors sense changes in the intestine and via an intrinsic reflex stimulate secretory cells to secrete hormones into the bloodstream. These hormones then act on remote cells, glands, organs and blood vessels to produce the desired result. The effects include the production of gastric enzymes, pancreatic juice and bile in response to distension and undigested food in the duodenum and ileum

Paracrine hormones acting on the GIT
Some of the many paracrine hormones acting on the GIT are shown in the Figure opposite. In general, receptors sense changes in the intestine and stimulate local hormone production. These hormones interact directly on local cells, glands and muscle to produce the desired result.

Neurocrine hormones acting on the GIT
Examples of neurocrine hormones acting on the GIT are shown in the Figure opposite. In general, nerves produce neurotransmittors which act directly upon the muscle cells, glandular cells and blood vessels they supply.

Movement of food through the GIT

Electrophysiology
There are two layers of smooth muscle, an inner circular and an outer longitudinal layer, which run along the entire length of the GIT.

* Gastro-intestinal smooth muscle cells are electrically coupled so they tend to work as a functional unit
* A resting membrane potential oscillates with a characteristic rhythm controlling the rate of regular contractions

Peristalsis
Contractions of the smooth muscles of the GIT wall which mixes and propels the contents of the lumen.

* These waves of contractions vary in frequency, averaging 13/min in the duodenum and 8/min in the ileum
* Hormones and neurotransmittors affect their force and strength. The vagus increases the rate of peristalsis

Migrating myoelectric complex (MMC)
The MMC is characterized by 70–90-min periods of quiescence, interrupted by periods of vigorous and intensely propulsive contractions lasting 3–6 min. These contractions sweep the stomach and small intestine clear of debris from the previous meal (the housekeeper of the bowel).

Swallowing

Swallowing is co-ordinated by the swallowing centre in the pons and medulla. Initiated by touch receptors in the pharynx, the swallowing reflex is an ordered sequence of contractions of muscles of the pharynx, upper oesophageal sphincter, oesophageal striated and smooth muscle and the lower oesophageal sphincter. (See Section 4.2, p. 349.)

Gastric motility

Relaxation of the lower oesophageal sphincter is caused by oesophageal peristaltic wave. This initiates receptive relaxation of the stomach, triggered by the movement of the pharynx.

- Distension of the stomach by food leads to increased secretion and motility mediated by local and vasovagal reflexes
- Contractions of the body of the stomach mix food with gastric juice
- More forceful contractions in the antrum cause a churning action
- The pyloric sphincter closes as waves arrive, allowing only small volumes (about 3 ml/min) into the duodenum
- Feedback by hormones and neurones ensure gastric emptying does not occur faster than the duodenum and jejenum can neutralize the gastric acid and process the chyme
- Gastric emptying takes 3-4 hours, liquid first, fat last
- The 'gastric slow wave' is a basic electrical rhythm every 20 s when feeding
- There are 10 min of activity every 100 min when fasting

Motility of the small intestine

The major contractile activity in the small intestine is segmentation which mixes and circulates the intestinal contents but it is not very powerful. This slow rate of transport allows adequate time for digestion and absorption.

Motility of the large intestine

In the proximal colon antipropulsive contractions predominate, allowing time for absorption of salt and water. In the transverse and descending colon haustral contractions mix and knead colonic contents to facilitate extraction of salts and water. Mass movements that occur in the colon 1–3 times daily sweep colon contents to the anus.

8. PEPTIC ULCERATION AND GASTRIC CARCINOMA

8.1 Peptic ulceration

Peptic ulcers are chronic, usually solitary lesions, occurring in the duodenum (80%), stomach (19%) or both (4%); 1% occur at other sites where gastric acid can damage the mucosa (e.g. oesophagus, gastro-enterostomy, stoma, jejunum, Meckel's diverticulum).

Epidemiology

* 0.8% of the population per year develop a duodenal ulcer
* 0.2% of the population per year develop a gastric ulcer
* The incidence is increasing worldwide but decreasing in developed countries
* The peak age for duodenal ulcer is increasing (35-44 years)
* Gastric ulcers occur in older age groups
* There is a 2:1 male:female ratio
* There is a higher mortality in the poor

Aetiology

* Peptic ulcers are caused by the action of gastric acid and pepsin on the mucosa of the gastrointestinal tract
* There is some controversy about whether it is an increased acid secretion or a decrease in mucosal defences that is more important
* It is thought that duodenal ulceration is mostly due to increased acid production
* Gastric ulceration, on the other hand, is thought to be mostly due to the breakdown in mucosal defence against acid and pepsin

---

Predisposing factors for peptic ulceration

* *H. pylori*
* Chemicals
* Associated disease
* Familial
* Gastrin hypersecretion

Helicobacter pylori infection

* *H. pylori* is a Gram-negative spiral micro aerophilic baccillus specific for human gastric mucosa that exists deep in the mucous layer
* It produces the enzyme urease creating an alkaline microenvironment
* *H. pylori* is probably causative in duodenal ulcer and may be associated with gastric ulceration (see table overleaf)

ASSOCIATION OF *H. PYLORI* AND PEPTIC ULCER

Clinical features	Cases with *H. pylori* infection (%)
Duodenal ulcer	90-100
Gastric ulcer	70-75
Dyspeptic symptoms but no visible ulcer	50
No symptoms (normal volunteers)	20

Chemicals
These chemicals have all been associated with an increased incidence of duodenal ulcers. They all decrease pyloric sphincter competence:

- Non-steroidal anti-inflammatory drugs
- Cigarettes
- Aspirin
- Alcohol

Associated diseases
Several diseases are associated with increased incidence of duodenal ulcers. They all increase serum calcium which stimulates gastrin production.

- Alcoholic cirrhosis
- Chronic renal failure
- Chronic obstructive airway disease
- Hyperparathyroidism

Familial
There is a three-fold increase in the incidence of duodenal ulcers in relatives. Duodenal ulcers are also most common in HLAB5 and blood group O patients

Gastrin hypersecretion
Zollinger-Ellison syndrome is an association between a gastrin-secreting tumour of the pancreas and gastric hypersecretion leading to gastroduodenal and jejunal ulceration. Gastric hypersecretion can also result from hyperplasia of the antral 'G' cells of the stomach.

Pathology and histology of peptic ulceration

Site

- 80% solitary
- 80% in duodenum
- 90% in first part of the duodenum on the anterior wall within a few centimetres of the pyloric ring
- 19% in stomach usually lesser curvature at the body/antrum border

Gross pathology
Chronic peptic ulcers have a standard virtually diagnostic gross and microscopic appearance.

- 50% are <2 cm diameter, 10% are >4 cm diameter (usually in stomach)
- Usually round or oval sharply punched out defect with straight walls and level margins (margin heaping is a sign of malignancy)
- Depth varies from superficial to deep penetrating muscularis mucosa; may perforate completely
- Base is usually smooth and clean with no exudate due to peptic digestion; vessels may project into base and lead to haemorrhage
- Underlying scarring causes spokes or spicules
- Surrounding mucosa usually oedematous and reddened

Histology

- **Zone 1**: superficial thin layer of necrotic fibrinoid debris
- **Zone 2**: active cellular neutrophil infiltrate
- **Zone 3**: active granulation tissue with mononuclear leucocytes
- **Zone 4**: solid fibrous or collagenous scar; local arteries thick and thrombosed

Clinical presentation

Duodenal ulcer

- Epigastric pain during fasting
- Pain at night (2–4 am)
- Relieved by food and antacids
- Relapsing and remitting, two weeks of symptoms every few months
- Penetrating posterior ulcers cause severe constant pain radiating to back
- 10% of duodenal ulcers are painless

Gastric ulcer

- Epigastric pain induced by eating
- Patient loses weight
- Nausea and vomiting more common than in duodenal ulcer
- Iron deficiency anaemia common

Investigations

Endoscopy
This is the gold standard as it diagnoses inflammation and gastric ulcers can be biopsied.

- 10% of all gastric ulcers are malignant
- At least six biopsies should be taken from the edge of any gastric ulcer seen
- Clo test can also be performed to test for *H. pylori*

Double contrast barium meal
This is usually done if endoscopy not possible.

- Barium meal will identify hiatus hernia and most ulcers but miss inflammation
- Biopsies are not possible

Tests for *H. pylori*
H. pylori infection can be tested for in a number of ways:

- Blood can be tested for antibodies
- Breath can be tested for urea
- Biopsied mucosa can be tested with a Clo test
- Biopsied mucosa can be examined by microscopy

Gastric acid secretion test
If there are multiple ulcers and Zollinger–Ellison syndrome is suspected, gastrin and penta-gastrin tests are useful.

8.2 Treatment of peptic ulcers

Treatment of peptic ulcers (summary)

- **Medical**
  Acid suppression
    H$_2$ blockers
    PPIs
  H. pylori treatment

- **Surgical (rare)**
  Gastric ulcer
    Billroth I and II
    Vagotomy, pyloroplasty and
      excision of ulcer
    Vagotomy, antrectomy and
      Roux-en-Y
  Duodenal ulcer
    Truncal vagotomy
    Selective vagotomy
    Highly selective vagotomy

Medical treatment

Acid suppression

H$_2$ blockers (e.g. ranitidine, cimetidine) heal 90% of duodenal ulcers in eight weeks. Recurrence rates on low-dose maintenance therapy is 13% at one year; 23% at two years.

Delayed healing in:

- Prior ulcer surgery
- Ulcer is >10 mm diameter
- Failure to eradicate *H. pylori*
- Smokers

Gastric ulcers are also treatable with H$_2$ blockers, but proton pump inhibitors (such as omeprazole) are more effective. H$_2$ blockers do not significantly decrease gastric ulcers in patients on non-steroidals, but do decrease duodenal ulceration.

Proton pump inhibitors (e.g. omeprazole, iansoprazole) heal 90% of duodenal ulcers in four weeks. Lower recurrence rates. Gold standard for gastric ulcer treatment with 80–90% healing rates at eight weeks.

H. pylori treatment

Triple therapy of omeprazole, metronidazole and amoxycillin or clavulanic acid for one week eradicates 90% of *H. pylori* infections.

- Patients should have endoscopy or barium before triple therapy
- *H. pylori* eradication should be used in first episode of ulceration
- Eradication should be confirmed six weeks after therapy by Clo testing, pathology or urea breath testing
- One year recurrence rate is <10%
- All patients with gastric ulceration should undergo repeat endoscopy after 6–8 weeks of therapy and the possibility of malignancy should be considered if the ulcer has not healed

Indications for elective surgery

- Failure of medical treatment (e.g. non-healing or frequently relapsing ulcer)
- Non-compliance with medication
- Complications or the reasonable expectation of complications (haemorrhage, perforation, obstruction)
- Any non-healed gastric ulcer — biopsies are not always reliable
- A giant gastric ulcer (>3 cm diameter) is not an indication for surgery, but must be removed if it has not healed after 6-8 weeks' medication

Operative treatment of gastric ulcer

The principles of surgery for a gastric ulcer are removal of the ulcer, with the gastrin secreting zone of the antrum. These operations are much less common now that proton pump inhibitors can treat so many ulcers successfully. The possible strategies are shown in the Figure opposite.

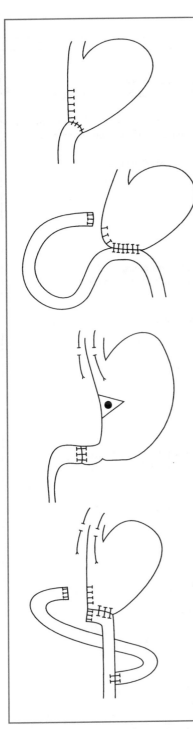

Billroth I partial gastrectomy
Removal of the distal third of the stomach and anastomosis to duodenum. Rarely performed for benign gastric ulceration but still used for ulcers of the lesser curve.

- <5% recurrence
- <1% mortality
- 85% are cured
- No need for vagotomy

Billroth II polya gastrectomy
Removal of distal two-thirds of stomach and gastro-jejunostomy.

- Even lower recurrence rate than Billroth I
- Higher post-operative morbidity
- 17-40% dumping
- Bilious vomiting, diarrhoea, weight loss, anaemia, metabolic bone disease
- Not used for elective surgery

Vagotomy, pyloroplasty and excision of ulcer
Used as an alternative if Billroth I is contraindicated.

Vagotomy, antrectomy and Roux-en-Y reconstruction
Generally reserved as a second operation for bilious vomiting.

Operative treatment of gastric ulcer

Operative treatment of duodenal ulceration

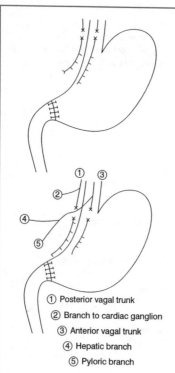

Truncal vagotomy and pyloroplasty
Cuts both vagal trunks at level of abdominal oesophagus.

- If stomach is denervated, this causes gastric stasis so a drainage procedure is needed (gastrojejunostomy or pyloroplasty)
- Similar complications to gastrectomy

Selective vagotomy and pyloroplasty
Denervation of stomach with preservation of nerve supply to the intact pylorus.

- Generally preserves coeliac and hepatic branches of the vagus
- Still needs a drainage procedure

① Posterior vagal trunk
② Branch to cardiac ganglion
③ Anterior vagal trunk
④ Hepatic branch
⑤ Pyloric branch

Highly selective/parietal cell/proximal vagotomy
Only branches to fundus and body are cut leaving antral nerves intact

- Does not disrupt coeliac, hepatic or pyloric branch
- No diversion procedure needed
- High recurrence rate

Operative treatment of duodenal ulcer

The principles of surgery for duodenal ulcer are reducing the acid secretions of the stomach by dividing the vagus nerve.

- If the vagus nerve is divided proximally, gastric stasis results, so a drainage procedure is needed
- Elective surgery for duodenal ulcer is seldom performed nowadays since medical treatment is successful
- The usual strategies are shown opposite

8.3 Complications of peptic ulceration

Complications of peptic ulceration are the fourth most common cause of peri-operative death.

Main complications of peptic ulceration

- Haemorrhage
- Gastric outlet obstruction
- Perforation
- Recurrent ulceration

Haemorrhage

Peptic ulceration is responsible for 70% of all upper GI haemorrhage. Mortality rate remains 5–10% despite advances in medical treatment because:

- One-third of patients with peptic ulcer haemorrhage have no previous history or diagnosis of peptic ulcer disease
- Increased prescription of non-steroidal anti-inflammatory drugs
- Increasingly elderly population

Clinical features
Presentation is haematemesis, melaena or rarely (in torrential bleed) blood per rectum. History and examination should concentrate on:

- Previous symptoms of peptic ulceration
- Alcohol abuse
- Cardiovascular disease and arrhythmias
- Bleeding tendency
- Medications, especially aspirin, non-steroidal anti-inflammatory drugs, anticoagulants

Re-bleeding is the principal cause of mortality in bleeding from a peptic ulcer. It can be predicted by:

- Fresh haematemesis or melaena in a stabilized patient
- Fall in blood pressure or rise in pulse in a stabilized patient
- Steady fall in haemoglobin over 24 hours

Investigations

Endoscopy is indicated in all cases, either as an emergency if bleeding is continued and uncontrolled, or after the patient is stabilized in all other cases. The aims of endoscopy are to:

- Identify the bleeding ulcer (or other cause of bleeding, e.g. varices)
- Identify major endoscopic stigmata (which indicate risk of re-bleeding and necessitates urgent therapy)
- Carry out endoscopic control of haemorrhage if major stigmata are present

Principles of management

The management of a bleeding gastric or duodenal ulcer is summarized in the figure opposite. The principles are as follows:

- After assessment and resuscitation, endoscopy can identify and often treat the bleeding point
- Emergency surgery treatment is reserved for unstable patients, a rebleeding ulcer or one that continues to bleed

---

MAJOR ENDOSCOPIC STIGMATA OF RECENT HAEMORRHAGE

Stigmata	Risk of ongoing bleed or re-bleed (%)
Pulsatile or oozing haemorrhage	> 85
Fresh clot on ulcer	85
Adherent clot on ulcer	50
Visible vessel in base of ulcer (e.g. dark spot, red spot, elevated tubular structure, defect in base of ulcer)	40

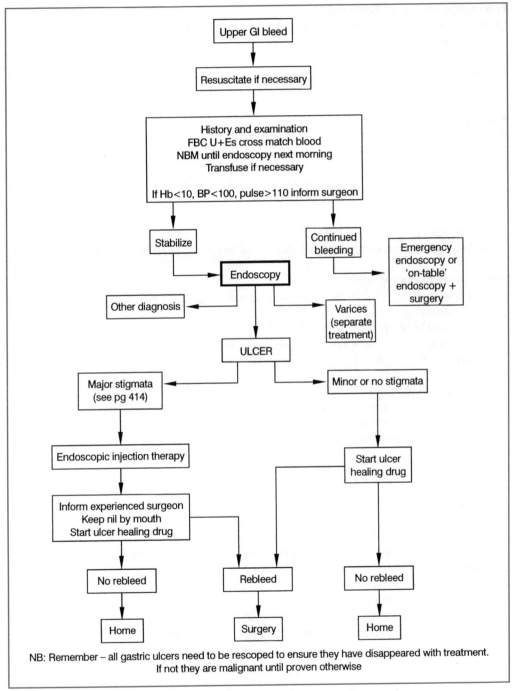

Summary of management of suspected non-variceal upper GI haemorrhage

Endoscopic control of haemorrhage

In the presence of major signs of recent haemorrhage, endoscopic therapy significantly reduces the risk of re-bleeding.

Methods include:

- Heater probe
- Bipolar electrocoagulator
- NdYAG laser
- Injection with: ethanol; variceal sclerosants; adrenaline

Typical dosage is 4 x 0.5-1 ml aliquots of 1:100,000 adrenaline into the four quadrants of the ulcer base.

Indications for emergency surgical treatment of bleeding peptic ulcer

- **Absolute indications**

  Patients with unstable vital signs who do not respond to intensive resuscitation

  Continued bleeding, particularly in the presence of a spurting vessel at endoscopy that does not stop with adrenaline

  Lesions that invariably re-bleed (aorta–enteric fistula)

- **Relative indications**

  One re-bleed in hospital (two re-bleeds in under 60-year-olds)

  A transfusion requirement of four units in 24 hours (over 50-years-old) or six units in 24 hours (under 50-years-old)

  Shortage of whole blood

Principles of emergency surgical treatment

- Stop bleeding by undermining bleeding vessel with a suture
- Conservative or definitive surgery depending on: patient's condition; experience of surgeon; cause of ulcer; previous medical treatment
- For bleeding duodenal ulcer, vagotomy and pyloroplasty or proximal gastric vagotomy is the definitive treatment
- For bleeding gastric ulcer, the definitive treatment is resection of ulcer to prevent re-bleeding and exclude malignancy — vagotomy is not needed

Perforation

Perforation from peptic ulcer is more common and more serious in the elderly age group (mortality of 20% in patients over 70) but can occur in younger patients also.

Clinical features
The classical presentation is sudden severe epigastric pain with developing peritonitis.

- 50% have no history of peptic ulcer disease
- 80% have a pneumoperitoneum on an erect chest X-ray
- After 12 hours bacterial peritonitis develops and the mortality rate increases with time

Principles of management

- Prompt diagnosis
- Vigorous resuscitation
- Early laparotomy
- In some cases conservative treatment is advised (see below)

Pre-operative care

- Fluid resuscitation
- Monitor urine output
- Correct electrolyte imbalance
- Nasogastric tube
- Antibiotics (e.g. cefuroxime and metronidazole)
- Analgesia (usually opioids)
- CVP measurement if in doubt about fluid replacement

Non-operative management
This is controversial.

- **Advantages**: reported mortality of less than 5% in selected patients; may be the only course of action in unfit patients; more popular now that proton pump inhibitors encourage rapid healing
- **Disadvantages**: up to 28% of patients eventually need surgery; may miss gastric cancer or perforation from another viscus (e.g. colon); needs regular assessment and surgeon ready to operate at any time if patient deteriorates
- **Mainstays of non-operative management**: nil by mouth; NG tube; IV fluid; broad-spectrum antibiotics; continued re-assessment.

Operative management of perforated duodenal ulcer
Simple closure by approximation of ulcer edges or use of omental patch is the most common procedure. Vigorous peritoneal lavage is essential. Definitive surgery is indicated provided

that the patient is cardiovascularly stable **and** no established peritonitis is present **and** a surgeon with sufficient experience is available.

If the patient perforated while awaiting definitive surgery or the patient perforated whilst on medical therapy, the procedure chosen is usually proximal gastric vagotomy or truncal vagotomy and gastro-enterostomy (see figure on p. 412).

Operative management of perforated gastric ulcer
This is much less common. Alternatives are:

* Simple closure
* Billroth I resection
* Truncal vagotomy with excision of ulcer and pyloroplasty
* Under-sewing of ulcer (e.g. if ulcer has perforated into the pancreas, resection is contraindicated)

Gastric outlet obstruction

Duodenal ulceration may cause stricturing and narrowing of the first part of the duodenum leading to gastric outlet obstruction, also called **pyloric stenosis**.

Clinical presentation
Uually projectile vomiting of undigested food but no bile, epigastric pain, weight loss, dehydration and electrolyte imbalances (hypochloraemic, hypokalaemic, metabolic acidosis).

Physical findings
May include palpable distended stomach, visible peristalsis and a succussion splash. In mild cases, the inflammation and obstruction may resolve with gastric lavage, acid suppression therapy and bed rest. More severe cases have hard fibrotic strictures with a dilated atonic stomach.

Management
Endoscopy is diagnostic and balloon dilatation may be therapeutic. Surgery should be deferred until fluid and electrolyte abnormalities have been corrected.

Surgical options are:

* proximal gastric vagotomy with duodenoplasty
* truncal vagotomy and gastro-enterostomy
* truncal vagotomy and antrectomy

Scarred gastric ulcers are rare nowadays but give rise to an 'hour glass' deformity and are treated by surgery.

Recurrent ulceration

This is most common following proximal vagotomy (25%) and least common after truncal vagotomy with antrectomy (0.5%).

Common reasons for recurrence include:

- Incomplete vagotomy
- Inadequate gastric resection
- Zollinger-Ellison syndrome
- Carcinoma
- Smoking
- *H. pylori*
- Hypercalcaemia
- Ulcerogenic drugs

Recurrence may occur months from the original operation and may present with bizarre pain. Treatment is with proton pump inhibitors and eradication therapy if necessary. 10% require surgical intervention — usually truncal vagotomy plus distal gastrectomy.

8.4 Post-operative complications

Dumping syndrome

This is a group of cardiovascular and gastrointestinal symptoms resulting from rapid gastric emptying after pyloroplasty or gastric resection.

- **Early dumping** features sweating, palpitations, dizziness, flushing, tachycardia, abdominal pain, nausea and diarrhoea within 5-45 minutes of eating. It tends to improve with time and small, dry meals. Subcutaneous somatostatin injections can limit symptoms.
- **Late dumping** is less common and tends not to feature the gastrointestinal symptoms. It occurs 2-4 hours after eating and is due to rebound hypoglycaemia. Small dry meals and glucose sweets help symptoms.

Diarrhoea

Severe diarrhoea occurs in 10% of patients post-truncal vagotomy. Less common with highly selective vagotomy. Treated by small meals, codeine and loperamide.

Alkaline reflux gastritis

Reflux of duodenal contents into the stomach leads to epigastric pain, bilious vomiting and weight loss. Treatment is with cholestyramine, antacids and occasionally Roux-en-Y gastro-jejunostomy.

Malabsorption

This is more likely after a Billroth II gastrectomy. Supplemental folic acid, iron, vitamin B12, calcium and vitamin D may be required.

Carcinoma of gastric remnant

Gastrectomy for benign disease predisposes to development of adenocarcinoma of the stomach three-fold over 20 years due to metaplasia. Prognosis is usually poor.

8.5 Gastric carcinoma

Gastric cancer is a common and important tumour. It is usually diagnosed too late for curative procedures in the UK, although it is detected earlier in countries such as Japan, where it is more common. The main surgical treatment modalities are partial and total gastrectomy

Incidence

- Third most cancer death in men in UK
- Very common in Japan
- Most common in the 50–70 age range and in lower social classes
- M:F/2:1
- Incidence is falling in Europe and the USA

Aetiology

Family history
Genetic factors are implicated by variations in races which persist despite emigration. The risk of stomach cancer is four times more in the relative of an affected patient than in those with no affected relative. Gastric cancer is most common in people with blood group A.

Environmental factors
Diet, alcohol and tobacco have been implicated in the cause of gastric cancer, but the links have not been proved.

Premalignant conditions
Four conditions have been shown to increase the incidence of cancer:

- **Gastric polyps**: adenomatous gastric polyps have a chance of malignant change, unlike hyperplastic polyps which rarely become malignant
- **Gastric ulcers**: the appearance of a gastric cancer in a chronic gastric ulcer has been recorded, but it is thought that this is usually due to an error in diagnosis
- **Chronic gastritis**: there is a known association between chronic gastritis and gastric cancer; 94% of superficial cancers are found in areas of gastritis
- **Pernicious anaemia**: the incidence of gastric cancer is raised in patients with pernicious anaemia

Pathology

Macroscopic
Cancer occurs most commonly in the antrum, lesser curvature and cardia and less commonly in the greater curve and fundus. There are four macroscopic appearances:

- **Malignant ulcer**: with raised, everted edges
- **Polypoid tumour**: proliferating into the stomach lumen
- **Colloid tumour**: a massive gelatinous growth
- The leather bottle stomach (**linitus plastica**): caused by submucosal infiltration of tumour with marked fibrous reactions producing a small, thickened contracted stomach

Microscopic
Tumours are all adenocarcinomas with varying degrees of differentiation. One method of classification (Lauren classification) divides these adenocarcinomas into intestinal and diffuse types:

- Intestinal type has a poor prognosis and is composed of malignant glands
- Diffuse type has a better prognosis and is composed of single or small groups of malignant cells

Spread
Local spread is often well beyond the visible tumour. The oesophagus or duodenum may be infiltrated and adjacent organs may be directly invaded.

Lymphatic spread is commonly along the nodes of the lesser and greater curves. Lymph drainage from the cardiac end of the stomach may invade the mediastinal nodes and thence the supraclavicular nodes of Virchow on the left (Troisier's sign). At the pyloric end, involvement of the subpyloric and hepatic nodes may occur. The Japanese Research Society for Gastric Cancer has designated four tiers of nodes as likely to be involved according to the location of the main tumour. These are groups of nodes whose involvement indicates increasingly advanced disease which correlates with survival.

Bloodstream dissemination occurs via the portal system to the liver and thence occasionally to the lungs and the skeletal system.

Transcoelomic spread may produce peritoneal seedlings and bilateral Krukenburg tumours due to implantation in both ovaries

Clinical features

The diagnosis is commonly made only when the disease is advanced. Symptoms are effects of the tumour, of secondary metastases or general features of malignant disease.

Local symptoms and signs

- Epigastric pain (which may radiate into the back, suggesting pancreatic involvement)
- Vomiting (especially with pyloric obstruction)
- Dysphagia (especially with tumours of the cardia)
- Perforation or haemorrhage in some cases
- Mass in upper abdomen on examination

Symptoms and signs of metastases

- Jaundice
- Abdominal distension due to ascites
- More rarely, chest infections or bone pain suggesting metastases of the lungs or skeleton
- Enlarged liver or nodes, jaundice or ascites on examination

General features

- Anorexia
- Weight loss
- Anaemia

Investigations

Barium meal
This investigation has 95% diagnostic accuracy in expert hands. The important radiological features looked out for are:

- A space occupying lesion
- An irregular stricture
- Evidence of 'leather bottle' stomach (linitis plastica), a small contracted indistensible stomach
- An ulcer with raised edges and surrounding infiltration
- Any lesion over 2 cm diameter should be regarded with suspicion

Shrinking of an ulcer and diminution of adjacent oedema on anti-ulcer treatment does not prove a diagnosis of benign ulcer

Gastroscopy
Combining radiology and endoscopy increases diagnostic accuracy to 98%. The advantage of fibre optic endoscopy is that a suspicious lesion can be biopsied. Biopsies from large malignant ulcers are notoriously difficult to take, as there are large areas of benign inflamed and necrotic material within the tumour. At least 6–8 biopsy specimens should be taken from the edge of the tumour.

Gastric cytology
Gastric cytology using gastric washings is now used only rarely. The cytology of smears taken through the gastroscope give a high yield of malignant cells.

Screening

In Japan the incidence of gastric cancer is high enough to justify population screening. This increases the proportion of patients diagnosed with early disease and has reduced the death rate from gastric cancer by 25%.

Differential diagnosis

There are five common diseases which give a similar clinical picture of slight lemon yellow tinge, anaemia and weight loss. These are:

* Carcinoma of stomach
* Carcinoma of caecum
* Carcinoma of pancreas
* Pernicious anaemia
* Uraemia

The principal differential diagnosis of gastric carcinoma is a benign gastric ulcer.

Management

Pre-operative optimization and staging
Optimizing lung function and nutritional status are important pre-operatively. An intensive care bed may have to be arranged. Full staging of the tumour is usually impossible until laparotomy (see table overleaf) but obvious spread such as liver metastases should be sought to help plan the surgery.

TNM STAGING SYSTEM FOR GASTRIC CARCINOMA

Stage	Clinical	Pathology	Five-year survival rate (%)
I	Radical resection	T_1, N_0, M_0	80
II	Radical resection	T_{2-4}, N_0, M_0	37
III	Radical resection	T_{X-4}, N_0, M_0	25
IVA	Palliative resection	$T_{X-4}, N_{1-3}, M_{0-1}$	9
IVB	No resection	T_4, N_{0-3}, M_{0-1}	2

Curative surgery

This is only applicable to those without widespread metastasis. Most patients in this country present with advanced disease with little prospect of surgical cure. The principles of curative surgery are:

- Removal of the lesion by partial or total gastrectomy
- Removal of lymph nodes to a level determined by the site and extent of the tumour
- Restoration of the continuity of the gastrointestinal tract
- Creation of a reservoir in the case of total gastrectomy

Radical gastrectomy is removal of the part of the stomach containing the lesion with at least 5 cm clearance on either side plus N_1 and N_2 nodes.

For **partial gastrectomy** the possible methods of reconstruction include Billroth I, polya and Roux-en-Y (see figure on p. 411).

Methods of reconstruction after a **total gastrectomy** include Roux-en-Y, gastrojejunostomy and variations of both of these. Five-year survival rates for radical gastrectomy vary according to stage (see table above).

Palliative surgery

Many patients with gastric cancer can only be offered palliation. The symptoms most commonly requiring palliative surgery are obstruction, haemorrhage and pain. The principles of palliative surgery are:

- Only perform surgery if it will significantly extend or improve quality of life
- The procedure should be tailored to the individual patient's symptoms and wishes
- The procedures available are bypass, intubation and exclusion (see figure opposite)

- Resection is the treatment of choice for obstruction and haemorrhage
- Resection is effective for ulcer-type pain but not for pain related to extragastric extension and metastatic disease

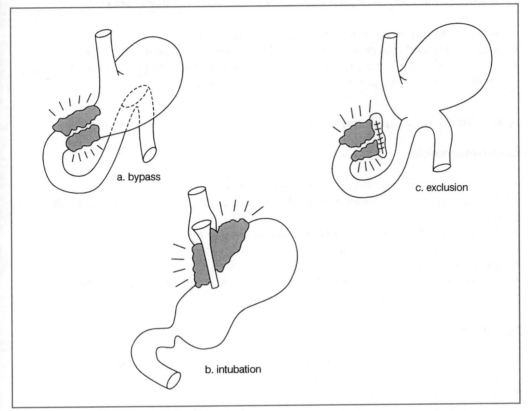

Palliative procedures for gastric cancer

Chemotherapy
Chemotherapy has been used as an adjuvant to surgery in advanced gastric cancer. Its effectiveness is still being evaluated.

Radiotherapy
This has not been proved conclusively to be a useful adjuvant for treatment of gastric cancer.

Post-operative management

This older group of patients often with co-morbidity have undergone a laparotomy and major surgery. They need careful post-operative care. Intensive care overnight is often indicated as post-operative ventilation and sedation have benefits for more frail patients.

Look for important immediate post-operative complications: chest infection, pulmonary embolus and anastamotic leak.

Total gastrectomies are associated with adverse long-term nutritional effects:

- Weight loss can be corrected by dietary supplementation
- Vitamin B12 and iron deficiency should be looked for and treated appropriately
- Malabsorption of fat and protein is common and absorption of glucose usually occurs, producing early hyperglycaemia and late hypoglycaemia

8.6 Other stomach tumours

Leiomyosarcoma

- 1–3% of all gastric tumours are leiomyosarcomas
- They originate from smooth muscle, direct spread is rare and lymph node involvement does not occur
- 75% of patients present with either haematemesis or melaena, and 60% of patients have a palpable abdominal mass
- Diagnosis is by endoscopy and radiology
- Surgery is curative involving wide local excision without lymphadenectomy
- The 5-year survival rate is in the region of 50%

Lymphoma

- The stomach is the most common extranodal primary site for non-Hodgkin's lymphoma
- It accounts for about 1% of gastric malignancy
- The mean age of presentation is 60 years and the symptoms are similar to those of gastric cancer
- 66% of the lesions are resectable and overall 5-year survival rate is 24%
- Radiotherapy is also used for adjuvant treatment, but chemotherapy has not been fully evaluated in gastric lymphoma

Squamous cell carcinoma

- Extremely rare
- Presentation and treatment is similar to adenocarcinoma

Carcinoid

- Rare
- If small they can be locally excised
- The prognosis is better than for other malignant gastric cancers

9. OTHER CONDITIONS AFFECTING THE STOMACH AND DUODENUM

9.1 Gastritis

Acute gastritis and stress ulcers

- Acute gastritis is a transient inflammatory response which is not associated with permanent gastric mucosal abnormality
- It tends to occur in response to specific insults, such as alcohol, drugs and dietary indiscretion
- Endoscopy shows inflamed mucosa which may bleed on contact
- Acute stress erosions are associated with severe burns (Curling's ulcers), brain damage (Cushing's ulcers), alcohol and non-steroidals
- They are 1–2 cm in size and found in the stomach and first part of the duodenum
- They differ from peptic ulcers because: they are multiple not single; they have no prediliction for the antrum and lesser curve; they do not reach the muscular propria
- The main surgical significance of acute gastritis is that it presents as acute abdominal pain and should be differentiated from peptic ulcer disease

Chronic gastritis

Chronic gastritis is very common. There are two main types:

Type A gastritis
Associated with parietal cell antibodies.

- Tends to have reduced acid secretion
- May lead to vitamin B12 malabsorption
- May present as pernicious anaemia
- Has a familial or genetic predisposition

Type B gastritis
Involves the pyloric region extending up along the lesser curve. Causes include:

- Duodeno-gastric reflux
- Post-gastric surgery
- Pernicious anaemia
- Chronic alcohol ingestion
- Non-steroidal drugs
- Cigarette smoking

The surgical significance of chronic gastritis is the increased risk of gastric carcinoma in patients with gastritis and its presentation with abdominal pain. In 90% of patients with a gastric cancer, atrophic gastritis with intestinal metaplasia can be demonstrated. Patients with known chronic gastritis may be at higher risk of developing cancer.

9.2 Congenital abnormalities of the stomach

Congenital hypertrophic pyloric stenosis is covered in Chapter 3, *Head, Neck, Endocrine and Paediatric*, Section 15.8, p. 290.

Gastric divertula

- True gastric divertula are rare, usually asymptomatic incidental findings on endoscopy or barium meal
- Surgical treatment is not usually needed, but the existence of these diverticula should be recognized so they are not confused with more serious pathology

Gastric duplication and cysts

- This is a tubular structure lined by gastric epithelium intimately applied to the wall of the stomach
- 15% communicate with the stomach but the majority have no outlet
- Do not usually present until the early teens, although they are present at birth
- Must be distinguished from hydatid cyst, dermoid cysts and enterogenous cysts
- Surgical treatment is not usually required, but a gastric duplication cyst can be opened and drained

Gastric mucosal diaphragm

- This is a rare defect which does not usually present until adulthood
- There is a mucosal diaphragm close to the pylorus with a small hole in it which can be enlarged endoscopically

Ectopic gastric mucosa

- This is most commonly found in a Meckel's diverticulum, where it may cause ileal ulceration
- Ectopic gastric mucosa has also been reported in the tongue, the duodenum and the biliary tract
- Conversely, ectopic pancreatic tissue can be present in the stomach wall

9.3 Congenital abnormalities of the duodenum

Duodenal atresia is covered in Chapter 3, *Head, Neck, Endocrine and Paediatric*, Section 14.6, p. 274.

Ectopic pancreas

- This abnormality results in a ring of pancreatic tissue around the second portion of the duodenum which may cause obstruction
- Ectopic pancreatic tissue can exist in the wall of the duodenum and may be seen on a barium meal
- Surgical treatment is not usually needed for ectopic pancreas unless it causes obstruction

Megaduodenum

- Enlargement of the first, second and proximal part of the third part of the duodenum is a rare condition
- Controversy exists as to whether this is an acquired or congenital disease, but it has been reported that Auerbach's plexus was absent from this section of the duodenum in one case
- This pattern of dilatation has also been seen after major surgery or after application of plaster cast to the trunk
- Megaduodenum has also been termed 'superior mesenteric artery syndrome' as the level of obstruction is the site where the duodenum is crossed by the superior mesentric artery
- The symptoms are bilious vomiting and a barium meal confirms the diagnosis
- Treatment is initially conservative with NG intubation and IV fluids, but occasionally bypass gastro-jejunostomy is necessary

Duodenal diverticula

- These are more common than gastric diverticula and arise close to the ampula of Vater
- Intraluminal diverticulum is a failure of recanalization leaving a sac in the lumen of the duodenum also arising from the region of the ampula of Vater
- These do not usually require surgical intervention but may cause confusion on diagnostic investigation

9.4 Gastric volvulus

The stomach can rotate in an organoaxial axis (60%) or mesenterioaxial axis (30%). It can occur at any age and has surprisingly mild symptoms of epigastric abdominal distension, retching and an inability to pass a NG tube. A paraoesophageal hiatus hernia is often associated with the organoaxial type of volvulus. Surgery involves repair of the paraoesophageal defect.

9.5 Ingested foreign bodies

Ingested foreign bodies which have successfully passed through the pharynx and the cardia will usually pass through the rest of the gastrointestinal tract and will not need surgery. Psychiatrically disturbed patients who ingest large numbers of unusual items should also be treated expectantly unless they develop evidence of perforation. A **trichobezoar** is a hairball caused by habitual chewing of hair. It can be large enough to fill the entire stomach, but is usually removable endoscopically. Collections of vegetable elements such as leaves and seeds may occur in post-gastrectomy patients where there is some obstruction to the efferent loop. Endoscopic removal is the first line of treatment of these also.

9.6 Duodenal tumours

Benign duodenal tumours are seen at 1% of endoscopies and include adenomas, leiomyomas, lipomas and carcinoid tumours. Presentation is usually gastrointestinal haemorrhage.

Malignant duodenal lesions are rare, but account for one-third of small bowel cancers. Adenocarcinomas, lymphomas and carcinoids are the most common types. Presentation is usually obstruction, jaundice due to obstruction of the ampula of Vater or a palpable mass. The five-year survival rate for all duodenal cancers is about 25%.

The duodenum is the most common extra-colonic site of tumours in patients with **familial adenomatous polyposis** and these patients should therefore be screened endoscopically.

9.7 Gastric operations for morbid obesity

Indications for surgery

Surgery in obese patients is dangerous and should only be considered when all other methods have failed and the patient is at significant risk from obesity.

Gastroplasty

There are many techniques for creating a mechanical barrier to the ingestion of food, usually using stapling devices. These procedures have a mortality of around 4% and a high rate of wound infection and hernia.

Gastric bypass

This procedure is not as commonly used as gastroplasty due to the technical difficulty and metabolic post-operative problems.

9.8 Trauma to the stomach and duodenum

Blunt external trauma

- Deceleration injuries, typically in road traffic accidents, can lead to rupture of the stomach or duodenum
- Rupture of the stomach is more likely if it is full and may occur as an isolated injury
- Rupture of the duodenum against the spine is more likely to be associated with injuries to the pancreas
- These injuries have a high mortality if untreated, and good management depends on prompt resuscitation, diagnosis and laparotomy, as covered in Chapter 3, *Trauma*, of the *MRCS Core Modules: Essential Revision Notes*

Penetrating injuries of the abdomen

These are usually caused by stab wounds and affect the stomach far more often than the duodenum. Recent management strategies involve a more expectant policy in patients without evidence of hypovolaemia or peritonitis (see Chapter 3, *Trauma,* of the *MRCS Core Modules: Essential Revision Notes*).

Iatrogenic perforation of the stomach and duodenum

Endoscopy and endoscopic procedures can result in perforation of the stomach and duodenum. Examples include:

- Over-inflation of a stomach with a necrotic lesion
- Use of NdYAG laser for endoscopic tumour ablation
- ERCP sphincterotomy
- Forcing the endoscope past a friable constricting tumour

Iatrogenic perforation can often be treated conservatively with nil by mouth, NG suction and IV fluids.

10. ABDOMINAL OBSTRUCTION

10.1 Intestinal obstruction

The term **intestinal obstruction** encompasses impedance to the normal passage of bowel contents through the small or large intestine.

*   **Mechanical obstruction**: caused by a physical blockage and can be complete or incomplete
*   **Functional obstruction**: caused by paralysis of intestinal transit
*   **Strangulated obstruction**: the absence of adequate blood supply
*   **Simple obstruction**: has an adequate blood supply
*   **Closed-loop obstruction**: colonic obstruction with a competent ileo-caecal which prevents air escaping proximally into the small intestine and thus accelerating large bowel distension

10.2 Functional obstruction

Functional obstruction is impedence to the normal passage of bowel contents in the absence of a mechanical obstruction. This may affect the small or large intestine. It is usually related to over-activity of sympathetic nervous system. The two most common clinical presentations are **paralytic ileus** and **pseudo-obstruction**.

Causes of functional obstruction

*   **Reflex inhibition of motor activity**
    Post-operative paralytic ileus
    Spinal injury
    Retro-peritoneal haemorrhage
    Head injury
    Chest infection

*   **Drug-induced**
    Tricyclic antidepressants
    General anaesthetics

*   **Mesenteric vascular diseases**
    Mesenteric arterial embolus
    Mesenteric venous infarction

*   **Metabolic**
    Hypokalaemia
    Hypothermia
    Diabetic ketoacidosis
    Uraemia

*   **Peritoneal sepsis**
    Peritonitis
    Pelvic and interloop abscesses

Paralytic ileus

This is most common after abdominal surgery when the normal short period of post-operative bowel inactivity is prolonged. It can be caused or exacerbated by any of the factors listed above. The small bowel undergoes massive distension along its length and as absorption of fluid from the lumen is impaired, salt and water are lost from the extracellular compartments.

Clinical features

- Recent history of operation or another recognized cause
- Typically effortless vomiting and abdominal distension on post-op day 2 or day 3
- No faeces or flatus passed
- Colicky pain is not usually a feature
- Silence on auscultation
- Plain abdominal film shows gas distended loops of small intestine and relatively empty colon
- There may be gas in the caecum and pelvic colon
- It is important to differentiate a paralytic ileus from a mechanical obstruction
- Mechanical obstruction tends to occur later in a post-operative phase and is usually associated with colicky abdominal pain and obstructive bowel sounds

Prevention
To prevent post-operative ileus avoid unnecessary exposure and handling of the intestine during surgery. It is also important to treat any infections and electrolyte imbalances promptly as they exacerbate the problem.

Treatment

- NG suction
- IV fluid replacement; the requirement for replacement fluid can be up to 7 L/day
- Replacement of lost electrolytes — potassium and sodium levels tend to drop which can perpetuate ileus
- Drug treatment stimulating peristalsis (e.g. cisapride) are controversial as they can be dangerous in mechanical obstruction which is often difficult to differentiate

Pseudo-obstruction

Clinical features
This presents as colonic obstruction, but a mechanical cause cannot be found.

- The patient is often elderly and bedridden
- The abdomen gradually distends and bowel actions cease; bowel sounds may remain and even sound obstructive
- There is little or no abdominal pain and no tenderness
- Abdominal X-rays show a similar picture to mechanical obstruction but gas may be seen in the rectum

Management
Once mechanical obstruction is excluded (usually a clinical judgement), management is conservative and includes:

- Correction of fluid and electrolyte imbalances
- Adequate oxygenation and nutritional support
- NG tube not necessary
- Passage of sigmoidoscope and flatus tube usually allow early decompression
- Colonoscopy is useful in investigating and decompressing the bowel
- Neostigmine has been shown to be effective in these patients

Complications

- In a grossly distended colon, especially in the presence of a competent ileocaecal valve, caecal rupture may occur
- Regular examination for caecal tenderness is recommended
- Laparotomy may be indicated if caecum becomes grossly dilated
- Caecal exteriorization may be required for decompression
- Caecal resection may be required if caecum is gangrenous
- Tube caecostomy is no longer a recommended procedure

10.3 Mechanical obstruction

This is a common surgical emergency which carries a reasonable prognosis if recognized and treated promptly. However, if cases present late, go undiagnosed or are resuscitated inadequately before surgery, they can lead to high mortality and morbidity. 80% of cases are small bowel obstruction, usually due to adhesions, hernias or intra-abdominal neoplasia. Large bowel obstruction is less common and is usually due to tumour, diverticular stricture or sigmoid or caecal volvulus.

Causes of mechanical obstruction

- **Extrinsic**
  Adhesions
  Hernia
  Volvulus
  Intussusception
  Inflammatory masses
  Neoplastic masses
  Congenital bands

- **Intrinsic**
  Crohn's disease
  Carcinoma
  Tuberculosis
  Congenital atresia

- **Luminal**
  Gallstones
  Foreign bodies
  Polypoid tumours
  Bezoars
  Parasites

Physiology

- Fluid and gas accumulate behind the obstruction
- Proximal bowel dilates
- Peristaltic activity increases (leads to colicky pain)
- Eventual inhibition of motor activity (protective mechanism)
- Strangulation is caused by increased intraluminal pressure or direct vascular occlusion by the obstructing lesion
- Venous compromise leads to oedema, which in turn results in arterial compression, ischaemia and intestinal necrosis
- This may result in perforation

Fluid sequestration

Even in simple (non-strangulated) bowel obstruction, large volumes of fluid can be sequestered in the dilated proximal bowel. Normally, 6–9 L of fluid enters the small intestine per day and 1–1.5 L enters the large intestine per day. The shifts of fluid from the intracellular to the extra-cellular space in obstruction leads to massive fluid and electrolyte imbalances and may lead to circulatory collapse, shock and death.

In strangulated bowel, the bowel wall oedema, intestinal ischaemia and migration of aerobic and anaerobic bacteria across the intestinal wall leads to further hypovolaemia, generalized sepsis and circulatory collapse.

Clinical signs and symptoms of mechanical obstruction

These vary depending on the level of the obstruction. The main aims of history, examination and investigation are to:

- Differentiate functional and mechanical obstruction
- Identify any strangulation or bowel ischaemia
- Assess fitness for surgery and resuscitation requirements

A careful history and examination should concentrate on the following findings:

Pain

- Typically colicky and referred to the central abdomen in simple small intestine and proximal colon obstruction (embryological midgut)
- It is referred to the central and lower abdomen in distal colon obstruction (embryological hindgut)
- Change from colicky to constant abdominal pain may indicate strangulation, ischaemic bowel and a more urgent need for surgery

Distension
More pronounced with large bowel obstruction than with proximal obstruction.

Vomiting

- Occurs early in patients with more proximal intestinal obstruction
- Initially composed of gastric or upper intestinal contents
- Later intestinal stagnation and bacterial overgrowth occur leading to effortless faeculent vomiting

Constipation
May be complete (no faeces or flatus) or incomplete (some faeces or flatus is passed). Constipation occurs early in colonic obstruction, but later in small bowel obstruction.

Tachycardia and hypotension

- May be due to hypovolaemia in simple obstruction which will usually respond to fluid resuscitation
- May be due to ischaemia and sepsis in strangulated obstruction which may be resistant to fluid resuscitation
- Management of septic shock pre-operatively is vital to good outcome

Temperature
A rise in temperature with tachycardia and peritoneal irritation may suggest intestinal ischaemia and/or perforation.

Dehydration
Decreased tissue turgor and dry mucus membranes.

Abdominal tenderness

- Simple obstruction leads to poorly localized tenderness which is usually not severe
- Bowel ischaemia causes focal peritonism with guarding over the affected bowel
- RIF tenderness in large bowel obstruction may indicate closed loop obstruction with imminent caecal perforation

Hernial orifices
As one of the most common causes of small bowel obstruction, it is essential to examine for an incarcerated or strangulated hernia at **all** the hernial orifices.

Bowel sounds
Obstructed bowel sounds are high-pitched with rushes. **Reduced** bowel sounds suggest bowel ischaemia.

Rectal examination
This is essential as it can help differentiate between functional and mechanical obstruction. In mechanical obstruction, the rectum is often empty and collapsed, but rectal tumours diverticular masses, pelvic malignancy or metastases may be felt.

Investigating mechanical obstruction

Blood tests

- FBC
- U&Es
- Amylase
- Cross-match

X-rays
Plain abdominal films are confirmatory in 60% of intestinal obstruction. Abnormally dilated, gas-filled bowel loops are seen.

In **small bowel obstruction** the features are:

- Bowel loops with bands (valvulae conniventes) which traverse the diameter of the gut
- Central bowel loops
- Pathological dilatation is present if bowel diameter exceeds 5 cm

In **large bowel obstruction** the abdominal films show:

- Bowel with bands (haustrae) which incompletely traverse the gut
- Dilated bowel tends to be peripheral not central
- Pathological dilatation is present if bowel diameter exceeds 8 cm
- Caecal dilatation is significant if greater than 10 cm

Specific causes of bowel obstruction may be seen in a plain abdominal film:

- **Gallstone ileus**: air in the biliary tree and a radio-opaque calculus near the ileocaecal valve
- **Sigmoid volvulus**: gross dilatation of the large bowel with the apex of the dilated loop arising from the left iliac fossa
- **Caecal volvulus**: gross dilatation of the large bowel in the right lower quadrant (coffee bean-shaped on plain films)
- **Hernia-induced obstruction**: distended bowel leading to either groin with a localized knuckle of gas-filled bowel in the region of the actual hernia sac
- **Foreign body-induced bowel obstruction**: radio-opaque foreign bodies may be seen

Contrast studies
If the patient is stable and urgent operative intervention is not indicated, contrast studies may help to diagnose the level and nature of the obstruction. Barium enemas are contraindicated in complete obstruction because:

- There is a risk of barium peritonitis if the bowel perforates
- Barium can block the suction channel of the endoscope

A single-contrast water-soluble contrast study (e.g. gastrografin) shows the level but not always the nature of the obstruction. An exception is intussesception which is shown as a 'coiled spring' appearance.

Computerized tomography (CT)
Double contrast CT can be used in the same circumstances as above, and identifies 95% of cases of obstruction. CT may show:

- The level of intestinal obstruction
- The cause of obstruction
- The viability of involved bowel; this is indicated by: circumferentially thickened, high attenuated bowel; congestive changes; haemorrhage in the local mesentery; size of closed loop obstruction ('U'-shaped configuration of dilated bowel and associated mesenteric vessels converging towards an apex)

Adhesions are normally a diagnosis of exclusion if no alternative cause is seen.

Ultrasound has a limited role as distended bowel obscures a good view. It can be used to diagnose intussusception in children when a 'target sign' is seen.

Conservative management of mechanical obstruction

Simple versus strangulated obstruction
Simple obstruction can initially be managed conservatively with fluid replacement and full investigations before planned definitive surgery if needed. Obstruction complicated by strangulation or ischaemia is a surgical emergency that should be operated on as soon as the patient is resuscitated. For this reason, it is important to assess those features which indicate the risk of strangulation, for example:

- Tachycardia
- Fever
- Tenderness and peritonism
- Leucocytosis
- Nature of obstruction (higher risk of strangulation in incarcerated hernias and an unscarred abdomen)

It is also important to re-assess the patient with simple obstruction regularly to ensure that any signs of strangulation are picked up early.

Non-operative treatment and resuscitation
Management of obstruction involves:

- **Nil by mouth**: intestinal rest and ensures the patient is ready for theatre at short notice
- **NG decompression**: decompresses the stomach (but not the intestine), reducing the risk of aspiration of gastric contents
- **Analgesia**: more important in strangulated cases
- **Oxygen**: with care in patients with chronic obstructive airway disease, monitoring saturation and arterial blood gases
- **IV fluid resuscitation**: vital whether or not early operative intervention is planned to prevent cardiac and renal complications

In more unwell patients or those with co-morbidity:

- Central venous monitoring
- Arterial blood gases

Surgical management of mechanical obstruction

General principles
The aims when operating on patients with intestinal obstruction are:

- Decompress obstructed bowel
- Correct the cause
- Maintain intestinal continuity
- Avoid iatrogenic injury

Decompress obstructed bowel
This can be done by:

- Milking intestinal contents back up the NG tube
- Using needle decompression
- Decompression via small enterotomy with 'savage' sucker
- Milking bowel contents through the proximal resection margin
- On-table lavage

Correct the cause
This cannot always be done at the first operation and depends on the specific cause. If the obstruction cannot be removed, a defunctioning ileostomy or colostomy is an alternative at the first procedure.

Maintain intestinal continuity
In some cases the bowel is not strangulated or if it is the ischaemia is reversible in which case no resection is necessary. It is often difficult to determine bowel viability intra-operatively. The most useful criteria are:

- Intestinal colour
- Bowel motility
- Presence of mesenteric arterial pulsation

Bowel of dubious viability is wrapped in warm, wet swabs and oxygen delivery is increased. If the bowel is deemed viable it is returned to the abdominal cavity, but if not it may need to be resected.

In the case of bowel resection, if an anastomosis is possible, it can be performed at the initial operation. Primary anastomosis should not be carried out if:

- Either bowel end is ischaemic
- There is tension on the anastomosis
- Peritoneal soiling with faeces or pus is present

If primary anastomosis is not possible, one or both bowel ends should be exteriorised rather than risk anastomotic disruption (see later).

Avoid iatrogenic injury
Distended bowel is friable and easily damaged.

Recurrent (post-operative) obstruction

In the early post-operative period, functional obstruction, i.e. an ileus, is more common than mechanical obstruction (i.e. adhesions, undetected distal obstruction, peri-anastomotic abscess or internal hernia). It is important to distinguish between them and CT may be useful in this setting. Adhesions may arise around areas of relative ischaemia. Various techniques have been suggested to prevent adhesions:

- Good surgical technique
- Peritoneal irrigation
- Avoidance of excessive packing with gauze
- Covering of anastomosis with omentum
- Pharmacological substances (e.g. bio-absorbable membrane such as sodium hyaluronidate-impregnated methyl-cellulose)
- Mechanical prevention — intestinal plication or small intestinal intubation
- Intestinal stenting in large bowel obstruction

The placement of an intraluminal stent is a relatively new technique which may become more common, especially in lesions of the descending colon and recto-sigmoid junction. It may be used in palliation of malignant colorectal obstruction or in allowing patients to avoid emergency surgery if temporarily medically unfit.

10.4 Other specific causes of mechanical obstruction

Sigmoid volvulus

A volvulus occurs when a segment of bowel twists through 360°. This often compromises the circulation of the affected segment. It always causes a closed loop obstruction. The term 'volvulus' usually applies to the large bowel, for example the sigmoid, the caecum and rarely the transverse colon, but volvulus of segments of the small intestine, especially in the presence of tumour or adhesions, may also occur.

Sigmoid volvulus is responsible for 4% of intestinal obstruction cases in the UK. It is more common in Africa and Asia, and more common in the elderly.

Predisposing factors include a redundant sigmoid colon and a history of chronic constipation ± laxative abuse.

The bowel twists in an anticlockwise direction. Circulation is impaired after one-and-half twists. It can lead to gangrene, perforation, peritonitis and death.

Patients are usually elderly, often senile or from a nursing home. There may be a history of constipation for many years. Acute abdominal pain, nausea and vomiting are followed by a distended abdomen and absolute constipation. The patient may develop peritonitis, toxaemia and tachycardia if bowel becomes gangrenous.

Plain AXR shows typical distended loop of large bowel full of air. The convexity lies away from the site of obstruction and a bird's beak narrowing of the colon points towards the site of obstruction.

Barium enema may be helpful in doubtful cases showing a typical 'ace of spades' deformity. Barium enema is contraindicated if gangrene is suspected.

Endoscopic decompression should be attempted as soon as possible with insertion of a flatus tube past the twist if possible and left *in situ* for 24 hours. This may obviate the need for an urgent operation.

Urgent surgery is indicated if the volvulus cannot be untwisted or if signs of gangrene develop. Reduction of the volvulus, followed by sigmoid resection is usually performed with primary anastomosis or exteriorization of the bowel ends.

Planned surgery after endoscopic decompression may be indicated in recurrent cases if barium studies confirm a grossly redundant sigmoid colon.

Caecal volvulus

This is less common than volvulus of the sigmoid colon ($<1\%$ of all cases of intestinal obstruction in the UK) and is usually due to a lax mesocolon with a mobile caecum. The clinical picture is that of a low small bowel obstruction. The caecum is visible and distended, lying in the midline or to the left of the abdomen.

Treatment is surgery with reduction of the volvulus. Right hemicolectomy, caecopexy and caecostomy have all been advocated.

Intussusception

This is described in the Chapter 3, *Head, Neck, Endocrine and Paediatric*, Section 15.9, p. 290, but can also present in adults with a tumour or lipoma the usual lead point.

Gallstone ileus

This is responsible for less than 1% of all cases of small bowel obstruction. The stone usually originates in the gallbladder, passes into the intestine through a cholecystoduodenal fistula or enters the duodenum through the common bile duct and lodges in the terminal ileum. It causes spastic contraction of the bowel, leading to intestinal obstruction.

Patients are usually elderly and may have a history of chronic cholecystitis. They usually present with symptoms of acute intestinal obstruction.

Plain AXR shows the features of intestinal obstruction. A gallstone may be seen in an unusual position. If the bile ducts or gallbladder are outlined by gas, a fistula is likely.

Surgical treatment is needed. The stone should be milked upwards into healthy bowel to avoid opening the bowel at the point where the stone has impacted as this area heals poorly. The cholecystoenteric fistula is usually scarred and at high risk of biliary leak if disturbed and the risk of further stones impacting is low, so the fistula need not be repaired and cholecystectomy is not necessary.

Radiation enteritis

External beam radiation can result in small intestine injury. Radiation-induced strictures often present at a delayed interval after radiotherapy. If it causes obstruction it is often subacute allowing time for careful assessment estimating the length of bowel affected and confirming the diagnosis.

Mechanical obstruction in children

*   Intussuception
*   Meconium ileus
*   Malrotation and volvulus neonatum

These are discussed in the Chapter 3, *Head, Neck, Endocrine and Paediatric*, Section 15, p. 285.

11. SYMPTOMS OF NON-ACUTE ABDOMINAL DISORDERS

11.1 Abdominal mass

A patient may present having noticed an abdominal mass or a mass may be noted on examination of a patient with related or unrelated symptoms. The causes are many and varied. The clinical objectives should be to identify the anatomical source of the mass and its pathology.

History

- Nature and rate of growth of the mass
- Presence of associated features, such as weight loss; jaundice; lymphadenopathy; upper GI or bowel symptoms

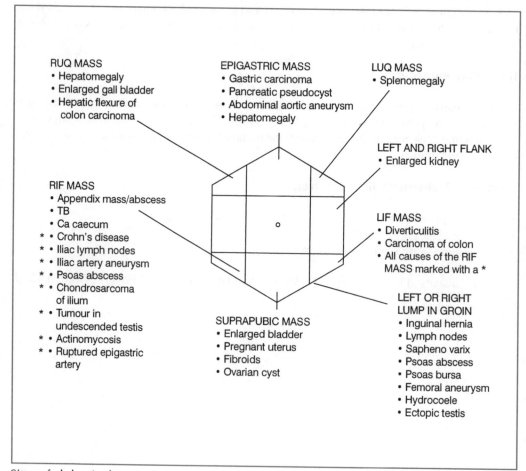

RUQ MASS
- Hepatomegaly
- Enlarged gall bladder
- Hepatic flexure of colon carcinoma

EPIGASTRIC MASS
- Gastric carcinoma
- Pancreatic pseudocyst
- Abdominal aortic aneurysm
- Hepatomegaly

LUQ MASS
- Splenomegaly

LEFT AND RIGHT FLANK
- Enlarged kidney

RIF MASS
- Appendix mass/abscess
- TB
- Ca caecum
* - Crohn's disease
* - Iliac lymph nodes
* - Iliac artery aneurysm
* - Psoas abscess
* - Chondrosarcoma of ilium
* - Tumour in undescended testis
* - Actinomycosis
* - Ruptured epigastric artery

LIF MASS
- Diverticulitis
- Carcinoma of colon
- All causes of the RIF MASS marked with a *

SUPRAPUBIC MASS
- Enlarged bladder
- Pregnant uterus
- Fibroids
- Ovarian cyst

LEFT OR RIGHT LUMP IN GROIN
- Inguinal hernia
- Lymph nodes
- Sapheno varix
- Psoas abscess
- Psoas bursa
- Femoral aneurysm
- Hydrocoele
- Ectopic testis

Sites of abdominal masses

Examination

- Position
- Shape
- Size
- Surface
- Edge
- Composition: consistency; fluctuation; fluid thrill; resonance; pulsatility; tenderness
- Association with enlargement of palpable organs

Investigations

Ultrasound scan is cheap, non-invasive and useful to image:

- Cystic masses and abscesses
- Liver, gall bladder, spleen, kidneys, bladder, aorta, ovaries and uterine masses

CT and **MRI** scans are invaluable especially for retroperitoneal masses. They also give additional information about the relations and operability of the mass as well as associated lymphadenopathy.

Specific investigations depend on the nature of the mass but may include:

- Contrast studies
- Endoscopy
- Radioisotope scans

Non-pathological abdominal masses

An abdominal mass may not always be pathological, for example:

- Distended urinary bladder
- Pregnant uterus
- Faeces-filled colon
- The abdominal aorta in a thin individual
- Riedel's lobe of the liver
- An ectopic kidney

Pathological abdominal masses are probably most usefully considered according to location, since this is usually the first reliable information that can be determined.

Generalized distension

The traditional 'six F's' is a useful list of common causes of generalized distension:

- Foetus
- Faeces
- Fluid: free (ascites); encysted (see table)

- Flatus
- Fat
- Fibroids and other solid tumours (see table)

CAUSES OF ASCITES

Increased portal venous pressure

Prehepatic	Portal venous thrombosis
	Compression of portal vein by lymph nodes
Hepatic	Cirrhosis of the liver
	Multiple hepatic metastasis
Post-hepatic	Budd–Chiari syndrome (thrombosis of hepatic vein)
Cardiac	Constrictive pericarditis
	Right heart failure
Pulmonary	Pulmonary hypertension
	Right heart failure

Hypoproteinaemia
Kidney disease associated with albuminuria
Cirrhosis of the liver
Cachexia of wasting diseases, malignancy and starvation
Protein-losing enteropathies

Chronic peritonitis

Physical	Post-irradiation
	Talc granuloma
Infection	Tuberculous peritonitis
Neoplasms	Peritoneal metastases
	Mucus-forming tumours (pseudomyxoma peritonei)

Chylous ascites
Congenital abnormalities
Trauma
Primary or secondary lymph gland disease

Cystic swellings which may cause abdominal distension

- Ovarian cysts
- Polycystic kidney
- Pancreatic cysts
- Hydatid cysts

- Hydronephrosis
- Urinary bladder
- Mesenteric cysts

Solid tumours which may cause abdominal distension

- Hepatomegaly
- Splenomegaly
- Pancreatic carcinoma
- Retroperitoneal lymphadenopathy
- Carcinoma of liver
- Retroperitoneal sarcoma
- Nephroblastoma (in children)

- Fibroids
- Large colon cancers
- Polycystic kidneys
- Carcinoma of kidney
- Perinephric abscess
- Ganglioneuroma (in children)

Organomegaly

There are certain abdominal organs which are specifically felt for on examination.

Hepatomegaly

The more common causes of hepatomegaly are listed in the table overleaf. The physical signs of an enlarged liver are as follows:

- Descends from the right costal margin
- You cannot get above it
- Moves with respiration
- Dull to percussion up to the level of the 8th rib in the mid-axillary line
- Edge can be sharp or rounded
- Surface can be smooth or irregular

Riedel's lobe is an extension of the right lobe of the liver down below the costal margin along the anterior axillary line. It is a normal anatomical variation which is often mistaken for a pathological enlargement of the liver or gall bladder.

CAUSES OF HEPATOMEGALY

Smooth generalized enlargement

With jaundice
Infective hepatitis
Biliary tract obstruction: gallstones;
  carcinoma of pancreas
Cholangitis
Portal pyaemia

Without jaundice
Heart failure
Cirrhosis
Reticulosis
Budd–Chiari syndrome
Amyloid

Knobbly generalized enlargement

With jaundice
Extensive secondary carcinoma
Cirrhosis

Without jaundice
Secondary carcinoma
Cirrhosis
Polycystic disease
Primary liver cancer

Localized enlargement

Riedel's lobe
Secondary carcinoma
Hydatid cysts
Liver abscess
Primary liver carcinoma

Splenomegaly

The spleen is almost always uniformly enlarged. The causes of an enlarged spleen are listed opposite. The physical signs of an enlarged spleen are:

- Appears from below the tip of the left 10th rib and enlarges along the line of the rib towards the umbilicus
- Is firm, smooth and usually spleen-shaped
- Often has a definite notch on its upper edge
- You cannot get above it
- Moves with respiration
- Is dull to percussion
- Cannot be balloted

CAUSES OF SPLENOMEGALY

Infection
Bacterial
Typhoid
Typhus
TB
Septicaemia

Spirochaetal
Syphilis
Leptospirosis

Viral
Glandular fever

Protozoal
Malaria
Kala-azar

Cellular infiltration
Amyloidosis
Gaucher's disease

Collagen diseases
Felty's syndrome
Still's disease

Cellular proliferation
Myeloid and lymphatic leukaemia
Pernicious anaemia
Polycythaemia rubra vera
Spherocytosis
Thrombocytopenic pupura
Mylosclerosis

Congestion
Portal hypertension
Hepatic vein obstruction
Congestive heart failure

Infarction
Emboli from
Bacterial endocarditis
Left atrium in atrial fibrillation
Left ventricle after myocardial infarction
Splenic artery or vein thrombosis
Polycythaemia
Retroperitoneal malignancy

Space-occupying lesions
Cysts
True solitary cysts
Polycystic disease
Hydatid cysts
Angioma
Lymphosarcoma
Lymphoma

Enlarged kidney
The common causes of enlargement of the kidney are listed overleaf. Physical signs of an enlarged kidney are:

- Is smooth and hemiovoid
- Moves with respiration
- Is not dull to percussion because of overlying colon
- Can be felt bimanually
- Can be balloted or 'bounced' between two palpating hands (this depends on the mass reducing into the loin)

Causes of enlargement of the kidney

- Hydronephrosis
  (may be bilateral in distal obstruction)
- Perinephric abscess
- Solitary cysts
- Polycystic disease (usually bilateral)

- Pyonephrosis
- Carcinoma of the kidney
- Nephroblastoma
  (occasionally bilateral)
- Hypertrophy

NB. A mobile or low-lying kidney may be easily palpable and so seem to be enlarged.

Enlarged gall bladder

An enlarged gall bladder is usually due to obstruction of the cystic duct or common bile duct. Obstruction of the cystic duct is usually by a gallstone and rarely by an intrinsic or extrinsic carcinoma. The patient is not jaundiced and the gall bladder will contain bile, mucus (a mucocoele) or pus (an empyema).

Obstruction of the common bile duct is usually by a stone or a carcinoma of the head of the pancreas. The patient will be jaundiced. Courvoisier's law states:

'In the presence of jaundice, the palpable gall bladder is unlikely to be due to stones'

This is because previous inflammation will have made the gall bladder thick and non-distensible. The exceptions are:

- Stones which form in the bile duct
- Stones in the cystic duct as well as a stone or carcinoma in the bile duct

The physical signs of an enlarged gall bladder are:

- Appears from beneath the tip of the right 9th rib
- Smooth and hemiovoid
- Moves with respiration
- You cannot feel a space between the lump and the edge of the liver
- Dull to percussion

A gall bladder mass is formed when omentum and bowel adheres to an acutely inflamed gall bladder. It is diffuse, tender and does not move much with respiration.

Abdominal aortic aneurysm

A normal aorta can be palpated in a thin individual. The size of the aneurysm can be estimated but should be confirmed by ultrasound. It is diagnosed by its expansile pulsation. Other enlarged organs or masses overlying the aorta may transmit pulsations, giving the false impression of an enlarged aorta, but these pulsations will not be expansile. The characteristics of an abdominal aortic aneurysm are:

- Smooth epigastric mass with distinct lateral margins
- Expansile pulsation
- May extend into the left or, less commonly, the right iliac arteries

NB. The aorta bifurcates at the level of the umbilicus.

11.2 Indigestion

'Indigestion' is an imprecise term used by patients to describe a number of symptoms. The term may mean epigastric pain, reflux, general abdominal discomfort, abdominal distension or nausea. A careful history can determine the exact nature of the symptoms and suggest a condition which may be responsible.

WHAT DO YOU MEAN BY INDIGESTION?

Symptoms	Suggests	Investigations
Burning retrosternal pain Worse on lying down or stooping May be referred to jaw or arms Associated with acid brash Worse with certain foods (e.g. citrus fruits)	Reflux oesophagitis	Barium meal or oesophagoscopy pH studies
Epigastric boring pain during fasting Pain at night relieved by food and antacids Relapsing every few months May radiate to back History of non-steroidal drug use	Duodenal ulcer	Endoscopy or barium meal *H. pylori* serology or breath test
Epigastric boring pain worse after eating Weight loss, nausea Associated with anaemia or melaena History of non-steroidal drug use	Gastric ulcer	Endoscopy or barium meal *H. pylori* serology or breath test
Right hypochondrial severe colic Radiating to right scapula Vomiting and sweating Worse after fatty food Patient fat, fair, female, fertile in her forties with a family history of gallstones Jaundice, pale stools, dark urine	Biliary colic	Ultrasound scan of gall bladder LFTs
Persistent severe pain in the right hypochondrium Fever, malaise Rebound tenderness Jaundice, pale stool, dark urine	Acute cholecystitis	Ultrasound scan of gall bladder FBC LFTs Amylase

Continues ...

Symptoms	Suggests	Investigations
Jaundice, fever, malaise, nausea, vomiting Vague upper abdominal pain Tender palpable liver	Hepatitis	Ultrasound scan of liver Immunological assay LFTs
Severe constant epigastric pain radiating to back Vomiting, malaise, tachycardia Generalized tenderness and guarding of abdomen History of gallstones or alcohol abuse	Pancreatitis	Ultrasound scan of biliary tree Amylase FBC, U&Es, Blood gases, CT of pancreas
Epigastric pain radiating to back Vomiting, dysphagia, haematemesis, melaena, anaemia, jaundice, ascites, weight loss Upper abdominal mass Supraclavicular nodes	Gastric or oesophageal cancer	Endoscopy and biopsy Ultrasound scan/CT of abdomen FBC
Central crushing chest pain radiating to neck and arm associated with exercise History of smoking or familial heart attack	Angina	ECG, cardiac enzymes Exercise stress test
Long-standing ache in abdomen Flatulence and intolerance to fatty foods, bloating loose stools, various non-colonic features such as back pain, headache, poor sleep	Irritable bowel syndrome	Large bowel investigations are usually normal Air insufflation at sigmoidoscopy reproduces pain
LIF pain, change in bowel habit, bloating, mucus or bleeding p.r.	Diverticular disease	Colonoscopy or barium enema
Change in bowel habit, blood or mucus p.r., weight loss, anaemia and malaise	Colonic carcinoma	Colonoscopy or barium enema FBC, Ultrasound scan of liver
LIF pain radiating to epigastrium worse after meals Diarrhoea, melaena, altered blood History of cardiovascular disease	Vascular insufficiency of the gut	Colonoscopy and biopsy Barium enema shows 'thumb printing'

453

11.3 Change in bowel habit

A change in bowel habit is an important and common manifestation of bowel disease. This symptom may result from a variety of causes, some of which are self-limiting and relatively innocuous and some of which may indicate a sinister cause.

A change in bowel habit may be defined as a sustained alteration in:

- Defaecation (frequency, periodicity or ease)
- Stool (consistency, appearance, presence of blood or mucus)
- Symptoms (pain on defaecation, tenesmus, feeling of incomplete evacuation)

The features characteristic of various disorders are covered in the relevant sections, but three symptoms deserve separate consideration. These are constipation, diarrhoea and bleeding per rectum.

Constipation

Causes of constipation

- **Organic obstruction**
  Carcinoma of the colon
  Diverticular disease
  Volvulus, hernias and intussusception
  Crohn's strictures

- **Adynamic bowel**
  Hirschsprung's disease
  Parkinson's disease
  Stroke
  Spinal cord injuries and disease
  Myxoedema
  Pseudo-obstruction

- **Diet**
  Dehydration
  Starvation
  Lack of fibre in diet

- **Painful anal conditions**
  Fissure *in ano*
  Prolapsed piles
  Perianal abscess

- **Drugs**
  Aspirin
  Opiate analgesics
  Anticholinergics
  Ganglion blockers
  Anticonvulsants

- **Habit/psychological**
  Dyschezia (rectal stasis
    due to faulty bowel habit)
  Depression
  Anorexia nervosa

- **Pelvic causes**
  Pregnancy and the puerperium
  Ovarian and uterine tumours
  Endometriosis

Presentation
Constipation is a symptom and cannot be considered as a diagnosis until all underlying causes have been excluded. It is defined as infrequent or irregular defaecation which may or may not be painful. The causes of constipation are legion but the more common causes are listed in the table on pp 452–453. The principle of management of constipation is the exclusion of each of the causes described. A careful history, including a drug history, gynaecological and psychological history and details of diet should be obtained. Examination should look for abdominal distension and masses. A rectal examination looking for fissures, painful piles or perianal sepsis is essential. Barium studies or colonoscopy must be undertaken to exclude organic obstruction. Bowel transit studies can identify an adynamic bowel. A thyroid function test, pelvic ultrasound or other specific tests may be indicated.

Special investigations
(See Section 12.2, p. 477 and Section 13.1, p. 520.)

- Defecating proctogram
- Electromyography
- Transit studies

Pathophysiology of primary constipation
Several pathophysiological derangements are seen in patients with intractable constipation in the absence of any obvious underlying cause. These abnormalities can co-exist.

- **A reduced anorectal angle**: during attempted defaecation
- **Functional rectal stenosis**: constipation due to anorectal spasm
- **Outlet syndrome**: a failure of the pelvic floor to relax on attempted defaecation
- **Pudendal neuropathy**: diagnosed by electromyography, common in multiparous women

Conservative treatment of constipation
Once the important causes of constipation have been excluded, the first line of management is lifestyle advice which may improve the symptoms. These include:

- ↑ fibre content in diet
- ↑ exercise
- Never ignore the need to pass stools
- Eat regular, healthy meals

If conservative treatment does not help, laxatives may be needed.

Laxatives
The main classes of laxatives are described in the table overleaf. Laxatives should be prescribed with caution. Bowel habit can be infrequent without doing any harm and not everyone needs to have a bowel movement every day. Prolonged use of some laxatives can lead to hypokalaemia and atonic non-functioning colon.

LAXATIVES

Type of laxative	Indications for use
Bulk-forming drugs Bran (Trifyba) Isphaghula husk (Fybogel) Methyl cellulose (Celevac) Sterculia (Normacol)	haemorrhoids anal fissures stomas diverticular disease irritable bowel
Stimulant laxatives Bisacodyl Danthron (Co-danthramer) Docosate sodium (Dioctyl) Senna Sodium picosulphate	the elderly drug-induced constipation avoiding straining bowel preparation for surgery or X-ray
Osmotic laxatives Lactulose Macrogols (Movicol) Lactitol	occasional use (e.g. post-operative) hepatic encephalopathy
Bowel-cleaning solutions Citramag Fleet phospho-soda Klean prep Picolax	bowel preparation before surgery or radiological investigation

Rectal laxatives
Stimulant
   Bisacodyl suppositories
   Glycerol suppositories
Softeners
   Arachis oil enemas
	post-operative

Osmotic
   Phosphate enemas (Fleet),
   Sodium citrate enemas
    (Fleet micro-enema, Micralax)
	bowel preparation before surgery
	  or radiological investigation
	impacted faeces in prolonged
	  constipation

The main indications for using laxatives are:

* Where straining will exacerbate a condition such as angina or haemorrhoidal bleeding
* In drug-induced constipation
* Before surgery and radiological procedures
* For expulsion of parasites after anthelmintic treatment
* In elderly patients or others with an adynamic bowel such as those with spinal injuries

Behavioural therapy
Behaviour therapy, bio-feedback training and psychotherapy may be useful in patients with severe idiopathic constipation or faecal soiling in children and adolescents. Patients learn how to control sphincter activity and establish a regular bowel habit.

Surgical treatment of constipation
This is a last resort in patients with severe intractable primary constipation and is usually restricted to specialist centres. Anorectal myectomy may be effective in the outlet syndrome but is contraindicated if colonic transit is slow. Colectomy and ileorectal anastomosis may be of benefit in patients with severe idiopathic slow transit constipation. Some specialist centres have fashioned a proximal colonic stoma through which regular antegrade colonic enemas can be performed. This is only offered to selected patients.

Diarrhoea

Diarrhoea can be defined as the passage of more than three loose stools a day. It is due to an increase in the stool water content. Causes of diarrhoea are listed overleaf. A careful history should determine if there is true diarrhoea (as opposed to faecal incontinence, irritable bowel, passage of blood or mucous) and if it is acute or chronic.

In **acute diarrhoea**, infective causes are likely and questions should include:

* Travel abroad
* Unusual food, such as seafood
* Diarrhoea in friends or family members

In **chronic diarrhoea**, irritable bowel syndrome, Crohn's disease and ulcerative colitis are likely, and colon cancer should be excluded especially in patients over 50 years of age. The investigation of diarrhoea is outlined below.

The treatment of diarrhoea depends on presentation. In acute diarrhoea the treatment is mainly supportive with oral or intravenous rehydration and replacement of electrolytes. Antibiotics are rarely indicated.

In chronic diarrhoea the treatment depends on the aetiology. Antimotility agents, such as loperamide (Imodium), diphenoxylate (Lomotil) and codeine, may be indicated in ulcerative colitis, Crohn's disease or short bowel syndrome. They are contraindicated in acute infective diarrhoea as they slow the clearance of infective agents.

Causes of diarrhoea

- **Specific infections**
  Food poisoning
    (Salmonella, Campylobacter
    Clostridium, Staphylococcus
    Shigella, Bacillus, Giardia)
  Dysentery
    (Amoebic, Bacillary)
  Cholera
  Viral enterocolitis

- **Loss of absorptive surface**
  Bowel resections and
    short circuits
  Sprue and coeliac disease
  Idiopathic steatorrhoea

- **Others**
  Pancreatic dysfunction leading to
    lipase deficiency
  Post-gastrectomy and vagotomy
  Anxiety states

- **Inflammation of the intestine**
  Ulcerative colitis
  Tumours of the large bowel
  Diverticular disease
  Crohn's disease

- **Drugs**
  Antibiotics
  Purgatives
  Digoxin

- **Systemic diseases**
  Thyrotoxicosis
  Uraemia
  Carcinoid syndrome
  Zöllinger–Ellison syndrome

Indications for antibiotic treatment in diarrhoea

- Severe cases of Shigella or
    Campylobacter jejuni
- Severe cases of *Clostridium difficile*
- Giardiasis

- Immunosuppressed patients,
    babies and the very old infected
    with Salmonella

Bleeding per rectum

Bleeding per rectum may be from upper or lower gastrointestinal tract. Chronic bleeding from the upper gastrointestinal tract usually presents as melaena, acute bleeding as a torrential bleed in association with hypovolaemia, shock and haematemesis. These upper gastrointestinal bleeds are most commonly due to peptic ulcer disease, oesophageal varices or gastric carcinoma, and are discussed in Section 8 of this chapter. This section will deal with lower gastro-intestinal haemorrhage. The causes of lower gastro-intestinal haemorrhage in different age groups is summarized below.

Causes of lower gastro-intestinal haemorrhage

- **Children**
  Meckel's diverticulum
  Juvenile polyps
  Inflammatory bowel disease
  Intussusception

- **Elderly people**
  Diverticular disease
  Angiodysplasia
  Adenomatous polyps
  Carcinoma
  Ischaemic colitis
  Inflammatory bowel disease
  Radiation proctitis

- **Adults**
  Inflammatory bowel disease
  Adenomatous polyps
  Carcinoma
  Arteriovenous malformation
  Hereditary telangiectasis
  Infective colitis
  Haemorrhoids
  Solitary rectal ulcer
  Anal fissure

The typical pattern of rectal bleeding in common cases is described below.

- **Bright red blood** is passed in patients with brisk haemorrhage or those with a distal colorectal lesion
- **Dark red blood**, mixed with faeces, is passed in patients with slow haemorrhage or those with lesions in the proximal colon

Haemorrhoids (see Section 13.2, p. 520)

- Bright red blood on the faeces and toilet paper
- May drip into toilet bowl
- Other rectal conditions should always be excluded before bleeding is assumed to be from haemorrhoids

Inflammatory bowel disease (see Section 12.3, p. 477)

- Small amount of blood mixed with mucus and faeces
- Associated with increased bowel frequency

Distal colorectal polyps and cancers (see Section 12.4 and Section 12.5, pp 489–514)

- Bright red blood or slightly altered streaks of blood passed
- May be associated with tenesmus, urgency or a feeling of incomplete defaecation

Proximal colon or caecal tumours (see Section 12.5, p. 498)

- May have occult bleeding only
- Commonly present with iron deficiency anaemia

Diverticular disease (see Section 6.2, p. 380)

- One of the most common causes of major lower gastrointestinal haemorrhage
- Often brisk and unheralded and can cause hypovolaemia and shock
- Typically the patient has a sudden urge to defaecate followed by the passage of a dark red stool
- The bleed may be repeated but usually stops spontaneously

Angiodysplasia (see Section 12.6, p. 514)

- Presents in a very similar manner to diverticular bleed and may occur in the presence of diverticulosis leading to a misdiagnosis
- Predominantly affects older people and can be difficult to identify by colonoscopy and arteriography

Management of minor lower gastrointestinal haemorrhage
This can usually be investigated and treated as an outpatient. An important principle is not to assume the bleed is due to (almost ubiquitous) haemorrhoids until more serious conditions such as neoplasia and inflammatory bowel disease have been excluded.

A sensible approach to management is:

- History and general examination
- Anorectal examination
- Proctosigmoidoscopy
- Colonoscopy or double-contrast barium enema
- Treatment of cause

Management of major lower gastrointestinal haemorrhage
This is usually best investigated and treated as an inpatient, at least initially. Important principles include:

- Resuscitation takes priority
- Upper gastrointestinal haemorrhage should be excluded
- Most bleeds stop spontaneously enabling investigations to be performed as an outpatient
- In the face of continued bleeding, endoscopy is not usually productive and efforts should be made to localize the bleeding point by isotope scanning or selective arteriography
- In life-threatening haemorrhage, a laparotomy is indicated whether or not the site has been identified

Irritable bowel syndrome

A number of patients who present with a change in bowel habits will have no organic disease discovered on investigation. Some of these will be found to have 'irritable bowel syndrome'. These patients present with a variety of symptoms which may include:

- Recurrent nausea
- Heartburn
- Epigastric fullness
- Distension and abdominal bloating
- Excessive flatus and p.r. mucus
- Abnormal bowel habit
- Loose or constipated stool, often of small volume
- Abdominal pain relieved by bowel movements

Patients may be subdivided into those with:

- Spastic constipation (abdominal pain related to disturbed bowel action)
- Painless diarrhoea

Irritable bowel syndrome is commonly associated with psychological or psychiatric disorders, such as:

- Anxiety
- Depression
- Neuroses
- Anorexia nervosa
- Munchausen's syndrome

The principles of management of irritable bowel are:

- Careful assessment — diagnosis can only be made when other causes of symptoms are excluded
- Look for psychopathological signs
- Be reassuring and sympathetic

Occasionally, patients may need:

- Anxiolytics (short-term)
- Antispasmodics
- Bulk laxatives
- Joint care with psychologist or psychiatrist

11.4 Intestinal fistulae

A **fistula** is an abnormal communication between two epithelialized surfaces.

An **intestinal fistula** is an abnormal communication between the intestinal tract and another epithelial surface.

An **internal fistula** is an abnormal communication between two internal epithelialized surfaces, such as the colon and the bladder or the duodenum and the gall bladder. In an **external fistula**, one of the epithelial surfaces is skin. The table below lists some different types of intestinal fistulae and their clinical presentation.

DIFFERENT TYPES OF INTESTINAL FISTULAE

Name	Between	Typical clinical presentation*
Enterocutaneous	Small intestine and skin	Discharging lesion (usually high output)
Enterovesical Colovesical	Small intestine or colon and bladder	Recurrent urinary tract infection Pneumaturia
Enterocolic Gastrocolic	Small intestine or stomach and colon	Diarrhoea, dehydration
Rectovaginal Colovaginal	Rectum or colon and vagina	Offensive vaginal discharge
Cholecystoduodenal Choledochoduodenal	Gall bladder or bile duct and duodenum	Often post-operative or after severe cholocystitis
Colocolic	Two areas of the colon	Diarrhoea
Colocutaneous	Colon and skin	Skin lesion discharging faeculent matter (usually low output)

*All may present with evidence of the underlying disease (such as weight loss, anaemia) or evidence of intra-abdominal sepsis (such as fever, tachycardia, abdominal masses or tenderness)

Aetiology

The box below shows the more common causes of intestinal fistulae. A fistula will tend to heal spontaneously in normal circumstances, but certain factors will inhibit spontaneous healing. These are:

- Distal obstruction
- Persistence of underlying disease (e.g. abscess, carcinoma, inflammatory bowel disease)
- Epithelialization of the fistulous tract
- Presence of foreign bodies, such as suture in the fistulous tract
- Loss of bowel continuity, such as occurs in anastomotic breakdown
- Malnutrition

Causes of intestinal fistulae

- **Iatrogenic**
  Anastomotic leakage
  Percutaneous abscess drainage
  Radiotherapy

- **Crohn's disease**
  Spontaneous
  Post-operative

- **Carcinoma**
  Direct invasion
  Abscess formation

- **Diverticular disease**

- **Embryological**

- **Traumatic**

Management

Management of a patient with an intestinal fistula depends on a number of factors, including the type of fistula, its underlying cause and the condition of the patient. It requires a methodical approach and a multi-disciplinary team. The aim of management is to obtain closure of the fistula while keeping the patient in good health.

After the initial resuscitation and stabilization of the patient, the important aspects of management can be remembered with the aid of the mnemonic 'SNAP':

Sepsis / Nutrition / Anatomy / Plan: conservative treatment or surgery

Special problems include skin care and haemorrhage.

Sepsis
A fistula is commonly associated with an abscess cavity that may lead to sepsis and death. Evidence of sepsis should be sought and treated as a matter of priority. The presence of an abscess is suggested by:

- Persisting pain
- Pyrexia
- Tachycardia
- Leucocytosis
- Falling serum albumin
- High urinary nitrogen

An abscess can be diagnosed by ultrasonography, CT or fistulography by use of contrast medium. Abscesses must be drained surgically or radiologically to control sepsis. The aim is to convert a complex cavity into a simple fistulous tract which may close spontaneously. No attempt to close the fistula surgically should be made at this stage. Antibiotics should be avoided unless there is evidence of cellulitis or septicaemia.

Nutrition
The nutritional support and monitoring of fluid and electrolytes should be addressed promptly in the management of patients with fistulae. Large amounts of fluid and electrolytes can be lost in a high fistula, and sepsis will increase metabolic requirements.

Multi-disciplinary team involved in management of intestinal fistulae

- Surgeons
- Stoma nurse
- Dietician
- Laboratory staff
- Radiologists

- Nutritional nurse
- Pharmacist
- Physiotherapist
- Medical staff
- Relatives

Recommended measures include:

- Documentation and analysis of fistula output
- Regular haematological and biochemical measurements
- Oral intake of food and fluids should be stopped to reduce both fistula output and intestinal secretions
- IV feeding allows intestinal 'rest' and provides adequate nutrition
- Total parenteral nutrition (TPN) is best given through a tunnelled dedicated central venous feeding line

TPN should supply energy, protein, minerals, trace elements and vitamins. Many of these nutrients can be measured in the serum. In the later stages of the high small bowel fistulae, jejunal enteral feeding may be considered.

Anatomy
Diagnosing the cause and extent of the fistula is important, but this should only be addressed once the patient is stable, any sources of sepsis are treated and the nutritional needs are met. The diagnostic methods used in determining the anatomy of the fistula include:

- Fistulography using contrast
- Barium studies of the large and small bowel
- Ultrasound scan
- CT scanning
- Injection of diluted methylene blue
- Biochemistry of fistulous output (differentiates between pancreatic, biliary, small bowel or urinary tract origin)

Plan
Once information is gained about the anatomy and cause of the fistula, the decision can be made about whether to treat the fistula conservatively or to proceed to surgery. Conservative management is indicated in fistulae which are likely to heal spontaneously.

Conservative management of intestinal fistulae

Approximately 60% of enterocutaneous fistulae will close within a month of conservative treatment after sepsis has been controlled if the patient is not malnourished. The principles of conservative management are:

- Drainage
- Skin protection
- Reducing fistula output
- Fluid and electrolyte support
- Nutritional support

Drainage is usually achieved by a drainage bag or, rarely, a sump suction system. Skin protection from the proteolytic enzymes in enterocutaneous fistulae is achieved with a number of adhesive devices and pastes under the guidance of an experienced stoma nurse. Fistula output is reduced by ensuring that the patient remains nil by mouth.

Drugs used to reduce secretions include:

- H_2 antagonists
- Proton pump inhibitors
- Somatostatin

Throughout a course of conservative treatment, fluid and electrolyte balance must be carefully monitored and maintained and nutritional support must be continued. If, after six weeks, a fistula that should have closed spontaneously has not, then the underlying reason for this must be sought and surgical treatment undertaken.

Surgical treatment of intestinal fistulae

The principles of surgical management of intestinal fistulae are as follows:

- Aims of surgery are to drain away any septic foci, relieve any distal obstruction and repair or resect the fistula
- Careful dissection of the adhesions and inflammatory masses is needed
- Temporary exteriorization of bowel may be necessary as primary anastomosis is not recommended in unfavourable conditions

Another indication for surgery is haemorrhage. Sudden and potentially fatal haemorrhage may occur from eroded vessels within the fistulous tract or associated abscess cavities. Urgent resection is sometimes required, although arterial embolization may be considered.

12. THE COLON

12.1 Anatomy and physiology

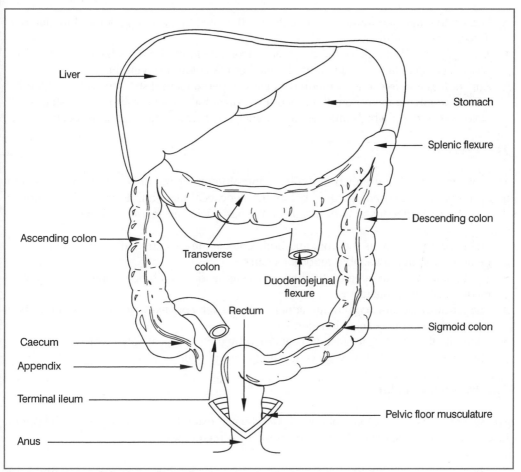

Gross anatomy of the large bowel

The mesenteries

- Transverse colon always has a mesentery (the transverse mesocolon)
- Sigmoid colon also has a mesentery (the sigmoid mesocolon)
- Rarely (in 12% and 22% of people, respectively) do the ascending and descending colon have a mesentery
- In most people the ascending and descending colon are plastered onto the posterior abdominal wall so they have posterior 'bare areas' devoid of peritoneum
- The transverse and sigmoid mesocolon carry blood vessels

The ascending colon

This is the first part of the colon, 15 cm long running from the ileocaecal junction to the hepatic flexure. It is usually retroperitoneal.

- Lies on the iliac and lumbar fascia between the lateral paracolic gutter and medial right infracolic compartment
- The longitudinal muscle of the colon is concentrated into three flat bands, the taeniae coli which sacculate or 'bunch up' the wall of the colon between them
- Appendices epiploicae are bulbous pouches of peritoneum distended with fat; blood vessels supplying them from the mucosa perforate the muscle walls causing areas of weakness through which mucous membranes can herniate causing diverticulae

The caecum

The caecum is the blind pouch of the large intestine projecting downwards from the commencement of the ascending colon below the ileocaecal junction. It lies on the peritoneal floor of the right iliac fossa, over iliacus and psoas fascia and the femoral nerve.

- The peritoneum covers the front and both sides of the caecum and continues up behind it forming a variable retrocaecal space
- The taeniae coli converge on the base of the appendix which opens into the postero-medial wall of the caecum
- The terminal ileum is commonly adherent to the left convexity of the caecum for about 2 cm below the ileocaecal junction
- Internally the ileocaecal junction is guarded by the ileocaecal valve which is not always competent, but may prevent reflux into the ileum

The transverse colon

The second part of the colon is about 45 cm long and extends from the hepatic to the splenic flexure in a loop suspended by its mesentery. It is intraperitoneal.

- The greater omentum, the transverse mesocolon and the transverse colon are fused, so the greater omentum appears to hang from the transverse colon in an apron
- The appendices epiploicae are larger and more numerous than on the ascending colon
- The splenic flexure is much higher than the hepatic flexure

The descending colon

The third part of the colon is 30 cm long and extends from the splenic flexure to the pelvic brim. It is usually retroperitoneal.

- It lies on the lumbar and iliac fascia like the ascending colon
- Appendices epiploicae are numerous and diverticulosis is common

The sigmoid colon

The fourth part of the colon is about 45 cm long, but its length varies, and extends from the descending colon at the pelvic brim to the upper end of the rectum in front of the third piece of the sacrum. It is intraperitoneal.

- The start of the rectum is defined by the end of the sigmoid mesentery which is the only distinction
- The taeniae coli are wider in the sigmoid and distally fuse to form a complete longitudinal coat
- The appendices epiploicae are most common here, as is the incidence of diverticulosis
- The sigmoid mesentery hangs from an upside down 'V'-shaped base which lies over the bifurcation of the common iliac artery; each limb is about 5 cm long (see the figure on p. 337).

Blood supply of the large bowel

Arteries
The blood supply of the large bowel is shown in the figure overleaf. The **superior mesenteric artery** supplies the appendix, caecum, ascending and proximal transverse colon. The **inferior mesenteric artery** supplies the rest of the transverse colon, the descending and sigmoid colon and the rectum. It anastomoses with the pudendal vessels in the anal canal.

Arterial disease of the aorta may occlude these arteries. The inferior mesenteric artery and the small arteries of the transverse colon are especially liable to atherosclerosis. The marginal artery is an artery near the gut wall which acts as an anastomosis between the inferior and superior mesenteric arteries. It may be absent or poorly developed.

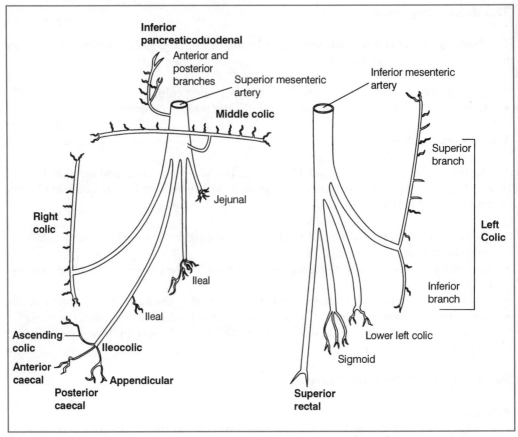

The superior mesenteric artery

The inferior mesenteric artery

Veins

The portal vein drains the blood from the large bowel (see figure opposite). Blood from the right side of the large bowel drains via the **superior mesenteric vein** and ends up in the right hepatic lobe due to the 'streaming' of blood in the portal vein. Blood from the left side of the large bowel drains via the **inferior mesenteric vein** into the splenic vein and ends up in the left hepatic lobe

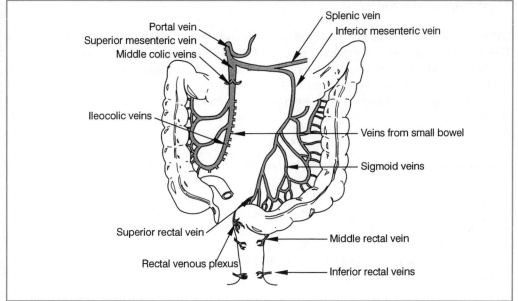

Venous drainage of the large bowel

Lymphatic drainage

- Lymphatic vessels tend to follow the arteries
- Left side of the large bowel drains via the superior mesenteric nodes to the para-aortic nodes
- Right side of the large bowel drains via the inferior mesenteric nodes to the superior mesenteric nodes and the pancreatic nodes
- There are smaller nodes located on the colonic wall and in the mesentery between the colon and the aorta

Nerve supply to the large bowel

The main pain receptors are transmitted via sympathetic components which pass along the arteries to the aortic plexi T_{10}–L_2 with vasoconstrictor nerves. The main motor fibres come from the vagus nerve to the proximal colon as far as the distal transverse colon.

- The distal large bowel receives its motor supply from the sacral outflows which run with the inferior mesenteric vessel
- In the bowel wall is an intramural plexus with connections from the extrinsic nerves
- The smooth muscle fibres are themselves in direct communication with each other by gap junctions

Physiology of the colon

The main functions of the colon are dehydration and storage of ileal effluent to form faeces. The movement of water electrolytes and metabolites is shown in the figure opposite. There are three main types of contraction involved in the mixing, absorption and transport of colon contents, shown in the figure below. An intrinsic nerve plexus is responsible for this contraction. If it is damaged (e.g. by trypanosomes in Chagas' disease or by drugs such as chlorpromazine or senna) or absent (e.g. in Hirschsprung's disease) severe constipation or obstruction results.

Various hormones and neurotransmitters can affect the intrinsic plexus and, therefore, colon motility.

- Cholecystokinin levels increase after meals and stimulate increased colonic activity
- Sleep ↓ colonic activity, stress ↑
- Many drugs have a potent effect on the colon (e.g. calcium channel blockers)
- Electrolyte imbalances such as low serum potassium concentrations can have a profound effect on smooth muscle function

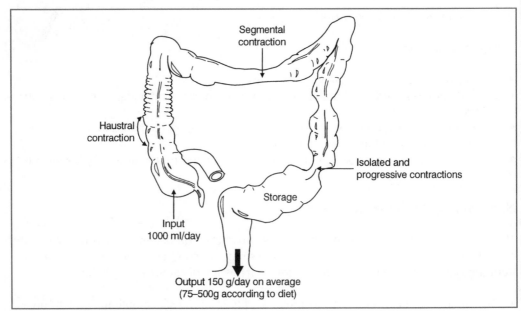

Activity of the large bowel

Movement of electrolyte and metabolites across the wall of the colon

12.2 Diagnosis of colorectal disease

History of colorectal disease

It is important to take a detailed history. The following points are worth eliciting:

- **General**
  Weight loss
  Jaundice
  Malaise
  Vomiting

- **Bowel habit**
  Altered frequency
  Constipation
  Diarrhoea
  Blood (bright red, dark,
    mixed in motion)
  Melaena
  Slime

- **Drugs**
  Laxatives
  Antidiarrhoeals
  Iron

- **Abdominal**
  Pain (constant or colic)
  Distension
  Borborygmi

- **Anal and perianal symptoms**
  Pruritus
  Pain on defaecation
  Prolapse
  Incontinence
  Discharge
  Tenesmus
  Swelling

- **Systemic manifestations of
    specific disease**
  Anaemia (neoplasia and
    inflammatory bowel disease)
  Dermoid cysts (Gardner's syndrome)
  Acanthosis nigricans
  Dermatomyositis
  Pyoderma gangrenosum } neoplasia
  Arthropathy
  Uveitis   } inflammatory
  Finger clubbing   } bowel disease

Examination of colorectal disease

Abdominal examination

- Distension
- Visible peristalsis
- Palpable mass
- Hepatomegaly
- Tenderness

Anorectal examination

- Inspection
- Pruritus ani
- Perianal warts, abscess, haematoma
- Prolapsing or thrombosed haemorrhoids
- Skin tags
- Anal fistulae and fissures
- Anal cancer
- Rectocoele
- Rectal prolapse
- Faecal soiling
- Inspect on straining
- Digital examination (see figure opposite)
- Inspect glove for blood, mucus, melaena or pus

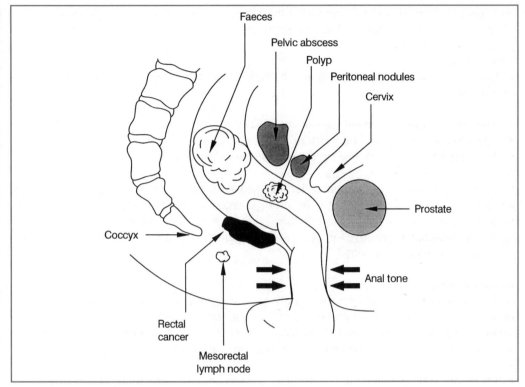

Findings on rectal examination

Investigation of colorectal disease

Proctoscopy
This enables inspection of the anal canal. It reveals haemorrhoids, anal and lower rectal polyps and tumours. Banding of haemorrhoids and biopsy of mucosa or tumours can be carried out via a proctoscope.

Sigmoidoscopy
Rigid sigmoidoscopy may be performed without bowel preparation or sedation in the outpatient clinic. The rigid sigmoidoscope is 20 cm long and allows visualization of the rectum. The tip of the sigmoidoscope should be advanced only when the lumen is visible. Sigmoidoscopy reveals abnormalities of mucosa (e.g. proctitis, inflammatory bowel disease) as well as mass lesions (polyps and tumours). Biopsies of mucosal lesions should be taken only below 10 cm for fear of rupture. Biopsies of any protuberant lesions which can be reached should be taken.

Flexible sigmoidoscopy uses fibre optic technology and a 60 cm long endoscope; 70% of colorectal carcinomas are within reach of the flexible sigmoidoscope. Sedation may be needed and specially trained staff maintain the equipment so they are less suited to an outpatient clinic. Biopsies may be taken of lesions or mucosa.

Colonoscopy
Colonoscopy is a skilled procedure which requires specialist training. Bowel preparation is needed, such as:

- Low-residue diet for a week before colonoscopy
- Clear fluids only for 48 hours before colonoscopy
- Strong purgative (two doses) on the day before colonoscopy

Colonoscopy is usually performed under light sedation. Antispasmodics (e.g. Buscopan) and analgesia (e.g. pethidine) may also be used. Oxygen saturation should be monitored by pulse oximetry. Experienced colonoscopists should reach the caecum in 90% or more of cases. Colonoscopy is sensitive for mucosal abnormalities and can facilitate biopsies, polypectomy and diathermy of lesions.

Barium enema
A **single-contrast** barium enema shows only gross abnormalities such as mechanical obstruction and may be used before emergency surgery to exclude pseudo-obstruction. A **double-contrast** barium enema is performed by insufflating air after evacuation of barium. This reveals fine mucosal detail and has better diagnostic accuracy.

Extra-colonic abnormalities, such as fistulae, are seen more clearly than on endoscopy. The right colon is revealed in patients in whom colonoscopists could not reach the caecum. However, biopsies and therapeutic snaring of lesions cannot be performed.

The distal 10 cm of the alimentary tract should be visualized by rigid sigmoidoscopy as lesions in this area may not be visualized by a barium enema. The choice of investigation depends on the local resources and expertise.

Ultrasonography
Useful for identifying liver metastases in patients with colorectal cancer. Rectal intraluminal ultrasonography may be useful in staging rectal tumours. Intra-operative ultrasonography is the most sensitive technique for identifying hepatic metastases.

CT and MRI
CT and MRI scans are ideal for identifying the local extent and distant spread of colorectal cancers. Contrast CT can be used to identify lesions in patients in whom endoscopy or barium enema are not successful.

Faecal occult blood tests (FOB)
This can be used to screen patients with iron deficiency anaemia for colorectal cancer. The faeces is smeared on a filter impregnated with guaiac acid. Hydrogen peroxide is added. The guaiac acid goes blue in the presence of haematin from haemoglobin. The test is not very specific as bleeding from haemorrhoids or fissures, or even high meat content in the diet can give false positives.

Microbiological tests
If infection is suspected, microscopy will show mobile amoebas and parasitic cysts in a fresh stool. Stool culture will grow bacterial pathogens. Toxins produced by *Clostridium difficile* may be identified in patients with pseudomembranous colitis.

Transit studies
Intestinal transit can be estimated by following the passage of a known number of ingested radio-opaque markers by plain X-ray. Delay in the transit is considered to be present if more than 80% of the markers are still present after 5 days. This test can be used to investigate constipation.

12.3 Inflammatory bowel disease

Inflammatory bowel disease (IBD) is a chronic gastrointestinal inflammation without identifiable cause. Several inflammatory bowel conditions also exist with a known cause, and these should be excluded.

- Infection
- Antibiotics (pseudomembranous colitis)
- Parasites
- Ischaemic colitis
- Radiation colitis

Crohn's disease

Although most commonly found in the terminal ileum, Crohn's disease may occur anywhere in the alimentary canal, from mouth to anus. It may be confined to the large bowel, or there may be involvement of both the small and large intestine. Perianal involvement is seen in 75% of patients.

Ulcerative colitis

This is a mucosal disease that almost invariably involves the rectum and then spreads more proximally in a continuous manner. Only 15% of cases extend more proximally than the splenic flexure. (This group has a greater risk of complications, including cancer.) In a few cases, the ileum is also affected (backwash ileitis).

PATHOLOGICAL FEATURES OF CROHN'S DISEASE AND UC

	Crohn's disease	Ulcerative colitis
Gross pathology	30% of cases only affect ileum 50% affect ileum and colon 20% affect only the colon	60% confined to rectum and sigmoid 25% extends to splenic flexure 15% more proximal than splenic flexure
	'Skip lesions' of abnormal areas intervening between normal mucosa	Continuous proximal spread from rectum — no 'skip lesions'
	Any part of alimentary canal affected from mouth to anus	Only large bowel affected with occasional 'Backwash ileitis' in extensive cases
Histology	Whole thickness of bowel wall affected Acute phase — swollen, red, ulcerated bowel Chronic phase — hosepipe thickening with fibrosis, luminal narrowing and obstruction Mucosa — cobblestone appearance Serosa — fatty encroachment Ulcers — may be very deep and fissuring causes adhesion and fistulae between bowel and adjacent structures	Usually limited to mucosa, not affecting muscularis propria Acute phase — swollen, red, ulcerated bowel Chronic phase — regeneration of epithelium; inflammatory pseudo-polyps Mucosa — atrophic apart from inflammatory pseudo-polyps Serosa — not affected except in toxic megacolon when all bowel layers are involved Ulcers — small and shallow
Microscopic features	Non-caseating epitheloid granulomas in 60–70% of patients Transmural inflammation Fissuring ulcers Lymphoid follicles Mucosal crypt distortion	Granulomas not typical Inflammatory infiltrate confined to lamina propria Crypt abscesses Crypt distortion Metaplasia and dysplasia — can be severe and predisposes to carcinoma

Epidemiology

Both Crohn's disease and ulcerative colitis (UC) are more common in developing countries and younger adults.

- Crohn's is more common in females but UC is seen in both sexes equally
- Incidence of UC is 26:100,000 of the population and is static
- Incidence of Crohn's disease is 6:100,000 and is rising

Aetiology

- 20–30% of patients with Crohn's or UC have a family history of IBD
- Aetiology is not clear in either disease but a post-infective theory has been postulated for Crohn's and autoimmune, environmental and dietary factors have been considered for UC

Pathology

The pathological features of Crohn's and UC are compared and contrasted in the table opposite. In severe cases it can be very difficult to distinguish between Crohn's and UC, even histologically.

Clinical features

- Bloody diarrhoea in otherwise fit patient is the most common presenting symptom of ulcerative colitis
- The presentation of Crohn's disease depends upon the area affected, but anal disease is a useful feature that indicates Crohn's disease (affects up to 75% of patients with Crohn's disease)
- Rectal Crohn's and UC can be difficult to differentiate
- The main clinical features of each disease are shown in the table overleaf; other clinical features are listed below

Typical features of Crohn's disease

- Stricture formation leading to chronic intestinal obstruction
- Local perforation
- Abscess
- Fistula to exterior or other organs
- Colitis leading to diarrhoea, mucus and bleeding
- Anal fissure, ulcers, infections and skin tags
- Extra-intestinal manifestations (see Table below)
- Anorexia, weight loss, malnutrition, anaemia, nausea

Typical features of ulcerative colitis

- Bloody diarrhoea with mucus, urgency and incontinence
- Constipation in cases of limited proctitis
- Cramping abdominal pain
- Anorexia, weight loss, malnutrition, anaemia, nausea
- Extra-intestinal manifestations (see table below)
- It is important to recognize patients with severe acute colitis: severe local symptoms; frequency more than 10 stools/24 hours with blood; wasting, pallor, tachycardia, pyrexia; tender, distended abdomen; these patients may progress to acute toxic dilatation of the colon and perforation

CLINICAL FEATURES IN UC AND CROHN'S DISEASE

Symptom	Crohn's disease	Ulcerative colitis
Bleeding	Sometimes	Common
Urgent defaecation	Sometimes	Common
Abdomen		
mass	Sometimes	Rare
spontaneous fistulae	Sometimes	Never
Anal region		
fissure	Common	Rare
ulceration	Common	Rare
infection	Common	Rare
lesions preceding bowel symptoms	Sometimes	Never

Extra-intestinal manifestations of inflammatory bowel disease

- **Related to disease activity**

  Skin
    Pyoderma gangrenosum
    Erythema nodosum
  Mucous membranes
    Aphthous ulcers of mouth
    and vagina
  Eyes
    Iritis
  Joints
    Activity related arthritis of
    large joints

- **Unrelated to disease activity**

  Joints/Liver
    Sacroiliitis, ankylosing spondylitis
  Biliary tree
    Chronic active hepatitis
    Cirrhosis
    Sclerosing cholangitis
  Renal
    Bile duct carcinoma
  Integument
    Amyloidosis in Crohn's disease
    Fingernail clubbing

Investigations

The aims of investigations are to:

- Make the diagnosis
- Assess the severity of disease

Sigmoidoscopy
Findings:

- Oedema of mucosa
- Contact bleeding
- Granularity of mucosa
- Ulceration with pus and blood

Similar in both Crohn's and UC apart from distribution of disease. Biopsy helps to distinguish between them. Sigmoidoscopy should not be performed in acute colitis — there is a risk of perforation.

Colonoscopy
Findings similar to sigmoidoscopy. Useful for assessing strictures and disease distribution. Biopsies should be taken. Avoid in acute colitis. Useful in surveillance for dysplasia and carcinoma.

Barium enema

Demonstrates extent of macroscopic disease. Useful for assessing strictures and disease distribution. Biopsies cannot be taken. Not appropriate in acute colitis due to the risk of perforation which would be complicated by barium. Good for distinguishing Crohn's disease from UC. Identifies fistulae not seen on endoscopy.

Barium enema findings in:

- **Crohn's disease**
  Discontinuous distribution
  ('skip lesion')
  Rectal sparing common
  'Cobblestone' appearance of
  mucosa
  'Rosethorn' ulcers
  Fistulae
  Strictures

- **Ulcerative colitis**
  Featureless 'hosepipe' colon
  Decreased haustra
  Affects rectum and spreads
  proximally
  Mucosal distortion
  Small ulcers and pseudo-polyps
  Shortened colon

Small bowel enema/barium meal

Useful in small bowel or ileocaecal Crohn's disease. The mucosal features are similar to those seen in the barium enema. In addition, long narrowed areas (Kantor's 'string sign' may be seen with proximal dilatation).

Blood tests

The blood tests help to assess the severity of inflammation and also the response to treatment.

- **FBC**: anaemia; leucocytosis in sepsis; platelets raised in acute Crohn's
- **ESR (Erythrocyte Sedimentation Rate) and CRP (C-reactive protein)**: are markers of inflammation raised in active disease
- **Serum albumin**: tends to be low in patients with active disease

Stool microscopy and culture

In order to differentiate between infective colitis and IBD.

Medical management

The mainstays of medical management of IBD involve:

- Anti-inflammatory medication
- Symptomatic control
- Replacement of nutrients, water and electrolytes

Anti-inflammatory medication

- **Oral 5-amino salicylic acid preparations** (e.g. mesalazine (Asocol), olsalazine): these are slow-release with few side-effects. Often they are the first line of treatment. Sulphasalazine (5-amino salicylic acid) and sulphapyridine suppress disease activity and maintain remission. Nausea, vomiting and skin rashes are side-effects.
- **Steroids** (e.g. prednisolone): used to control exacerbation of widespread colitis. Well-known side-effects include peptic ulceration, osteoporosis, Cushing's syndrome and psychiatric effects. Withdrawal may lead to recurrent attacks. Modified release budesonide causes fewer side-effects. Prolonged high-dose steroids are undesirable and may be an indication for surgery.
- **Topical**: these are particularly useful in acute attacks of ulcerative colitis as the disease is often restricted to the rectum. 5-amino salicylic acid preparations and steroids are available in suppositories, enemas and foam enemas.

There is some controversy over whether antibiotics have any effect. Metronidazole is sometimes prescribed, but in general antibiotics should only be given if specifically indicated for managing bacterial overgrowth in the small bowel or for treating the infective complications of Crohn's disease and perianal Crohn's.

Symptomatic control

- **Antidiarrhoeal agents** (such as codeine phosphate, diphenoxylate preparations (Lomotil) and loperamide): may be necessary to control distressing and debilitating diarrhoea

Replacement of nutrients, water and electrolytes
Iron may be needed in chronic cases. Nutritional supplements may be needed if markers such as albumin are low.

- **Parenteral nutrition**: in severely malnourished patients
- **Intravenous fluids**: in acutely unwell, dehydrated patients
- **Potassium supplementation**: may be necessary in acutely unwell patients with severe diarrhoea

Surgical management

Indications for surgery

- To restore health in patients with chronic disease (e.g. in nutritional failure)
- To eliminate the risks of side-effects of steroids in patients requiring long-term high doses of steroids
- Premalignant change on colonoscopic surveillance

- Patients at high risk of developing cancer (ulcerative colitis with early onset, extensive colonic involvement and continuous symptoms)
- To treat complications (usually emergency surgery) e.g. perforation, severe haemorrhage, toxic dilatation (>6 cm megacolon), stricture causing obstruction, fistulation or abscess formation, sepsis, acute severe attack, need to defunction diseased bowel with an ileostomy.

Principles of surgery in inflammatory bowel disease
Because of the differences between Crohn's disease and UC, the principles of surgery are not the same.

In **Crohn's disease**, surgery should be as limited as possible and be reserved for patients with a specific operable problem. This is because:

- Crohn's disease is relapsing and recurrent and can affect the entire length of the gastrointestinal tract; it cannot be 'cured' by surgery.
- Patients may have a lifetime of the disease so it is important to leave as much functioning bowel as possible; 40% of patients operated on for Crohn's of the small bowel need further surgery within 10 years.
- Complications such as post-operative sepsis and fistulation are common
- Conservative treatment, limited bowel resection or bowel-preserving procedures, such as stricturoplasty or balloon dilatation, is commonly employed in Crohn's disease

By contrast, in **ulcerative colitis** radical surgery is often performed. This is because:

- Ulcerative colitis is restricted to the large bowel and is always continuous with the diseased rectum; removal of the diseased segment may well cure the patient.
- Patients are at risk of death from perforation or toxic megacolon, so prompt radical surgery is indicated in this condition.
- Patients with long-standing active ulcerative colitis have >1/10 risk of developing carcinoma of the colon, which panproctocolectomy prevents; this complication is relatively rare in Crohn's disease.

Proctocolectomy with ileostomy
This has been a traditional operation for ulcerative colitis. It eliminates all disease and risk of malignancy. It leaves the patient with a permanent ileostomy. It is still the procedure of choice in many middle-aged and elderly patients. An intersphincteric approach is used when removing the rectum to avoid damage to the pelvic autonomic nerves.

Sphincter-preserving proctocolectomy with ileal pouch
This is popular in younger patients with ulcerative colitis.

- The rectum is excised leaving the anal canal with an intact sphincter mechanism
- A pouch is constructed from a duplicated or triplicated loop of ileum
- The pouch is anastomosed to the dentate line
- The desired result is complete continence; results are often good but there is usually frequency of stools (at least 4–6/day)

Patients with Crohn's disease are not usually suitable for a pouch as recurrence may affect the ileum used to form it.

Colectomy with ileorectal anastomosis
This is used in both ulcerative colitis and Crohn's disease to avoid an ileostomy.

- The best results are in disease where the rectum is not affected or only mildly affected
- 33% of patients have a good result; 33% of patients have an intermediate result and 33% of patients have a poor result
- Poor results are usually because of recurrent rectal disease, perianal Crohn's with fistulation or rectovaginal fistulation

In failed cases, a proctectomy is usually indicated.

Subtotal colectomy with ileostomy and mucous fistula
This is the operation most indicated in emergency surgery for conditions such as:

- Acute severe attack of colitis resistant to medical therapy
- Perforations
- Toxic megacolon
- Obstruction due to stricture
- Severe haemorrhage
- Fistulation leading to sepsis

Advantages include:

- Restores health of patient with minimum surgical trauma
- Spares sick patient morbidity of pelvic dissection
- Leaves an intact rectum and anal sphincter for future restorative surgery
- Makes available a specimen for firm histopathological diagnosis

Complications of inflammatory bowel disease

Complications of inflammatory bowel disease

- **Ulcerative colitis**
  Toxic megacolon
  Perforation
  Haemorrhage
  Malignant change

- **Crohn's disease**
  Small bowel strictures
  Fistulation
  Perianal sepsis
  Perforation

Toxic dilatation (megacolon)

- Acute severe ulcerative colitis can lead to toxic megacolon
- Such patients should be jointly managed by a physician and a surgeon
- Management involves daily review, medical treatment and nutritional fluid and electrolyte replacement
- Sigmoidoscopy, biopsy and stool cultures are required
- Colonoscopy and barium enema are contraindicated
- Daily plain abdominal films assess degree of dilatation of the colon
- Toxic megacolon is suggested by a colon diameter >6 cm
- Surgery is indicated in toxic megacolon
- Subtotal colectomy with ileostomy and mucous fistula is the safest emergency option (see above)
- Left untreated, toxic megacolon leads to perforation, sepsis and high mortality

Perforation
Ideally, under close joint management, perforation should be avoided by early referral for surgery. Perforation secondary to IBD has a high mortality. Pre-operative diagnosis and management of perforated large bowel is covered in detail later in this chapter. Again, a subtotal colectomy with ileostomy and mucous fistula is the safest operation.

Haemorrhage

- Bleeding may be acute or chronic with progressive anaemia
- It is more common in ulcerative colitis than in Crohn's
- Massive bleeding is rare
- When it occurs, the bleeding site is often in the rectum
- Emergency surgery is indicated in continued life-threatening bleed
- Severe recurrent anaemia may contribute to the indications for an elective colectomy

Malignant change in ulcerative colitis

There is a very significant increase in the incidence of colonic carcinoma. Tumours are more likely than those in non-colitic bowel to:

- Affect a younger age group
- Be anaplastic
- Be multiple
- Be masked by the symptoms of colitis

The risk is greatest in:

- Long-standing colitis
- Continued rather than episodic disease
- Disease affecting the whole large bowel
- Patients affected since childhood

12% of patients with colitis of 20 years' duration are likely to develop malignancy. Patients with long-standing, active or widespread colitis should therefore have a regular colonoscopy to monitor for dysplasia and early invasive cancer. These patients should also be considered for prophylactic surgery, especially as they are in a group who also probably suffer more severe and debilitating symptoms.

Malignant change in Crohn's disease

There is thought to be a very slight increased risk of colon cancer in patients with Crohn's disease. However, prophylactic colectomy is not usually performed. In long-standing Crohn's disease, adenocarcinoma may develop in the affected small intestine (the ileum in two-thirds of cases). This complication is rare and the prognosis is poor.

Strictures in Crohn's disease

Strictures are more likely to occur in Crohn's disease than in ulcerative colitis due to its transmural pathology.

- In **inflammatory** strictures causing small bowel obstruction, steroids and low residue diets may improve symptoms
- In **fibrous** strictures, however, surgery is indicated

Stricturoplasty overcomes obstruction while preserving intestine in patients with multiple short segments of disease. Resection of diseased small bowel and caecum is indicated in obstructed patients with poor response to medical management. If surgery is delayed in such patients, fistulation may occur. Balloon dilatation of strictures is another bowel preserving method of overcoming obstruction.

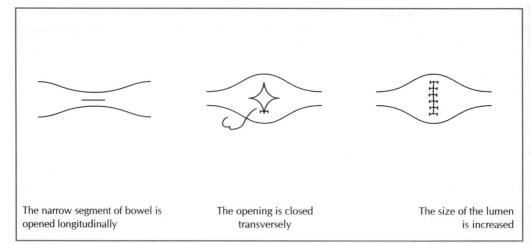

| The narrow segment of bowel is opened longitudinally | The opening is closed transversely | The size of the lumen is increased |

Stricturoplasty in Crohn's disease

Fistulae in Crohn's disease

Fistula formation is present in 15–30% of patients with Crohn's disease. It is less common in ulcerative colitis because the ulceration is limited to the mucosa and not transmural.

Types of Crohn's fistulae include:

- External (enterocutaneous)
- Internal
- Enterovesical
- Enterovaginal
- 'High-low' gastro-intestinal

Contrast studies, including barium enemas, barium meals and sinograms, can identify the fistula. Fistulae will occasionally respond to medical treatment, but surgical resection of the diseased bowel and fistula is usually required to achieve a cure.

The principle of fistula surgery is to resect the diseased bowel and fistula *en bloc* and repair the secondary defect in the healthy organ or bowel. Primary anastomosis should be performed under favourable conditions. In sepsis or malnourished patients, delayed anastomosis should be considered.

Perianal complications in Crohn's disease
Up to 75% of patients with large bowel Crohn's disease have an anal lesion. These include:

- Fissure
- Anorectal sepsis (perianal abscess and fistulae)
- Ulceration
- Oedematous skin tags
- Stenosis of the anorectal junction
- Rectovaginal fistulae

Complex perianal abscesses and fistulae can be difficult to manage and supralevator abscesses may lead to proctectomy. Operations on fistulae should be avoided. Acute abscesses should be drained. Long-term treatment with metronidazole reduces the number of exacerbations. Occasionally, wide excision of the affected perineum, followed by skin grafting or flap repair, is performed once the acute sepsis has resolved. Rectovaginal fistulae may be repaired successfully but some need proctectomy eventually. Haemorroidectomy should be avoided in Crohn's disease if possible as it may be complicated by perianal sepsis.

Inflammatory bowel disease in children
See Chapter 3, *Head, Neck, Endocrine and Paediatric*, Section 15.12, p. 293.

12.4 Benign colonic tumours

Polyps

The term 'polyp' is very non-specific. A polyp is an abnormal elevation from an epithelial surface. It may be:

- Pedunculated (have a head and stalk)
- Sessile (no stalk but may be flat or villous)
- Acquired
- Inherited
- Symptomatic
- Non-symptomatic
- Part of a 'polyposis syndrome' (see later)
- Neoplastic
- Non-neoplastic
- Benign
- Malignant

Benign polyps can be classified according to embryological origin, or as neoplastic and non-neoplastic (see box overleaf).

Classification of benign colonic tumours

- **According to embryological origin**

  Epithelial
  Adenoma
    tubular
    tubulovillous
    villous
  Metaplastic polyp

  Mesodermal
  Lipoma
  Leiomyoma
  Haemangioma
  Other rare tumours

  Hamartoma
  Juvenile polyp
  Peutz–Jeghers polyp

- **Neoplastic/non-neoplastic**

  Neoplastic
  Adenoma
  Benign lymphoma
  Lipoma
  Leiomyoma
  Fibroma
  Haemangioma

  Non-neoplastic
  Metaplastic polyp
  Hamartomatous polyp
    Juvenile polyp
    Peutz–Jeghers polyp
  Inflammatory polyp

Tumour
The term 'tumour' is also very non-specific, meaning only 'swelling' It is often used interchangeably with 'neoplasm'.

Neoplasm
A neoplasm is a new growth arising from uncontrolled and progressive cell multiplication. It can be benign or malignant.

Cancer
Cancer is the common term for all malignant tumours.

Malignant versus benign
This is often a difficult distinction to make but, in general, malignant tumours are non-differentiated, locally invasive and prone to metastasis. The rate of growth also helps to make the distinction.

Non-neoplastic polyps

Metaplastic polyps
Also known as **hyperplastic polyps**.

- The most common type of polyp found in the rectum
- 2–5 mm in diameter, usually flat-topped and the same colour as the mucosa

There is no evidence that they develop dysplastic or neoplastic change. Clinically they are seen and biopsied on sigmoidoscopy and if large, may occasionally give rise to symptoms

Hamartomatous polyps
These are malformations in which the normal tissues of a particular part of the body are arranged haphazardly usually with an excess of one or more of its components. There are two types of colonic hamartomas:

- **Peutz–Jeghers** polyps are found in patients with the rare familial Peutz–Jeghers syndrome. The syndrome consists of pigmentation around the lips associated with characteristic intestinal polyps. The polyps are most common in the small intestine but can occasionally occur in the colon. The polyps are often present in childhood with intussusception or bleeding and are widespread and, therefore, hard to treat. They have a very low-grade malignant potential.
- **Juvenile polyps** are the most common polyps in children. They occur anywhere in the large bowel but are usually in the rectum. They occur in children under 10 and present as prolapse through the anus or bleeding. They are not pre-malignant and are easily treated by excision.

Inflammatory polyps
These are essentially normal mucosal tags in the colon of any patient suffering from a chronic inflammatory disease of the bowel. They occur commonly in ulcerative colitis or Crohn's disease.

Benign neoplastic polyps

- **Benign lymphoma**: the most common non-epithelial benign tumour of the colorectum; usually a single reddish purple polyp of varying size; differentiated from malignant lymphoma by the well-defined germinal centre on histology; simple local excision is the treatment.
- **Lipoma**: relatively rare in large bowel; tends to present in caecum and right colon; varies in size, may be multiple and does not tend to undergo malignant change; may cause intussusception or be confused with a neoplastic tumour on contrast studies or colonoscopy; may need resection to make the histological diagnosis.
- **Leiomyoma**: rare smooth muscle tumours; histological differentiation between benign and malignant is very difficult.

- **Fibroma**: rare colonic tumour arising from submucous layer; hard, mobile pedunculated, covered by intact epithelium; may contain muscle or glandular tissue; rarely undergoes malignant change.
- **Haemangioma**: these vascular lesions need to be differentiated from angiodysplasia; they can cause profuse rectal bleeding.
- **Adenomas**: important because they are the most common neoplastic polyp of the large bowel; they can develop into carcinoma. They are dealt with in more detail below.

Adenomas of the colon

Pathology
An adenoma is a benign neoplasm of the large bowel glandular epithelium. There are three microscopic categories of adenoma:

- **Tubular adenomas**: commonly multiple and may co-exist with a carcinoma; their malignant potential is less than a villous adenoma; they may be pedunculated or sessile and are usually small (<2 cm)
- **Villous adenomas**: often large and sessile with a shaggy frond-like surface; they may extend into a 'carpet-like' lesion; they are more prone to malignant transformation and are found more commonly in the rectum
- **Tubulovillous adenoma**: an intermediate form containing features of both morphological types

Incidence
About 33% of the population have an adenoma at post-mortem (M > F). 66% of all colorectal adenomas occur distal to the splenic flexure. This distribution is not the case in multiple polyposis coli syndrome or in elderly patients. Adenomas occur at any stage, increase with advancing age and, typically, present at the age 55–60 years.

The adenoma–carcinoma sequence

'Dysplasia' refers to the following changes in the epithelial cells:

- Increase in mitotic figures
- Pleomorphism of the nuclei
- Loss of polarity
- Formation of several layers

60% of adenomas show mild dysplasia, 30% show moderate dysplasia and 10% show severe dysplasia (also called 'carcinoma *in situ*').

- 'Carcinoma *in situ*' in an adenoma still confined to the mucosa is not a cancer
- 'Malignant transformation' occurs when these abnormal epithelial cells invade through the muscularis mucosa to enter the submucosa

Virtually all pathologists believe that adenomas can go through the various grades of dysplasia to frank malignancy — the so-called '**adenoma–carcinoma sequence**' but the evidence is circumstantial.

Evidence of the adenoma–carcinoma sequence includes:

* Similar distribution on left side of colon of adenomas and carcinomas
* High incidence of adenomas when a carcinoma is present
* Carcinoma patients with adenomas are twice as likely to develop another carcinoma as those with no adenomas
* Epidemiology of adenomas and carcinomas are similar
* Experimental carcinogens produce colorectal cancer and induce adenomas
* Histological examination of carcinomas show elements of benign adenomas in many cases
* Histological examination of 'benign' adenomas show carcinomas in 3–4%
* Familial adenomatous polyposis coli patients will always develop carcinoma (see later)

Clinical features of adenoma
Adenomatous polyps can present in a number of ways:

* Detected on routine screening
* Bleeding, fresh or altered depending on site
* Change in bowel habit, such as diarrhoea or mucus
* Prolapse of rectal polyp
* Intussusception may present as colic or an acute abdomen
* Tenesmus, mucus and incontinence with large rectal polyps

Diagnosis
Rectal examination:

* Villous tumours are often difficult to feel because of their soft consistency
* Non-villous pedunculated lesion may be palpable
* Focal malignant invasion may be felt as areas of hardness within the polyp

Endoscopy:

* Rigid sigmoidoscopy should detect polyps up to 25 cm from the anal verge
* Flexible sigmoidoscopy should detect polyps up to 60 cm from the anal verge and detection is three times as high as with a rigid instrument
* Colonoscopy detects polyps anywhere in the large bowel

After detection of a polyp, the rest of the bowel must be examined either by colonoscopy or barium enema.

Management of rectal adenomas
Once a polyp has been detected it should be removed so that its histology can be determined and to prevent the adenoma–carcinoma sequence.

- **Endoscopic removal**: the best method to remove most rectal adenomas via a sigmoido-scope using a diathermy snare
- **Endoscopic diathermy**: not ideal as it may not destroy the whole tumour and does not allow histological analysis (may be the most suitable in certain cases)
- **Transanal excision**: may be performed under local or general anaesthesia via a Park's self-retaining anal retractor. The tumour is removed by sharp dissection and diathermy taking care not to disrupt the underlying rectal muscle. The mucosal defect is then repaired.
- **Laparotomy**: may be necessary for large adenomas and is similar to those procedures used for low rectal carcinomas (e.g. abdomino-perineal resection or proctectomy and colo-anal anastomosis).

Management of colonic adenomas
Endoscopic removal is often possible via a colonoscope, but if a polyp is too large then colonic resection is necessary. Diathermy snare is used for pedunculated polyps. Piecemeal resections may be necessary for large sessile polyps.

Laparotomy
The indications are:

- Too large or sessile for endoscopic removal (usually >3 cm)
- A symptomatic adenoma inaccessible to endoscopist
- A partially removed polyp which histology shows to be malignant

The options at laparotomy are:

- **Operative colonoscopic polypectomy**: in which the surgeon helps the colonoscopic removal of the polyp by manipulating the bowel through an abdominal incision. The bowel is not opened.
- **Colotomy and polypectomy**: in which the bowel is opened and the polyp removed. This is rarely indicated as colonic resection is usually safer if a tumour is too large to be removed endoscopically.
- **Colonic resection**: with primary anastomosis

Follow-up after polypectomy for adenoma
This is controversial but the general principles are:

- After removal all patients must be followed-up by endoscopy
- Whole colon must be visualized — if not possible on colonoscopy, a barium enema should be employed to exclude other polyps
- If the polyp proves to be non-neoplastic (metaplastic or inflammatory), no follow-up is needed
- Follow-up endoscopy should be more frequent if malignant features are seen on a histology
- If symptoms develop before scheduled endoscopy follow-up, prompt investigation is indicated

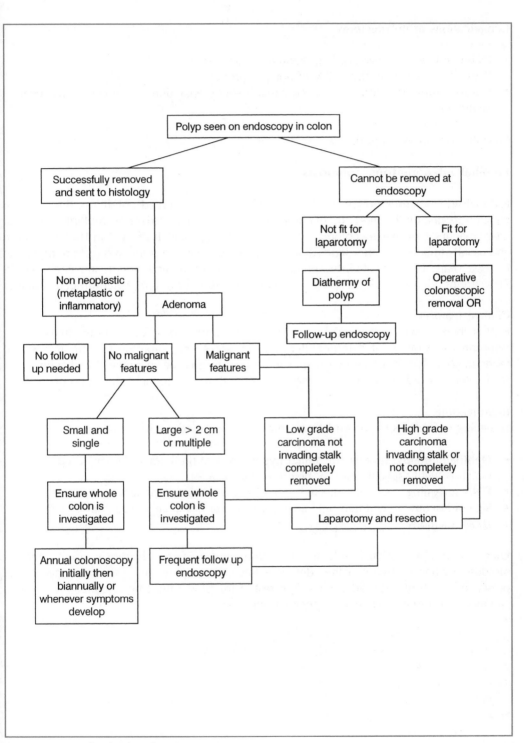

Management of colonic adenoma

Complications of polypectomy

- Bleeding (2% have haemorrhage requiring transfusion)
- Perforation (occurs in 0.2–0.7% of polypectomies)
- Gas explosion (should not occur now that bowel preparation with mannitol has been abandoned)

Overall mortality is about 0.05%.

Familial adenomatous polyposis

Familial adenomatous polyposis (FAP) is a dominantly inherited condition, the gene for which is carried on the short arm of chromosome 5. It is characterized by multiple colorectal adenomas and typical extra-colonic stigmata (see box opposite). It affects 1 in 10,000 liveborn and usually hundreds or thousands of adenomas develop in the colon and rectum during the teenage years. Left untreated, the progression to colorectal carcinoma is inevitable within 20 years of adenomas developing. FAP is responsible for 1% of all colorectal cancers.

Clinical features
FAP is increasingly diagnosed by screening of children of affected individuals before symptoms can occur. If it is not identified by screening, symptoms occur in the late teens or 20s. The most common presentations are change in bowel habit with loose stool, blood or mucus p.r. Patients may present with a carcinoma of the colon or rectum.

Investigations
Screening in relatives of known FAP patients can be carried out in a number of ways:

- **Ophthalmoscopy**: reveals congenital hypertrophy of the retinal pigmented epithelium which is highly specific for FAP before polyps develop
- **DNA screening**: identifies affected individuals with 95% confidence
- **Sigmoidoscopy**: in children until adenomas appear has largely been superseded by the above methods

Diagnosis in new patients with new mutations and no family history is usually by sigmoidoscopy and biopsy after the adenomas become symptomatic. FAP is assumed in the presence of 100 or more adenomas. The rest of the bowel must be visualized to exclude carcinoma before management is decided upon.

Extra-colonic manifestations of FAP

- Hamartomatous polyps in the stomach
- Dental cysts
- Retinal pigmentation

- Adenomas of the duodenum
- Osteomas of the jaw
- Epidermoid cysts
- Desmoid tumours, usually in the abdomen

Management

Because of the inevitability of malignant transformation, surgery is indicated in all patients with FAP. There are three options for prophylactic surgery:

- **Panproctocolectomy and end ileostomy**: has the advantage of removing all the affected bowel, but the disadvantage of a permanent stoma. It is becoming less acceptable to this usually young group of patients.
- **Colectomy and ileorectal anastomosis**: in this procedure, the rectum is spared so the patient retains relatively normal bowel function. The main disadvantage is recurrence of disease. Rectal adenomas may regress after surgery, and regular surveillance with removal of polyps endoscopically as necessary can be satisfactory. Development of rectal cancer, however, remains a risk which cannot be completely eliminated and which some patients are not prepared to accept.
- **Proctocolectomy with ileal pouch and ileoanal anastomosis**: in this procedure, all the affected bowel is removed but an ileostomy is avoided. This option is becoming more popular. The disadvantages are poor functional results and the risks of a large and relatively complex operation.

All FAP patients require long-term follow-up no matter which operation they have undergone because of the extra-colonic manifestations, especially ampullary tumours of the duodenum.

Other polyposis syndromes

Apart from FAP, other polyposis syndromes are rare and not as clinically significant. They are listed overleaf.

Classification of polyposis syndromes

- **Neoplastic**
  Familial adenomatous polyposis
  Turcot's syndrome
  Lymphosarcomatous polyposis
  Leukaemia polyposis

- **Inflammatory**
  Ulcerative colitis
  Crohn's disease
  Other inflammatory polyposis:
    amoebiasis
    schistosomiasis
    eosinophilic
  Granulomatosis
  Histoplasmosis

- **Hamartomous**
  Juvenile polyposis
  Peutz–Jeghers syndrome
  Neurofibromatous polyposis
  Lipomatous polyposis
  Cronkhite Canada syndrome
  Cowden's disease

- **Others**
  Metaplastic
  Pneumatosis cystoides intestinalis

12.5 Colorectal cancer

Epidemiology

Ca colon is the second most common cause of death from malignancy in the UK after lung cancer. More common in western Europe and North America than in developing countries. Less than 5% of patients are under 40 years old, and the peak incidence is in people aged 70–80 years. F > M (marginally).

Aetiology

The exact cause is unclear but both environmental and genetic factors are thought to be involved. Immigrants from an area of low incidence to an area with a high incidence soon become just as prone to develop the disease as the indigenous population. The following environmental factors have been implicated:

Dietary and digestive factors

- **Lack of fibre**: thought that reduced speed of transit exposes gut mucosa to potential carcinogens
- **High fat diet**: thought to favour bacterial flora which can degrade bile salts into carcinogens

- **High levels of bile acids**: bile salts have a direct effect on mucosa and are degraded into carcinogens
- **Previous cholecystectomy**: not proven conclusively, but may lead to an increased production of degraded bile salts

Inflammatory bowel disease
12% of patients with ulcerative colitis of 20 years' duration are likely to develop malignant change. Accounts for about 1% of all cases of colorectal carcinoma. May be a small, but not clinically significant increase in the incidence of colorectal carcinoma in Crohn's disease.

Uretero-sigmoidostomy
This technique for urinary diversion is less commonly performed now as carcinoma of the sigmoid developed more often in these patients.

Irradiation
Pelvic irradiation increases risk of developing rectosigmoid carcinoma.

Genetic factors
75% of cases of colorectal cancer are sporadic; 1% are in patients with pre-existing inflammatory bowel disease (see p. 487). The remaining 24% are associated with genetic factors (see figure below).

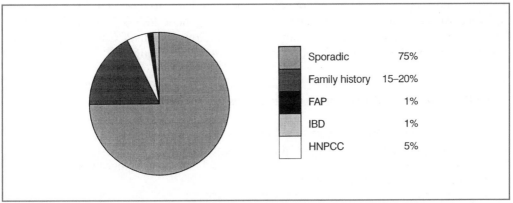

Sporadic	75%
Family history	15–20%
FAP	1%
IBD	1%
HNPCC	5%

Risk factors associated with new cases of colorectal cancer

Family history
Some families have a higher incidence of colorectal cancer due to:

- Familial adenomatous polyposis (see p. 496)
- Hereditary non-polyposis colon cancer (HNPCC)
- Other familial colon cancer (essentially a diagnosis of exclusion of the first two conditions)

Several genes have been identified as contributing to hereditary colorectal cancer. They include:

- Tumour suppressor genes, such as APC, p53 and DCC
- Oncogenes, such as Ras
- Mismatch repair genes, such as hMSH2 and hMLH1

It is unlikely that specific mutations are responsible for most of the cases of colonic cancer that run in families. FAP and HNPCC are two hereditary cancers for which molecular genetic testing is available.

HNPCC (hereditary non-polyposis colon cancer)
HNPCC is a type of inherited colon cancer which accounts for 5% of new cases of colorectal cancer per year. It is due to mutations in four different mismatch repair genes whose products normally repair damaged DNA. Mutations in the mismatch repair gene hMSH2 accounts for 31% of HNPCC families; hMLH1 for 33% and hPMS1 and hPMS2 for 5% between them. HNPCC is characterized by: average age of diagnosis 45 years or younger; tumours more likely to develop in the proximal portion of the colon (unlike sporadic colorectal cancers); tumours which show a rapid transformation from benign to malignant case; and the presence of extra-colonic cancers (i.e. endometrial cancer in 20–40%; ovarian cancer in 10%; gastric cancer in 6%; biliary tract cancer in 4%; urinary tract cancer in 2%; brain tumours in 1% and small bowel cancers in 1%).

Patients with a strong family history of colon cancer are likely to have HNPCC if they fit the so-called **Amsterdam criteria** (see below). Molecular genetic testing is the only means of properly classifying the patient and family. Patients confirmed as HNPCC should have regular colonoscopy and the rest of the family should be offered screening.

Amsterdam criteria for clinical diagnosis of HNPCC

- Three or more family members with colorectal cancer
- Colorectal cancer extends over two or more generations
- One affected family member is a first-degree relative of the other two
- One or more affected before the age of 45
- Exclusion of Familial Adenomatous Polyposis (FAP)

Pathology

Distribution of colorectal tumours
The distribution of carcinoma is shown in the figure overleaf. 75% of tumours are situated in the rectum and sigmoid colon (i.e. within reach of flexible sigmoidoscopy). Patients with familial colon cancer FAP or HNPCC have a higher incidence of right-sided tumours. Approximately 3% of patients with a primary carcinoma will have another (synchronous) tumour present at the time of presentation. Approximately 75% of patients with a primary carcinoma will have associated benign adenoma. 3% of patients with a successfully treated colon cancer will develop a further colorectal tumour within 10 years (metachronous tumour).

Classification of colorectal tumours
98% of all cancers of the large bowel are adenocarcinomas. The other (rare) tumours of the large bowel are carcinoid, primary and secondary lymphoma and leiomyosarcoma. This section deals only with adenocarcinomas. They can be classified as follows:

- Papilliferous
- Ulcerating
- Annular (circumferential, obstructing lesion)
- Diffuse infiltrating
- Colloid tumour (produce excess mucus)

Grading of colorectal tumours
Colorectal tumours are graded histologically I–IV according to the degree of differentiation of cells:

- Grade I is well-differentiated (20%)
- Grades II and III are moderately differentiated (60%)
- Grade IV is anaplastic (20%)

Spread of colorectal tumours

Direct spread
More common laterally than longitudinally:

- 2 cm longitudinal clearance is usually adequate; 5 cm is recommended
- Eventually involves adjacent viscera

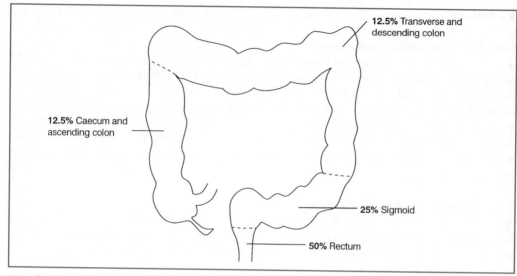

Distribution of carcinoma within the large bowel

DUKE'S PATHOLOGICAL STAGING OF COLORECTAL CANCER

Duke's stage	Extent of tumour	Five-year survival rate (%)	
		Rectum	**Colon***
A	Confined to bowel wall	91.9	70–80
B	Through bowel wall, lymph nodes not involved	71.3	
C	Lymph nodes involved, no other metastases, highest node not involved	40.0	30–40
C_2*	Lymph nodes involved, no other metastases, highest node involved	26.5	
D*	Distant metastases	<16.4	

*Not included in Duke's original staging but often used

Lymphatic spread

- Via lymphatics which run with supplying arteries
- To regional lymph nodes, para-aortic nodes and thence to the thoracic duct

- Supraclavicular nodes may be involved in advanced cases
- Upward spread is more likely for rectal carcinomas than lateral spread or spread down to lower lymphatics; this makes sphincter-saving operations more practicable

Blood-borne spread

- Portal vein spreads metastases to the liver
- 30% of patients have liver metastases at presentation
- Also to the lungs (5% of cases), adrenal glands, kidneys and bones

Trans-coelomic spread

- Produces deposits of malignant nodules throughout the peritoneal cavity
- This occurs in 10% of patients after resection
- Spread to the ovaries form metastatic deposits termed 'Krukenberg tumours'

Implantation
This method of spread is possible, although uncommon. Recurrences occur in wounds, suture lines, colostomies and laparoscopy port sites.

Staging

Pathological staging
Colorectal cancers are staged primarily on the pathological characteristics of the resected specimen. Duke's system is the accepted classification in the UK, although it was originally described only for rectal tumours (see table). There are other pathological staging systems, including the TNM system.

Clinical staging
There are three main prognostic groups following surgery:

- **Incurable because of distant metastases**: as shown by histology or imaging
- **Incurable because of residual local disease**: histological examination shows tumour at resection margin of specimen; specimen perforated or adherent to adjacent viscera
- **Curative operation**: in which all demonstrable tumour has been removed

Clinical presentation

- **General effects of malignant disease**: anaemia, anorexia, weight loss
- **Symptoms of secondary disease**:
  liver metastases: jaundice; ascites; hepatomegaly;
  lung metastases: incidental finding on CXR; pleural effusion; recurrent chest infection;
  other: e.g. lymphadenopathy, bone pain

- **Local effects**:
  right colon tumours (usually proliferative, soft and friable): change in bowel habit; altered blood p.r.; right-sided mass; abdominal pain and perforation; more likely than left-sided tumours to be occult and symptomless;
  left colon tumours (usually annular and constricting): change in bowel habit; constipation and obstruction; abdominal colic and perforation; more overt bleeding and mucus p.r.; 25–30% of patients with left colon tumours present as an emergency — usually obstruction or perforation;
  rectal tumours: bleeding is the presenting complaint in 60% of patients; change in bowel habit, including mucus; tenesmus; palpable prolapsing mass; symptoms worse in the morning

Due to these early warning symptoms, rectal tumours are much less likely to present as an emergency. Spread to other pelvic organs is common and can cause fistulae, urinary tract symptoms or bone pain.

Examination
In a patient with suspected colorectal cancer, clinical examination should concentrate on:

- Presence of a mass (either per abdomen or per rectum)
- Evidence of intestinal obstruction
- Evidence of spread (hepatomegaly, ascites, jaundice, supraclavicular lymph nodes)
- General effects of malignancy (e.g. weight loss, anaemia)

Investigations

Sigmoidoscopy: most rectal tumours should be detectable on rigid sigmoidoscopy; the rest of the large bowel must be investigated in order to exclude adenomas or synchronous tumours.

Colonoscopy: a complete investigation of the large bowel.

Double-contrast barium enema: useful for visualizing the right side of the large bowel; the lesion is shown as a filling defect or 'apple core' stricture.

The presence or otherwise of distant metastases can greatly influence the prognosis and hence the surgical management of the patient.

- **Ultrasound**: will reveal metastases in the liver
- **Chest X-ray**: will reveal lung metastases
- **CT scan**: may be useful to show the extent of the tumour, its invasion into local organs and spread to lymph nodes.

Complications of colorectal cancer

Obstruction
More common in the left colonic tumours which tend to be annular and constricting. The luminal contents are also more solid than on the right, predisposing to absolute constipation. A tumour may obstruct by acting as the apex for volvulus or intussusception. Patients present with colicky, central lower abdominal pain, distension and absolute constipation.

Perforation
May occur through a carcinoma or proximal to it. The caecum is the most common area of perforation, especially in the presence of a competent ileocaecal valve. Perforation may result in generalized faecal peritonitis or a localized abscess. Mortality is high and surgical long term cure is much less likely in a perforated carcinoma.

Fistula formation
Direct invasion of a colorectal tumour into a neighbouring organ, such as the bladder or vagina can cause a fistula. Vesicocolic fistulae present with pneumaturia and recurrent urinary tract infections. Rectovaginal fistulae present with faeculent vaginal discharge. A fistula of the transverse colon and the stomach or duodenum may present with faecal vomiting. Fistulae caused by colorectal cancer can be difficult to distinguish from those caused by diverticular disease.

Other complications include:

- Haemorrhage
- Appendicitis (secondary to caecal carcinoma)
- Colocolic intussusception (carcinoma causes 50% of all adult intussusceptions)
- Invasion into adjacent organs

Principles of surgery for colorectal cancer

Principles of surgery for colorectal cancer

- Pre-operative preparation
- In the curable elective case aim for wide resection of tumour with regional lymphatics
- In the obstructed emergency case aim for primary relief of the obstruction followed by elective surgery if necessary
- In the incurable case aim to relieve present or potential obstruction and alleviate symptoms
- Post-operative care is vital

Preoperative preparation

- **Optimize fitness**: the patient's general condition may influence the choice of procedure; liaise with medical/anaesthetic staff
- **Define extent of tumour**: the presence of distant metastases may influence the choice of surgical procedure
- **Imaging**: of the lung and liver; the extent of local spread should also be quantified as pre-operative adjuvant therapy to de-bulk the tumour may be useful
- **Bowel preparation**: bowel lumen bacteria are the chief source of sepsis in bowel surgery. In elective cases, three days of a liquid-only diet and two sachets of sodium picosulphate in the 24 hours before the surgery is one regime commonly used. In emergency, obstructed cases, on-table lavage may be performed.
- **Prophylactic antibiotics**: metronidazole and cephalosporin at induction and for at least three doses post-operatively
- **Counselling and consent**: the diagnosis, results of investigations, planned procedure, possible outcomes and complications and risks of mortality should be made clear to patients and, if they agree, their relatives. The chances of a colostomy should always be explained, and if it is thought to be likely, and time allows, a stoma nurse should be involved in the pre-operative counselling.

In the curable elective case, one should aim for wide resection of the tumour, together with the regional lymphatics.

- **Non-obstructed cancer of the right colon**: treated by right hemicolectomy with primary anastomosis (see Figure A opposite)
- **Non-obstructed cancer of the left colon**: treated by left hemicolectomy with primary anastomosis (see Figure B)
- **Non-obstructed cancer of the transverse colon**: is treated by a transverse colectomy (rarely) or an extended right or left hemicolectomy
- **Non-obstructed cancer of the sigmoid colon**: treated by sigmoid colectomy (see Figure C)
- **Non-obstructed low rectal tumours**: usually treated by abdomino-perineal excision and end ileostomy (see Figure D) — selected tumours or small tumours associated with liver metastases may be treated by transanal excision
- **Non-obstructed high rectal tumours**: are treated by an anterior resection.

The advent of stapling devices has meant that lower tumours are able to be resected with successful anastomoses. The discrediting of the '5 cm' rule means that a 5 cm longitudinal clearance is no longer considered necessary, since tumours which have spread further than 1 cm usually have distant metastases.

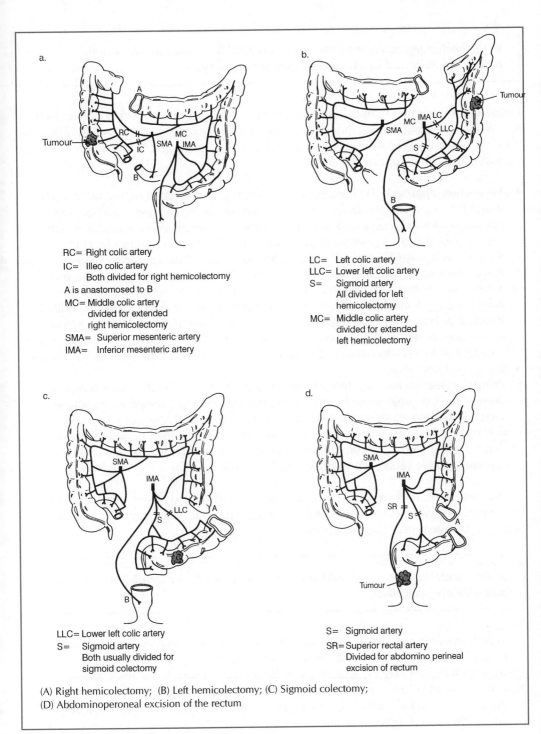

a.

RC= Right colic artery
IC= Illeo colic artery
   Both divided for right hemicolectomy
A is anastomosed to B
MC= Middle colic artery
   divided for extended
   right hemicolectomy
SMA= Superior mesenteric artery
IMA= Inferior mesenteric artery

b.

LC= Left colic artery
LLC= Lower left colic artery
S= Sigmoid artery
   All divided for left
   hemicolectomy
MC= Middle colic artery
   divided for extended
   left hemicolectomy

c.

LLC= Lower left colic artery
S= Sigmoid artery
   Both usually divided for
   sigmoid colectomy

d.

S= Sigmoid artery
SR= Superior rectal artery
   Divided for abdomino perineal
   excision of rectum

(A) Right hemicolectomy; (B) Left hemicolectomy; (C) Sigmoid colectomy;
(D) Abdominoperoneal excision of the rectum

Large bowel resection for cancer

> **In the obstructed emergency case, one should aim for primary relief of the obstruction followed by elective surgery if necessary.**

Right-sided obstructing tumours are often suitable for an emergency right hemicolectomy and primary anastomosis — this is because the small intestine is not usually distended proximal to the ileocaecal valve. The management of obstructing left-sided tumours is more controversial. Three approaches are available:

- **Three-stage approach**: (1) Primary decompression; (2) Resection of tumour at a later date; (3) Closure of colostomy. This has the advantage of a simple initial life-saving operation allowing the patient to recover before the more extensive resection which can be undertaken by a senior surgeon on an elective list. Unfortunately, cumulative mortality is about 20% and 50% of patients never have their colostomy closed.
- **Hartmann's procedure**: primary resection with delayed anastomosis. Approach achieves dual objectives of relieving the obstruction and resecting the tumour while avoiding the potential complications of an anastomosis under sub-optimal conditions. Reversal of Hartmann's has a high complication rate and 10% mortality, therefore many patients end up with a permanent colostomy. Primary resection and formation of a mucous fistula or double-barrelled colostomy (Paul Mikulicz procedure) can simplify the second operation.
- **Primary resection and anastomosis**: this approach ensures the definitive operation is done at the first laparotomy but the anastomosis is done in sub-optimal conditions. On-table lavage and subtotal colectomy can reduce the incidence of sepsis and discrepancy between dilated proximal bowel end and collapsed distal bowel end. A defunctioning loop ileostomy can give the anastomosis time to heal and involves a relatively simple procedure to reverse it.

Obstructing rectal tumours are comparatively rare and not usually as curable so primary decompression with a colostomy is often most appropriate until the tumour can be assessed and a management plan decided upon.

> **In the incurable case one should aim to relieve present or potential obstruction and alleviate symptoms.**

- Resection of the primary tumour offers the best palliation. It relieves obstruction, reduces the risk of future obstruction and reduces future metastatic spread.
- Bypass procedure may be appropriate if the primary tumour is not resectable.
- Defunctioning colostomy is less traumatic and relieves obstruction in frail patients.
- Radiotherapy and chemotherapy may give temporary alleviation. Radiotherapy is particularly useful in rectal tumours.

- Stenting is becoming more widely practised in low obstructing lesions.
- Local techniques for rectal cancer include electrocoagulation, contact irradiation, local excision and laser treatment.

Post-operative care after colonic or rectal resection is important.

- **Hydration and monitoring electrolytes**: IV fluids needed until normal oral intake has resumed; hypokalaemia due to diarrhoea or high stoma output should be avoided to minimize ileus
- **Prophylactic antibiotics**: three post-operative doses of cefuroxime and metronidazole are often given
- **Analgesia**: patient-controlled analgesia, epidural or regular opiates are important to minimize post-operative pain
- **Catheterization**: to monitor urine output and avoid urinary retention in the post-operative period; beware denervated bladder which leads to more longstanding retention
- **Careful nursing and dressing of wound**: patients should be nursed in a low sitting position, except for after an abdomino-perineal resection in which case they are nursed on the side. The wound should be carefully observed and kept clean and dry. Abdominal sutures usually can be removed at days 10–14.
- **Physiotherapy**: chest physiotherapy to prevent atelectasis; early mobilization to prevent urinary retention and deep vein thrombosis
- **Deep vein thrombosis prophylaxis**: subcutaneous heparin and anti-thromboembolic stockings
- **Care of colostomy**: initially an ileostomy drainable bag over the colostomy; stoma therapist must be involved to fit permanent device; patients taught how to care for stoma
- **Counselling and informing patients**: histology of specimen, what was done at the operation, plans for future surgery and prognosis should be explained to the patient and relative; follow-up should be arranged (see p. 513)

Post-operative complications

General complications include:

- Cardiorespiratory
- Deep vein thrombosis
- Pulmonary embolus
- Post-operative renal failure

Specific complications include the following:

- **Anastomotic leak**: typically occurs 7–10 days post-operatively. Along with cardiorespiratory problems, this is the major cause of post-operative mortality. The risk is higher in low anastomoses. The surgeon and surgical technique are other major factors. The results of anastomotic leak or dehiscence are pelvic abscess, peritonitis, fistulation or death.
- **Anastomotic stricture**: caused by either recurrence or fibrosis and tends to present later
- **Wound infection and dehiscence**: as with any laparotomy, the wound is less likely to heal if the patient is elderly with co-morbidity and unwell at the time of surgery. Risk of wound infection is higher in colorectal surgery and is minimized by bowel preparation, pre-operative optimization of the patient, prophylactic antibiotics and meticulous technique. Perineal wound is especially prone to infection, abscess, pressure necrosis and primary or secondary haemorrhage.
- **Intestinal obstruction**: due to herniation of small bowel through lateral space; adherence of bowel to wound closure; adhesions between loops of bowel; oedema of colostomy; anastomotic stricture
- **Urinary retention**: due to post-operative pain; prostatic obstruction; denervation of bladder
- **Injury of urinary tract**: ureteric injury leading to hydronephrosis, pyonephrosis, urinary fistula. Bladder injury during anterior dissection. Urethral injury during perineal dissection may lead to fistula or stricture.
- **Sexual dysfunction**: impotence due to injury of nervi erigentes more common after abdomino-perineal excision (50%) than after anterior resection (20%). Failure of ejaculation due to damage to presacral nerve. Dyspareunia in females due to fibrosis around the vagina.
- **'Phantom rectum'**: after abdomino-perineal resection, this distressing sensation of an uncomfortable rectum still present occurs in 50% of patients.

Colostomy complications
(See Section 3.3, p. 344):

- Bleeding
- Prolapse
- Retraction
- Stenosis
- Skin excoriation
- Parastomal hernia
- Fistulation

Altered bowel function

Bowel frequency and incontinence are more likely the lower the colorectal anastomosis; 70% of patients with a coloanal anastomosis have normal continence. Function tends to improve with time, up to one year after the operation.

Results of surgery for colorectal cancer

- 70–80% of colonic cancers are amenable to resection
- 20–30% of patients have disseminated disease at presentation
- Post-operative five-year survival rate is 50–70% overall, but this varies depending on several factors

A worse prognosis is expected in:

- High Duke's stage
- Emergency presentation, especially perforation
- Young patient
- Short history of disease
- Development of complications
- Low rectal tumours
- Anaplastic tumours

Local recurrence is thought to be due to:

- Lateral spread beyond excision margin
- Spread into mesorectum
- Residual cancer in regional lymph nodes
- High Duke's stage
- Low rectal tumours

80% of local recurrence occurs within two years post-operatively. Local recurrence presents as pelvic pain, leg pain, urinary symptoms, changes in bowel habit or recurrence seen at follow-up endoscopy. Distant metastases are most commonly seen in the liver but also in the lungs.

Adjuvant therapy for colorectal cancer

Radiotherapy

Radiotherapy is used for rectal cancer rather than colonic cancer because there is:

- A defined anatomical location
- Less risk of small bowel injury

Radiotherapy reduces local recurrence but does not affect distant metastases or survival.

Radiotherapy only benefits those with a high risk of local recurrence and does not have benefit in early disease which has been adequately resected. The advantages and disadvantages of pre-operative and post-operative radiotherapy are shown in the table below.

Radiotherapy instead of surgery may be suitable if patient is unfit for surgery and symptomatic (e.g. with pain, imminent obstruction, bleeding or mucus from a low rectal tumour).

ADVANTAGES AND DISADVANTAGES OF PRE-OPERATIVE AND POST-OPERATIVE RADIOTHERAPY

Pre-operative radiotherapy	Post-operative radiotherapy
Advantages	
Reduces local recurrence rates	Reduces local recurrence rates
Converts an inoperable bulky tumour to an operable one, increasing chance of curative resection	Pathology and stage of tumour are known so patients with early disease which is completely resected, can be excluded
Tumour is easily targeted and small bowel injury can be avoided	Does not delay surgery so is appropriate in emergency (e.g. obstructed cases)
If surgery is done at an appropriate time afterwards, post-operative complications are not increased	
Short course is effective	
Irradiated bowel is then resected	
Compliance is high	
Disadvantages	
Does not prolong survival or reduce distant metastases	Does not prolong survival or reduce metastases
Patients may be included who turn out at laparotomy to have early disease, although no benefit is shown for these patients	Small bowel is more likely to be in the field so injury is more common
Post-operative morbidity, wound sepsis and mortality is higher if surgery is not done soon after radiotherapy	Course is prolonged (4/5 weeks) and may be delayed by surgical complications
	Irradiated bowel (including anastomosis) is left in and may develop radiation colitis
	Compliance is low due to post-operative morbidity, patient frailty etc.

Chemotherapy

The National Cancer Institute in the USA has advocated that all patients with Duke's stage 'C' colon cancer should be treated with 5-Fluorouracil (5FU) and levamisole for one year after surgery. This regime has been shown to reduce both recurrence (by 40%) and mortality (by 33%). A 5FU and folinic acid combination has also been used. The QUASAR study in the UK is investigating the benefits of post-operative chemotherapy in Duke's stage 'B' cancer. Other methods of administering chemotherapeutic agents are being studied (e.g. intraportal vein infusion at laparotomy (the AXIS trial) and hepatic artery infusion).

Follow-up for colorectal cancer

The aims of follow-up after surgery for colorectal cancer are to:

- Check for post-operative complications
- Identify recurrence or metastatic disease
- Detect metachronous tumours
- Ensure appropriate adjuvant therapy has been performed

There are several methods for identifying recurrence or metastatic disease:

- **Endoscopy**: the most common method with regular colonoscopy recommended to detect recurrence or metachronous tumours. Barium enema is an alternative.
- **Imaging of the liver or pelvis by CT or ultrasound**: can be useful but is not done routinely in all centres
- **Carcinoembryonic Antigen (CEA)**: a tumour marker which can be used to predict recurrence

Some centres recommend a 'second look' laparotomy if CEA levels become raised after regular measurements. Clinical review, including questioning about bowel habit, pain, jaundice, etc. and examination of scar and abdomen for nodules, masses, ascites or hepatomegaly should be done but is not very sensitive. Liver resection may be possible for patient with metastases and this is more successful if detected early by liver ultrasound or carcinoembryonic antigen.

Screening for colorectal cancer

Regular screening by colonoscopy is advocated in high-risk groups, such as patients with:

- Active longstanding ulcerative colitis
- Familial cancer syndromes, such as FAP and HNPCC or strong family history
- Previous cancer of the colon
- Previous adenomatous polyps

Sporadic cancers account for about 90% of all cases of colorectal cancer, and it has been suggested that the general population should be screened over a certain age. The two methods now available for screening are **faecal occult blood test** (FOBT) and **flexible sigmoidoscopy**. It is generally thought that colonoscopy is too expensive with too low acceptability to patients to be a good screening tool.

Faecal occult blood testing (FOBT)

In one FOBT, a sample of faeces is smeared on a test card impregnated with guaiac. Hydrogen peroxide is added in the laboratory and a colour change indicates the presence of blood. Patients who test positive are then sent for colonoscopy or barium studies. There are several different FOBTs and they are variously sensitive and specific. In general, sensitivity is low — FOBT fails to detect 20–50% of cancers and 80% of polyps. Specificity is also low — false positive results are yielded by other conditions, such as haemorrhoids, peptic ulcer or anal fissures and by ingestion of meat and some vegetables. There is no associated morbidity but the test can be unacceptable to some patients. Some studies have shown a 33% reduction in colorectal cancer-related mortality, although these have been FOBT with high false positives and, therefore, high negative colonoscopy rates.

Flexible sigmoidoscopy

Several studies are looking at the practicality of using flexible sigmoidoscopy as a screening tool for colorectal cancer in the general population. This is more expensive than FOBT, has a lower acceptability to patients and has a small associated morbidity. It can only screen the distal bowel, but 70% of colon cancers occur within the reach of a flexible sigmoidoscope. It is highly sensitive, especially compared with FOBT. It can endoscopically remove polyps and biopsy tumours. Other pathologies, such as inflammatory bowel disease, can be diagnosed.

12.6 Other colorectal conditions

Vascular malformations

Vascular malformations can cause colonic bleeding. The two main types of vascular malformations in the colon are **angiodysplasia** and **haemangiomas**.

Angiodysplasia

Colonic angiodysplasia consists of small, submucosal vascular swellings of unknown aetiology and unclear histology. They may occur sporadically, or in association with hereditary telangiectasia of the skin and mouth in Osler–Weber–Rendu disease. There is an association with aortic valve disease. Bleeding p.r. can present as anaemia, positive FOBTs, recurrent small bleeds or a torrential acute bleed. The lesions are more common in the right colon in elderly patients. Diagnosis is by colonoscopy showing spider naevi-like lesions. In major haemorrhage selective mesenteric angiography shows a characteristic 'blush' lesion. Coagulation via colonoscope may be curative for small lesions. Extensive troublesome areas of angiodysplasia may need resection.

Haemangiomas

These are usually cavernous or giant haemangiomas and involve the whole thickness of the bowel wall. They commonly occur in the rectum and present with bleeding p.r. Colonoscopy or angiography can reveal the lesion. Electrocoagulation or sclerotherapy may control symptoms. Surgery may be required for more extensive lesions.

Ischaemic disease of the large bowel

Ischaemic bowel disease is becoming more frequent with an ageing population. The causes are listed below. Patients can present with transient episodes of abdominal pain (clinically similar to diverticular disease or gastroenteritis), or with ischaemic strictures usually near the splenic flexure. Treatment in mild cases is essentially supportive, with the diagnosis made by barium enema or colonoscopy. Surgery is rarely needed unless the stricture causes an obstruction.

More typically a middle-aged or elderly patient presents with acute abdominal pain, rapid deterioration and shock. The clinical signs of generalized peritonitis (abdominal distension and systemic shock) usually indicate laparotomy at which the diagnosis will be made. Other investigations are notoriously non-specific.

- AXR may be normal at first and later show progressive dilatation
- Blood tests show leucocytosis, raised packed cell volume, metabolic acidosis and raised amylase and transaminases
- Barium enema and angiography are of no value in these severe cases

Treatment in severe cases involves aggressive resuscitation and laparotomy with resection and exteriorization of the bowel end. Primary anastomosis is contraindicated. There is a high mortality.

Causes of ischaemic disease of the large bowel

- Spontaneous arterial thrombosis
  (e.g. atheroma of inferior mesenteric artery. Can be precipitated by embolus or low flow states.)
- Small vessel disease
  (e.g. polyarteritis, Buerger's disease, systemic lupus erythematosus (SLE), atheromatous disease, diabetes)
- Venous occlusion
  (e.g. extensive venous thrombosis — hypercoagulable state or idiopathic)

- Iatrogenic ischaemia
  (e.g. ligation of inferior mesenteric artery at its origin during aneurysm repair or colonic surgery)
- Low flow states
  (e.g. sepsis, heart failure, shock)
- Intestinal obstruction
  (e.g. obstructing carcinoma)
- Idiopathic infarction

Irradiation bowel disease

Radiotherapy for uterine or bladder cancer can result in irradiation bowel disease, the effects of which are summarized below. Rectal resection and coloanal anastomosis may be successful if the sphincter has not been damaged and recurrent tumour has been excluded.

Effects of irradiation bowel disease

- Ulceration
- Fistula formation
  into vagina
  into bladder

- Stricture formation
- Radiation proctitis
  Bloody diarrhoea

Infective bowel disease

Although strictly speaking a medical complaint, infective bowel disease can present as abdominal pain, change in bowel habit, diarrhoea and bleeding p.r. It is, therefore, important to be aware of the differential diagnosis in order to avoid inappropriate surgery.

Amoebic dysentery

Caused by protozoan *Entamoeba histolytica*. Pathology is colonization of colonic wall causing ulceration. Clinical presentation includes:

- Fluctuating, bleeding diarrhoea
- Chronic dysentery
- Amoebic appendicitis

Ulcers may be mistaken for carcinoma on colonoscopy. Fresh stool microscopy shows protozoa. Treatment is antibiotics and amoebicides.

Bacillary dysentery (shigellosis)

Caused by endotoxin-producing Shigella bacteria. Pathology is infection of colon, leading to coagulopathy or haemolytic anaemia due to endotoxins. Clinical presentation includes:

- Abdominal pain and diarrhoea
- Systemic sepsis, coagulopathy and haemolytic anaemia
- Epidemic disease usually with a contact history

Colonoscopy shows discrete ulcers, inflammation and formation of a membrane. Diagnosis is by stool culture. Treatment is supportive with antibiotics reserved for severe cases.

Schistosomiasis

Caused by Schistosoma trematode worm which is carried by the freshwater snail. The trematode burrows into the skin, enters the blood supply and grows into egg-laying adults. Symptoms depend on the site of the eggs which can be the bowel, lung, brain, spinal cord or urinary tract. Colonoscopy shows ulceration and barium enema shows an immobile, regular colon. Repeated stool microscopy may show the parasites. Rectal biopsy is often diagnostic. Treatment is by the drug praziquantel.

Pseudomembranous colitis

Caused by *Clostridium difficile* following the use of antibiotics, such as clindomycin, ampicillin or tetracycline. The pathology is overgrowth of the bowel with clostridium which produces an inflammatory toxin. The clinical picture varies from diarrhoea to severe colitis. Colonoscopy shows epithelial necrosis and a white pseudomembrane. Clostridium toxin can be measured in stool. Rectal biopsy shows the characteristic histology of a pseudomembrane. Treatment is vancomycin or metronidazole.

Other colonic infections

Campylobactor enterocolitis and *Yersinia enterocolitis* predominantly involve the small intestine but may occasionally cause colitis.

Intussusception is discussed in Chapter 3, *Head, Neck, Endocrine and Paediatric*, Section 15.9. Diverticulitis is discussed in Section 6.2, p. 380. Large bowel obstruction is discussed in Section 10, p. 432. Caecal and sigmoid volvulus are discussed in Section 10.4, p. 441.

13. ANAL AND PERI-ANAL CONDITIONS

13.1 Anatomy and physiology of the rectum and anus

Anatomy of the rectum and anus

Rectum

The rectum commences at the level of the third piece of the sacrum where it is continuous with the sigmoid colon. It is about 13 cm long and ends where the longitudinal muscle coats are replaced by the sphincters of the anal canal (the anorectal junction) at the pelvic floor. There is a complete outer layer of longitudinal muscle over the rectum — the taeniae coli coalesce. There are no appendices epiploicae.

The rectum has no intraperitoneal mesentery. Peritoneum covers the upper third of the rectum at the front and sides, the middle third only at the front. The lower third is below the level of the peritoneum which is reflected to form the rectovesical or rectouterine pouch.

Posterolateral relations at risk in rectal operations include the sympathetic trunk, pelvic and splanchnic nerves, the rectal vessels and the anterior rami of the lower three sacral and coccygeal nerves. The blood supply is derived from:

- The superior rectal artery (the terminal branch of the inferior mesenteric artery)
- The median sacral artery (from the internal iliac artery)
- The middle rectal artery (from the internal iliac artery)
- The inferior rectal arteries (from the internal pudendal branch of the internal iliac artery)

All these vessels supply all layers of the rectum and anastomose freely. Veins correspond to the arteries and anastomose freely with one another; this is a portosystemic anastomosis.

Lymphatics run with the branches of the superior and middle rectal and the median sacral arteries. The three main groups of nodes are along the:

- Median sacral artery in the hollow of the sacrum
- Middle rectal artery on the side wall of the pelvis
- Inferior mesenteric artery and upwards to the para-aortic nodes

The sympathetic nerve supply is derived by branches from the hypogastric and coeliac plexuses. The parasympathetic supply is from S2 S3 S4 by the pelvic splanchnic nerves

Anus

The anal canal is the last 4 cm of the alimentary tract. There are two layers of circular muscle making up the wall, an internal anal sphincter of smooth muscle and an external anal sphincter of skeletal muscle. The intersphincteric groove is the area between the external and internal sphincters (see figure opposite). It used to be called 'Hilton's white line'. The anorectal junction is at a 90° angle at the pelvic floor where the puborectalis muscle forms a sling around the bowel and is continuous with the external sphincter. The mucous membrane in the anal canal forms horizontal folds called anal valves above which submucosal anal glands secrete mucus. Infection in these glands produces anal abscesses and fistulae.

The pectinate or dentate line is just above the level of the anal valves, some way above the intersphincteric groove (see figure opposite). The colorectum is lined with columnar epithelium as far as the dentate line in the middle of the anal canal, where sensitive squamous epithelium takes over. The pecten is the area between the dentate line and the intersphincteric groove where the epithelium is transitional. Above the dentate line the mucosa is derived from endoderm, below it is derived from ectoderm. This is relevant for blood and nerve supplies and lymph drainage.

Blood supply is, as for the rectum, from the superior, middle and inferior rectal vessels and the median sacral arteries. The veins correspond to the arteries and the site of the portosystemic anastomosis is in the upper third of the anal canal. The rectal venous plexus forms three cushions in the 3, 7 and 11 o'clock positions which assist the sphincter in maintaining watertight closure of the canal. Haemorrhoids are varicosities at these sites.

Lymph drainage from above the dentate line drains to the internal iliac nodes and from below the dentate line drains to the palpable superficial inguinal group. Sympathetic nerve fibres from the pelvic plexus cause contraction of the internal sphincter. Parasympathetic impulses from the pelvic splanchnic relax the internal sphincter. The external sphincter is supplied by somatic inferior rectal branches (S2) of the pudendal nerves. These nerves also provide sensory supply for the lower end of the canal which is very sensitive.

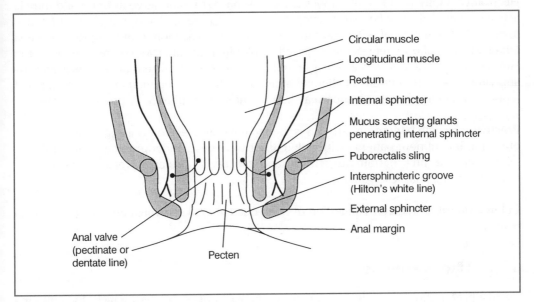

Coronal section of the anal canal

Physiology of the rectum and the anus

Defaecation
The rectum is normally empty until left colonic motility is enhanced (e.g. by awakening or eating breakfast). Faeces enter the rectum and the person is called to stool. Anorectal sensation permits discrimination of solids from gas. Sitting or crouching straightens out the anorectal angle allowing faeces to be passed to the anal canal. The anal sphincter is under voluntary control with a normal pressure of 45–90 mmHg which can be doubled voluntarily (squeeze pressure). If the passage of stool is not voluntarily stopped, faeces may be passed from as far as the splenic flexure. The diaphragm, abdominal wall and levator ani contract to aid defaecation. The average daily volume passed is 150 ml. The rectum can accommodate 400 ml maintaining a low rectal pressure. Chronic tolerance of faeces in the rectum may be associated with severe constipation.

Anorectal function tests

Assessment of anorectal physiology helps with the diagnosis and management of patients with faecal incontinence, sphincter injuries, rectal prolapse and abnormalities with defaecation.

Anal manometry uses an air or water-filled balloon system to measure resting (internal sphincter) and squeeze (external sphincter) pressures; 24-hour ambulatory manometry can be performed.

Rectal compliance is measured by filling a rectal balloon and recording the volume and pressure at first sensation and noting the maximum capacity the patient will tolerate.

Electromyography with fine electrodes assesses sphincter motor nerve function and muscle activity. Concentric needle electromyography can map the sphincter muscle in a traumatized anus. The rectoanal reflex test looks at the normal reduction in resting pressure when filling a rectal balloon, representing the reflex inhibition of sphincter contraction (absent in Hirschsprung's disease), rectal prolapse and incontinence. Anal sensation is measured by applying an electric current or thermal stimulus to the anal epithelium until the patient reports sensation. Loss of sensation may be present in incontinence or post-operatively.

Proctography with barium suspensions is used to measure the anorectal angle which may be obtuse in incontinent patients with pelvic floor weakness. Videoproctogram records the expulsion of a thick barium suspension and can reveal prolapse, rectocoeles and the function of ileo anal reservoirs.

Colonic transit is studied by ingestion of radio-opaque markers which are viewed by serial AXRs.

13.2 Haemorrhoids

Internal haemorrhoids or 'piles' are varices of the superior rectal veins which drain into the inferior mesenteric vein. Normally this venous plexus helps to form the anal cushions which aid continence and are found at the 3, 7, and 11 o'clock positions in lithotomy above the dentate line. As these internal piles enlarge they can prolapse through the anus.

'External haemorrhoids' is a non-specific term that should not be used. It is applied to several conditions:

- **Perianal haematoma** or **thrombosed perianal varices**: thrombosis of the external haemorrhoidal plexus beneath the skin of the distal anal canal below the dentate line
- **Sentinel pile**: is a tag of skin at the outer edge of a fissure *in ano*
- **Perianal skin tags**: are usually formed by resolved prolapsed internal haemorrhoids

Classification

Different texts use different methods of classification but this is one common classification:

- **First-degree haemorrhoids**: confined to anal canal — bleed but do not prolapse
- **Second-degree haemorrhoids**: prolapse on defaecation — reduce spontaneously or may need digital replacement
- **Third-degree haemorrhoids**: remain persistently prolapsed outside the anal margin

Predisposing factors

- Idiopathic
- Pregnancy
- Cardiac failure
- Excessive use of purgatives
- Chronic constipation
- Portal hypertension (rare)

Clinical features

Symptoms

- Noted incidentally on examination (i.e. symptomless)
- Bleeding: painless; fresh blood; on paper or splash into pan; around motion not mixed in
- May produce anaemia but this is rare and another cause should be sought
- Mucus discharge
- Pruritus
- Prolapse: on defaecation; on exercise; needing digital replacement; permanently prolapsed
- Thrombosis
- Painful swelling

Signs

- Skin tags may be present around anus
- Prolapsed piles, or piles prolapsing on straining. Prolapsed piles are usually at the 3, 7 and 11 o'clock positions. Often include tissue from above and below the dentate line. Usually dark red or purple covered with pale areas of squamous metaplasia. It is important to differentiate piles from a prolapsed rectum (see later).
- On proctoscopy dark haemorrhoidal tissue is seen
- Piles may flop into the lumen of the scope
- Abdomen should also be examined for pelvic mass or enlarged liver

Differential diagnosis

- Fissure *in ano*
- Perianal haematoma due to trauma
- Perianal or ischiorectal abscess
- Tumour of the anal margin
- Prolapsing rectal polyp

Management

Exclusion of other pathology
Rectal bleeding or unexplained anaemia should not be attributed to haemorrhoids unless other, more serious, causes are excluded. Depending on the symptoms and age of the patient, sigmoidoscopy, colonoscopy, gastroscopy or contrast studies may be appropriate. Predisposing causes, such as pelvic malignancy or an abdominal mass, should also be excluded by careful examination.

Conservative treatment
Asymptomatic piles should not be treated. First-degree piles may respond to increasing fibre in the diet or prescribing bulking agents. Patients may not want intervention once they are reassured that their symptoms are not due to anything more serious than piles. Thrombosed strangulated piles may be treated conservatively with analgesia, bed rest, elevated legs and an ice-pack or by surgery.

Injection sclerotherapy
Injection of a sclerosant via a proctoscope can be done as an outpatient. This is suitable for first- and second-degree piles; 2–3 ml of 5% phenol in almond oil is injected into each pile above the dentate line. The injection is into the submucosal layer. Further injections may be required. The procedure should be painless and follow-up should be arranged for six weeks.

Rubber band ligation
Strangulation of piles with a rubber band applied via a proctoscope can also be done as an outpatient. Various methods, including using forceps or a suction device to grasp the haemorrhoid can be used. No more than three bands should be applied as an outpatient at one time. Sloughing off of the strangulated pile may be accompanied by bleeding which the patient should be warned about. This method is suitable for second-degree piles. The patient should be reviewed in six weeks.

Lord's procedure
Manual dilatation of the anus under general anaesthetic involves the insertion of four fingers into the anal canal for four minutes. This procedure has largely fallen into disrepute due to the high incidence of subsequent incontinence of flatus or even faeces. Some consultants still recommend it for second- and third-degree piles.

Surgery

Only about 5% of piles need to be treated by haemorrhoidectomy. These are large, third-degree piles which may straddle the dentate line or be too large to band. The most common method is the Milligan–Morgan haemorrhoidectomy which involves dissection, transfixion and excision of the three main piles, preserving the intervening skin and leaving the wounds open. Thrombosed, strangulated piles which present as an emergency may be treated conservatively (see above) or may be treated by immediate haemorrhoidectomy. Acute perianal haematoma may be treated conservatively in the same way, or may be incised and evacuated under local or general anaesthetic.

Post-operative complications

Acute retention of urine
Due to post-operative pain.

Stricture
Occurs if the surgeon has failed to leave a bridge of epithelium between each excised haemorrhoid.

Haemorrhage
Bleeding may be reactionary within 24 hours of the operation. Secondary bleeding, often due to infection, occurs on post-operative days 7 or 8. Bleeding may not be apparent externally if blood fills the rectum. Patient may need transfusion, examination under anaesthetic or packing of anal canal.

13.3 Anal fissures

Anal fissures (or fissure *in ano*) are common. M = F/30–50 years. The lesion is a longitudinal tear of the squamous lined lower half of the anal canal from the anal verge towards the dentate line. Most fissures lie in the mid-line posteriorly, but anterior fissures are seen in women. Aetiology is unknown, both constipation and high sphincter pressures are more common in patients with an anal fissure, but these might be the result of the fissure rather than the cause. Fissures are the most common anal lesion in Crohn's disease and may often be multiple in these patients.

Clinical features

- Pain on defaecation (90% of patients) often lasting for 1–2 hours afterwards
- Minor bright red bleeding on the paper after wiping
- Constipation, probably secondary to pain, in 20% of patients
- Pruritus occurs in 50% of patients
- Watery discharge in 20%

On inspection, the split in the anal canal can be seen when the skin is gently retracted. A sentinel pile occurs when the skin at the base of the fissure becomes oedematous and hypertrophied. Rectal examination may be impossible but it is useful to assess degree of spasm

Management

- Glyceryl trinitrate paste has recently been shown to be the best first-line treatment for anal fissures
- Dilatation of the anus under general anaesthetic is effective but can lead to incontinence of flatus or faeces
- Lateral sphincterotomy involves the division of the distal internal sphincter up to the dentate line lateral to the anal orifice, leaving the sphincter undisturbed; it can also lead to incontinence
- Long-term high fibre diet should always be advised
- Rectal examination and proctoscopy to exclude an anal cancer is mandatory, and may necessitate a general anaesthetic if the fissure is still painful after initial treatment

13.4 Anorectal abscesses

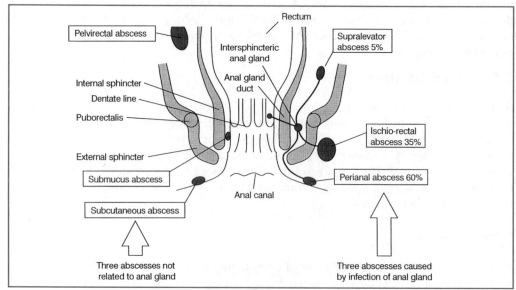

Coronal section of anal canal showing causes of anorectal abscesses

The most common and most clinically important anorectal abscess is that caused by infection of the anal glands.

Other anorectal abscesses include:

* **Subcutaneous/perianal abscess**: results from infection of a hair follicle, sebaceous gland or perianal haematoma. The pus will grow skin flora and not enterococci.
* **Submucous abscess**: results from an infected fissure or laceration of the anal canal or infection after injection of a haemorrhoid
* **Pelvirectal abscess**: results from spread from a pelvic abscess. Relatively rare.

Pathogenesis

Apart from the abscesses described above, most anorectal abscesses are the result of infection of one of the 10–12 anal glands. Since the gland body lies in the inter-sphincteric space, this is where the abscess usually starts. As the abscess expands, the pus may track longitudinally to present as a perianal, ischiorectal or supralevator abscess (see figure opposite).

Tracking can also occur circumferentially leading to a 'horseshoe' extension. This can be at the level of the intersphincteric space, the supralevator space or (most commonly) the ischiorectal space. A chronic intersphincteric abscess may occur if the cavity becomes walled-off by fibrosis.

Clinical features

* Pain: severe and worse on defaecation
* Fever and inguinal lymphadenopathy
* Swelling and redness: may be absent

It may not be possible to do a rectal examination until the patient is under general anaesthetic. It is important to determine whether there have been any previous episodes, or if the patient has any associated conditions, such as inflammatory bowel disease, hidradenitis suppurativa or tuberculosis.

Treatment

An abscess should be incised and drained under general anaesthetic. Antibiotics are unlikely to abort the infection once the symptoms have been present for 24 hours. The procedure is performed as follows.

Surgical procedure
The patient is in lithotomy position under general anaesthetic.

* Sigmoidoscopy is performed to exclude inflammatory bowel disease
* Proctoscopy is performed to look for an internal opening

- Abscess is drained by an incision over the point of maximal tenderness (usually in the perineum)
- Loculi are broken down with a finger
- Pus is sent for culture and sensitivity
- Abscess cavity is deroofed by removing a disk of skin to prevent early closure of the wound
- Cavity is then packed with a ribbon gauze, usually soaked in betadine or proflavin

Antibiotics should only be given to patients at high risk of infection, such as diabetics and the immunocompromised. It is inadvisable to probe for, or lay open, a fistula at this stage since the anatomy may not be easily identified and a false passage may be created.

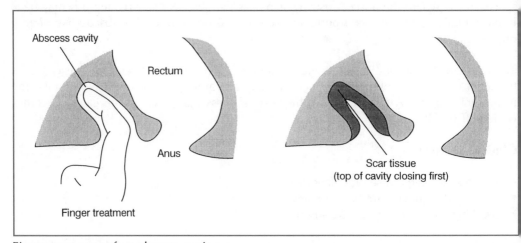

Finger treatment of an abscess cavity

Post-operative care
The pack is changed after 24 hours with analgesia. Some surgeons recommend finger treatment to keep the cavity open in preference to gauze packing (see figure above). The patient may be discharged when the wound can be managed at home.

Follow-up
If an associated fistula is suspected, a routine examination under anaesthetic 10 days later to look for it should be arranged. Factors suggesting an associated fistula include:

- A recurrent abscess
- Growth of enteric rather than a cutaneous organism in the pus culture
- Pus draining from an internal opening seen on proctoscopy

Chronic intersphincteric abscess

Chronic intersphincteric abscess is a separate pathological entity from anorectal abscess.

- Occurs when an intersphincteric abscess cavity becomes walled-off by fibrosis and does not track to the exterior
- May remain dormant for long periods with acute exacerbations
- Clinical presentation is episodes of anal pain without evident discharge, redness or swelling
- Pain usually resolves spontaneously after a few days
- Internal opening lies posteriorly in the mid-line in 66% of cases

The abscess is identified on bidigital palpation and is usually tender and about 1 cm in diameter. In cases where the internal opening is evident, a probe can be passed into the abscess which can be laid open. Alternatively, the abscess can be dissected out.

13.5 Anorectal fistulae

A fistula is an abnormal communication between two epithelialized surfaces.

- 80% of recurrent anorectal abscesses are associated with a fistula
- Most fistulae start as an abscess, others develop insidiously or are due to Crohn's disease, trauma, tuberculosis or carcinoma

Pathology

A fistula *in ano* has an internal opening (usually single) and an external opening (which may be multiple) connected by the primary track. The internal opening is usually at the level of the anal glands and, in 33% of cases, is tiny or stenosed. The track of most fistulae runs below the puborectalis and is more straightforward to treat. In complex fistulae, secondary tracks may run in the supralevator space or within the ischiorectal fossa. Fistulae with a main track running above the puborectalis are more difficult to treat.

Clinical features

- Intermittent acute abscess formation
- Discharge of pus from the external opening
- Rectal examination reveals induration around the tracks and abscesses
- The primary track is identified by the presence of the internal opening usually felt as an area of induration at the level of the anal crypts
- In 66% of patients, the internal opening lies in the mid-line posteriorly
- In the remainder, the internal opening lies in the anterior quadrant

Lateral openings are very rare in fistulae not associated with Crohn's disease. Goodsall's rule (shown in the figure below) usually applies. The presence of secondary tracks should be checked for by palpating the levator ani above the anorectal junction.

Features of a complex fistula include:

- Recurrent trouble after surgery
- Multiple external openings
- Induration felt above puborectalis
- Probe from external opening passes upwards instead of to anus

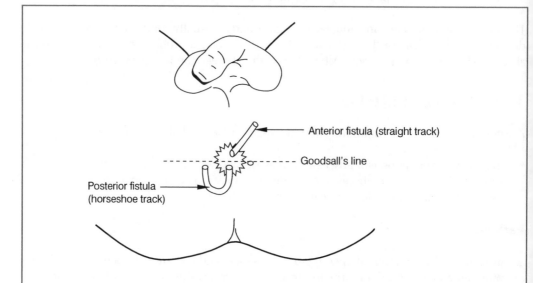

Anterior fistula (straight track)

Goodsall's line

Posterior fistula (horseshoe track)

Goodsall's rule: if the external opening of a fistula lies *behind* a line drawn transversely across the anus the track should curve in a horseshoe-like manner towards the internal opening in mid-line posteriorly. If the external opening of a fistula lies *in front of* the line the track tends to pass radially in a straight line towards the internal opening.

Goodsall's rule

Treatment

The principle of surgical management is to lay open the primary track and to drain any secondary tracks. It is important to maintain faecal continence by avoiding transection of puborectalis muscle. The common **intersphincteric fistulae** lie well below puborectalis and can be laid open and packed. The rarer **suprasphincteric** and **high transphincteric fistulae** pass superior to the puborectalis and so should be treated by a Seton suture as immediate laying open has a high risk of incontinence (see Figure opposite).

The Seton can be tied **tightly** with the aim of producing a slow division of the muscle over a period of weeks. Alternatively, a **loose** Seton drains any infection and allows healing to occur. It is then removed several weeks later, leaving a simple track which should heal. Treatment of complex fistulae with secondary tracks can be difficult and magnetic resonance scanning or intraoperative methylene blue can be helpful in defining the anatomy.

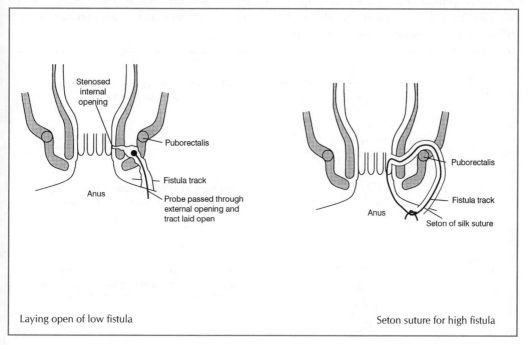

Laying open of low fistula   Seton suture for high fistula

Treatment of anorectal fistulae

Crohn's perianal fistulae

70% of patients with Crohn's disease have perianal symptoms. Fistulae tend to be multiple, with more oedema and may be less painful. Treatment is more conservative as surgical wounds tend to be slow to heal and the fistulae tend to be complex. Control of the intestinal Crohn's disease medically is a priority.

13.6 Pilonidal sinus

A pilonidal sinus is a subcutaneous sinus which contains hair, most commonly found in the natal cleft associated with chronic inflammation and acute abscess formation. The condition is common and affects young adults. There are rare variants of the pilonidal sinus in other sites (e.g. the webs of barbers' fingers, the axilla, the lumbar region in children). The latter are congenital and extend to the neural canal and dura.

Pathology

Perianal pilonidal sinuses are thought to be an acquired condition, starting at the onset of puberty when the hair follicles become distended and inflamed (see figure below). The sinus usually consists of a mid-line opening or openings in the natal cleft about 5 cm from the anus. The primary track (lined with squamous cell epithelium) leads to a subcutaneous cavity containing granulation tissue and usually a nest of hairs. Secondary openings can be seen often 2.5 cm lateral from the mid-line pits.

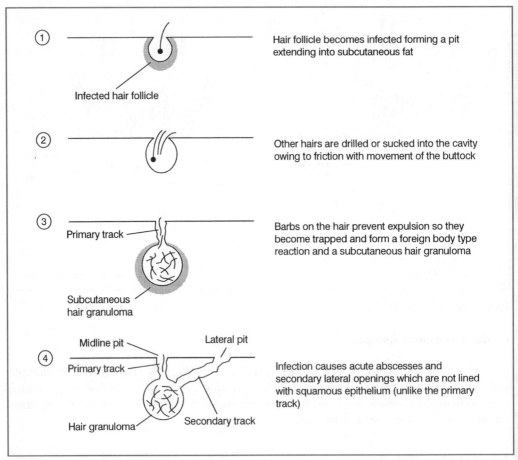

Formation of a pilonidal sinus

Clinical features

Patients are usually between the age of puberty and 40 years (75% male). Patients are often dark and hairy and may be obese. 50% present as emergencies with an acute pilonidal abscess. The rest have intermittent discomfort and discharge. Examination reveals the characteristic mid-line pit or pits which may have hair protruding. Lateral pits may be present.

Treatment

Incision and drainage

An acute pilonidal abscess needs incision and drainage under GA with follow-up. Later treatment of the pilonidal sinus may be required when the abscess cavity has healed if there are residual problems (33% of patients require further treatment).

Excision of pits and laying open of sinus

This is usually done under GA. The mid-line pits and lateral openings are excised with a small area of surrounding skin. The cavity is curetted and packed loosely with a gauze ribbon. Frequent changes of dressing and close supervision are needed post-operatively. Regular rubbing with a finger avoids premature closure. Meticulous hygiene and shaving are important. Shaving may be stopped once the wound has healed.

Excision with primary suture

Some surgeons recommend excision of sinus with primary suturing of the defect. The advantages and disadvantages are shown below. The proportions of wounds healed at two months are similar for both forms of treatment.

Advantages and disadvantages of laying open (versus primary closure) of pilonidal sinus

- **Advantages**
  Effective in most hands
  Shorter period in hospital
  Healing by secondary intention
  leaves broad, hairless scar which
  reduces recurrence

- **Disadvantages**
  Slower healing
  Open wound delays return to work
  Active wound care with frequent
  wound dressing

Recurrence

Occurs in up to 50%. Causes include:

- Neglect of wound care (e.g. shaving, finger treatment)
- Persisting poorly drained tracks
- Recurrent infection of hair follicle
- Mid-line scars

13.7 Pruritus ani

Irritation and itching around the anus (pruritus ani) is a common and frustrating symptom which can be difficult to treat. The symptoms can be caused by a variety of conditions (see table opposite) which must be excluded, but the majority of patients have no discernible cause.

Clinical features

- Men are more commonly affected than women
- Symptoms are worse at night and in hot weather
- Scratching affords short-term relief but worsens the situation by causing excoriation

A full history, excluding the general medical disease and skin disorders listed in the table opposite, is essential. An anorectal examination may reveal anal tags, fissures, haemorrhoids or other potentially treatable causes. If the reddened skin has a clearly demarcated margin, fungal infection should be suspected. It is confirmed by microscopy of skin scrapings. Threadworms may be seen on examination of fresh stool.

Management

The principles of treatment are:

- Identify and treat secondary causes
- Give advice about personal hygiene (see table opposite)
- Maintain patient's confidence
- Avoid frequent unproductive clinic visits

Symptomatic relief with local applications of soothing lotions, such as calamine lotion or short courses of topical corticosteroids. In chronic cases, a dermatological opinion might be helpful.

CAUSES OF PRURITUS ANI

Idiopathic 50%

General medical diseases	Diabetes
	Myeloproliferative disorders
	Obstructive jaundice
	Lymphoma
Skin diseases	Eczema
	Psoriasis
	Lichen planus
	Allergic eruptions
Perianal disease	Fissure
	Carcinoma
	Crohn's disease
	Infection: fungal; yeast; worms
	Sexually transmitted diseases (see later)
Local irritants	Sweat
	Mucus (due to prolapse, polyp or cancer)
	Pus (e.g. in fistula)
	Faeces (e.g. diarrhoea, incontinence, poor anal hygiene)
	Chemicals (e.g. local anaesthetics or antibiotics)

Advice for patients with pruritus ani

- Wash after defaecation
- Use moist toilet tissue and dab rather than rub
- Wear cotton undergarments
- Wear cotton gloves at night to reduce the damage from subconscious scratching
- Avoid medicated or scented soaps
- Use only prescribed hypoallergenic ointments
- Avoid highly seasoned or spicy foods

13.8 Rectal prolapse and proctalgia fugax

There are three main types of rectal prolapse.

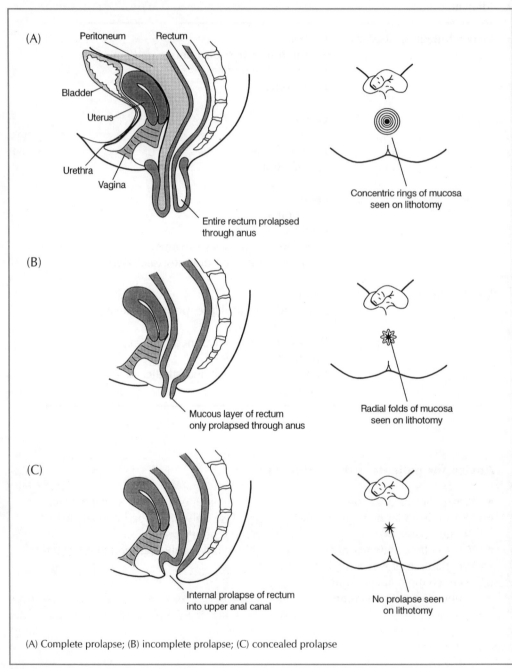

(A) Complete prolapse; (B) incomplete prolapse; (C) concealed prolapse

Three types of rectal prolapse

- **Complete prolapse**: the full thickness of the rectum prolapses through the anus. The prolapse thus contains two layers of rectum with an intervening peritoneal sac which may contain small bowel.
- **Incomplete prolapse**: the prolapse is limited to two layers of mucosa; this is often associated with haemorrhoids
- **Concealed prolapse**: there is an internal intussusception of the upper rectum into the lower rectum; this prolapse does not emerge through the anus

Pathology

Incomplete prolapse can occur in children or adults. It is caused by excessive straining in children and is associated with haemorrhoids in adults (see below). Complete prolapse tends to occur in older adults (F:M–6:1) and is associated with weak pelvic and anal musculature or a floppy redundant sigmoid colon (see below).

CAUSES OF RECTAL PROLAPSE

Incomplete prolapse	Complete prolapse
Children	
Excessive straining	
Constipation	
Cystic fibrosis	
Adults	
Haemorrhoids	Idiopathic intussusception of rectum
After anal surgery	Lack of fixation of rectum to sacrum
Atony of anal sphincters	Weak pelvic and anal musculature
	Floppy redundant sigmoid colon

Clinical features

Children
In children, prolapse is usually noticed by a parent after defaecation. It is usually easily reduced and must be differentiated from colonic intussusception and prolapsing polyps.

Adults
In adults, the presentation is of a prolapsing mass. Initially the prolapse is related to defaecation, later it can occur on standing, coughing or sneezing. Initially it reduces spontaneously, later it may require digital replacement. Other symptoms include bleeding, mucous discharge and faecal incontinence.

On examination the prolapse may not be seen at rest but a patulous anus, large anal orifice or poor anal tone may be noted. The prolapse may be evident on straining. Complete rectal prolapse has concentric rings, whereas mucosal prolapse has radial folds (see figure on p. 534). If >5 cm of bowel emerges, it will invariably be a complete prolapse.

Differential diagnosis includes:

- Large haemorrhoids
- Prolapsing rectal tumour
- Prolapsing anal polyp
- Abnormal perineal descent
- Anal warts

An acute, painful irreducible or strangulated prolapse may present as an emergency.

Management

Incomplete prolapse
Involving only the mucosal layer of the rectum, treatment is similar to that of haemorrhoids. Injection sclerotherapy, mucosal banding or formal haemorrhoidectomy may all be successful. The results are less satisfactory in patients with poor anal sphincters.

Complete prolapse
Conservative treatment with bulk laxatives is indicated in patients too frail for surgery or with only occasional episodes of prolapse. Abdominal rectopexy is the most popular treatment for patients fit enough for laparotomy. The rectum is mobilized and attached to the sacrum by prosthetic material which relieves incontinence in 60% of patients but causes constipation in 60%. Other procedures are described in the shaded box opposite.

Acute strangulated prolapse
Can usually be reduced with analgesia. Rarely, a patient presents with a gangrenous prolapse requiring urgent rectosigmoidectomy.

Children
Dietary advice, toilet training and treatment of constipation will usually resolve the prolapse. An operation is rarely necessary.

Operations for complete rectal prolapse

- **Perineal operations**

  Perineal sutures
  This insertion of an encircling
    suture used to be popular in
    frail patients but has poor
    results
  Delorme's procedure
  The rectal mucosa is excised
    and the underlying rectal muscle
    is plicated with sutures; long term
    results are not very satisfactory
  Perineal rectopexy/resection
  Perineal rectosigmoidectomy may
    be combined with a rectopexy
    and repair of pelvic floor and
    coloanal anastomosis

- **Abdominal operations**

  Abdominal rectopexy
  The treatment of choice in most
    patients well enough for
    laporotomy (see text)
  Anterior resection rectopexy
  Resection of the redundant sigmoid
    loop and upper rectum gives superior
    results but carries a significant
    morbidity risk

Solitary rectal ulcer

Solitary rectal ulcer is a chronic recurrent ulcer on the anterior wall of the rectum associated with bleeding, discharge of mucus and discomfort. There may be up to three ulcers, 7–10 cm above the anal verge, which are shallow with white, grey or yellow bases and surrounding hyperaemic mucosa. This rectal ulcer is believed to be caused by repeated mucosal trauma due to prolapse into the anal canal during straining and defaecation.

The anterior rectal mucosal prolapse can be shown by defecating proctography (see figure overleaf). These patients usually use their fingers to aid defaecation but this probably does not cause the ulcer. Principles of management include:

- Exclusion of other pathology (by biopsy if necessary)
- Treatment of constipation
- Conservative treatment if symptoms are tolerable
- Rectopexy may be effective if indicated
- Profuse haemorrhage may occur necessitating urgent surgery

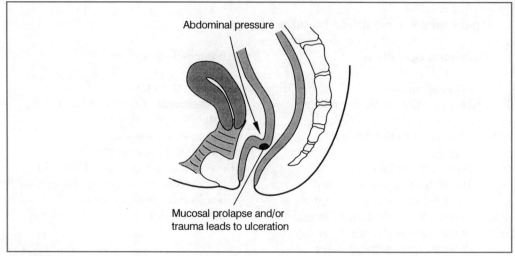

Possible aetiology of solitary rectal ulcer

Proctalgia fugax

Benign condition affecting young men with anxiety.

- Attacks of pain in the rectum, perineum or urethra
- Not related to defaecation; occurs at night
- Responds to smooth muscle relaxants, such as nitrates

Management involves:

- Exclusion of organic disease
- Explanation and reassurance
- Analgesics, antispasmodics
- Glyceryl trinitrate
- Puborectalis stretch by patient during attack

13.9 Faecal incontinence

Faecal incontinence is the involuntary loss per anum of flatus or faeces. Patients find this symptom distressing and embarrassing.

Pathology

Maintenance of anal continence depends on:

Major factors

- Anal sphincters with normal anatomy and function
- An acute anorectal angle (maintained by puborectalis)
- A capacious and distensible rectum
- Bulky and firm faeces
- Intact rectal and anal sensation (mostly the pudendal nerve)

Minor factors

- Vascular anal cushions above the dentate line
- Cyclic retrograde propulsion (15/min)

The causes of faecal incontinence can thus be classified as **diarrhoea, neurological** or **mechanical** (see box below).

Causes of faecal incontinence

- **Diarrhoea**
  Inflammatory bowel disease
  Functional bowel disease

- **Mechanical**
  Sphincter ring disruption:
    trauma
    congenital
  Fistula:
    extra-rectal
    rectovaginal

- **Neurological**
  General neurological diseases
    (e.g. multiple sclerosis)
  Dementia
  Age
  Spinal trauma
  Pudendal nerve neuropathy
  Faecal impaction

History

Patients must be questioned directly and sensitively. The factors to ask about are:

- **Call to stool**: often altered in neuropathy
- **Urgency**: suggests voluntary muscle weakness
- **Consistency of stool**: to exclude diarrhoea or impaction
- **Difficulty wiping**: indicates lax sphincter or prolapse
- **Leakage**: indicates low resting sphincter tone which suggests internal sphincter deficiency

- **Urinary incontinence**: usually co-exists in obstetric damage to the pudendal nerve and pelvic floor
- **Obstetric history**: difficult deliveries often result in pudendal nerve damage
- **Anal surgery**: especially anal dilatation or surgery for a fistula which may have damaged the anal sphincter

Examination

The factors to look for are:

- Perianal soiling
- Gaping of the anus: suggests low resting sphincter tone and poor internal sphincter function
- Descent of the anal verge below the ischial tuberosities suggesting weakness of the pelvic floor
- Rectal prolapse
- Scars: indicating underlying muscle division

On rectal digital examination, the factors to look for are:

- **Low anal tone**: on inserting a finger suggests poor internal sphincter tone
- **Anorectal angle**: formed by the puborectalis sling which is felt as a muscular sling
- **Squeeze test**: poor squeeze means damaged voluntary muscle either directly or due to pudendal neuropathy
- **Faecal masses**: impacted in the rectum may interfere with the anorectal mechanism
- **Tumours**

Endoscopy may reveal proctitis which reduces rectal capacity, increases sensitivity and causes diarrhoea.

Investigations

(See p. 520):

- Anal manometry
- Rectal compliance
- Electromyography
- Defecating video proctography
- Anal ultrasound: gives an image of the anal sphincter and shows sphincter defects, such as scarring by obstetric or surgical trauma
- Barium enema or colonoscopy: important to exclude tumours or proctitis

Treatment

Conservative
Exclude causes of diarrhoea and bowel disorders, such as colitis, polyps or tumours. Solidify stools with drugs, such as codeine phosphate if stools are loose. Identify cause of incontinence.

Physiotherapy
If there is good muscle bulk and the voluntary contraction is shown to be weak, pelvic floor strengthening excises can be useful.

Rectopexy
If a rectal prolapse is identified, it should be repaired before any work is undertaken on the anal sphincter.

Overlapping sphincter repair
If direct obstetric or surgical trauma has caused identifiable scarring, sphincter repair can be curative in 85% of patients (see figure below).

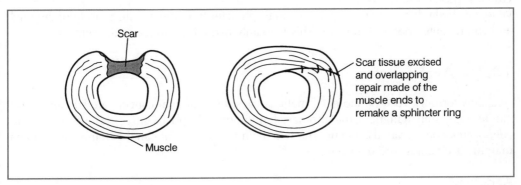

Overlapping sphincter repair

Post-anal repair
If neuropathic damage has occurred, the pelvic floor is lax and the sphincter mechanism has descended, this will cause loss of the anorectal angle which contributes to incontinence. Post-anal repair seeks to recreate this angle by opposing muscles behind the rectum, thus taking it upwards and forwards (see figure overleaf). It is successful in 50% of patients.

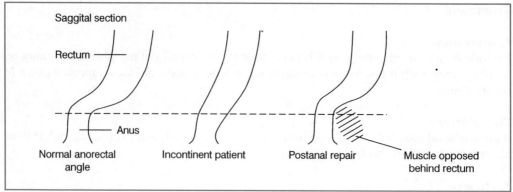

Post-anal repair

Colostomy
For a few patients, if other treatment has failed, a colostomy may be more acceptable than continued incontinence.

Gracilis muscle transplant
Work has been done on creating a new anal sphincter from the gracilis muscle of the thigh and an implanted nerve stimulator. This is mainly carried out in specialist centres.

13.10 Anal cancer

Accounts for only 10% of anorectal malignancies. 80% of anal cancers are squamous cell carcinomas, but malignant melanomas, lymphomas, Kaposi's sarcoma and anal gland adenocarcincomas can also occur. The two main types are **anal canal carcinomas** and **anal margin carcinomas** (see opposite).

Aetiology

Certain groups of people are predisposed to anal cancer:

* Male homosexuals
* People who practise anal sex
* People with a history of genital warts

It is postulated that human papilloma virus predisposes to anal cancer as it does to cervical cancer.

Clinical features

- Patients are usually in their 50s or 60s
- Common presentations are bleeding, pain, swelling and ulceration around the anus
- Late cases can present with disturbed bowel habit, incontinence and rectovaginal fistulae
- Many patients have enlarged inguinal lymph nodes but only 50% of palpable glands contain tumour

Differential diagnosis include:

- Anal papilloma
- Anal warts
- Anal fissures
- Haemorrhoids

Examination under anaesthesia (EUA) is usually necessary. The important features to note are:

- Arising from anal margin or anal canal
- Greater or less than 5 cm in diameter
- Local spread to surrounding structures
- Take biopsy specimens

Anal margin cancers versus anal canal cancers

- **Anal margin cancers**
  Arise below the dentate line
  Visible at the anus
  Tend to behave like basal cell
    skin carcinomas
  Spread to inguinal lymph nodes
  More common in men
  More likely to be treatable with
    local excision

- **Anal canal cancers**
  Arise above the dentate line
  Not visible at the anus
  More locally invasive with a
    poorer prognosis
  Spread to superior haemorrhoidal
    lymph nodes
  More common in women
  More likely to be treated with
    radiotherapy

Treatment

The principles of treatment for anal cancer have been changing as trials are carried out. The overall five-year survival is about 50%. Generally, there are four main treatment strategies.

Local resection
This is indicated in small tumours (< 2 cm diameter) of the anal margin with no invasion of the anal sphincter. Less than 5% of anal cancers fulfil this criteria.

Radiotherapy
Radiotherapy has largely replaced radical surgery for first-line treatment in most anal cancers. The initial radiotherapy field includes the tumour and inguinal lymph nodes and the course lasts about 4–5 weeks. Women suffer artificial menopause and men become azoospermic. There is a temporary desquamation of the perineum. A radioisotope boost is given to the primary tumour under general anaesthetic. 50% of tumours are cured by radiotherapy, but some may need further surgery. Some treatment regimes combine chemotherapy with radiotherapy.

Radical abdomino-perineal resection
This surgery, which leaves the patient with a permanent colostomy, used to be the traditional treatment for most anal cancers. This procedure is now usually reserved for cases in which radiotherapy fails or is contraindicated. Patients with obstructive cancers may benefit from a colostomy while they undergo radiotherapy.

Chemotherapy
5 Fluorouracil and mitomycin have been used in combination with radiotherapy or surgery. Evidence supporting their use is controversial and side-effects include thrombocytopenia and agranulocytosis. Chemotherapy is particularly useful in aggressively metastasizing tumours, which may spread to the bones, abdominal lymph nodes or the brain.

13.11 Sexually transmitted anorectal diseases

Can affect women and heterosexuals but most commonly seen in homosexuals. Patients are best managed by a genitourinary physician but may present to a colorectal surgeon with anorectal symptoms. It is important to be able to differentiate these conditions from surgical disorders. In general, investigation of proctocolitis should include those features listed opposite.

Investigation of proctocolitis

- **Test**
  Stool microscopy

  Rectal swabs
  Sigmoidoscopy and rectal biopsy

- **Looking for**
  Protozoa and bacteria, cryptosporidium
  and atypical mycobacteria
  Viruses (e.g. *Herpes simplex*)
  Cytomegalovirus and Kaposi's sarcoma

Gonorrhoea

Caused by *Neisseria gonorrhoeae*, a Gram-negative diplococcus. The organism is spread by anal intercourse and contamination from vagina to anus in women. There is a 5–7-day incubation period. Symptoms include:

- Asymptomatic (the majority)
- Pruritus ani
- Mucopurulent discharge
- Tenesmus
- Bleeding
- Joint pains
- Proctitis

Diagnosis is by anal swabs for microscopy and culture. Treatment is with amoxycillin for patient and partners. Eradication of infection should be confirmed after two weeks.

Chlamydia

Caused by *Chlamydia trachomatis*, an intracellular organism. The organism is spread by anal intercourse. Symptoms include:

- Asymptomatic (common)
- Mucopurulent discharge
- Bleeding
- Pain
- Tenesmus
- Fever
- Inguinal lymphadenopathy
- Proctitis

Diagnosis by anal swab in special Chlamydia culture medium. Treat with tetracycline or erythromycin for patient and partners. Rectal stricture is a rare complication.

Syphilis

Caused by *Treponema pallidum*, a spirochaete. The organism is spread by anal intercourse. Symptoms include:

- **Primary syphilis** (2–6 weeks after infection): anal chancre (looks like a fissure); inguinal lymphadenopathy
- **Secondary syphilis** (6–8 weeks after primary chancre): condylomata lata (warty mass around anus); discharge; pruritus
- **Tertiary syphilis** (rare): rectal gumma (can be mistaken for tumour); tabes dorsalis; severe perianal pain; paralysis of sphincters

Diagnosis is by the VDRL assay (Venereal Disease Research Laboratory) which is positive in 75% of patients with primary syphilis. Other serological tests are the Fluorescent Treponema Antibody test (FTA) and the Treponema Pallidum Haemagglutination Assay (TPHA). Treat with intramuscular penicillin. Follow-up serological tests are repeated periodically for a year after treatment to confirm eradication.

Herpes

Herpes is caused by *Herpes simplex* virus. 90% of anal infections are due to herpes simplex type 2 and 10% to type 1. The organism is spread by anal intercourse. If the infection is ulcerative and lasting more than a month in an HIV patient it is diagnostic for AIDS. There is a 1–3-week incubation period. Symptoms include:

- Burning pain
- Mucoid or bloody discharge
- Malaise and fever
- Vesicles, pustules and ulcers around the anus
- Lesions too painful to be examined without general anaesthetic
- Proctitis and erythema on sigmoidoscopy

Diagnosis is by viral culture of vesicular fluid. Treat with acyclovir (oral or IV) continued until all mucocutaneous surfaces have healed. Partners should also be treated.

Anal warts

Anal warts are caused by human papilloma virus, usually types 6, 16 and 11. Spread by anal intercourse, direct spread from genitals or may be sporadic with no history of anal intercourse. Symptoms include:

- Asymptomatic — patient notices warts and presents
- Itching and discomfort
- Discharge
- Bleeding

On examination white, pink or grey lesions occur around anus, perineum and inside anal canal. There may be associated lesions on the penis or vulva. There may be a few scattered papillomas or bulky confluent lesions.

Proctoscopy should be performed and patients should be screened for other sexually transmitted disease. Diagnosis is clinical and treatments include:

- Chemical topical agents, such as podophyllin
- Surgical excision or diathermy

Partners should be treated. Papilloma infection is thought to predispose to anal cancer, but this is rare.

HIV-associated anorectal problems

Patients with HIV infection are susceptible to anorectal problems such as:

- Haemorrhoids
- Fissures
- Perianal abscess
- Fistulae
- Kaposi's sarcoma
- Proctocolitis due to herpes; cytomegalovirus; Cyptosporidium; isosporiasis; *Mycobacterium avium*; Shigella; Campylobacter; *E. histolytica*

14. DISEASES OF THE BILIARY TRACT AND PANCREAS

14.1 Jaundice

Jaundice is defined as an elevation of the serum bilirubin (normal 9 mmol/L). Clinically detectable at 35 mmol/L. Bilirubin metabolism is outlined in the figure overleaf. Jaundice is usually classified as pre-hepatic, hepatic or post-hepatic (see table on p. 549).

In clinical practice, the hepatic and post-hepatic forms often co-exist. For example, cholestasis may produce secondary damage to the liver (biliary cirrhosis). Conversely, liver cirrhosis or metastatic disease may cause bile duct compression.

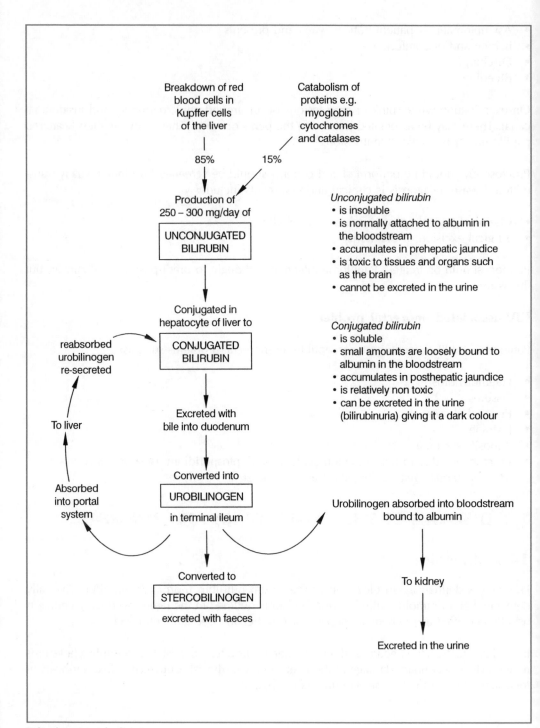

Bilirubin metabolism

CLASSIFICATION OF JAUNDICE

	Pre-hepatic	Hepatic jaundice	Post-hepatic (obstructive) jaundice*
Causes	Spherocytosis Haemolytic anaemia Pernicious anaemia Incompatible blood transfusion	Hepatitis Cirrhosis Drugs Toxins (e.g. phosphorous chloroform), Liver tumours (primary or secondary)	*Obstruction in the lumen* — gallstones *Obstruction in the wall* — atresia, traumatic stricture, tumour of bile duct, chronic cholangitis, sclerosing cholangitis *External compression* — pancreatitis, tumour of pancreas
Jaundice	*Mild jaundice Bilirubin rarely >100 mmol/L unconjugated*	*Variable jaundice May be conjugated or unconjugated*	*Variable jaundice Bilirubin may exceed 1000 mmol/L conjugated*
Urine	*Normal colour Bilirubin not present Urobilinogen raised*	*Dark Bilirubin may be present*	*Dark Bilirubin present*
Stool	*Normal colour Increased urobilinogen*	*Normal colour*	*Pale stools Stercobilinogen down*
Alkaline phosphatase ALP	Normal	*Mildly raised Very high in primary biliary cirrhosis*	*Very high*
Amino transferases ATi	Normal	*Typically very high especially in acute viral hepatitis or cirrhosis*	*Normal or moderately raised*
Prothrombin time	Normal	*Prolonged and not correctable with vitamin K*	*Prolonged but correctable with vitamin K*

*May lead to secondary liver damage causing misleading results so can be difficult to distinguish from hepatic jaundice.

History of a jaundiced patient

- **Important aspects**
  Recent travel
  Drug addiction
  Joint pains
  Anorexia
  Malaise

  Alcohol addiction

  Fat intolerance
  Recurrent right upper quadrant pain

  Weight loss
  Constant epigastric boring pain

  Family history of blood disorders

  Bruising tendency

  Pale stool, dark urine
  Pruritus

- **Suggests**
  Hepatitis

  Cirrhosis

  Gallstones

  Malignancy

  Haemolytic disorders

  Hepatocellular damage

  Obstructive jaundice

Examination of a jaundice patient

- **Important aspects**
  Spider naevi
  Palmar erythema
  Finger clubbing
  Ascites

  Splenomegaly
  Prominent abdominal wall veins

  Xanthomata
  Kayser Fleischer rings in iris
  Large knobbly liver

- **Suggests**
  Stigmata of chronic liver disease

  Portal hypertension and cirrhosis

  Biliary cirrhosis
  Wilson's disease
  Malignant disease

Investigation of jaundice

A simplified scheme for investigating jaundice is shown opposite. Many diagnostic tools can aid in the diagnosis of the cause of the jaundice. These are described in the following pages.

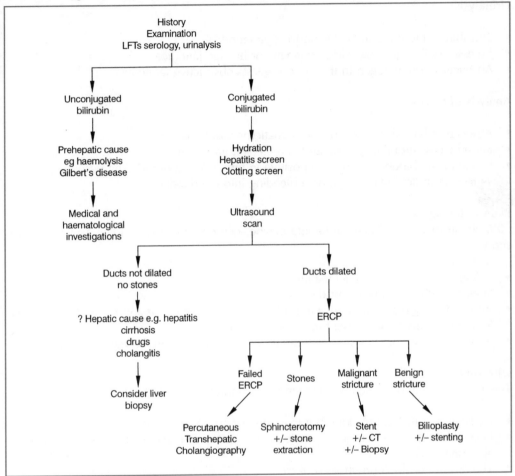

A plan for investigating the jaundiced patient

Blood tests
Serum bilirubin is raised by definition. The presence of raised conjugated bilirubin suggests that the jaundice is either hepatic or post-hepatic.

LFTs are useful in determining the degree of hepatic damage. The results of serum biochemistry in jaundiced patients are shown in the table on p. 549.

Haematological investigations (red blood cell fragility, Coombs' test, reticulocyte count) can confirm haemolytic cause.

The **PT** should be checked before any invasive investigations are performed.

Similarly, a **hepatitis screen** should be performed before invasive procedures if possible.

Urinalysis

- Bilirubin in the urine indicates obstructive jaundice
- Excess urobilinogen suggests pre-hepatic or hepatic jaundice
- Absence of urobilinogen in the urine suggests obstructive jaundice

Analysis of faeces

- Absence of bile pigments indicates hepatic or post-hepatic cause
- Raised faecal urobilinogen suggests pre-hepatic jaundice
- Faecal occult blood tests may be positive in the presence of bleeding oesophageal varices or an ampullary carcinoma bleeding into the duodenum

Plain radiographs
10% of gallstones are radio-opaque and maybe seen on a plain AXR. Plain X-rays may also show:

- Calcification in chronic pancreatitis
- Lung metastases in malignant disease
- An air cholangiogram if there is a fistula between the intestine and biliary tree, or if gas forming organisms are present in severe cholangitis
- An enlarged gall bladder may be seen as a soft tissue mass in the right upper quadrant

Ultrasound
This is an essential baseline investigation in a jaundiced patient. It can show:

- Gallstones in the gall bladder (but may miss stones in the duct)
- Dilated bile ducts (a common hepatic duct of >8 mm diameter at the porta hepatis is abnormal)
- The level of obstruction (in 90% of cases)
- The cause of obstruction may be diagnosed but the degree of accuracy varies
- Intra-hepatic tumour deposits, abscesses, cysts or cirrhosis can be diagnosed and biopsied under ultrasound control
- A mass in the pancreas can be assessed and measured but may be difficult to diagnose
- Splenomegaly
- Upper abdominal varices
- Alteration in portal flow dynamics associated with hypertension, compression or invasion
- Lymph node enlargement
- Ascites

Endoscopic retrograde cholangiopancreatography (ERCP)

ERCP has revolutionized the investigations of the biliary tree. It allows diagnostic and therapeutic access to both the bile and pancreatic ducts. ERCP can identify:

- Details of ductal anatomy
- Level of obstruction
- Nature of obstruction
- Stones and stricturing tumours
- Congenital ductal abnormalities
- Acquired abnormalities, such as early chronic pancreatitis

Biopsies may be taken and therapeutic measures, such as sphincterotomy, stone extraction, dilatation and stenting of strictures, can be performed

Percutaneous transhepatic cholangiography (PTC)

PTC is cannulation of an intrahepatic bile duct with a fine bore needle under radiological control, and injection of contrast. Provides a useful alternative if ERCP is unavailable or not technically feasible. Is invasive, may cause biliary leakage and does not provide information about the pancreas. Useful in delineating intrahepatic duct strictures and anastomoses between the biliary tree and jejunum.

CT

Useful when:

- Ultrasound findings are equivocal (e.g. view obscured by gas or ascites)
- ERCP is equivocal or unsuccessful
- Staging and assessing tumour operability
- Looking for invasion/compression of arterial and portal systems
- Radiological biopsies of tumour masses are required

IV contrast is usually used, but arterial portography by selective catheterization of the coeliac and superior mesenteric vessels can be performed.

ERCP

- **Pre-procedure**
  Check clotting
  Patient starved for 6 hours
  Trained endoscopic team essential
  Oxygen, suction and ERCP equipment in fluoroscopic room

- **Contrast medium**
  Non-ionic to reduce pancreatitis (usually iodine)
  Low concentration to visualize stones in bile duct
  Higher concentration to visualize pancreatic ducts

- **Procedure**
  Left lateral position
  Local anaesthetic throat spray
  Intravenous sedation
  Intravenous broad-spectrum antibiotics
  Hyoscine butyl bromide given to reduce duodenal peristalsis
  Side viewing duodenoscope introduced by mouth
  Ampulla identified
  Selective cannulation of both bile and pancreatic ducts
  Visualization by radiography
  Overfilling of pancreatic duct avoided

- **Therapeutic modalities available**
  Sphincterotomy
  Stone extraction
  Balloon dilatation of strictures
  Stenting of tumours

- **Causes of failure to cannulate bile duct**

Duodenal diverticulum	Ampullary stenosis
Previous surgery	Sub-ampullary tumour
Impacted stone	Technical difficulty

- **Complications of ERCP**

Mild self-limiting pancreatitis (3%)	Bacteraemia
Severe life-threatening pancreatitis (0.1%)	Septicaemia
Contrast reactions	Perforation and haemorrhage in therapeutic cases

MRI

Magnetic resonance imaging (MRI) is used increasingly to image the biliary tree and some clinicians are of the opinion that it may supersede ERCP as a diagnostic tool in the future. It has the advantage of being non-invasive and can be used to diagnose:

- Biliary obstruction
- Common bile duct stones
- Malignant bile duct obstruction

Also used to stage and assess tumour operability. Enables biopsies to be taken.

Radionucleotide scanning

A gamma-emitting isotope, which is taken up by the liver, is injected into the patient. Depending on the choice of isotope, different areas are imaged and captured by a gamma camera, for example:

- Technetium 99m sulphur colloid is taken up by the Kupffer's cells of the reticulo-endothelial system of the liver and spleen
- Gallium 67 citrate is useful to detect hepatomas
- Technetium-labelled WBCs can demonstrate liver abscesses
- Technetium 99m labelled iminodiacetic acid compounds (99m-HIDA) is secreted in the bile and so outlines the biliary tree

Radionucleotide scanning has been largely supplanted by ultrasound, CT and ERCP in recent years.

Arteriography

Although not used to investigate the biliary system directly, selective arteriography of the hepatic, coeliac and superior mesenteric arteries can give valuable information before hepatic or pancreatic surgery. Arteriography provides information about:

- Anatomical variants
- Vessel compression
- Vessel invasion
- Tumour operability

Therapeutic embolization can also be employed for vascular non-operable tumours.

Barium studies

Not routine investigations in jaundiced patients but can give information about:

- Duodenal distortion due to adjacent tumours
- Gastric carcinoma
- Oesophageal varices

Oral cholecystogram
Not generally helpful in jaundiced patients as the uptake and excretion of the dye is impaired in the damaged liver.

Management of jaundice

Depends on the underlying cause. In general, while investigations are being carried out, it is essential to preserve renal function with adequate hydration and monitoring of urinary output then proceed to definitive treatment.

14.2 Anatomy of the liver

Gross anatomy

At 1.5 kg the liver is the largest gland in the body. It is wedge-shaped and has an upper diaphragmatic surface and a postero-inferior visceral surface. It consists of four lobes — **right, left, quadrate** and **caudate**. The diaphragmatic or upper surface is:

- Convex and lies under the diaphragm
- Made up of anterior, superior, posterior and right surfaces
- Mostly covered by peritoneum, by which it is attached to the diaphragm

Viewed from the diaphragmatic surface, the left and right lobes of the liver are divided by the **falciform ligament**, a double fold of peritoneum attaching the liver to the diaphragm (see figure opposite).

The postero-inferior or visceral surface is moulded to adjacent viscera, is irregular in shape, and lies in contact with the abdominal oesophagus, stomach, duodenum, right colic flexure, right kidney, right adrenal gland and gall bladder.

Viewed from the visceral surface, the left and right lobes of the liver are divided by an 'H'-shaped arrangement of structures formed by the:

- Fissure for the ligamentum venosum
- Ligamentum teres
- Porta hepatis (the crossbar of the 'H')
- Inferior vena cava
- Gall bladder

The caudate and quadrate lobes of the liver lie within the limbs of this 'H' (see figure opposite).

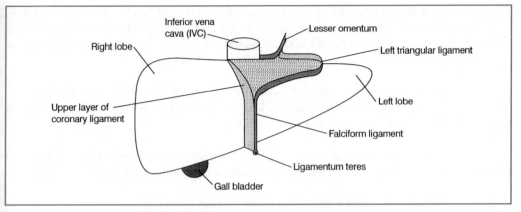

Anterior view (front) of the liver. This shows the right, anterior and superior parts of the diaphragmatic surface of the liver.

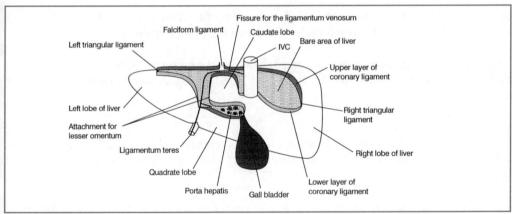

Posterior (back) view of the liver. This shows the posterior part of the diaphragmatic surface and the visceral surface of the liver.

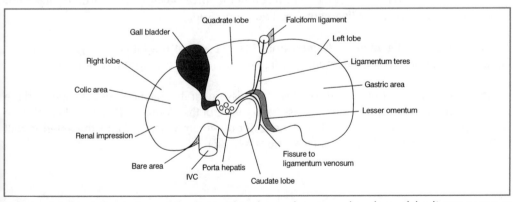

Inferior (undersurface) view of the liver. This shows the visceral surface of the liver as seen at laparotomy when looking into the abdomen with the lower border of the liver retracted up towards the costal margin.

The **ligamentum teres** is the obliterated remains of the left umbilical vein which, *in utero*, brings blood from the placenta back to the foetus. It runs from the umbilicus in the free edge of the falciform ligament and passes into a fissure on the visceral surface of the liver to the porta hepatis.

The **ligamentum venosum** is the fibrous remnant of the foetal ductus venosus which shunts blood from this left umbilical vein into the inferior vena cava, short circuiting the liver. It runs in a fissure on the visceral surface.

The porta hepatis is the hilum of the liver. It lies in the free edge of the lesser omentum and is 5 cm long. The contents of the porta hepatis are (from anterior to posterior):

- Left and right hepatic duct forming the common hepatic duct
- Hepatic artery
- Portal vein

Sympathetic nerve fibres from the coeliac axis, parasympathetic nerve fibres from the vagus and lymphatic vessels and lymph nodes also lie in the porta hepatis.

The **caudate** and **quadrate** lobes are anatomically part of the right lobe of the liver but, as they are supplied by the left hepatic artery and portal vein, they are functionally part of the left lobe.

Peritoneal attachments
The liver is enclosed in peritoneum except for a small posterior bare area. The peritoneum is reflected from the liver on to the diaphragm and stomach in a double layer forming various ligamentous attachments (see figure on p. 557).

The **falciform ligament** is a two-layered fold of peritoneum ascending from the umbilicus to the anterior and superior surface of the liver. It contains the ligamentum teres.The **upper layer of the coronary ligament** is formed from the right leaf of the falciform ligament and extends around the bare area of the liver meeting the **lower layer of the coronary ligament** to form the **right triangular ligament** (see figure opposite).

The **left triangular ligament** is formed from the left leaf of the falciform ligament and is continuous with the lesser omentum (see figure on p. 557, posterior view of liver).

The **lesser omentum** arises from the edges of the fissure for the ligamentum venosum and the porta hepatis and passes down to the lesser curvature of the stomach. The porta hepatis (see figure opposite) runs in the free edge of the lesser omentum where it forms the anterior wall of the epiploic foramen (the entrance to the lesser sac).

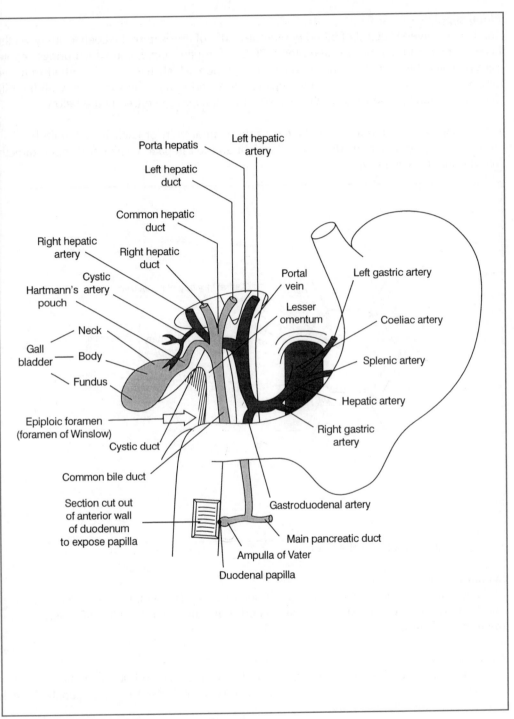

Structures entering and leaving porta hepatis

Blood supply
The liver receives 1500 ml of blood per minute; 30% of this is from the coeliac artery via the hepatic artery carrying oxygenated blood; 70% is from the portal vein which brings venous deoxygenated blood rich in the products of digestion which has been absorbed from the gastrointestinal tract. Branches of the hepatic artery and portal vein run along with the bile ductules forming portal triads at the corners of each liver lobule (see figure below).

Arterial and venous blood is conducted to the central vein of each liver lobule by liver sinusoids. The central veins drain into the right and left hepatic veins which open directly into the inferior vena cava.

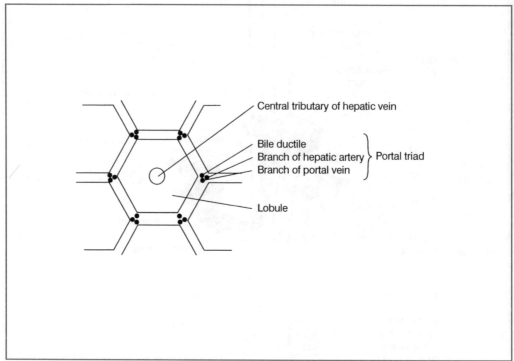

Arrangement of lobules of the liver

Lymph vessels
The liver produces more than a third of all body lymph. The lymph vessels leave the liver via the porta hepatis. The draining lymph nodes are the coeliac nodes and the posterior mediastinal nodes.

Nerve supply
The nerve supply of the liver is derived from the sympathetic and parasympathetic nerves by way of the coeliac plexus. The anterior vagal trunk gives rise to a large hepatic branch which passes directly to the liver.

Physiology of the liver

The liver performs many vital functions which are summarized below. They fall into the categories of **metabolism, excretion, bile secretion, storage** and **vitamin D activation.**

Metabolism
The portal venous system delivers the products of digestion to the liver where they are metabolized into a form which can be utilized by the body:

* **Fats**: 30% of chylomicrons from intestinal lacteals are transported to the liver to be made into triglycerides, phospholipids and cholesterol
* **Proteins**: are broken down by the liver into their constituent amino acids producing ammonia as a byproduct; the liver also synthesizes all non-essential amino acids; from these amino acids, the liver synthesizes 25 g/day of plasma proteins and enzymes, including serum albumin, prothrombin 2, fibrinogen and blood clotting factors
* **Carbohydrates**: the liver is responsible for the storage and release of glucose in the form of glycogen; glycogenolysis releases glucose into the blood when the blood glucose level is low: gluconeogenesis converts amino acids, lipids and carbohydrates into glucose if needed

Excretion
Ammonia is formed by the breakdown of proteins and is converted into urea and excreted via the urea cycle. The basic reaction in the liver needs a lot of energy in the form of ATP.

Lipid-soluble substances, such as drugs, hormones, bilirubin, steroids and phenols, are made soluble and then conjugated with glucuronic acid, glycine or glutathione. **Protein hormones** also get inactivated in the liver. **Bacteria and foreign particles** are removed from the bloodstream by filtration. **Cholesterol** is produced as a side-effect of fat metabolism. The bile is the only route of excretion of cholesterol so the liver is responsible for the regulation of serum cholesterol.

Bile secretion
The production and re-circulation of bile is summarized later in this chapter (pp 580–582).

Storage
Apart from glycogen, the liver is an important store of iron, ferritin and vitamins, including A, D and B12.

Vitamin D activation
Vitamin D is converted to 25-hydroxycalciferol essential for calcium absorption and metabolism.

14.3 Cirrhosis of the liver

Cirrhosis is a group of conditions in which there is chronic hepatic injury with healing occurring by regeneration and fibrosis. This fibrosis leads to further cell damage and destruction of hepatic architecture progressing to liver failure and portal hypertension.

The causes of cirrhosis are many and some are listed in the shaded box below. The most common are alcohol, viral hepatitis, primary biliary cirrhosis and, in the tropics, schistosomiasis and secondary biliary cirrhosis.

- **Primary biliary cirrhosis** is a distinct clinical entity thought to have an autoimmune pathogenesis. It occurs mainly in middle-aged women.
- **Secondary biliary cirrhosis** is caused by damage or compression of the bile duct, leading to recurrent cholangitis.
- **Schistosomiasis** is very common in South America, Africa, the Middle East and East Asia. It is a parasite carried in fresh water snails and infestation causes fibrosis, leading to portal hypertension but not a true cirrhosis.

Cirrhosis is diagnosed by ultrasound and CT scan but can only be confirmed on histology. Abdominal surgery is very hazardous in a patient with cirrhosis as it leads to an increase in ascites, haemorrhage and renal failure. The main complications of cirrhosis are liver failure, ascites and portal hypertension.

Causes of cirrhosis of the liver

- **Portal**
  Alcoholic
  Nutritional (protein deficiency)
  Post-hepatic
  Idiopathic

- **Congenital**
  Haemochromatosis
  Wilson's disease
  α1-antitrypsin deficiency
  Galactosaemia
  Type IV glycogen storage disease

- **Drug-induced**

- **Idiopathic**

- **Biliary**
  Primary biliary cirrhosis
  Secondary biliary cirrhosis

- **Cardiac**
  Congestive cardiac failure

- **Other**
  Chronic active hepatitis
  Schistosomiasis
  Sarcoidosis
  Viral hepatitis

14.4 Portal hypertension and oesophageal varices

Pathogenesis

The normal portal pressure is between 80 and 150 mm of water (5–10 mmHg above IVC pressure). Portal hypertension is an acute or chronic increase in this pressure. Portal hypertension results from an obstruction in the portal tree and the causes are classified according to the site of the block (see the shaded box below).

Causes of portal hypertension

World-wide, post viral hepatitis is the most common cause.
In developed countries, alcoholic cirrhosis is the principle cause.

- **Pre-sinusoidal**

Extrahepatic	*Intrahepatic*
Portal vein thrombosis	Schistosomiasis
Splenic vein thrombosis	Chronic active hepatitis
Arteriovenous fistula	Early primary biliary cirrhosis
Tropical splenomegaly	Congenital hepatic fibrosis
Immunological (lupoid)	Sarcoidosis
Occlusion by tumour or	Toxins
pancreatitis	Idiopathic

- **Sinusoidal**

Cirrhotic	*Non-cirrhotic*
Post-viral hepatitis (B, C, D)	Acute alcoholic hepatitis
Alcoholic	Cytotoxic drugs
Metabolic (e.g. Wilson's disease)	Vitamin A intoxication
Drugs (e.g. methotrexate)	
Cryptogenic	

- **Post-sinusoidal**
  Budd–Chiari syndrome
  Veno-occlusive disease
  Caval abnormality
  Constrictive pericarditis
  Tumour invasion of hepatic vein

The four important effects of portal hypertension are:

- Development of a collateral portosystemic circulation
- Splenomegaly
- Ascites
- Hepatic failure and its sequelae

There are four main areas of portosystemic anastomosis that become developed in portal obstruction. These are:

- **Between the left gastric vein and the oesophageal veins**: forming oesophageal varices
- **Between the superior and inferior rectal veins**: forming haemorrhoids
- **Along the obliterated umbilical vein to the superior and inferior epigastric veins**: forming a caput medusae
- **Retroperitoneal and diaphragmatic anastomoses**: which may cause intraoperative hazards

Oesophageal varices and resulting gastrointestinal haemorrhage are the most serious complications of portal hypertension.

Splenomegaly occurs because of:

- Portal congestion
- Leucopenia and thrombocytopenia causing hypertrophy of the splenic substance itself

Ascites is due to a combination of:

- Raised portal pressure (not enough to cause ascites on its own)
- Low serum albumin
- ↑ Aldosterone activity with sodium retention
- ↑ Lymphatic pressure in the cirrhotic liver resulting in lymph transudation

Clinical features of portal hypertension

Because of its range of effects, portal hypertension can present in many ways:

- Haemorrhage from bleeding oesophageal varices or haemorrhoids
- With signs of hepatic failure: jaundice; CNS effects; stigmata of liver disease
- A cause of ascites
- A cause of splenomegaly
- A cause of hepatomegaly

Because of its catastrophic effect, haemorrhage from bleeding oesophageal varices is the most significant surgical presentation of portal hypertension.

Haemorrhage from oesophageal varices

Oesophageal varices account for 50% of deaths from upper gastrointestinal bleeding, although they cause only 10% of cases. Whilst the patient is being resuscitated, certain investigations should take place — others should be delayed until the patient's condition stabilizes (see the shaded box below).

Investigations for patients with bleeding oesophageal varices

- **Immediate**
  FBC
  Clotting indices
  Blood grouping and cross-matching
  U&Es
  LFTs
  Hepatitis screen (B and C)
  Upper gastrointestinal endoscopy
  CXR
  Urine and blood culture
  Liver biopsy
  Mesenteric angiography $\Big\}$ If indicated
  CT scan or MRI

- **Subsequent**
  Auto-antibodies
  Serum copper and caeruloplasmin
  Serum iron, iron binding, ferritin
  α1-antitrypsin
  α-fetoprotein
  Abdominal ultrasound
  Ascitic fluid microbiology
  Ascitic fluid cytology
  Wedged hepatic vein pressure

The management should be carried out in high-dependency units with specialized teams. The principles are:

- Control the acute bleeding
- Prevent recurrent bleeding
- Treat underlying condition

Control of variceal haemorrhage

Immediate resuscitation takes priority. The airway should be protected. Central venous access is often indicated. Blood, fresh frozen plasma and platelets are usually needed. Catheterization to monitor urine output. Over-expansion of the circulation may cause a dangerous increase in portal venous pressure. Prevention of complications or the early recognition and treatment of these is important.

565

Complications of variceal haemorrhage

- Aspiration
- Hepatic encephalopathy
- Ascites
- Malnutrition
- Infections from enteric organisms

- Pneumonia
- Hypoxia
- Renal failure
- Alcohol withdrawal

Drug treatment of oesophageal varices

Somatostatin is a hormone that reduces splanchnic and hepatic flow. **Octreotide** and **lanreotide** are longer-acting synthetic analogues of somatostatin. **Vasopressin** causes generalized vasoconstriction but its use is controversial. It is given in combination with glyceryl trinitrate under close cardiac monitoring. **Terlipressin** is an analogue of vasopressin which has a longer action and fewer systemic effects.

Balloon tamponade

Insertion of a double-ballooned Sengstaken–Blakemore or Minnesota tube into the oesophagus controls variceal bleeding temporarily by direct compression at the bleeding site. Use of balloon tamponade is recommended in:

- Massive bleeding preventing endoscopy
- Stabilizing patients awaiting definitive therapy
- Patients being transferred to a specialist unit

It should not be used in patients with a large hiatus hernia.

Sclerotherapy of varices

Injecting sclerosant, such as ethanolamine, into bleeding varices is usually undertaken at the initial emergency endoscopy to control acute bleeding. It is successful in 70–90% of cases, and may be repeated the following week to prevent re-bleeding. If two attempts of sclerotherapy fail, a more major intervention is indicated. Complications include:

- Fever
- Retrosternal discomfort
- Dysphagia
- Ulceration
- Stricture
- Local perforation

Variceal banding

Banding produces better control of bleeding than sclerotherapy with lower morbidity and reduced re-bleeding. It is not as suitable for the acutely bleeding patient, due to technical limitations. Banding is therefore recommended for second or subsequent endoscopy sessions to eradicate varices initially treated by sclerotherapy.

Intrahepatic shunt

Trans-jugular intrahepatic porto-systemic shunt (TIPSS) is a radiological technique for creating a porto-systemic shunt via the trans-jugular route.

Indications for TIPSS

- Uncontrolled acute variceal bleeding
- Failed endoscopic therapy
- Surgery contraindicated by poor hepatic function or general condition
- Recurrent variceal bleeding
- Patient intolerant of endoscopic therapy
- Patients awaiting liver transplants

- Under local or general anaesthetic, the right hepatic vein is cannulated by a percutaneous jugular route and the liver punctured to gain access to the portal vein
- The track is then dilated with a balloon catheter and a stent of 8–12 mm diameter is placed to maintain patency

The principle is to reduce the portal pressure gradient by short circuiting the liver. TIPSS is contraindicated in:

- Right-sided heart failure with an elevated central venous pressure
- Polycystic liver disease
- Severe acute progressive hepatic failure

Complications of TIPSS

- **Life-threatening (1–2% incidence)**
  Haemoperitoneum
  Haemobilia
  Acute hepatic ischaemia
  Cardiac puncture
  Pulmonary oedema
  Septicaemia

- **Late complications**
  Shunt thrombosis (30–50% within
    one year)
  Portal or splenic vein thrombosis
  Chronic haemolysis
  Deterioration in liver function
  Encephalopathy
  Re-bleeding of varices
    (due to shunt inefficiency)

- **Minor complications**
  Local puncture site haematoma
  Pain
  Puncture of other abdominal organs
  Transient arrhythmias
  Hypotension
  Migration of the stent
  Haemolytic anaemia
  Fever
  Reactions to contrast materials

Extrahepatic shunt

In long-term elective treatment, extrahepatic shunt or oesophageal transection are the alternatives to repeated sclerotherapy. The aim of extrahepatic shunt is to decompress the whole or part of the portal venous circulation. These shunts require a surgical procedure and are indicated in patients with failed endoscopic treatment. The three main extrahepatic shunts are:

- **Total shunt** (portocaval): the whole of the portal venous circulation is fully decompressed. In total shunts, there is no portal vein flow into the liver. The incidence of encephalopathy is high.
- **Partial shunt** (narrow diameter portocaval): the whole of the portal venous circulation is partly decompressed with a narrow (8–10 mm) non-expansile graft. Some portal flow continues so post-operative encephalopathy is reduced. This procedure can be done without extensive dissection and so is preferable to a total shunt for both uncontrolled acute and recurrent bleeding.
- **Selective shunt** (distal splenorenal): an isolated part of the portal circulation is fully decompressed. This is not advocated in an acute situation because of its technical complexity.

Oesophageal transection

The aim of oesophageal transection is to interrupt the gastric oesophageal porto-systemic anastomosis. Early oesophageal transection has compared favourably with injection sclerotherapy, but it requires a laparotomy and dissection in the presence of established portal hypertension and opening of the stomach, all of which may be hazardous in the acutely bleeding patient. The procedure is as follows:

- Anterior gastrotomy
- Stapling gun passed up into the oesophagus
- Vagus nerve identified and excluded
- Lower oesophageal wall tied into stapling line
- Gun fired to transect and re-anastomose the oesophagus simultaneously

Problems include:

- Bleeding gastric varices require further devascularization
- May be more hazardous than simple partial shunt
- Chances of sepsis are increased by opening stomach
- Recurrent bleeding is more likely than with shunts

Liver transplantation
Liver transplantation may be the preferable option for intractable portal hypertension. It is not suitable in cases of pre-hepatic obstruction with good liver function or in cases with a persisting underlying cause.

14.5 Liver neoplasms

Benign liver tumours (rare)

- **Adenoma**: associated with use of the OCP. It presents incidentally or with bleeding following rupture. Treatment is removal if it is expanding or there is doubt about the diagnosis.
- **Focal nodular hyperplasia**: these discrete sub-capsular lesions have an obscure aetiology and are usually symptomless. Growth can cause pain, rupture can cause bleeding.
- **Angioma**: these benign mesenchymal tumours can cause bleeding or be mistaken for metastatic tumours.

Primary malignant liver tumours (rare)

- **Hepatocellular carcinoma** (hepatoma): is rare in the UK/USA but world-wide it is common. Most cases arise in cirrhotic livers, usually due to viral hepatitis or alcohol. The tumour forms a large solitary mass or multiple foci throughout the liver. Distant metastasis is late. The clinical picture is hepatomegaly, bloodstained ascites, rapid progression and prognosis is poor.

- **Cholangiocarcinoma**: much less common. An adenocarcinoma arising from the intrahepatic bile duct system. Predisposing factors include: primary sclerosing cholangitis; anabolic steroids; liver fluke infestation. Usually presents with jaundice, poor prognosis.
- **Angiosarcoma**: either primary or a secondary spread from the spleen. It is a rare, malignant vascular tumour. Predisposing factors include: cirrhosis; arsenic; vinyl chloride and anabolic steroids.

Metastatic disease of the liver

By far the most common liver neoplasm, especially from colorectal cancer. The metastatic deposits can arise by portal or systemic blood, or direct spread. The clinical effects are:

- Hepatomegaly (large, hard, irregular liver)
- Jaundice (due to liver destruction and intrahepatic duct compression — hepatic or post-hepatic)
- Hepatic failure
- Portal vein obstruction producing oesophageal varices and ascites
- Inferior vena cava obstruction producing leg oedema

Diagnosis is by ultrasound but other investigations which help assess the extent of the tumour and plan management include:

- Serum biochemistry
- HIDA scans
- CT scans
- Percutaneous liver biopsy
- Arteriography and venography

Treatment of liver cancer

Surgery
Most treatment strategies for liver cancer are centred on metastatic liver disease. Surgical resection is the only potentially curable treatment for liver metastases with a five-year survival rate for colorectal metastases approaching 40%. However, only 20% of such lesions are deemed resectable. The main features indicating resectability are shown opposite.

Features associated with successful resection of liver cancer

- **Likely to be successful**
  Three or fewer tumours
  No portal vein invasion
  No hepatic vein invasion
  Pseudocapsule present
  No extrahepatic metastases

- **Controversial**
  Clear resection margins (> 1 cm)
  No more than one lobe involved

Resection is based on liver segments which allow more adequate margins. Staged resection can be performed to avoid liver insufficiency in large resections. Intra-operative vascular occlusion techniques allow excision of lesions lying near the vena cava.

Chemotherapy

Primary hepatomas have been treated with 5-Fluorouracil and adriamycin with some success. The use of chemotherapy for colorectal cancer is well-documented. Following resection of liver metastases, 60–70% of patients will develop recurrent disease. Systemic and intraperitoneal chemotherapy after liver resection has not been shown to improve survival. Recent studies have concentrated on other techniques which include:

- Intra-arterial chemotherapy through the hepatic artery
- Portal vein infusion
- Implantable infusion pumps

Limitations include:

- Development of extrahepatic metastases
- Toxicity such as biliary sclerosis
- Aftercare demands on patients
- Cost

Immunotherapy

Tumour-specific immunotherapy regimes have been attempted in advanced disease resistant to conventional therapy.

Other treatment modalities

Mainly experimental or used as part of a multi-modality treatment. **Hepatic artery chemoembolization** is not widely used. **Portal vein embolization** can decrease the likelihood of liver insufficiency occurring after extensive liver resection by inducing hypertrophy in the future remnant liver. This is used especially in hilar cholangiocarcinoma.

Brachytherapy in which radioactive implants are placed at laparotomy has been used to decrease recurrence in selected patients after surgical resection. **Cryotherapy**, **alcohol injection** and **laser** are also used to manage residual inaccessible lesions during liver resections. **Hepatic artery ligation** theoretically restricts tumour growth and reduces pain but is not often used. **Hepatic artery embolization** has been used for malignant endocrine tumours.

Post-operative surveillance

Patients with tumours that commonly spread to the liver should be monitored after excision of the primary. Post-operative colorectal carcinoma patients should have regular liver ultrasonography and measurement of tumour markers. Detecting hepatic metastatic disease at an early stage has a major impact on resectability rates. Some authors suggest that all patients with colorectal liver metastases should be assessed by a liver surgeon as apparently irresectable disease may be treated with other modalities.

14.6 Liver trauma

The liver is the most frequently injured intra-abdominal organ. Mechanisms include:

- **Penetrating injuries**: knife and gunshot wounds
- **Blunt injuries**: deceleration in falls from a height or road traffic accident
- **Compression injuries**: from a blow to the abdomen

There is a hepatic injury scale which grades the liver damage from Grade I (small laceration or subcapsular haematoma) to Grade VI (avulsion, incompatible with survival).

Assessment

The initial management should be along ATLS guidelines (see *MRCS Core Modules: Essential Revision Notes*, Chapter 3, *Trauma*). Immediate laparotomy is indicated in:

- A gunshot wound to the abdomen
- A stab wound to the abdomen in a haemodynamically unstable patient
- Clinical evidence of intra-abdominal bleeding in a haemodynamically unstable patient

Otherwise, the following investigations may be useful:

- Ultrasound
- Diagnostic peritoneal lavage
- CT
- Laparoscopy

The results of these will guide management.

Non-operative management of liver injury

80–90% of all cases are Grade I or II injuries which require minimal or no operative treatment; 50–80% of liver injuries stop bleeding spontaneously. The selection criteria for non-operative management include:

- Haemodynamically stable (the most important)
- No peritoneal signs
- Good quality CT scans and an experienced radiologist
- Facilities to monitor patient on ITU
- Facility for immediate surgery if needed
- Low-grade hepatic injury with <125 ml free intraperitoneal blood
- No other intra-abdominal injuries

Principles of non-operative management include:

- Continual re-assessment, including re-scanning
- Correcting clotting abnormalities
- Blood transfusion as needed
- Immediate surgery if indicated

Operative management of liver injuries

If surgery is indicated, it should not be delayed. Successful outcome depends on:

- Experienced liver surgeon
- Adequate blood, platelets, fresh frozen plasma and cryoprecipitate
- An intensive care unit
- Diagnostic back-up

If any of these requirements are absent, the patient should be transferred to a liver unit after initial control of haemorrhage.

The surgical techniques include:

- Initial control of bleeding by manual pressure on the liver, portal triad or aorta
- Resuscitation and assessment while bleeding is controlled
- Mobilizing liver
- Definitive surgery or packing

Retrohepatic venous injuries occur in around 10% of hepatic trauma and are very difficult to repair. Total vascular exclusion, venovenous bypass and atriocaval shunting have all been used to control bleeding during surgical repair.

Complications of liver trauma

Complications occur in nearly 66% of patients with liver trauma. Haemorrhage is the most common cause of re-operation. If more than 6 units of blood are needed in the first 12 hours post-operatively, re-laparotomy is indicated. Sepsis occurs in 10%. Biliary fistula occurs in 5% and is more common after resection. It usually ceases spontaneously but ERCP and stenting may be necessary.

14.7 Acute infections of the liver

Liver abscesses

Possible sources of infection are:

- **Arterial**: as part of a general septicaemia (unusual)
- **Portal**: from an area of suppuration drained by the portal vein
- **Biliary**: resulting from an ascending cholangitis
- **Spread**: from adjacent infection such as subphrenic abscess or acute cholecystitis
- **Trauma**: followed by secondary haemorrhage

The clinical features of a liver abscess include:

- High swinging temperature and rigors
- Abdominal pain and a tender palpable liver
- Jaundice

Ultrasound scan is usually diagnostic. A CXR shows:

- Elevation of the right diaphragm
- Right pleural effusion
- Basal pulmonary collapse
- Fluid level below the diaphragm

CT scans and isotope liver scans may also be helpful. Blood cultures should be taken before antibiotics are commenced. Antibiotic treatment should be targeted to the causative organism.

If a localized abscess is identified on ultrasound, percutaneous aspiration under ultrasound control is often successful. Surgery is indicated if the abscess ruptures, causing peritonitis, or percutaneous aspiration fails.

Liver abscesses secondary to severe cholangitis may require urgent bile duct drainage, usually by endoscopic sphincterotomy. Abscesses due to *Entamoeba histolytica* are a special type of portal infection. An enzyme produced by the protozoa destroys the liver tissue. Metronidazole is the antibiotic of choice.

Hydatid cysts

Occur as a result of liver infestation with *Echinococcus granulosus*, a parasite of dogs, sheep and man. Clinical features are often non-specific and include pain, incidental findings or jaundice. The active cyst may:

- Rupture into the peritoneal cavity, alimentary canal or biliary tree
- Become infected
- Press on intrahepatic bile ducts and produce obstructive jaundice

Investigations include:

- Ultrasound or CT scan
- Serological tests specific for hydatid antibodies

Eosinophilia and plain abdominal films are not diagnostic but may arouse suspicion. Treatment with albendazole may shrink or cure the cysts. Calcified asymptomatic cysts are usually dead and should be left alone. Enlarging subcapsular cysts are likely to cause complications and may need surgery. At laparotomy, aspiration with or without cyst excision is recommended but recurrence is likely.

Viral hepatitis

This is essentially a medical condition, but its surgical implications include:

- Sequelae such as hepatocellular carcinoma, cirrhosis, portal hypertension
- Risks of transmission to the surgeon
- Differential diagnosis of jaundice

There are several separate viral agents:

- **Hepatitis A**: spread by the faecal–oral route and by nasal droplets. Children and young adults are usually affected
- **Hepatitis B**: transmitted by inoculation with contaminated syringes or a transfusion of blood or plasma from an infected patient. The blood in these subjects contains the Australia antigen and is highly infective. Any age may be infected.
- **Hepatitis C**: similar in transmission to type B

Both Hepatitis B and C can lead to chronic infection, cirrhosis and tumour formation. There is a prodromal period of a few days with anorexia, fever, malaise and vomiting. The patient becomes jaundiced with dark urine. The liver is palpable and tender. Treatment is supportive with rest, a low fat diet and avoidance of alcohol. Complications include:

- Hepatic failure
- Massive liver necrosis (rare)
- Relapse
- Post-hepatic cirrhosis

Hepatitis B is a risk to hospital workers who should all be immunized.

Congenital abnormalities of the liver

Riedel's lobe is a projection of normally functioning liver tissue downwards from the right lobe of the liver. May cause diagnostic difficulties by giving a false impression of hepatomegaly. **Polycystic liver** may result in gross hepatomegaly but liver function is rarely compromised. May be associated with polycystic disease of the kidneys and pancreas.

14.8 Anatomy and physiology of the gall bladder and bile ducts

Anatomy of the biliary system

Bile capillaries lying in the portal triads at the corners of the liver lobules collect bile and drain it into branches of the hepatic duct. The right and left hepatic ducts fuse in the porta hepatis to form the 4 cm long **common hepatic duct**. This joins with the cystic duct (also 4 cm long), draining the gall bladder, to form the common bile duct (10 cm long). The common bile duct commences about 4 cm above the duodenum then passes behind it to open at a papilla on the medial aspect of the second part of the duodenum. The common bile duct usually joins the main pancreatic duct in a dilated common vestibule, the ampulla of Vater. Occasionally, the bile and the pancreatic ducts open separately into the duodenum. The opening of the ampulla is guarded by the muscular sphincter of Oddi. The structures in the hilum of the liver are arranged in the free edge of the lesser omentum forming the anterior boundary of the foramen of Winslow (see figure on p. 559).

The gall bladder
The gall bladder normally holds 50 ml of bile. It functions as a bile reservoir and concentrator. It lies in a fossa separating the right and quadrate lobes of the liver. The duodenum and transverse colon lie inferior to it and an inflamed gall bladder can ulcerate or fistulate into either of these structures. The muscular sac is divided into a fundus, body and neck which opens into the cystic duct via a dilated Hartmann's pouch (see figure on p. 559). Gallstones commonly lodge in Hartmann's pouch, which may not be present in a non-pathological gall bladder.

The mucosa of the biliary tree is lined by columnar cells and bears mucus-secreting glands. The gall bladder is supplied by the cystic artery which is usually a branch of the right hepatic artery. The cystic artery lies in a triangle (**Calot's triangle**) formed by the inferior border of the liver, the cystic duct and the common hepatic duct.

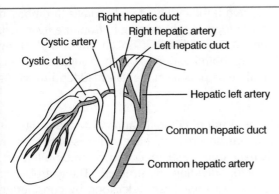

Right hepatic duct
Right hepatic artery
Cystic artery
Left hepatic duct
Cystic duct

— Hepatic left artery

— Common hepatic duct

— Common hepatic artery

a. Normal anatomy
Calot's triangle is formed by the inferior border of the liver, the cystic duct and the common hepatic duct. This is usually where the cystic artery can be found.

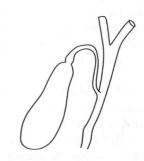

b. A long cystic duct (7%)
Joins the hepatic duct low down behind the duodenum

c. Absent cystic duct
The gall bladder opens directly into the common hepatic duct

d. Double gall bladder
The result of a rare bifid embryonic diverticulum from the hepatic duct

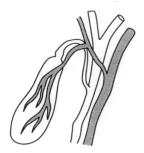

e. Anterior right hepatic artery (25%)
R hepatic artery crosses in front of the common hepatic duct

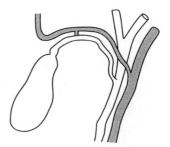

f. Recurrent right hepatic artery (7%)
Can be mistaken for a cystic artery

Anomalies in biliary anatomy

Gangrene of the gall bladder is rare because even if the cystic artery becomes thrombosed in acute cholecystitis, there is a rich secondary blood supply coming in from the liver bed. Gangrene may occur in the unusual event of a gall bladder on an abnormally long mesentery undergoing torsion which will destroy both its sources of blood supply. There is no vein accompanying the cystic artery. Small veins pass from the gall bladder through its bed directly into the liver.

Errors in gall bladder surgery are frequently the result of failure to appreciate the variations in the anatomy of the biliary system (see figure on previous page). This is why it is so important to identify clearly the common hepatic duct, cystic duct and common bile duct, together with the cystic and hepatic arteries before dividing any structure. The gall bladder and ducts are subject to numerous anatomical variations best understood by considering their embryological development. During development of the biliary tree, the ducts and gall bladder are temporarily solid due to proliferation of the epithelial lining. If recanalization fails to occur, this can lead to atresia of the gall bladder, bile duct or hepatic duct. Most commonly, biliary atresia occurs at the level of the porta hepatis.

Embryological development of the liver and gall bladder

In week 3 of gestation, the liver bud appears as an outgrowth of endodermal epithelium at the distal end of the foregut (see figure opposite). The hepatic cell strands of the liver bud penetrates the mesodermal septum transversum that lies between the pericardial cavity and the stalk of the yolk sac. The connection between the liver bud and the foregut (the bile duct) gives rise to a ventral outgrowth which will form the gall bladder and cystic duct. The epithelial liver cords mingle with the vitelline and umbilical veins forming the hepatic sinusoids. They also form the parenchyma and lining of the biliary duct. The mesoderm of the septum transversum forms the haemopoietic cells, Kupffer's cells and connective tissue cells.

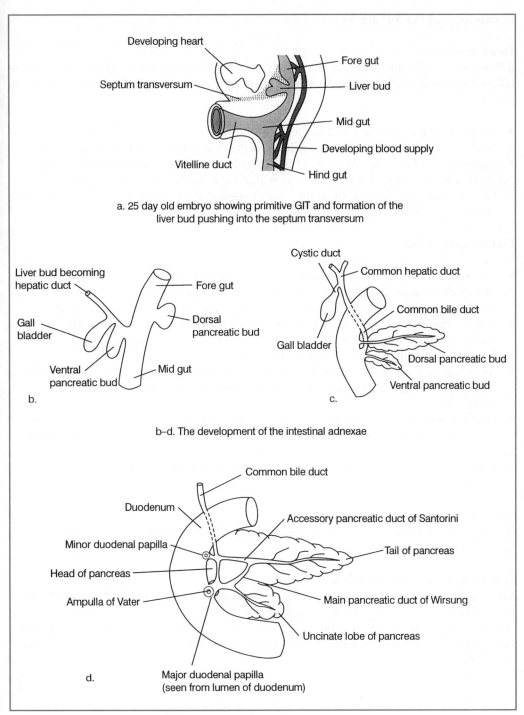

Developing heart

Septum transversum

Fore gut

Liver bud

Mid gut

Developing blood supply

Vitelline duct

Hind gut

a. 25 day old embryo showing primitive GIT and formation of the
liver bud pushing into the septum transversum

Liver bud becoming
hepatic duct

Fore gut

Gall
bladder

Dorsal
pancreatic bud

Ventral
pancreatic bud

Mid gut

b.

Cystic duct

Common hepatic duct

Common bile duct

Gall bladder

Dorsal pancreatic bud

Ventral pancreatic bud

c.

b–d. The development of the intestinal adnexae

Common bile duct

Duodenum

Accessory pancreatic duct of Santorini

Minor duodenal papilla

Tail of pancreas

Head of pancreas

Ampulla of Vater

Main pancreatic duct of Wirsung

Uncinate lobe of pancreas

d.

Major duodenal papilla
(seen from lumen of duodenum)

Embryology of the pancreas and biliary tree

579

Physiology of the biliary tree

Function of bile
Bile is a fluid with various constituents secreted by the liver into the duodenum through the biliary tract. Excess bile is stored between meals in the gall bladder. The functions of bile are:

- Excretion of pigments and cholesterol
- Neutralizing of stomach contents arriving in the duodenum with bicarbonate
- Digestion of fats — bile salts consist of a fat soluble hydrocarbon ring with several charged groups around it so it can mix with fat and water. It increases fat solubility by emulsifying the fat leading to the easier digestion of fat by water soluble lipases to glycerol, glycerides and fatty acids in micelles.

Composition of bile

- **Bile salts or acids** (50% of dry weight of bile): are synthesized from cholesterol and are mostly cholic acid and chenodeoxycholic acid. Four grams per day are secreted, mostly to be reabsorbed in the ileum (see later). They aid in the digestion of fats.
- **Bile pigments**: are purely excretory products of haemoglobin breakdown. The liver transforms the unconjugated bilirubin, which is insoluble, to soluble conjugated bilirubin by conjugating it with glucouronic acid.
- **Inorganic salts**: mostly sodium chloride and sodium bicarbonate. The concentration of bicarbonate ions is high and allows for the neutralization of gastric acid in the duodenum.
- **Phospholipids**: hepatocytes secrete phospholipids like cholesterol and lecithins. This is the major route for cholesterol excretion, and excess cholesterol in the bile predisposes to gallstones.
- **Water**: 97% of bile is water. Some is reabsorbed in the gall bladder which concentrates bile.

Control of bile secretion
A complex combination of hormonal, neural and feedback mechanisms, summarized in the figure opposite.

Enterohepatic circulation of bile
Bile is secreted into the duodenum by contractions of the gall bladder. In the small intestine, bile acids first emulsify dietary fat and then form mixed micelles with the products of fat digestion. In the terminal ileum, bile acids are reabsorbed. Finally, they are taken up by the hepatocytes by a secondary active transport mechanism and re-secreted into bile (see figure on p. 582).

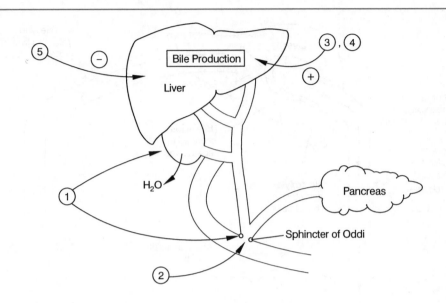

(1) **CCK**:
- Contracts the gall bladder
- Opens the sphincter of Oddi
- Is secreted in response to acid calcium, fatty acids and amino acids in the duodenum

(2) **Cephalic reflux**:
- Opens sphincter of Oddi in response to food in mouth

(3) **Secretin**:
- Increases hepatic bile production; increases water and bicarbonate content

(4) **Vagus**:
- Acts as secretin; stimulated in the cephalic and gastric stages of digestion

(5) **Level of bile salts**:
- High level of recirculators bile salts decreases new production in the liver (feedback mechanism).

Control of gall bladder secretion

581

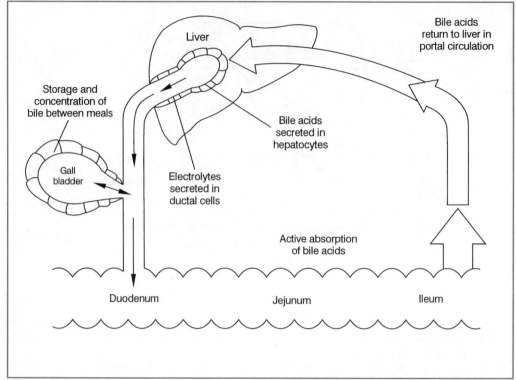

Enterohepatic circulation of bile

14.9 Gallstones

Incidence

- 10% of British women in their 40s have gallstones F:M–2:1
- Incidence increases with age and certain nationalities (e.g. Mediterranean)
- The saying that gallstones occur in fair, fat, fertile females of 40 is inaccurate but a useful reminder of the typical patient

Pathogenesis

There are three common varieties of gallstones:

- **Cholesterol stones** (20%): occur as solitary stones, in pairs or as multiple mulberry stones. May be associated with high cholesterol, pregnancy, diabetes and the contraceptive pill. The 'strawberry gall bladder' is cholesterosis of the gall bladder with a mucosa studded with submucous collections of cholesterol. Bile salts and phospholipids hold insoluble cholesterol in suspension so a decrease of either increases gallstones.

- **Bile pigment stones** (5%): small, black, irregular, multiple, gritty and fragile stones. Occur in excess of circulating bile pigment (e.g. haemolytic anaemia).
- **Mixed stones** (75%): these are multiple, faceted and may collect in similar-sized groups (generations of stones). Originate because of precipitation of cholesterol.

Other predisposing factors include:

- Excess mucus production of gall bladder
- Infection of biliary tract
- Metabolic factors
- Stasis (e.g. in pregnancy)
- Ileal dysfunction (prevents re-absorption of bile)
- Obesity, hypertriglyceridaemia
- Chronic liver disease

Pathological effects of gallstones

Silent
The majority of gallstones are asymptomatic.

Obstruction of the cystic duct
A gallstone may become impacted at the exit of the gall bladder or in the cystic duct. This causes a chemical cholecystitis because water is absorbed from the bile in the gall bladder and it becomes concentrated. This is usually sterile at first but then becomes secondarily infected from organisms secreted from the liver into the bile stream. Occasionally, if the gall bladder is empty of bile when outlet obstruction occurs, mucus secretion continues and distends the gall bladder, forming a mucocoele.

Movement of a stone into the common bile duct
May be asymptomatic. May distend the cystic duct causing colicky pain. May obstruct the common bile duct causing jaundice and proximal distension.

Ulceration of a stone through the wall of the gall bladder
Usually ulcerates into the duodenum or colon. Impaction of the stone in the distal ileum results in intestinal obstruction (gallstone ileus).

Other effects:

- Acute pancreatitis
- Chronic pancreatitis
- Carcinoma of the gall bladder

Clinical presentation of gallstones

Biliary colic
This is pain resulting from distension of the gall bladder outlet or duct system when a stone becomes impacted. Typical clinical features include:

- Right hypochondrial or epigastric pain
- Episodic
- Radiating to the lower pole of the right scapula
- Restless patient rolling in agony
- Sweaty, nauseous, vomiting
- Intermittent jaundice with pale stools and dark urine

The episode may resolve when the stone is passed along the duct or falls back into the gall bladder. Differential diagnosis includes renal colic, intestinal obstruction and angina.

Acute cholecystitis
Inflammation of the gall bladder due to chemical or bacterial cholecystitis is a sequela of obstruction of the biliary tree by gallstones in 95% of cases. Typical clinical features include:

- A history of previous dyspepsia, fat intolerance or biliary colic
- Right upper quadrant pain becoming more severe, constant and localized after a day or two
- Fever, toxaemia, leucocytosis, rigors

On examination, rebound tenderness and guarding in the right upper quadrant, Murphy's sign (see Section 5.5, p. 365). A mass may be palpable.

Complications include:

- Empyema of gall bladder
- Perforation of the gall bladder, causing peritonitis
- Obstructive jaundice, even if ductal stones have passed, due to local oedema
- Acalculus acute cholecystitis can occur in 5% of cases: if a single causative stone has been passed; in typhoid fever; in gas gangrene infection

Differential diagnoses include acute appendicitis, perforated duodenal ulcer, acute pancreatitis, right-sided basal pneumonia.

Chronic cholecystitis — 'gall bladder dyspepsia'
Almost always associated with gallstones which repeatedly inflame the gall bladder, resulting in fibrosis and thickening of the entire gall bladder wall. Long-standing dyspeptic symptoms punctuated by episodes of cholecystitis are typical. Differential diagnoses include peptic ulceration, hiatus hernia and angina.

Stones in the common bile duct may present with any combination of:

- No symptoms
- Biliary colic
- Obstructive jaundice
- Biliary cirrhosis
- Cholangitis
- Cholecystitis

Differential diagnoses of stones in the common bile duct include:

- With jaundice (75%): malignant obstruction (e.g. cancer of the pancreas); acute hepatitis; other causes of jaundice (see table on p. 549):
- Without jaundice (25%): renal colic; intestinal obstruction; angina

Investigations

These are described in detail in Section 14.1, p. 547, on investigation of the jaundiced patient. Ultrasound scan, liver function tests and ERCP are the mainstays of diagnosis of gall bladder disease. CT scan may be useful in obstructive jaundice with malignancy suspected.

Management of gallstone disease

Acute cholecystitis

The principles of treatment of an acute cholecystitis attack include:

- Admission to hospital
- Pain relief with opiates
- Nil by mouth
- IV fluids
- Broad-spectrum antibiotics
- Elective cholecystectomy 6 weeks after discharge

Elective cholecystectomy is recommended after an attack of cholecystitis because:

- There is a high risk of recurrent attacks
- There is a risk of life-threatening complications, such as perforation of the gall bladder, pancreatitis or obstructive jaundice in future attacks

Cholecystectomy is not generally performed during an acute attack because:

- 90% settle on conservative treatment
- Dissection is more difficult when the gall bladder is acutely inflamed
- The condition of the patient for surgery is not optimal when septic and dehydrated

Cholecystectomy is indicated in acute cholecystitis in:

• Failure of conservative treatment
• Development of a dangerous complication, such as empyema, perforation or fistulation

Some surgeons advise early surgery rather than delayed cholecystectomy for acute cholecystitis.

Chronic cholecystitis

If a patient is diagnosed as having chronic cholecystitis, an elective cholecystectomy is indicated.

Stones in the common bile duct

The majority of cases resolve on conservative treatment. Subsequent elective cholecystectomy can then be performed. If jaundice is persistent or progressive, particularly in the presence of high fever, an urgent procedure is needed (ERCP and sphincterotomy or an open operation).

The symptomless stone

There is controversy over the management of asymptomatic gallstones. If left alone, only 7% of asymptomatic gallstones needed surgery for gallstone-related disease within 5 years, so prophylactic surgery is not indicated. However, 44% of symptomatic patients with gallstones required surgery, thus justifying a cholecystectomy.

Medical treatment of gallstones

All patients with gallstones are advised to keep to a low-fat diet. Oral bile salts (e.g. chenodeoxycholic acid) are used to dissolve small, non-calcified stones in a functioning gall bladder in patients not suitable for surgery. Disadvantages include:

• Prolonged treatment for months is necessary
• Attacks of biliary colic as fragments of stone are passed
• Recurrence is common

Lithotripsy (ultrasonic destruction of small stones) is possible and can be combined with percutaneous aspiration of debris under ultrasound control. These methods have limited applications.

Cholecystectomy

Open cholecysectomy is being replaced by the laparoscopic operation except when contraindicated. The operative time and cost of equipment is less in an open procedure, but the mean hospital stay and time to return to work is less in the laparoscopic procedure.

Open cholecystectomy

- **Pre-operatively**
  Ultrasound and liver function tests and clotting screen
  Exclude peptic ulcer disease and hiatus hernia if diagnosis in doubt
  Encourage weight loss and smokers to stop
  Decide if intraoperative cholangiogram is likely

- **Incision**
  Usually right subcostal (Kocher's)

- **Procedure**
  Thorough laparotomy, especially duodenum, caecum and oesophageal hiatus
  Packs behind liver to lift it forward
  Free duodenum and hepatic flexure of colon from gall bladder
  Clamp on fundus and clamp on Hartmann's pouch
  Divide peritoneum over cystic duct
  Identify hepatic duct, common bile duct, cystic duct and cystic artery
  Divide cystic artery between ligatures
  Perform cholangiogram if indicated
  Divide the cystic duct between ligatures
  Dissect the gall bladder from the liver bed (antegrade removal)
  In difficult cases (e.g. fibrotic or acutely inflamed gall bladder) the dissection can be
    fundus first (retrograde removal)
  Ensure haemostasis
  A drain may be placed next to the liver bed

- **Closure**
  In layers with non-absorbable sutures
  Clips to skin

- **Post-operatively**
  Analgesia, early chest physiotherapy, oral fluid day 1
  Drain out at 24 hours if <100 ml drainage
  Home day 5 if all well

- **Operative hazards**
  Damage to hepatic or common bile ducts
  Damage to hepatic artery

- **Complications**
  Haemorrhage from slipped tie or from gall bladder bed
  Biliary leak
  Missed stone in bile duct or cystic duct stump
  Biliary stricture from damage to biliary tree

Laparoscopic cholecystectomy

- **Pre-operatively**
  As with open cholecystectomy, plus
  Ensure there are no contraindications to laparoscopic cholecystectomy
  Consent patient for conversion to an open operation

- **Procedure**
  Induce a pneumoperitoneum through a 10 mm subumbilical incision (see p. 339)
  Three further incisions are made under laparoscopic vision:

  > 10 mm incision in the mid-line just below the xiphisternum
  > 5 mm incision in the mid-axillary line on the transpyloric plane
  > 5 mm incision in the anterior axillary line 5 cm below the costal margin

  Perform a laparoscopic survey of the entire abdomen
  Identify the structures of Calot's triangle as in the open operation
  Divide the cystic artery between ligaclips
  Perform cholangiogram if indicated
  Divide cystic duct between ligaclips
  Dissect gall bladder from the liver by a combination of blunt dissection
   and cautery
  Check the liver bed for haemostasis
  Remove the gall bladder through the subumbilical or subxiphisternal port
  A drain can be brought out through one of the right-sided ports
  The abdomen is exsufflated and the instruments withdrawn

- **Closure**
  Close linea alba in 10 mm incisions with non-absorbable sutures or P.D.S.
  Skin clips

- **Post-operatively**
  Fully mobilized and eating by the next day
  Home after 24 hours if all well

- **Operative hazards**
  Requiring conversion to an open operation (should be < 5%)
  Injury to the bowel or great vessels during insufflation
  Damage to common bile duct, portal vein or hepatic artery
  Failure to complete procedure
  Common duct stones
  Carbon dioxide retention due to absorption of intraperitoneal carbon dioxide
  Accidental perforation of the gall bladder and scattering of calculi

- **Complications**
  As for open operation

Relative contraindications to laparoscopic cholecystectomy

- Jaundice
- Acute pancreatitis
- Cirrhosis
- Previous upper abdominal surgery
- Surgeon not familiar with
  equipment or technique

- Ductal calculi
- Acute cholecystitis
  (empyema/gangrene)
- Morbid obesity
- Pregnancy

Intraoperative cholangiography

There has been a great deal of debate about whether cannulation of the biliary tree and contrast radiography during cholecystectomy is necessary. The argument for intraoperative cholangiography is that it:

- Defines anatomical variations
- Confirms that the duct about to be divided is the cystic duct
- Visualizes stones in the common bile duct (occurs in 10% of cholecystectomies) which, if overlooked, would lead to persistent obstructive jaundice and risk of post-operative cholangitis and bile leak

Some surgeons suggest that an intraoperative cholangiography should only be performed on selected patients including those with:

- Abnormal common bile duct seen on ultrasound
- Wide cystic duct seen on operation
- An elevated alkaline phosphatase or bilirubin within the 6 months preceding the operation
- Difficulty in identifying anatomy or suspicion of intraductal stones during the operation

The options available to the surgeon who finds a stone in a bile duct during a laparoscopic cholecystectomy are:

- Leave it and do a post-operative ERCP
- Convert to an open procedure
- Attempt laparoscopic retrieval using balloon, basket, cholendoscope or by performing a laparoscopic choledochotomy

Endoscopic retrograde cholangiopancreatography (ERCP)
ERCP is described in detail in Section 14.1, p. 547. This technique has revolutionized the treatment of choledocholithiasis (stones in the common bile duct). The common bile duct is successfully cleared in 94% of cases, usually using a balloon, basket or sphincterotomy.

Pre-operative ERCP is an alternative to intraoperative cholangiogram, but it is expensive and carries a morbidity so is not done as routine. Surgery is preferred to ERCP in difficult cases, such as:

* Aberrant anatomy
* Periampullary diverticulum
* Prior surgery
* Difficult stones, such as >15 mm; intrahepatic; impacted; multiple
* Stricture associated with the stone

14.10 Other disorders of the biliary tree

Carcinoma of the gall bladder

Pathology
Carcinoma of the gall bladder is rare. F:M–4:1. 90% are adenocarcincomas, 10% are squamous cell carcinomas. Associated with gallstones in 95% of cases. Spreads to the liver, either directly or via the portal vein and via lymphatics to the porta hepatis.

Clinical features
Either discovered incidentally during cholecystectomy or presents with a picture closely resembling chronic cholecystitis.

Treatment
Hepatic resection and tumour excision is the only chance of cure, which is poor unless a small localized tumour is found incidentally at an early stage.

Gall bladder disease in children

The development of the gall bladder and biliary tree are discussed in Section 14.8, p. 576. The main childhood disorders are:

* Extrahepatic biliary atresia
* Choledochal cysts
* Inspissated bile syndrome (can occur secondary to haemolysis)
* Spontaneous perforation of the common bile duct (rare)
* Acute gall bladder distension (often following respiratory tract infections)
* Benign inflammatory tumours of the bile ducts

Primary sclerosing cholangitis

A chronic fibrosing inflammatory condition of the bilary tree affecting young adults. It affects intrahepatic and extrahepatic ducts. The gall bladder and the pancreas may also be affected. Of unknown origin but associated with ulcerative colitis in 50–70% of cases. Patients may be at increased risk of developing bile duct carcinoma. Presentation is usually progressive jaundice and right upper quadrant pain. Cholangiography shows strictures. LFTs show a high alkaline phosphatase. Immunological studies are also useful. Treatment is symptomatic with an average survival of 5–7 years.

Benign bile duct stricture

These are most often post-operative or associated with gallstones. Other causes include parasitic infestations, acute cholecystitis, chronic pancreatitis and sclerosing cholangitis. Investigations are aimed at identifying the level of the stricture and excluding a malignant cause. Percutaneous transhepatic cholangiography is useful as ERCP cannot image the bilary tree proximal to the stricture. Ultrasound is less invasive.

Bile duct carcinoma

One of the 10 most common cancers in France but less common in the UK. Unlike carcinoma of the gall bladder, it affects men and women equally. Predisposing factors include:

- Bile duct stones (in 20–30%)
- Sclerosing cholangitis
- Ulcerative colitis
- Cysts of the bile duct
- Parasitic infestation

They are adenocarcinomas and appear macroscopically as a small nodule, a papillary lesion or a diffuse stricture; 50% occur in the hepatic duct. 50% in the cystic and common bile duct.

Clinical features
Jaundice (90%), pain (30%), ascites (40%), anorexia, weight loss and anaemia.

Investigations
Depend on presentation, site of tumour and planned management and include:

- Ultrasound
- Transhepatic cholangiography
- ERCP

- Angiography
- CT
- FNAC can be obtained under ultrasound or ERCP control

Management
Curative surgery:

- Potentially curable lesions are surgically resected
- This operation has a high morbidity and mortality
- Distal tumours have a higher resectability rate

Palliation
80–90% of patients have incurable lesions. The aim is to relieve obstruction. Techniques include:

- Bypass procedures, such as hepaticojejunostomy or Roux-en-Y
- Intra-operative insertion of internal or intero-external stents
- Percutaneous biliary stenting
- Percutaneous biliary drainage
- Endoscopic transpapillary stenting
- Radiotherapy

In frail, older patients with concurrent disease, non-operative measures are preferred.

14.11 Anatomy and physiology of the pancreas

Anatomy

Gross anatomy
The pancreas lies retroperitoneally in the transpyloric plane. Divided into head, neck, body and tail. The head lies in the C-shaped curve of the duodenum. It has an uncinate process which hooks behind the superior mesenteric vessels. The neck lies in front of the superior mesenteric and portal veins. The body passes to the left and upwards behind the lesser sac forming part of the stomach bed. The lesser sac can become distended with fluid from acute pancreatitis forming a pseudo-cyst. The tail lies within the spleno-renal ligament touching the hilum of the spleen. The pancreatic duct of Wirsung drains the majority of the pancreas into the major duodenal papilla. It is joined by the common bile duct at or before the ampulla of Vater. The uncinate process is drained by the accessory duct of Santorini which opens into the duodenum at the minor duodenal papilla. Although the uncinate lobe is an inferior part of the pancreas, it drains into the minor duodenal papilla which is 2 cm above or proximal to the major ampulla due to development reasons (see figure on p. 579).

The important posterior relations of the pancreas are:

- Inferior vena cava
- Superior mesenteric vessels
- Crura of the diaphragm
- Coeliac plexus
- Left kidney and adrenal gland
- Splenic artery (along the upper border of the pancreas)
- Splenic vein, inferior and superior mesenteric veins draining into the portal vein behind the neck of the pancreas
- The common bile duct

A neoplasm at the head of the pancreas can, therefore, cause obstructive jaundice, portal vein obstruction or inferior vena cava obstruction.

Blood supply
Blood supply is from the splenic and pancreaticoduodenal arteries. The corresponding veins drain into the portal system, the lymphatics drain largely to superior mesenteric nodes.

Embryology
The embryology of the pancreas is shown in the figure on p. 579. It develops from a large dorsal bud from the duodenum and a smaller ventral bud from the common bile duct. The ventral bud swings round posteriorly to fuse with the dorsal bud, trapping the superior mesenteric vessels between the two parts. The ducts of these two buds of the pancreas then communicate and that of the smaller takes over the main pancreatic flow to form the main duct, leaving the original duct of the larger portion of the gland as the accessory duct (see figure on p. 579).

Rarely the two developing segments of the pancreas completely surround the second part of the duodenum (annular pancreas) and may produce duodenal obstruction. Ectopic pancreas nodules can be found in the stomach or small intestine.

Structure
The pancreas is lobulated and encapsulated. The lobules are made up of serous secretory cells draining via their ductules into the main ducts (exocrine glands). Between these alveoli lie the islets of Langerhans which secrete insulin, not into the ducts but directly into the circulation (endocrine glands).

Exocrine pancreas: the structure of the exocrine pancreas resembles that of the salivary glands and accounts for 98% of the volume of the pancreas.

- Acinar cells form acini which each drain into an intercalated duct forming the functional unit of the exocrine pancreas

- Acini are organized into lobules which drain via intra and extra lobular ducts into the pancreatic duct
- The pancreas is innervated by branches of the vagus nerve which stimulates secretion of both acinar and islet cells
- Post-ganglionic sympathetic nerves from the coeliac and superior mesenteric plexus tend to be inhibitory to secretion

Endocrine pancreas

- The endocrine cells of the pancreas reside in the islets of Langerhans
- These tiny (100 nm diameter) clusters of specialized cells account for less than 2% of the volume of the pancreas
- They have a good blood supply and are innervated by the vagus and sympathetic nerves
- The islets consist of separate types of cells secreting hormones
- Insulin from β cells
- Glucagon from α cells
- Somatostatin from δ cells
- Pancreatic polypeptide from F cells

Physiology of the exocrine pancreas

The pancreas acts as an exocrine gland secreting pancreatic juice into the duodenum via pancreatic ducts.

Summary of pancreatic physiology

- **Exocrine pancreas**
  Pancreatic juice
  Acinar (enzymes)
  Ductile (water, bicarbonate, sodium)

- **Endocrine pancreas**
  Insulin
  Glucagon
  Somatostatin
  Pancreatic polypeptide

Exocrine pancreatic secretion
Composition of pancreatic juice:

- **Acinar secretion** (digests duodenal contents): trypsinogen, chymotrypsinogen, procarboxylase, procarboxypeptidases, phospholipase, amylase, lecithin, sodium chloride, water
- **Ductile secretion** (increases pH of duodenal contents): bicarbonate, sodium ions, water

Secretion of pancreatic juice

Digestive enzymes are stored in an inactive form to prevent autodigestion. Granules containing inactive proenzymes fuse with cell membrane and exocytose. Trypsinogen is converted to trypsin by enterokinase in the duodenum. Trypsin then converts the other inactive enzymes into their active forms. The duct cells secrete bicarbonate in exchange for chloride ions. The bicarbonate concentration increases as the secretion rate increases.

Stimulation of pancreatic secretion

- **Parasympathetic vagal stimulation**
  In response to cephalic and
  gastric phase

- **Secretin**
  In response to acid in the   ↑ Ductal alkaline aqueous
  duodenum   component

- **CCK**
  In response to peptides, amino   ↑ Acinar enzyme components
  acids, fatty acids in the duodenum

Physiology of the endocrine pancreas

As well as acting as an exocrine gland, the pancreas also acts as an endocrine gland, secreting several hormones directly into the bloodstream from the islets of Langerhans.

Insulin from β cells

The main effects of insulin are to promote fuel storage. It is:

- Glucoregulatory
- Antilipolytic
- Antiketogenic
- Anabolic

Insulin consists of two straight-chain peptides held together by disulphide bands. Secretion is stimulated by:

- Glucose
- Protein
- Gastrointestinal peptides
- Cholinergic and beta-adrenergic stimuli

Its release is inhibited by circumstances requiring fuel mobilization, such as fasting or exercise. Insulin inhibits:

- Adipose tissue lipolysis
- Ketogenesis
- Hepatic glycogenolysis
- Gluconeogenesis
- Glucose release
- Muscle proteolysis

Insulin stimulates:

- Muscle glucose uptake
- Storage of glucose as glycogen
- Protein synthesis

Insulin acts through a plasma membrane receptor with tyrosine kinase activity. This leads to modulation of the activities of enzymes involved in glucose and fatty acid metabolism. Insulin also affects gene expression of numerous enzymes and proteins.

Insulin decreases plasma levels of:

- Glucose
- Free fatty acids
- Ketoacids
- Branch chain amino acids

Insulin deficiency (diabetes mellitus) leads to:

- Hyperglycaemia
- Loss of lean body mass
- Loss of adipose tissue mass
- Growth retardation
- Metabolic ketoacidosis

Glucagon from α cells

Glucagon is a single chain polypeptide released in response to hypoglycaemia and to amino acids. Glucagon promotes mobilization of glucose by stimulating hepatic glycogenolysis and gluconeogenesis. It also increases fatty acid oxidation and ketogenesis. The mechanism of action is modifying enzyme activities by phosphorylation. cAMP is its second messenger. Glucagon increases plasma levels of:

- Glucose
- Free fatty acids
- Ketoacids

The insulin/glucagon ratio controls the relative rates of glycolysis and gluconeogenesis. The two hormones have antagonistic effects at numerous steps in hepatic metabolism.

Somatostatin

Somatostatin is a neuropeptide produced by the delta cells. It reduces the rate of digestion by decreasing:

- Motility of the gastrointestinal tract
- Gastrointestinal secretions
- Digestion and absorption of nutrients
- Secretion of insulin and glucagon

It is secreted in response to meals and avoids overload of the portal venous system with the products of digestion.

Pancreatic polypeptide

This is the least clearly understood of the pancreatic hormones. It is a small polypeptide, secreted from the F cells of the islets of Langerhans. Its production is stimulated by a drop in blood sugar, protein and fasting. It slows food absorption and helps regulate the variations in the rate of digestion.

14.12 Pancreatitis

Acute pancreatitis is an acute inflammation of the pancreas typically presenting with abdominal pain and raised pancreatic enzymes in the blood and urine. It can be:

- Mild
- Severe (with derangement of one or more body systems)
- Fulminant (with life-threatening multisystem failure within 48 hours)
- Complicated

Chronic pancreatitis is a continuing inflammatory disease, characterized by irreversible morphological change and typically causing pain and/or permanent loss of function.

Aetiology and predisposing factors

This has long been remembered by the medical student mnemonic

'GET SMASH'D'

Gallstones and alcohol account for 80% of cases in the UK.

Aetiology and predisposing factors of pancreatitis

Gallstones and bilary tract disease (40% of cases)
Ethanol (alcohol) related (40%)
Toxins and drugs (e.g. steroids, thiazides, diuretics, oestrogens and azathioprine)

Surgery or trauma including ERCP
Metabolic (e.g. primary hyperparathyroidism, uraemia, diabetic coma, hyperlipidaemia, pregnancy)
Autoimmune and inherited
Snake bite and infections
Hypothermia
Duodenal obstruction

Pathology

- **Initiation of condition**: acinar damage by activitated pro-enzymes either due to hyper-secretion and ductal obstruction or reflux of duodenal content back into pancreatic ducts
- **Pancreatic necrosis**: once the initial insult has occurred, proteolytic enzymes damage blood vessels leading to ischaemia and haemorrhage. Further enzymes from the ischaemic pancreas leak into the bloodstream causing systemic effects.

The main enzymes liberated in pancreatitis are **trypsin, lipase** and **amylase**. There are three pathological types of pancreatitis:

- Oedematous
- Haemorrhagic $\left.\vphantom{\begin{array}{c}1\\1\\1\end{array}}\right\}$ which may be focal, segmental or total
- Necrotizing

Clinical features

Peak incidence is at 60 years of age. Alcoholic pancreatitis is more common in men, whereas gallstone pancreatitis is more common in women. Clinical features are systemic and local (see the shaded box opposite) but the typical presentation is an acute abdomen in a systemically unwell patient. Differential diagnoses include:

- Acute cholecystitis
- Peritonitis
- Peptic ulcer disease
- High intestinal obstruction
- Myocardial infarction

Clinical features of pancreatitis

- **Local**
  Epigastric pain radiating to the back
  Acute abdomen — tender, rigid, silent abdomen with distension
  Jaundice due to pancreatic oedema/gallstone
  Ascites
  Abscess formation
  Grey Turner's and Cullen's signs

- **Systemic**
  Shock due to retroperitoneal fluid loss and vasoactive substances from pancreas
  Respiratory failure due to pleural ARDS and effusions
  Renal failure due to hypovolaemia and direct effects of enzymes

- **Metabolic changes**
  Hypocalcaemia
  Hypoglycaemia
  Hypomagnesemia

Investigations

- **Serum amylase**: over 200 Somogyi units is abnormal; over 1000 units is virtually diagnostic; peritonitis can also cause elevated amylase
- **Other blood tests**: FBC (↑WCC); U&Es; LFTs; albumin; magnesium; glucose
- **Urinary amylase**
- **Erect CXR and AXR**
- **USS**: shows gallstones and pseudo-cyst but difficult to visualize pancreas
- **CT scan**: shows pancreas more clearly than ultrasound
- **Blood gases**: hypoxia occurs in severe cases

Management
Acutely this should comprise immediate resuscitation and assessment. Mainstays include:

- Analgesia
- Nil by mouth
- NG tube
- IV fluids
- Oxygen
- Antibiotics
- Catheterization
- Sliding scale insulin regime

Later management is divided into **systemic** and **local** management. **Systemic** management supports and monitors the various systems:

- Cardiovascular system may need central venous pressure monitoring, and ionotropes in severe cases
- Renal failure may necessitate dialysis
- Respiratory failure may lead to ventilation
- Metabolic problems may indicate IV calcium gluconate or IM magnesium
- Total parenteral nutrition may be needed

Local long-term management centres on:

- Promoting pancreatic blood flow with dextran and steroids
- Suppressing pancreatic secretions with anticholinergics, glucagon and NG aspiration
- Counteracting vasoactive enzymes using apoprotein (controversial)

Antioxidants may also have a role.

Surgery is best avoided unless:

- Diagnosis is in doubt
- Deterioration continues
- Operable complication develops

ERCP may be indicated (e.g. if an obstructing stone is impacted in the bile duct).

Local complications of pancreatitis

- Phlegmon (non-suppurative inflammatory mass)
- Oedema
- Generalized effusion/infected effusion/localized effusion — this usually fills the lesser sac forming a pseudo-cyst
- Ascites
- Abscess (usually sterile)
- Necrosis
- Pseudoaneurysm

Ranson's criteria

This severity scale of pancreatitis is used as a research tool and correlates well with prognosis and chance of admission to ICU. It is also used clinically to indicate the severity of the attack.

Ranson's criteria

- **On initial assessment**

1. Age more than 55
2. WCC >16
3. Glucose >20
4. LDH >350
5. AST >250

- **Within 24 hours**

1. Haematocrit fall >10%
2. BUN > 8 mg/dl
3. Calcium <8 mg/dl
4. PaO$_2$ <60 mmHg
5. Base deficit >4 m
6. Fluid sequestration >600 ml

The higher the score, the worse the prognosis

14.13 Pancreatic carcinoma

Incidence

A common, lethal metastasizing ductal adenocarcinoma. The fourth most common cancer in the UK. Incidence is increasing rapidly. Peak incidence at 60–80 years. Predisposing factors include:

- Smokers
- Diabetics
- Coffee drinkers
- Adenomas of the ampulla
- Familial adenomatous polyposis
- Gardner's syndrome

Pathology

Most commonly ductal adenocarcinomas; 70% occur in the head, 20% in the body and 10% in the tail. Macroscopically it is a big, grey white diffuse tumour with ill-defined borders. The tumour tends to spread into and along the main pancreatic duct (of Wirsung) and along the bile duct. It is aggressively invasive locally, spreading to the duodenum, local lymph nodes, the portal vein and nerve sheaths. It metastasizes to the liver. Rarer types of tumour include:

- Carcinoma *in situ*
- Intraductal carcinoma
- Papillary carcinoma
- Adenosquamous carcinoma
- Osteoclast (giant cell) carcinoma
- Cyst adenocarcinoma
- Lymphoma

Carcinoma of the pancreas is one of the periampullary tumours but should be differentiated from the other malignancies in that area:

- Ampullary carcinoma
- Duodenal carcinoma
- Lower bile duct carcinoma

These other periampullary tumours present similarly but have a much better resection and survival rate when compared with pancreatic carcinoma.

Presentation

Typical clinical features of pancreatic cancer include:

- Weight loss (91% of cases)
- Jaundice (71%)
- Pain (83%)
- Malaise (34%)
- Pancreatitis (5% — usually in a young age group)

Tumours of the head of the pancreas tend to present with obstructive jaundice, nausea, weight loss and weakness. A palpable mass may be felt in the right upper quadrant since, unlike in gallstone disease, the gall bladder tends to be normal, thin-walled and distensible (see Courvoisier's law, p. 450). In tumours of the body and tail, only 20% present with jaundice. Pain, diabetes and hepatomegaly can indicate a tumour in this site. They tend to present late. Trousseau's sign is a migratory superficial thrombophlebitis associated with pancreatic cancer.

Diagnosis

This relies upon clinical suspicion of vague symptoms such as:

- Upper abdominal pain and backache with a negative ultrasound and endoscopy
- Unexplained weight loss with no other signs
- Pancreatitis in the absence of gallstones
- Newly diagnosed diabetic with dyspepsia

Suspicion should increase with the age of the patient.

Investigations

- **USS**: shows dilatation of ducts in obstructive jaundice and excludes gallstones but is not very good at visualizing the retroperitoneal pancreas
- **ERCP and biopsy:** probably the single most useful investigation in periampullary tumours
- **Contrast CT**: gives valuable information about the spread of the disease.
- **MRI scan, angiography** and **percutaneous biopsy:** under radiological control can all be useful
- **Laparoscopy** and **intraoperative ultrasound**: have also been used
- 90% of inoperable cases should be identified prior to laparotomy
- 80% of jaundiced patients should have ERCP stenting if possible

Surgical management

The principles of surgery are different for cancers of the head (**periampullary cancers**) and cancers of the **body and tail** of the pancreas. Both need meticulous pre-operative preparation (see the shaded box below).

Pre-operative preparation for pancreatic cancer

- **Clotting**
  Deranged clotting can be corrected with vitamin K

- **Endotoxaemia**
  This can be minimized with
    IV mannitol
    oral bile salt
    lactulose

- **Thrombosis**
  Subcutaneous heparin may be required when clotting is corrected

- **Sepsis**
  Intraoperative IV antibiotics

- **Drainage**
  Biliary obstruction should be relieved by
    ERCP stent or external draining
    Surgery is more hazardous if the bilirubin is >150 units

Periampullary cancers

This term encompasses true cancers of the head of the pancreas, duodenal cancers, ampullary cancers and low bile duct cancers.

Overall, periampullary cancers have a resection rate of 40%. Whipple's resection is the preferred technique (see figure opposite). Ampullary carcinomas can be locally resected. 'Pylorus saving' operations reduce post-operative dumping and ulceration. No benefit has been shown in performing a total pancreatectomy.

The 5-year survival rates are approximately:

- 60% for ampullary carcinomas
- 20% for true carcinoma of the head of the pancreas
- 50% if there is no nodal involvement

Carcinoma of the body and tail

- Late presentation leads to an overall resection rate of less than 7%
- Prognosis is poor — most patients are dead within five months
- Cystadenocarcinomas are rare but have a 5-year survival rate of 50% if resected
- Adjuvant therapy has no proven role

Palliative management

Symptomatic treatment aims to alleviate problems such as:

- Obstructive jaundice
- Pain
- Duodenal obstruction

Modalities of treatment include:

- ERCP intraluminal stenting
- Bypass procedures
- Chemical splanchectomy
- Coeliac block
- Radiation
- Chemotherapy

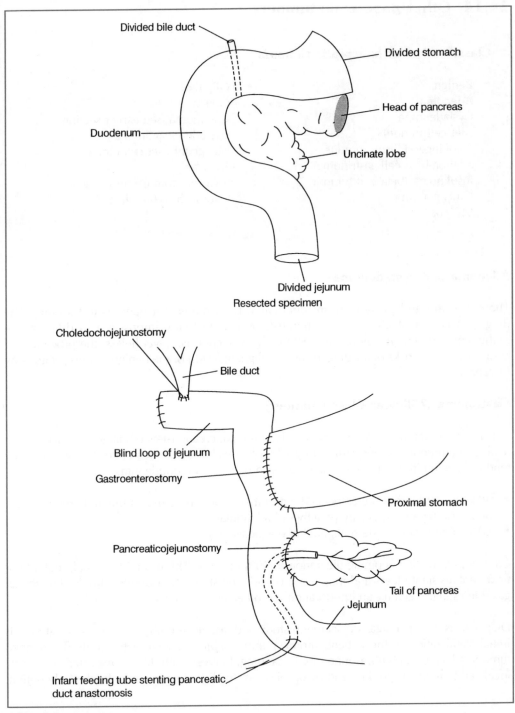

Divided bile duct

Divided stomach

Head of pancreas

Duodenum

Uncinate lobe

Divided jejunum

Resected specimen

Choledochojejunostomy

Bile duct

Blind loop of jejunum

Gastroenterostomy

Proximal stomach

Pancreaticojejunostomy

Tail of pancreas

Jejunum

Infant feeding tube stenting pancreatic
duct anastomosis

Whipple's operation

14.14 Other pancreatic tumours

Classification of pancreatic tumours

- **Benign**
  Adenoma
  Cystadenoma
  Islet cell tumours
    Zöllinger–Ellison tumour
      (non-beta cell gastrinoma)
    Insulinoma (beta cell tumour)
    Glucagonoma
    VIPoma

- **Malignant**
  Primary
    Carcinoma (see earlier section)
    Cystadenocarcinoma
    Malignant islet cell tumour
  Secondary
    Invasion from carcinoma of
      stomach or bile duct

Adenoma and cystadenoma

These are rare and present in an identical way to malignant pancreatic tumours. The diagnosis is almost always post-operative as it is virtually impossible to differentiate malignant and benign lesions pre-operatively. Resection is, nevertheless, the procedure of choice due to the risks of misdiagnosing a malignant lesion or the benign lesions progressing to cancer.

Gastrinoma (Zöllinger–Ellison tumour)

This is a rare tumour of the non beta cells of the pancreatic islets of Langerhans which can lead to overproduction of gastrin. Only 17% of cases have a single pancreatic tumour. They tend to have multiple metastases and can also occur in the duodenum.

- 30% of gastrinomas are associated with other endocrine tumours (multiple endocrine neoplasia type I) especially parathyroid adenomas
- 60% of gastrinomas are malignant at diagnosis

Clinical presentation is peptic ulceration in 90% of cases. These can be normal, multiple or treatment-resistant ulcers and may occur outside the stomach or duodenal bulb. Diarrhoea, gastrointestinal bleeding and perforation are other presentations.

Diagnosis is by a pentagastrin secretion study and fasting serum gastrin levels. Treatment is initial stabilization of the patient, proton pump inhibitors and resection only if a defined tumour is localized by ultrasound or CT scanning. In those with diffuse, metastatic or poorly localized tumours, vagotomy and pyloroplasty or total gastrectomy may be the only option.

Insulinoma

Twice as common as a gastrinoma but still rare (annual incidence of $1:1 \times 10^6$ of the population). Unlike gastrinomas, most insulinomas are solitary tumours of the beta cells of the pancreas. Clinical presentation is due to hypoglycaemia, including:

- Episodes of disturbed consciousness
- Episodes of odd behaviour
- Patient feels well between attacks

Diagnosis is by:

- Blood glucose
- Plasma insulin
- Glucagon test
- Ultrasound
- CT

Treatment is excision due to the malignant potential of the tumours. Finding the tumour, even if localized by imaging techniques, can be difficult as they may be as small as 5 mm in size. If the tumour cannot be found, a distal pancreatectomy may be indicated.

Glucagonoma

Tumours of the pancreatic α cells of the pancreas are extremely rare. Present with a bullous rash and diabetes. Treatment as for insulinoma.

VIPoma

Vasoactive intestinal peptide secreting tumours are very rare and present with:

- Watery diarrhoea
- Hypokalaemia
- Achlorhydria

Plasma VIP levels are raised and resection of the tumour is curative.

Cystadenocarcinoma

A rare tumour, 90% occur in middle-aged females. Slow-growing. May present as an abdominal mass or obstructive jaundice. If technically feasible, resection should be undertaken. If not, prolonged survival may occur even in untreated malignant cases as the tumour is not very aggressive.

14.15 Other disorders of the pancreas

Pancreatic cysts

The classification of pancreatic cysts is seen in the shaded box below. Present as firm, large, rounded upper abdominal swelling. Initially, the cyst is apparently resonant because of the loops of gas filled bowels in front of it but as it increases in size it becomes dull to percussion. True cysts require surgical excision. False cysts are drained. This may be performed internally by anastomosis into the stomach or into the small intestine. Percutaneous drainage under ultrasound control can also be achieved.

Classification of pancreatic cysts

- **True (20%)**
  Congenital polycystic disease
    of the pancreas
  Retention
  Hydatid
  Neoplastic (cystadenoma/
    cystadenocarcinoma)

- **False (80%)**
  A collection of fluid in the
    lesser sac
  After trauma to the pancreas
  Following acute pancreatitis
  After perforation of a posterior
    gastric ulcer (rare)

Pancreatic trauma

Can result from blunt or penetrating trauma and is associated with other injuries in 90% of cases. Classified into:

- **Minor**: injury does not involve main ducts
- **Intermediate**: distal injury ± duct disruption
- **Major**: injury to the head of the pancreas or pancreaticoduodenal injury

Retroperitoneal injury is notoriously difficult to diagnose clinically, with minimal clinical findings.

Some non-specific investigations which may suggest pancreatic injury are:

- Raised serum amylase
- Plain abdominal film: air bubbles — along right psoas margin, along upper pole of right kidney, along lower mediastinum; obliteration of the psoas shadow; scoliosis; ground glass appearance due to filling of lesser sac with fluid; gastrografin swallow may show duodenal rupture
- During laparotomy, the lesser sac should be explored if retroperitoneal injury is suspected

Minor and intermediate pancreatic injury may be treated by simple haemostasis and drainage. Major injury may need distal pancreatectomy and splenectomy or pancreatico-duodenectomy. Post-operative care is important, as more mortalities are due to late complications such as sepsis or secondary haemorrhage.

The pancreas in cystic fibrosis

Cystic fibrosis is the most common inherited disorder in Caucasians. It affects many organ systems, especially the lungs. The abnormally viscous mucus secretion causes progressive exocrine pancreatic insufficiency. Pancreatic enzymes may be taken orally to supplement the failing pancreas. Surgery is rarely needed unless stenosis develops in the lower bile and pancreatic ducts.

Chapter 5
Urinary System and Renal Transplantation

CONTENTS

15. Benign prostatic hyperplasia (BPH) 678

16. Carcinoma of the prostate 684

17. Testicular tumours 692

18. Tumours of the penis 698

19. Genito-urinary trauma 702

20. Renal transplantation 709

21. Transplantation immunology 716

Urinary System and Renal Transplantation

1. EMBRYOLOGY

1.1 Nephric system

The nephric system develops from the lateral side of the internal cell mass as:

- Pronephros
- Mesonephros
- Metanephros

Pronephros

- Extends from 4th to 14th somites
- Consists of 6–10 tubular pairs
- Disappears by fourth week, but its duct persists

Mesonephros

- Mesonephric tubules develop from intermediate mesoderm caudal to pronephros and give rise to the glomeruli
- Mesonephric tubules connect with the primary nephric duct to form the mesonephric duct; this forms in the fourth week and reaches maximum size by the ninth week

Metanephros

- Originates from the intermediate mesoderm and mesonephric duct
- Arises opposite the 28th somite
- Gives rise to the ureteral bud — grows cephalad, forming ureter as it does so
- Acquires mesoderm around its tip which enlarges and differentiates as upwards (cephalad) migration occurs
- The cephalic end of the ureteral bud forms the pelvicalyceal system, and pushes into the proliferating cortex (from mesoderm)

1.2 Vesico-urethral unit

- Blind end of hindgut expands to form the cloaca, which is separated from the outside by the cloacal membrane
- Lies in ectodermal depression (proctodeum)
- Divides into ventral (urogenital sinus) and dorsal portions (rectum) by the seventh week
- Urogenital sinus receives mesonephric ducts
- Common caudal end of the mesonephric duct becomes absorbed into the urogenital sinus so that mesonephric duct and ureteral bud have independent openings by the seventh week
- This absorption introduces mesodermal tissue into the surrounding endoderm of the urogenital sinus; this 'foreign' tissue becomes the trigone
- Opening of the mesonephric duct migrates downwards and medially (to become ejaculatory duct)
- Opening of ureteral bud migrates upwards and laterally (to become the ureteral orifice)
- Gives rise to the bladder, part of the urethra in males and the whole urethra in females

Prostate

Develops as multiple solid outgrowths of the urethral epithelium above and below the entrance of the mesonephric duct. It begins development at the eleventh week as five distinct groups and is complete by 16 weeks. Five groups of epithelial buds form five 'lobes' which fuse.

1.3 Gonads

- Initially sexually undifferentiated
- Primitive sex glands appear at fifth week within a localized region of thickening known as the urogenital ridge
- Sixth week: the gonad consists of a superficial germinal epithelium and an internal blastema
- Seventh week: differentiated into the testis (increases in size and moves caudally) or ovary (gains a mesentery)

Descent of the testis

- **Third month**: testis located retroperitoneally in the false pelvis
- **Gubernaculum**: extends from the lower pole of the testis to the scrotum; guides testis into the scrotum
- **Seventh month**: testis crosses inguinal canal
- **Eighth month**: testis at external ring
- Descends into the scrotum by birth; undescended testes common in pre-term infants and most minor cases will descend spontaneously (see Chapter 3, *Head, Neck, Endocrine and Paediatric*, Section 14.7, p. 280)

Descent of the ovary

- Becomes attached to the tissues of the genital fold by the gubernaculum and uterovaginal canal and gives rise to the ovarian ligament and round ligament respectively
- The mesentery, which descended with the ovary, becomes the broad ligament

1.4 Genital duct system

- Pronephric duct (**Wolffian duct**) grows caudally to join the ventral cloaca and gives rise to the urethral bud
- In the **male** it forms the epididymis, vas deferens, seminal vesicles and ejaculatory ducts; the Mullerian duct degenerates leaving the appendix, testis and prostatic utricle
- In the **female** the Mullerian duct forms the fallopian tubes, the uterus and most of the vagina; the Wolffian duct remains rudimentary

External genitalia

After the eighth week external sex differentiation occurs. Three small protuberances on the external aspect of the cloacal membrane central genital tubercle and genital swellings on either side form the external genitalia in both sexes.

2. ANATOMY AND PHYSIOLOGY OF THE GENITO-URINARY TRACT

2.1 Anatomy of the kidneys

- Lie on psoas, therefore oblique
- Right kidney lower due to the liver above it
- Kidney supported by perirenal fat. Gerotas fascia (perirenal fascia) — tough membrane which encloses both the kidney and adrenal.

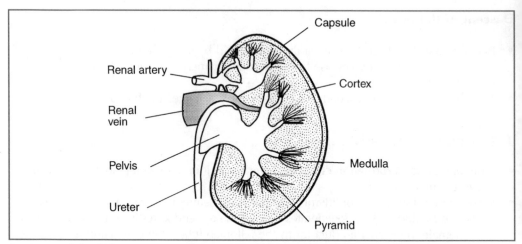

Anatomy of the kidney

Arterial supply

Supplied by renal artery (direct aortic branches — usually one each side). Usually lies behind the renal vein. May have more main branches or may divide before reaching the hilum. The main artery divides into anterior and posterior branches. The posterior branch supplies the mid-segment of the posterior surface. The anterior branch supplies the entire anterior surface and both lower and upper poles. There may be a separate upper pole vessel (can cause PUJ obstruction). Renal arteries are end arteries, therefore occlusion results in infarction.

Venous drainage

Usually a single vein which lies in front of the artery, but they can be multiple. The left renal vein receives the left gonadal vein. The right renal vein (being nearer to the inferior vena cava) is shorter and therefore harder to dissect.

Lymphatic drainage

Drainage into para-aortic/lumbar lymph nodes.

Pelvicalyceal system

Eight to twelve minor calyces are indented by the medullary pyramids. These unite to form two to three major calyces which join to form the renal pelvis. This may be intra- or extra-renal. The renal pelvis or the upper ureter usually lies behind the renal artery at the hilum of the kidney.

2.2 Anatomy of the ureters

The ureters lie on the psoas muscle and pass retroperitoneally down to lie over the sacroiliac joints. They then swing laterally adjacent to the ischial spines before turning medially to join the bladder at its base. In females the uterine arteries are in close proximity to the distal ureters which can be damaged during gynaecological procedures. In males the vas deferens leave the internal inguinal ring and sweep over the pelvis side walls anterior to the ureters. They lie medial to the ureters before joining the ducts of the seminal vesicles, penetrating the base of the prostate to become the ejaculatory ducts.

Blood supply

- **Upper third**: renal arteries
- **Middle third**: gonadal ± common iliac arteries
- **Lower third**: branches of the common iliac, hypogastric, inferior and superior vesical and middle rectal arteries
- Veins follow arteries

Lymphatic drainage

To para-aortic nodes and pelvic nodes along the internal iliac artery.

2.3 Anatomy of the bladder

Hollow muscular organ which has a storage function (400–500 ml in adults). When empty it lies behind the symphysis pubis, but in children it lies higher. Internal sphincter under involuntary control. Composed of smooth muscle and situated at the bladder neck. Innervated by α–receptors. Genital sphincter thought to be separate entity. Concerned with the preservation of prograde ejaculation. External sphincter lies distal to verumontanum at apex of prostate. Composed of striated muscle and under voluntary control.

Relations

- **Males** — posterior: seminal vesicles, vasa deferentia, ureters and rectum
- **Females** — posterior: uterus and vagina

The dome and posterior surfaces are covered by peritoneum.

Blood supply

Superior and inferior vesical arteries (from the internal iliac artery). Smaller branches from the obturator and inferior gluteal arteries (plus branches from the uterine and vaginal arteries in the female).

Lymphatics

Vesical, external iliac, internal iliac and common iliac nodes.

2.4 Anatomy of the prostate

See Section 15, p. 678, on benign prostatic hyperplasia.

Anatomy

- Fibromuscular and glandular organ lying inferior to the bladder
- Normal prostate weighs approximately 20 g
- Contains prostatic urethra (2.5 cm in length)
- Anteriorly supported by puboprostatic ligaments
- Inferiorly supported by urogenital diaphragm
- Perforated posteriorly by ejaculatory ducts which empty through the verumontanum on the floor of the prostate just proximal to the external urinary sphincter

Zonal anatomy

- Classic description by McNeal (1972): anatomical zones — central, peripheral, transitional, anterior, fibromuscular

Blood supply

Arterial
Derived from the inferior vesical, internal pudendal and middle rectal arteries.

Venous
Drainage into peri-prostatic plexus, connecting with the deep dorsal vein of the penis and the internal iliac veins.

Nerve supply

Richly innervated by both sympathetic and parasympathetic nerve plexi.

Lymphatic supply

Drainage into the internal iliac, sacral, external and vesical lymph nodes.

2.5 Anatomy of the testis

Covered by tunica albuginea (TA) and invaginated anterolaterally by a 'visceral' membrane known as the tunica vaginalis (under which fluid accumulates in a hydrocoele).The 'parietal' layer lines the inner scrotal wall. The TA sends fibrous septa into the testis, separating it into approximately 250 lobules.

Blood supply

- **Testicular artery** — direct aortic branches, just below origin of renal arteries.
- Testicle receives some blood supply from the artery to the vas deferens.
- **Left testicular (gonadal) vein** drains into **left renal vein**, whereas on the **right** it drains directly into the **IVC**.
- *Unilateral* varicocoele almost always on left because higher pressure in left renal vein than IVC, left kidney higher, left testis lower, vasoconstrictor substances from adrenal gland may contribute as can rudimentary valves at the opening into the renal vein.
- The finding of a left varicocoele necessitates an ultrasound of the left kidney as tumour thrombus within the left renal vein can occlude the terminal testicular vein and cause a varicocoele.

2.6 Anatomy of the penis

- Two **corpora cavernosa** (the main body of the penis), corpus spongiosum (surrounds the urethra)
- Each corpus cavernosum is surrounded by a tough fascial sheath — the **tunica albuginea** (it has an inner circular and an outer longitudinal layer which move on each other during an erection and occlude the emissary or perforating veins which run perpendicular and through these two layers)
- All three are surrounded by a **Buck's fascia**
- **Colles fascia**, which is continuous with Scarpa's fascia, lies beneath the skin and fat
- The proximal ends of the corpora cavernosa are attached to the pelvic bones, just anterior to the ischial tuberosities

Blood supply

Two cavernous arteries supply the corpora cavernosa, the **bulbourethral artery** supplies the corpus spongiosum and urethra and the **deep penile artery** supplies the glans. Venous drainage collects in the subtunical plexus that is subject to compression during erection. This, and the emissary veins (see above) form the veno occlusive mechanism of erection. Most of this venous drainage is by the superficial and deep dorsal veins into the internal pudendal vein.

Lymphatics

- **Skin**: superficial inguinal nodes
- **Glans**: external iliac nodes
- **Deep urethra**: internal iliac and common iliac nodes

2.7 Physiology of the kidney

Tubular physiology

The renal tube has many reabsorptive and secretory functions (see figure below); these are energy-consuming and hence tubular cells are those most vulnerable to ischaemic damage (the ATN of ischaemic acute renal failure).

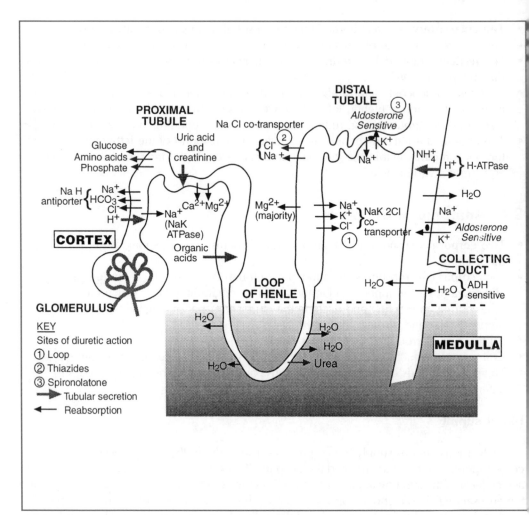

Schema of a nephron, showing tubular physiology

Proximal tubule

50% of filtered sodium is re-absorbed within the proximal tubule (via Na K ATPase); the Na H antiporter secretes H^+ into the lumen and is responsible for 90% of bicarbonate and some chloride reabsorption. All of the filtered glucose and amino acids are re-absorbed here. Other important characteristics are:

- Phosphate re-absorption occurs under the influence of parathormone (PTH)
- Some important drugs are secreted into the tubular filtrate here: trimethoprim, cimetidine, most β-lactams and most diuretics (note that diuretics such as thiazides, amiloride and loop diuretics are highly protein-bound and are not filtered at the glomerulus)
- Creatinine and urate are secreted into the lumen

Loop of Henle

The medullary concentration gradient is generated here; the medullary thick ascending limb (mTAL) is impermeable to water. 40% of sodium is re-absorbed (via the Na K 2Cl co-transporter). Loop diuretics compete for chloride-binding sites on this transporter.

Distal tubule

In this segment of the nephron 5% of sodium is re-absorbed (Na Cl co-transporter); thiazide diuretics compete for these chloride-binding sites. As loop diuretics increase sodium delivery to the distal tubule, their combination with a thiazide (e.g. metolazone) can provoke a massive diuresis in resistant oedema. There are aldosterone receptors in both the distal and collecting tubules (see below).

Collecting duct

Aldosterone-sensitive sodium channels are responsible for 2% of all sodium re-absorption; spirolactone binds to the cytoplasmic aldosterone receptor. Atrial natriuretic peptide (ANP) is also anti-aldosterone in action. Other important collecting duct functions include:

- H^+ secreted into lumen by H-ATPase, so forming ammonia/NH_4^+ (urinary acidification)
- Anti-diuretic hormone (ADH) increases water re-absoption by opening water channels; lithium enters the collecting duct cells via the sodium channels and inhibits the response to ADH (hence, nephrogenic diabetes insipidus (NDI) results)

623

2.8 Physiology of the bladder

Normal vesical innervation

- Syncytium of smooth muscle fibres
- Two sphincteric units: internal involuntary smooth muscle sphincter at bladder neck (sympathetic innervation); external voluntary striated sphincter from the prostate to the membranous urethra in males and at the mid-urethra in females
- Voluntary external sphincter maintains a constant tonus and is the primary continence mechanism — the tone can be temporarily increased by the voluntary contraction of the pelvic floor muscles
- Parasympathetic innervation originates in the S2–4 segments — cholinergic post-ganglionic fibres supply both the bladder and sphincter
- Sympathetic nerves originate at T10–L2 and innervate the smooth muscle of the bladder base, internal sphincter and proximal urethra
- Somatic motor innervation originates in S2–3 and travels to the external sphincter via the pudendal nerve
- Somatic afferents are carried by the pudendal nerve
- Visceral afferents are carried by the sympathetic and parasympathetic nerves to respective spinal areas

Normal vesical function

- During bladder filling sacral reflexes increase urethral pressure maintaining continence
- To void, inhibition from higher centres is removed and the micturition reflex occurs
- Micturition reflex commences with urethral relaxation as noted by EMG silence in the pudendal nerves
- Within 3–5 s of the urethral pressure dropping, a sustained detrusor contraction occurs
- Detrusor then relaxes and urethral pressure is restored
- The micturition reflex is co-ordinated from the pontine mesocephalic centre situated in the brainstem — efferents pass down the spinal tracts to the detrusor and pudendal nuclei in the sacral segments of the spinal cord
- Afferent impulses into the pontine centre include bladder stretch receptors and mucosal receptors, and sensory input including cold, visual and auditory information, and higher centres
- The detrusor nucleus (the parasympathetic S2–4 centre in the dorsal horn) is responsible for co-ordinated detrusor contraction
- The pudendal nucleus (situated in the anterior horn of the same segment) is the spinal nucleus for somatic efferents to the sphincter and is responsible for control of co-ordinated sphincter mechanisms
- The detrusor and pudendal nuclei together comprise the sacral centre

3. IMAGING

3.1 Radiography

Basic principles

X-rays are electromagnetic waves with photon energy. Different tissues absorb X-rays to varying degrees. Radio-opaque contrast highlights lumens and enhances soft tissues.

Basic equipment

- High-voltage electric generator
- X-ray tube
- Collimating device
- X-ray film

Patient preparation and safety

- Ensure female patients are not pregnant
- Bowel preparation for elective IVUs
- Ensure no contrast allergy

Contrast

Overall incidence of adverse events (AEs) 5%. Most are minor (nausea, vomiting, rash, flushing); 1:40,000 mortality. Non-ionic agents cause fewer AEs but are more expensive. Used in patients with previous serious reactions or a strong history of allergies. If known AE and contrast mandatory, cover with steroids.

Plain kidneys, ureter, bladder (KUB) X-ray

- Supine abdominal film to include kidneys, ureters and bladder
- Simple; preliminary radiograph preceding other investigations (e.g. IVU)
- Demonstrates bone, spine and soft tissue abnormalities
- Specifically: renal outlines (size, position), nephrocalcinosis, stones, sacral abnormalities (spina bifida)

Intravenous urogram (IVU)

Principle
Preliminary plain KUB, injection of iodine-based contrast (300 mg/kg) given as bolus or infusion, usually an immediate film (nephrogram), then 5- and 20-minute films (pyelogram).

Special films

- **Delayed films** (if obstruction present)
- **Compression** (to further fill upper tracts)
- **Prone films** (to assist emptying of renal pelvis)
- **Post-micturition films** (to assess bladder emptying and to demonstrate a 'standing column' of contrast in obstruction)
- **Frusemide IVU** (addition of frusemide may distinguish a 'baggy' system from an obstructed one)
- **Tomography** (swinging of the X-ray arm whilst emitting X-rays in a partial semi-circle to highlight an area of interest)

Contraindications
Pregnancy, contrast allergies, renal failure, patients on metformin (must stop 24 hours before — otherwise causes lactic acidosis).

Retrograde urography

Injection of contrast into ureter at cystoscopy. Usually performed under general anaesthesia, but local anaesthetic is also possible. Useful for a suspicious area not ruled out by other investigations (i.e. a possible filling defect in a poorly functioning non-excreting kidney). Also useful on-table, prior to ureteroscopy to identify stone position and patient anatomy.

Percutaneous antegrade urogram

Percutaneous needle (under ultrasound or CT guidance) into pelvicalyceal system and injection of contrast or injection of contrast into an already sited nephrostomy tube.

'Loopograms'

Useful for surveillance and the detection of upper tract tumours following cystectomy and urinary diversion for muscle-invasive TCC of the bladder (must visualize upper tracts intermittently). Applies to any urotheliocutaneous fistula.

Cystography

Direct or indirect (see Section 3.5, p. 629). Contrast instilled into bladder via catheter, bladder filled. Catheter removed, patient voids (micturating cystogram). Useful to detect vesico-ureteric reflux and genuine stress incontinence (bladder base descent on lateral stress views, ideally use leak point pressures). Essential in boys where posterior urethral valves are suspected.

Urethrography

Useful in diagnosis and management of strictures. In trauma patients when urethral rupture suspected (use water-soluble contrast).

Vasography

Investigation of male infertility. Contrast injected into ductal system (directly into ejaculatory duct) or, more commonly into vas deferens after surgical exposure.

Lymphangiography

Oily contrast into lymphatic vessel in foot. Highlights inguinal, pelvic and retroperitoneal lymphatic system. Not often used but may show non-enlarged lymph nodes infiltrated with tumour, otherwise not seen on conventional imaging.

Venography

Being replaced by CT and MRI, especially in involvement of the renal vein or IVC with renal cell carcinoma. Useful in the diagnosis of renal vein thrombosis (persistent dense nephrogram).

3.2 Ultrasonography (US)

General principles

- Sound frequencies >20 Hz (beyond human hearing — *ultra*sound)
- Frequencies most commonly used 3.5–10 MHz
- Ultrasound waves generated by piezoelectric crystals which emit ultrasound waves when they are deformed by an electrical voltage, and vice versa, therefore they also act as sound receivers
- Reflections give rise to grey-scale images
- Moving structures (e.g. blood flow) produces a Doppler effect; Doppler shift determined, so flow direction and velocity can be shown as a trace (spectral Doppler) or as colour (colour Doppler)

Uses

Kidneys, ureters, bladder

- 3.5–5.0 MHz transducers in longitudinal or transverse planes
- Size and cortical thickness determined

- Detects stones, tumours, hydronephrosis, cysts (simple or complex)
- Useful in bladder outflow obstruction: upper tract dilatation, post-micturition volume, bladder wall thickness, presence of significant intravesical prostate or a middle lobe
- Transplanted kidneys: obstruction, blood flow, lymphatic or peri-nephric collections
- Renal vein thrombosis, renal artery thrombosis, patency of arteriovenous fistulae in dialysis patients

Prostate

- Transrectal ultrasound scan (TRUS): visualizes prostate and associated structures (e.g. seminal vesicles, ejaculatory ducts)
- Measures prostatic size (when planning transurethral resection of prostate (TURP) versus open prostatectomy or calculating PSA density)
- Can easily differentiate between peripheral zone (where most cancers arise) and transitional zone (where BPH originates); identifies high bladder neck or significant middle lobe
- Identifies hypoechoic areas (suspicious) and directs biopsy needle
- Must give antibiotic cover; small (but severe) incidence of systemic sepsis
- Used in brachytherapy to plan and direct the appropriate number and position of radioactive seeds

Testes

- High-frequency ultrasound (5–10 MHz gives good soft tissue resolution)
- Colour Doppler shows real-time flow characteristics (useful for diagnosis of epididymo-orchitis but not reliable enough to exclude torsion)

3.3 Computerized tomography (CT)

Standard, weighted images, contrast-enhanced, spiral. Multiple uses in diagnosis and facilitating treatment (e.g. tumour staging, CT-guided biopsy etc.).

NB. Will identify 'all' stones if cuts fine enough (<5 mm). Fat is black (angiomyolipoma, i.e. has negative Hounsfield units). Also useful when ultrasound fails in obese patients or those with significant bowel gas.

3.4 Magnetic resonance imaging (MRI)

- Relies on atoms containing odd number of protons/neutrons which spin and produce a small magnetic field
- Application of strong magnetic field causes low-energy orientation in direction of external magnetic field

- Additional short pulses of radio waves are absorbed causing elevation to high-energy orientation
- When pulse ends, protons return to low-energy orientation emitting the same radio waves as they are absorbed; this energy is detected and transformed into images
- Magnetic resonance images are reflections of hydrogen densities in various body tissues
- Weighted images also employed

Same uses as CT, but better definition of soft tissue. Addition of gadolinium (extracellular contrast agent mainly excreted by glomerular filtration) to define both anatomy and function (useful in obstruction and renal tumours).

- **Advantages**: no X-rays, large field of view, good soft tissue resolution
- **Disadvantages**: cost of machinery and service, metallic objects contraindicated (e.g. metallic surgical clips), claustrophobia

3.5 Nuclear medicine

General principles

- Radiopharmaceuticals, scintillation cameras, computer software
- Technetium-^{99m} (^{99m}Tc) or iodine^{131} (^{131}I)
- Traces of radionuclide provides photon flux
- Safe, non-invasive, allergic reactions uncommon (low dose). Radiation dose lower than conventional X-rays
- Usually given intravenously, therefore enters target organ physiologically
- Thallium-drifted sodium iodide crystal — circular and clear
- Photon interacts with crystal to produce visible light photons
- Collimator (has parallel channels of lead) accepts only those photons which travel end-on
- Photomultiplier detects end-on visible light, released by the crystal and accepted by the collimator
- Spatial location of incident photon determined

DMSA scan

- ^{99m}Tc-DMSA (technetium-^{99m} dimercaptosuccinic acid)
- Used for cortical imaging
- i.v. dose 71 µCi/kg
- 50% is bound to renal proximal tubular cells within four hours
- Images taken after this show details of parenchyma
- Useful to demonstrate scarring (photopenic areas), tumours, trauma
- Can calculate differential function

DTPA scan

- ^{99m}Tc-DTPA (technetium-^{99m} diethylenetriamine penta-acetic acid)
- i.v. dose 171 μCi/kg
- Used for 'excretory' imaging (rapidly excreted in urine)
- Select region of interest (usually kidney, but also lower ureter in an indirect cystogram)
- Given in conjunction with frusemide (0.5–1 mg/kg)
- Number of counts at any one time measured
- Curves calculated from sequential counts and displayed as a graph of tracer activity versus time
- Useful in the diagnosis of obstruction (e.g. PUJ obstruction), where tracer not adequately excreted or may further accumulate, leading to 'flat' or 'rising' curves
- Gives estimate of divided renal function, but in obstruction this can be unreliable. The placement of a percutaneous nephrostomy for several weeks prior to performing this study may show improved function, and in borderline cases (i.e. in PUJ obstruction with a poorly functioning kidney) may help to distinguish whether pyeloplasty or nephrectomy should be performed.
- Can be used to perform an **indirect cystogram** — following a DTPA scan, the bladder naturally fills with radionuclide. An area of interest is placed over the distal ureters. Reflux can therefore be detected when the patient voids (requires toilet training).
- A **direct cystogram** uses radionuclide instilled in the catheterized bladder, instead of conventional contrast and avoids the use of X-rays

MAG-3 scan

Gives information of differential function and excretion. Useful in the measurement of renal blood flow. Commonly used in children.

Bone scan

- ^{99m}Tc-methylene diphosphonate (MDP)
- Absorbed into surface of bone crystals
- Intercalates into crystal imperforation
- Correlates with vascularity
- Use is combined with plain X-rays (to differentiate between 'hot spots' and degenerative disease)

NB. Metastases from prostate cancer are usually **osteosclerotic** on plain X-ray.

Adrenal scintigraphy

- **Adrenal cortex**: uses cholesterol as basis for steroid synthesis
- **Radiolabelled cholesterol** is therefore used for imaging
- **Adrenal medulla**: metaiodobenzylguanidine (MIBG) scans used particularly in the diagnosis of pheochromocytoma

Xenon washout

In selected centres, used to measure penile blood flow in patients with erectile dysfunction.

3.6 Other future investigations

PET scans

- F-18 fluorodeoxyglucose Positron Emission Tomography
- Increasingly used to detect micrometastases
- Relies on malignant cells having higher turnover, therefore a faster metabolism with an increased consumption of glucose

Monoclonal antibodies

Specific antibodies attach and highlight a specific target. Currently experimental.

4. URINARY TRACT INFECTIONS (UTIs)

Definitions of urinary tract infections

- Simple or uncomplicated
- Recurrent infection due to reinfection or persistence of cause
- Complicated due to abnormal anatomy or foreign body

EPIDEMIOLOGY OF URINARY TRACT INFECTIONS

Age group	Percentage	M:F Ratio
Neonatal	1	1.5:1
Pre-school	1–2	1:10
School	1–2	1:30
Reproductive	2–5	1:30
Elderly	20–30	1:5 to equal over age 65

4.1 Aetiology and pathology

Mode of entry

- **Ascending**: most common; females at greater risk than males (shorter urethra)
- **Haematogenous**: uncommon; Staph.; TB
- **Direct extension**: inflammatory bowel disease; fistulae

Urinary pathogens

E. coli represents 90% of community acquired infections. In hospital, *E. coli* represents 50%, the rest are made up of:

- Klebsiella
- Enterobacter
- Citrobacter
- Serratia
- Pseudomonas
- Enterococcus

Uropathogens are organisms virulent enough to cause infections in the absence of abnormalities in the urinary tract.

There are 150 strains of *E. coli* — six are consistently seen in urinary tract infections.

Virulence of urinary pathogens

Adherence

Mediated by pili or fimbriae. Pathogenic *E. coli* adhere more intensely to epithelial cells than those from normal faecal flora. There are four types of pili thought to contribute to pathogenecity:

- **Type 1 pili**: expressed by all strains of *E. coli*. Agglutination of guinea-pig erythrocytes inhibited by D-Mannose (Mannose sensitive)
- **Type 2 pili**: attaches strongly to urothelium. Agglutination of human erythrocytes not inhibited by D-Mannose
- **X-pili**
- **P-pili**

Bacterial capsular polysaccharide (K antigen)

Presence of K antigen may help resist phagocytosis.

Bacterial haemolysis

Haemolysans are cytotoxic peptides. Toxic to erythrocytes, PMNs, monocytes and fibroblasts. Eighty per cent of pyelonephritic strains express genes for haemolysans, c.f. 20% faecal strains.

Aerobactin

Required for multiplication. Strains with aerobactin more likely to have P-pili.

Defence mechanisms

Urine

- Mechanical effect of flushing
- High osmolality of urine
- Concentration of urea, organic acids and low pH
- Tamm–Horsfall protein: a glycoprotein excreted by ascending loop of Henle and CT binds Type 1 pili and allows excretion
- Urinary immunoglobulins IgA and IgG inhibit adherence
- Prostatic antibacterial factor (PAF)

Perineum

Lactobacillus, corynebacteria and streptococci reduce adherence and inhibit multiplication of uropathogens.

Bladder

- Efficient emptying of bladder
- Bladder mucopolysaccharide layer GAGs are hydrophilic and bind a layer of water,
  ? protective role

Abnormalities affecting defence mechanisms

- **Obstruction**
  Interferes with emptying of kidney,
    ureter or bladder
  Increased pyelonephritis at all ages
    with obstruction

- **Diabetes**
  3x more likely to have UTI if female
  Immunocompromised ↓ urinary Abs
    ↑ adherence

- **Pregnancy**
  5% incidence of bacteriuria

- **Foreign bodies**
  Cause of persistent bacteriuria
  Indwelling catheters: daily incidence
    of infection up to 10% per day

- **Elderly**
  Increased in incidence with age
  10–20% of elderly at home have UTI,
    higher in nursing homes
  Over age 65, M:F incidence similar
  Senile vaginitis

- **Calculi**

4.2 Evaluation

History

- Much more common in females (except in infants under 3 months and in elderly patients in residential homes where sex incidence is equal)
- Usually symptomatic: presents with dysuria and irritable bladder (frequency, urgency, nocturia)
- May be asymptomatic, especially in elderly and in patients with long-term catheters
- Ask about PMU/FH stones (Proteus infections), obstructive voiding symptoms in men and sensation of incomplete emptying (residual urine)
- Ask about previous infections ? documented
- Childhood infections persisting into adulthood suggest presence of underlying abnormality, i.e. vesico-ureteric reflux
- Infections in boys raises suspicion of posterior urethral valves

Blood/urine tests

- MSU
- Glucose
- Creatinine, U&Es
- FBC (↑ WCC)

Routine imaging

- Plain KUB
- Renal tract USS with post-micturition residual volume

Special imaging

- DMSA scan (scarring from reflux nephropathy)
- DTPA/MAG-3 scan (if obstruction suspected, i.e. PUJ obstruction)
- Cystography: direct, catheter introduced into bladder and filled with contrast or isotope, voiding demonstrates reflux; indirect, following a DTPA or MAG-3 scan, bladder fills with isotope. γ-camera placed over distal ureters and patient voids. Does not grade reflux but useful for 'screening'. ↓↓ dose of radiation, but requires toilet training therefore unsuitable for children under 2 years
- IVU if USS suggests anatomical abnormality

4.3 Management

Cystitis

- Treat active infections (three days of antibiotics is usually sufficient)
- Exclude anatomical abnormality
- 'Standard cystitis advice' (drink fluids, void before and after intercourse, wipe from front to back)
- Treat any underlying condition (i.e. bladder stone, residual urine)
- Recurrent UTIs (i.e. ≥3 infections/12-month period) often require a prolonged course (6 months) of low-dose prophylactic antibiotics

Pyelonephritis

- 'Simple' pyelonephritis requires a two-week course of antibiotics
- Severe or persisting temperature requires urgent renal USS to exclude obstruction
- Recurrent pyelonephritis suggests vesico-ureteric reflux, PUJ obstruction or a renal tract calculus

Pyonephrons/peri-renal abscess

- Urgent drainage required (percutaneous nephrostomy or insertion of JJ stent)
- Once infection settled, treat underlying cause

Acute prostatitis/epididimyitis

- Acute bacterial infection
- 4-week course of 4-Quinolone (e.g. ciprofloxacin 500 mg p.o. b.d.)
- Prostatic abscess requires draining, usually with TURP

Antibiotic prophylaxis

- Prior to any instrumentation of the GU tract
- Usually use IV gentamicin, but any antibiotic with Gram-negative cover will suffice
- Special care required in patients with prosthetic materials, especially heart valves (as in other systems)
- Prior to prostate biopsy, usually use oral agent with good penetrance into the prostate (e.g. ciprofloxacin, ofloxacin) plus add metronidazole. Give for five days (start one day before biopsy)
- Should delay surgery if MSU positive; exception is the case of UTI secondary to infected calculi, where sterilization is not usually possible

Complications

- Stone formation (esp. Proteus)
- Renal scarring (children with vesico-ureteric reflux)
- Recurrence
- Persistence
- Relapse
- Gram-negative septicaemia

5. URINARY TRACT CALCULI

5.1 Aetiology and pathology

Stone formation requires supersaturated urine. Urine is acidic in the morning and alkaline after meals.

- **Ksp (solubility product)** above this: metastable (easily soluble). Capable of initiating crystal growth and epitaxy (deposition of one crystal type on another, for example, calcium oxalate crystal deposition on urate).
- **Kfp (formation product)**: unstable solutions. Spontaneous homogenous nucleation occurs.

Types of stone

- Calcium
- Phosphate
- Struvite
- Xanthine
- Matrix

- Oxalate
- Urate
- Cysteine
- Silicate

- **Calcium**: excess absorption: sarcoid, milk-alkali, hyperparathyroidism, Vit D.
  Bone disease: hyperparathyroidism, osteolytic lesions, multiple meyloma.
  Treatment: cellulose phosphate, thiazides, low ca diet, increase fluids (all stones), orthophosphate (inhibits Vit D synthesis).
- **Oxalate**: inflammatory bowel disease, chronic diarrhoea, surgical bypass (Ca loss, therefore unchecked oxalate absorption). Can treat with oral Ca supplements. Low citrate (inhibits stone formation) hypoK, hypoMg, fasting, RTA I.
- **Struvite**: triphosphate stones Mg, Amm, Phos. ppt in alkaline urine. Associated with urea splitting organisms (urease) i.e. proteus, pseudomonas, klebsiella, mycoplasma. Staghorn calculi.
- **Urate**: radiolucent. Gout, myeloproliferative disease, ileostomy (diarrhoea-acid urine-ppt urate). ppt acid urine. Rx fluids, alkaline urine allopurinol.
- **Cysteine**: very hard stones. 0.45 density of ca stones. COLA (auto ress). ppt acid urine. Treatment: fluids, alkalinise urine, D-penicillamine.
- **Xanthine**: rare. Congenital deficiency of xanthine oxidase. Radiolucent.

5.2 Evaluation

History and examination

- Asymptomatic (majority of renal calculi)
- Loin pain (usually intermittent)
- Acute ureteric (renal) colic (ureteric calculi)
- Haematuria (usually microscopic)
- UTI (esp. Staghorn calculi — Proteus UTIs)

Investigation

Most only investigate second stone, multiple stones, family history, children, Afro–Caribbean women, nephrocalcinosis or if solitary kidney. Need **serum Ca**, urate. **24-hour collection** of Ca, oxalate, phosphate, urate, citrate, volume.

Imaging

IVU, US, CT (useful for fat contrast allergic patients), retrograde urography, DMSA (function). DTPA (obstruction)

5.3 Management

Treatment depends on size and location.

Options: watchful waiting (if septic with obstructing calculus needs nephrostomy urgently).

Extra-corporal shock wave lithotripsy (ESWL)

- Several types of machine; three types commonly in use
- Original spark gap (e.g. Dornier HM3) — most powerful, but requires general or spinal anaesthesia and patient must be submerged in a water bath
- Electromagnetic (e.g. Modulith or Lithostar) — most common in use, relies on an AC current which repels diaphragms against a plate under the patient
- Piezoceramic (e.g. Piezolith) — current causes deformation of crystals sited on the concave surface
- F1 is the energy source; F2 is the focal point
- Useful for stones <2 cm diameter in the kidney (1 cm if in lower pole calyx), upper or lower ureter
- Calcium monohydrate, bushite and cysteine stones usually too hard to break
- Difficulties in treating stones in mid-ureter (difficult to image, transverse processes overlie) and in obese patients (F2 too short, most tables do not accommodate patients >300 kg); also stones in horseshoe kidneys
- Absolute contraindications — pregnancy, aortic aneurysms which lie in the 'blast path'
- Caution in patients with pacemakers (piezoceremic safe)

Ureteroscopy

- **Rigid**: useful for stones in lower and mid-ureter; most difficult in younger men (pelvis narrower)
- **Flexible**: scopes expensive; expertise needed to operate; used in conjunction with energy source which fits in the working channel and bends (laser or EHL)

Ureteric stents

- Useful for preventing pelvic stones from obstructing kidney at PUJ
- Prophylactic stenting of kidney stones >1 cm prior to treatment
- Inserted following planned or accidental ureteric opening (e.g. following open removal of a stone)

Percutaneous nephrolithotomy (PCNL)

- Percutaneous puncture directly into calyx or renal pelvis
- Track dilated over guide wire, usually to 26F
- Used for stone bulk >2 cm or in patients with spinal deformities
- Larger stones may require ESWL afterwards to residual fragments ('sandwich technique')
- Can use all energy sources as channel of nephroscope is straight

Open surgery

- **Nephro- or pyelolithotomy**: particularly if underlying PUJ obstruction which can be treated as well
- **Ureterolithotomy**: particularly for impacted middle ureteric stones

Laparoscopy

Via trans- or extraperitoneal (retroperitoneal) approach. Most useful for large, impacted mid-ureteric stones.

Nephrectomy

If differential function <15% (assuming normal global renal function).

Stone breaking equipment

- **Lithoclast**: ball-bearing bounces back and forth in chamber; vibrating probe; like pneumatic drill. Newer version has flexible probe and suction channel.
- **Ultrasound**: sonic vibration of probe; generates +heat, therefore should not use in ureter; water irrigation required. Probe has suction channel to remove fragments.
- **EHL**: local spark has mini-lithotripsy effect. Can cause serious tissue injury, therefore not recommended for use in ureter.

- **Laser**: usually pulsed holmium as source; fibre transmits energy; can bend fibre up to 'critical angle'. Holmium energy absorbed by water and causes plasma bubble at stone surface; rapid expansion leads to shock wave and stone fragmentation. Generates very high local temperature which also causes stone dissolution. Coumarin lasers (e.g. Coumarin Green) have little effect on tissues, therefore are very safe to use. Drawbacks are expense and total specificity for use with stone disease.

Prevention

In general encourage fluids. Specific conditions: refer to endocrinologist as management complex. Certain stones can be prevented or even dissolved by changing the pH of urine.

6. RENAL TUMOURS

6.1 Benign tumours

Previously rarely detected ante-mortem.

Renal adenomas

Renal adenomas are the most common benign parenchymal lesion. They are small well-differentiated glandular tumours of renal cortex. Usually asymptomatic and diagnosed at autopsy (incidence 7–22% autopsy study). No clinical, histological or immunohisto-chemical differentiation from RCC.

Treatment
Observation versus surgery.

Renal oncocytoma

- Spectrum of behaviour from benign to malignant
- Histology: large epithelial cells with finely granular eosinophilic cytoplasm
- Also occur in adrenal, salivary, thyroid and parathyroid glands
- Represent 3–5% of renal tumours
- M:F 2:1

Macroscopically have well-defined fibrous capsule and are tan or light brown. Rarely demonstrate necrosis cf RCC and are usually solitary and unilateral. Cell of origin not clear ? proximal convoluted tubule cells. Grade 1 well-differentiated benign behaviour. Grade 3 poorly differentiated (may have RCC intermixed). Diagnosis usually pathological. Clinically, pain and haematuria less than 20%. 'Spoke-wheel' appearance on CT and angiography.

Treatment

Radical nephrectomy. If diagnosis can be made by aspiration and tumour <4 cm — partial nephrectomy.

Angiomyolipoma (renal hamartoma)

Rare benign tumour seen in two populations, i.e. tuberose sclerosis or normal population, though histology is similar. Angiomyolipomas seen in 50–80% of patients with tuberous sclerosis and are typically bilateral and asymptomatic. Those occurring in the normal population are usually unilateral and larger. 25% may present with spontaneous rupture and haemorrhage. Macroscopically they are unencapsulated and are yellow to grey lesions. There are three major histologic components: mature fat cells, smooth muscle and blood vessels. Extra-renal deposits represent multicentricity, not metastatic potential. Easily diagnosed on ultrasound (highly echogenic) and CT (black, i.e. negative Hounsfield units) due to high fat content.

Treatment

- **Asymptomatic**: <4 cm diameter, yearly CT; >4 cm diameter six-monthly CT
- **Symptomatic or complication** (bleeding, pain): embolization, partial nephrectomy, total nephrectomy (usually necessary if bleeding severe)

Leiomyomas

Leiomyomas are found in smooth muscle areas of kidney, i.e. capsule and pelvis. There are two groups: multiple small cortical lesions and larger, solitary lesions often diagnosed pathologically.

Haemangiomas

Haemangiomas are small vascular tumours which may be multiple (12%) but rarely bilateral. May present with intermittent haematuria and are diagnosed with angiography or endoscopy.

Lipomas

Uncommon deposits of mature adipose cells arising from capsule or peri-nephric tissue, asymptomatic, diagnosed on CT.

Juxtaglomerular tumour

A juxtaglomerular tumour is very rare, and causes significant hypertension. Arises in pericytes of afferent arterioles and contains renin secretory granules. Nephrectomy or partial nephrectomy cures hypertension.

6.2 Renal cell carcinoma

Renal cell carcinoma (RCC) represents 3% of all adult cancers. It occurs most commonly in the 40–
60 age group (M:F 2:1).

Aetiology

* Is not well understood
* Associated with von Hippel–Lindau (vHL) syndrome, horseshoe kidneys, adult poly-cystic disease and acquired renal cystic disease (CRF)
* Chromosomal studies indicate abnormality on chromosome 3p may account for familial and sporadic form. This is also the location of the VHL tumour supressor gene.

Known risk factors of renal cell carcinoma

* Smoking
* Shoe industry
* Exposure to cadmium, petroleum products and asbestos
* First-degree relatives with RCC

* Analgesic abuse
* Leather tanners
* Possibly also caffeine, diuretics, obesity and exogenous oestrogens

Pathology

* Originates from proximal renal tubular epithelium
* Macroscopically tumour is yellow to orange
* Clear cell type (yellow due to lipids) versus granular type (grey to white)
* Larger tumours show necrosis, haemorrhage and calcification
* No true capsule but may demonstrate pseudo-capsule

Most often RCC is mixed adenocarcinoma with clear cells, granular cells and occasionally sarcomatoid cells. Other types are papillary (10–14% — 40% multifocal, but not on other side, not associated with VHL gene abnormalities) and chromophilic.

Pathogenesis

Vascular tumours that spread via direct invasion through renal capsule into peri-nephric fat and adjacent viscera, or by direct extension into the renal vein. Metastases are to lung, then liver, bone, ipsilateral nodes, adrenal and other kidney.

Staging of renal cell carcinoma

Aim to select appropriate therapy and provide prognostic information. Include history, examination, FBC, U&Es, LFTs, Ca, ALP and MSU, CXR, CT abdomen and pelvis. Bone scan not indicated unless bone pain or abnormal ALP/Ca.

ROBSON STAGING

Stage 1   Tumour within renal parenchyma
Stage 2   Tumour involves peri-nephric fat but within Gerota's fascia (includes adrenal)
Stage 3a Tumour involves main renal vein or IVC
Stage 3b Tumour involves regional lymph nodes
Stage 3c Tumour involves both local vessels and nodes
Stage 4a Tumour involves adjacent organs other than adrenal
Stage 4b Distant metastases

TNM STAGING

T_x	Primary tumour cannot be assessed
T_0	No evidence of primary tumour
T_1	Tumour <7 cm within kidney
T_2	Tumour >7 cm within kidney
T_{3a}	Tumour invades adrenal or peri-nephric tissues but within Gerota's fascia
T_{3b}	Tumour extends into renal vein or IVC below diaphragm
T_{3c}	Tumour extends into supradiaphragmatic IVC
T_4	Tumour invades beyond Gerota's fascia
N_0	Regional lymph nodes cannot be assessed
N_1	Metastasis in single lymph node
N_2	Metastasis in two or more lymph nodes
M_x	Presence of distant metastasis cannot be assessed
M_0	No distant metastasis
M_1	Distant metastasis

Grading

Multiple pathological grading systems exist, limiting usefulness. Fuhrman (grades I–IV) most commonly used.

Signs and symptoms

- Great variety of presenting symptoms
- Classic triad (pain, mass and haematuria) present in only 10–15%
- 60% have macro- or microscopic haematuria
- 40% have pain or mass or both
- Symptoms of metastatic disease or secondary effects of malignancy
- Incidental finding on imaging or other investigations
- Left variocoele
- Para-neoplastic syndromes

Para-neoplastic syndromes

- **Erythrocytosis**
  3–10% of patients
  Related to erythropoietin
  produced by tumour or
  regional hypoxia of normal
  tissue

- **Hypercalcaemia**
  3–13%
  Humoral substances similar to
  parathyroid hormone identified
  also caused by bony metastasis

- **Also syndromes due to ACTH**
  glucagon, prolactin, insulin
  and gonadotrophins

- **Hypertension**
  Up to 40% of patients
  Related to renin secretion

- **Non-metastatic hepatic dysfunction
  (Stauffer's syndrome)**
  Abnormal LFTs
  Prolonged PT
  Fever, fatigue, weight loss resolves
  after nephrectomy
  ? Hepatotoxin

Laboratory findings

- Anaemia (30%)
- Haematuria (60%)
- ESR raised (up to 75%); ESR > 40 = worse prognosis
- Para-neoplastic phenomena (see shaded box)

Radiology

- **Intravenous pyelogram**: in isolation, 75% accurate, calcification highly suspicious
- **Computed tomography**: gold standard; more sensitive than US or IVP; enhancing mass, though less so than surrounding parenchyma; consider renal hilum, renal vein (RV), inferior vena cava (IVC), adrenals, lymphatic structures, and adjacent organs (± chest). Bosniak classification of renal masses.
- **Ultrasound**: non-invasive; 98% accurate in defining simple cysts; complementary to CT; proper study identifies renal vein and IVC in > 90%
- **Angiography**: largely replaced by CT; demonstrates neo-vascularity, contrast pooling plus renal vein involvement; AV fistula; procedure has morbidity (complications of Seldinger technique); useful for defining vascular anatomy, particularly if partial nephrectomy contemplated
- **Magnetic resonance imaging**: better than CT at demonstrating RV and IVC involvement (gold standard for IVC assessment) otherwise equivalent to CT for staging
- **FNAC**: limited role in evaluation of renal cell carcinoma; for diagnosis where non-surgical Mx is appropriate; evaluation of masses in solitary kidneys; chronic abscess versus cystic carcinoma (aspirate and inject contrast)

Cytology: in general, haematuria needs evaluation with urinary cytology.

Treatment of renal cell carcinoma

Localized disease

- Radical nephrectomy is treatment for localized disease
- *En bloc* dissection of kidney and enveloping fascia, ipsilateral adrenal proximal ureter and lymph nodes to area of vessel transection was originally described
- Role of lymph node dissection: randomized study indicates no survival difference with LN dissection and increased transfusion requirement
- Pre-operative renal artery embolization not shown to decrease blood loss; complications to other organs, other kidney; post-infarction syndrome: flank pain, fever, leucocytosis; reserved for large tumours with abnormal vasculature; palliation for pain, haemorrhage or para-neoplastic phenomena
- 5–10% of RCC have some degree of IVC involvement
- IVC involvement alone does not confer poor prognosis ($T_{3b}N_0M_0$ similar to T_2)
- May require cardio-pulmonary bypass for proximal extension into right atrium

For bilateral RCC (3%) or solitary kidneys or ↓ renal function or non-functioning contralateral kidney, alternatives include partial nephrectomy. Some perform partial nephrectomy in normal kidneys if < 4 cm and confined to upper or lower pole (Novick). Survival unchanged, but local recurrence 6–8%, therefore need close surveillance.

Disseminated disease

- Up to one-third have metastatic disease at presentation
- Radical nephrectomy may be effective palliation for pain, haematuria or para-neoplastic syndromes (embolization should be tried first)
- Solitary metastases may be treated by combined nephrectomy and excision (NB. Patients with delayed solitary metastases have improved survival over those whose solitary metastasis presents initially)
- Radical nephrectomy is often required prior to immunotherapy to reduce tumour bulk

Radiotherapy
Palliation of metastatic disease in brain, bone and lungs (temporary tumour sterilization).

Hormonal therapy
Early studies demonstrated response to progesterone, androgens and anti-oestrogens, but not confirmed by larger series and, at best, effects minimal.

Chemotherapy
Resistant tumour to single and multiple agent treatment, probably due to multi-drug resistance (MDR) gene in tumour which inactivates chemotherapeutic agents.

Biologic response modifiers
BCG, interferons and IL-2. IL-2 most effective single agent; may be given i.v. (high bolus — significant morbidity) or s.c. (low-dose, at home); combination therapy most effective.

Prognosis of renal cell carcinoma

- T_1 disease: 80–100% five-year survival
- T_2–T_{3b}: 60%
- M_1: 0–20%; few patients survive >2 years; median survival 6–12 months

6.3 Other malignant renal tumours

Nephroblastoma (Wilms' tumour)

- Peak incidence in third year of life
- M:F ratio 1:1
- 5% bilateral
- Familial (15–20%) and sporadic forms

Autosomal dominant with variable penetrance; younger and more frequently bilateral.

- Histology demonstrates blastemal, epithelial and stromal elements
- Anaplastic cells, clear cells and rhabdoid tumours have poor prognosis
- Macroscopically they are large, multi-lobulated and grey or tan in colour
- Tumour spread via direct extension, haematogenously via renal vein or via lymphatics to lungs (85–95%) and liver (10–15%)
- Usually present with mass, abdominal pain, anorexia, nausea, vomiting, fever and haematuria.

Treatment
Surgery for resectable lesions, plus combinations of chemotherapy and radiotherapy relating to stage. Overall survival is approximately 90%.

Sarcoma of the kidney

Primary sarcomas are rare, representing 1–3% of all malignant renal neoplasms most commonly present in fifth decade, with slight male predominance. Common presentation is with flank pain and/or weight loss. Mainly leiomyosarcomas (50%), but also fibro-sarcomas, liposarcomas etc. Radical nephrectomy for localized disease is only effective therapy.

Transitional cell carcinomas

See Section 7.

Secondary renal tumours

- Frequent site for metastatic spread for solid and haematological tumours
- Primary site is lung (20%), breast (12%), stomach (11%) and renal (9%)
- Lymphoma and non-Hodgkin's lymphoma metastases also occur

7. UROTHELIAL CANCERS

7.1 Bladder carcinomas

Incidence

- M:F ratio 2.7:1
- Average age at diagnosis 65 years — 85% localized and 15% metastasized
- 80% of invasive tumours present *de novo*

Pathogenesis

Multi-step phenomenon:

Initiator or metabolite → alteration in cellular DNA → malignant cell → protein formation

Promoters → proliferation of abnormal cells

Oncogenes (H-RAS) and tumour supressor genes (p53, Rb)

Bladder cancer initiators or promoters

- Smoking
  (α and β naphthylamine)
- Cyclophosphamide

- Benzidine
- Aromatic amines
- Physical trauma
  (catheters, infection, calculi)

p53: tumour suppressor gene located on 17p. *In general,* 'wild type' (normal) p53 is undetectable on immunochemistry due to its short t½. 'Mutant' p53 has a longer half-life, therefore is detectable, i.,e. p53-positive. p53 positivity is associated with high grade, muscle invasive tumours.

Wild type p53 acts by inducing p21 (WAF-1), a cyclin-dependent kinase inhibitor, which causes slowing of the cell cycle to allow DNA repair, if possible. It can also direct damaged cells to apoptosis by altering the bax/bcl2 ratio.

Risk industries
Chemical, dye, rubber, petroleum, leather, printing.

STAGING OF BLADDER CARCINOMAS

UICC

T_{is}	*In situ*	N_0	no nodes
T_a	confined to epithelium	N_1	single node <2 cm
T_1	invades into lamina propia	N_2	single node 2–5 cm or
T_{2a}	superficial muscle		multiple nodes <2 cm
T_{2b}	deep muscle	N_3	any nodes >5 cm
T_{3a}	microscopic perivesical	M_0	no metastases
	invasion	M_1	metastases
T_{3b}	macroscopic perivesical		
	invasion		
T_{4a}	contiguous organs (prostate etc.)		
T_{4b}	fixed to pelvic side wall		

Histopathology

Normal
Urothelium: 3–7 layers of transitional cell epithelium; rests on basement membrane; lamina propia contains loose connective tissue and muscularis mucosa; muscularis propia inner and outer longitudinal fibres; middle circular fibres.

Adventitia.

Papilloma

- Papillary tumour on stalk having normal number of layers (3–7) of cells that maintain polarity
- Only small number progress

TCC

- 90% of bladder tumours
- Papillary/exophytic, sessile, or ulcerated
- Three grades based on urothelial architecture: cell size; pleomorphism; nuclear polarization; hyperchromatism; mitoses

Carcinoma *in situ* is flat, non-papillary anaplastic epithelium. Many progress to invasive disease.

Frequency of tumour invasion, recurrence and progression correlates with grade (and stage — see later). Progression is noted in:

- 10–20% Grade 1
- 19–37% Grade 2
- 33–67% Grade 3
- Survival: low-grade 98%, 10 years; high grade 35%

Non-TCC

- **Adenocarcinoma**: 2% of all bladder cancers. Primary adenocarcinomas may arise from cystitis and metaplasia. Urachal adenocarcinomas occur at the dome. Five-year survival poor.
- **SCC**: 5–10% of bladder tumours; associated with chronic infection, vesical calculi and catheters (2–10% paraplegics); bilharzial infection; often invasive at diagnosis
- **Undifferentiated carcinomas**: rare; no mature epithelial elements
- **Mixed**: combination of transitional, glandular, squamous

---

Rare epithelial and non-epithelial cancers

- Villous adenomas, carcinoid, melanoma (ep)
- Direct extension from prostate, rectum, cervix etc.

- Phaeos, lymphomas and mesenchymal tumours (non-ep)
- Metastases from melanoma, lymphoma, stomach, breast, kidney, lung

---

Clinical findings in bladder cancer

Symptoms

- Haematuria is presenting feature in 90%
- Vesical irritability: frequency, urgency and nocturia
- Symptoms of metastatic disease: bone pain, flank pain etc.

Signs

- Nil
- Mass or bladder wall thickening
- Hepatomegaly, lymphadenopathy
- General signs of malignancy

Laboratory investigations

- **Routine**: haematuria; uraemia; anaemia
- **Urine cytology/cytometry tests**: detection depends on adequacy of specimen, grade and volume of tumour. Flow cytometry (if available) detects 80% of all bladder cancers, 50% papillomas, 82%, 89% and 90% of Ta, TIS and invasive lesions, respectively. Certain urine tests may be useful in some circumstances but are not sensitive enough to replace cystoscopy (e.g. BTA tests detects bm complexes), NMP-22, FDPs.
- **Cell surface antigens**: blood group Ag lost in BT correlating with stage and grade; bladder carcinoma cell Ag lost correlating with stage and progression rates
- **Imaging IVP, U/S, CT, MRI, retrograde urography**: advantages and disadvantages; limitations of detecting nodal disease; bone scan and CXR
- **Cytology/transurethral resection (TUR)**: initial diagnosis, staging and complete excision of low-stage lesions; may perform differential cytology, random Bx now versus later (Hicks 1982, described seeding)

Management of bladder cancer

Defined by two separate but related processes: **recurrence** and **progression**. Progression greater biological risk, but recurrence has significant morbidity. Treatment options determined by:

- Tumour stage
- Grade
- Multiplicity
- Recurrence pattern

Tumour stage at presentation

- T_a or T_{is} 50–70% of bladder tumours superficial at presentation
- T_1 28%
- T_2 24%
- M_+ 15%

Grading

- Grade 1   43%
- Grade 2   25%
- Grade 3   32%

Superficial tumours rarely metastasize, but may progress or recur.

Progression

T_a <6%, T_1 45%

- Grade 1: 10–20% progress
- Grade 2: 20–40%
- Grade 3: 30–60%

Recurrence

Related to grade, number, size and history of disease. Risk with:

- T_1, multiple (>4 cm), large (>5 cm), high-grade
- CIS or dysplasia away from tumour site

Initial treatment

- T_{is}: biopsy and intravesical BCG for six weeks followed by repeat cytology and cystoscopy ± biopsy (contraversial)
- T_a: transurethral resection (TUR) alone and surveillance (single, low-grade, not recurrent)
- T_a: TUR and intravesical chemo/immunotherapy (large, multiple, recurrent or high-grade) initially (single dose within 24 hours), or at three months (either single dose if previous solitary tumour of 6-week course if previously multiple). Maintenance immunotherapy (BCG) can be given for 'nuisance' recurrences that fail conventional treatment — beware toxicity (26% versus 9%, severe toxicity — maintenance vs 6-week, BCG arm – SWOG study)
- T_1: TUR and ± intravesical chemo/immunotherapy. Recurrence of G3T1 disease: either maintenance, BCG or cystectomy (particularly if T_{1b} + T_{is})
- T_2–T_4: radical cystectomy with ileal conduit, catheterizable stoma, orthotopic bladder reconstruction or rectal pouch implantation. Partial cystectomy (particularly tumours of dome). Radical radiotherapy (in general long-term results not comparable to radical cystectomy).
- Any T, N_+, M_+: systemic chemotherapy or palliative surgery or radiotherapy

Treatment

Intravesical chemotherapy

- Majority of superficial bladder cancers recur
- Intravesical chemotherapy as a therapeutic or prophylactic measure
- Instillations increase efficacy whilst decreasing morbidity
- All give local side-effects, predominantly irritative symptoms
- Increase efficacy by increasing contact time and concentration
- May respond to one agent after another has failed
- **Mitomycin C** (anti-tumour, antibiotic alkylating agent); inhibits DNA synthesis

40–80% have complete response; irritative symptoms and palmar rash 6%; a single dose within 24 hours of TURBT reduces recurrence
- **Thiotepa** (alkylating agent): 55% response; side-effects cystitis and myelosuppression in 10%
- **Doxorubicin**: 40% response rate
- **BCG** (attenuated strain of *Mycobacterium bovis*): immunologically mediated; binds to fibronectin receptors of bladder urothelium; upregulates MHC expression on tumour surface and induces immune-type response; most efficacious agent for CIS; 40–70% response overall; side-effects local irritative; haemorrhagic cystitis (7%); systemic infection (2%)

Surgery

- **TUR or ablation**: initial form of treatment
- **Partial cystectomy**: few patients are true candidates; localized invasive cancers on lateral walls, dome or in diverticulum; local recurrences common
- **Radical cystectomy**: removal of anterior pelvic organs; ± urethrectomy in men (if +ve prostate biopsy); urinary diversion or reconstruction; adjuvant chemotherapy improves survival if lymph nodes found to be positive (Skinner), but not widely accepted

Radiotherapy
Alternative to surgery in deeply invasive lesions, 15% have significant bowel, bladder or rectal complications. Local recurrence is 40–70%.

Chemotherapy

- Single or combination of agents
- MVAC, CMV
- Complete response 13–35%
- Median survival only one year

7.2 Ureteral and renal pelvic cancers

bladder: ureter: renal pelvis = 51:1:3

Importance

Risk of bladder TCC after upper tract TCC is 30–50%. Risk of contralateral tumour 2–4%. However, the risk of upper tract tumour following TCC bladder is low (<2%).

Bladder surveillance must be performed following diagnosis of upper tract tumour.

Aetiology

Same as TCC bladder plus: NSAID abuse, Balkan nephropathy and thorotrast (contrast media no longer used).

Staging

Same as TCC bladder except:

- T_2 only — extends into muscle (no a or b)
- T_3 only — extends through wall into fat (no a or b)

Treatment

- **Nephroureterectomy**: resect cuff of bladder or 'rip and pluck' (resect ureteric orifice endoscopically and pull)
- **Local resection/ablation**: if solitary kidney

8. HAEMATURIA

Classification of haematuria

- Microscopic (85%) versus Macroscopic (15%)
- Painless (tumour more likely) versus Painful (UTI or stone)
- Acute versus Chronic
- Initial versus Terminal versus Complete

8.1 Aetiology

- **Renal**: stone, tumour, TB, trauma, pyelonephritis, glomerulonephritis, loin-pain haematuria syndrome
- **Ureter**: tumour, TB, stone, trauma
- **Bladder**: tumour, stone, cystitis, foreign body, trauma (catheter), TB, schistosomiasis, interstitial cystitis
- **Prostate**: BPH (never assume this), carcinoma of the prostate, prostatitis
- **Urethra**: tumours, warts, stone

8.2 Evaluation

History

- Ask about risk factors and other effects of the above
- Consider schistosomiasis in patients who have recently been to endemic areas and ask about swimming in fresh water
- Consider symptoms of secondary spread and the general effects of malignancy when considering a possible tumour cause

- Determine which classification (see shaded box opposite)
- As with bleeding elsewhere, consider general causes, such as genetic (haemophilia) or acquired disorders (thrombocytopaenia, liver disease), drugs

Examination

- Consider the general status of the patient i.e. anaemia (conjunctiva), uraemia (glomerulonephritis), cachexia (tumours)
- Specifically, palpate kidneys and perform digital rectal examination (DRE)

Investigations

In general terms **all patients** with any degree of haematuria should be investigated. Specific investigations if any of above suspected (e.g. CXR in TB):

- FBC to assess severity
- U&Es to exclude underlying renal failure
- Clotting ± LFTs
- MSU to confirm (exclude haemoglobinuria) and to exclude UTI
- Urine cytology (mostly positive in cases of invasive TCC and carcinoma *in situ*, but may 'miss' superficial TCC)
- Intravenous urogram (probably more sensitive than ultrasound at detecting urothelial tumours). Can use ultrasound **and** plain KUB (ultrasound may miss smaller stones), particularly in younger patients. Ultrasound better at detecting small renal tumours, but these do not usually cause haematuria.
- Flexible cystoscopy (under local anaesthesia)
- 24-hr urinary protein collection and phase contrast microscopy (>20% dysmorphic RBCs) if medical cause suspected or if above tests are negative and haematuria persists

8.3 Management

- Of the underlying condition
- Anaemia to be corrected before any surgery or shortly afterwards and patient optimized, as with any procedure

Positive cytology is almost always associated with an underlying high-grade urothelial neoplasm or carcinoma *in situ*. Failure to detect an abnormality in the presence of positive cytology is an indication for a repeat specimen. If this is positive the patient should have a rigid cystoscopy under GA. Differential cytology can be obtained from the bladder and both ureters. In addition bilateral retrograde pyelograms, bilateral ureteroscopy and an EUA can be performed.

Macroscopic haematuria is not an indication for catheterization, unless the patient develops clot retention or there is evidence of clots within the bladder (e.g. on ultrasound), where irrigation with bladder washouts can be commenced using a large three-way catheter.

Persistent haematuria should be managed by GA cystoscopy, bladder washout and dia-thermy (if appropriate). If life-threatening, options following this include installation of alum, prostaglandins or formulin (under GA), embolization or ligation of the internal iliac arteries (usually leads to erectile dysfunction), radiotherapy (efficacy not proven) or as a last resort, cystectomy and urinary diversion.

9. CONGENITAL ABNORMALITIES OF THE KIDNEY AND URETER

9.1 Anomalies of the kidney

Agenesis

- Bilateral agenesis is rare (only 400 cases)
- Solitary kidney — ureteral bud fails to develop or does not reach metanephros and thus kidney atrophies
- Ureter absent 50% of time with solitary kidney
- Many cases are now recognized as regressed multicystic kidneys (following improved ante-natal scanning)

Hypoplasia

A small kidney. Unilateral or bilateral hypoplasia is associated with foetal alcohol syndrome and cocaine exposure.

Supernumerary kidneys

More than three kidneys very rare.

Dysplasia and multicystic kidney

- Multicystic kidney of the newborn is usually unilateral, non-hereditary and characterized by an irregularly lobulated mass of cysts — the ureter is usually absent or atretic
- Thought to be due to lack of reciprocal induction of uretic bud and mesonephric mass
- Contralateral PUJ obstruction or reflux occurs in ≈ 20%
- Dysplasia is also seen with ureteral obstruction or reflux early *in utero*
- Histologic findings include primitive glomeruli, ductules, tubules, cartilage, and primitive ducts

Adult polycystic kidney disease

- Autosomal dominant
- Bilateral 95%
- Symptoms from age 40
- Cysts of liver, spleen, pancreas and 'berry' aneurysms of Circle of Willis
- Progressive renal impairment secondary to enlarging renal cysts
- Cysts form due to defects in the development of the nephrons and collecting tubules
- Macroscopically enlarged kidneys with cysts scattered through parenchyma; fluid is amber or occasionally haemorrhagic

Symptoms
Pain due to size; obstruction; haemorrhage or sepsis; renal failure.

Signs
Palpable kidneys; hypertension in 70%; sepsis.

X-rays
IVP characteristic 'spider' deformity.

Complications include infected cysts, renal failure. Usually dialysis-dependent within 5–10 years of diagnosis.

Simple cyst

- ? congenital or acquired. Uncommonly seen in ante-natal scanning, therefore probably acquired
- Simple cyst: thin smooth walls, absence of internal echoes, posterior acoustic enhancement
- Pain may be due to bleeds, infection, pressure or obstruction
- Percutaneous drainage may be combined with injection of contrast material ± sclerosant
- Larger cysts recur after sclerosant
- Bosniak class I (classification of CT-detected cysts)

Renal fusion

One in 1000 have some form of renal fusion — the most common is **horseshoe kidney**. Fusion occurs early, thus kidneys seldom ascend to the normal position. Normal rotation cannot occur, therefore each pelvis lies on the anterior surface and some degree of ureteral obstruction is common. Often asymptomatic, though occasionally associated with GI symptoms, infection or hydronephrosis.

Radiology

- **Horseshoe**
  Axis of kidney is parallel to the spine
  Renal pelvis lies anteriorly
  (lower pole calyces medial to ureter)

- **Crossed renal ectopy with fusion**
  Two renal pelvises and two ureters
  (one ureter crosses the mid-line)

- **Fused pelvic kidney**
  Two separate pelvises and ureters

Ectopic kidney

Simple ectopy
A low kidney on the correct side that failed to ascend normally. Situated in the pelvic brim or pelvis (rarely in the chest). During ascent, the vascular supply to the kidney is locally derived until it reaches its final position, therefore blood supply is from adjacent vessels. Prone to obstruction or infection.

Crossed ectopy without fusion
On the opposite side without fusion.

Abnormal rotation
Normal loin position but the renal pelvis remains anterior.

Medullary sponge kidney

Autosomal recessive defect characterized by ectasia of the distal collecting tubules. Usually bilateral. Infection and nephrocalcinosis are the common complications.

Calyceal diverticulum

A calyceal diverticulum is an out-pouching of part of a minor calyx into the adjacent renal parenchyma; it is lined by transitional epithelium. A calyceal diverticulum may be multiple, and can occur anywhere in the kidney. There is a similar incidence in children and adults.

Megacalycosis

Megacalycosis is a non-obstructive condition in which the calyces are dilated, malformed, and often increased in number in the absence of ureteropelvic junction obstruction or enlargement of the renal pelvis. The usual presenting symptoms in children are urinary tract infections, which are not necessarily related. It is more common in males.

9.2 Anomalies of the ureter

Ureteral atresia

The ureter may be entirely absent, or may end blindly due to failure of the ureteral bud to form from the mesonephric duct, or by an arrest in its development prior to its contact with the metanephros. It results in an absent or multicystic kidney (lack of reciprocal induction).

Duplication of the ureter

Common congenital malformation — some form of duplication in 0.9% in autopsy series (1944). Autosomal dominant with incomplete penetrance; females > males.
Incomplete form is caused by branching of the ureteral bud prior to it reaching the metanephros. **Complete form** is caused by the presence of two ureteral buds.

Weigert–Meyer law

The ureter draining the upper segment usually inserts infero-medially (and is often obstructed), whereas the ureter draining the lower segment usually inserts supero-laterally (and often demonstrates reflux)

Many present with recurrent infections. The ureter to the upper pole may be ectopic with an insertion distal to the external sphincter or outside the urinary tract, resulting in continuous urinary incontinence.

Ureterocoele

A ureterocoele is a sacculation of the terminal portion of the ureter; it may be orthotopic or ectopic.

- **Orthotopic ureterocoeles** are usually associated with single ureters, whereas **ectopic ureterocoeles** most often involve the upper pole of duplicated ureters
- F:M of 7:1 and 10% are bilateral
- Aetiology is unclear
- May present with infection, bladder outlet obstruction, incontinence, calculi formation or a ureterocoele may prolapse (cecoureterocoele)

Treatment options range from endoscopic incision or resection (de-roofing), to open hemi-nephrectomy ± ureterectomy (± common sheath re-implantation) to excision of the ureterocoele, vesical reconstruction and ureteral reimplantation (ureterocoeles). Often contain a stone.

NB. In a complete duplex system, both ureters are distally enclosed in a common sheath.

Ectopic ureteral orifice

An ectopic ureteral orifice mostly occurs with ureterocoele and duplication.

- Single ectopic ureters can occur
- Genital tract anomalies are frequently associated

The anatomical arrangement and the relative renal function will dictate the management.

Retrocaval ureter

Retrocaval ureter occurs where the embryological normal right ureter becomes trapped behind the vena cava because of abnormal development of the abdominal blood vessels. It is caused by persistence of the posterior cardinal vein as the major portion of the infra-renal inferior vena cava. There are two types:

- Upper ureter and renal pelvis are almost horizontal as they pass behind the vena cava — generally no obstruction
- Ureter descends normally to approximately L3, then it curves upwards in the shape of a reverse J to pass behind and around the vena cava — obstruction usually results

Hypospadias, epispadias and bladder extrophy are covered in Chapter 3, *Head, Neck, Endocrine and Paediatric*, Section 14.7.

10. PELVI-URETERIC JUNCTION OBSTRUCTION

Definition: *Stenosis of the renal pelvis outlet*

Effect: distension of the renal pelvis with potential impairment of renal function.

- Peak incidence in children within the first 6/12
- More common in boys (5:2)
- More common on left side (5:2)
- Between 11% and 40% bilateral
- Most common cause of antenatal hydronephrosis
- Otherwise, bimodal age distribution: teens (alcohol) and elderly (diuretics)

10.1 Aetiology and pathology

Congenital

- Dysfunctional segment of ureter. Thought to be due to disruption of the neuromuscular segment during embryonic recannalization

- Extrinsic compression by vessels or fibrous bands
- Kinks

Acquired

- Stones
- Stricture (secondary to inflammation, passage of stone, infection (TB), instrumentation etc)
- Extrinsic compression (retroperitoneal fibrosis, enlarged lymph nodes)

10.2 Evaluation

Clinical

Depends on age of patient:

- **Infants**: palpable abdominal mass; failure to thrive (FTT); feeding problems; pyrexia of unknown origin (PUO); recurrent UTIs
- **Children**: intermittent loin pain; haematuria, palpable kidney
- **Adults**: pain on drinking fluids or alcohol, recurrent UTIs, palpable kidney

Investigations

Investigations vary with clinical situation:

- IVP
- Ultrasound
- Nuclear medicine scans (DTPA or MAG-3)

NB. Retrograde pyelogram only useful to ensure ureter is normal. Should only be performed at time of pyeloplasty. Performing earlier risks infection.

10.3 Management

Adults

Mild
No symptoms or infection. Observe with yearly MAG-3/DMSA scans.

Moderate and severe
Pain, infection, stones or renal impairment. Surgical intervention required.

Pyeloplasty:

- **Anderson–Hynes**: for large baggy pelvises and the most commonly performed
- **Culp**: if ureteric insertion not too high
- **YV plasty**: simplest technique

Percutaneous nephrostomy and endopyelotomy

Retrograde pyelotomy (acusize, endoburst, laser). Nephrectomy (if kidney has poor (<15%) function).

The results from surgery excellent (>90%) in terms of functional preservation and relief of symptoms. Minimally invasive techniques (80% at best) but results comparable when re-do operations performed. X-ray changes may never completely resolve, but if size of kidney improves, especially in child — can assume a good result.

Children

Indications for surgery:

- Bilateral PUS obstruction
- Obstructed renogram with half-life >20 minutes
- <40% split function on affected side
- Recurrent episodes of pyelonephritis

Complications of surgery

- Infection
- Urinary fistula: common, resolves in 5–10 days

11. VESICO-URETERIC REFLUX (VUR)

Primary reflux is due to an inadequate valve mechanism at the VUJ not associated with obstruction or a neuropathic bladder.

Secondary reflux is that which occurs secondary to obstruction, neuropathic bladder or distortion of the trigone.

Incidence of vesico-ureteric reflux

- Children with no history of UTI   Rare
- Children with history of UTI

Girls overall	14%
Boys overall	29%
<1 year	70%
<4 years	25%
<12 years	15%
Adults	8%

NB. 50% of children with a documented UTI will have VUR

11.1 Aetiology and pathology

Primary

Shortened submucosal tunnel.

Secondary

- Lower pole of duplex
- Ureteral ectopia without ureterocoele
- Cystitis (acute bacterial, radiation, interstitial)
- Elevated intravesical pressure (neuropathic bladder, detrusor instability, detrusor–sphincter dyssynergia)
- Prune Belly syndrome
- Posterior urethral valves ('pop-off') — PUVs
- Iatrogenic (TURP, bladder neck surgery)

97% of children with renal scars show evidence of VUR. Scarring may be due to reflux of sterile urine with abnormally high pressures, or by reflux of infected urine at normal pressures.

Pig studies showed intra-renal reflux and subsequent scars in polar areas in the absence of infection. In the presence of *E. coli* in these animals the scarring was more widespread and severe. Clinical studies suggest that intra-renal reflux of infected urine leads to scarring.

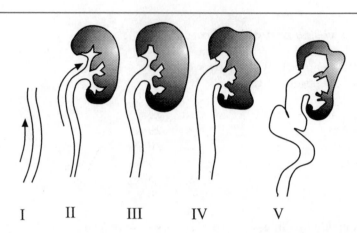

I II III IV V

(I) Ureter only; (II) Ureter and pelvis, no dilatation; (III) Mild dilatation, no forniceal blunting; (IV) Moderate dilatation, forniceal blunting, preservation of papillary impressions; (V) Gross dilatation, tortuosity of ureter, blunting of calyces.

International reflux classification

Pathology

Kidney
Affects tubular function (concentrating ability), predominantly affects glomerular function only if there has been parenchymal damage.

Renal growth
Growth of kidneys with VUR is stunted in the absence of prophylactic antibiotics — ? catch-up renal growth.

Hypertension (HT)
Renal failure: 10–30% of children with end-stage renal failure (ESRF) kids have scarring that may have been due to VUR. VUR may be a factor in 20–30% of adults with ESRF. Long follow-up of severe VUR; 80% have renal scarring; 29% have either renal insufficiency, proteinuria or HT.

11.2 Evaluation

- 20–30% of siblings have reflux on micturating cytourethrogram (MCU)
- 67% of offspring of an affected parent have VUR
- MCU and ultrasound
- Nuclear cystogram is a reasonable alternative for females (need to visualize urethra in boys to exclude PUVs)
- Abnormal ultrasound → DMSA scan

- All studies must be performed after UTI has cleared
- DMSA at least three months after clearance of UTI
- MCU at least three weeks after clearance of UTI

Nuclear medicine studies

- **Direct** (i.e. inject isotope into bladder)
- **Indirect** (i.e. DTPA or MAG-3 scan, then wait for bladder to fill, place camera over lower ureters and ask patient to void). Note: children must be toilet trained. Non-standardized grading system (mild, moderate, severe). Lower radiation dosages. Good for follow-up in both sexes and for screening of families. Not good for bladder pathology and male urethra (e.g. bladder diverticula).

DMSA

To visualize cortical tissue and measure renal function. More sensitive than IVP for picking up scarring.

Endoscopy

Types of ureteric orifice: normal, horseshoe, stadium and golf-hole (worst). The conclusion of the International Reflux Study Committee (IRSC) was that there was poor correlation between the endoscopic findings and resolution of reflux.

11.3 Management

Treatment

Medical
Monitor with cultures, MCU or nuclear cystogram and DMSA. Failure: persistence beyond puberty; breakthrough infections; new or increased scarring; deterioration of function; non-compliance. Studies have shown no disadvantage in medical versus surgical therapy except risk of pylonephritis is 2.5x higher with medical management.

Surgical
In UK primary treatment is medical except for grade V reflux or bilateral grades III–V reflux that presents late, i.e. >6 years. Failure of medical treatment is also an idication for surgery. Many different types of ureteric re-implantation (can be broadly divided into intra- and extra-vesical repairs); 95–99% success. Low rate of secondary obstruction. STING procedure losing favour — migration of Teflon particles and results not equal to surgery.

Prognosis

Reflux

Will disappear spontaneously in many children (Ducat, 1983); 63% of Grade II, 53% of Grade III and 33% of Grade IV will resolve spontaneously if infection is controlled.

International Reflux Study Committee (IRSC)

- **Unilateral**: Grade IV resolves in 61%
- **Bilateral**: Grades III–IV resolved in only 9% in five years

Resolution beyond adolescence is unlikely. Renal scarring rarely occurs in refluxing children if sterile urine is maintained. Long-term antibacterial therapy is usually safe and well tolerated. Re-implantation has a high success rate; 95–98% in normal-calibre ureters. Reflux that persists in adolescence or adulthood is unlikely to resolve (worse implications for females than males).

IRSC

Randomized under-nines with Grade IV reflux to medical or surgical treatment. Bilateral Grade IV was unlikely to resolve within five years. Clinical cases of pyelonephritis higher in the medical group. The number of scars was the same but surgery group scarred early and medical group scarred evenly throughout the five years. Surgery had a very high success rate (IVP was used to document renal scarring).

12. THE NEUROPATHIC BLADDER

There are many systems of classifying the neuropathic bladder in existence.

Classification systems for neuropathic bladder

- **International Continence Society**
Detrusor	Normal, hyper-reflexic or hypo-reflexic
Striated sphincter	Normal, hyperactive or incompetent
Sensation	Normal, hypersensitive or hyposensitive

  Allows individual classification of urinary dysfunction

- **Wain, Benson and Raezer**
  Failure to empty; failure to store

Continues ...

... Continued

- **Millard** (*Australian Continence Journal*, Sept 1995)

  Supra-pontine lesion   Hyper-reflexic bladder, normal voiding, normal sensation

  Supra-sacral lesion   Hyper-reflexic bladder, detrusor-sphincter dyssynergia, loss of sensation

  Infra-sacral lesion   Acontractile bladder, isolated sphincter obstruction, loss of sensation

12.1 Aetiology and pathology

Neurological lesions affecting bladder function

Supra-pontine lesions

- Loss of central inhibition and loss of central facilitation of micturition
- The bladder is hyper-reflexic, with normal co-ordinated voiding and normal sensation
- Symptoms are frequency, urgency, nocturia and urge incontinence

Common causes include CVA, MS, encephalitis and meningitis, dementia, Parkinson's disease, cerebral SOLs, epilepsy. Treatment depends on patient co-operation and includes anti-cholinergic agents, timed voiding, continence appliances and IDCs as a last resort.

Supra-sacral lesions

Lesions between the pons and the sacrum cause a hyper-reflexic bladder and there is usually detrusor-sphincter dyssynergia. Depending on whether the lesion is complete or incomplete, there may also be loss of bladder sensation.

If the lesion is thoracic or cervical and complete, the patient will neither have a desire to void sensation nor a feeling of fullness, and will be unable to perceive temperature or pain from the bladder. If the lesion is below T10, where the sympathetic nerves from the bladder enter the cord, a feeling of fullness and some pain and temperature sensation may be preserved.

Common causes include trauma, herniated disks, tumour, vascular lesions, MS, syringomyelia, and myelitis. Management options are multiple and depend on the nature of the lesion and the period of time since the lesion occurred.

Spinal shock

A stage of flaccid paralysis following severe injury to the spinal cord or conus medullaris. May last from a few weeks to six months (usually 2–3 months). With time, the reflex excitability of striated muscle progresses until a spastic state is achieved. Smooth muscle is much slower to develop this hyper-reflexic activity and thus urinary retention is the rule initially after spinal injury. The return of sacral reflexes is usually detectable by leakage around the catheter, return of the bulbo-cavernosus reflex of return of spontaneous erections.

Autonomic dysreflexia

Autonomic dysreflexia is sympathetically mediated reflex behaviour triggered by sacral afferent feedback to the spinal cord. Seen with spinal cord injuries at the cervical or high thoracic level (above the sympathetic outflow from the cord). Hypertension, bradycardia, sweating, pilo-erection and headache may result from pelvic autonomic afferent activity (over-distension of bladder, bowel or erection) and somatic afferent activity (ejaculation, spasm of lower extremities, insertion of a catheter). The headache can be severe and the hypertension life-threatening.

Management is by awareness of condition and prevention with nifedipine prior to cystos-copy. Acute haemodynamic effects may be managed by removal of stimulus, α-blockers, atropine. Peripheral rhizotomy has been used to prevent recurrent episodes.

Sacral and infra-sacral lesions

The bladder and urethra are isolated from the sacral and pudendal nuclei. Bladder is areflexic but of low compliance — as the bladder fills, the pressure rises until the leak-point pressure is reached (usually around 50 cm H_2O) and this is determined by the residual urethral tone. McGuire demonstrated that continuous bladder pressure above 40 cm H_2O caused upper tract deterioration.

Common causes include sacral centre lesions (trauma, polio and herpes zoster, radiation and surgery); conus-medullaris lesions; cauda equina lesions; autonomic neuropathies (DM, tabes dorsalis, pernicious anaemia, collagen diseases). Pelvic nerve injury (AP resection, Wertheim hysterectomy, radiotherapy, cordoma, pelvic/sacral fracture.

Ideal management is clean intermittent self-catheterization $\pm$ anticholinergics.

12.2 Evaluation

Examination

- Establish level of lesion
- Assess reflexes
- Assess sensory and motor deficits

Investigations

- UA/MSU
- U&Es

Radiology
Periodic IVP and cystograms to assess for hydronephrosis, scarring, calculi. Consider ultrasound as alternative for ongoing evaluation of upper and lower tracts.

Cystoscopy
Exclude stricture, calculi, trabeculation, diverticulae, secondary changes due to indwelling catheters, chronic infection.

Urodynamics
Uroflowmetry, cystometry, urethral profilometry, electromyography and fluoroscopic studies.

Aim to assess the function of the detrusor, the function of the external sphincter and sensation.

Urodynamic studies
Filling
Determine residual volume (in neuropaths, RV is NOT drained), unstable constrictions, bladder compliance and end-filling pressure. Determines whether bladder is 'safe' or 'unsafe' (>40 cm water end-filling pressure).

Voiding
Flow rate, detrusor pressure at maximum flow, dyssynergic voiding, abdominal straining.

NB. Filling rates in patients with neuropathic bladders should be <10 ml/min (50–100 ml/min in normal adults). If unstable contractions, stop study and continue after 5 min. In neuropaths, filling is commenced on top of residual volume (i.e. after bladder is not drained) in contrast to 'normal' urodynamics.

12.3 Management

Aims:

- Continence
- Preservation of renal function
- Avoidance of infection

Management

- **Early**
  Urethral or CIC during spinal shock
    phase
  Initial urodynamics study
  Assess capacity, pressures, DSD
  Baseline imaging

- **Late**
  Urethral catheter
  Suprapubic catheter
  CIC ± anticholinergics
  External drainage devices and tapping
  Surgery
  Sphincterotomy
  Stent
  Diversion
  Augmentation
  Electrical stimulation ±
    posterior rhizotomy

Complications

- **Infection**: renal amyloidosis
- **Hydronephrosis**: sexual dysfunction and fertility
- **Calculi**: autonomic dysreflexia
- **Squamous cell carcinoma**: in patients with long-term catheters (up to 2–10%)

13. URINARY INCONTINENCE

Incidence:

- 2.5–5% men
- 10–25% women

More than 50% of women have complained of incontinence at some time, 40% of elderly women and 50% of nursing home residents.

Definitions:

- **Incontinence**: the involuntary loss of urine which is a social or hygienic problem and can be objectively demonstrated
- **Genuine stress incontinence (GSI)**: involuntary loss of urine when the total intravesical pressure exceeds maximum urethral pressure in the absence of detrusor activity
- **Urge incontinence**: involuntary loss of urine associated with a strong desire to void — motor or sensory
- **Overflow incontinence**: intravesical pressure exceeding urethral pressure associated with distension in the absence of detrusor activity
- **False incontinence**: i.e. vesico-vaginal fistula

Complications:

- **Medical**: rashes; ulcers; UTIs and septicaemia; falls and fractures
- **Social implications**: embarrassment; isolation; depression
- **Community implications**: institutionalization; cost
- **Transient incontinence**: delirium; UTIs; atrophic vaginitis/urethritis; drugs; psychiatric disorders; polyuria; impaired mobility; constipation; childbirth
- **Chronic incontinence**

Classification of chronic incontinence

- **Failure to store**
  Bladder
  Urge incontinence
  Detrusor overactivity
  Decreased compliance
  Sensory urgency
  Reflex incontinence
  Supra-sacral
  Supra-pontine — dementia etc.
  Outlet:
    GSI, urethral instability,
    post-prostatectomy and pelvic surgery
  Trauma:
  Fracture pelvis, ectopic outlet —
  fistula, ectopic ureter, extrophy

- **Failure to empty**
  Bladder
  Neurogenic
  Myogenic
  Psychogenic or idiopathic
  Outlet:
    Anatomic: prostate, bladder neck, urethral stricture
    Functional: smooth or striated sphincter dyssynergia

Other classifications of GSI

Raz classification
Anatomic (urethral hypermobility) or intrinsic sphincteric defect (ISD).

McGuire classification

- I Minimal hypermobility, VLPP 90–120 cm H_2O
- II Marked hypermobility, VLPP 60–90 cm
- III Prior failed bladder neck suspension, VLPP < 60 cm

NB. VLPP = Valsalva Leak Point Pressure. Mean Urethral Closure Pressure also used. In general, < 20 cm water = ISD.

13.1 Aetiology and pathology

Female

- Pure GSI 30–40%
- Anatomical 90–95%
- ISD 5–10%
- Pure urge 20%
- Mixed 40–50%

Male

- Post-TURP (~50% have some urge component)
- Overflow
- Urge
- Trauma, pelvic surgery, radical prostatectomy (<2% complete incontinence, many have stress incontinence which improves with pelvic floor exercises or bulking agents)

13.2 Evaluation

History

- Type: urge, stress or mixed
- Degree of leakage (i.e. number of pads)
- Relation to activity, position and state of bladder fullness
- Timing of onset and course of progression
- Associated dysuria, haematuria
- Past medical, surgical and obstetric/gynaecological history
- Medications
- Bladder diaries
- Bowel function
- Prolapse (splinting, evacuation, etc.)

Examination

- Pelvic support
- Prolapse: cystocoele, rectocoele enterocoele, vault, UV prolapse and mobility of vaginal wall
- Atrophic vaginitis, SI demonstrated
- Abdominal examination, palpable bladder
- Neurological examination

Investigations

- Urine microbiology
- Renal function
- Radiology: upper and lower tracts
- Urodynamics: PVR, flowmetry. Filling and voiding phases. Valsalva leak point pressures (McGuire). Fluoroscopy (video-urodynamics). CMG $\pm$ urethral pressure profilometry (UPPs) (urodynamics)

Indications for urodynamics
Complex incontinence, neuropathic bladders, previous surgery and prior to surgery in most patients.

13.3 Management

Treatment of genuine stress incontinence (GSI)

Treatment of the incontinent patient

- **Non-surgical treatment of GSI**
  Kegel exercises:
    50–80% improvement in the
    short term
  Behavioural modification
    fluid restriction
    timed voiding
    avoidance of irritants
    60–70% will show some improvement
  Electrical/electromagnetic devices
    intravaginal devices
    electromagnetic chairs
  Drug therapy
    oestrogens for atrophic vaginitis no more
    effective than placebo in normal population
  Alpha-agonists have major side-effects
    and little efficacy

- **Surgical treatment of GSI**
  Distinguish between urethral hypermobility (anatomic) and intrinsic sphincteric defect (ISD), although isolated ISD is unusual
  Types of treatment
  Retropubic colposuspension
  Transvaginal suspensions
  Slings (fuscin into, rectus abdominus)
  Transvaginal tape (TVT)
  Peri-urethral injections
  Urinary diversion
  NB. Operation selection will also be dependent on presence of prolapse

SUCCESS RATES AFTER SURGERY

	12 months	48 months
Retropubic colposuspension	84%	84%
Transvaginal suspensions	80%	67%
Anterior repair	70%	61%
Slings	82%	83%

(Leach ICS, 1995)

Success rate of TVT-data now to 5 years. 'Significant improvements' maintained at $\simeq$ 80%.

NB. Success rates are highly variable. When evaluating data and comparing, beware of 'improvement'. Many female urologists consider success as complete continence.

Complications of surgery

- Urinary retention
- Osteitis pubis (1% — MMK)
- Post-operative urgency, sling 20%, retropubic 4%

Treatment of intrinsic sphincteric deficiency (ISD)

- Injection of bio-compatibles into the bladder neck
- Sling
- Artificial urinary sphincter (AUS)

Treatment of mixed GSI/ISD

Therapy is directed at treating the predominant symptom. Poorer results cf pure GSI.

Treatment of detrusor instability

- Bladder training (60–80% response after 3 months), includes timed voiding, progressive holding and pelvic floor exercises (inhibit onset of detrusor contraction)
- Drugs (oxybutynin, tolterodine, probanthine)
- Electrical stimulation
- Neuromodulation
- Surgery: augmentation, detrusor myomectomy
- Diversion (severe intractable incontinence)

14. ACUTE RETENTION OF URINE (AUR) AND BLADDER OUTLET OBSTRUCTION (BOO)

14.1 Acute retention of urine (AUR)

Causes of AUR

Prostate

- BPH (common)
- Carcinoma of the prostate
- Prostatitis
- Prostatic infarction

Bladder

- Detrusor atonicity (primary failure, anticholinergic drugs or drugs with anticholinergic adverse effects)
- Bladder stone

Neuropathic

- Spinal shock
- Any cause of a lower motor neurone lesion
- Autonomic dysfunction
- CVA, Parkinson's

Urethra

- Stricture (uncommon)
- Stone
- Trauma (do not catheterize if suspected)

General

- Immobility
- Constipation (common)
- Alcohol or diuretics
- Certain drugs
- Stress (sympathetic overactivity)

Risk factors

- Increasing age
- Large prostate
- Significant symptoms
- Lower flow rates

Evaluation of acute retention of urine

History
NB. Must catheterize patient before taking detailed history.

- Symptoms of BPH (BOO, LUTS) preceding
- History of constipation, especially in elderly
- History of reversible precipitating factors (e.g. recent excess of alcohol, commencement of diuretics or other drugs)

Examination
Confirm diagnosis. Perform digital rectal examination *after* catheterization, as a full bladder pushes the prostate downwards and exaggerates its size. Assess rectal tone, yellow tinge of uraema.

Investigations

- FBC (renal failure may lead to anaemia of chronic disease)
- U&Es (if elevated, try to obtain a previous result to determine baseline function)
- CSU
- U/S KUB

NB. Do *not* perform PSA, as retention causes elevation. Also PSAs should only be performed after explaination of the significance of an elevated result, the need or not for biopsy, and the possible treatments, if appropriate, of organ-confined disease.

Treatment

General

- Catheterize
- Expect a post-obstructive diuresis if the U&Es are abnormal
- Monitor hourly urine output
- Match input to output + 20 ml/h for insensible losses
- Monitor K^+
- Perform daily weight, and start reducing fluids when weight stabilizes

- Patients with severe renal failure may need dialysis, so refer early to a renal physician, if appropriate
- Stop aspirin, if operation likely
- Treat constipation if found on digital rectal examination (DRE)

Specific
When renal function stabilizes and patient optimized:

- Consider if appropriate for a **trial without catheter** (TWOC)
- Patients suitable include those with a reversible precipitating cause or little or no prior symptoms
- Success rates of TWOC are improved by commencing α–blockers 48 hrs before and after removal of catheter
- Patients with renal impairment, severe symptoms prior to retention or complications of BPH are not suitable for a TWOC and require definitive treatment
- Definitive treatments are the same as BPH (see Section 15, p. 678)
- Patients with a CVA should have a TWOC after several months

14.2 Bladder outlet obstruction (BOO)

Aetiology of BOO

Anatomical — male

- Bladder neck tumour
- Bladder stone
- Bladder neck stricture
- Ureterocoeles
- Benign prostatic hyperplasia
- Cancer of the prostate

Full counselling, including on:

- Prostatitis
- Urethral stricture
- Posterior urethral valves
- Cancer of the urethra
- Meatal stenosis

Anatomical — female

- Bladder neck suspension surgery
- Urethral masses

- Cystocoele
- Cancer of the cervix

Functional

- Smooth sphincter dyssynergia (rare)
- Striated sphincter dyssynergia
- Neurological
- Non-neurological

Pathophysiology

- Detrusor hypertrophy
- Hyperplasia
- Collagen deposition
- Trabeculation
- Saccules and diverticulae
- Trigonal hypertrophy

Leads to:

- Detrusor instability 53–80%; BPH — down to 20% post-TURP (Abrams)
- Decreased bladder compliance
- Hypocontractility
- Detrusor hyperactivity and impaired contractility

Other terms

- **Benign prostatic enlargement (BPE):** clinical finding of enlargement
- **Benign prostatic hyperplasia (BPH):** histological diagnosis
- **Lower urinary tract symptoms (LUTS):** obstructive, irritative symptoms

15. BENIGN PROSTATIC HYPERPLASIA (BPH)

15.1 Aetiology and pathology

Aetiology

- Role of testis: androgens permissive
- Ageing
- Prostatic growth factors — epithelial and stromal interactions

Pathology

Franks classification
Five types of nodule:

- Stromal
- Fibromuscular
- Muscular
- Fibroadenoma
- Fibromyoadenoma

McNeal's zones

- Peripheral zone (capsule)
- Central zone (pierced by ejaculatory ducts)
- Transitional zone (surrounds the mid-prostative urethra)
- Anterior fibromuscular zone

Greater increase in stroma compared with epithelial component (from 2:1 to 5:1). Hyperplasia of peri-urethral glands in the transitional zone.

Incidence

- **Micro BPH**: 30–40, 8%; 60–70, 70%; 70–80, 80% (Autopsy studies, Berry, 1984)
- **Prostatism**: 41–50, 26%; 71–80, 80% (Vacurg)
- **Weight**: >20 g, symptoms, Q_{max} <15 ml/s, 40% >65 years
- **Lifetime risk for surgical intervention**: 29% by age 80

15.2 Evaluation of BPH

History

Irritative symptoms:

- Frequency
- Urgency
- Nocturia

Obstructive symptoms:

- Incomplete emptying
- Intermittency
- Weak stream

- Hesitancy
- Dribbling
- Straining
- Double voiding

AUA symptom score severity scale of lower urinary tract symptoms using seven questions scoring 0–5

- 0–7 mild
- 8–20 moderate
- 21–35 severe
- Correlates with bothersomeness
- Reasonable re-test reliability

Complications

- Retention (acute, chronic)
- Renal failure
- Urinary infection
- Bladder stones
- Haematuria (never assume a prostatic origin)

Examination

- Abdominal examination
- Genitalia
- DRE (digital rectal examination)

Investigations (basic)

- U&Es, glucose
- Prostate specific antigen (PSA) (controversial — should only be performed after counselling the patient and in general should *not* be performed in men with life expectancy <5 years)
- Mid-stream urine (MSU)
- Flow rate
- Residual volume

Investigations (additional)

- Urodynamics: if suspect low voiding pressures, predominately irritative symptoms, other abnormalities (e.g. detrusor-sphincter dyssynergia), CNS abnormalities or previous pelvic surgery, i.e. previous prostative/bladder neck surgery, younger men

- Upper tract imaging (not recommended routinely)
- Cytology: if predominantly irritative symptoms, to exclude carcinoma *in situ* of the bladder as a cause

15.3 Management of BPH

Conservative therapy

- Reduce fluid intake if excessive (very common)
- Reduce caffeinated (diuretic and bladder irritant) and alcoholic drinks
- Adjust lifestyle
- Suitable for patients with mild symptoms

Medical therapy

5-alpha reductase inhibitors

- Finasteride is currently the only drug in this class
- Inhibits conversion of testosterone to DHT in stromal and basal epithelial cells
- 25–35% improve in terms of symptom score
- Very modest improvement in flow rates
- Lepore (1996) no better than placebo (study looked mainly at smaller prostates) — Veterans Administration study
- Works best in larger glands (>30–40 g)
- Decreases prostatic bleeding
- If taken long-term (i.e. 4 years), decreases incidence of acute urinary retention and the need for surgery by about half (PLESS trial)

Alpha-blockers

- **α1 blockers**: prazosin, terazosin, alfusocin
- **α1c blockers**: tamsulosin (theoretical advantage but selectivity clinically not proven)
- Change in symptom score and flow rate, but nowhere near comparable to TURP ('gold standard')
- Side-effects are headache, dizziness, retrograde ejaculation, hypotension

Surgical therapy

Transurethral prostatectomy (TURP)

- **Early complications**: transfusion (<1%); blocked catheter; failed TWOC (5%); secondary haemorrhage; urosepsis (2–5%); epididymitis; hypothermia; TUR syndrome

- **Late complications**: bladder neck contracture (2%); urethral strictures (2–3%); incontinence (1–2%); impotence, unreliable figures, studies quote 0–40%, AUA study found 13.6% (wide confidence interval); retrograde ejaculation (70–80%)

TURP mortality of 0.2% in 1989 (AUA); sepsis then cardiovascular complications main causes. Repeat TUR 12% at eight years (Roos).

Transurethral incision of prostate (TUIP)

'The most under-utilized operation in urology'

Orandi (1973) published 40 patients claiming TUIP an alternative to TURP. Indications for surgery essentially similar, plus:

- Small prostates (<30 g)
- High-risk patients
- Younger patients (relative preservation of prograde ejaculation)

Soonawalla (1992) randomized 220 patients (prostates <30 g) to TURP versus TUIP:

- Less operating time
- Lower transfusion rate
- No significant difference in flow rate improvement

Reichmann (1993) no difference in symptom scores between two groups. Retrograde ejaculation in 70% of TURP cf 38% TUIP.

Open prostatectomy
Indications:

- Size of gland (>80–100 g)
- Presence of diverticulae or large calculi (can also be treated)
- Co-existing urethral disease
- Musculo-skeletal disease preventing lithotomy position
- Transfusion rate ~15%
- Transvesical or retropubic approach

Complications:

- Longer length of stay
- More respiratory complications, less mortality than TURP (Roos)
- Significantly more bleeding, transfusions
- Bladder neck contracture (~2%)
- Impotence 15–20%
- Retrograde ejaculation in most patients

Transurethral electrovaporization of prostate (TUEVP)

An electric current causes vaporization and desiccation in combination to remove hyperplastic prostatic tissue.

* **Advantages**: haemostatic; only small risk of TUR syndrome; efficacious; early catheter removal
* **Disadvantages**: slower procedure; long-term data poorly reported

Laser prostatectomy

Nd:YAG or holmium:

* Interstitial coagulation
* VLAP
* Resection
* Enucleation

* **Advantages**: efficacious (70% improvement in symptom scores and flow rates); haemostatic; reduced incidence of impotence, retrograde ejaculation; day-case procedure; no TUR syndrome.
* **Disadvantages**: increased irritative symptoms; cost of fibres and laser machine; prolonged catheter drainage and delay in ultimate outcome; re-operation rate higher than TURP; no tissue for pathology; high rate of bladder neck strictures.

Transurethral microwave thermotherapy

* Radiating heat energy generates temperatures >45 °C causing sterile necrosis
* Improvements in pressure/flow study, symptom scores and flow rates significantly poorer cf. TURP in randomized controlled studies (AUA, 1995)
* Potential advantage of being an office-based procedure
* Sedation only, avoiding GA (not new high energy versions)

Transurethral needle ablation of prostate (TUNA)

* Uses thermal therapy in the form of low radiofrequency waves to create areas of necrosis by heating transition zone to >45 °C
* Flow rates: 20–60% improvement
* Symptoms: 40–70% improvement
* Interstitial variant infuses hypertonic saline for bigger lesions and shorter treatment time

High intensity focused ultrasound (HIFU)

* A form of acoustic energy that can be sharply focused to cause coagulative necrosis but avoiding thermal injury to intervening and adjacent tissue

- Temperatures of 80–200 °C can be achieved
- Results are limited and treatment times excessive
- Bladder, testis, kidney and prostate have been subjected to HIFU therapy

Stents

- Permanent (Urolume™) or temporary (Memokath™)
- Rarely used now
- Problems with dislodgement, encrustation and difficult to remove (permanent)

16. CARCINOMA OF THE PROSTATE

- One in 18 males will be diagnosed with prostate cancer prior to the age of 75 years
- Lifetime risk of mortality from cancer of the prostate is only one in 70 (1/20 risk of CV disease)
- Autopsy studies of prevalence: 30% — 50 years; 70% — 80 years
- Incidence of prostate cancer has risen by 60–75% in the western world in the last 15 years, but has been declining in USA since 1992 (?aggressive early treatment and case selected screening)

16.1 Aetiology and pathology

Risk factors

- **Race**: high in Black Americans, low in Far East
- **Familial**: 5% autosomal dominant; 43% of carcinoma of prostate prior to 55 years of age; one first-degree relative 2x; three first-degree relatives 11x
- **Saturated fat**: animal and epidemiological evidence
- **Vitamin D**
- **Phyto-oestrogens**: soybean, grains
- **Vasectomy**: JAMA 1.7x RR (not reproduced by others)
- **Vitamin E**: may be protective

Classification of carcinoma of the prostate

- **Epithelial**
  Adenocarcinoma from acini (95%)
  Atypical adenocarcinoma
  Primary or secondary ductal
  Endometrioid
  Mucinous
  Transitional cell carcinoma
  Squamous cell carcinoma

- **Non-epithelial**
  Carcinosarcoma
  Sarcoma
  Rhabdomyosarcoma
  Fibrosarcoma
  Lymphoma
  Small cell

- **Secondary**
  Contiguous from bladder, colorectal etc.
  Metastatic leukaemia, melanoma, kidney etc.

Macroscopic appearances

- 70–80% peripheral zone, 20–30% central zone, 10–15% transition zone
- Firm yellow orange or grey white nodules

Histology

- Adenocarcinoma arises from epithelium of prostatic duct acini
- Normal appearance is double layer of organized glandular tissue with fibromuscular stroma
- Gleason grade is a reflection of glandular differentiation and architecture, not cytological appearance
- Invasion is characterized by absence of basal cell layer
- Prostatic intraepithelial neoplasia (PIN) is most likely a precursor of CaP: 35% of PIN biopsies will demonstrate invasive Ca on biopsy 3–6 months later; 80% of CaP has associated PIN. Fragmentation of basal cell layer
- Gleason sum: 2–4 well-differentiated; 5–6 moderately differentiated; 7–10 poorly differentiated
- Gleason grade correlates well with progression/prognosis
- Gleason grade given either as a combined score (as above) or as the most common differentiation followed by the second most common, i.e. a tumour that is mostly poorly differentiated with significant areas of moderate differentiation would be a Gleason 5 + 3 or combined Gleason sum of 8

16.2 Evaluation

- Commonly diagnosed on transrectal ultrasound (TRUS) guided biopsy — hypoechoic areas
- <5% of cancer of the prostate diagnosed following TURP (removes transition zone only)
- Sextant biopsies standard (40% isoechoic or hyperechoic)
- May present with effects of secondary spread, i.e. pathological fracture etc.

Staging by TNM or Jewett

- **Digital rectal examination (DRE)**: subjective; fails to diagnose T_{1c} tumours; poorly discriminates between T_2 and T_3 tumours; false positives: prostatitis, calcifications, BPH etc (50% nodules benign-Jewett)
- **TRUS**: identifies the 60% of cancers which are hypoechoic; facilitates accurate sampling for biopsy; accuracy of diagnosis seminal vesicle involvement is 77–85%
- **CT**: useful for identifying gross lymph node involvement; consider for high PSA (>20) or high Gleason grade.
- **MRI**: expensive; more accurate than TRUS for identifying extracapsular spread and seminal vesicle invasion.

See Section 7, p. 649, for staging.

Pelvic lymphadenectomy

- Symptomatic lymphocoele <3%
- Laparoscopic or mini-laparotomy technique
- Risk of positive LNs where PSA <10 and Gleason score ≤6 was <1% (Narayan)

Bone scan

- Tc^{99m} radio-isotope
- False positive rate of less than 2%
- PSA <10 bone scans positive 0.5%, <20 ~0.8% (Oesterling)

Ploidy: aneuploidy associated with high-grade tumours and less favourable prognosis.

Prostate specific antigen (PSA)

- Proteolytic enzyme — main role is liquefaction of ejaculate
- Free and bound form (PSA-ACT and PSA-MG)
- Half-life ~2–3 days
- Many monoclonal Ab assays currently in use
- Must counsel patients before measuring, including explanation of PSA, TRUS and

complications and treatment options if cancer detected. Do not measure without patient's consent and, in general, should not be measured in patients >75 years or if significant co-morbidity, i.e. life expectancy <5 years.

Variability of PSA measurements

- Up to 23.5% variation (range 4–10) 2–3 weeks apart (*J Urol*, 1987)
- ↑ after ejaculation
- ↑ with prostatitis, UTI, retention, BPH and CaP, TURP
- ↓ by 50% with finasteride
- No change with DRE, catheter, cystoscopy or TRUS (without biopsy)

Prostate cancer detection

Level of prostate-specific antigen (PSA)

- **PSA >4.0**: sens 40–90% Positive preditive value (PPV) ~33%; spec 60–90%
- **PSA >10**: sens 35–100%; spec 40–90%
- The greater the PSA, the greater the likelihood of finding cancer within biopsy specimens

PSA density (PSAD)

- Benson (1992) serum PSA/prostate volume (>0.15 CaP likely)
- 1 g BPH 0.3 ng/ml PSA (~10x less than CaP)
- Variability in volume calculation, therefore disappointing

PSA velocity (PSAV)

- >0.75 ng/ml/year on three consecutive measurements (Carter)
- Problems again with volume and inherent variability of PSA

Free/Total — ratio
Less than 25% indicates increased likelihood of a tumour, particularly when the PSA lies between 4 and 10 ug/L.

Age-specific values of PSA

- 2.5 ng/ml: 40–49 years
- 3.5 ng/ml: 50–59 years
- 4.5 ng/ml: 60–69 years
- 6.5 ng/ml: 70+ years

16.3 Management

- Diagnosis
- Pathology — PIN versus invasive disease
- Staging: DRE, PSA, TRUS with sextant biopsy, CT, MRI, pelvic lymphadenectomy, bone scan
- Treatment

What does 'treatment' mean?

- Radical treatment of localized disease
- Hormonal treatment
- Observation (especially for small low-grade tumours)
- Palliative treatment

Treatment of organ-confined (localized) disease

Rationale for treatment
Clinically detected cancer of the prostate progresses inevitably. Treatment is effective if detected early. Treatment is relatively safe. Although small, well-differentiated tumours can be treated conservatively (see, watch and wait), moderately and poorly differentiated tumours have an increased 5- and 10-year disease-specific survival if treated with radical prostatectomy. Poorly differentiated tumours show a survival benefit with radical radiotherapy (SEER data).

Treatment options for localized disease

- Watch and wait
- Radical prostatectomy
- Radical radiotherapy
- Brachytherapy
- Cryotherapy

Watch and wait
Two major studies and a meta-analysis have shown that small, well-differentiated tumours have a high 10-year survival rate with no treatment.

- Avoids morbidity associated with radical treatments
- No randomized trial comparing all treatment options, but difficult to randomize as patients have their own views on which treatment they want
- Most would consider this option in patients >75 years
- Monitor with PSA and DRE

Natural history of CaP largely not understood. Observation does not preclude definitive treatment at a later stage. Molecular biological techniques required to identify indolent tumours. Emotional concerns of living with 'untreated cancer'. Criticisms of these studies are most tumours were small and well-differentiated in older patients (shorter life expectancy).

Radical prostatectomy

Highest rate of 'cure' — excellent results for low-stage, low-grade disease (but these also do well with watch and wait). Large retrospective studies (SEER) show benefit over other treatments for moderately and poorly differentiated tumours.

- Definitive staging
- Early risks are bleeding, DVT, rectal injury and lymphocoele — up to 1% mortality
- Other complications: incontinence — mild 30%, severe 2–5%; impotence — 40–100%; bladder neck contracture
- Up to 50% will have PSA failures, therefore selection essential (see Partin's tables below)
- T_{1c} — 70% organ-confined, 20% positive margins
- UCLA/Mayo/Washington: T_1–T_2 — 80% progression-free survival (PFS) at five years, 70% PFS at 10 years
- 'Partin's tables' predict likelihood of positive margins, seminal vesical or lymph node involvement following surgery

Radical radiotherapy

- Results for radiotherapy better than watchful waiting, especially poorly differentiated tumours with 5–10-year life expectancy
- Impotence and incontinence significantly less than for RP
- Risks are radiation cystitis and proctitis (acute and chronic)
- Usually 6-week radiotherapy course. Fractionation daily for 5 working days per week
- Less effective in the presence of high-grade disease, larger tumour volume/stage

Brachytherapy

Implantation of radioactive iodine (or palladium) seeds within the prostate, placed transperineally under general anaesthetic.

- Higher dose of radiation possible than external beam
- Ten-year retrospective data suggests viable treatment option (although tumours treated solely with brachytherapy were well differentiated and therefore not likely to progress)
- Initial series indicated 48% incontinence rate in patients with previous TURP, therefore should avoid in these patients
- Only two visits needed: planning TRUS and implantation of seeds
- Cannot treat prostates > 50–60 gm with brachytherapy alone as pubic arch prevents implantation; also middle lobes and intravesical prostates difficult to treat
- Recent data suggests that it is not an effective treatment (D'Amico)

Cryotherapy

- Localized freezing leading to tissue destruction
- Still considered by most to be experimental
- Results influenced by patient selection
- Local control rates of 75% to 85% at the time of a 1–2-year evaluation reported, and 33% of patients have a PSA value in the undetectable range at 12 months (Cogen, *J Urol*, 1995)
- Advantages are low rate of impotence and incontinence, ability for re-treatment, relatively low operative morbidity
- Additional complications include fistulae, perineal pain, UTIs and ureteric obstruction

Hormonal treatment of prostate cancer

Clinical indications

- Early treatment of non-localized CaP
- Delayed treatment of non-localized CaP (MRC study suggests delaying treatment tends to increased complications and decreased survival — particularly in locally advanced non-metastatic disease)
- Treatment of failed definitive local therapy
- Debatable role of maximum androgen blockade (latest meta-analysis suggests no benefits)
- No role for neo-adjuvant radiotherapy for RP, evidence regarding combined hormones and DXT for locally advanced disease indicates a survival benefit (Bolla — but no control arm of hormones alone) and Pilpich (downstages and ? sensitizes T_3 tumours prior to DXT)
- Locally advanced T_3 prostate cancer now treated actively as survival improved and complications reduced (MRC study); most treat with long-term hormones and DXT (Bolla, Pilpich)
- Intermittent androgen therapy (reduces SEs in muscle wasting and osteoporosis and may increase time to development of hormone escape)
- Anti-androgen monotherapy (may allow preservation of erections — serum testosterone not affected). Used in locally advanced disease. In metastatic disease study shows inferior to orchidectomy, therefore not licenced

Agents

- Orchidectomy
- Oestrogens (with aspirin — risk of thromboembolic complications)
- LHRH agonists
- Steroidal anti-androgens (CPA)
- Non-steroidal anti-androgens (flutamide, bicalutamide)
- Second-line therapy

Advantages

- Generally well tolerated
- Very effective for hormone-sensitive tumours
- Effective Rx for aged and medically unfit
- Treatment of systemic disease
- May be used as adjuvant Rx after failure of local definitive Rx
- MRC study showed survival advantage in early versus delayed hormonal treatment in locally advanced tumours, also complications (ureteric obstruction, spinal cord compression etc.) less severe and frequent in both locally advanced and metastatic disease

Disadvantages

- Mean period of response is 18 months
- Causes impotence and loss of libido
- Testicular atrophy, gynaecomastia, hot flushes, osteoporosis and lethargy may result
- Expensive (medical therapy)

Palliative treatment of prostate cancer

Hormone refractory disease

- Median survival 6–9 months
- Conventional chemotherapy largely ineffective
- Flutamide (partial agonist) withdrawal benefit
- Suramin, ketoconazole and liarozole, somatostatin
- Isolated external beam DXT, hemi- and whole-body radiation, strontium 89 or bisphosphonates for bone pain
- Treatment of complications: urinary retention, ureteric obstruction
- Palliative care: NSAIDs, opiates

Treatment of complications

- **Bone pain**: external beam radiotherapy if hot spot confirmed on bone scan and plain X-ray (osteosclerotic lesions)
- **Hot flushes**: small dose (50 mg o.d.) cyproterone acetate
- **Iron/blood transfusions**: for symptomatic anaemia
- **'Channel' TURP**: for poor flow/urinary retention
- **Analgesia**: if required
- **Support**: family, MacMillan nurses etc.

Newly developed treatments

- Intermittent androgen therapy
- Finasteride + flutamide

17. TESTICULAR TUMOURS

Classification of testicular tumours

- **Primary**
  Germ cell (95%)
    Seminomas
    Non-seminomatous
      teratoma
      embryonal cell tumour
      yolk sac tumour
      choriocarcinoma
      mixed cell type
  Non-germ cell (5%)
    Leydig cell
    Sertoli cell
    Gonadoblastomas

- **Secondary**
  Lymphoma
  Metastatic (rare)

17.1 Germ cell tumours

- 4:100,000 males per year
- Lifetime risk 1:500
- 90–95% germ cell
- 5% non-germ cell

Increase in five-year survival rates: 78% in 1974–1976; 91% in 1980–1985.

There is a marked variation between countries, races and socio-economic classes. Higher in Scandinavia, lower in Japan. Slightly more common right versus left (increased risk of cryptorchidism on right). 1–2% of primary testicular tumours are bilateral (50% of these in men with unilateral or bilateral cryptorchidism). Incidence is 1:450 normal testis. Incidence increased if previous history of maldescent, atrophic testis or previous tumour on contralateral side.

Aetiology

- Cryptorchidism (one in 20 intra-abdominal testes, one in 80 inguinal develop malignancy)
- CIS (intra-tubular germ cell neoplasia)
- Maternal oestrogens
- 12p chromosome duplications
- Prolonged sitting (adjusted for social class)

Types of germ cell tumour

- Seminomas
- Teratoma
- Embryonal cell carcinoma
- Yolk sac tumour
- Choriocarcinoma

Seminomas
Three subtypes:

- Classic or typical
- Anaplastic
- Spermatocytic

Classic seminoma represents 85% of all seminomas. Most common in 30–40-year-olds. Macroscopically grey nodules. Microscopically monotonous sheets of large cells with clear cytoplasm and densely staining nuclei. Syncytiotrophoblastic elements present 7–10% of cases and account solely for elevated βHCG.

Teratoma
May be seen in children and adults. Macroscopically, the tumour appears lobulated and contains cysts of gelatinous or mucinous material. Mature teratomas may have elements resembling benign structures derived from ectoderm, mesoderm and endoderm. Immature teratoma consists of undifferentiated primitive tissue.

Embryonal cell carcinoma
Often extensive haemorrhage and necrosis; pleomorphic.

Yolk sac tumour

- Pure form in infants — good prognosis
- Mixed outcomes in adults
- Alpha-FP production

Choriocarcinoma
Pure form is rare. These are small lesions within the testis with central haemorrhage. Microscopically demonstrate syncytia and cytotrophoblastic elements. Clinically the lesions behave in an aggressive fashion with early haematogenous spread. β–HCG production.

Patterns of metastatic spread

Germ cell tumours generally spread in a stepwise lymphatic fashion to para-aortic nodes. Right side tumours spread to the interaorto-caval area at the renal hilum. Left side tumours spread initially to the para-aortic area at the level of the left renal hilum. Invasion of the epididymis or spermatic cord may alter lymphatic drainage patterns (external iliac and obturator nodes), the tunica albuginea or scrotum (inguinal nodes), or previous surgery may alter patterns. Visceral metastases may be seen in advanced disease. Choriocarcinomas may be associated with early haematogenous spread.

Clinical staging of germ cell tumours

UICC TNM classification becoming widely used.

UICC TNM classification of testicular tumours

- **T — primary tumour**
  T_x cannot be assessed
  T_0 no evidence of primary tumour
  T_{is} intratubular cancer
  T_1 testis and epididymis, **no** vascular/lymphatic invasion
  T_2 testis and epididymis **with** vascular/lymphatic invasion or invades through to turnica vaginalis
  T_3 invades spermatic cord
  T_4 invades scrotum

- **N — regional lymph nodes**
  N_x cannot be assessed
  N_0 no regional lymph node metastases
  N_1 single <2 cm
  N_2 single >2 cm, <5 cm, multiple <5 cm
  N_3 >5 cm

- **M — distant metastasis**
  M_x cannot be assessed
  M_0 no distant metastasis
  M_{1a} non-regional lymph node or pulmonary metastases
  M_{1b} non-pulmonary visceral metastases

Symptoms

Most common symptom is painless enlargement of the testis. Typical delay from initial recognition of the lesion by patient to definitive therapy is 3–6 months. Acute pain may be present in 10%. Ten per cent present with symptoms related to metastatic disease:

- Back pain (RPLN involving nerve roots)
- Cough or dyspnoea (lung)
- Anorexia, nausea, vomiting (retroduodenal)
- Bone pain (skeletal)
- Lower extremity swelling (caval obstruction)

Signs

- A mass or testicular enlargement in the majority of cases
- Hydrocoele may be present
- Bulky retroperitoneal disease on abdominal examination
- Other regional and distant LNs
- Hepatomegaly
- Gynaecomastia in 5%

Laboratory findings and tumour markers

- Anaemia
- Abnormal LFTs
- Renal impairment with ureteral obstruction

Biochemical markers

- **AFP**
  High levels in foetal serum
  Beyond one year only present in
    trace amounts
  Present in varying degrees of
    non-seminomatous germ cell
    tumour (NSGCT)
  Never present in pure seminoma

- **LDH**
  Cellular enzyme
  Shown to correlate with tumour
    burden in NSGCT
  Useful prognostic marker

- **hCG**
  Alpha and beta units
  Beta can be assayed
  Commonly elevated in NSGCT
  Elevated in 7–10% of seminomas
    (syncytiotrophoblastic elements)

- **PLAP and GGT**
  Not used in clinical practice

Imaging

Primary accurately assessed by scrotal ultrasound. Defines mass, site, extent and assesses hydrocoeles.

Staging with CXR and CT chest-abdo-pelvis.

Differential diagnoses

*   Epididymitis and epididymo-orchitis
*   Hydrocoele
*   Spermatocoele
*   Haematocoele
*   Granulomatous orchitis
*   Varicocoele
*   Epidermoid cyst (intra-testicular benign lesion)

Treatment

Inguinal exploration, clamping of spermatic cord and orchidectomy.

Low-stage seminoma

*   Highly radiosensitive — 95% of all localized seminomas cured with orchidectomy and prophylactic retroperitoneal radiotherapy
*   DXT in low doses is well-tolerated and minimal side-effects
*   Low volume retroperitoneal disease is similarly managed, with salvage
*   CRx for relapses (90% survival) — N_1 disease
*   Trial of carboplatin versus prophylactic DXT (current)

High-stage seminoma

* N_2 or greater, or those with raised AFP, Rx with primary chemotherapy
*   Sensitive to platinum-based regimens (commonly BEP in 3–4 cycles)
*   90% of stage III with chemotherapy achieve complete response — residual masses warrant excision (20% residual disease)
*   Survival 35–75% depending on series and CRx regimes

Low-stage non-seminomatous germ cell tumours (T_1–T_4, N_0, M_0)
Surveillance (UK)
Only 30% relapse:

- Complications of retroperitoneal lymph node dissection (RPLND)
- Early detection of relapse does not alter prognosis
- Can give two cycles of BEP if 'high-risk' (vascular invasion, high stage or embryonal elements — most use only vascular invasion)

Retro-peritoneal lymph node dissection (RPLND) (USA)
Relapse after RPLND only 10%:

- 3–4 cycles of BEP if relapsed
- Less intensive follow-up
- Consider for poorly compliant, geography etc.

Localized disease survival 96–100%.

High-stage non-seminomatous germ cell tumours
Primary platinum-based combination chemotherapy after orchidectomy. May require surgery for resection of residual masses. Histology of post-chemotherapy excised masses:

- 40% fibrosis
- 40% differentiated teratoma
- 20% residual cancer

70% of patients with high volume disease may still be cured.

17.2 Non-germ cell tumours

Only 5–6% of all primary testis tumours are non-germ cell tumours:

- Leydig cell tumours (bimodal age distribution, may produce testosterone)
- Sertoli cell tumours (bimodal age distribution, involves Sertoli cells which 'nourish' tubules and contribute to 'blood–testis' barrier)
- Gonadoblastomas

Lymphoma is the most common testicular tumour over age of 50.

Metastatic tumours are rare.

18. TUMOURS OF THE PENIS

Primary

Common in undeveloped world and associated with poor hygiene and an intact prepuce.

Epithelial

- **Benign**: condyloma acuminata, papilloma, haemangioma, naevi, sebaceous cyst
- **Pre-malignant**: erythroplasia of Queyrat, Bowen's disease, Buschke–Löwenstein tumour, balanitis xerotica obliterans
- **Malignant**: SCC, BCC, melanoma

Mesenchymal
Benign, malignant, Kaposi's.

Lymphoma

Secondary

TCC, prostate, colon, renal, testis lymphoma, leukaemia.

18.1 Benign and pre-malignant lesions of the penis

Benign lesions

Condyloma acuminata (genital warts)
Histology is connective tissue stroma with keratin covered papillary fronds. Associated with human papilloma virus (HPV) 6 and 11 (compared with 16 and 18 for Ca).

Treatment
Cryotherapy, podophyllin, fulguration or laser.

Pre-malignant lesions

Buschke–Löwenstein giant condyloma
Similar histology to normal condyloma, but locally invasive and destructive. Usually on glans and/or prepuce. Associated with HPV 6 and 11.

Treatment
Surgical excision.

Balanitis xerotica obliterans

Dry sclerosing inflammation of the glans/prepuce/meatus. May extend to fossa navicularis. Associated with phimosis and balanitis. Histology is hyperkeratosis, oedema and collagen deposition in the upper dermis, inflammation in the mid-dermis. May progress to leukoplakia and SCC.

Treatment

Topical steroids $\pm$ meatotomy and circumcision.

Leukoplakia

Histology is hyperkeratosis with a disorderly arrangement of keratinocytes and atypia. Macroscopic appearance is that of white plaques. Often co-exists with squamous cell carcinoma (SCC).

Treatment

Biopsy and careful follow-up.

18.2 Malignant lesions of the penis

CIS of the penis

Encompasses erythroplasia of Queyrat (E of Q), Bowen's disease, Bowenoid papulosis.

- **E of Q**: a red/velvety, well-marginated lesion confined to the glans. Histology is CIS showing atypical cells with mitoses, basement membrane intact. Treatment is 5 FU or excision.
- **Bowen's disease**: CIS at any site of the penis or prepuce, same histology as E of Q. Dull red plaque with crusting and oozing. Treatment is as for E of Q.
- **Bowenoid papulosis**: CIS histology with multiple round red brown papules. Often occurs in younger patients (20s and 30s). Associated with HPV-16; risk of cervical Ca in partners.

Squamous cell carcinoma of the penis

Incidence and epidemiology

- 6.6/100,000 Zimbabwe; 0.1/100,000 Israeli Jews; 0.1–0.8/100,000 US
- 12% of cancers in Uganda; 0.4% in the US
- Incidence stable over last 25 years
- Rare < 55 years, highest incidence > 75 years

Aetiology

- **Circumcision**: extremely rare in circumcised males; increased incidence in delayed circ cf neonatal circ (Muslim boys); in West, similar rates between circ and non-circ
- **Phimosis**: common co-existing abnormality (up to 50%)
- **STDs**: up to 20% of patients with SCC; no causal relationship found
- **Hygiene**: lower incidence with better hygiene
- **Socio-economic**
- **Smegma**: debris of desquamated epithelial cells and secretions from Tyson's glands; phimosis allows retention of smegma
- **Viruses**: HPV DNA in 31% of Ca penis; types 16 and less so 18; ? HPV binds p53 allowing cellular proliferation

Pathology

Gross
Commonly glans or prepuce. Ulcerated in 85%, secondary infection in 90%, palpable nodes inflammatory in 50%. Appearance exophytic, ulcerating or scirrhous.

Histology
Loss of polarity and normal maturation from base. Pleomorphism ± keratin pearls.

Spread
Initially controlled by Buck's fascia and tunica of corpora.

Lymph drainage
Glans: deep inguinal to iliac nodes. Prepuce and shaft: sup. inguinal to deep inguinal. Abundant L-R crossover. Haematogenous spread at Dx uncommon.

Clinical presentation

- Mass/lump/nodule 47%; ulcer 35%; bleeding 17%
- Glans 48%; prepuce 21%; both 9%; shaft 2%

Investigations

- 1% toludine + 1% acetic acid detects CIS
- Biopsy
- CXR, abdo-pelvic CT

Staging

- **T**
  - T_{is} CIS
  - T_a Epithelium
  - T_1 Sub-epithelial connective tissue
  - T_2 Corpus cavernosum/spongiosum
  - T_3 Urethra or prostate
  - T_4 Adjacent organs

- **N**
  - N_1 Single superficial inguinal node
  - N_2 Multiple or bilateral superficial inguinal nodes
  - N_3 Deep inguinal or pelvic nodes

- **M**
  - M_0 No metastases
  - M_1 Metastases

Treatment

Treatment of the primary neoplasm and inguinal nodes.

Primary neoplasm

- **Stage T_{IS}**: multiple confirmatory biopsies to rule out invasion. Small non-invasive lesions may be locally excised. Circumcision may suffice for preputial lesions. Other alternatives are topical 5 FU, radiotherapy and NdYAG or CO_2 laser, cryotherapy and Mohs micrographic surgery.
- **Stage T_a and T_1–T_4**: amputation by partial or total penectomy is the gold standard. Glans and distal shaft — partial penectomy with 2 cm margin necessary to prevent local recurrence. Radiotherapy for small distal lesions where organ conservation important can be delivered by external beam (penis surrounded in wax block) or brachytherapy by implantation of irradium needles as the use of a dual/penile sheath (outer sheath removed for voiding). Proximal shaft involvement requires total penectomy and perineal urethrostomy radiotherapy, lasers and Mohs micrographic surgery also described.

Treatment of inguinal nodes
Nodes affect prognosis more than tumour grade. 50% of enlarged inguinal nodes at presentation are caused by inflammation and infection, therefore a six-week course of antibiotics is prescribed, following which the nodes are reassessed. Persistent lymphadenopathy should be considered metastatic and bilateral ilio-inguinal node dissections performed (as 85% of patients with palpable nodes post antibiotics had positive nodes, MSKCC 1987).

20–50% of patients with palpable nodes and positive pathology achieve five-year disease-free survival (rises to 80–90% when single nodes are involved).

If lymphadenopathy resolves with antibiotics, observation is warranted for low stage tumours (T_{IS}, T_a and T_1). Resolving lymphadenopathy in higher stage tumours warrants limited node sampling (incidence of occult metastases in clinically normal nodes ranges between 2% and 25%).

Patients who have initially impalpable nodes but who subsequently develop palpable nodes should undergo a unilateral ilio-inguinal node dissection, although the treatment of lymph nodes in penile cancer is controversial. Extensive disease (any M_1) may warrant palliative chemotherapy or radiotherapy.

Survival depends on node status.

- 5-year survival for node negative disease ranges between 65% and 90%
- Positive inguinal nodes reduces this to 30–50% and iliac nodes to 20%
- No 5-year survivors are reported for M_1 disease

19. GENITO-URINARY TRAUMA

Principles

- 'Resuscitate' patient as per trauma guidelines
- GU tract well protected (except external genitalia in males) by musculoskeletal system and viscera
- Mobility makes shearing injuries less likely
- Do not insert urinary catheters in patients with blood at the external urinary meatus, history of pelvic trauma or a high-riding prostate on examination p.r.
- 10% of all traumatic injuries involve GU system

19.1 Renal trauma

- Protected, as above plus ribs. Cushioned by perirenal fat within Gerota's fascia and are mobile (vertical, 1–3 ribs)
- Renal trauma present in 10% abdominal trauma

Evaluation

History
From witness if unconscious. Blunt (90%) versus penetrating (10%), vehicle speed, driver versus pedestrian, nature of injury (deceleration), size of gun etc. Pre-existing renal abnormality makes injury more likely (hydronephrosis, tumour, cystic disease, vascular abnormalities).

Mechanism of injury

- RTAs, sports injuries, falls
- Sudden deceleration stretches renal artery and may produce tear resulting in subintimal dissection and thrombosis
- Children at higher risk of injury — have larger kidneys which are less well-protected
- Penetrating trauma associated with other injuries in 80–85%; greatest determinant of mortality is the presence of associated injuries

Examination
Bruising, stab wounds, rib fracture etc. **Look for associated injuries.**

NB. Thoracic trauma may involve kidneys.

Urinalysis
Dipstick — rapid and economical.

NB. The degree of haematuria does not predict severity of renal injury.

Catheterize patient (if no blood at urinary meatus, otherwise urethrogram first) and test urine for blood.

American Association for the Surgery of Trauma classification

(Moore et al. *J Trauma* 1989)

- **Grade I:**   contusion — with haematuria (macro or micro)
- **Grade II:**   non-expanding subcapsular or perinephric haematoma
- **Grade III:** laceration <1 cm (without urinary extravasation)
- **Grade IV:**   laceration >1 cm or any laceration extending into the collecting system
- **Grade V:**   main vessel injury with contained haemorrhage; completely shattered kidney; avulsion of renal hilum (renal devascularization)

Investigations

Investigate all penetrating injuries, macroscopic haematuria, children and patients with microscopic haematuria and a systolic BP < 90 mmHg or patients with a known pre-existing renal abnormality (renal injury more likely), e.g. hydronephrosis.

High-dose IVU

- Rapid bolus of 1 ml/lb bodyweight 30% iodinated contrast medium
- Films at 1, 5, 15 and 30 minutes
- Confirms presence of two functioning kidneys, demonstrates renal outlines and an intact collecting system
- Non-visualization caused by congenital absence or ectopia, severe hypertension, obstruction, renal artery/vein thrombosis, avulsion or spasm of the renal pedicle, non-function (e.g. chronic pyelonephritis, 'burnt-out' PUJ obstruction)
- Tomograms increase sensitivity for parenchymal lacerations, devitalized segments and intrarenal haematomas and should be performed immediately if renal injury seems likely from the urogram

CT

- Greater sensitivity and specificity (parenchymal injury, extravasation and non-viable tissue)
- Provides information on associated injuries
- Detects perirenal, retroperitoneal injuries and haematoma; defines arterial injury
- Spiral CT quick, but may need to do second delayed films and need to see contrast in the collecting system

Arteriography

- Use limited
- If non-visualization on IVU and CT
- Renal artery thrombosis most common cause

Indications for surgery

- Uncontrolled bleeding
- Associated injuries
- Non-viable parenchyma
- Renovascular injuries
- Major urine leak (large collecting system lacerations, PUJ disruption)

Surgery

- Use mid-line transperitoneal approach (reduces renal loss)
- Sling (control) renal arteries prior to opening the retroperitoneum (increased renal salvage rate)
- If laparotomy performed for other reasons absolute indications for opening retroperitoneum are an expanding or pulsatile haematoma
- If imaging not performed use single-shot on-table IVU primarily to demonstrate presence of functioning contralateral kidney
- Attempt renal conservation, particularly if other kidney non-functioning (may need single shot IVU on table to confirm, if no prior imaging)
- Debride dead tissue (until bleeding occurs)
- Renorrhaphy (penetrating > blunt) — primary closure ± surgicel, coverage with omentum for larger defects when capsule destroyed
- Partial nephrectomy: excise non-viable tissue and ligate vessels (4/0 Chr catgut)
- Try to preserve capsule for coverage, if not use omentum
- Reconstruction with synthetic mesh, free peritoneal or free fat grafts
- Attempt watertight closure by closing renal capsule or applying omentum etc.
- Vascular injuries: repair of segmental arteries unsuccessful ∴ partial nephrectomy, total nephrectomy more likely if vascular injury
- 18% multiple renal injury (mostly parenchymal and renal vessel), nephrectomy required in 11.3% (McAninch, *J Urol* 1991)
- Drain retroperitoneum if collecting system entered (risk of infection of haematoma)
- No difference in renal salvage with blunt versus penetrating injuries
- Treat secondary haemorrhage with embolization

Follow-up

- Patient followed up by ultrasound
- IVU if collecting system injury (extravasation)
- Hypertension, if present usually disappears by week six

Complications of renal trauma

- Urinoma, abscess, pyelonephritis
- Hydronephrosis (large haematoma + extravasation)
- AV fistula (uncommon, after penetrating injuries)
- Hypertension (in 1% due to ↓flow in devitalized tissues, or from renal artery stenosis)
- Ileus (RP haematoma)
- Calculus formation
- Secondary haemorrhage

19.2 Ureteric injuries

Least-injured organ in GU tract (mobile, small calibre, protected and surrounded by retroperitoneal fat).

Aetiology

External trauma

- Penetrating 92% (gunshot, stab)
- Blunt 8% (RTAs, falls); more common in children and associated with PUJ disruption (greater mobility of spine — flexion/hyperextension injury in RTAs)

Iatrogenic trauma
Only 20–30% recognized at time of injury. Delay leads to increase in nephrectomy:

- **Urological**: ureteroscopy
- **Gynaecological**: hysterectomy, laser endometriosis, tubal ligation, oophorectomy, colposuspension; commonly when ureter crosses pelvic brim or posterior to broad ligaments or ovarian vessels
- **Colorectal**: AP resection
- **Vascular**: aortic/iliac grafts

Evaluation

Haematuria absent in >30% overall; present in >90% external trauma; present in 11% iatrogenic injuries. Early signs are non-specific (pain, low grade fever, ileus, ↑creatinine). Delayed signs are prolonged ileus, obstruction, leakage, anuria, sepsis and fistula.

Imaging

- **IVU**: non-visualization — hypotension or associated renal injury, extravasation, ureteral dilation or deviation, presence of contralateral kidney
- **CT**: only useful if associated injuries
- **Retrograde ureteropyelography**: an attempt should be made to pass a guide wire ± urethroscopic visualization
- **Intra-operative**: visual inspection, IV or retrograde methylene blue

Classification of ureteral injuries

- **Grade I**: haematoma or contusion
- **Grade II**: laceration <50% transection
- **Grade III**: laceration >50% transection
- **Grade IV**: complete transection with <2 cm devascularization
- **Grade V**: complete transection (avulsion) with >2 cm devascularization

Management

- Release tie/suture at operation or at laparoscopy within 24 hours; stent ureter
- Beware of associated injuries (>90% with penetrating trauma)
- Surgical repair (debride, ureteral mobilizsation, spatulated end–end anastomosis, isolate from associated injuries, JJ stent, drainage near but not directly on anastomosis, closed suction)
- Percutaneous nephrostomy
- Ureteral ligation and percutaneous nephrostomy ('bail out procedure')
- Ureteral intubation (tube through laceration and bring out to skin)

Surgical techniques

- **Lower ureter**: reimplant, psoas hitch
- **Middle ureter**: Boari flap, end-end anastomosis (see above)
- **Upper ureter**: transureteroureterostomy, ureterocalylostomy
- **Ureteral replacement** (ileal ureter): not recommended in acute setting (contamination and lack of bowel preparation)
- **Autotransplantation**

Follow-up

- Ureteric stents removed at 10 days
- IVP
- DTPA renography

Complications

- Urinary extravasation
- Fistula
- Stricture (Rx balloon, incision, open surgical revision)
- Infection

19.3 Bladder trauma

- 86% due to blunt abdominal trauma, 14% penetrating injuries
- 89% associated with pelvic fracture; pelvic fracture associated with bladder laceration in 9%, posterior urethral injury in 2% and both in a further 1%
- 95% have gross haematuria
- If no blood at ext. meatus perform cystogram with > 300 ml contrast. Must obtain post-drainage films. Intraperitoneal contrast highlights bowel loops. Extraperitoneal injuries contained contrast and tear drop deformity of bladder secondary to pelvic haematoma.
- Injury is extraperitoneal or intraperitoneal. If both present, mortality is 60% (due to force of injury).
- Intraperitoneal injuries characteristically occur during fall when bladder full (bursts at weakest point — dome)
- Extraperitoneal injuries caused by anterior pubic arch fracture or by trauma when bladder empty
- Explore all penetrating and intraperitoneal injuries; repair extraperitoneal injuries at time of laparotomy for other cause, otherwise treat conservatively
- Treat extraperitoneal injuries with 10 days of catheterization; perform cystogram after this. Large extraperitoneal or persistent injuries may need repair. Must not disturb pelvic haematoma ∴ bladder opened anteriorly and repair performed intravesically.

19.4 Urethral trauma

- Anterior (penile or bulbar urethra) or posterior (prostate or membranous urethra)
- Anterior injury — straddle injury. Butterfly bruising on perineum (if Buck's fusila penetrated, otherwise confined to penis)
- Posterior injury — associated with pelvic fracture (>90% of cases). High riding prostate felt on rectal examination
- DO NOT CATHETERIZE, especially if blood at meatus
- Call urologist
- Perform urethrogram with 25 ml water-soluble contrast
- If injury confirmed site suprapubic catheter
- Repair is usually carried out after 3–6 months

19.5 Testicular trauma

Manage conservatively if small haematoma and no testicular rupture. If large haematoma or testicular rupture, explore. Evacuate haematoma, debride necrotic seminiferous tubules and close ruptured tunica albuginea. Drain scrotum. Patient wears scrotal support for one week (as with all scrotal surgery). Dislocation injuries may occur (testis becomes 'dislocated' into inguinal canal). Treatment is sedation and manipulation. Failure is an indication for formal open exploration and replacement.

20. RENAL TRANSPLANTATION

Renal transplantation is the preferred treatment for end-stage renal failure (ESRF).

20.1 End-stage renal failure

Incidence

- Men > Women — Blacks > Whites
- 250 cases per million

Causes

- **Adults**: diabetes (34%) > hypertension (29%) > glomerulonephritis (14%)
- **Children**: glomerulonephritis (38%) > congenital disorders (19%) > collagen vascular diseases (10%)

'Permanent renal failure' — GFR < 10 ml/min (children < 6 ml/min).

Treatment

- Haemodialysis, chronic ambulatory peritoneal dialysis (CAPD), renal transplantation
- Transplantation most cost-effective and allows return to normal life. Survival advantage over other methods *but* patients may be selected, resulting in bias. Live related donors have best results (↑10%). Also, less waiting and less recipient morbidity. Cadaveric donors most common. 'Quality' of kidneys decreasing as road safety improves (i.e. more kidneys from older 'medical' patients). Also 'non-heart beating' donors.
- CAPD initially preferred in children. Growth failure prevented with recombinant growth hormone

(See also Chapter 4, *Intensive Care*, in the *MRCS Core Modules: Essential Revision Notes*.)

Deaths

- Heart disease > sepsis > stroke
- Patients on dialysis have accelerated arteriosclerosis

History of renal transplant

- First human renal transplant 1933. Anastomosis to femoral vessels with cutaneous ureterostomy. Patient produced a small amount of urine but died after 48 hours.
- Donor-specific blood transfusions (DST). Used in past. Increased immune tolerance **but** post-introduction of cyclosporin, minimal effect and increases risk of virus transmission (now abandoned).

20.2 Selection of recipients

General

- Diagnosis of primary disease
- Beware increased risk of recurrence in transplanted kidney (especially focal golomerular sclerosis and haemolytic uraemic syndrome). Type I hyperoxaluria rapidly recurs in transplanted kidneys and is best treated with combined liver and kidney transplant.
- Rule out infection (dental sepsis, ? immunization status, prophylactic cholecystectomy in patients with gallstones as cholecystitis and immunosuppression lethal). High risk of morbidity in patients with chronic active hepatitis receiving immunosuppression.
- Ensure fit for anaesthesia
- Must be compliant with post-op immunosuppressive medication
- Must have two cancer-free years from last treatment (except low-grade TCC bladder, superficial melanomas, BCC and Cis cervic)
- Ensure anatomy suitable for transplant and evaluate arteriopathies

Urologic evaluation

- Consider recipient bladder and outflow
- Consider need for pre-transplant nephrectomy

History
Tumours, stones obstruction, reflux, infection, previous GU surgery.

Examination
Scars, sites of CAPD catheters (both make extra-peritoneal access more difficult).

- MSU, ultrasound, KUB with post-micturition residual (if patient produces urine)
- Evaluate difficult cases with voiding cystourethrography, urodynamics or cytoscopy
- Consider ureteric implantation in native bladders in some 'diverted' patients
- Augmentation cytoplasty may be required pre-op. Gastrocytoplasty preferred over enterocytoplasty, which causes metabolic acidosis.
- TURP/TUIP pre-op. If oliguric, insert suprapubic catheter in sterile water to prevent scarring or obliteration of prostatic fossa. Can also teach self-catheterization with bladder instillation and subsequent voiding.

Recipient testing

- Initially screen with ABO blood types
- HLA matching. HLA-A,B and DR important in transplantation. Best match, all six alleles in common (zero mismatch)

- Matching 'seen' from recipient serum (e.g. recipient A2; B1,15; DR3,5 and donor A2,3; B11,15; DR3 is a 1, 1, 0 mismatch)
- Recipient serum mixed with donor lymphocytes (cross-match)

Pre-transplant nephrectomy

Indications
Uncontrolled hypertension, renal calculi/obstruction, severe proteinuria, persistent antiglomerular antibodies, acquired cystic kidney disease (6–30x malignancy, esp. if kidney > 150 g), polycystic kidney disease with infection, severe haematuria or gross enlargement (preventing transplantation). Small kidneys best removed by vertical lumbotomy.

20.3 Selection of donors

Principles

- Minimize warm ischaemic time
- Preserve renal vessels (end-arteries)
- Preserve ureteral blood supply
- Ensure compatibility

Live related donors

Principles

- Donor must have near normal renal function after donation
- Keeps 'better' of two kidneys
- Consider right kidney donation in women of childbearing age (pregnancy preferentially causes right hydronephrosis)
- Exclude: patients with mental disorders; renal disease; high operative risk; significant transmissible diseases; ABO incompatibility; positive cross-match

Special investigations

- HIV
- HTLV-I
- Hepatitis
- CMV (some centres do not transplant serum-positive donors with seronegative high risk (i.e. > 50 years, diabetic) recipients. Prophylaxis with acyclovir or ganciclovir may be required.
- Syphilis
- IVU
- Isotope renography
- Arteriography

Procedure

- 25 g mannitol over 1 hour at time of skin incision
- IV fluids 1 l/hr (maintain diuresis)
- Confirm diuresis (by ureteric transection) before clamping vessels
- Post-nephrectomy, place kidney in ice-cold solution and perfuse

Post-operatively

- Creatinine clearance up to 80% pre-op level
- No increase in hypertension
- 0.03% mortality
- 0.23% permanent complication

Brainstem dead (cadavaric) donors

Pre-conditions of brainstem death

- Comatose and ventilated
- Diagnosis certain
- Must have structural brain damage (e.g. head injury, subarachnoid haemorrhage, meningitis, neurological symptoms)
- Exclude: reversible causes (e.g. hypothermia, alcohol, drugs, metabolic causes)

Brainstem reflexes

- Performed by two doctors independent of retrieval team
- Vestibulo-ocular reflex (20 ml ice-cold water on either side. Must look in ear to ensure tympanic membrane intact)
- GAG reflex (usually have ET tube, so can place smaller tube down lumen of ET tube)
- No response to pain
- No response to corneal stimulation
- No grimacing
- Apnoea test: pre-oxygenate prior (to ensure hypoxic damage does not occur during test). No respiratory movement when arterial $PaCO_2$ >6.65 kPa.

Donation criteria

- No diabetes
- No malignancy except primary brain tumours and treated skin malignances
- No generalized bacterial or viral infections
- Normal renal function (ideally)
- Negative VDRL, hepatitis, HIV, HTLV
- Blood cultures if hospitalized for >72 hours must be negative
- >18 months age (technical difficulties)

Retrieval

- Aim to maintain BP >90 mmHg systolic and urine output >0.5 ml/kg/hr
- Total mid-line approach preferred over cruciate incisions as most are multiple donors

Kidney preservation

- Warm ischaemic injury due to failure of oxidative phosphorylation and cell death due to ATP depletion
- ATP required for Na/K pump
- Na therefore enters cells resulting in cellular swelling
- Anaerobic glycolysis and acidosis occurs
- Lysosomal enzymes activated
- Reperfusion causes oxidation of hypoxanthine (a product of ATP degradation) to xanthine with the formation of free radicals which cause further cell damage
- Cellular energy requirements reduced by hypothermia
- Perfusion with hyperosmolar solutions reduced by hypothermia
- Perfusion with hyperosmolar solutions reduces cellular swelling
- Perfusion fluids contain electrolyte concentrations similar to those inside the cell, therefore if fluid does enter cell, it has a similar electrolyte composition

University of Wisconsin solution

- Used in all organ transplants
- Contains impermeable solutes, to minimize cellular swelling (lactobionate, raffinose and hydroxyethyl starch)
- Phosphate used for buffering H^+ ions
- Adenosine, used in ATP synthesis
- Glutathione used as free radical scavenger
- Allopurinol inhibits xanthine oxidase (inhibits free radical formation)
- Magnesium and dexamethasone — membrane-stabilizing agents
- Max. 72 hours storage time

20.4 Recipient operation

Kidney prepared on bench. Culture of fluid medium taken. Fat removed. Vessels identified. Arterial patch trimmed. Operation planned

NB. Right kidneys technically more difficult due to short renal vein.

- Prophylactic antibiotics on induction, continued until results of culture known
- Kidney transplanted into either iliac fossa (extra-peritoneal)
- No preference; either kidney to either side
- Side dictated by existing scars (adherent peritoneum), catheters (CAPD) or previous transplants
- Patient catheterized with three-way tap (to fill bladder intra-operatively and facilitate ureteric implantation)
- Spermatic cord preserved in males
- Lymphatics tied or clipped to reduce post-op lymphocoele
- i.v. heparin (30 U/kg) given before vessel clamping
- During anastomosis, mannitol (0.5–1 g/kg) given to act as free radical scavenger and to promote diuresis
- Recipient given crystalloid infusion ± albumin (promotes early function)
- Renal artery usually anastomosed to internal iliac (end–end or end–side)
- Can use external iliac (end–side) or common iliac (end–side)
- When pelvic vessels unsuitable, use splenic or native renal arteries (and renal vein or IVC)
- Renal vein usually anastomosed to external iliac vein (end–side)
- Ureter usually anastomosed by extravesical approach tunnelling some length under detrusor muscle, thus creating an anti-reflux mechanism
- Ureter stented to reduce incidence of anastomotic strictures
- Ureter can be joined to diverted systems (e.g. to the base of an ileal conduit)
- Drainage is usually performed

Paediatric transplants

- Use mid-line incision
- Anastomosis to common iliac artery or aorta and IVC (adult kidneys usually available)
- Kidney placed in retroperitoneal space behind caecum
- Renal vein is usually too long and must be shortened to prevent kinking and thrombosis
- 100–150 ml packed RBCs often given before releasing clamps

Post-operative management

- Match fluid input with output plus insensible losses
- Monitor renal function
- Obtain Doppler ultrasound at 48 hours — fluid collections, hydronephrosis and ensure adequate blood flow
- If oligoanuria occurs, obtain 2x weekly isotope renograms until urine output improves
- Continue prophylactic heparin until mobile
- Remove ureteric stent at six weeks

20.5 Complications of renal transplant

Rejection

- Hyperacute
- Accelerated
- Acute
- Chronic (see Section 21.1)

Vascular complications

- Kinking, thrombosis: more common on right due to long artery and short vein
- Hyper-acute rejection
- Hypercoagulable state of recipient (e.g. protein C, S or antithrombin III deficiency)
- Renal artery stenosis (causes hypertension)

Complications of immunosuppressive treatment

- Complications of steroid treatment (i.e. poor wound healing, thin skin, easy bruising, striae, hyperglycaemia, hypertension, buffalo hump, moon face, confusion, psychosis, peptic ulcer, obesity, hypokalaemia)
- Increased incidence of infections (inc. opportunistic infections)
- Increased incidence of malignancy

Lymphocoele

Similar creatinine concentration as serum. Small — observe. Large —create window in peritoneum to allow drainage.

Urine leak

Can be initially managed by diverting urine with percutaneous nephrostomy. Large leaks need surgical exploration.

Ureteral stricture

Caused by devascularization (periureteral tissues) during retrieval or bench dissection. Balloon dilation usually short-term benefit. Often requires reimplantation $\pm$ boari flap. Can use native ureter or ileal interposition.

UTIs

Common (immunosuppression, catheters).

Vesicoureteric (VU) reflux

Treat as VU reflux in 'normal' subjects.

Tumours

Immunosuppressed patients more likely to develop tumours. Most common are skin cancers followed by lymphomas.

Hypertension

Common. Due to immunosuppressive medication, intrinsic renal disease and rejection.

Transplant nephrectomy

Indications are symptomatic rejected kidney or asymptomatic rejected kidney where risk of development of anti-HLA antibodies exists for a future transplant. Operation difficult after first month. Often subcapsular nephrectomy required. Cyclosporin stopped post-op, prednisolone reduced, **but** azathioprine **must** be continued for one month because some residual 'foreign' tissue is left behind.

21. TRANSPLANTATION IMMUNOLOGY

21.1 Principles of transplant rejection

Hyper-acute rejection

Occurs immediately after renal revascularization or within 24 hours. Irreversible process mediated by pre-formed circulating cytotoxic antibodies (from previous antigen exposure in pregnancy, blood transfusion or prior transplant). Activates clotting system and causes intra-renal thrombosis and renal infarction. Incidence rare with cross-match screening.

Accelerated rejection

Occurs 4–7 days after transplantation. Mediated by both humoral and cellular components. Usually does not respond to treatment.

Acute rejection

Occurs within weeks to months (usually 3–6 months). 'Flu-like symptoms accompany graft tenderness. Suspect also if fever, hypertension, poor urine output, fluid retention and poor tubular function. Biopsy confirms diagnosis (mononuclear cell infiltration and vasculitis). Treated by high-dose pulses of prednisolone (5 mg/kg/day) for five days, tapering down to the maintenance dose. Failure is treated with antilymphocyte antibody preparations (e.g. OKT3 = monoclonal antibody).

Chronic rejection

Gradual decline in renal function with hypertension and proteinuria. Accounts for 90% graft losses. Tubular atrophy, interstitial fibrosis and vascular changes (intimal proliferation and glomerulosclerosis) confirmed on biopsy. Not responsive to therapy.

Immunosuppression

Triple therapy most popular. Allows reduced doses, therefore less side-effects with same efficacy. Prednisolone, cyclosporin and FK506. Cyclosporin may be unnecessary in HLA-identical sibling transplants. Glucocorticoids commenced at higher doses and reduced during first six months. Antilymphocyte antibodies (e.g. OKT3) sometimes given in first two weeks as induction therapy (spares nephrotoxic use of cyclosporin or FK506). Beware drug interactions.

21.2 Cellular basis of rejection

T-cell stimulation

- Recognition of foreign proteins
- Expressed on MHC proteins on surface of antigen presenting cells (APCs)
- **Direct recognition**: donor antigen on surface of donor APCs
- **Indirect recognition**: processed donor antigen presented by recipient (self) APCs

T-cell antigen receptor (TCR)/CD3 complex

- Clonally variant TCR α–β peptide chains recognize antigen with MHC
- Clonally different CD3 chains initiate intracellular signals when recognize antigen

CD4 and CD8 proteins

- CD4 protein binds to HLA II
- CD8 protein binds to HLA I

Signal transduction

- TCR/CD3 and CD4/CD8 proteins activate intracellular tyrosine kinases
- Tyrosine-kinase phosphorylases phospholipase Cγ_1 activating it
- PCγ_1 initiates hydrolysis of PIP$_2$ to form IP$_3$ and diacylglycerol
- IP$_3$ mobilizes calcium from intracellular stores

- Calcineurin activity increased in presence of calcium and participates in signal transduction
- CsA and FK506 inhibit phosphatase activity of calcineurin and cause immunosuppression

Graft alloreactivity

Cytokine production and expression of cell surface receptors on transcellular molecules leads to antigen-specific and graft-destructive T-cells.

21.3 Immunosuppressive drugs

CsA and FK506

- CsA is a small fungal cyclic peptide
- FK506 is a macrolide
- Both block T-cell activation by similar mechanisms
- Form heterodimeric complexes with their respective cytoplasmic receptor protein
- CsA binds cyclophilin, FK506 binds FK binding protein (FKBP)
- Both complexes bind calcineurin and inhibit its phosphatase activity
- Inhibits nuclear regulatory proteins and T-cell activation genes encoding cytokines and their receptors (e.g. IL-2) and proto-oncogenes (e.g. H-ras, c-myc)
- Primary mechanism is inhibition of expression of IL-2

Corticosteroids

- Inhibit T-cell proliferation and T-cell-dependant immunity
- Inhibit cytokine gene transcription by forming heterodimeric complexes with intracellular gene-coding receptor protein

Azathioprine

- Purine analogue
- Functions as purine antagonist and therefore inhibits cellular proliferation

Rapamycin

- Antibiotic
- Binds to FKBP
- Blocks IL-2 and other growth-factor mediated signal transduction

Mycophendate Mofeti

- Semi-synthetic derivative of a fungal antibiotic
- Mycophenolic acid is active metabolite

Mizoribine

- Imidazole nucleoside blocks purine synthesis pathway
- Inhibits mitogen-stimulated T- and B-cell proliferation

15-deoxyspergualin, brequinar sodium, leflunomide

Still being evaluated in clinical trials.

OKT3

- Binds to ε chain of T-cell CD3 proteins and modulates T-cell antigen receptor/CD3 complex
- Initially causes fever, capillary leak syndrome, pulmonary oedema, nephropathy, hypotension and encephalopathy
- Recipients may generate antibodies to OKT3 and reduce its efficacy

Other immunosuppressive therapy

Principle: *Multiple drug therapy with synergistic effect*

Prophylactic antibiotic induction

- Monoclonal antilymphocyte antibodies (e.g. OKT3)
- Polyclonal antilymphocyte antibodies
- Used as induction therapy 7–14 days after transplantation
- Reduces incidence of early rejection
- Used in high-risk patients (i.e. transplants)

Vasodilator therapy

- CsA causes intense intra-renal vasospasm
- Transplant kidneys may be damaged by calcium dependant ischaemic and reperfusion injuries
- Addition of a calcium antagonist (diltiazem, verapamil, nifedipine) improves graft survival

21.4 Cross-match testing

HLA

- Genes located on short arm of chromosome 6
- Class 1 on surface of all nucleated cells and platelets (HLA-A, B, C)
- Class 2 (HLA-DR, DQ) on surface of B-cells, monocytes/macrophages and dendritic cells
- Graft survival higher in HLA-matched patients

Test recipient serum for antibodies to donor HLA antigens (donor lymphocytes) in presence of rabbit serum (source of complement).

T-cell cross-match

- Recipient cytotoxic antibodies to donor Class I antigens = positive T-cell cross-match
- Transplantation contraindicated
- 80–90% hyper-acutely rejected

B-cell cross-match

- Not a contraindication
- Graft survival decreased by 7% (primary), 15% (retransplant) if cross-match positive

Flow cytometry

Detects complement and non-complement fixing antibodies. Positive test results in reduces graft survival.

Transplant tolerance

Clonal anergy

- Antigen-reactive cells present but not functional
- Thought to be due to incomplete signalling
- Thought to be main mechanism of tolerance in transplantation

Clonal deletion

- Self-antigen — reactive cells detected mostly in thymus (negative selection)

Glossary

aa	Amino acids	ESR	Erythrocyte sedimentation rate
ABGs	Arterial blood gases	ESRF	End-stage renal failure
ADH	Antidiuretic hormone	ESWL	Extra-corporal shock wave lithotripsy
ALL	Acute lymphoblastic (leukaemia)	EUA	Examination under anaesthesia
AML	Acute myeloblastic (leukaemia)	FAP	Familial adenomatous polyposis
AUA	American Urological Association	FBC	Full blood count
AUS	Artificial urinary sphincter	FOBT	Faecal occult blood testing
AXR	Abdominal radiograph	FTT	Failure to thrive
bcl2	b cell lymphoma	GFR	Glomerular filtration rate
BCC	Basal cell carcinoma	GIT	Gastro-intestinal tract
BOO	Bladder outlet obstruction	GOJ	Gastro-oesophageal junction
BPE	Benign prostatic enlargement	GOR	Gastro-oesophageal reflux
BPH	Benign prostatic hyperplasia		
		Hb	Haemoglobin
Ca	Carcinoma	HIFU	High intensity focused ultrasound
CAPD	Chronic ambulatory peritoneal dialysis	HNPCC	Hereditary non-polyposis colonic cancer
CCF	Congestive cardiac failure		
CDH	Congenital dislocation of the hip	IBD	Inflammatory bowel disease
CLL	Chronic lymphocytic leukaemia	ICP	Intra-cranial pressure
CML	Chronic myeloid leukaemia	IRSC	International Study Committee
CT	Computerized tomography	ISD	Intrinsic sphincteric deficiency
CRP	C-reactive protein	IVU	Intravenous urogram
CXR	Chest X-ray		
		LIF	Left iliac fossa
DOS	Diffuse oesophageal spasm	LOS	Lower oesophageal sphincter
DSA	Digital subtraction angiography	LUTS	Lower urinary tract symptoms
DST	Donor-specific blood transfusion		
DVT	Deep vein thrombosis	MAGPI	Meatal advancement and granuloplasty
ECST	MRC European Carotid Surgery Trial	MALT	Mucosa-associated lymphoid tissue
EPO	Erythropoietin	MAS	Minimal access surgery
ERCP	Endoscopic retrograde cholangiopancreatography	MDR	Multi-drug resistance

721

MESS	Mangled extremity severity score	TRUS	Transrectal ultrasound scan
MMC	Migrating myoelectric complex	TRH	Thyroid releasing hormone
MUA	Manipulation under anaesthetic	TSH	Thyroid stimulating hormone
MRI	Magnetic resonance imaging	TUEVP	Transurethral electro-vaporization of prostate
NASCET	North American Symptomatic Carotid Endarterectomy Trial	TUIP	Transurethral incision of prostate
NDI	Nephrogenic diabetes insipidus	TURP	Transurethral prostatectomy
OA	Osteoarthritis	UC	Ulcerative colitis
ORIF	Open reduction plus internal fixation	US	Ultrasound
		USS	Ultrasound scan
		UTI	Urinary tract infection
PAF	Prostatic antibacterial factor	VMA	Vanillylmandelic acid
PCNL	Percutaneous nephrolithotomy	VQ scan	Ventilation perfusion scan
PDGF	Platelet derived growth factor		
PE	Pulmonary embolus	WCC	White cell count
PET	Positron emission tomography		↑ Increased
PIN	Prostatic intra-epithelial neoplasia		↓ Decreased
PoP	Plaster of Paris		
p.r.	per rectum		
PSA	Prostate specific antigen		
PTC	Percutaneous transhepatic cholangiography		
PTFE	Poly-tetrafluoroethylene		
PTH	Parathyroid hormone		
PUO	Pyrexia of unknown origin		
PVD	Peripheral vascular disease		
RA	Rheumatoid arthritis		
RIF	Right iliac fossa		
RPLN	Retroperitoneal lymph nodes		
RSD	Reflex sympathetic dystrophy		
RTA	Road traffic accident		
SCC	Squamous cell carcinoma		
SIRS	Systemic inflammatory response syndrome		
SOM	Suppurative otitis media		
SVR	Systemic vascular resistance		
TA	Tunica albuginea		
TBG	Thyroxine binding globulin		
TBPA	Thyroxine binding pre-albumin		
TPN	Total parenteral nutrition		

Bibliography

Berne RM, Levy MN. *Principles of Physiology*, 2nd edition. Mosby International 1996.

Borley NR, Mortonsen N. Inflammatory bowel disease. *Surgery* 16(7): 157–165, July 1998.

Botterill ID, Finan PJ. Diverticular disease. *Surgery* 16(7): 145–150, July 1998.

Botterill ID, Finan PJ. Surgery for diverticular disease. *Surgery* 16(7): 150–153, July 1998.

Botterill ID, Sagar PM. Intestinal obstruction. *Surgery* 16(10): 221–228, October 1998.

Browse NL. *An Introduction to the Symptoms and Signs of Surgical Disease*, 3rd edition, Arnold 1997.

Burnand KG, Young AE. *The New Aird's Companion in Surgical Studies*, 4th edition. Churchill Livingstone 1998.

Calne R, Pollard SG. *Operative Surgery*. Gower Medical Publishing, 1991.

Dow G, Leaper D. Abdominal stomas. *Surgery* 12(1): 1–7, January 1994.

Ellis H. *Clinical Anatomy, A Revision and Applied Anatomy for Clinical Students*, 9th edition, Blackwell Science, 1997.

Ellis H, Calne R. *Lecture Notes on General Surgery*, 9th edition, Blackwell Science, 1998.

Garden RS, Low angle fixation of femoral neck. *Journal of Bone and Joint Surgery* 43(B): 647–663, 1961.

Geoghegan JG, Scheele J. Treatment of colorectal liver metastases. *British Journal of Surgery* 86(2): 158–169, February 1999.

Helfet et al. MESS (Mangled Extremity Severity Score) Limb salvage versus amputation, preliminary results of the Mangled Extremity Severity Score. *Clinical Orthopaedics and Related Research* 256: 80–86, 1990.

Irving M, Carlson GL. Interocutaneous fistulae. *Surgery* 16(10) 217–222, October 1998.

Jones DJ, Irving MJ. *ABC of Colorectal Diseases*, 2nd edition, BMJ, 1999.

Khan S, Sutton R. Portal hypertension and oesophagogastric varices. Surgery 15(8): 175–181, August 1997.

Mitchell L et al. *Journal of Bone and Joint Surgery* 40(A): 41, 1958.

Mahadevan V. The Pathophysiology of Bowel Strangulation and Gangrene in Hernia. STEP Course, Systems Modules A–E, The Royal College of Surgeons of England.

McArdle CS. Colorectal cancer. *Surgery* 16(12): 265–271, December 1998.

McRae R. *Practical Human Anatomy*, Lloyd Luke Medical Books, 1982.

McRae R. *Clinical Orthopaedic Examination*, 3rd edition, Churchill Livingstone, 1996 .

Medical Research Council, Memorandum 45, Aids To The Examination Of The Peripheral Nervous System, London HMSO, 1976.

RCS. *Clinical Guidelines on the Management of Groin Hernia in Adults*. Report from a Working Party convened by The Royal College of Surgeons of England.

Sadler TW. *Langman's Medical Embryology*, 6th edition, Williams & Wilkins, 1990.

Salter RB, Harris WR. Injuries involving epiphyseal plate. *Journal of Bone and Joint Surgery* 45(A): 587–621, 1963.

Scholefield JH, Northover JMA. Anal cancer. *Surgery* 16(12): 281–284, December 1998.

Sharma V, Williamson R. Endocrine tumours of the pancreas. *Surgery* 16(12): 271–275, December 1998.

Sinnatamby CS. *Last's Anatomy (Regional and Applied)*, 10th edition, Churchill Livingstone, 1999.

Singh S, Knight MJ. Biliary anatomical abnormalities and their surgical importance. *Surgery* 15(8) 188–191, August 1997.

Snell RS. *Clinical Anatomy for Medical Students*, 6th edition, Lippincott Williams, 1986.

Stern PJ. In: *Fracture of the Metacarpals and Phalanges in Operative Hand Surgery*, ed DP Green. Churchill Livingstone, 1993.

Thomas WEG, Investigation of the biliary tree and the jaundiced patient. *Surgery* 15(8): 183–182, August 1997.

Treacy PJ, Johnson AG. Complications of peptic ulceration. *Surgery* 15(12): 269–273, December 1997.

Treacy PJ, Johnson AG. Presentation and management of peptic ulceration. *Surgery* 15(12): 265–269, December 1997.

Whittaker RH, Borley NR. *Instant Anatomy*, 2nd edition, Blackwell Science, 2000.

Index

PASTEST REVISION BOOKS

MRCS Core Modules: Essential Revision Notes   1 901198 36 7
Ed. J Elkabir & A Khadra
MRCS System Modules: Essential Revision Notes   1 901198 41 3
Ed. C Parchment Smith & C Hernon

These new books give a unique presentation of the key elements of all subjects covered in the Core and Systems Modules syllabus. Unlike conventional textbooks, the essential facts in each subject are presented in note form with special attention given to areas which are often poorly understood. Designed to make learning easier, no candidate should be without these excellent books.

- Vital facts presented in user-friendly format
- All areas of the syllabus covered in concise note form
- Diagrams, lists, illustrations and bullet points to aid learning

MRCS Core Modules: MCQs and EMQs   1 901198 09 X
A Williams, C Chan, T Hennigan & L Barker
MRCS System Modules: MCQs and EMQs   1 901198 10 3
A Williams, C Chan, T Hennigan & L Barker

These two books have been devised to comprehensively cover all aspects of the Core and System Modules necessary for the exam. Extensive explanations are provided for each question and are presented in an easily accessible format.

- Over 300 new MCQs and EMQs covering each of the Modules in its own section
- Similar in content and level of difficulty to current exam questions
- Expert advice on successful examination technique

MRCS Core Modules: Practice Papers   1 901198 45 6
C Chan
MRCS System Modules: Practice Papers   1 901198 46 4
C Chan

Compiled by a team of experienced surgeons, these new books feature five Practice Papers, providing an excellent framework for study and revision for those preparing for the written component of the MRCS exam.

- Answers and detailed teaching notes for each question
- Similar in content and level of difficulty to current exam questions
- Expert advice on successful examination technique

To order any of the above titles, please contact PasTest on:

01565 752000

PasTest Ltd, FREEPOST, Knutsford, Cheshire WA16 7BR
Fax: 01565 650264; E-mail: books@pastest.co.uk
or order on-line at www.pastest.co.uk

PASTEST REVISION COURSES FOR MRCS

Feeling in need of a helping hand towards success in your exams?

PasTest has over twenty-five years' experience in helping doctors to pass first time, with specially tailored courses to make the most of your valuable revision time.

Over 4000 candidates attend our courses each year at centres throughout the UK. To give you the most up-to-date information and help you to achieve the best results, we constantly update and improve our courses based on feedback from those who attend.

Our course material is continually updated to ensure the best possible revision for the exam. You will receive hundreds of exam-type MCQs and EMQs, with explanations and detailed handouts, and mock exam practice.

- **Two-day MCQ/EMQ courses**
  Intensive revision in either Core Modules or Systems Modules. An opportunity to study over the weekend — ideal if you are unable to take study leave.

- **Three-day MCQ/EMQ courses**
  Following feedback from previous MRCS candidates, we have extended the two-day course to include extra teaching time for the more complex areas.

- **Clinical and Viva courses**
  Run in association with various hospitals, our two-day clinical and viva courses offer small teaching groups to provide you with the best help possible.